HARVARD HISTORICAL STUDIES

PUBLISHED UNDER THE DIRECTION OF
THE DEPARTMENT OF HISTORY

FROM THE INCOME OF

THE HENRY WARREN TORREY FUND

VOLUME XXX

THE FRANCO-RUSSIAN ALLIANCE

1890-1894

BY

WILLIAM LEONARD LANGER

1967

OCTAGON BOOKS, INC.

New York

Printed in U.S.A. by
NOBLE OFFSET PRINTERS, INC.
NEW YORK 3, N. Y.

TO THE MEMORY OF

ARCHIBALD CARY COOLIDGE

PREFACE

IN the pre-war European system the Franco-Russian Alliance played a rôle similar to that of the Austro-German Alliance of 1879. Each served as the kernel of an international group, into which other powers were drawn and around which the smaller states gravitated. Reference to their importance, then, would be quite gratuitous, and no excuse need be offered for a detailed monographic study of the circumstances attending the conclusion of either one of them. In the case of the Franco-Russian Alliance there has been no exhaustive treatment to date. At the time of its consummation it attracted a great deal of attention from political writers, for the secrecy of the terms stimulated curiosity and the anomaly involved in a combination between the democratic French Republic and the Muscovite autocracy demanded explanation. French writers in particular lost no time in reviewing the making of the agreement, which, they felt, had restored their nation to its rightful place in the European scene. The more important contemporary accounts, like those of Cyon, Hansen and Daudet, were based at least in part upon direct personal knowledge or upon confidential information. But under the circumstances they could not be other than one-sided and incomplete.

The scientific study of the great international alliance systems could hardly begin until the texts of the various agreements and the documents bearing upon the negotiations were published after the world war. The French *Yellow Book* of 1918 on the Franco-Russian Alliance called forth such articles and books as those of Packard, Darmstaedter and Welschinger, in which the subject was reviewed in the light of the new material. But the French collection was so incomplete that anything like an exhaustive treatment was still impossible.

Meanwhile the deluge of material from the German side began to divert the attention of scholars to the problems of German foreign policy. A number of excellent books were published on

the Austro-German Alliance and on various aspects of Bismarckian and Wilhelminian diplomacy. Only in recent years
has the discussion of the question of war responsibility again
focussed attention upon the history of the Franco-Russian pact.
The year 1925 saw the publication of the present writer's two
articles on the making of the alliance, in the *Slavonic Review*,
and of an admirable study of the military convention by Eugen
Fischer in the *Preussische Jahrbücher*. Otto Becker's book,
Das russisch-französische Bündnis appeared before the end of
the year. Since then the literature on the subject has been
enriched by Koerlin's study of the background of the alliance
and by Michon's history of the pact to 1917. Nothing need be
said of Senator Owen's *The Russian Imperial Conspiracy*, which
is a thoroughly perverted and unscholarly production, not to be
taken seriously by the profession.

The present writer has worked at this subject intermittently
for the past eight years. With a draft treatment he went to
Vienna in 1921 and spent the entire winter examining the
documents of the period in the Vienna archives. The results of
these investigations were embodied in a doctoral dissertation
presented to the Faculty of Arts and Sciences of Harvard Univ-
ersity in 1923, under the title *The European Alliances during the
Chancellorship of Caprivi*. It was thought at that time advisable
not to publish it in book form until the German documents for the
period, which were just appearing, could be made use of. As a
matter of fact volumes seven to ten of the German publication
added little to what the author had learned from the Austrian
archives, but the articles published in the March and June numbers of the *Slavonic Review* for 1925 were meant as an abstract
of the subject as the author viewed it after an examination of the
new material. Since then many months have been spent in
continued research and much time devoted to an attempt to
clarify certain obscure questions with the aid of less familiar
material, especially the periodical press and the newspapers.
The whole monograph has been rewritten from the ground up, so
that in its present form it bears little resemblance to the original
dissertation.

It will be seen from this that the author has worked out the present book quite independently of other investigators. The large mass of critical writing on special phases of the problem has, of course, been carefully considered, but no other writer has covered the same ground and in the majority of cases the author had already examined the material for himself and reached his own conclusions. In general these were not far different from the conclusions of other contributors, but few references have been made to secondary treatments, since there was rarely an obligation to be acknowledged. This applies even to Becker's book, which is the second volume in a series entitled *Bismarck und die Einkreisung Deutschlands*. The book is also based in part upon Austrian archive material and is a splendid contribution—one of the best diplomatic studies, in fact—but the title alone indicates that the whole problem is approached from the standpoint of German policy.

Becker's object is to show how the Bismarckian policy was nullified by his successors, thereby making possible the formation of the hostile combination of France and Russia. In a general way the present writer is in accord with his argument, but in this monograph the aim all through has been not to isolate the alliance and not to examine it from the standpoint of any one government or any one policy. The object has been rather to place it in its European setting and to explain it as the product of the general international situation. The author has chosen a rather strict chronological approach in the hope of bringing out more clearly the interaction of different forces and different events. He has made a particular effort to illuminate the position and policy of England and has investigated, for the first time, the bearing of questions of sea power upon the development of international relations in this period. It is his hope that something has been added to our knowledge of the circumstances and conditions which led to the conclusion of the alliance and that the attitude and mentality of the statesmen and nations has to some extent been revived. For, after all, a just appreciation of the past can be gained only if the events of the past are viewed with the eyes of the actors. The author has scrupulously avoided the injection of post-war notions into the discussion of the subject.

It may be objected that a definitive treatment of the problem cannot be undertaken until the historian has more authentic material from the French, English and especially the Russian archives. The author has, of course, felt the dearth of Russian material very keenly in all stages of the work. But there is some consolation in the thought that the historian can never hope for exhaustive source material. The effort to reconstruct the past is worth making if the data available is reasonably abundant and relevant. The study here presented would never have been written unless the writer had been convinced that the material is quite sufficient to clear up the fundamental problems. He cannot believe that the publication of new material would destroy the basic lines of the argument.

In pursuing an investigation of this kind the writer is bound to put himself under obligation to many persons who have aided him in one way or another. The author can never forget the cordiality with which he was received in Vienna so soon after the war and the unremitting kindness shown by the authorities of the Austrian archives. Neither can he forget the generosity of his teacher and very good friend, Professor Alfred Francis Pribram, who first introduced him to the methods of archive work. To Professor Sidney B. Fay and Mr. Donald McKay he is obliged for their careful reading of the proof. But his greatest debt must always be to his teachers at Harvard—to Professor Robert H. Lord, who guided the work in its initial stages, and above all to the lamented Professor Archibald Cary Coolidge, whose knowledge and understanding of European diplomacy were unrivalled. He never wavered in his interest and never hesitated to sacrifice his time in discussion and suggestion. No words can express the author's debt to him.

WILLIAM L. LANGER.

Cambridge, Mass., April 10, 1929.

CONTENTS

CONTENTS

THE FRANCO-RUSSIAN ALLIANCE

CHAPTER I

THE BISMARCKIAN SYSTEM

WHEN William II ascended the imperial German throne in June 1888, he became the head of the predominant nation of continental Europe. He inherited from his father and grandfather not only a united Germany but also the greatest political genius of modern times, Prince Otto von Bismarck, who had effected the unification of a large part of central Europe under the aegis of Prussia, and had lifted the young empire to the paramount position in Europe. Germany was at that time connected by alliances and agreements, directly or indirectly, with Austria-Hungary, Italy, Russia, England, Serbia, Rumania, and Spain, while a number of the remaining powers revolved in the orbit of the so-called Bismarckian system.

This great international organization, this system of alliances and engagements unprecedented in European history, was in part due to chance and in part due to necessity, but above all it was the work of the master-builder in the Wilhelmstrasse. It was sheer political insight and understanding that enabled him to recognize not only the interests of his own state, but the interests and aims of others. It was by keen exploitation of the position and policies of others that he succeeded not only in preserving peace for the infant German Empire but in making the whole world of international affairs centre in Berlin.

The successive victories of Prussia over Denmark, Austria and France in 1864, 1866 and 1870 had overturned the balance of power as it had previously existed in Europe and compelled all the great powers to readjust their foreign policies to meet a new situation, the outstanding characteristics of which were the eclipse of France and the reorganization of central Europe under unified leadership. Of the European nations the one least affected was undoubtedly England, since, by virtue of her geographical position and overseas interests, she was a world power

3

rather than a European power. The German question can hardly
be said to have played a very important part in English policy
before 1870, and the English were, generally speaking, well-
satisfied to see the power of Napoleon III broken and an old
rival, France, relegated for the time being, at least, to a second-
rate position. Once assured that Bismarck did not mean to
pursue his conquests, once convinced that he had no designs on
Belgium or the Channel ports, the English statesmen were willing
enough to maintain cordial, and, if need be, intimate relations
with Berlin.

Their chief interests, however, lay in the Near and Middle,
and even the Far East, while their chief enemy in all these
fields was Russia. The policy of the Crimean War had not been
wholly futile, and the principle of the integrity of the Turkish
Empire was still stoutly maintained by many Englishmen. In
any case it was felt that to allow the Russian advance to proceed
unchecked in either the Near or Middle East would be the death
knell of England's imperial position. English policy, therefore,
was consistently directed towards the weakening or paralyzing of
Russia. France was a secondary enemy, and from the nature of
things would be held in check by Germany, but against Russia it
was harder to find allies, and Russia was practically unapproach-
able so far as England was concerned. The Austrians, to be sure,
were also the opponents of Russia, but only in the Near East.
England and Austria were, after 1870, consistently on friendly if
not intimate terms, but Austrian aid in itself would hardly have
sufficed to check Russia, and besides, the Austrian statesmen were
constantly on the alert lest they might find themselves drawing
the chestnuts out of the fire for England. Had the English been
able to enlist Germany in an openly anti-Russian policy they
would undoubtedly have been glad to do so. Failing this, however, it was logical that the foreign office should devote its
efforts to keeping Russia involved in Europe to such an extent
that she would be forced to take her eyes off the Indian frontier.
England's chances of success were infinitely better if the clash
came in the Balkans, than if it came in Afghanistan. In any case,
it was to England's interest to hold aloof from binding agreements

on the continent, and to temporize until the first shot had been fired before she threw the weight of her power into the scales. She had nothing to fear from continental coalitions, though naturally she looked askance at any arrangement which might afford Russia protection in the West while an attack was launched against India. Of all possible combinations the most dangerous one would be not a Russo-German, but an Austro-Russian agreement, in so far as the latter might lead to a settlement of differences in the Balkans or even coöperation in the Near East to the detriment of England's interests.

Of France comparatively little need be said. Her prestige shattered, her government shaky, her army and finances in a chaotic state, the vanquished nation was compelled for years to play a secondary rôle and to submit to the organization of Europe without her and against her. A valiant attempt was made to preserve some show of greatness and to uphold the colonial tradition, especially in the Mediterranean. This meant rivalry with England and with Italy, and this antagonism was a constant factor in French politics. But France's eyes were unalterably riveted on the German frontier, on the "hole in the Vosges." Quite apart from the sentiment of *revanche*, which in Bismarck's time never had a serious chance of realization, the French statesmen were constantly haunted by the fear of an attack by Germany, of a war of revenge, designed to crush the nation for all time. The very existence of this fear dictated the principle on which French policy hinged.

France was forced by her very position to seek an ally, and the very rudiments of statesmanship demanded that that ally should be in the East, in the rear of the enemy. In the past the French had sought the alliance of Turk, Swede or Pole, and they had on occasion cultivated close relations with Russia. After 1870 this latter power, of course, could alone be considered as a possible ally, and offhand one would think that community of interest between the two nations would in itself have created a sort of informal pseudo-alliance, a tacit understanding of mutual support in case either became the subject of attack by Germany or even became involved in war through its own provocation.

This theory of a *de facto* alliance between France and Russia after 1870 has frequently been developed by political writers. It should, however, be carefully noted that such a tacit understanding, even had there been one, would have been of very questionable value. In any case the indisputable fact is that French statesmen themselves considered it from their viewpoint wholly inadequate. Its disadvantages really outweighed its advantages, for without a written *de jure* alliance there was not the slightest guarantee that France would not be left in the lurch by her pseudo-ally at the most critical moment. Every extraordinary mission from Berlin to St. Petersburg gave rise to rumors of negotiations by which Germany was to receive from her eastern neighbor a free hand against France in return for allowing the Tsar freedom of action in the Near East. It is perfectly obvious that Germany could, at almost any moment, reach an arrangement with Russia to this effect, and indeed this is the fundamental principle underlying the famous Reinsurance Treaty of 1887.

The conclusion to be drawn, then, is that French statesmen were compelled by the force of circumstances to angle for a really substantial Russian alliance. In the beginning they hardly dared pursue their object openly, and it may well be doubted whether they could ever have mustered sufficient courage while Bismarck was at the helm. The risk was too great, and even with a definite Russian promise of immediate help there always remained the danger that the German chancellor, from whom such an important development could hardly be kept secret, might cut the Gordian knot and demolish the French defense before the ponderous Russian machine could be set in motion. There was more justification for the French dread of a "preventive" war than for Bismarck's *cauchemar des coalitions*.

Of all the European great powers Italy certainly played the least significant rôle in the period from 1870-1890. Newly united and composed of extremely diverse provinces, the government was confronted with almost insuperable domestic problems. Economically the nation was poor, and dependent on the trade with France. But the Italian statesmen could not refrain from imperialist ambitions in the Mediterranean, with the result that they soon ran foul of Italy's Latin sister and for years were on the very worst terms with the French Republic. Under these conditions the Italian government was forced to rely above all on English friendship, and statesmen of all parties were scrupulously careful to dissipate any clouds that might arise on that part of the political horizon. To be sure, they were the supplicants, and they knew that England could never be depended upon to do more than defend the far-flung Italian coast from French attack.

For protection on the land side they had to look to the central powers. An alliance with Germany was the logical solution, especially since Germany as a Protestant power could then be reckoned upon to throw the tremendous weight of her influence against any French or even Austrian plans to restore to the Pope his temporal possessions. So urgent was the need for this alliance that the Italians, after the French occupation of Tunis in 1881, were unable to resist the German demand for the inclusion of Austria in the pact. This meant shelving irredentism at least as a government policy, but then, irredentism was a luxury the Italian government could have ill-afforded in any case. Relations with the old traditional enemy could never be based on higher considerations than those of interest, nor could the Italian statesmen ever reconcile themselves entirely to the thought that Austria would be of no value in furthering Italian hopes in the Mediterranean while, on the other hand, the Danubian monarchy was anything but a negligible obstacle in the way of the nascent Italian ambitions in the Adriatic and the Balkans. At times the Italian statesmen had lent a willing ear to the temptation of a Russian alliance, but the risks were too great. Such a policy would have led inevitably to German hostility and above all to the estrangement of England. After all, it could at least be said for the Austrian alliance that it carried with it the whole-hearted approval of the English government.

The international position of the Austro-Hungarian Monarchy was an exceedingly difficult one after 1870. With the defeat of France all hope of revenge on Prussia had vanished and an entirely new orientation of Austrian foreign policy became necessary.

In the southwest the monarchy was bounded by an outspokenly hostile Italy, still seething with irredentist agitation. In the northwest was the young and powerful German Empire, the master-mind of which, for all the Austrians could know, might be planning to crown his work of German unification by the conquest of the German *Kronländer* on the upper Danube. Finally, beyond the Carpathians lay the great Russian incubus, still mindful of Austria's "treason" in 1854 and more determined and better prepared than ever to lay its heavy hands on the Balkans, the last region of expansion open to the Austrians after the loss of Italy and Germany. Austria was completely isolated, for the sympathy of England could not be reckoned upon to pass the Platonic stage, and furthermore would have proved of very little value in the face of a Russo-German combination. The road to salvation for Austria, therefore, lay in the prevention of such a combination, which might lead to the break-up of her own polyglot empire and the conquest of the Near East by Russia. Indeed, it may be said that Austria's policy was always on the defensive, seeking to protect herself and to enlist the support of others in furthering her interests in the Near East.

In eastern Europe the great Russian Empire was easily the controlling factor in European politics after 1870. Alone of the continental great powers Russia had not suffered from the wars which shook Europe in the 'sixties. Since the Crimean War extensive reforms had been undertaken, and though the revolutionary movement was steadily gaining impetus after 1870 it can hardly be said that the Nihilists, who constantly threatened the person of the autocrat, had as yet made any appreciable impression on the autocratic system.

In international affairs Russia gained rather than lost by centralized control, and the Tsar had at his command a huge army upon the loyalty of which he could depend. The Russian and Prussian royal families had long been united by marriage and by close personal friendship, and Bismarck's successes in the years preceding the Franco-Prussian War were due in no small measure to the benevolent neutrality of his eastern neighbor. But the Prussian wars had profoundly altered the situation, even as it affected Russia. The defeat of Austria and France was unquestionably a source of personal satisfaction to the Tsar, but it soon became painfully obvious to the statesmen on the Neva that there was a limit beyond which the process of German aggrandizement must not go. It could not be to Russia's interest to have the hegemony of France replaced by a German one much nearer her frontier. Indeed, the very unification of Germany involved a weakening of Russian influence in central and western Europe. Even under these altered circumstances, however, it was still in the Russian interest to cultivate the friendship of Germany. Politically the two nations were nowhere in direct conflict, while Germany might prove very helpful in furthering Russian desires. In spite of their disappointment by Austria in 1854 the Russians at first confidently expected that Germany would repay the services rendered by cordially supporting Russian ambitions, especially during the Near Eastern crisis of 1876-1878.

Russian policy was distinctly one of expansion—in the Near East, in the Middle East and to a slighter extent in the Far East. In all these areas England was an obstacle—in the Middle and Far East, at least, she was the only important impediment. In the Near East Austria was the immediate rival, but there too England loomed in the background. The services which Germany could render Russia in furthering her plans of expansion were numerous and varied. In the first place she could stand aloof and permit the Russians to settle the score with Austria if the latter were to make an attempt to block the Russian advance in the Balkans. In the second place she could help bar the road against the British by insisting on the maintenance of the principle of the closure of the Straits against foreign warships in time of peace. This would give Russia an opportunity to seize Constantinople and control the Straits before the English squadrons could pass the Dardanelles. Finally, Germany could be of supreme assistance to Russia by promising benevolent neutrality and perhaps by keeping Austria in order while Russia was engaged in war with England on the Indian or Chinese frontier. Add to this the common interest of the two powers in keeping the

Poles in subjection, and their common interest in upholding the monarchical principle against the subversive revolutionary movements of the West, and it should be quite evident that the advantages of the German alliance, consecrated by a long and successful history, far outweighed the possible advantages to be derived from any other combination.

Only in case Germany failed her, only in the event that the Germans should refuse to give the support which the Russians expected, could the French alliance become attractive. It must not be forgotten that, while Russia could not look on indifferently while Germany weakened France further, there was absolutely no inducement for the Russians to go beyond this perfectly negative attitude. The French government was regarded as revolutionary, atheistic and corrupt, and even in the political sphere there was nothing to be gained from the French alliance. To be sure, France was, like Russia, the rival of England. But the spheres of French and Russian interest did not coincide, nor was it likely that the infant republic, weak and tottering, would be ready to engage in a duel with so formidable an opponent, especially when it could be predicted almost with certainty that Germany would not look on indifferently. Russia could not aid France effectively in the Mediterranean, much less in Africa or in Indo-China, while France, in turn, could do nothing against Austria in the Balkans, much less against England in Middle Asia or in the Far East. Contact in the Mediterranean would have been the *sine qua non* of effective common action, and it is hard to see how France was to gain by a Russian conquest of Constantinople or by the appearance of Russia as a sea power in the Mediterranean. Only against Germany were the two powers natural allies, and even in this respect their interests were anything but identical.

The discussion of Germany's position and policy has been left to the last, partly because her central position made her more or less the natural focus for the policies of others, but even more because it was the statesmanship of Bismarck which discerned the interests, ambitions and tendencies of the others and based upon them a great international system which aimed at protecting the young state against war and at the same time secured for it the decisive voice in European affairs.

The great chancellor's policy after 1870 was founded upon a few essential principles. He desired peace for the infant empire, because only by the prevention of war could he hope to consolidate the new structure and ground it securely on the basis he had chosen. This does not mean that Bismarck was a pacifist. There were times when he unquestionably would have welcomed war between other powers in order to divert their attention and relieve the pressure on the inner lines. But he regarded Germany as a saturated nation, and we know that he never seriously considered even such plans as the complete unification of the German peoples by the acquisition of the Baltic provinces of Russia or the German provinces of Austria, let alone such Pan-German fantasies as the annexation of Holland or the Flemish part of Belgium. In brief it may be said, then, that the cornerstone of his policy was to keep Germany out of war and to prevent all wars in which Germany might become involved.

The policy of peace, in Bismarck's view, rested of necessity upon the policy of isolating France. He never expected the French to take their defeat in good part, and on frequent occasions expressed his conviction that even without the loss of Alsace and Lorraine the French would have cherished the idea of revenge. However that may be, no one can dispute the fact that Bismarck was genuinely apprehensive of a French attack. There was, perhaps, never a real danger of such a development in the twenty years before his fall, but in any case Bismarck realized that the French were constrained to seek allies, and he devoted his best efforts to frustrating all attempts in that direction.

A further danger to peace, as Bismarck saw it, lay in the position of Austria-Hungary. It was hardly thinkable that the disruption of the Dual Monarchy should take place without a general European War, and what was more important yet, he believed that the break-up of the Danubian state would prove as disastrous to German interests as to those of the Hapsburgs themselves. It would leave the Russians without an effective rival in the Balkans, and presumably would result in the estab-

lishment of a sort of Russian protectorate over the Slavs of the
monarchy. Russia would have no rival on the continent but
Germany, and Bismarck had a veritable horror of finding himself
alone with Russia on the one side and a France thirsting for
revenge on the other. He stood unalterably by his assertion
that the maintenance of the Dual Monarchy as a great power
was of vital interest to the German Empire.

Finally there was a principle of Bismarckian policy which derived naturally from his anxiety to prevent wars into which Germany might be drawn. Germany's geographical position was
such that almost any European war might necessitate her participation. To avoid such a contingency the powers must be encouraged to settle their disputes outside of Europe. The wars
which were constantly threatening on the continent were a new
Franco-German War, an Austro-Russian War, and an Anglo-
Russian War. To prevent a Franco-German War or an Austro-
Russian War was the immediate object of the great chancellor's
continental policy. As for the impending Russo-English conflict, his great aim was to prevent its being fought out in Europe,
in the Near East, where it might involve Austria and so Germany.
He consistently threw his influence into the scale to divert the
European powers to extra-European fields. The more the great
powers could be interested in colonial enterprise, the more their
conflicts could be transferred to Africa, Asia or the Pacific, the
more relieved he was. To deflect the pressure on the centre, this
was one of Bismarck's cardinal principles.

There was nothing of the theorist about the German chancellor, and he certainly did not begin the second phase of his great
career with the idea of organizing Europe in a series of alliances
and agreements to isolate France and maintain the peace. As a
matter of fact international alliances in times of peace had not
been customary among European powers, excepting in the face
of impending conflict. There is no evidence that Bismarck in
the first years after 1870 sought to build up a coalition, even of
the most rudimentary type, although he certainly knew that he,
and the German Empire with him, were regarded with profound
distrust, even by some of his earlier friends.

The so-called Alliance of the Three Emperors in its original form of 1872-1873 was exactly what its name implies. It was not so much the result of Bismarck's efforts as of the desire of Andrássy to escape the dangerous isolation of Austria, and of the anxiety of the Tsar lest the Austro-German friendship should become too firmly established to the detriment of Russia. It was essentially a monarchical understanding, the object of which was to preserve the peace and the monarchical principle at a time when both alike were menaced. Bismarck seems to have accepted it without enthusiasm and without sanguine hopes for its future. In these early years he appears to have relied mainly on the traditional friendship between Russia and Prussia to keep France isolated. In the England of Gladstone he had no confidence and the efforts of Austria he evidently regarded with indifference.

The first steps in the construction of the Bismarckian system go no further back than the famous War Scare of 1875, on which occasion Russia, supported by England, intervened to preserve the peace between the two enemies of 1870-71. The details need not detain us here. What is really important is the fact that the incident revealed to Bismarck the real attitude of the powers. The action of England was of minor significance, but the interference of Russia in behalf of France was a development which certainly astonished and disillusioned the German statesman. In future he was on his guard, and in the documents of the succeeding period it becomes increasingly evident that the former element of trust and confidence had disappeared from Russo-German relations to a marked degree.

This was the more unfortunate for Russia because, in the Eastern crisis that immediately followed the War Scare, she soon found herself in conflict with her pseudo-ally Austria. All attempts to effect a settlement on the basis of the Alliance of the Three Emperors proved futile, despite the support lent by Bismarck. The Russian government was rapidly drifting into war with Turkey, and the English, now under the leadership of Disraeli, were assuming a more and more outspoken opposition, thereby also encouraging the Austrians in their resistance to the Russian policy.

In view of these circumstances the position of Germany was not an enviable one. Without direct interests in the Near East herself she was forced to stand by while a crisis developed which threatened to embroil half of Europe and eventually to involve the disinterested states as well. Before long, in the summer of 1876, Bismarck found himself confronted with what amounted to a demand by Russia that he support her against Austria and England—that he repay Russia for the friendly services given before 1870. The German statesman was in a quandary. He sympathized with Russian hopes in the Near East and was willing to support Russian policy and demands not only against the Turks, but against the English. In return, however, he desired an assurance that Germany should not suffer for her attitude. In the first place Germany must be guaranteed against a French attack, possibly supported by England—she must have a guarantee of Alsace-Lorraine. In the second place she must be assured that a Russian victory over the Turks would not develop into a Russian victory over Austria. Through an unfortunate misunderstanding the demand for a Russian guarantee of Alsace-Lorraine in return for a free hand in the East was never presented in due form. All that the Russians were told was that Germany could not promise to remain neutral while Austria was defeated and deposed from her position as a great power— perhaps even dismembered.

The blow was a severe one for the Russian statesmen. In a way they never overcame their disappointment and surprise at Bismarck's "ingratitude." Bismarck himself urged other solutions, and repeatedly suggested a general pacification on the basis of reciprocal compensation at the expense of Turkey. To these suggestions neither the Austrians nor the English were ready to listen. The crisis went from bad to worse, and in the end the Russians, forced by circumstances and by public opinion to go to war, were obliged to protect their lines of communications by far-reaching concessions to Austria.

The period of international tension following the Russo-Turkish War of 1877-78 was, if anything, more severe than the one that preceded it. The Russians had been completely victorious and, naturally enough, meant to reap the fruits of success. The temptation to forget the obligations assumed towards Austria was, of course, a strong one, while, on the other hand, it is readily comprehensible that both Austria and England should stand forth in defence of their interests. Against the one-sided Treaty of San Stefano—an error in statesmanship if there ever was one—the cabinets of Vienna and London rose in common protest. They had been negotiating for the better part of a year but had made no progress beyond agreeing on the rudimentary points of a common program. The English had hoped to involve the Austrians to such an extent that retreat along the road of separate agreement with Russia would no longer be possible. The Austrians, on the other hand, were filled with distrust, fearing lest they be left in the lurch by "perfidious Albion" and preferring, finally, to entrench themselves behind their agreements with Russia. Only when the Russians appeared inclined to disregard these arrangements did the Austrians come out in open opposition, and only then did England show real determination.

As for Bismarck, he had been in a dilemma for some time. For once in his life he did not see quite clearly. At times he appears to have hoped that England and Austria would take common military action, and by defeating Russia relieve central Europe from the Slavic incubus for some time. But in the end the danger to Germany of an Austro-Russian conflict appeared too great, especially at a time when Italy was threatening Austria in the rear and France was passing through a domestic crisis which made the future absolutely uncertain. It was Bismarck himself who finally mediated between England and Austria on the one hand and Russia on the other, and it was the German chancellor who, at the Congress of Berlin, exerted himself to the utmost to send the various delegations home satisfied.

The gratification of England and Austria is easy enough to understand. Even France returned from the Congress with a promise of support in Tunis. On the other hand sympathy cannot be denied the Russians and the Italians. The latter, to be sure, had taken no part in the conflict, but they felt entitled to some

compensation on an occasion when everyone seemed to be getting
something for nothing. The Trentino and Trieste, they thought,
would have been a fair return for the Austrian occupation of
Bosnia and Herzegovina and the extension of Austrian influence
in the Balkans. But their case was wholly secondary. The
Russians could fairly claim that they had been deprived of the
results of victory. Their gains had been considerable, to be sure,
but the Treaty of Berlin looked lean indeed as compared to the
Treaty of San Stefano. The indignation of the educated classes
and especially of the Panslavists, knew no bounds, while the
diplomats, anxious to exonerate themselves and unwilling to
admit that they had been obliged to capitulate to the demands
of the arch-enemies, England and Austria, found it convenient to
make Bismarck the scapegoat. There was, however, a good
measure of sincerity in their plea. They genuinely felt that the
German chancellor had ill-requited their benevolent attitude in
the period before 1870.

The assertion that Bismarck had already, before 1875, made
his choice between Austria and Russia in favor of the former is
certainly a debatable one. It would, perhaps, be more correct
to say that he never made a choice one way or another. What is
clear is merely that he felt menaced by the growing hostility of
Russian officialdom and Russian opinion, and was genuinely
alarmed by the concentration of Russian troops in Poland.
When Russian discontent reached its zenith in the famous
Briefohrfeige of August 1879 and news reached Bismarck of
the approaching resignation of Andrássy he decided to take protective measures before it was too late. The news of Russian
soundings in Paris sufficed to determine him.

But it is easy to overestimate Bismarck's enthusiasm for the
Austrian alliance. His master's obstinacy compelled him to
utilize every argument and to paint the projected combination
in the brightest colors. As a matter of fact he probably even
then would have preferred the Russian alliance, for Austria,
notoriously a weak, if not a moribund state, was not a particularly desirable ally and could be of comparatively little use, if
any, in case of a Franco-German conflict. The point to be em-

phasized was that, at the moment, the Russians themselves seemed to have renounced the connection with Germany while the Austrian alliance had at least one attractive aspect: it would bring England informally to the Bismarckian side. Even then, be it noted, Bismarck not only maintained friendly relations with the repentant Russian diplomats, he even exerted himself to disarm the apprehensions of the French. Above all, he took great care not to engage himself in the Near Eastern dispute. The Austro-German Alliance in no way bound Germany to support Austrian policy in the Balkans. It was a distinctly negative agreement, and left Germany as free as ever to negotiate for her security in the West on the basis of concessions to be made to Russia in the East.

Even if, in October 1879, Bismarck had hopes of drawing England into the Austro-German combination, his expectations were necessarily exploded with the advent of a new Gladstone ministry in 1880. Wrapped up in domestic problems, the new cabinet, with its Austrophobe leader, could not be reckoned upon to support a policy like the one Disraeli had initiated. Whatever may have been his plans, Bismarck recognized the necessity of returning to his original position, the alliance with Russia, insisting, however, that Austria be included in order to facilitate the settlement of Balkan conflicts and in order to prevent a duplication of German treaty obligations.

The Three Emperors' Alliance of June 1881 must certainly be regarded as the classic example of one solution of the dilemma arising from Germany's geographical position. Throughout a compromise, it represented the maximum good at the smallest price. Each one of the signatory powers derived substantial benefits from it and it was thoroughly in accord with the interests of each. Russia, who, in her isolation, had originally broached the suggestion, received an assurance that a union of Bulgaria and Eastern Rumelia would not be opposed, and therewith she gained one of the points most hotly contested at Berlin. This in itself was a defeat for Austria and especially for England. In addition Russia was assured of German and Austrian neutrality in case of a war between England and Russia. Finally, the reaffirmation of the principle of closure of the Straits gave her security against a possible English campaign in the Black Sea.

As for Austria, her gains were no less great, and it is difficult to understand the hesitancy of Austria in accepting the agreement. To be sure, it put an end to the prospect of monopolizing German friendship and exploiting it against Russia, but it did actually protect Austria against Russian aggression, it did secure her rear in the event of an Austro-Italian War, and it did obtain for her in advance the assent of Russia to the annexation of Bosnia and Herzegovina. After all, the union of Bulgaria and Eastern Rumelia would be not nearly so dangerous to Austria as an extension of the Bulgarian frontier to the west, and the treaty did stipulate that Austria must maintain neutrality in a war between Russia and Turkey only if Russia first negotiated with her allies an agreement as to the results of the war. In other words, Austria was protected against a repetition of the San Stefano incident.

Bismarck's own gains were no less than those of his two neighbors. The Alliance of the Three Emperors whitewashed over the Near Eastern question at least as effectively as possible, while there was reason to hope that the mutual concessions made by both Russia and Austria would diminish the hostility of the two, and that the provision for consultation in case of Balkan difficulties would prevent future tension before it had developed far. But for Bismarck the outstanding feature was the fact that by the alliance he was given security in the East in case Germany became involved in war with France. Indeed, under the treaty of 1881 Germany could claim Russian neutrality even if she embarked on a war of aggression against France. And the price he paid was nothing more than a promise to remain neutral in the event of an Anglo-Russian war, which, in all probability, would be fought in Asia. The treaty was indeed a masterpiece and the German chancellor, repeatedly confronted with the problem of western as against eastern orientation, could never have asked for more than the maintenance of this combination of conservative great powers, dominating the continent and so powerful that it might conceivably have attracted into its orbit every other continental power. Diplomatically even England could be defeated at every turn by such a coalition, and it may well be doubted whether England could ever have successfully resisted it by force of arms.

Compared with the Three Emperors' Alliance the significance of the Triple Alliance of 1882 grows very dim. In its original form it was merely a side issue for Germany. Italy was not a great factor in international affairs nor was her military position a strong one. She had been treated shabbily enough by the other powers at Berlin in 1878 and had made the fatal error of opposing French policy in Tunis. In the crisis of 1881 the Italian statesmen learned to their consternation that the French had not only the English but the Germans behind them. Like the Russians in 1881 they were forced to seek protection, and, turning as supplicants to the only possible group, they were sent home from Vienna with little more than a promise of support in case of an attack by France. There was no guarantee of Rome and no assurance of support in Mediterranean aspirations. For years the Italians remained what they had been, essentially a negligible factor. On the other hand the Austrians were, by the treaty, assured of Italian neutrality in case of conflict with Russia, and Bismarck had the satisfaction of knowing that in the event of a French attack on Germany the Italian armies would at least engage a few army corps in the South, and that even if Germany were the aggressor the French would be obliged to leave an army of observation on the Italian frontier.

The early years of the 'eighties may with justice be called the years of triumph for Bismarck. His position was practically unassailable. In 1881 the Serbs, discontented with the preference shown by Russia for Bulgaria, concluded an alliance with Austria which made Serbia practically a protectorate of her neighbor for eight years. In 1883 Rumania, equally dissatisfied by the Russian policy in 1878 and dreading Russian influence to the South, also concluded a defensive agreement with Austria to which Germany adhered. Add to this the fact that Germany and France were on exceptionally good terms and that Bismarck was enabled to exploit this situation in order to lay the foundations of the German colonial empire, and it is difficult to see what more the great German statesman could desire. Safely secured on the continent by a network of reinsurance treaties he was able to guarantee the peace to Germany further by diverting potential trouble-makers to non-European fields. By sending the English to Egypt and thus embroiling them with France he established a control over English policy which he never again lost. One might almost say that by encouraging Russian activity in the Middle East and by protecting Russia against the consequences of her action he laid an equally firm hand on Russia's future policy. Never before or after did he have the balance so firmly in his control.

The weakness of the system lay in the fact that it was based on the hope that Austria and Russia would remain satisfied with a compromise in matters of the Near East. It was a problem over which no statesman had ever secured the mastery, and Bismarck was hardly more successful than his predecessors or successors. With the aspirations of the nationalities and the welter of interests a permanent solution always proved impossible, even by force of arms. The revolution at Philippopolis in September 1885 was the outcome of years of intriguing and subterranean wire-pulling, and when the explosion finally came it blew up the Three Emperors' Alliance and placed everything once more in jeopardy. What made the Bulgarian crisis of 1887 especially ominous for European peace was that it coincided with a reopening of the great problem of western Europe—that of Franco-German relations. The so-called Franco-German entente of the early 'eighties had been merely an interlude, a period of reason, a truce during which the two antagonists had shelved their great difference and had coöperated cordially and to their mutual advantage. With the fall of Ferry in March 1885 the situation had begun to change. The demons of revenge were once more in the ascendant and before long France was in the throes of the Boulangist movement.

As in the years 1875-1878 Bismarck at first did his utmost to patch over matters. Repeatedly he urged a territorial division of the Balkans into a Russian and an Austrian sphere of influence. But the Russians were skeptical and the Austrians flatly refused to entertain the suggestion. What began as a Bulgarian difficulty soon attained the magnitude of a first-rate European crisis, and before long every power—and they were all concerned, more or less—began to seek support for its own position. Bismarck, once more in a serious predicament, found himself assailed by both Austria and Russia, each demanding that the weight of his influence be utilized to turn the scales in her favor. At the same time the developments in the West called for uninterrupted attention.

The crucial stage in the situation was reached in August 1886, when the kidnapping of Prince Alexander of Bulgaria opened the whole question of that country's position and the problem of Russian influence in the Balkans. England, once more under a Conservative ministry, stood shoulder to shoulder with Austria in supporting the anti-Russian party in Bulgaria, while the Russians began preparations to assert what they considered their rights. Bismarck, as of old, sympathized with the aspirations of Germany's eastern neighbor and was out of patience with his Austrian ally, who rejected every reasonable suggestion of a compromise. He had no intention of embroiling himself with Russia or of allowing himself to be dragged at the chariot wheels of Austrian policy in the Near East, especially at a moment when trouble threatened from France and rumors were rife of Russian approaches to the French government for an alliance. The activities of Déroulède in France and of Katkov in Russia made it obvious that Russia, in order to safeguard her interests, might take a rash step. Never since 1870 had the war clouds lowered so threateningly both in the East and West.

Bismarck was ever on the watch to protect Germany from exploitation in the interest of others, but he was never loath to reverse the policy and engage others to shoulder a burden in order to relieve his own state. Certainly he never showed more resourcefulness than in 1887 and never exhibited so complete a mastery of ways and means. The expiration of the Triple Alliance and of the Three Emperors' Alliance gave him ample opportunity to put his ideas into practice. The guiding principle of his policy in these anxious months may be stated in very few words: to secure support for Austrian demands and interests elsewhere, and thus to make it possible to hold Russia by making the necessary concessions.

The first step was the consummation of the First Mediterranean Agreement concluded between England and Italy on February 12, 1887 and adhered to by Austria on March 24, 1887. The fundamental principle involved was the preservation of the *status quo* in the Mediterranean, Adriatic and Black Seas, while specifically Italy offered to support English policy in Egypt in return for an English promise of support for Italian policy in North Africa. Bismarck had sponsored the agreement, and its existence made it easier for him to satisfy the demands of the Italians, who, in view of the tension between Germany and France, meant to exploit the situation in order to obtain better terms under the treaty of the Triple Alliance.

According to the stipulations of the new treaty, as signed on February 20, 1887, the Austrians were obliged to promise the Italians compensation for any acquisitions made by Austria in the Balkans, while Germany promised to support Italy in her North African policy. Bismarck even went so far as to guarantee Italy support in case she felt obliged to take action against France, either in North Africa or in Europe, to forestall French action in the western Mediterranean. He furthermore promised not to object to Italy's seeking "territorial guarantees with respect to France for the security of the frontiers of the Kingdom and of her maritime position," which meant, of course, the annexation of Nice or Savoy. The concessions made by the German chancellor were, be it noted, practically illusory, for by securing the support of England for Italian interests in the Mediterranean he had made a Franco-Italian War more than unlikely, whereas by the renewal of the Triple Alliance he had retained Italy as an ally against France in case of serious developments. The *status quo* in the West was further strengthened by the exchange of notes between Italy and Spain on May 4, 1887, adhered to by Austria on May 21. Therewith a new satellite came into the system and France was deprived of one more possible ally, even though an insignificant one.

The great problem, however, was to maintain intact the wire to St. Petersburg. The Russians themselves realized that their interest lay in the alliance with Germany, but they obstinately refused to have anything more to do with Austria. The compromise as laid down in 1881 and renewed in 1884 had proved entirely unworkable, and they desired, if possible, to remain free in the future from any obligations to their rival in the South. Bismarck, naturally enough, would have preferred the old arrangement *à trois*, but in any case he could not afford to fly in the face of Russia or to drive her into the arms of France by refusing support to ambitions with which, at heart, he was in sympathy. He therefore agreed to a separate treaty between Germany and Russia, and after difficult negotiations the famous and much disputed Reinsurance Treaty was signed in Berlin on June 18, 1887.

In the debate which has gone on uninterruptedly since the publication of this treaty in 1918 scholars have frequently lost sight of the fact that the treaty really hinged on the problem of reinsurance. It was a security pact like that of 1881 and like most of the other Bismarckian agreements. In the original Russian draft provision was made for the maintenance of German neutrality in case Russia became involved in war with a third power, while Russia, on her part, made the same promise of neutrality in the event of war between Germany and a third power.

On the face of it this left the advantage with Russia, who was secured on her west flank in a war with either Austria or England or both, while Germany was protected in the East only in case of war with France. But Bismarck felt that the guarantee against war on two fronts was worth the difference. War between Germany and France was more threatening than an English or Austrian war with Russia, and he relied on his own statesmanship to prevent the latter contingency. In the later negotiations Bismarck was, of course, obliged to make a reservation for the eventuality of a Russian attack on Austria, in which case the *casus foederis* of the Austro-German Treaty of 1879 would have obtained. Thereupon the Russian negotiator insisted upon making the same reservation in respect to a German attack upon France. Bismarck was profoundly discouraged, but he set so high a value upon the promise of Russian neutrality in a French war of revenge against Germany, that he not only accepted the Russian redaction, but also the clauses by which Germany recognized Russia's rights in the Balkans (especially her preponderant and decisive influence in Bulgaria, and the principle of the closure of the Straits) and promised moral and diplomatic support in case the Tsar should deem it necessary to take steps to guard the entrance of the Black Sea, "the key to his Empire."

By the Reinsurance Treaty Bismarck had consolidated his position with regard to France. He could face developments in that quarter with equanimity, his only fear being that possibly the Tsar would be unable to resist the pressure of Katkov, the Panslavists and other Francophil groups in Russia, and be forced by public opinion to take the side of France, even if the latter were the aggressor. What had not yet been provided for adequately was the defense of Austrian interests against Russia. The Austrians were calling more and more loudly for German support, but this Bismarck had no intention of giving. He had refused it on earlier occasions and he meant to refuse it in the future. His theory had always been that Russia must find satisfaction somewhere, and that a compromise could be found which would satisfy the aspirations of the two rivals in the Balkans. He had recognized the Russian claims partly because it was necessary in order to prevent a Franco-Russian coalition and partly because he believed that the vital interests of Austria would not be impaired. All of which does not mean that he objected to Austria's maintaining her own views. What he insisted on was that Austria should not reckon on German support, but should seek the assistance of the powers whose interests were similar. His influence was at Austria's disposal in any attempt to attain this end, and it was largely due to his efforts that the Second Mediterranean Agreement was signed between England, Austria and Italy on December 12, 1887.

This document was much more specific than the earlier engagement. It dealt exclusively with the East and reaffirmed the maintenance of the *status quo*. Turkey was neither to cede her sovereign rights in Bulgaria nor her rights over the Straits. The three contracting powers agreed to assist the Porte in upholding these principles and in protecting the independence and integrity of the Turkish Empire. In case of adverse action by Turkey they agreed to occupy parts of the Ottoman territory to enforce respect for the principles laid down.

The Second Mediterranean Agreement was obviously directed against Russia and was intended to forestall action on her part. Bismarck had enlisted the aid of England and of his own allies in creating a situation by which he was relieved from fulfilling the promises he had made to Russia, just as, earlier in the year, England had been induced to support the Italian policy in the western Mediterranean. But both agreements were distinctly in the interest of the signatory powers. Bismarck had simply taken advantage of an existing community of interest. Therein lay his statesmanship. The year which had opened so ominously for Germany saw Bismarck, at its close, in complete mastery of the situation. Both France and Russia had been completely checkmated, peace was assured and the burden of maintaining it had been in large measure assigned to Germany's friends.

The winter of 1887-1888 was still critical, but appearances in this case were distinctly misleading. It was natural that the great powers, exhausted by a prolonged period of tension, should have been irritable. How much France or Russia knew of the Mediterranean agreements is not clear, but in any case they were aware of their existence. Both chafed and yet neither dared make a move. Subconsciously at least they felt that they were surrounded and that to stir would be fatal. As of old there was a tendency to lay the blame on Bismarck, and in this case at least the natural impulse was true. It was to be years before the bitterness and passion passed off, but the immediate danger was over, and when William II came to the throne in June 1888 he could safely rely on his great servant to protect the state and to guide it through the last stage of the crisis.

CHAPTER II

THE DÉBUT OF WILLIAM II

BISMARCK had been enabled to follow a consistent policy because he could, in the last resort, always rely on his master's approval. The old Emperor, imbued though he was with a profound belief in the value of Russian friendship, had been persuaded to assent to the Austro-German Treaty and had, on occasion, been induced to acquiesce in what seemed at times like a really hostile policy towards Russia. It was extremely unfortunate for Bismarck and for Germany that at a moment so crucial as that of the Bulgarian crisis two changes of ruler became necessary within the brief period of three months.

Frederick III, who succeeded his father in March 1888, was married to an English wife who had long exercised a powerful influence over him. Far from being Russophil, he dallied with the ideas of English liberalism and was generally reckoned a member of the group, composed chiefly of high military men, who were inclined to support Austria in the Near East and to seize the opportune moment to remove the Russian menace by force of arms.[1] Bismarck had never enjoyed the confidence of the new ruler and had every reason to fear complications. In the very first crown council under the presidency of the new Emperor he deemed it necessary to summarize his whole policy and to warn his master of the dangers involved in a change of front. Austria, he pointed out, must not take action until England could be induced to give up her traditional passivity, until the English cannon boomed on the Bosporus as they had in the Crimean War. But as a concession to the sentiments of Frederick he discreetly added that, if Austria nevertheless became involved in war with Russia, Germany might at first "play dead," but in

---

[1] On the attitude of Frederick III see the anonymous pamphlet: *Videant Consules ne quid Respublica Detrimenti capiat* (Cassel 1890) p. 38.

the end would be forced to intervene to prevent the annihilation of her ally and the disappearance of Austria as a great power.[2]

The chancellor's precautions were hardly necessary. Frederick was known to be mortally ill, and was wisely determined not to dismiss Bismarck and not to initiate a new policy during the brief lease of life which was given him. Being unable to speak, he nodded approval of Bismarck's remarks, though Prince William, the heir to the throne, listened attentively without giving a sign of assent.[3]

It was, indeed, an open secret in Berlin that the young Crown Prince adhered to the party of action, and this constituted the real danger to Bismarck's system.[4] The young heir, at that time only twenty-eight years old, was a problematical character, and had long caused anxiety to his parents. His early domestic life had been anything but happy and by the time he had reached manhood he found himself in open conflict with both father and mother. Both seemed to him too Anglophil, and by way of reaction he had drifted more and more into the point of view of his grandfather, which, in a modified way, was also that of Bismarck. In 1884 he had been sent on a special mission to the Tsar, and in the following years he had written to his autocratic cousin letters filled with passion and hatred of Russia's enemy, England.[5] But he had had no real training in foreign affairs. It was only with reluctance that his father, who evidently regarded him as mentally unbalanced and abnormally immature,

---

[2] Robert, Freiherr Lucius von Ballhausen: *Bismarck-Erinnerungen* (Stuttgart 1920) pp. 442-443. Similarly a despatch to Vienna, February 26, 1888: "Wir bleiben für Oesterreich sichere Bundesgenossen und können es in der Gefahr nicht im Stich lassen" (*Die Grosse Politik der europäischen Kabinette 1871-1914*, edited by Johannes Lepsius, Albrecht Mendelssohn Bartholdy and Friedrich Thimme. Berlin 1922-1926. [Hereafter cited as G. P.] Vol. X, p. 216 footnote).

[3] Lucius *loc. cit.*

[4] Fürst Chlodwig zu Hohenlohe-Schillingsfürst: *Denkwürdigkeiten* (Stuttgart 1907) II, pp. 428, 437.

[5] These letters are reprinted in the *Krasny Arkhiv* II, 1922, pp. 118-129. Extracts may be found in Sir Sidney Lee's: *Edward VII* vol. I (New York 1925), pp. 485, 510-511. On Prince William's visit to Russia in 1884 see G. P. III, nos. 631-632.

had consented to his receiving instruction at the foreign office.[6] Even then he was not drawn into affairs as he should have been, and, being easily led in spite of his autocratic leanings, he soon fell under the influence of the young army officers with whom he lived in comparative seclusion at Potsdam.[7]

The military circles were almost without exception pro-Austrian and anti-Russian in their outlook. They saw only the massing of Russian troops in Poland, and based their conclusions on the fanatically Germanophobe outbursts of the Russian press. Like their great master, Moltke, they believed in the advisability of a "preventive" war, and in the winter of 1887-88 had done all in their power to bring about a modification of the Austro-German Alliance to provide for German aid in an offensive war against Russia.[8] Prince William appears to have become converted to their view through the influence of Count Waldersee, the chief of staff, and largely as a result of a visit he paid to the Tsar at Brest Litovsk in September, 1886, from which he returned deeply impressed with the hostility of the Russians and with the error of Bismarck's policy.[9]

[6] Otto, Fürst von Bismarck: *Gedanken und Erinnerungen* III, (Stuttgart 1921) pp. 1 ff.

[7] See among others Eduard von Wertheimer: Ein k. und k. Militärattaché über das politische Leben in Berlin 1880-1893, (*Preussische Jahrbücher*, September 1925, p. 278).

[8] Graf Alfred von Waldersee: *Denkwürdigkeiten* I (Stuttgart 1922), pp. 331-356; Graf Alfred von Waldersee: *Aus dem Briefwechsel* (Berlin 1928) I, *passim*; Egon C. Corti: *Fürst Alexander von Battenberg* (Vienna 1920) p. 316; Philipp, Fürst zu Eulenburg-Hertefeld: *Aus 50 Jahren* (Berlin 1923) p. 153; and the documents printed in G. P. VI, chapter xxxviii. See also Wertheimer in *Preussische Jahrbücher*, September 1925, pp. 267-268.

[9] This is according to the Kaiser's own account: *Ereignisse und Gestalten 1878-1918* (Leipzig 1922) pp. 12-15. On the visit see G. P. V, no. 985. The actual conversion, however, seems to have come later, in 1887. Eulenberg p. 139, reported the Prince as still Russophil in June, 1887, and the Bismarck-Salisbury correspondence of November, 1887 (G. P. IV, nos. 930 ff.) shows that he was still so regarded in London. On the other hand the Prince was talking about the possibility of war with Russia in August, 1887 (Josef Maria von Radowitz: *Aufzeichnungen und Erinnerungen* [Berlin 1925] II, p. 274), and was said to have urged Bismarck in November 1887 not to allow the favorable moment for settling the score with Russia to slip by (Széchényi to Kálnoky, July 12, 1890, in the Vienna Archives, henceforth cited as V. A.). By December 1887 the Prince was already completely under the influence of Waldersee (Eulenburg p. 150).

The chancellor could hardly fail to note this development or to appreciate the necessity of leading back the heir to the throne to the true faith. Personally the relations between the two men left nothing to be desired, and so Bismarck was enabled to seize the earliest opportunity to set his young charge aright in a friendly but very serious fashion. William had made marginal notes on a despatch from Vienna of April 28, 1888, in which the German ambassador had reported on the prevailing pessimism in Austrian governmental circles. The Austrian minister, Count Kálnoky, believed that Russia's preparations in the West would be complete in one or two years, after which the pacific Russian foreign minister, M. de Giers, would be "blown" away and the war party in St. Petersburg would gain complete control over the Tsar. "Perhaps," he added, "the officers of the Austrian and German staffs were right after all when, last autumn, they advised the annihilation of Russia's forces before these could become too dangerous."[10] The comments of Prince William left no doubt that he held the same view. He did not believe that the Russians would go into the Balkan "trap" and regarded with the greatest scepticism the combinations devised by Bismarck to checkmate Russia.[11]

Bismarck's reply indicates how alarmed he was by these sentiments. He pointed out that if, on the Emperor's death, German policy were to be changed so radically, a different attitude must be adopted toward Russia immediately. Germany must seek to provoke a war as soon as possible. The prince quailed somewhat before this exposition of the consequences, but in his reply to Bismarck, which, characteristically, he first submitted to Waldersee, he still insisted that, if the domestic developments in Russia were to make the Tsar powerless, Russia and France would inevitably come together and war would then be certain as soon as the two powers felt themselves sufficiently prepared. "Under the circumstances," he added, "the value of

[10] This, and the other documents mentioned in this connection, may be found in G. P. VI, nos. 1339-1341.

[11] Though in November 1887 Bismarck had written to Salisbury that the English-Italian-Austrian entente had the full approval of Prince William (G. P. IV, no. 930).

Germany's allies becomes greater and greater. To bind them to us without allowing them to influence us will be the great and, I admit, the difficult task of a wise German policy."[12]

The exchange of notes on this occasion is of supreme importance. In Prince William's marginalia and especially in his reply to Bismarck's comments may be found the germs of his own future policy. They go a long way towards explaining the events of the next two years, and it is to be particularly noted that in no sense do they indicate a conversion to the Bismarckian view. Waldersee himself might have written the reply to Bismarck, and no one appreciated the fact more thoroughly than the chancellor himself. Apparently he was at a loss to know just what to do. It seems that it was at this time that he communicated to the Crown Prince and to some of the leaders of the military group the provisions of the Reinsurance Treaty, in order to convince them of the improbability of a Franco-Russian Alliance, at least until the expiration of the treaty in June, 1890.[13] It would even appear that, for a moment, he considered forcing the issue by provoking France, while Russian neutrality could still be relied upon.[14] In any case new and more stringent passport regulations were introduced in Alsace-Lorraine, and when the Italians, fearing an attack on Spezzia by the French fleet, appealed for help he sent |to |Paris |a warning couched in unnecessarily sharp terms.[15]

For the moment, however, the crisis passed away. The accession of William II in June, 1888 in no way endangered the chancellor's position, and he hoped, so long as he could retain it, to be able to defend his policy against the intrigue and sub-

[12] The Prince's reply was first published in Bismarck's *Gedanken und Erinnerungen* III, pp. 136 ff. Cf. the draft as given in Waldersee: *Denkwürdigkeiten* I, pp. 395-398.

[13] There is no indication that Prince William knew of the treaty prior to May 1888 (G. P. VI, no. 1341). Waldersee also knew of it (See Aus den Erinnerungen des Generalfeldmarschalls Grafen Waldersee, *Deutsche Revue*, June 1921, p. 222).

[14] Waldersee: *Denkwürdigkeiten* I, pp. 387, 399, 400, 401, and the very interesting utterances of Bismarck on May 13 in Lucius p. 452.

[15] G. P. VI, nos. 1278-1281; Francesco Crispi: *Memoirs* (New York 1913) II, pp. 293, 349; Hohenlohe II, pp. 434-435; Lord George Hamilton: *Parliamentary Reminiscences and Reflections, 1886-1906* (London 1922)., pp. 139-140.

terranean machinations of the hostile group.[16] At first he began by humoring his new sovereign. The speech from the throne in June contained a reference to the Austro-German Alliance as an inheritance of German history, while no particular mention was made of Russia.[17] At the same time Bismarck permitted the mission of Waldersee to Vienna to announce the accession of the new Emperor, and raised no objection to the exchange of warm letters between Berlin and Vienna.[18] The result was that he succeeded in persuading his master to pay his first visit, not to Francis Joseph, but to Alexander III. In the masterly instructions drawn up for William's guidance he strongly emphasized the necessity of upholding the Austrian alliance, but also insisted that Russia must not be unnecessarily antagonized, and that Russian designs on Constantinople and the Bosporus must not be opposed so long as Austria was not directly menaced by them. Herbert Bismarck was sent along to see that no *faux pas* were made.[19]

Outwardly, and in its strictly personal aspect, the visit was undoubtedly a success, but William returned more distrustful of Russian policy than ever.[20] Though he may have subscribed

[16] On Waldersee's views see Eissenstein's report of November 5, 1887 in Wertheimer (*Preussische Jahrbücher*, September 1925, p. 268), in addition to Waldersee's *Denkwürdigkeiten* and *Briefwechsel*. Waldersee somewhat later summarized his political views as follows: "Mein politisches Glaubensbekenntnis geht einfach dahin für Deutschland so lange als möglich die Segnungen des Friedens erhalten zu sehen und gerade zu diesem Zweck scheint es mir unumgänglich notwendig unsere Beziehungen zu Oesterreich-Ungarn immer intimer zu gestalten und einer Macht wie Russland unausgesetzt zu mistrauen da wir doch alle wissen dass fast alle Männer in massgebenden Stellungen in Petersburg wie in Moscow einen Kampf gegen Oesterreich-Ungarn und Deutschland als einen heiligen Krieg ansehen würden" (Eissenstein to Kálnoky, August 15, 1890 in V. A.).

[17] Wilhelm Schüssler: *Bismarcks Sturz* (Leipzig 1921) p. 197. Lucius p. 468, says that as Bismarck read the draft to the ministers his regret that he could not say more for Russia was very evident.

[18] G. P. VI, no. 1342. The correspondence is reprinted in the *Neue Freie Presse* July 31 and August 7, 1921. See also Waldersee: *Denkwürdigkeiten* I, pp. 407-410.

[19] Bismarck's instructions in G. P. VI, no. 1343.

[20] On the success of the visit see the reports of Herbert Bismarck and of General von Schweinitz (G. P. VI, nos. 1345-1347). Also Lucius p. 477; Hohenlohe II, pp. 445, 446, 449; J. F. Baddeley: *Russia in the 'Eighties'* (London

to Bismarck's theory that Russia would be weakened rather than
strengthened by the possession of Constantinople and the Bosporus, he appears to have feared that the Russian attack would
be by land as well as by sea, and that it would involve the re-
appearance of a Russian army in Bulgaria, to the detriment of
Austrian interests. Bismarck agreed that the Russians undoubtedly were planning an assault on the Turkish capital and
that the necessary military and naval preparations would be
complete by 1890, though he refused to believe that the attempt
would be made until the international situation was favorable,
and doubted whether an advance through Bulgaria would be
essayed.[21]

The question hung fire for the time being, but as the winter
of 1888-1889 drew near the old fear of an attack by Russia in
the spring once more became dominant in the official circles
of Berlin. Outwardly the relations between Germany and Russia
had in no way improved since 1887. The Russians had forbidden
foreigners to acquire land in Russia and had passed various other
measures of Russification which were obviously directed at the
German influence. Bismarck had replied by a regulation forbidding the Imperial Bank to accept Russian securities as col-
lateral. In Poland the concentration of Russian troops continued, and on both sides of the frontier the newspapers were
engaged in accusations and recriminations. Certain it is that
the note of intimacy, cordiality and confidence had gone out of
Russo-German relations, and nothing but cold self-interest
remained as the basis of the alliance.

The Russians were still unable to free themselves from the
feeling that Germany should do something positive to solve the
Bulgarian question in their favor, and the Tsar appears to have
believed that, after the imperial visit, German policy would be

1921) p. 402. On the Kaiser's distrust see Bismarck: *Gedanken und Erinner-
ungen* III, p. 142; Eulenburg p. 201. The same attitude is reflected by B.
Bülow's remark to Take Jonescu towards the end of 1888 (Take Jonescu: *Some
Personal Impressions* [New York 1920] p. 207).

   [21] Bismarck to William II, August 19, 1888 (G. P. VI, no. 1350).

more obliging.[22] When these hopes proved illusory the Russian government continued its armaments with redoubled vigor and began to negotiate a large conversion loan in Paris. Even General von Schweinitz, who was cool-headed and a sincere friend of Russia, began to fear for the future, and Bismarck himself seems to have been genuinely alarmed.[23] The danger, as he saw it, was not so much from a direct Russian attack, as from a victory of Boulangism in France, resulting in a war of revenge against Germany, in which Russian public opinion would force the Tsar to participate.[24] The German chancellor had little confidence in the support to be expected from Austria and Italy[25] and in January 1889 he instructed Count Hatzfeldt, the German ambassador at London, to make direct overtures to Lord Salisbury suggesting a defensive alliance against France to be concluded for three years.[26]

It may well be doubted whether he even hoped for a favorable reply, but there can be little question that in case of acceptance he would have considered the situation saved. He suggested that the treaty be submitted to the English parliament, and thus made public in order to leave in the minds of the French no doubt that Germany and England would stand shoulder to shoulder in case of an attack directed against either. The English reply was evasive, as might have been expected, but with the failure of this attempt Bismarck believed it more than ever

[22] Eygermont's reports from St. Petersburg, August 13 and 27 1888 (Wilhelm Köhler: *Revanche-idee und Panslawismus* [Berlin 1919] pp. 239-244). Also Pourtalès to Bismarck, October 9, 1888 (G. P. VI, no. 1353).

[23] Waldersee: *Denkwürdigkeiten* II, pp. 17, 19, 28. Cf. also Radowitz II, p. 290.

[24] G. P. IV, no. 943. On the whole subject of the war-scare in the spring of 1889 see the interesting discussion in Gaetano Salvemini: *La Politica Estera di Francesco Crispi* (Rome 1919) pp. 61 ff.

[25] In October 1888 Herbert Bismarck told the Council that the basis of the Austrian alliance was crumbling because the alliance was losing its internal strength (Lucius p. 480). See the similar statement made later by Reuss: "Fürst Bismarck hielt wenig von der Bundestüchtigkeit Oesterreichs, und sah in diesem Bündnis nicht das Äquivalent für die Gefahren, denen wir, zwischen Russland und Frankreich eingeklemmt, ausgesetzt sein könnten" (G. P. VII, no. 1381.).

[26] For the negotiations see G. P. IV, nos. 942 ff. Also Waldersee: *Denkwürdigkeiten* II, pp. 38, 39, 47.

necessary to secure the neutrality of Russia. Waldersee and
others actually believed that he was inclined to drop Austria
entirely and draw still closer to Russia.[27] The victory of the
Russophil parties in Rumania and Serbia in the spring of 1889,
followed by the Tsar's toast of May 30, 1889, in which he referred to the Prince of Montenegro as his only true and faithful
friend, led to a general feeling in the West that Russia was preparing for action.[28] Various expedients were suggested. Crispi, the
Italian premier, favored the establishment of a Balkan league
consisting of Serbia, Bulgaria and Rumania, while the Kaiser
was disposed to encourage the Turks to resist Russian influence.[29]
But Bismarck refused to change his views in regard to Russian
policy in the East. Here he was, as ever, disposed to favor the
Tsarist aspirations, especially as their realization would alleviate
the danger of a Franco-Russian Alliance. Unfortunately for
him he made no secret of his attitude, and did not even attempt
to conceal his views about Austrian policy. Thus he incurred
the outspoken hostility of those who distrusted Russia and who
believed in bolstering up the existing alliances.[30] Late in May
the Kaiser declared that Bismarck was taking the matter too
lightly: "If Bismarck is unwilling to act against the Russians,
our ways must part. I have already told him through Herbert
that my patience with Russia is at an end."

The test of strength came in the summer of 1889. The Russian
government, desiring to convert an issue of railroad bonds,

[27] Waldersee: *Denkwürdigkeiten* II, pp. 36 ff. On January 21, 1889 Waldersee writes in his journal: "Der Kanzler hofft, sich Russland nähern und Oesterreich fallen lassen zu können." Similarly Bismarck's observations to Schweinitz
in October 1888 (*Briefwechsel* p. 256).

[28] Lucius p. 493, reports Bismarck's uneasiness. Cf. also Radowitz II, p.
296, and Waldersee: *Denkwürdigkeiten* II, pp. 43, 45; the Belgian reports printed
in Köhler pp. 257-259; and Villaume's report of June 4, 1889 (G. P. VI, no. 1356).

[29] Crispi II, pp. 379-386. Waldersee: *Denkwürdigkeiten* II, pp. 14, 52.
Eulenburg p. 224. Radowitz II, p. 296 found Waldersee and other military men
convinced of the necessity of war with Russia and fearful lest Bismarck, grown too
old to change his views, would allow the favorable moment to pass. The Kaiser
posed as the leader of this group.

[30] Radowitz II, p. 297. Cucchi, on a mission to Berlin in July, noted in Bismarck "a certain coldness toward Austria" (Crispi II, p. 413). See also Hohenlohe
II, p. 456, and especially Eulenburg p. 284; Schweinitz: *Briefwechsel* pp. 256-257.

wished to have them admitted to the Berlin exchange. Bismarck could see no reason for refusing their quotation, and felt that a prohibition would be the equivalent of a slap in the face for Russia. The Kaiser, on the other hand, supported by Waldersee, maintained that the German people must not be allowed to supply the enemy with money for additional armaments which, it appeared to him, were destined for use against the central powers. Bismarck, in seclusion at Varzin, could do nothing to counteract the influences which were working against him. In his letter to Bötticher of June 26 he pleads that good relations with Russia be maintained at least until the German armaments could be completed and, if possible, until England were better prepared and her coöperation could be counted upon with certainty. It was all of no avail. Bismarck was given to understand that his policy was too "Russophil."[31] All he could do was to open another attack on Waldersee in the semi-official press.

In August the Kaiser paid a visit to England and was accorded an unprecedented reception. The English statesmen, no less disturbed by the designs of Russia than were other statesmen of western Europe, made every effort to encourage the young sovereign in his suspicions or to win him over to the English point of view.[32] Knowing his great interest in naval affairs they flattered him by an appointment as admiral of the fleet. From this time on the Kaiser, who hitherto had been anti-Russian, became pro-English as well. In expressing his appreciation he referred to the English fleet as the greatest in the world, and one "which, if the political situation should require it, would be able to force its way through the Dardanelles."[33] Bismarck hardly

---

[31] This incident is well treated in Schüssler p. 38. See further Georg, Freiherr von Eppstein: *Bismarcks Entlassung* (Berlin 1920) pp. 95-118; Bismarck: *Gedanken und Erinnerungen* III, p. 142. Waldersee's influence comes out distinctly in his *Denkwürdigkeiten* II, pp. 54-60, and *Briefwechsel* I, pp. 297 ff. See also the exhaustive treatment of this point in Ernst Gagliardi: *Bismarcks Entlassung* (Tübingen 1927) vol. I, pp. 245 ff., based in part on unpublished reports.

[32] On the Kaiser's early Anglophobia and the friction resulting from attempts made by the English royal family to interfere in German domestic affairs in 1888 see Lee: *Edward VII* vol. I, pp. 262, 365, 484, 485, 643-653.

[33] On being notified of the appointment William exclaimed: "It is enough to make me quite giddy." His letter of appreciation, dated August 17, 1889, is re-

exaggerates when he says in his reminiscences: "The uniform of admiral of the fleet may be regarded as the symbol of a new chapter in the foreign policy of the Empire."[34]

It may be safely said that by this time the chancellor no longer had a real hold on his master. When and how the decisive conflict would arise was merely a matter of time and chance. Bismarck even then seems not to have believed that he would be dismissed, but Sir Charles Dilke, who visited him in September, found the great man "evidently discontented with the emperor" and apparently on "bad terms" with him, while the minister, Lucius von Ballhausen, an unusually keen observer, wrote in October that the chancellor's position was no longer as secure and influential as it had been in the time of William I.[35] Waldersee, on the other hand, noted with glee that the Kaiser had become quite convinced that nothing could be done with Russia by peaceful means, and quoted the following statement made by his sovereign: "I have formed my opinion and no longer speak with the chancellor about it, for he has his own view and we can no longer agree."[36]

That the real state of affairs was not unknown abroad is shown by what transpired during the visit of Alexander III to Berlin in October. The Tsar came "imbued with the idea that Germany was preparing an attack against him."[37] The Kaiser's trip to England and his plan to go to Constantinople, as well as the recent visit of Francis Joseph to Berlin, had made him very suspicious. He feared that Germany had allied herself with England and that an alliance with Turkey was projected to complete the coalition, the ultimate object of which was to attack Russia. Austrian policy in Bulgaria appeared to him as

printed in Lee pp. 653-656, where a full account of the visit is given. The letter did not become known until later (Hohenlohe II, p. 465), but the essentials of the text were reported by Széchényi to Kálnoky, April 26, 1890 (in V. A.).

[34] Bismarck: *Gedanken und Erinnerungen* III, p. 146.

[35] Stephen Gwynn and Gertrude M. Tuckwell: *The Life of the Rt. Hon. Sir Charles Dilke* (New York 1917) II, pp. 305-306; Lucius p. 503.

[36] Waldersee: *Denkwürdigkeiten* II, p. 69.

[37] Greindl report October 23, 1889 (Köhler pp. 264-265). For the Tsar's early suspicions of the Kaiser see *ibid.* pp. 218, 227, 229.

the preliminary of an occupation of Serbia.[38] His suspicions centered on the military influences in Berlin and he complained bitterly to Bismarck, especially of Waldersee, whose name is said to have passed the imperial lips no less than eight times in the course of the conversation. The Tsar furthermore expressed doubts regarding Bismarck's continuance in office.[39] The chancellor did his best to reassure his visitor, and reiterated his indifference to Balkan affairs.[40] Apparently he succeeded in convincing Alexander of his own intentions and set his mind at rest in regard to German policy so long as he was at the helm.[41]

Even though the international situation was but little altered by Alexander's visit, the relations between the Kaiser and his chancellor were profoundly affected and again took a turn for the worse. William, at first rather uncompromising in his attitude, yielded to the representations of Bismarck and went to the other extreme. Imbued with great confidence in his own personal magnetism he hoped to accomplish by himself what the statesmanship of his minister had hardly succeeded in bringing about. Carried away for the moment by the Tsar's cordiality in leaving, he invited himself to the Russian manoeuvres in the following summer.[42] Bismarck, when the news was broken to him, immediately remonstrated, because, so he tells us, he realized the in-

---

[38] Bismarck to Solms, Hatzfeldt and Reuss, October 15, 1889 (G. P. VI, no. 1358); O. Gradenwitz: *Bismarcks Letzter Kampf* (Berlin 1924) pp. 64-66, quoting letters of Marschall; Radowitz II, pp. 300 ff.; L. Raschdau: Zur Vorgeschichte des Rückversicherungsvertrages, in *Deutsche Rundschau* May 1924, p. 126.).

[39] Lucius p. 504; Waldersee: *Denkwürdigkeiten* II, pp. 70-73; Gradenwitz pp. 64-66; Bismarck in the *Neue Freie Presse*, June 23, 1892.

[40] Lucius p. 504; Greindl report October 23, 1889 (Köhler pp. 264-265).

[41] Bismarck himself doubted whether the Tsar would be able to resist the influence of Pobiedonostsev "und Consorten" (Brauer, Marcks, Müller: *Erinnerungen an Bismarck* [Stuttgart 1915] p. 59; Gradenwitz p. 65.).

[42] Bismarck: *Gedanken und Erinnerungen* III, pp. 144-145; Hermann Hofmann: *Fürst Bismarck 1890-1898* (Leipzig 1914) vol. I, p. 16; G. Egelhaaf: *Geschichte der Neuesten Zeit* (Stuttgart 1920) I, p. 229 (on information from Herbert Bismarck); Waldersee *Denkwürdigkeiten* II, p. 72; Eulenburg p. 286; General von Schweinitz: *Denkwürdigkeiten* (Berlin 1927) II, p. 392. The personal intercourse of the two rulers is reported by Lerchenfeld, March 29, 1890 (*Süddeutsche Monatshefte* December 1921, p. 171). Wolkenstein to Kálnoky, December 18, 1889 (in V. A.) reports Schweinitz as saying: "Der Kaiser war anfänglich zu schroff und steif, später viel zu liebenswürdig und entgegenkommend."

compatibility in the character of the two men and feared misunderstandings would arise if they were too much in each other's
company. The Kaiser, who had honestly tried to please his
chancellor, was extremely irritated, for he expected to be praised
for his efforts to conciliate the Tsar.[43] Evidently he felt that the
old man could not be satisfied and that he would raise objections
to anything that was done without consulting him.[44] Immediately after this incident William left for Athens and Constantinople, despite Bismarck's objections.[45] During the trip he
repeatedly sent glowing telegrams to the chancellor, but these,
like his hearty New Year's greetings of January 1, 1890, in no
way indicate a change in attitude towards Bismarck's policy.
At best they show a desire to maintain friendly personal relations.

We know that the Kaiser's visit to the Near East was not
inspired by hopes of a political nature. He had long been anxious
to acquaint himself with the terrain and the conditions, and he
took a keen interest in the military and naval situation in the
eastern Mediterranean.[46] Without a doubt his sympathies were
with those who opposed the Tsarist advance on Constantinople,
but it is hardly likely that he had any clear conception as to
what attitude the Germans should take. His meeting with the
Prince of Wales at Athens, his inspection of the English squadron
at the Piraeus and finally his sojourn at Yildiz were distinct
tactical errors.[47] Despite Bismarck's assurances the Tsar's suspicions were aroused and he made no effort to conceal his irritation. He sent no New Year's greetings and made disparaging

[43] Bismarck: *Gedanken und Erinnerungen* III, pp. 144-145; Hofmann I,
pp. 16 ff.; Egelhaaf I, p. 229.

[44] On October 26 the Kaiser's uncle, the Grand Duke of Baden, told Hohenlohe
that his nephew was thoroughly sick of Bismarck (Hohenlohe II, p. 459).

[45] Wilhelm II: *Ereignisse und Gestalten* p. 23; Bismarck's account to Lvov
(*Novoie Vremia* May 10, 1890); E. Jäckh: *Kiderlen-Wächter* (Stuttgart 1924)
I, p. 88.

[46] The Kaiser had been intent on a trip to the East as early as 1885, and had
been encouraged by Radowitz, the ambassador in Constantinople. On this whole
subject see Radowitz: *Aufzeichnungen* II, pp. 249, 287, 288, 294, 300-307.

[47] At Athens and on later occasions the Kaiser pointed out to the Prince of
Wales that the English Mediterranean squadron was insufficient and inferior to
the French (Lee: *Edward VII* vol. I, pp. 657-658).

remarks about his fellow-sovereign, whom he described as "an ill-bred and faithless youngster."[48] Sooner or later these utterances found their way to Berlin, and Bismarck considered it his duty to withhold from his master all reports which might serve to increase the tension. It was dangerous strategy, however, for while Bismarck was in retirement on his estates, Waldersee and Holstein, one of the undersecretaries who had surreptitiously left the Bismarckian fold, saw to it that the young ruler was always well-supplied with material of an inflammatory nature. Waldersee received private reports of Russian troop movements and these, together with political correspondence and newspaper clippings furnished by Holstein, he submitted to the Kaiser.[49]

It was just at this time, in January, 1890, that the conflict between the Kaiser and his chancellor regarding domestic policies was coming to a head. It is unnecessary to enter upon the various phases of a crisis which lasted intermittently until Bismarck's dismissal in March. It need only be recalled that the fundamental difference of opinion which antedated the whole dispute about social legislation and ministerial procedure necessarily contributed to making the breach an irreparable one. It is one of the ironies of fate that the conflict should have come at a moment when the foreign policy of the empire called for a momentous decision. The famous Reinsurance Treaty was due to expire in June, 1890 and negotiations had already been opened by the Russians. The Tsar had apparently decided in favor of renewal as early as December, 1889, and on February 10, 1890, Count Shuvalov, the ambassador at Berlin, scenting the danger of Bismarck's fall, had discussed the matter with the German chancellor.[50] Bismarck expressed his complete satisfaction with

---

[48] Bismarck: *Gedanken und Erinnerungen* III, pp. 83-85 indicates that even worse things were said. See also Waldersee: *Denkwürdigkeiten* II, pp. 116-117.

[49] The wisdom of Bismarck's policy in this respect may well be questioned. At any rate the Kaiser had a just grievance, for important despatches from St. Petersburg, Vienna and Bucharest were withheld. See especially Schweinitz II, p. 402; Eulenburg pp. 224 286, 289, and Waldersee: *Denkwürdigkeiten* II, pp. 85-89 *passim*; also Waldersee: Erinnerungen (*Deutsche Revue* June 1921, pp. 222, 223).

[50] It had been decided by the Russians to open negotiations in April. See S. Goriainov: The End of the Alliance of the Three Emperors (*American Historical*

the treaty and suggested its indefinite continuation, because, he said, the text of the agreement is "the expression of a fixed and unchanging situation."[51] The Kaiser was informed of this conversation and gave his consent to the renewal.[52] The question immediately arises: Why was this consent given, when the Kaiser was notoriously anti-Russian and was half disposed to take measures to support Russia's enemies? The answer is not easy, and one is driven to the conclusion that William's attitude was entirely due to his own uncertainty. He had no coherent plan to suggest as a substitute for Bismarck's policy and when the time for decision came he wavered and then yielded.[53]

A month later the crisis recurred in an even more violent form. During the acrimonious debate between the Kaiser and his chancellor on March 15 the tension was at its height, and at that very moment the problem of foreign policy once again came to the fore. The uneasiness which had been prevalent in Berlin military circles ever since 1887 had, if anything, been on the increase since the beginning of 1890.[54] Large conversions of the Russian debt were being carried out, and on February 23 it was announced that in Paris the new issue had been oversubscribed some seven or eight times.[55] The German ambassador at St. Petersburg reported that the result of the various conversions since 1888 was that the Russian ministry of finance had at its disposal over 200,000,000 marks in cash, which was to be deposited in London and Berlin, subject to immediate withdrawal when called for. While it was recognized that the purpose of this fund was to raise the value of the ruble, it was feared that

---

Review January 1918, pp. 340-341); V. N. Lamsdorf: *Dnievnik, 1886-1890* (Moscow 1926) pp. 226, 239, 247 ff. and G. P. VII, p. 3 footnote; Schweinitz II, p. 397.

[51] Goriainov p. 342.

[52] Herbert Bismarck to William II, March 20, 1890 (G. P. VII, no. 1367).

[53] This is the view advanced by Wilhelm Mommsen: Bismarcks Sturz (*Archiv für Politik und Geschichte* vol. I, 1923, pp. 483-484.).

[54] See especially Eulenburg p. 286, who notes, on January 8, 1890, that much alarm was felt in the German embassy at St. Petersburg and refers to a letter from Reuss expressing the fear that Russia would attempt to reach a separate agreement with Austria against Germany.

[55] Schulthess: *Europäischer Geschichtskalendar* 1890, p. 282. *London Times* March 3, 1890.

the military circles in Russia regarded it merely as a war fund and that, in a critical moment, the minister of finance might lose all control over its disposition.[56] The international atmosphere was charged with rumors. It was generally expected that Russia's naval and military preparations would be complete in the spring. She had a numerical superiority of some 90,000 men in Poland[57] and was massing troops on the Rumanian front.[58] England strengthened her Mediterranean force and Rumania decided to reorganize the defences of Bucharest, while all Europe waited breathlessly to see if the visit of the Serbian premier, Pašič, to St. Petersburg would result in the formation of a Balkan league directed against Austria.[59]

Such was the situation when, on March 15, a bundle of twenty reports arrived in Berlin from Raffauf, the German consul in Kiev. He had long been one of the government's chief sources of information and the letters were immediately submitted to Bismarck, who, on the following day, sent five of them, dealing with military matters, to the Kaiser. One of them, dated March 3, reported the preparations being made for the summer manoeuvres in Volhynia. Others were of earlier date, and from this the Kaiser concluded that they had been withheld from him. Enraged at Bismarck he sat down and penned a most extraordinary note. The Russian menace, he declared in his marginalia, was greater than any ever made by one state against another in time

[56] Széchényi to Kálnoky, March 15, 1890 and, after a talk with Berchem, March 16, 1890 (in V. A.).

[57] *London Times*, February 15, 25, and March 17, 1890.

[58] *London Times*, February 21, 1890.

[59] Even the Turkish government gave orders that four first-class ironclads be fitted for active service immediately. Pašič was received in St. Petersburg by the Tsar and by Giers. He was reported to have said that Russian statesmen had assured him of Russia's intention of soon showing her good will "by acts." The *Times* correspondent in Vienna reported that "Pašič is engaged in nothing less than a conspiracy against the monarchy." On all this see especially G. P. IX, nos. 2073-2094 *passim*, and the *London Times*, January 29, March 1, 13, 14, 1890; *Saturday Review* March 15, 1890; *Spectator* March 15, 1890. In an interesting article in the *Nouvelle Revue* for February 1, 1890 de Hutin predicted that the Russians would begin by an attack on Afghanistan, where they could easily defeat England.

of peace. The Russians, he believed, could march to Vienna without meeting serious opposition:

> "It is perfectly clear from the reports that the Russians are strategically concentrating their forces and are on the point of declaring war. I deeply regret that so few of the Kievan reports were sent to me. You might have called my attention to this dreadful menace long ago. It is high time to warn the Austrians and to take countermeasures. Under the circumstances my trip to Krasnoe is, of course, out of the question. The reports are excellent."[60]

Bismarck replied to this outburst immediately and at some length, attempting to show that the Russians had been concentrating troops for at least three years and that this did not constitute a menace to Germany. Austria, he argued, no doubt had more reliable information on these matters than the German consul at Kiev, and furthermore the Austrian government had already taken extensive precautionary measures in the past. In view of the pending negotiations for the renewal of the Reinsurance Treaty Bismarck insisted that there was no cause for uneasiness.

It is clear that Bismarck had no faith whatsoever in the rumors of an attack to be launched on Germany or Austria. Along with others he expected the Russians to take action in 1890, but not to the west or southwest. In his opinion the Russians would choose the sea route, against the Bosporus, Constantinople or even Bulgaria.[61] In any event he relied upon the English and Italians to assist the Austrians if they felt called upon to oppose such an advance. In fact, he felt certain that even the French would object to a Russian attack on Constantinople.[62]

[60] On the whole incident see Bismarck: *Gedanken und Erinnerungen* III, pp. 88 ff., 100; G. P. VI, nos. 1360-1362; Eppstein pp. 183 ff., 193; Lerchenfeld p. 161; J. von Eckardt: *Aus den Tagen von Bismarcks Kampf gegen Caprivi* (Leipzig 1920) p. 51; Eulenburg p. 236; Gradenwitz pp. 61, 160-161; Scholz: *Erlebnisse* pp. 111 ff.

[61] Bismarck to William II, August 19, 1888 (G.P. VI, no. 1350); Hohenlohe II, p. 461 (December 18, 1889). That he still thought so in 1891 appears from the *Hamburger Nachrichten* April 10, 1891 (in Hofmann I, pp. 349-350).

[62] Hohenlohe II, p. 461; Bismarck to William II, August 19, 1888 (G. P. VI, nos. 1206, 1343, 1350); Berchem memorandum March 25, 1890 (G. P. VII, no. 1368). Cf. Hans Rothfels: Zur Geschichte des Rückversicherungsvertrages

But it seems that Bismarck took the whole matter too serious-ly. The evidence would indicate that the Kaiser's note was only the first of several extraordinary actions for which he was re-sponsible in the following days. It is almost impossible to say whether he was playing a well-considered game with the avowed intention of getting rid of the chancellor, or whether he had by this time entirely lost his head.[63] Given the character of William II one would incline to the latter view and point out that the genuineness of his alarm is proved by the fact that the reports were turned over to the general staff and copies sent to Vienna for communication to Count Kálnoky.[64] On the other hand the serenity of the Emperor during the following days lends color to the hypothesis that his note was merely a tactical move. Bismarck's reply was convincing, but no attention was paid to it. The equanimity of the ruler was positively appalling. On the evening of this very day, while awaiting Bismarck's resignation, the Kaiser turned the pages while Count Eulenburg sang Norse ballads. He interrupted only once in order to whisper: "Now the resignation has arrived." Then the singing continued.[65]

The break had, indeed, become complete. Bismarck, who had originally considered laying down all his offices excepting control of foreign affairs, was forced by the incident of the Kiev reports, to

---

(*Preussische Jahrbücher* March 1922, p. 281) and the same author's *Bismarcks englische Bündnispolitik* (Stuttgart 1924) p. 102.

[63] Bismarck himself believed he had convinced his master (G. P. VI, no. 1362) but, from the fact that no attention was paid to him, Gradenwitz (p. 162) argues the first explanation with some effect. The Kaiser himself told Schweinitz at the time that he had suffered greatly and that his hair had turned gray (Schwei-nitz II, p. 402). Later he wrote Francis Joseph that he had spent many sleepless nights thinking of the dismissal. Shuvalov, the Russian ambassador, on the other hand, could not avoid asking himself whether the young emperor "was in his normal state" (Goriainov p. 343).

[64] G. P. VI, no. 1360 footnote. Evidently they made no effect. It is interest-ing to note that even after Bismarck's dismissal Kálnoky did not regard the Rus-sian troop movements with serious apprehension though he shared the belief that an assault upon Constantinople might be tried (Radowitz II, p. 327; G. P. IX, no. 2074).

[65] Eulenburg p. 237. Of course he was mistaken when he believed the resig-nation had actually arrived.

give up even this plan.[66] Since his resignation of the foreign
ministry placed the future of the Russian treaty in jeopardy this
development must have been a particularly severe blow. This
perhaps accounts for the fact that in later years the international aspect of the crisis rankled most in his mind.[67] On the
afternoon of this same eventful 17th of March he explained to
the cabinet that, quite aside from domestic affairs, he could no
longer retain his position because he could not subscribe to the
Kaiser's policy towards Russia.[68] In his resignation he states
the situation very clearly: "I could not," he declares, "retain
even the ministry of foreign affairs after the recent decisions arrived at by Your Majesty, for by so doing I should be calling
into question all the successes obtained in our Russian policy
during the reigns of your two predecessors, in spite of unfavorable
circumstances."[69]

As a matter of fact the Kaiser had no new Russian policy to
suggest. To be sure he found it desirable to strengthen his own
position by emphasizing the disagreement, especially in speaking
to the military men. On the evening of March 18 he told his
commanders "that Russia is about to occupy Bulgaria with
military forces and desires the neutrality of Germany," but that
he had promised the Austrian Emperor that he would be a faithful ally and that he would keep his word. The occupation of
Bulgaria would mean war with Austria and he did not intend to

[66] The plan was considered during the crisis in February (Lucius pp. 510-
512; Széchényi to Kálnoky, February 7 and 13, 1890, in V. A.).

[67] O. Hammann: *Zur Vorgeschichte des Weltkrieges* (Berlin 1919) pp. 43-44;
Deutsche Weltpolitik (Berlin 1925) p. 35. According to Herbert the chancellor
refused to resign voluntarily because he was anxious to wind up the matter of the
treaty (Radowitz II, p. 314).

[68] Bismarck: *Gedanken und Erinnerungen* III, p. 92; Lucius pp. 522-523;
Gradenwitz p. 149; Scholz pp. 110 ff. Bismarck gave Shuvalov the same explanation (Goriainov p. 343); Schweinitz II, p. 396, 399. From Lamsdorf
pp. 272 ff. it appears that Shuvalov accepted the chancellor's arguments with
reservations, suspecting a ruse to enlist Russian support in the crisis. It is interesting to note that Rowland Blennerhassett gave a fairly correct account of the
conflict on foreign policy in the *Nineteenth Century* for April 1890, pp. 706 ff.

[69] Bismarck: *Gedanken und Erinnerungen* III, pp. 98 ff., and in numerous
other places.

leave Austria in the lurch.[70] "I am through with the Russians and with Tsar Alexander" he had told his enraptured friend Waldersee on the preceding day.[71] Shortly after, the Kaiser's uncle, the Grand Duke of Baden, told Hohenlohe that William suspected Bismarck of wishing to conduct German policy according to his own plans, which were unknown to the ruler. Bismarck, he continued, meant to give up Austria and the Triple Alliance and effect an understanding with Russia.[72] Besides, the chancellor had been blackening the imperial reputation in the eyes of foreign diplomats and had described his sovereign as "a sort of crazy blockhead."[73]

To the diplomats, however, the young Emperor spoke in very different terms. He insisted that foreign policy had nothing to do with the crisis, and that the only significance of the Kievan reports lay in the fact that Bismarck had withheld information from him and had acted too independently. The Kaiser even went so far as to assert that he had been left in ignorance of the negotiations with Russia.[74] As a matter of fact nothing shows more clearly than these negotiations how completely the Kaiser was at sea, and how uncertain he was in his mind just what should be done now that Bismarck had gone.

Shuvalov had left for St. Petersburg on February 27 and was back in Berlin on March 17 with full powers to renew the existing treaty for six years.[75] When informed of the impending resignation of the chancellor he had declared that before re-

---

[70] Hohenlohe II, p. 466; Waldersee: *Denkwürdigkeiten* II, pp. 118-119.

[71] Waldersee: *Denkwürdigkeiten* II, p. 117.

[72] Hohenlohe II, p. 465.

[73] Széchényi to Kálnoky, April 13, 1890 (in V. A.); Hohenlohe II, p. 469.

[74] Radowitz II, pp. 315 ff.; Schweinitz II, p. 399. On March 19 the German representatives abroad were informed that the change would in no way affect Germany's foreign policy (Crispi: *Memoirs* II, p. 431). This is also the burden of the Kaiser's long letter to Francis Joseph on April 3 (*Oesterreichische Rundschau* 1919, p. 100 ff.). See further the Kaiser's remarks to Hohenthal, the Saxon representative (*Deutsche Rundschau* 1922, p. 168).

[75] But it was to be considered permanent. Even in 1887 the Russians had proposed its conclusion for five years (G. P. VII, no. 1366; in no. 1370 Giers speaks of having agreed to renewal for five years, but this may have been a slip. See also Schweinitz II, p. 396).

opening the discussion he must await further instructions. Herbert Bismarck reported these developments to the Kaiser on March 20, but misrepresented the facts to the extent of asserting Russia's unwillingness to renew the treaty with the new chancellor.[76] The object of these tactics is perfectly clear. Bismarck himself seems to have believed that he could not be dispensed with for long[77] and furthermore quite reasonably supposed that after the Kaiser's violent Russophobe outbursts the Reinsurance Treaty would be dropped. His son Herbert had no desire to remain in office under a new chief, but appears to have hoped to force the Kaiser's hand by leaving him completely in the lurch and by shouldering him with responsibility for the breach with Russia.[78]

Great must have been the surprise and joy in the Bismarck house when the Kaiser expressed his astonishment at Shuvalov's attitude. In the marginal notes on Herbert Bismarck's report the Kaiser indicated that he was quite prepared to renew the treaty as suggested. Had the Bismarcks now played their hand well, they might yet have seen the treaty safely renewed. But instead of utilizing the favorable attitude of the Kaiser they apparently assumed that the road was perfectly clear. Herbert Bismarck insisted that Shuvalov was unwilling to negotiate with

[76] The Bismarcks always insisted that Shuvalov had declared the unwillingness of the Russians to renew the alliance with a new chancellor (see G. P. VII, nos. 1366-1367; Bismarck: *Gedanken und Erinnerungen* III, pp. 90, 101, 105-6; Hofmann I, p. 113; Bismarck interview in the *Neue Freie Presse* October 27, 1896). There is no evidence to substantiate this. Shuvalov told the Kaiser on March 21 that "he had been obliged to suspend negotiations because of not knowing who were the persons with whom he was to conduct them" (Goriainov p. 343). The later negotiations make it obvious that the Russian government, at least, had no compunctions about negotiating with another chancellor. It is interesting to note that Schweinitz recognized the ruse on the part of Bismarck. It does appear, however, that Shuvalov, in conversation with Herbert Bismarck, had enlarged on the difficulties of negotiating with new men (Schweinitz II, p. 400).

[77] Bismarck: *Gedanken und Erinnerungen* III, p. 105; Lerchenfeld p. 167; Hohenthal pp. 167, 170; Eulenburg p. 252.

[78] Herbert Bismarck's determination to resign was made known on the morning of March 17 (Radowitz II, p. 312; Waldersee II, p. 118; Schweinitz II, p. 399). The text of Herbert's resignation is in Gradenwitz pp. 178 ff. In it Herbert calls attention to the difficulties of convincing the powers that no change in foreign policy was intended.

the new chancellor and, knowing that the Kaiser was anxious for him to remain at the foreign office in order to avoid the appearance of a change of policy, he insisted on handing in his resignation. The Bismarcks were nourishing a vain hope that by sheer pressure they could force the Kaiser to retract.[79]

But events took a very different turn. The young Emperor decided to clear the situation himself, and in his usual abrupt manner sent to Shuvalov and had him waked at one in the morning in order to invite him to the palace for breakfast at eight. The ambassador, believing that something had happened to his master, appeared promptly at the appointed time.[80] He was received "with a kindness and cordiality beyond all expression."

"Sit down and listen to me," said the Kaiser. "You know how much I love and respect your sovereign. Your emperor has been too good to me for me to do otherwise than inform him personally of the situation created by the events which have just taken place. Tell his Majesty, then, that I have parted with my old chancellor, for it was truly impossible to keep on working with him in view of the state of his health and the excitable condition of his nerves. Herbert Bismarck told me last evening that you were authorized by your sovereign to pursue the negotiations respecting the renewal of our secret treaty, but that at present you had abandoned them. Why? I beg you to tell His Majesty that on my part I am entirely disposed to renew our secret treaty, that my foreign policy remains and will remain the same as it was in the time of my grandfather. That is my firm resolve. I shall not depart from it." Assured by Shuvalov that he was merely awaiting new instructions, the Kaiser concluded: "Nothing has changed, then, and I

---

[79] Shuvalov somewhat later expressed the opinion that the Bismarcks tried to use the negotiations with Russia as a lever to bring pressure on the Kaiser (Lamsdorf p. 302). Herbert Bismarck handed in his resignation on March 21, after his father's had been accepted, but it should be noted that as late as March 25 the Bismarcks expected their candidate, Alvensleben, to be appointed minister of foreign affairs (Radowitz II, pp. 319-320). As late as the afternoon of the 26th Herbert and Schweinitz tried to persuade Alvensleben to accept (Schweinitz II, p. 403).

[80] There is a serious discrepancy of dates here. Goriainov (p. 343) says Shuvalov was waked "in the night of March 21," while Schweinitz (G. P. VII, no. 1373) later sent home a copy of Shuvalov's report dated March 21 in which the ambassador says "hier matin l'Empereur m'a invité de venir chez lui." Obviously the conversation took place on the morning of March 21, for it was certainly after the correspondence between Herbert Bismarck and the Kaiser on March 20; Schweinitz II, p. 400 also indicates that the conversation took place on the morning of March 21.

rely upon your friendship to lay the situation before your emperor, assuring him that nothing has changed either in my personal sentiments toward him or in my policy towards Russia."[81]

It would be difficult to imagine a more consistent misstatement of the facts. About the only true part of the Kaiser's declaration was his assertion that no change in policy was intended. He, the man who for years had antagonized Bismarck on the point of the policy towards Russia, and who at heart no doubt was determined to stand by Austria and her friends in opposing Russia, had neither the strength of will nor the power of his convictions. He had been anxious to get rid of his mentor and had made the most of their disagreement on foreign affairs, but once the immediate aim was accomplished he dared not do otherwise than to continue the policy which he had so long denounced. The one thing uppermost in William's mind in the critical days following Bismarck's dismissal was the almost pathological fear that his action would be construed as a change in foreign policy and that it would lead to the international complications which, while his great chancellor was at the helm, he had regarded with equanimity. He announced in a published telegram that the course would remain unchanged and he never tired of assuring foreign diplomats to the same effect.[82]

Meanwhile the mines were being laid which, in the end, were to blow up the Reinsurance Treaty, in spite of the Kaiser. The men who had plotted Bismarck's fall and who had worked incessantly towards that end knew exactly what they wanted and they, at least, were logical. The military men could affect foreign policy only indirectly, but in the Wilhelmstrasse itself there sat a man who was entirely of their mind and knew how to work carefully in the dark. Baron Fritz von Holstein's personality has been the subject of numerous essays.[83] "The man with

---

[81] Goriainov pp. 343-344. This account tallies with Schweinitz' version of Shuvalov's report (G. P. VII, no. 1373); see also Schweinitz II, p. 400, and Lamsdorf pp. 283 ff., where Shuvalov's reply to the Kaiser is given *verbatim*.

[82] See note 72. Apparently the Kaiser was also haunted by the fear that Bismarck would publish the imperial note on the Kievan reports (Gradenwitz pp. 167-168).

[83] See Maximilian Harden: *Köpfe* (Berlin 1910) I, pp. 89-147; Eckardt pp. 3-5; Hermann, Freiherr von Eckardstein: *Lebenserinnerungen passim*; O. Ham-

the hyena's eyes," as he was known by his contemporaries, was an odd nature, very retiring and mysterious, thirsty for power and yet shrinking from responsibility. He had served under Bismarck when the latter was ambassador at St. Petersburg, and for the past fifteen years had been in the foreign office, where he was regarded as the chancellor's most trusted henchman and was much feared. Although at first a sincere admirer of Bismarck he had, during the last years, become somewhat critical of the existing policy, which he considered too involved and too unsteady.[84] Apparently he had never approved of the Reinsurance Treaty, which appeared to him as a betrayal of the Austro-German Alliance, and he did not at all subscribe to the Bismarckian policy of "grovelling before Russia."[85] In his opinion not only the Berlin Congress, but also Bismarck's efforts to prevent a clash between England and Russia in 1885, were serious errors.[86] Personal friction had developed in the last months, and Holstein was enough of a vindictive nature to take his revenge, no matter by what means, but preferably by intrigue.[87]

Holstein had played for Bismarck's fall only in an indirect way, by supplying Waldersee with reports which the chancellor desired to withhold from the Emperor. But once the crisis had:

mann: *Der neue Kurs* (Berlin 1918) pp. 58 ff.; Prinz Alexander zu Hohenlohe *Aus meinem Leben* chapter xii; Raschdau (*Deutsche Rundschau* December 1924); Rath (*Deutsche Revue* October 1909); *London Times* May 10, 1909; Gooch: Baron von Holstein (*Cambridge Historical Journal* I, pp. 61-84). Richard Frankenberg: *Die Nichterneuerung des deutsch-russischen Rückversicherungsvertrages* (Berlin 1927) makes out the strongest indictment of Holstein and his intrigues in 1890.

[84] Harden I, p. 100. Bismarck, while not unaware of Holstein's attitude, seems to have greatly underrated his importance.

[85] Harden *ibid.* Also Széchényi to Kálnoky, January 18, 1890 (in V. A.) speaks of Holstein's "Abneigung gegen Russland und seine stets wachsame Besorgnis einer über seine Wünsche hinausgehende Annäherung an dasselbe." He adds that Holstein was delighted by the Kaiser's determination to stick firmly by the Austrian alliance.

[86] Hohenlohe II, p. 507; Eckardt p. 24.

[87] Radowitz II, p. 326; Eulenburg p. 245. It is interesting to note that as late as August 1889 Holstein refers to himself in a letter as a "Bismarckianer" (Waldersee: *Briefwechsel* I, p. 317).

come Holstein was the first to desert the Bismarckian ship.[88] The great statesman's dismissal opened up for him the prospect of undisputed control in the foreign office. He may have had something to do with Caprivi's nomination, and he certainly was anxious for the replacement of Herbert Bismarck by some inexperienced man. Marschall was undoubtedly his nominee.[89]

But it was not enough to get the Bismarcks out—it was necessary to keep them out, and this could best be accomplished by effecting a change of men. Holstein was sincerely patriotic, no doubt, but the letters he wrote to Eulenburg in these days show conclusively that the motives for his actions at this time were predominantly personal and selfish. On March 22 he reports the confusion as terrible and expresses great anxiety lest Herbert Bismarck should remain in office: "I certainly wish Herbert well," he writes, "but not at the expense of the prize now at stake."

His first move was to induce Caprivi to call a conference at the foreign office, on March 23, to reconsider the question of the treaty with Russia. Those present besides the new chancellor and Holstein were the undersecretaries Berchem and Raschdau, who had undoubtedly been primed by their domineering chief.[90] It turned out that those present were unanimously opposed to the renewal of the treaty, but here again the reasons adduced seem extraordinary, to say the least. There was no substantial objection to the policy of which the treaty was the expression. Criticism centered rather on the existence of the written agreement itself. It was argued that under the treaty all the advantages accrued to Russia. Her claims in Bulgaria were recognized by those present as being legitimate and it was admitted that a

---

[88] See especially his letters to Eulenburg, published by Vindex Scrutator (J. Haller) in Der Tag November 4, 1920. Also Radowitz II, p. 326.

[89] Radowitz II, p. 326, says that Holstein had known Caprivi for some time and had been in touch with him recently (probably since the crisis of February). See also Bismarck: Gedanken und Erinnerungen III, p. 31; Lerchenfeld p. 171; Hohenlohe p. 466.

[90] Raschdau: Das Ende der deutsch-russischen Rückversicherung (Der Tag October 17, 1920); "Vindex Scrutator" in Der Tag November 4, 1920; Eckardt p. 53; L. Raschdau in Deutsche Rundschau May, 1924, p. 113. Among the best accounts of the nonrenewal of the treaty are those of Bornhak in the Archiv für Politik und Geschichte II, pp. 570-582 (1924), and of Frankenberg.

Russian advance on Constantinople would hardly be objectionable to Germany. But it was dangerous to have this on paper. Russia might at any time reveal the agreement to Austria or England and thus disrupt the Triple Alliance. Bismarck himself might, in a vengeful moment, divulge it and thus place his successors in an awkward position. Furthermore the treaty was not compatible, at least in spirit, with the obligations of Germany under other alliances. At the same time Germany gained nothing by the pact, for there was nothing in the wording of it to make a Franco-Russian Alliance impossible. All told the alliance was a dangerous thing, more likely to lead to war than to preserve peace. It was a product of Bismarckian ingenuity and complicated Germany's international relations to such an extent that no one who lacked Bismarck's genius and prestige could hope to make the system function.[91]

These considerations, fully developed in a memorandum drawn up by Berchem, decided Caprivi, who from the start seems to have been thoroughly frightened by the complexity of the Bismarckian system and who appears to have had genuine moral scruples in the matter.[92] The members of the conference therefore decided to recommend the nonrenewal of the treaty to the Kaiser. A suggestion made by Raschdau that the German government make its acceptance conditional on certain changes in the text and on the publication of the document and thereby induce Russia to reject it, was turned down.[93]

"I believe that even Machiavelli himself might have been able to learn from Holstein's involved tactics in those days," wrote Count Eulenburg later.[94] Certainly there can be no doubt that he was a master of cunning. He had entirely neglected Herbert Bismarck and had, on the other hand, fully informed Marschall, who did not become foreign minister until the younger Bis-

---

[91] Berchem memorandum March 25, 1890 (G. P. VII, no. 1368); cf. the extract of the draft in Eckardt p. 53; also Harden I, p. 102.

[92] Bismarck: *Gedanken und Erinnerungen* III, p. 106; Hohenlohe II, p. 519; A. v. Tirpitz: *Erinnerungen* (Leipzig 1919) p. 26; Marschall in the Reichstag November 16, 1896.

[93] Raschdau in *Der Tag* October 17, 1920.

[94] Eulenburg p. 245.

marck's resignation on March 26.[95]   In any case Holstein had
succeeded in completely forestalling any action by the Bismarcks.
All available information would indicate that the ex-chancellor
and his son were over-confident after the Kaiser's declaration in
favor of the treaty. Herbert offered his resignation on March 21,
but with the expectation that Alvensleben would be appointed as
his successor. During these days he evidently appeared but rarely
at the foreign office. Bismarck himself showed astonishing lack
of energy and was certainly quite unaware of Holstein's intrigues.
He liked Caprivi and hoped to convince him with but little difficulty.[96] The new chancellor was regularly invited to breakfast
at the Bismarcks',[97] but little attempt was made to educate him
in questions of foreign policy. When, on the very day of the
foreign office conference, March 23, Bismarck raised the question
of the Russian treaty, Caprivi was reticent and finally replied
evasively that while his host might be able to juggle five balls
successfully other people would do well to confine their efforts to
two. He must, he said, have time to consider the problem.[98]

[95] G. P. VII, no. 1369, footnote; XXX[1], no. 10989 where Marschall, in a letter
of December 4, 1911, asserts that he refused to consider the position unless the
treaty were dropped.   Marschall was a close friend of the Austrian ambassador
and made no secret of his disapproval of Bismarck's Russian policy.   His sympathies for Austria and the Triple Alliance were well-known (Széchényi to Kálnoky,
March 24, 29, April 19, June 4, 1890 in V. A.).

[96] See note 77. It is said that William I once considered Caprivi as a possible
successor to Bismarck and recommended him to his grandson (Blowitz: *Memoirs*
p. 296, who says he was told the story by Münster). Bismarck spoke of Caprivi as
a man of considerable force and one likely to prove more obstinate than he himself
had been (Lucius p. 452; Széchényi to Kálnoky, March 16, 1890, in V. A.) There
can be no doubt that Bismarck was highly pleased by the appointment (Radowitz
II, pp. 314, 321; Kardorff letter March 21, 1890, in *Deutsche Revue* 1917, p. 53;
Hohenthal in *Deutsche Rundschau* 1922, p. 169; Széchényi to Kálnoky March
22 and 25, 1890, in V. A.) and retained his high opinion of Caprivi personally,
(Hammann: *Der neue Kurs* p. 17). For other very favorable estimates of Caprivi
passed at the time of the crisis see Waldersee: *Denkwürdigkeiten* II, pp. 103, 118,
119; Lerchenfeld pp. 167, 169; *The Letters of the Empress Frederick* (London
1928) pp. 411-413; and the Kaiser's own opinion (Letter to Francis Joseph April
3, 1890, in *Oesterreichische Rundschau* 1919, p. 107).

[97] Eckardt p. 59.

[98] Eckardt p. 52; Radowitz II, p. 323. Bismarck claimed (*Gedanken und
Erinnerungen* III, p. 114; Waldersee: *Denkwürdigkeiten* II, pp. 199, 202) that he
had only one short talk with Caprivi and that he was not at all consulted in the

With that the efforts of the Bismarcks seem to have stopped. Herbert evidently knew nothing of what had been decided until just before the acceptance of his resignation on March 26.[99] But the opposing faction made the best of its opportunities. Nothing had been said of the decision of March 23, because it was deemed necessary first to convert General von Schweinitz, the ambassador to Russia.[100] This was accomplished by means of the Berchem memorandum on March 27, and on the same day Caprivi and Schweinitz together laid their arguments against the renewal of the treaty before the Kaiser.[101] The Kaiser showed little hesitancy about making up his mind, and with incredible levity dismissed the matter with the simple declaration: "Well, it cannot be done, much as I regret it."[102] It seems that even then he shirked the responsibility and on the following day made remarks to Shuvalov which led the latter to believe that all was not lost, that negotiations would be continued at St. Petersburg and that the matter might be arranged at a later date by some alterations in the text.[103]

matters at issue, but Lerchenfeld (p. 168) reports that on March 23 the two men had a long talk in which Bismarck "developed the whole situation."

[99] He actually did discuss the situation with Caprivi on March 26, but only after learning that Holstein had anticipated him and that the decision had practically been made (Bismarck: *Gedanken und Erinnerungen* III, p. 106; Harden I, p. 102; Eckardt p. 52; "Vindex Scrutator" in *Der Tag* November 4, 1920).

[100] It is barely possible that the decision of the conference of March 23 was reported to the Kaiser before the conversion of Schweinitz, and that the Kaiser insisted on first hearing the opinion of the ambassador. In any case it appears that the Kaiser instructed Caprivi to talk the matter over with Schweinitz (G. P. VII, nos. 1391-1392, retrospective letters of Berchem and Holstein).

[101] G. P. VII, no. 1369; Schweinitz II, p. 404. Evidently the Kaiser had already half made up his mind not to renew the treaty, and was only waiting for Schweinitz' decision (see William II: *Ereignisse und Gestalten* p. 45; G. P. VII, no. 1391). On Schweinitz' attitude see further Holstein's letter of March 27, 1890 (*Der Tag* November 4, 1920); Harden I, p. 102; Hammann: *Der neue Kurs* p. 36; Eckardt p. 53 note. It appears from Schweinitz' *Denkwürdigkeiten* II, p. 392 that already in November 1889 the ambassador was dubious as to the desirability of renewing the treaty.

[102] Holstein memorandum June 10, 1904 (G. P. VII, no. 1392).

[103] Radowitz II, p. 323; G. P. VII, no. 1370, from which it appears that Shuvalov had wired home that the negotiations had been "suspended," etc. This was Schweinitz' suggestion. Evidently the Kaiser felt obliged to tone down his communication, in view of the statements he had made to Shuvalov on March 21.

The scene now shifted to St. Petersburg, where Schweinitz arrived on March 31. He immediately went to call on M. de Giers, the Russian foreign minister. The errand was a delicate one, for Giers had long been known as an advocate of the agreement with Germany and had himself once admitted that his position depended on the maintenance and success of this policy.[104] The Russian statesman was, then, in a serious quandary. He had been watching events in Berlin with an anxious eye, and when the great news of Bismarck's resignation reached the Russian capital on March 18 he said to the Austrian ambassador:

"Prince Bismarck was pacific and monarchical in his sentiments. One knew with whom one was dealing. Today we find ourselves before the unknown. But it will be prudent not to overemphasize our regrets, for it is necessary to avoid their being interpreted as a sign of distrust of the German Emperor."[105]

Knowing William's views he was, naturally enough, very much preoccupied, and the Tsar himself suspected that the resignation of the great chancellor would prove the prelude to a change of policy.[106] On receiving Schweinitz just before the latter's departure for Berlin on the 19th, Alexander made no secret of his regret and showed a genuine appreciation of Bismarck's policy, especially towards Russia.[107] Now that he was gone the Russians

These had been reported to Caprivi by Schweinitz, and the new chancellor called the Kaiser's attention to the contradiction (Schweinitz II, p. 406.)

[104] Herbert Bismarck to his father, March 30, 1884 (G. P. III, no. 629.). Cf. also Schweinitz II, p. 411.

[105] Wolkenstein to Kálnoky, March 19, 1890 (in V. A.). Prince Lobanov spoke in almost identical terms and suggested that the Kaiser's ear trouble had affected his brain. As early as March 5 Giers had expressed his doubts as to the wisdom of the Kaiser's labor policy, and had, indeed, questioned his ability to rule (Wolkenstein to Kálnoky, March 5, 1890, in V. A.). Giers had been kept well-informed of the development of the crisis in Berlin (Schweinitz II, p. 398; Lamsdorf pp. 272 ff.).

[106] G. P. VI, no. 1365. The explanation for this lies in the fact that Shuvalov had reported Bismarck's statement to the effect that relations with Russia were a factor in the disagreement (Goriainov p. 343; Lamsdorf pp. 272 ff.; G. P. VII, no. 1370; Schweinitz II, pp. 396, 399.).

[107] G. P. VI, no. 1365; also Wolkenstein to Kálnoky, March 19, 1890; Aehrenthal to Kálnoky, April 3, 1890 (in V. A.); Schweinitz II, pp. 397, 399, 410 ff. The Tsar was particularly worried by the thought that Waldersee might succeed Bismarck.

realized that, after all, he had been a sincere advocate of peace, and they began to regret that the opportunities he had offered them had not been utilized. In future, instead of the tried old statesman, it would be necessary to deal with a young and impetuous monarch, whose ambitions and military inclinations were sufficient cause for anxiety. While Bismarck was still in power the Kaiser had not been taken too seriously, but his vigor in dealing with a man of Bismarck's calibre placed him in a new light. There was no knowing but what, on occasion, he might deal quite as summarily with Russia. Under the circumstances the Russians decided on a policy of reserve and determined to await developments. The Tsar reminded the Kaiser, through Schweinitz, of the projected visit to Russia and the Russian press was instructed not to show too much sympathy for Bismarck.[108]

It was with great relief, then, that Giers read Shuvalov's telegram of March 21 recording his conversation with the Kaiser and the latter's determination to renew the treaty. The Tsar, too, was well impressed, and noted: "Nothing more satisfactory could be looked for. We shall see by the sequel whether deeds correspond to words."[109] Instructions for the ambassador in Berlin were immediately drawn up, but just as they were ready a new telegram arrived from Shuvalov, on March 30, in which he announced the failure of the negotiations.[110] Just what Shuvalov reported we do not know, but it seems that, speaking with Schweinitz after his second talk with the Kaiser, he indicated that the negotiations had been merely postponed.[111] In any case Schweinitz found Giers still hopeful on the evening of March 31.

[108] This is the summary of a number of reports. See G. P. VI, nos. 1364-1365; also Wolkenstein to Kálnoky, March 25, 1890; Aehrenthal to Kálnoky, April 3 and 16, 1890 (in V. A.). Cf. also the St. Petersburg letter in *Mémorial Diplomatique* March 29, 1890, p. 197.

[109] Goriainov p. 344; G. P. VII, no. 1370; Schweinitz II, p. 405; Lamsdorf p. 286.

[110] G. P. VII, no. 1370; Lamsdorf pp. 291 ff. The despatch of the instructions had been delayed by Shuvalov's report that negotiations were to be transferred to St. Petersburg (*ibid.* pp. 239 ff.). Shuvalov was informed of the new turn of events by Schweinitz on March 28 (Schweinitz II, p. 405).

[111] Lamsdorf p. 297.

The German ambassador tactfully explained the situation, pointing out that, although the treaty would not be renewed, no change in policy was intended, even in respect to Germany's attitude towards Russian claims in Bulgaria.[112]

Giers was struck with consternation. The vision of Russia entirely isolated in the face of the Triple Alliance and England rose before his eyes. He could not believe what he heard, and recalled to Schweinitz what the Kaiser had said to Shuvalov on the 21.[113] The Tsar, however, received the news with greater equanimity. He certainly distrusted the Kaiser, and evidently felt relieved that the situation had now cleared. While he assured Schweinitz that he relied upon the Kaiser's declarations of good intentions towards Russia, he noted on Giers' report: "The new chancellor's views about our relations are very significant. It appears to me that Bismarck was right when he said that the policy of the German Emperor would alter from the day that he, Bismarck, should retire."[114]

Giers, however, was determined to continue the negotiations if possible. Moved by deep apprehension he reopened the subject twice in the following six weeks, pointing out that any scrap of paper would do—an exchange of notes or of imperial letters.[115] On May 15 he finally suggested to Schweinitz that Russia would be willing to renew the treaty without the secret protocol and without the declaration of Germany's recognition of Russia's preponderant and decisive influence in Bulgaria. Schweinitz, who appears never to have been more than half-converted to the new course, reported to his government and recommended acceptance of the Russian offers.[116]

[112] G. P. VII, no. 1370.

[113] G. P. VII, no. 1370. On Giers' apprehensions see Goriainov pp. 344-346; G. P. VI, nos. 1364-1365. Also Wolkenstein to Kálnoky, March 25, 1890; Aehrenthal to Kálnoky, April 3, 16, 1890; Schweinitz II, p. 409.

[114] G. P. VII, no. 1371; Goriainov p. 344. Schweinitz II, p. 407 reports Giers as saying that, in contrast to himself, Alexander had never been much interested in the treaty. The Tsar did not even mention the treaty to Schweinitz.

[115] G. P. VII, nos. 1372, 1379.

[116] G. P. VII, no. 1372; Schweinitz II, p. 412. From G. P. VII, no. 1370 it appears that Giers had, from the beginning, been willing to drop the protocol. From Lamsdorf, passim, it is clear that the protocol had been the work of Shuvalov,

The whole problem was, indeed, reconsidered in Berlin, and memoranda were drawn up by Holstein, Marschall, Kiderlen and Raschdau.[117] The tenor of these was that even without the protocol and without the recognition of Russia's claims in Bulgaria the treaty would bind Germany to insist on the principle of closure of the Straits. This would be detrimental to English interests, and the English, who had never forgiven Germany's action in maintaining the principle in 1885 during the Afghan crisis, would be estranged if Germany persisted on supporting the Russians in this matter. The argument hinging on the incompatibility of the Russian treaty with Germany's other agreements was also disinterred, but above all the fear of possible divulgence of the treaty by Russia and the consequent disruption of the Triple Alliance came out more clearly than ever. Russia, it was argued, is evidently preparing for action in the Near East, and consequently is anxious to prevent Germany's siding with England and Austria. With the treaty secure Russia could, at the crucial moment, reveal the agreement to Austria and thus throw the whole anti-Russian coalition into confusion.

Schweinitz was directed to lay the situation before Giers once more.[118] Caprivi, he was to say, intended to maintain the existing good relations with Russia and to pursue a "simple and transparent" policy, which "would give no occasion for misunderstanding." But there was to be no treaty. On hearing this Giers was more disconsolate than ever. His first impulse was to attempt new negotiations through the Emperors or through Shuvalov at Berlin, but he was finally convinced that such action would be futile.[119] Nothing more was done, and on June 18, 1890 the Reinsurance Treaty automatically lapsed.

that Giers had always regarded it as dangerous and that he was absolutely set on getting rid of it (see esp. pp. 226, 239). While in St. Petersburg in March Shuvalov had tried to rescue the protocol, but had failed (pp. 267, 291 ff.).

[117] G. P. VII, nos. 1374 ff.; Raschdau in *Deutsche Rundschau* May 1924, pp. 113-114.

[118] G. P. VII, no. 1380; Goriainov p. 344.

[119] G. P. VII, no. 1382. Shuvalov's arguments dissuading Giers from reopening negotiations in Berlin are summarized in Goriainov pp. 345-346 and Lamsdorf pp. 310 ff., 322 ff. He was so offended at what seemed to him like the

In considering the motives that underlay this important step in German foreign policy one must constantly bear in mind that William II took little part in the discussions of the question. It can hardly be doubted that he had lost faith in Bismarck's Russian policy long before and that he heartily disapproved of the treaty.[120] But he had decided to renew it because he dreaded the consequences of Bismarck's disappearance. Not until Schweinitz had been won over did he finally accept the arguments adduced by his ministers.

It is on the Kaiser's advisers, then, that the responsibility rests. Of these Holstein certainly must be held chiefly accountable. It is well-known that in his mind the treaty was closely bound up with the "Bismarck dynasty," and it is obvious that he regarded the nonrenewal of the treaty as the best way to preclude Bismarck's return.[121] But it is also clear that Holstein disapproved of the treaty in principle, and of the whole Bismarckian policy which culminated in the treaty. No one has ever called Holstein's patriotism in question, and it may be conceded that he was genuinely sincere in his attitude on this occasion. His personal ambitions happily coincided with his convictions.

As for the other ministers, some were unquestionably influenced by their chief, but this fact is of minor significance. It can hardly be supposed that Caprivi could be convinced by anything short of sound arguments, and besides that we know that men like Radowitz and even Schweinitz and Reuss, all of them thoroughgoing Bismarckians, were opposed to the renewal of the treaty.[122]

It is worth reviewing briefly the arguments adduced against

double-dealing of the Germans that he thought for a moment of resigning, and he never forgave the Kaiser in this matter (Schweinitz II, pp. 405-406, 413).

[120] Cf. Marschall's letter of December 4, 1911 in G. P. XXX¹, no. 10989: "Noch viel schärfer (als Caprivi) hat Seine Majestät den Vertrag verurteilt."

[121] This comes out most clearly in the letters published by Haller in *Der Tag* November 4, 1920.

[122] Caprivi told Radowitz on March 27, 1890 that he had taken office only on condition that Bismarck's foreign policy be continued. Radowitz nevertheless advised against the treaty (Radowitz II, pp. 322-323). The attitude of Schweinitz has already been discussed (Schweinitz II, p. 404). For Reuss' opinion see G. P. VII, no. 1381.

the renewal of the treaty. The Berchem memorandum of March 25, 1890 evidently reflects all the opinions submitted in the conference of March 23.[123] In general four main objections were raised to the treaty: it was incompatible, in spirit more than in letter, with the Triple Alliance and Germany's obligations to Rumania under the agreement of 1883, and it was inconsistent with Germany's policy towards other states. Second, the very existence of the secret treaty gave Russia a weapon she might use to disrupt the Triple Alliance. She might at any time divulge the agreement and thus discredit Germany in the eyes of her allies and friends. Then again, the advantages under the treaty were almost exclusively on the side of Russia. Lastly, the pact so complicated the German policy that no one lacking the genius and prestige of Bismarck could hope to avoid conflicting obligations under the various treaties.

There is no escape from the logic of these arguments.[124] The Reinsurance Treaty was undeniably incompatible with the letter as well as the spirit of the separate German-Italian Treaty of 1887 and particularly with Germany's obligations to Rumania, and it was unquestionably true that the treaty was irreconcilable with the policy of Germany towards England since 1887. There is, to be sure, something to be said for Bismarck. Almost every treaty will show defects if subjected to a minute legalistic examination.[125] The German chancellor's ultimate object was always the maintenance of peace, and he had surely succeeded during his last three years of office in suppressing every danger of conflict in Germany's obligations. Not having a direct interest in the Near East he did not hesitate to sponsor the Mediterranean Agreements, the object of which was to enable his allies to defend their interests in the Near East with the assistance of England, a power equally interested. On the other hand he

[123] The Berchem memorandum is in G. P. VII, no. 1368.

[124] There is a useful review and criticism of these arguments, written in a Bismarckian sense, by Pürschel: Das Ende des Rückversicherungsvertrages (*Vergangenheit und Gegenwart* XV, 1925, pp. 144-159), and a very minute and painstaking analysis, also written from a thoroughgoing Bismarckian standpoint, in Frankenberg.

[125] Cf. G. P. IV, no. 852.

had no compunctions about promising his support to Russia in the latter's Near Eastern projects. Technically he was disloyal to both sides, for he encouraged both.[126] But he trusted to his own ability to maintain this perfect balance which prevented either side from making progress.

It can hardly be maintained, however, that Bismarck was disloyal to Austria.[127] He had consistently taken the stand that Germany was under no obligation to support the Austrian policy in the Balkans. He had repeatedly warned the Austrians against reckoning on his support, and he always insisted that an agreement which gave Germany some control over Russian policy would prove beneficial to Austria as well.[128] As a matter of fact, the Austrians, while they did not actually know of the treaty, suspected some sort of German-Russian agreement, and there is no evidence that, when informed of the Reinsurance Treaty after its lapse, the Austrian emperor or his ministers showed either surprise or chagrin.[129]

[126] The disloyalty to England is often overlooked, but compare Count Julius Andrássy: *Bismarck, Andrássy and their Successors* (Boston 1927) p. 149: "The treaty was unfair for Salisbury too," and p. 150: "Bismarck deceived Russia rather than us and England."

[127] Certainly the accusation of double-dealing launched against Bismarck, (notably by the Kaiser in his letter to Francis Joseph June 12, 1892) represents a gross exaggeration.

[128] Hofmann II, p. 378 and numerous other references. As a matter of fact Bismarck was determined to save Austria from destruction even if she were the aggressor against Russia, and in spite of the Reinsurance Treaty (G. P. VI, nos. 1191, 1197; X, p. 216 note and especially Lucius p. 442). It was really a question of disloyalty to Russia, not to Austria. On the other hand it appears from a later report of Hatzfeld (G. P. IX, no. 2395) that Bismarck also considered sacrificing Austria, if necessary, to buy Russian neutrality in a Franco-German War.

[129] The treaty was not actually revealed to the Austrians until the Kaiser's meeting with Francis Joseph at Rohnstock on September 1, 1890 (Pribram: *Die Geheimverträge Oesterreich-Ungarns 1879-1914* vol. I, p. 209; G. P. XXX¹, nos. 10987, 10998; Eckardt p. 55; Hammann: *Der missverstandene Bismarck* [Berlin 1921] p. 58.) On the Austrians' suspicions compare Molden: Kálnoky (in *Allgemeine deutsche Biographie* XXI, pp. 16-17), and the following: "Sowohl der Vater als auch der Sohn waren Russland gegenüber mehr oder minder engagiert, oder doch zum wenigsten mit Bezug auf diese Macht nicht ganz frei" (Széchényi to Kálnoky, April 19, 1890, in V. A.). The newspaper and other citations adduced by P. Mahn: *Kaiser und Kanzler* (Berlin 1925) pp. 155-156 to prove that the treaty was known in Vienna, are inconclusive. That the Austrians fully appre-

The provisions of the treaty with Russia were undoubtedly in most flagrant conflict with Germany's obligations to Rumania, and it was on this account that Schweinitz finally agreed to vote against renewal.[130] Apparently the contradiction had not occurred to Bismarck, and it may be assumed that had he known it he would have modified the agreement with Rumania.[131] After all, Germany had merely "acceded" to an Austro-Rumanian pact, and the importance of Rumania to Germany was as nothing compared with that of Russia.[132] It should also be pointed out that Bismarck did not consider a Russian violation of Rumanian territory probable. The Russians, he was convinced, would advance in the Near East by sea, in order not to expose themselves to Austrian or Rumanian attack in the rear.[133]

The second argument, centering about the danger of divulgation by Russia, was certainly one of the most potent in the view of the statesmen gathered in conference on March 23.[134] The idea has been ridiculed by many writers, and Bismarck himself pointed out that Germany had never insisted on secrecy; that, indeed, Germany could only gain if the matter were to come out.

ciated the German position is shown by a despatch of Kálnoky August 18, 1887 (quoted by W. N. Medlicott: The Mediterranean Agreements of 1887—*Slavonic Review* June 1926, p. 78).

[130] G. P. VII, no. 1392; Schweinitz II, p. 404-405; Eckardt p. 53 footnote; Hammann: *Der missverstandene Bismarck* pp. 59-60. O. Becker: *Das französisch-russische Bündnis* (Berlin 1925) pp. 58-59 attempts to show that the Reinsurance Treaty was not necessarily incompatible with the Rumanian Treaty.

[131] Bismarck's determination to draw a sharp line between Germany's various obligations is evident from G. P. V, nos. 1087, 1100; VI, nos. 1184, 1190, etc.

[132] Cf. Bismarck's low estimate of the treaty in 1888: "Ich sehe in demselben eine Steigerung eher unsrer Passiva als unsrer Activa, und habe unsere Akzession dazu durchaus nicht aus dynastischem Interesse, sondern nur aus Konnivenz für die oesterreichische Politik bei Seiner Majestät befürwortet" (G. P. VII, no. 1464 note).

[133] See note 60. It is interesting to note that while Berchem took the contrary view (G. P. VII, no. 1368) Caprivi appears to have agreed with Bismarck (G. P. VII, no. 1379).

[134] Holstein's remark in Harden I, p. 100: "We cannot expect anything tangible from it and if it becomes known we shall be branded as deceitful fellows." See also Holstein's letter of March 27, 1890 (*Der Tag* November 4, 1920); Schweinitz II, p. 404.

But this line of approach misses the point entirely.[135] The prestige of Bismarck was so great that no Russian statesman, or any other of the time, had the courage to attempt beating him at his own game. The Benedetti incident of earlier days had made a lasting impression on the diplomatic world and the German chancellor was looked upon as a man who could all too easily turn the tables on anyone audacious enough to attempt tricking him. It was not to be expected that the same awe should be shown of his successor. A second and more important point is that Russia's interest in maintaining the secrecy of the treaty existed only so long as Russia was intent on preserving the *status quo*. Once she took action she would be obliged to lay every conceivable mine to blow up the coalition opposing her, and there was at least a possibility that, by divulging the treaty, she might estrange Austria and England from Germany.[136] Under such circumstances a Russian statesman who failed at least to make the attempt would have deserved dismissal for incompetence and timidity. Now it must be remembered that in Berlin in March 1890 practically everyone, including Bismarck, expected Russia to take action in the near future. The great chancellor may have regarded the situation with equanimity. His successors could not.

The question of the comparative advantages derived from the treaty by the two contracting powers was evidently of secondary importance. At any rate it was a complex problem. On the face of it, there can be no dispute that Russia appeared as the chief beneficiary. While Germany was guaranteed only Russian neutrality in case of a French attack, Germany promised Russia neutrality in case of an Austrian or English attack and furthermore recognized Russia's "preponderant and decisive" influence in Bulgaria, and promised support on three points: in reëstab-

---

[135] It may be doubted whether Bismarck was wholly sincere in this. After all, he knew perfectly well that the Tsar could not think of divulging the treaty, partly on account of the Katkov opposition and partly for fear of sacrificing all hope of French aid in a crisis. For Bismarck's utterances on the subject see G. P. V, no. 1099; VI, no. 1345; Hofmann II, p. 374, etc.

[136] G. P. VII, no. 1381. This fear was prevalent in some circles in Berlin even before Bismarck's dismissal (Eulenburg p. 286).

lishing a regular and legal government in Bulgaria; in upholding the Russian view as to the closure of the Straits; and in enabling the Tsar to take measures he might deem necessary to guard the "key of his empire."

This discrepancy was, however, more apparent than real. In the first place, some of the clauses of the secret protocol had been inserted at Bismarck's suggestion, and represented a gratuitous gift, so to speak.[137] But even in the essentials it is obvious that an assurance of Russian neutrality in case of a French attack was of at least as great importance to Germany as a similar guarantee of German neutrality in the event of an Austrian or English attack was to Russia.[138] Without the agreement Germany was constantly exposed to a joint attack by France and Russia. To be sure, the treaty did not exclude the possibility of a Franco-Russian Alliance, but it did prevent Russia from concluding an offensive agreement with France against Germany,[139] and there was practically no prospect of France embarking upon a war of revenge so long as she could not be certain of Russian support. Bismarck himself repeatedly emphasized the fact that the treaty, by leaving Germany the possibility of a more extensive agreement with Russia, safeguarded the former against pressure from Vienna or attempts by Austria or England to make Germany their tool against Russia in the Balkans.[140]

On the other hand Russia was not exposed to attack by Austria so long as the latter could not count on German support in such

[137] Goriainov, *passim*; M. N. Pokrovski: Russko-Germanskie Otnoshenia (*Krasny Arkhiv* I, pp. 96 ff., 124). Giers never attached much importance to these concessions, and even Paul Shuvalov was under no illusions as to their "caractère théoretique et purement éventuel." Schweinitz (II, p. 404), however, objected to the protocol and meant to vote against its renewal even if Bismarck remained in office.

[138] See important utterances of Bismarck on this point in G. P. V, no. 1100; Hofmann I, 102, 114, etc.; Radowitz II, p. 314. In 1887 Bismarck believed that Russia would not intervene even in a Franco-German War (Eulenburg p. 134).

[139] Hofmann I, p. 107. Schweinitz concurred in this opinion, both in 1887 and in 1890 (G. P. V, no. 1093; VII, nos. 1370, 1373.)

[140] Bismarck: *Gedanken und Erinnerungen* III, p. 263. See especially the long review of the Russian considerations, dated August 1879, in the *Krasny Arkhiv* vol. I, pp. 78 ff.

an aggressive enterprise.[141] The assurance of German neutrality in case of a Russo-English contest was undoubtedly of greater value, but even so it should be remembered that there was slight danger of England taking the aggressive. Her interest was to maintain the *status quo* and check Russia rather than to advance herself. The treaty did, indeed, give Russia the opportunity of taking the offensive in Bulgaria and of choosing her own time. But the Mediterranean Agreements of 1887 were designed to meet just this eventuality.[142] Germany had no cause for apprehension.

On one point the statesmen who followed Bismarck were quite agreed. They believed that the whole Bismarckian system was too complicated for anyone but the master-builder himself.[143] It has been pointed out by some writers that the problem was not so difficult as it appeared, and that at least a man of Holstein's ability might have continued to run the engine after Bismarck had left it in perfect condition.[144] This might have been true if the political outlook had been clear, but the expected advance of the Russians threatened to test the German system, and in view of this possibility the new chancellor and his advisers thought it wise to extricate themselves from all embarrassing entanglements, and to concentrate on a simple, straightforward policy.[145]

By way of summarizing the preceding observations it might be said that, on the whole, the arguments used on March 23 and embodied in the Berchem memorandum were tenable and sound. If the treaty in its existing form was worth renewing it should have been worth Bismarck's retention in power. It is hardly just to blame Caprivi and his subordinates for deciding against

---

[141] Hofmann II, p. 383; Hans Plehn: *Bismarcks auswärtige Politik nach der Reichsgründung* (Munich 1920) p. 313.

[142] See especially Felix Rachfahl: Der Rückversicherungsvertrag, etc. (*Weltwirtschaftliches Archiv* July 1, 1920, particularly pp. 63-64, 75).

[143] Cf. among others Schweinitz II, p. 404; Hammann: *Der neue Kurs* p. 35; Raschdau (*Grenzboten* 1918, pp. 25 ff.); Marschall in G. P. XXX¹, no. 10989.

[144] Heinrich Friedjung: *Das Zeitalter des Imperialismus* (Berlin 1919) I, p. 122; Plehn p. 330; Rothfels: *Preussische Jahrbücher* 1922, p. 290 note 2; Richard Fester: *Deutsche Rundschau*, October 1920.

[145] Cf. Hammann: *Deutsche Weltpolitik* p. 32: "Der Verzicht war ein Fehler, wenn Bismarck blieb, er war eine notwendige Vorsicht, wenn er ging."

the treaty after Bismarck's dismissal. The real blunder lay in the dismissal of Bismarck, in putting off the pilot who alone was able to sail the ship. The Kaiser might assert that the course would remain the same, but he soon found out that the rocks were too dangerous for his unpracticed hand and that a divergence was absolutely necessary.

Fortune gave the Kaiser and his new ministers an extraordinary opportunity to retrieve the error of Bismarck's dismissal before any harm had been done. The occasion was the new offer of Giers in May, when the Russian minister suggested the renewal of the treaty without the protocol and without the German recognition of Russia's preponderant and decisive influence in Bulgaria. In this revised form the treaty might still have involved for Germany a conflict with her other agreements, but it certainly equalized the terms and removed any suggestion of disloyalty to Austria. In other words, the new suggestion of Giers altered the situation materially, and necessitated a reconsideration of German policy. It is highly interesting to examine the arguments advanced on this occasion. We have memoranda by Holstein, Marschall, Kiderlen, Raschdau and Caprivi, and these embody some important and enlightening considerations.[146] Holstein's brief is concerned almost entirely with the idea that even in its revised form the treaty would bind Germany to support Russia in her view of the closure of the Straits, that this view was diametrically opposed to the English view, and that by divulging the treaty Russia could at any time drive a wedge between Germany and England. Kiderlen enlarged on the same subject, and expatiated on the dangers of such obligations, as shown during the Afghan crisis of 1885. Raschdau and Caprivi dilated on the fact that the treaty, after all, would be of little value to Germany, for even in the event of a French attack on Germany the Tsar could not allow France to be entirely crushed, and would be forced by public opinion to intervene. But what appears most clearly from these documents is that the German statesmen were above all apprehensive lest Russia should utilize the secret treaty as a charge with which to blow up the

[146] G. P. VII, nos. 1374 ff.

Triple Alliance and the Anglo-German friendship. The objection was not to the treaty as such, but to *any* secret treaty.[147] Raschdau advised making the renewal of the agreement contingent on its publication, firmly convinced that the Russians would reject such a public treaty as worthless for their purposes. This suggestion was passed over, and Holstein apparently did not press his own view that an open agreement might be possible.

It is difficult to find much justification for the German policy on this occasion. Even if the Russians were planning an attack on Constantinople and the Straits and desired the treaty for this purpose, one fails to see why Germany should have been so concerned. In 1885 both Austria and Italy, to say nothing of France, had sided with Germany in supporting the Russian view of the Straits agreements as against the English. The German statesmen were really placed in the position of having to choose between Russia and England or Austria.[148] They had no obligations to England and Bismarck had always carefully avoided making himself the catspaw of the island empire or any other power. Caprivi and his advisers knowingly cut the wire to St. Petersburg. They cast a substantial treaty with Russia into the discard for the Platonic friendship of England. To be sure, the treaty was still incompatible with the other agreements, but Giers had expressed a willingness to accept even an informal paper—an exchange of notes, or even of imperial letters. What he was mostly concerned with was the recognition of the Russian claims in Bulgaria and the promise of support in maintaining the closure of the Straits. His offer was almost conclusive proof that Russia, if she took action at all, would do so by sea, not through the Balkans.

[147] This is borne out in striking fashion by an entry in Schweinitz' diary (quoted by Becker p. 59). From this it appears that on March 27 Caprivi was more opposed to the treaty without the protocol than with, for he regarded the existence of the protocol as the one guarantee that the Russians would not divulge the treaty.

[148] Writing retrospectively in 1911 Marschall (G. P. XXX¹, nos. 10987, 10989, 10998) attempts to justify the German policy in 1890 by arguing that to support the Russian Straits policy would have been disloyal to Austria. This reasoning is quite unconvincing in view of the fact that in 1885 Austria upheld the Russian interpretation of the treaties. Giers had, by May, dropped the features of the treaty that might have been objectionable from the Austrian viewpoint.

Giers had opened the door wide for negotiations. The Germans closed it with a bang.

It has been necessary to enter in so great detail upon the story of the nonrenewal of the Reinsurance Treaty, because its importance was well-nigh epochal. Throughout the whole negotiations the German statesmen acted as a group of theorists, a group of hair-splitting lawyers. Nowhere is there an indication that they realized the possible psychological effects of their action. They showed no appreciation whatsoever for the Russian view. They were concerned entirely with a consideration of the possible dangers of renewing the treaty. They forgot to take into account the possible dangers of not renewing it. Bismarck had tossed in bed many a sleepless night, haunted by the spectre of a Franco-Russian Alliance and a war on two fronts. His successors comforted themselves with the argument that the danger of a Franco-Russian Alliance was steadily diminishing, and that in any case the French would never consent to the abandonment of the Straits to Russia.

The Russians could not be expected to understand the motives underlying the German policy. They could not know of the possible contradictions in Germany's numerous obligations, nor could they suppose that the Germans had suddenly concluded that the treaty was not advantageous to them. Bismarck had never made a secret of the value he attached to the agreement. At the same time it should be remarked that there is not a trace of evidence that the Russians meant to utilize the treaty to sow dissension between Germany and her allies or friends. As for Caprivi's declarations that Germany's attitude was unchanged but that the new policy must be simple and transparent, this argument seemed unconvincing to the Russians. All they knew was that, after the Kaiser had explicitly declared in favor of renewal, the German attitude had suddenly changed. While Caprivi insisted that Germany would continue to recognize Russia's position in Bulgaria, he steadfastly refused even the most informal written declaration to that effect. No concessions could overcome the German obstinacy. It was but human to seek an explanation for this extraordinary conduct.

We have a pretty detailed account of the reaction of the Russians to these events. The Tsar declared himself content and received the news with equanimity.[149] This may have been due to his natural dislike of the Germans and his aversion to written agreements. He had long felt that the Germans had not been playing him entirely fair, and his dignity prevented his showing regret even if he felt it.

But Giers, the foreign minister, made no effort to conceal his apprehension. For eight years he had fought the Pan-Slav agitation and had defended the alliance with Germany. He recognized the value of the treaty for Russia, not so much for what was written, as for the fact that it embodied friendly relations and served as a check on Austria and England. Now he saw himself isolated, confronted by the Triple Alliance and a hostile England on friendly terms with Germany. He actually begged for a mere scrap of paper, and when this was refused he could no longer evade the conclusion that Germany intended a change of policy after all—she evidently meant to extend her support of Austria, and was probably hoping for the accession of England to the Triple Alliance, thus completing the bulwark that obstructed Russia's advance on Constantinople. The nonrenewal of the Reinsurance Treaty thus necessitated a reconsideration of Russian policy.[150] If plans had been laid for action in the spring of 1890 they had to be given up for the time being. Russia was, for the moment, on the defensive, watching developments and preparing to guard against any hostile steps that might be taken by the enemy.

[149] Goriainov p. 344.
[150] Cf. Schweinitz II, p. 422: "Hierzu war es (Russland) nicht nur berechtigt, sondern sogar gezwungen."

CHAPTER III

THE NEW COURSE

THE position of the new chancellor was a very difficult one, not only in respect to domestic policy, but also in regard to foreign affairs. In questions of international relations he was wholly inexperienced and it was only with profound reluctance that he had agreed to assume the responsibilities of the new position.[1] Like most of the military men he was imbued with the idea of an inevitable war between Germany on the one hand and Russia and France on the other. Not that he was a *Kriegshetzer* like Waldersee, but he was decidedly pessimistic of the future, believed in keeping his powder dry and in cultivating the friendship of anti-Russian powers like England, while at the same time straining every nerve to maintain close connections with Germany's allies and contributing so far as possible to the consolidation of the entente between these powers and the island empire.[2]

Marschall von Bieberstein, the new foreign minister, was also quite inexperienced in international affairs, but was known to sympathize with the Austrians as against the Russians, this being also the attitude of Holstein, who at last found himself without a rival in the foreign office so far as knowledge of foreign affairs and German policy was concerned.

It may be said without fear of contradiction that neither the Kaiser nor Caprivi intended a change of front in Germany's relations with her neighbors. Indeed, the dictates of common sense demanded that all appearance of change should be avoided. But it was only natural that the powers should feel uneasy and

[1] Caprivi was known as an able and energetic administrator, but only in official circles. On Caprivi's reluctance to assume the position see his letters in the *Deutsche Revue* 1922, pp. 140 ff. He told the Prussian Diet on April 15, 1890 that he felt he was beginning with a deficit.

[2] Lucius p. 269; Tirpitz pp. 23-26; Hans Delbrück: *Bismarcks Erbe* (Berlin 1915) p. 184; Irmer: *Völkerdämmerung im Stillen Ozean* (Leipzig 1915) p. 49, and the evidence in G. P. *passim*.

suspicious. The Kaiser enjoyed a reputation for belligerent tendencies, and it was believed unlikely that he would dismiss a statesman of Bismarck's calibre and international prestige unless he intended to start off on a new tack. Anxiety, however, was much less prevalent in Germany, Austria and Italy than in the countries outside the Triple Alliance.[3] Already on March 22 Lerchenfeld could remark that in Vienna and Rome the excitement had largely subsided.[4] This was probably due to the efforts of the German government and of the Kaiser. The German representatives abroad were informed that the resignation of the chancellor had nothing to do with foreign affairs, and letters were despatched to the sovereigns.[5] A full account of the crisis was given to Francis Joseph, and the Austrians before long were apparently convinced and satisfied.[6]

Of the apprehension of Giers and of Russian official circles mention has already been made. In Paris the government circles were no less disturbed. Freycinet tells us that, while Bismarck had never showed any affection for France, his policy had been based on German interests and not on personal prejudice.[7] With the great chancellor out of the way it was feared that the young emperor's likes and dislikes would be decisive and that his warlike proclivities would be given full rein. The French press, too,

---

[3] Schweinitz II, p. 408; Wilhelm Mommsen: *Bismarcks Sturz und die Parteien* (Stuttgart 1924). Cf. the political review in the *Rassegna Nazionale* April 1, 1890, and the article "Der Rücktritt des Fürsten Bismarck und das Ausland" in *Preussische Jahrbücher* volume 65, pp. 577 ff. (1890); *Mémorial Diplomatique* March 22, 1890. *London Times* March 20, 1890: "There is something that jars upon the feelings in the readiness with which public opinion in Germany and Austria has acquiesced in the retreat of the Great Chancellor."

[4] Lerchenfeld p. 167; Eduard von Wertheimer: Bismarcks Sturz (*Preussische Jahrbücher* June 1921, pp. 333-334).

[5] Crispi: *Memoirs* II, p. 431, 433. The German government assured the Italians that no attempt would be made to restore the temporal power.

[6] The correspondence with Francis Joseph in the *Oesterreichische Rundschau* 1919, pp. 100 ff. Kálnoky instructed the Austrian representatives to join their German colleagues in reassuring the foreign governments (Deym to Kálnoky March 27; Kálnoky to Aehrenthal April 12, 1890).

[7] Charles de Freycinet: *Souvenirs 1878-1893* (Paris 1913) pp. 437-440; Hoyos to Kálnoky March 27, 1890 (Wertheimer in *Preussische Jahrbücher* June 1921, p. 333); *Spectator* March 22, 1890. *London Times* March 19, 1890.

spoke in a very appreciative vein and on the whole recognized frankly that Bismarck had worked for the maintenance of peace.[8]

The English, on their part, were inclined to assume a detached attitude of watchful waiting. Lord Salisbury and the conservative press had viewed the Kaiser's social experiments with distrust, and they were distinctly sceptical as to Germany's future.[9] The famous cartoon "Dropping the Pilot" brings this out most clearly. "The greatest change at all possible in the personnel of European statesmanship excites interest, indeed, but no particular alarm," wrote the *Saturday Review*.[10]

"We cannot but think that Prince Bismarck's resignation will prove, on the whole, and perhaps by degrees, unfavorable to continued peace," remarked the *Spectator*,[11] for the "awe of Bismarck's unbending character and terribly large views was very deep," and "this, the removal of an overhanging source of dread or reverence, will be the main result of Prince Bismarck's resignation, and it must in some degree, so to speak, loosen the bonds of Europe.. All the frogs will be feeling as if the stork had flown away."

And a week later the same paper was more pessimistic yet:

"We are wholly unable to take the optimistic view of the situation on the continent.. The great fly-wheel of the machine has been removed, and if there is not a crash, it will be due to Providence, not to the engineers."

---

[8] Schoen's report (G. P. VI, no. 1363). Valbert, in the *Revue des Deux Mondes* (April 1, 1890) wrote very characteristically: "L'Europe a fini par s'accoutumer à M. de Bismarck, par le connaître et le comprendre. Pendant ces quinze dernières années, il lui avait donné par intervalles de vives alertes, lui avait fait passer de mauvais moments. A la longue elle s'était aperçue que ses incartades n'étaient, le plus souvent, que des manoeuvres destinées à influencer les electeurs ou les votes du parlement, que son éloquence était plus noire que son âme, que tant qu'il vivrait et gouvernait il n'y aurait plus de grande guerre européenne. Aujourd'hui tout est rémis en question." See summary of French press comment in *London Times* March 21, 1890.

[9] Deym to Kálnoky March 20, 27; April 23, 1890. Cf. also Wertheimer in *Preussische Jahrbücher* June 1921, p. 333. On his return from Berlin Prince Edward reported to Salisbury that he had found the Kaiser very anxious to be on good terms with the English. The premier passed this on to the Queen with the characteristic comment: "So long as it lasts, this mood is very valuable, but will it last?" (Lee I, p. 662.)

[10] *Saturday Review* March 22, 1890.

[11] *Spectator* March 22, 1890.

"We seem to be entering on stirring times," wrote Mr. Stead, the well-known editor of the *Review of Reviews*; "It will be well if we emerge without a spill, for the German coach has lost its brake."[12]

The general reaction, then, was one of apprehension and uncertainty, rather than one of alarm. What complicated the situation, from the German point of view, was the growing friction with England resulting from the activities of German explorers in eastern and central Africa. The rivalry of the two nations had, by April 1890, assumed dangerous dimensions, and the English press was beginning to indulge in very acrimonious remarks, not to say recriminations.[13]

This development was by no means pleasing to either the English or the German governments. The former had for years done its utmost to preserve good relations with Berlin, and had not forgotten the lesson taught by Bismarck in 1884, namely that the price of indispensable German support in the Egyptian question was full consideration and recognition of Germany's legitimate ambitions in the colonial field. Ever since 1887 the French and the Russians had been coöperating in a loose way to keep the Egyptian question open and to stir up the Sultan against the English. At this very moment the Porte submitted a new draft for a convention providing for evacuation, and the French were raising difficulties for the English proposal to convert the Egyptian debt.[14] The object of this projected conversion was to

---

[12] *Review of Reviews* April 1890, p. 256.

[13] The friction on these matters went back to the early part of 1889 (see G. P. IV, no. 946, VIII, nos. 1672 ff.; Waldersee II, p. 131; Hohenlohe II, pp. 470-471; Deym to Kálnoky April 9, 13, May 13, June 5, 1890). The English press was uniformly bitter in its comments. According to the *Saturday Review* (May 3, 1890) the action of the Germans was of "the most vexatious, unwarrantable and unfriendly character." There is a good brief account of the various points in dispute by Francis de Winton in the *Nineteenth Century* for May, 1890. Already in December 1889 tentative discussions had been opened between England and Germany (G. P. VIII, nos. 1672 ff). Evidently Bismarck's fall had postponed negotiations.

[14] Mme. Adam, one of Bismarck's most inveterate enemies, suggested in the *Nouvelle Revue* of May 1, 1890 that the situation was excellent for reopening the Egyptian question, while England and Germany were at odds in Africa. On the negotiations see G. P. VIII, nos. 1775 ff.; Freycinet pp. 450-452.

raise the necessary funds for the reconquest of the Sudan, a step which became more urgent the more precarious the English hold upon Egypt itself became.[15]   The idea of a Cape to Cairo route was much in vogue even at that time, and it was believed that the Germans, as well as the French, were considering the conquest of all equatorial Africa.   Lord Salisbury had, therefore, from the very beginning advocated an amicable arrangement. In the general confusion he could not afford to sacrifice German support at a time when the Egyptian question was troublesome, and when there were all sorts of rumors and indications of coming complications in the Near East.[16]

The new men in Berlin were no less anxious for an agreement for they could not think of facing the future with England hostile while Russia was estranged.[17]   Moreover, the Kaiser and his counsellors believed that English support of the "League of Peace" was absolutely indispensable for the continued existence of that League itself.[18]   William II, who, in his earlier years had been notorious for his Anglophobe views, had recovered from them in a remarkably short time after his accession to the throne. The differences between him and the Prince of Wales, his uncle, had been patched over, and the appointment as admiral of the fleet had completed the conversion of the young ruler from his pro-Russian sympathies to the English view.[19]   In the critical

---

[15] G. P. VIII, nos. 1778-1779. The connection between the Heligoland Treaty and England's Egyptian policy has been ably set forth by Adolf Hasenclever: Zur Geschichte des Helgolandvertrages (*Archiv für Politik und Geschichte* November 1925).

[16] This point is interestingly developed in the *Spectator* May 31, June 14, 1890. It should also be remembered that the perennial dispute between England and France regarding the fishing rights on the Newfoundland coast had become acute in the spring of 1890.

[17] For a moment they seem to have feared that England and France would come to an agreement on the conversion of the Egyptian debt (G. P. VII, no. 1543).

[18] William, even before his accession, had given his approval to the Mediterranean Triplice and after his appointment as Admiral of the Fleet in 1889 he took his position very seriously and frequently dispensed advice to the English admiralty, particularly in regard to its Mediterranean squadron (Lee I, pp. 657-658; Lord George Hamilton: *Reminiscences* pp. 139-140).

[19] On the Kaiser's early Anglophobia see Bismarck: *Gedanken und Erinnerungen* III, pp. 134-135; Lucius p. 244; Waldersee: *Denkwürdigkeiten* I, p. 247, and

days of March, 1890, the Prince of Wales was his nephew's guest in Berlin, the future King George V was decorated with the order of the Black Eagle, and the happy reunion was made an occasion for high-sounding imperial speeches in which William recalled the Anglo-German comradeship in arms at Waterloo and expressed hope for the future coöperation of the strongest navy in the world with the continent's strongest army.[20]

Till the end of his days Bismarck seems to have believed that English influence played some part in his dismissal.[21]   There is no adequate evidence to substantiate his suspicions, but the old chancellor had on numerous occasions been compelled to struggle against the English family influence, and one can readily understand that the presence of Prince Edward in Berlin during the crisis should have roused distrust.[22] It should be remembered, however, that Bismarck's attitude towards the English government was entirely distinct from his sentiments towards the royal family.   It would be going too far afield to attempt a review of his entire English policy, but it is perfectly evident that in the great statesman's calculations England had played a rôle subordinate only to that of Russia.[23] The whole of German policy after 1870 may be described as an attempt to hold the balance

especially his correspondence with Alexander III in 1884-1885 (*Krasny Arkhiv* II, pp. 118-129). On his reconciliation with Prince Edward see especially Lee I, pp. 651 ff.

[20] Hohenlohe II, p. 463; Lee I, p. 661.

[21] Hofmann I, pp. 106-7; Penzler: *Fürst Bismarck nach seiner Entlassung* VII, p. 139. Lee I, p. 659, thinks Edward was invited to Berlin in view of the Kaiser's determination to dismiss Bismarck. There is nothing to support this conjecture.

[22] Especially the question of the Battenberg marriage in 1888 (Bismarck: *Gedanken und Erinnerungen* III, chapter iii; Corti, chapter xi; G. P. chapter xlii), and the attempt made by Queen Victoria to influence William II, soon after his accession (William II: *Ereignisse* pp. 21-22; G. P. VI, no. 1346). The Prince of Wales had also attempted on occasion to interfere in German policy (see G.P. VI, no. 1346 and above all Lee pp. 262, 365, 643-644, 646 ff., 649).

[23] The two most important and scholarly surveys of Bismarck's policy towards England are those of Felix Rachfahl: *Bismarcks englische Bündnispolitik* (Freiburg 1922) and of Hans Rothfels, with the same title (Stuttgart 1924). Cf. also the admirable discussion in Otto Becker: *Bismarcks Bündnispolitik* (Berlin 1923), chapter iii; and F. Frahm: England und Russland in Bismarcks Bündnispolitik (*Archiv für Politik und Geschichte* VIII, pp. 265-431, 1927).

between the two traditional enemies, Russia and England. At one time Bismarck would incline more to the one, then more to the other, but he was always as anxious to prevent a break with the one as with the other. At times, when the situation in the East seemed particularly black and hopeless, he even went so far as to suggest or propose an alliance with England, and he had, in 1887, succeeded in associating the island empire with Germany's allies in what was known as the "Eastern" or "Mediterranean Triplice." Very likely this arrangement fully realized the rôle which Bismarck desired England to play in European politics.[24] Without prejudicing his agreement with Russia he thus secured for Austria a measure of support in Balkan questions which Germany was unwilling to give, and for Italy the necessary naval protection against France which Germany was unable to give.[25]

It is obvious, then, that in seeking to maintain close relations with England the men of the New Course were honestly attempting to follow the principles laid down by their great predecessor. The danger lay in a possible overdoing of friendly demonstrations and in the fact that Russia, no longer in possession of any written agreement with Germany, would necessarily view with greater apprehension than before any indications of a closer rapprochement. This was what actually happened in the case of the so-called Heligoland Treaty of June 1890, and therein lies its larger significance in general European developments.

The story of the actual negotiations need not detain us here.[26]

---

[24] See especially his masterful review of his policy in the despatch to Reuss and Hatzfeld April 20, 1887: "Wir können in dem dreiseitigen Bündnis mit Oesterreich und Italien weder die Türkei noch England brauchen..." (quoted by Trützschler von Falkenstein: *Bismarck und die Kriegsgefahr des Jahres 1887* [Berlin 1924] pp. 88-89; see also G. P. IX, no. 2117 with footnote).

[25] Cf. Despatch to Vienna February 28, 1888 (G. P. X, no. 2555 footnote): "Die drei Mittelmeermächte bilden ein in friedlichem Sinne wirkendes Gegengewicht gegen solche orientalische Bestrebungen Russlands, welche ihre gemeinsamen Interessen bedrohen könnten, ohne die unsrigen zu berühren."

[26] A long account was published in the *Reichsanzeiger* on July 30, 1890; the pertinent documents are in G. P. VIII, chapter li. The reports of Deym to Kálnoky May 13, June 10, 18, 1890 also throw some light on the discussions.

They were taken up seriously in May, 1890, and it soon appeared that the main points in dispute were those concerning the western frontier of German East Africa and the protectorate over Zanzibar and Witu, the one a great emporium, the other a well-known base of munitions supply. Neither side showed much inclination to yield until Salisbury finally suggested the cession of Heligoland in return for Witu and the Zanzibar protectorate. The Germans held out to the end on the question of the boundary in the west and finally won their point, cutting off the English from direct connections between the north and south. But they were only too ready to accept Heligoland in return for concessions in Zanzibar and Witu.

The idea of acquiring the rocky island in the North Sea was by no means a new one in Germany.[27] It appears that Caprivi had long advocated it, and that he considered the North Sea-Baltic Canal of little value so long as the island remained in the hands of a foreign power. Soon after taking over the position of chief of the admiralty in 1883 he had raised the question and had succeeded in persuading Bismarck to take steps towards securing its cession to Germany. Advances were made to England in May, 1884, Germany agreeing to build a harbor on the island if England would agree to give it up.[28] For some unknown reason the negotiations were dropped, and it was not until March, 1889 that the question was again raised, this time informally by Herbert Bismarck and Hatzfeld. Salisbury, however, showed little enthusiasm, and the Bismarcks deemed it expedient to allow the matter to rest. By this time the Kaiser had become one of the most passionate supporters of the project, and it was

[27] For the earlier history of the question see especially von Hagen: *Geschichte und Bedeutung des Helgolandvertrages* (Munich 1916) and the same author's *Bismarcks Kolonialpolitik* (Gotha 1923).

[28] England had been casually sounded on the matter in 1873 (Sir Edmond Fitzmaurice: *The Life of Lord Granville* [New York 1905] II, p. 113). On Caprivi's policy in 1883 see his letter in the *Deutsche Revue* 1922, p. 251 and Hammann: *Der neue Kurs* p. 20. For the negotiations of 1884 see Fitzmaurice II, pp. 351-361, and G. P. IV, nos. 738-741. Széchényi to Kálnoky August 7, 1890 reports that in 1883 the German admiralty considered the extension of the Kiel Canal to Jade Bay, so that ships might be sent from Kiel to Wilhelmshaven without passing Heligoland.

only with great difficulty that he was dissuaded from raising the subject in conversation during his trip to England in the summer of 1889.[29]

Once Salisbury suggested the exchange of Heligoland for African territory the German government laid chief emphasis on this point. It was not merely a matter of sentiment, but a question of strategy. The government was fully aware of its value and regarded its possession as almost indispensable.[30] Not that it was looked upon as a menace while in English hands, or that it was intended as a fortress against the English fleet.[31] Few, if any German writers even considered the possibility of war with England, but Heligoland was considered as a menace because, in a Franco-German war, with England neutral, it would have served as a convenient coaling station and shelter for a French blockading fleet.[32]

The English, though they suggested the cession, were very hesitant about giving up the island. The country was superstitious about abandoning territory in Europe and some members of the government, at least, were not entirely convinced of the advisability of abandoning the outpost.[33] Salisbury himself spoke of the island as a mere sandbar, which, sooner or later, would be undermined and washed away, and finally the naval

[29] G. P. IV, nos. 946, 950, 951; William II: *Ereignisse* p. 10.

[30] G. P. IV, nos. 739, 946; VIII, nos. 1680, 1681. Curiously enough the German admiralty in 1890 appears to have attached little value to the island (Tirpitz p. 59; Delbrück pp. 134-135). Vice-Admiral Batsch's interesting article in the *Deutsche Rundschau* October 1890, pp. 120-130, bears this out. See the discussion in various opinions in Manfred Sell: *Das deutsch-englische Abkommen von 1890* (Berlin 1926), pp. 38 ff.

[31] Tirpitz p. 59. Bismarck himself believed a war with England to be almost inconceivable (G. P. II, p. 351, and his talk with Kingston of the *Daily Telegraph* on June 10, 1890, in Penzler I, p. 105).

[32] G. P. IV, nos. 775, 949; also Vice-Admiral Henk in *Hamburger Nachrichten* June 19, 1890.

[33] A. E. *Gathorne-Hardy, a Memoir* (London 1910) II, p. 318, shows that there were rather animated cabinet meetings on the subject on June 3, 8 and 11. See also G. P. VIII, nos. 1684, 1688. Greenwood in the *Contemporary Review* (August 1890) objected violently to the cession, and Colonel Maxse, the ex-governor of the island, declared in the *Daily Graphic* that for £1,000,000 Heligoland could be made into a "Gibraltar of the North."

authorities, after careful investigation, decided that even in a
war with Germany it could not be defended unless it were
heavily fortified and unless a strong detachment of the fleet
were stationed there to protect it. Taken all in all it would
hamper rather than promote the effective action of the English
fleet.[34] The mistake of the English was not so much in ceding
the island as in ceding it to Germany.

The Heligoland Treaty certainly did much to remove possible
sources of conflict between England and Germany and it did
put an end to the growing irritation on both sides.[35] On the
whole the agreement was well received by both peoples. In
England there appears to have been an understanding between
the government and the opposition leaders.[36] There was no
serious objection raised in parliament, and the press was almost
unanimous in declaring the bargain a good one. According to
Stanley, who had led the journalistic opposition to Germany's
colonial encroachments, England had secured a new pair of
trousers for an old suspender button.[37] Sir Harry Johnston
openly stated that he viewed the agreement with "great satisfaction."[38] On the German side the *Kolonialmenschen* were,

[34] Lord George Hamilton p. 140-142, who, as first lord of the admiralty in
1890, was chiefly responsible. Salisbury's opinion in G. P. IV, no. 949. The *Saturday Review* (June 21, 28, 1890) thought the island "of very little practical importance to England.. It has been long known that the island, except for the two
purposes of sentiment and smuggling, is of very dubious value and that its only
possible military or naval use would come in at conjunctures which would make
it practically useless." On July 12, 1890 the same paper wrote that the government had the "overwhelming majority of naval and military experts behind it."
The *Spectator* (June 21, 1890) declared Heligoland "of no earthly value to any
power" and remarked: "If there is any knowledge of geography left in our countrymen, that settles the acceptance of the treaty."

[35] Even Bismarck admitted that the agreement had this good side, though he
protested against the abandonment of Zanzibar (*Gedanken und Erinnerungen* III,
Chapter xi; Busch: *Bismarck* (London 1898) III, p. 353; Hofmann I *passim*, for
Bismarckian utterances in the *Hamburger Nachrichten*).

[36] There is an excellent investigation of this and other points in connection
with the English policy in Hasenclever: Zur Geschichte des Helgolandvertrages
(*Archiv für Politik und Geschichte* November 1925).

[37] Friedjung I, p. 138.

[38] Sir Harry Johnston in *Fortnightly Review* July 1890, p. 124. The *Saturday
Review* (June 21, 1890) declared: "The bargain is a thoroughly good bargain and

of course, rabid in their denunciations of the government's indifference, but the public at large was deeply gratified by the
acquisition of Heligoland.[39]

But the good points of the agreement were counterbalanced
by some bad effects, from which Germany was eventually to
suffer. The statesmen in Berlin had been very anxious to conciliate England and this anxiety appears clearly in the discussions
regarding the Reinsurance Treaty, especially in May. What
they failed to realize was that the Tsar would view this new turn
with great and even unreasonable distrust. Shuvalov, reflecting
the Bismarckian view, had begun by reporting the anti-Russian
tendencies of the Kaiser, and stated frankly that in his opinion
the nonrenewal of the treaty was in part at least traceable to
the Kaiser's desire to draw nearer to England. The unusual
demonstrations connected with the presence of the Prince of
Wales in Berlin gave color to these suggestions, and other minor
events appeared to strengthen the suspicions of the Russians.[40]
In May a bill was introduced in the Reichstag calling for an increase of 18,000 men for the army, the reasons for the demand
given by the government being the recent military acts passed in
France and the augmentation of Russia's forces.[41] At the same
time the Kaiser went to Königsberg and delivered two unmistakably belligerent speeches, in one of which he promised the
members of the East Prussian diet that he would allow no one
to lay hands on the province, and that he who dared do so would
find the Kaiser opposing him like a rock of bronze.[42] A month
later, on the eve of the anniversary of Waterloo, came the pub-

---

the best thing of the kind that any English government has made since Lord Bea-
consfield made the Suez Canal a mainly English property.«

[39] See the summary of press comment in *Preussische Jahrbücher* volume 66
(1890), pp. 90-91, and the monographic study by Sell: *Das deutsch-englische Abkommen von 1890.*

[40] Wolkenstein to Kálnoky March 25, 1890; Aehrenthal to Kálnoky April 3, 16
1890. See also G. P. VI, nos. 1364-1365; Goriainov pp. 344-346, 349.

[41] Speech from the throne May 6, 1890. On the impression made upon the
Tsar see Goriainov pp. 348-49. Evidently the Russians believed that Waldersee
was now the real master in Berlin (Waldersee II, pp. 128-129).

[42] J. Penzler: *Reden Kaiser Wilhelms II* (Leipzig n. d.) volume ii, pp. 113-116.

lication of the Heligoland Treaty, coincident with the expiration of the Reinsurance Treaty.[43]

The Tsar was "deeply hurt and angered" by the Kaiser's speeches, which he regarded as a warning for him not to follow in the footsteps of Napoleon. So exasperated was Alexander that the Austrian ambassador could report: "The love felt here for Kaiser William is already quite half-hearted and weak," and Schweinitz went so far as to tell his colleague that in his opinion the Austrians stood better in St. Petersburg than the Germans.[44]

To top it all came the Kaiser's visit to England in August. The reception given him was a very hearty one, and the newspapers, which had been enthusiastic in June now became almost rhapsodical. There was undoubtedly a good deal of calculation behind the press comments, for it was in the English interest to picture Anglo-German relations as more intimate than they actually were. But the Tsar could read in almost any English paper editorials that must have sounded very significant to him. The *Morning Post*, generally regarded as a governmental organ, welcomed the Kaiser as "the most sincere exponent of the only true peace policy" and announced that "the period of England's isolation is over," while the *Times* expressed the opinion that England and Germany should always be allies. The *Daily Telegraph* went even further, and stated "that everywhere in Europe the (Heligoland) Treaty is regarded as the prelude of a not formal but nevertheless sound Anglo-German Alliance." The *Saturday Review* on June 28, 1890, spoke of the treaty as having gained for Germany not only Heligoland, but the "fast alliance with England" and the *Review of Reviews* declared in July

[43] The Tsar was particularly grieved by the cession of Heligoland to Germany. He had apparently hoped that it would be given to Denmark, which planned, in that case, to exchange it for part of Northern Schleswig (Deym to Kálnoky September 24, 1890). Vlangali, the assistant of Giers, complained bitterly to Morier, the English ambassador, and prophesied that England would pay dearly for her action in the future war between England and Germany, which he regarded as inevitable (Wolkenstein to Kálnoky June 25, 1890).

[44] Wolkenstein to Kálnoky May 20, 28, June 12, 1890. Cf. St. Petersburg letter in *Mémorial Diplomatique* May 24, 1890.

that the net effect of the treaty was "to pose England before the world as the informal ally and exceeding good friend of Germany, not only in Africa, but also in Europe." *Punch* published a cartoon showing the Kaiser and the Prince of Wales toasting each other. The legend read in part: "Nay Kaiser, 'tis not the actual Triple, but the conceivable Quadruple that perturbs the importunates...No Statecraft's Scarlet Seals, or scrawly Imperial Signs-manual need we for our amicable Treaty."[45]

Similar sentiments were voiced by the continental press. The *Wiener Politische Korrespondenz* wrote : "this visit may be described as, in a way, a supplement to the treaty of peace which unites Germany, Austria-Hungary and Italy, as at least a moral strengthening of the principles which form the basis of the Triple Alliance." Naturally enough the French newspapers exerted themselves to picture the situation as black as possible. There was much talk of secret clauses in the Anglo-German agreement, by which England supposedly promised Germany naval support in the Baltic in return for German support in Egypt.[46] Even a moderate writer like Gabriel Monod came to the conclusion that "it is difficult to avoid seeing in the treaty a partial accession of England to the Triple Alliance and a design on the part of the two nations to make common cause, in some degree, against France and Russia."[47]

[45] *Punch* July 11, 1891.

[46] The British government was interpellated in the house on June 27 as to whether there existed in the treaty a secret article providing for coöperation in time of war. The point was developed in the Paris *Temps* and *Figaro* and in many other papers. See *Preussische Jahrbücher* volume 66 (1890), pp. 90-91 and especially Mme. Adam in *Nouvelle Revue* July 15, 1890. Apparently the French government also suspected the existence of secret clauses (G. P. VIII, no. 1690). As a matter of fact, as a result of the treaty, the German representatives were instructed to support England in the Egyptian question (G. P. VIII, no. 1784).

[47] *Contemporary Review* July 1890, p. 34.

CHAPTER IV

THE NEAR EASTERN PROBLEM AND THE BEGINNINGS OF THE FRANCO-RUSSIAN ENTENTE

No one can find fault with the Russian statesmen for considering a reorientation of their policy after the events of March and June, 1890. Their position, simply stated, was this: Since 1870 they had been confronted with the problem of German hegemony on the continent, the obvious cure for which was an alliance with France, provided such an alliance could be obtained without excessive sacrifices. On the other hand Russian policy had met an apparently insurmountable obstacle in the antagonism of England, and this, if anything, was a more serious matter than the preponderance of Germany. For the Russian policy of intervening in central European affairs had of necessity come to a close with the unification of Germany in 1870.[1] So far as the continent was concerned the aspirations of the St. Petersburg government were confined to the Near East. It was obvious to any keen observer that the ultimate aim of the Tsar must be the control of the Bosporus and Dardanelles, with or without the possession of Constantinople[2]. It was an age-old policy even in 1890, and the Russian statesmen had pursued it unswervingly, varying their methods but never wavering in their determination to attain the goal. Economic as well as moral and political considerations were behind this policy, and it was almost as important for Russia as existence itself.

Since the period of the Crimean War the policy of the Tsars and their ministers had been based upon indirect action, in the hope of circumventing the opposition of the European powers. The plan was gradually to gain control of the Balkans and thus

[1] Schweinitz, November 9, 1886 (G. P. VI, no. 1206).

[2] Cf. G. P. V, nos. 978, 991, 1062. European diplomats were almost unanimous in declaring Alexander's ultimate goal to be the control of the Straits.

to construct a road to Constantinople. The Montenegrins and the Serbians had been supported by the Russians, and since 1877 attention had been concentrated on Bulgaria. But all the way through this plan had been foiled by the Austrian government, which had taken an ever livelier interest in the Near Eastern problem since the events of 1859-1866, which excluded the Hapsburgs from Italy and Germany. No doubt the attitude of the Viennese authorities had much to do with the determination of the Russians to shift their interest from Serbia to Bulgaria, just as the opposition of the Austrians was primarily responsible for the failure of the Russian attempt to establish a virtual protectorate over Bulgaria in the period following 1878. But it should be noted that in all this the Germans played no part. Bismarck had affirmed and reaffirmed that Germany had no direct interest in the Balkans and he had openly stated that he could see no objection to the acquisition of Constantinople by the Tsar.[3] There was no cause for friction here, and all that the Russians could hold against Bismarck was the conclusion of the Austro-German Alliance of 1879, a purely defensive arrangement which in no way involved German support of the Austrian ambitions in the Balkans. If the Russians resented this arrangement it was perhaps chiefly because of the realization that it had resulted primarily from their own blundering and from the bluster of a small group of Pan-Slav militarists, and because there was always the possibility that the agreement might be extended to include German coöperation with Austria against Russia.[4]

As a matter of fact Bismarck had always held aloof from the Balkan imbroglio, and had repeatedly rejected Austrian appeals

[3] Among other utterances see Bismarck's remark to Shuvalov in 1887 (*Krasny Arkhiv* I, p. 96): "L'Allemagne n'aurait rien à redire en vous voyant maîtres des détroits, possesseurs de l'entrée du Bosphore et de Constantinople même." It is not quite clear as to what Bismarck's intentions were in regard to the Dardanelles, though apparently he was willing to let the Russians have the key as well as the lock (G. P. VI, no. 1207). In the Reinsurance Treaty there is talk only of the "entrance to the Black Sea." See the discussion of this point in Rothfels: *Bismarcks englische Bündnispolitik* p. 102, and in Frankenberg p. 21, note 4.

[4] Cf. the interesting statement in *Preussische Jahrbücher* volume 65 (1890) p. 579 to the effect that Russian ill-will was really due to Germany's unwillingness to come out openly with Russia against England, Austria and Italy.

for assistance. On the contrary he had attempted to mediate between the two rivals, at times through the Three Emperors' League, at times through his suggestion of a direct compromise: the western Balkans for Austria, the eastern Balkans for Russia.[5] It might even be said that his encouragement of Russian designs on Constantinople was based on the theory that direct acquisition of the ultimate goal would obviate Austro-Russian rivalry for the control of the Balkans, which, for the Russians, was only a means to an end. The Russians certainly looked upon his suggestions in this light. During the most critical period of the negotiations preceding the Congress of Berlin the Russians presented in Vienna a so-called "maximum program" which provided for the abandonment of the western Balkans to Austria. In 1886 and 1887 they were inclined to accept Bismarck's partition proposals, which involved a similar abandonment of the western Balkans.[6]

Why were these different propositions rejected by Andrássy and his successors? In part, no doubt, because the Austrians desired to exclude the dangerous Russians from the Balkans entirely. A weak Turkey or a group of infant Slavic states would be more comfortable as neighbors.[7] On the other hand it was felt that if Russia once had a foothold in the Balkans the Slavic provinces would be irresistibly drawn from Austria, with the resulting disruption of the Empire.[8] For Austria the atti-

---

[5] G. P. III, nos. 603, 636, 637, 639, 643; V, no. 972; IX, no. 2085. This whole matter is discussed in detail by Eduard Heller: *Das deutsch-oesterreichisch-ungarische Bündnis in Bismarcks Aussenpolitik* (Berlin 1925) pp. 107 ff. At times, as in 1887, Bismarck even tried to effect a compromise between England and Russia, though he naturally desired that Austria be included (G. P. IV, nos. 908-909; no. 1036).

[6] On various occasions between 1887 and 1890 the Russians had expressed a willingness to compromise on the Bulgarian question, reducing their demands more and more (G. P. IX, no. 2084. J. V. Fuller: *Bismarck's Diplomacy at its Zenith* [Cambridge 1922] pp. 283 ff).

[7] G. P. IX, no. 2077. Besides, the advent of the Russophil party in Serbia in 1889 made the Austrians more cautious than ever about Bulgaria (G. P. IX, no. 2084).

[8] Cf. G. P. X, no. 2497, Eulenburg to Hohenlohe November 8, 1895: "Oesterreich kann nicht Russland in Konstantinopel dulden oder Russlands Monopol auf die Durchfahrt durch die Dardanellan gestatten, weil sich die Balkanstaaten

tude of England was well-nigh decisive. So long as Austria could not count on German support in the Near East she was absolutely dependent on England. Without England the Austrians could do little to prevent the whole Balkan peninsula from falling under Russian influence.

The object of English policy had for the better part of a century been the blocking of Russia's attempts to gain control of the Straits and Constantinople. There were some Englishmen who believed this policy outworn and unessential, but with the majority and with the people it had become a sort of religion.[9] The nation had gone to war on this point in 1854 and Disraeli was determined to do so again in 1878. But the English had always been impressed with the difficulty of checking

(insonderheit Bulgarien) sofort um dieses neue russische Zentrum kristallisieren würden, respektive der oesterreichische Einfluss im Adriatischen Meere verloren ginge." G. P. XI, no. 2680, where Goluchowski says: "Wenn Russland in Konstantinopel festen Fuss fasse, werde sich der russische Einfluss bis nach Dalmatien hin geltend machen." G. P. XII[1], no. 2931, where Deym says: "Auch das Zugeständnis bedeutender territorialer Landabtretungen bis nach Saloniki würde keine hinreichende Kompensation bieten, noch weniger wenn dies in der schon früher einmal zur Sprache gebrachten Form einer Teilung der Interessen-sphären zu Russland und Oesterreich beabsichtigt werden sollte," for Austria would not be able to digest these territories and Russia would eventually win them over and perhaps even absorb Bosnia and Herzegovina. G. P. XXX, no. 1098: Goluchowski 1903: "Wenn Russland in Konstantinopel steht, ist Oesterreich nicht mehr zu regieren, denn die zentrifugalen Elemente würden es auseinandersprengen." See also Count Julius Andrássy: *Bismarck, Andrássy and their Successors* (Boston 1927) pp. 128-130: "If Russia should become master of the strong strategic base of the Black Sea, her progress could not be arrested by any artificial paper frontier: like an ink-blot on a piece of blotting paper it would spread until it had covered the whole region."

[9] Salisbury in July 1890, however, confessed to Münster that one of his objects in concluding the Heligoland Treaty was to check the growth of a Russian party (G. P. VIII, no. 1703). Cf. Quis: Who Shall Inherit Constantinople? (*National Review* December 1890, pp. 558-563), a defense of the traditional policy. Hajo Holborn: *Bismarcks europäische Politik zu Beginn der siebziger Jahre* (Berlin 1925) pp. 94-97 prints an interesting report of Münster (January 24, 1875) showing that even then there were English statesmen who opposed the traditional policy. Cf. further Rothfels: Das Wesen des russisch-französischen Zweibundes (*Archiv für Politik und Geschichte* III, p. 151 (February 1925), and Preller: *ibid.* July 1925, p. 67; Medlicott: The Mediterranean Agreements (*Slavonic Review* June 1926, p. 68) and the same author's article: Lord Salisbury and Turkey (*History* October 1927).

Russia in a military sense. An actual clash might come when once the Russians were at Constantinople itself, but if the Russian action came quickly and unexpectedly the Dardanelles might be closed before the English squadrons could pass.[10] It was obviously advisable to check the Russian advance by land as well as to prepare for a sudden attack by sea. Therefore the English statesmen consistently supported the Austrian policy in the Balkans, in which they themselves had only an indirect interest. In return the Austrians were compelled to support the English policy in respect to Constantinople, though the question of the Straits and the Turkish capital was one of secondary importance to them compared with the problem of Russian influence in the Balkans.[11] Had the Austrians assented to a compromise settlement with Russia in regard to the Balkans they would immediately have lost the backing of the English, and without German support they would have been at the mercy of the Russians.[12]

In brief it may be said that, so far as European affairs were concerned, the Germans were in no sense opponents of the Russian aspirations.[13] Indeed, the hopes of a peaceful solution depended upon Germany. The Austrians, on the other hand, resisted the Russians in the question of the Balkans, while the English were the prime movers in checking the Russian advance to the ultimate goal—the Straits and Constantinople. Since 1876 and especially since 1886 the Russian hopes had been completely

[10] G. P. IX, nos. 2087 ff.

[11] G. P. IX, no. 2079. The Austrians were determined to leave the initiative to England if the Russians were to threaten Constantinople, just as England insisted on allowing Austria to take the lead in Bulgarian matters. All the way through the Austrians showed themselves loath to come out too openly against Russia, especially on Mediterranean matters (see Medlicott in *Slavonic Review* June 1926, p. 86).

[12] Similarly the Austrians practically forced the English into the Second Mediterranean Agreement by threatening to conclude a compromise with the Russians (G. P. IV, no. 918).

[13] This comes out again and again in the later volumes of the German documents, for example in connection with the Armenian crisis of 1895-97, the Bosnian crisis of 1908, and the Tripolitan War in 1911. Cf. for example G. P. X, no. 2945, XI, no. 2670, XII[1], no. 2924, XVIII[1], no. 5392, XXV[2], no. 8859, XXVI[1], nos. 9057, 9061, 9079, and chapter cxcix *passim*, XXX[1] chapter ccxxxvi *passim*.

wrecked by the close coöperation of Austria and England, their complete understanding having found its expression in the Mediterranean Agreements of 1887. In the last count the one irreconcilable enemy of Russia was England.[14] Their antagonism in Europe was essentially a Mediterranean antagonism, and this, in turn, was only one aspect of the Asiatic rivalry between the two powers which extended from Constantinople eastward to the Yellow Sea. In 1890 the burning point was in the Near East, the tension diminishing as one passed to Central Asia and the Indian frontier and thence to China.

How did the Russians attempt to meet this English opposition? There were various methods and they were all tried at different times. Direct action by war had failed in 1877-1878. The next best way was obviously to attempt to isolate England. This was certainly the idea underlying the various proposals of compromise made to the Austrians, just as the ultimate object of the Reinsurance Treaty, as viewed from the Russian side, was to obviate the possibility of Germany's joining the hostile coalition, for it excluded the idea of German support for the Austrians in the Balkans[15] and, what was even more important, it excluded the possibility of Germany's adopting the English view of the question of the Straits and Constantinople and gave Russia insurance against German attack on her western frontier in case England and Russia came to blows.

But there was one other power to be considered in any policy of isolating England, and that power was France. For years the French had taken a stand analogous to that of England so far as questions of the Near East were concerned. Their interests were not equally great, but they were similar, and in 1854 the French had fought shoulder to shoulder with the English against the

---

[14] Cf. Quis: Who Shall Inherit Constantinople? (*National Review* December 1890, pp. 559). Medlicott in *Slavonic Review* June 1926, p. 68, quoting Russian Embassy Archives.

[15] Cf. Giers to Mohrenheim August 20, 1883: "Notre accession (à l'entente établie entre l'Allemagne et l'Autriche) y a donné un caractère négatif et défensif qui en a brisé la pointe eventuellement dirigée contre nous, et en a fait, pour le moment, une garantie du maintien de la paix..." (quoted from Russian Embassy Archives, London, by Medlicott in *Slavonic Review* June 1926, p. 67).

Russians.[16]   After 1870 France, to be sure, played a less significant part, but on every occasion she sided with England against
Russia, or at least failed to support the Russians. Bismarck, we
know, believed that if the question of Constantinople were to be
raised in an acute form the French would be found in opposition
to Russia.[17] It cannot be proved, but it seems likely that the
various unofficial soundings taken by the Russians in Paris in
1879 and notably in 1886 were meant as first steps in a policy to
estrange France and England. At any rate they always came at
times of acute Anglo-Russian friction in periods of relatively
good feeling between Germany and France. They go a long way
toward explaining the anxiety of the English not to break entirely with France. In any case the English would never seriously consider any of Bismarck's suggestions which involved a
policy hostile to France.[18]

[16] The Russo-French antagonism in the Near East is competently discussed
by A. Leroy-Beaulieu: La France, La Russie et l'Europe (Paris 1888) pp. 59 ff.
See also Rothfels: Archiv für Politik und Geschichte February 1925, p. 151.

[17] Cf. Bismarck's talk with Saburov July 22, 1879 (Krasny Arkhiv I, p.
68): If the Russians had occupied Constantinople and the English had succeeded
in passing the Dardanelles "l'Angleterre vous aurait fait la guerre pour sûr, l'Autriche peut-être et la France probablement." Similarly G. P. VI, nos. 1206, 1207,
1209, 1220, 1343, 1350; Schweinitz believed the French might consent to the
locking of the Bosporus to foreign warships, but not to free passage for Russian war
craft through the Dardanelles, "wenigstens solange nicht, als diese Mittelmeer-
macht nicht die ganze Staatsraison der Revanche unterordnet." Bismarck appears
to have encouraged the Russians' aspirations in part in order to create an antagonism between France and Russia (G. P. VI, no. 1209). Cf. also the article by a Former
Ambassador: Die russisch-französische Allianz, in Deutsche Revue October 1891.
The French attitude continued more or less unchanged until the time of the World
War, though after 1905 the French allowed the English to assume the odium of
resisting Russian desires. Even Delcassé in 1915 objected to abandoning both
sides of the Straits to Russia (see the present writer's articles on the Straits question
from 1904 to 1912 in the English Historical Review January 1929 and the Political
Science Quarterly September 1928, as well as B. Shatzky: La Question de Constantinople et des Détroits (Revue d'Histoire de la Guerre Mondiale October 1926,
January 1927.)

[18] Holborn pp. 75, 84 shows that even in 1875 the Russian flirtation with
France was essentially meant to isolate England rather than Germany. It should
be pointed out that Russia and Germany had a common interest in preventing an
Anglo-French entente, Russia because of hostility to England, Germany because
of hostility to France. Hence Russia regularly supported the French in the Egyptian question, while Germany backed England.

There was, indeed, but slight possibility of a Franco-Russian Alliance before 1890. Looked at theoretically such a combination might appear logical enough, but only if one assumes that Germany was the common enemy.[19] Such was not the case in the 1880's. In France the group of irreconcilable *Revanchards* undoubtedly looked upon the alliance with Russia as the sole hope of salvation, but the saner French statesmen realized the impracticability of the revenge movement and many were unable to reconcile their republican principles with the tenets of Russian autocracy. They could not help but see that Russia had no interest in securing Alsace-Lorraine for France and that an alliance could probably be obtained only by the renunciation of France's traditional policy in the Near East. Even then the alliance would inevitably lead to the hostility of England and would drive the latter power into the arms of Germany.[20] Bismarck would certainly regard a Franco-Russian combination as directed against Germany and might well be expected to precipitate a general war in which France would bear the brunt of the fighting and almost certainly pay the costs.

The Russians, indeed, showed no desire for a French alliance against Germany. They were unwilling to see France again defeated and further weakened, but that was all.[21] So long as

[19] German diplomats never tired of pointing out that in case of a conflict between Russia and Germany the former could count on French support in any event and without assuming obligations (see for example G. P. VII, nos. 1489, 1491).

[20] G. P. III no. 455; IV, no. 712. This may explain the rejection of the Russian suggestions by the French in 1879 and 1886, the details of which are unknown. Even in June 1890 Münster believed that the French statesmen still distrusted the Russians and would scrutinize rather carefully any concrete proposals made to them. At any rate he claims to have given Ribot a real fright by referring to the Franco-Russian Alliance as though it existed (G. P. VII, no. 1400). The argument against the alliance is very ably set forth by Gabriel Monod in *The Contemporary Review* July 1890, p. 32, and the whole problem is brilliantly discussed by A. Leroy-Beaulieu: *La France, la Russie et l'Europe.*

[21] Cf. Shuvalov's utterance in May, 1887 (*Krasny Arkhiv* I, p. 116): Russia can not allow either France or Germany to be mortally wounded, with the interesting explanation: "La France nous était nécessaire comme Puissance Navale dans des complications d'avenir." It should be noted that in the original Russian draft of the Reinsurance Treaty Russia made no reservation as to neutrality in a Franco-German War. To be sure this draft was the expression of Shuvalov's personal views,

Bismarck abstained from aggression he had no cause for fear. The Hohenzollern and Romanov houses were united by close dynastic ties and the two nations had the common memory of a hallowed comradeship in arms against the French in 1813-15. Prussia and Russia were bound by community of interest in the Polish question, and the conservative principle of opposition to the revolution, which had underlain the Holy Alliance, was still potent and found renewed expression in the Three Emperors' Alliance of 1873 and 1881. The Russian autocrat was filled with disgust and hatred for the Republican radicalism of France and his dislike was enhanced by the aversion of a deeply religious nature to the so-called "atheism" which appeared to be inseparable from political "revolution."[22]

In matters of policy the gulf separating Russia from France was no less marked.

"A rapprochement with France," says a Russian memorandum of August 1879, "can be based only on the supposition of a permanent antagonism between that power and Germany. Our friendship can be necessary for France only for the attainment of revenge. But it would be hazardous to reckon too much upon the duration of this antagonism. The situation is one in which we risk finding ourselves between two chairs. For Bismarck has more than one string to his bow. He might, some day, put forth some new Benedetti 'convention' to indemnify France, or he might indeed exchange Lorraine for some non-French province, if he saw therein a means for avoiding a war from which he is not certain of emerging victorious. A rapprochement between ourselves and France could only encourage him in these ideas. In that case we should have exerted ourselves merely to reverse the whole course of modern history to our own detriment and without securing a new ally; for France, disinterested by some territorial acquisition or by the retrocession of Alsace-Lorraine, would no longer need us."

The writer continues by pointing out the advantage of Franco-German tension for Russia and recalls the fact that Russo-German friendship would always be an obstacle to Austro-German

---

but the fact remains that the difficulty lay not so much in Russia's unwillingness to desert France as in Germany's unwillingness to abandon Austria.

[22] For a few choice utterances concerning the French Republic by Alexander III and Giers see G. P. III, nos. 617, 621; IV, nos. 760, 761; V, nos. 978, 1118, 1122; VI, nos. 1205, 1210, 1218.

coöperation. Finally, the friendship of Germany relieves Russia of the fear of attack on her west front.[23]

These are general considerations of European politics, but they go far towards explaining the Russian policy after 1870. Russia stood to gain by the continuance of the Franco-German antagonism. She intervened to save France in 1875, but she had no interest in joining France to settle the Alsace-Lorraine problem to Germany's disadvantage. Abstracting the question of European preponderance, the alliance with Germany was of much greater value to Russia than an alliance with France would have been. No wonder that all Russian statesmen after 1870, including Gorchakov and Alexander III (neither of whom could be accused of pro-German proclivities), stood by the traditional connection with Germany, despite the sad experiences of 1876-1878 and 1885-1887, despite the German alliance with Austria, and despite all the virulent animosity and all the persuasive eloquence of a Katkov. No wonder that Giers was anxious to renew the Reinsurance Treaty even after Bismarck had gone.[24]

As a matter of fact there had been more friction than friendship in the relations between France and Russia from 1870 to 1890, especially after the advent of the Republicans in 1877-79.[25]

---

[23] *Krasny Arkhiv* vol. I (1922) pp. 78 ff. Cf. also the argument of Arsenieff in the *Messager d'Europe* October 1890, directed against the alliance, and the remark of a Russian diplomat, quoted by Leroy-Beaulieu (p. 47): "En prenant l'Alsace-Lorraine Bismarck travaille pour nous; Strasbourg et Metz à l'Allemagne, c'est, pour la prochaine guerre, la France à notre dévotion."

[24] Giers' policy was essentially that of the Three Emperors' Alliance and he personally would have liked to see it renewed in 1887 (G. P. V, no. 1093; cf. also G. P. III, nos. 617, 626; V, no. 1003). Cyon's whole book on the Franco-Russian entente is an indictment of Giers' German sympathies. Cf. also Henri Welschinger: *L'Alliance Franco-Russe* (Paris 1919) pp. 37, 53. One must reread the Russian documents on the conclusion of the Reinsurance Treaty (*Krasny Arkhiv* I, pp. 92 ff.) to appreciate the motives underlying Russia's policy. In September 1887 Giers, speaking of the improved relations with France, nevertheless added: "Das verhindere aber nicht, dass das gute Einvernehmen mit Deutschland der 'Pivot' der russischen Politik bleiben müsse und für Kaiser Alexander auch nach wie vor sei" (G. P. VI, no. 1217).

[25] Cf. the account by E. de Cyon: La France et la Russie (*Nouvelle Revue* April 15, 1890) and his book: *Histoire de l'Entente Franco-Russe* (Paris 1895). There is an excellent brief account of the history of Franco-Russian relations and a well-considered review of the obstacles to an alliance in the St. Petersburg letter

Gambetta was originally filled with a deep-rooted aversion to the "barbarian" autocracy and Jules Ferry preferred the coöperation with Germany to the friendship with Russia.[26] There had been acrimonious disputes regarding the extradition of revolutionary plotters, and at times relations were all but broken off.[27] When, in moments of crisis, the Russians had taken unofficial soundings in Paris they had received no encouragement. Indeed, their advances were reported to Bismarck by the French ministers themselves.[28]

It was only in the years immediately preceding Bismarck's fall that a gradual change took place. The critical year 1887 marks the turning point, for the various agreements concluded in that year created a situation which made a certain degree of coöperation between France and Russia not only natural, but imperative.[29] For the first time since 1870 the two burning

in the *Deutsche Revue* May 1891. The history of Franco-Russian relations from 1879 to 1890 is exhaustively studied, with aid of recent material in Kurt Koerlin: *Zur Vorgeschichte des russisch-französischen Bündnisses* (Halle 1926).

[26] Paul Deschanel: *Gambetta* (Paris 1920); Alfred Rambaud: *Jules Ferry* (Paris 1903); Gwynn and Tuckwell: *Life of Sir Charles Dilke* I, p. 454; II, p. 477. On Gambetta's attitude see also Koerlin, chapter iv.

[27] Ernest Daudet: *Histoire Diplomatique de l'Alliance Franco-Russe* (Paris 1894) pp. 138-142.

[28] On the Russian soundings of 1879 see G.P. III, nos. 461, 477, 479, 482, 513, 515; Hohenlohe II, p. 275; *Krasny Arkhiv* I, p. 88; H. Galli: *Dessous Diplomatiques* (Paris n. d.) p. 160, note. On the Russian proposals of 1886 see G. P. IV, no.903; V, nos. 1001, 1004, 1007; VI, nos. 1200-1204, 1210, 1211. It appears that Grévy and Flourens rejected similar offers in January 1888 (G. P. VI, nos. 1176, 1220). Giers flatly denied that any official advances were made either in 1879 or 1886: "C'est une alliance qui ferait horreur à l'Empereur" (G. P. VI, no. 1210).

[29] In February 1887, at the height of the crisis, Lord Ampthill reported Bismarck as having an attack of nerves every time he saw the names France and Russia together in a newspaper (Köhler p. 20). It was just at this time that the agitation for the alliance came to a head in both countries, led by Katkov and Cyon on the one hand, and by Déroulède and Mme. Adam on the other (cf. Cyon: *Histoire de l'Entente Franco-Russe passim*). According to a report of Schweinitz of February 10, 1887 (H. Trützschler von Falkenstein: *Bismarck und die Kriegsgefahr des Jahres 1887* [Berlin 1924] p. 64) the French ambassador enquired of Giers what attitude Russia would take in a war between France and Germany, but the Russian minister refused to discuss the matter (See also Goriainov: *American Historical Review* XXIII, p. 332). A month later there appear to have been Russian sugges-

questions of European politics, that of Franco-German relations and that of the Near East, entered upon an acute phase at one and the same moment. In order to preserve the peace Bismarck engineered a series of agreements which were detrimental to both France and Russia. The Mediterranean Agreements of February and December, concluded between England, Austria and Italy, provided for the preservation of the *status quo* in the Mediterranean, both west and east. They made impossible an extension of French power in North Africa and checked the Russian advance on Constantinople.[30] In the same way Germany, under the terms of the renewed Triple Alliance, assumed obligations towards Italy in respect to the maintenance of the *status quo* in North Africa. But the soul of the Mediterranean coalition was not Germany. It was England, the opponent both of French and Russian expansion.[31] The Germans, it should be remembered, concluded with Russia the Reinsurance Treaty of June, 1887, which in no way jeopardized Russian policy in the Near East, but rather encouraged it.[32] Germany was the enemy only of France, while England was the enemy of both France and Russia.

It was but natural, then, that the two powers which were threatened should attempt to coöperate against the common antagonist. We do not know when the existence of the Mediterranean Agreements became known to them, but certainly

tions made in Paris in regard to the Bulgarian question, the French returning a dilatory reply (see Fuller p. 159).

[30] The most recent account, with some new material, by W. N. Medlicott: The Mediterranean Agreements of 1887 (*Slavonic Review* V, no. 13, pp. 66-68, June 1926).

[31] Medlicott (*op. cit.*) shows that Germany played an even smaller part than has been supposed and that England's chief difficulty was in enlisting the support of Austria. The first Mediterranean Agreement was essentially an Anglo-Italian pact and even then the Italians had desired to incorporate a clause providing for mutual aid if either party became involved in war with France (See G. P. IV, nos. 886-887). The Austrians took part only reluctantly (see especially Medlicott p. 74). It is interesting to note that at the height of the Bulgarian crisis in the autumn of 1887 both France and Russia made attempts to buy off the English opposition and thus wreck the whole hostile coalition (see Fuller pp. 233 ff.).

[32] It has, indeed, been claimed that Russia concluded the Reinsurance Treaty solely with the possibility of war with England in view (Fuller p. 197).

they suspected some hostile arrangements at an early date.[33] In the late spring of 1887 they acted together for the first time in wrecking the Drummond-Wolff Convention.[34] The object quite clearly was to attack England in her most vulnerable position, Egypt, and to secure the support of the Turks against the Mediterranean group. The policy failed to accomplish anything in 1887, but it did cause great uneasiness in England, where the implications of Franco-Russian coöperation did not escape notice.[35] Just as Bismarck during the 1880's had influenced British policy and secured British support by selling his approval of English policy in Egypt, so now France and Russia

[33] Lord Newton: *Lord Lyons* (London 1913) II, p. 399. Lyons wrote on March 29, 1887, "that the French are horribly afraid of our being led to join the Italo-Austro-German Alliance and that they have been urged by Russia to exert themselves to prevent this." It appears from Medlicott p. 87 that the Russians knew of the pact before the end of December 1887 and by February 1888 had realized that it was directed against them. The opposition of the three powers to the proposed Ernroth regency in the autumn of 1887 had been more than sufficient evidence of close understanding between them (see Fuller pp. 217 ff). Speeches by Crispi, Kálnoky and Salisbury in October and November revealed the close understanding (Fuller pp. 251 ff). In October 1887 Giers remarked that the English, Austrians and Italians were triumphant at Constantinople and had checked Russian influence at the Porte (G. P. VI, no. 1218). See also E. Bourgeois and G. Pagès: *Les Origines et les Responsabilités de la Grande Guerre* (Paris 1921) pp. 234-235. G. Salvemini: *La Politica Estera di Francesco Crispi* (Rome 1919) pp. 59-60 says in February 1888 the French government, through an indiscretion at the Italian court, learned of the existence of the Italo-German military convention.

[34] Fuller pp. 199 ff.; Radowitz: *Aufzeichnungen* II, pp. 267-268, from which it appears that Bismarck believed this action to be the personal work of the French and Russian ambassadors rather than of the governments. On the other hand it should be noted that in November 1886 the French notified Bismarck of their intention to seek Russian support against England in the Egyptian question. They evidently hoped Bismarck would be benevolently neutral. As a matter of fact the German chancellor gave his full approval (G. P. VI, nos. 1202, 1233). His attitude changed only when Gladstone was succeeded by Salisbury (see Fuller pp. 201-202).

[35] Cf. Köhler p. 200, July 9, 1887: "Le fait le plus important et le plus sérieux de la convention, c'est qu'elle fait sortir la France de son isolement et qu'elle a fait constater avec ostentation l'union politique intime Franco-Russe, restée jusqu'à ces derniers temps à l'état d'aspirations reciproques, plus ou moins platoniques." Also *Neue Freie Presse* July 20, 1887: "Nicht Frankreich hat einen diplomatischen Sieg über England in Konstantinopel davongetragen, sondern Russland" (quoted by Fuller p. 201).

were attempting to weaken the general position of England by striking in the same quarter.

It was a serious matter, not only from the political, but from the strategical point of view, for if the French were to take the second step and approve the Russian designs on Constantinople there would be no further obstacle to a juncture of the French and Russian squadrons in the eastern Mediterranean.[36] The Russians had been building a strong squadron in the Black Sea ports,[37] the fortifications of the Bosporus and Dardanelles were in very poor condition, the Turkish fleet in a state of decay.[38] The French squadrons at Toulon were very strong, nearly, if not quite, the equals of the British Mediterranean fleet. The issue would at least be doubtful in a conflict between the English and the Italians on the one hand and the French and Russians on the other, especially as the English would be taken on the flanks.[39]

[36] See the brilliant argumentation by Cyon (*Nouvelle Revue* April 15, 1890) in which he attempts to prove, not only that England is the enemy, but that Russian control at Constantinople would be beneficial rather than detrimental to French interests: "L'accès libre de la Russie à la Mediterranée est pour la France d'un intérêt vital, et, disons-le hardîment, plus considérable encore que la possession de l'Alsace et de la Lorraine.....L'hégémonie de l'Allemagne n'est qu'un accident passager....Mais un ennemi autrement sérieux, un adversaire autrement implacable pour la France, est et a toujours été l'Anglais....C'est dans la Mediterranée que l'isolement de la France la menace des plus grands dangers, et il ne prendra fin que quand la Russie, maîtresse des détroits, fera flotter son pavilion maritime à côté du drapeau de la France. Il n'y a donc aucun antagonisme, mais au contraire une identité complète entre les intérêts français et les visées politiques poursuivies par la Russie. Sans la destruction de la marine russe operée pendant la guerre de 1854, l'Angleterre n'aurait pas pu s'emparer de l'Egypte; ce sera peut-être grace à la flotte russe de la mer Noire que la terre des Pharaons recouvrera son indépendance." See also Cyon's article in *Nouvelle Revue* August 15, 1890, and his *Histoire de l'Entente Franco-Russe* pp. 141 ff.

[37] Russia had in the Black Sea in 1890 three first-class battleships, six gunboats and forty-three torpedo boats, and was rapidly building more (*Annual Register* 1890, p. 341).

[38] G. P. IX, nos. 2083, 2087, 2094. In 1890 the Turks had only six armored ships of over 5000 tons and of these only the *Mesudieh* and the *Hamidieh* had been built later than 1865 (Brassey: *Naval Annual* 1890, p. 340). The Turk ships had not left the Golden Horn since 1878 (Lefevre: Constantinople Revisited, in *The Nineteenth Century* December 1890, p. 937).

[39] See *Saturday Review* July 26, 1890, editorial; and an article in the *Neue Militärische Blätter* May 1891. It is interesting to note that the problem set for the French naval manoeuvres in 1890 was how to stop a hostile squadron escaping

No wonder that the English hastened to revise their building program by laying down the famous two-power standard.[40] No wonder that the Turks were alarmed and applied for membership in the Triple Alliance.[41] No wonder that Spain hastened to conclude an agreement with Italy and England, and no wonder, finally, that Bismarck scrupulously kept aloof from this Mediterranean imbroglio.[42] So long as the conflict could be relegated to the Mediterranean Germany would be safe, and England would of necessity be forced, in protecting her own interests, to protect also those of Austria which Bismarck was unwilling to defend, and those of Italy which, without a fleet, he was unable to defend.

European politics from 1887 to 1890 were essentially Mediterranean politics. Everything hinged on the solution of the problems centering in the Mediterranean Basin. If the saner French statesmen opposed Boulangism and disapproved of the Revanche

from the Mediterranean and making for the Channel (*Saturday Review* August 30, 1890). We learn from Lee's biography of Edward VII (volume I, pp. 658) and from Lord George Hamilton's *Reminiscences* that in 1889 and 1890 the Kaiser was repeatedly calling the attention of the English to their precarious position in the Mediterranean.

[40] Trützschler von Falkenstein pp. 80 ff. quotes a number of reports of 1886-1887 on the condition of the British military and naval forces and suggests that Bismarck's attitude towards England may have been influenced by considerations of this nature. See Manning: *Life of Sir William Henry White* (London 1923) pp. 234, 243, 244, and Hamilton chapter xii, from which it is evident that the Naval Defence Act was the result of alarm over a possible Franco-Russian naval combination. Bismarck's remarks to Booth in November 1887 also show how heavily he stressed the naval considerations (John Booth: *Persönliche Erinnerungen an den Fürsten Bismarck* [Hamburg 1899] p. 72).

[41] Trützschler von Falkenstein pp. 88 ff.

[42] On the position of Spain see especially Trützschler von Falkenstein pp. 70 ff. Text of the agreement in Pribram, A. F.: *Die politischen Geheimverträge Oesterreich-Ungarns* (Vienna 1920) I, pp. 48 ff. Cf. further A. Mousset: *L'Espagne dans la Politique Mondiale* (Paris 1923) pp. 66-72; *Neue Frie Presse*, June 10, 11, 15, 1904; XXX: La Nuova Alleanza (*Nuova Antologia* vol. 106, p. 514, August 1, 1903); Gabriel Maura Gamazo: *Historia Crítica del Reinado de Don Alfonso XIII* (Barcelona, n. d.) vol. I, pp. 60 ff.; and most recently: Conde de Romanones: *Las Responsabilidades políticas del Antiguo Regimen* (Madrid, 1924) pp. 15 ff., and A. Marvaud: La Politique Extérieure de l'Espagne (*Revue des Sciences Politiques*, Jan.-Mar. 1927); P. Silva: Aspetti e Fasi del Problema del Mediterraneo Occidentale (*Nuova Rivista Storica* July-October 1924, pp. 408 ff).

movement it was at least in part because they recognized the hopelessness of such a policy. The assistance of Russia would be highly questionable and even with that assistance victory would by no means be certain. In any case France would be the chief sufferer.[43] On the other hand, if the French brought pressure, both economic and political, upon Italy in an attempt to drive her from the Triple Alliance, there was at least some prospect of success. A return to Franco-Italian friendship would not only relieve France from the menace of German-Italian military co-öperation on the continent, but would also mean the liberation of French policy in North Africa and would signify a decisive blow at the British position in Egypt and therewith in the entire Mediterranean. The balance of power would shift definitely to the French side. Consequently the principle of French policy was, logically enough, to continue pressure directly upon Italy and at the same time to undermine the Italian position in North Africa and in Abyssinia, for, in a sense, the Italian policy in Abyssinia was merely one aspect of the British policy in Egypt.[44]

In the same fashion Russian policy was necessarily actuated by a desire to isolate England. The Russians were naturally interested in the French attempts to wean Italy from her connections, but they were themselves in a better position to conciliate Austria by offering concessions in the Balkan question. Meanwhile they worked behind the scenes, disputing with England the diplomatic position at Constantinople, essaying at times the organization of a Balkan league as a means of bringing pressure upon Austria and Turkey alike, coöperating with France in op-

---

[43] The Russians appreciated the French attitude and Giers in March 1887 expressed doubt whether the French would accept an alliance if it were offered them: "Elle veut être bien avec nous et profiter de l'apparence d'une entente, mais elle ne voudrait pas s'exposer aux dangers d'une guerre contre vous; et puis, qu'est ce qu'elle pourrait nous donner en Orient?" remarked Giers to Schweinitz (G. P. VI, no. 1212; see also no. 1220.) The military dangers of an alliance are well brought out in Leroy-Beaulieu pp. 111-112.

[44] *Mémorial Diplomatique* April 12, 1890, pp. 232-233 for a good discussion of this aspect of the problem. Also the Italian memorandum of July 14, 1895 (G. P. X, no. 2369 annexe).

posing the British action in Egypt and even taking a rather significant part in creating difficulties for Italy in Abyssinia.[45]

Such was the situation in 1890. Europe was only outwardly calm. Below the surface the machinations and intrigues went on uninterruptedly, both France and Russia delivering one blow after another in their attempts to smash the Mediterranean coalition. Up to the time of Bismarck's dismissal they had been unsuccessful, and in a sense there was little prospect of success so long as the great man dominated the scene and held together the various powers which he had brought into the "League of Peace" to preserve the *status quo*.[46]

The disappearance of the Iron Chancellor of itself meant a significant change. Both in France and in Russia it was believed that the Triple Alliance would soon collapse.[47] The new men in Berlin appear to have been apprehensive on this score. Hence their desire to "simplify" the Bismarckian system and hence the abandonment of the Reinsurance Treaty. In the period following March 1890 they were of necessity concerned with the stability of the alliance and were bound to make every effort to render it attractive to the other members. The French and the Russians on the other hand quite naturally redoubled their efforts to undermine the system. They were still acting more or less independently, and it was only gradually that they came together. Coöperation became almost imperative after the non-

[45] There is some evidence that Russia tried to draw Italy over to her own side in 1879, 1882 and 1886 (G. P. III, nos. 461, 513, 543-544; IV, nos. 847, 850; VI, no. 1208). In May 1890 Giers engineered the visit of the Italian Crown Prince to Russia (Wolkenstein to Kálnoky May 21, 1890 in V. A.) and at the same time the Russian chargé in Italy appears to have encouraged agitation against the renewal of the Triple Alliance (Eissenstein to Kálnoky August 1, 1890). At the Anti-Slavery Conference of 1889-1890 both France and Russia refused to recognize Italy's right to speak in behalf of Abyssinia. On Russian policy in Abyssinia see Vicomte de Constantin: Une Expédition Religieuse en Abyssinie (*Nouvelle Revue*, February 1, 15, 1891) and especially Elets: *Imperator Menelik i Voina evo s Italie* (St. Petersburg 1898); F. Crispi: *La Prima Guerra d'Africa* (Milan 1914).

[46] Daudet: *Histoire Diplomatique de l'Alliance Franco-Russe* (p. 328) specifically says that the alliance became possible "parce que M. de Bismarck n'était plus au pouvoir."

[47] Köhler p. 84, note 1; G. P. VI, no. 1364; Schweinitz II, p. 407; *Moscow Gazette* March 20, 1890; *Mémorial Diplomatique*, March 22, 1890.

renewal of the Reinsurance Treaty and the Anglo-German Heligoland Treaty had given rise to the impression that Germany had joined or was about to join the Mediterranean group. Such an adhesion on the part of the Germans would make them direct enemies of the Russian plans and would justify an agreement with France aimed at Germany as much as at England and her Mediterranean satellites.

The events of 1891 and the conclusion of the Franco-Russian Entente of August can be understood only if the various points at issue in 1890 are clearly grasped. If one takes first the German side, it is necessary to point out that, in spite of all appearances to the contrary, no actual change in policy was intended. The Kaiser was certainly Russophobe in his outlook and was not inclined to accept the Bismarckian doctrine that Constantinople should be left to the Russians. He was interested in Turkey and the Near East, though rather from the economic than from the political standpoint. But there is no evidence that he intended to come out openly against Russia. Either because of timidity or because of common sense (it matters not which) he meant to confine himself to a secondary rôle. He would no longer encourage the Turks to fortify the Dardanelles against the English. On the contrary he would utilize his position to encourage an agreement between England and Turkey, thus removing the Egyptian question as a field of Franco-Russian coöperation. Similarly he would abandon the Bismarckian attitude of complete disinterestedness in respect to the Austrian policy in the Balkans. He would support Austrian interests so far as possible without coming into open conflict with Russia. In regard to the Straits question itself he would not flatly repudiate the Bismarckian policy, but he would not bind Germany formally by a written agreement.[48]

This policy with its shift of emphasis had been forecast in the Kaiser's visit to England in the summer of 1889 and by his trip to Constantinople shortly after. It is clearly expressed in the

---

[48] Writing retrospectively in December 1911 Marschall emphasizes the difference in the Bismarckian and post-Bismarckian policy of Germany in Near Eastern matters (G. P. XXX¹, nos. 10987, 10989).

nonrenewal of the agreement with Russia and in the refusal of
the German government to accept any substitute arrangement
which would have bound it in respect to the Straits. It may be
further traced in the German attitude towards the Bulgarian
problem in the summer of 1890 and in the discussions which took
place during William's visit to Russia in 1890.

In Bulgaria the regime of Stambulov had reached its full development. Relying upon the good will and perhaps on the
support of Austria and England the dictator was pursuing a
ruthless and even aggressive policy. He not only nipped the
notorious Panitza conspiracy in the bud, but dared to defy the
Russians by executing the ringleader.[49] The press of St. Petersburg raved and ranted but the government could not afford to
press the point. Since the whole Bulgarian question was distinctly one of secondary importance Giers carefully avoided
challenging Austria.[50]

A more important question was that of the recognition of
Ferdinand. This was, naturally enough, the goal which Stambulov had set for himself. The logical way to begin was to secure
the recognition of the suzerain, Turkey, and negotiations towards
this end were carried on in the spring of 1890. In the summer
Ferdinand paid a visit to Austria.[51]

This in itself was enough to make the Russians uneasy. But
the attitude of the German government was such as to change
their uneasiness to apprehension. When Shuvalov appealed to
Marschall for support in bringing pressure on the Porte to prevent
recognition, he was given an evasive reply.[52] In June, 1890, when
Stambulov succeeded in securing the appointment of three Bul-

[49] There was considerable evidence that the Russian minister in Bucharest
and perhaps even the Russian government was implicated in the plot (Wolkenstein
to Kálnoky March 13, 1890; Kálnoky to Wolkenstein February 23, 1890) though
Giers denied this (Wolkenstein to Kálnoky February 13, 1890 in V. A.).

[50] G. P. IX, no. 2075.

[51] G. P. IX, no. 2075. Vulkovič was sent to Constantinople in March (Schulthess: *Europäischer Geschichtskalendar* 1890, p. 293).

[52] G. P. VII, no. 1610; IX, no. 2143. Marschall simply reiterated that Germany regarded the existing situation in Bulgaria as contrary to the Treaty of
Berlin and therefore illegal. The Russians brought pressure on the Porte to
prevent recognition (Memorandum, June 27, 1890 in V. A.).

garian bishops for Macedonia, the German ambassador at Constantinople joined his English, Austrian and Italian colleagues in strengthening the Porte against the protests of the Russian representative.[53]

All this does not mean that a radical change had taken place in German policy, but it was a perceptible departure from the Bismarckian attitude, a departure dictated by the German desire to strengthen the Triple Alliance by supporting Austria in minor issues of Balkan affairs. Not only the Austrians but the English were agreeably surprised by the unwonted readiness of the German government to accept the anti-Russian view.

"The attitude of the German Cabinet in the question of the Bulgarian bishops has proved that a very considerable change has taken place in the views of the German government in regard to Bulgaria," noted Kálnoky with satisfaction.[54]

The Tsar had determined in the spring to reserve judgment on the German policy until he had had the opportunity of dis-

[53] G. P. VII, no. 1610; Schweinitz II, p. 413; Széchényi to Kálnoky July 26; Eissenstein to Kálnoky July 31, 1890 in V. A.; Nelidov had threatened "serious consequences" if the appointments were made. A full account of Bulgarian developments in the *Annual Register* 1890, pp. 345-348, and in *Parliamentary Papers, Turkey no. 2* (1891).

[54] Marginalia on report from Eissenstein August 1, 1890 in V. A. In the question of recognition the German government had actually taken the initiative in proposing joint pressure on Bulgaria to keep quiet, and coöperation at Constantinople to secure proper consideration for Bulgaria's desires. Francis Joseph was so surprised that he underlined the whole passage of the report (Report from Berlin June 25, 1890 in V. A.). Towards the end of July there were rumors that Stambulov was planning a *coup d'état* and the deposition of Ferdinand in his absence. Holstein hastily offered the Austrian government assistance in preventing such a move. The Austrians were greatly astonished by this new interest (Széchényi to Kálnoky July 30, 31, 1890; Kálnoky to Széchényi August 1, 1890; Eissenstein to Kálnoky August 1, 1890 in V. A.). The English ambassador in Berlin also thought that German policy in regard to Bulgaria had undergone "a very noticeable change" (*ibid*). In November 1890 Holstein suggested that the Sultan be encouraged not to make further concessions to the Armenian church, which led the Austrian chargé at Berlin to write home: "Das Axiom von den Knochen des pommerschen Landwehrmannes ist hier *ad acta* gelegt worden und wenn man auch bei Behandlung orientalischer Angelegenheiten sich noch eine grosse Reserve auferlegt, so ist doch unbedingt ein viel regeres Interesse für alle Vorgänge auf der Balkanhalbinsel wahrzunehmen" (Eissenstein to Kálnoky November 15, 1890 in V. A.). Cf. also *Annual Register* 1890, p. 333.

cussing the situation with William personally. The imperial visit took place on August 17, and for five days the two monarchs were together at Narva. The Kaiser was by no means enthusiastic about the visit and was above all else anxious to avoid friction and embarrassing questions.[55] In order to reassure Germany's allies the semi-official press announced in advance that the visit was not meant to have political importance and that no agreements detrimental to Germany's friends were being contemplated.[56] The questions likely to be discussed were carefully gone over in the German foreign office and evasive replies had been decided upon.[57]

Viewed from the standpoint of the personal relationship between the two sovereigns the visit was undoubtedly a success, due, apparently, to William's excessive amiability which at times seems to have bordered on the obsequious.[58] But all this was of secondary importance. The apprehensions of the Russians were in no way allayed. The two Emperors talked over the dismissal of Bismarck and probably also the failure of the Germans to renew the Reinsurance treaty.[59] Apparently there was also

[55] Hohenlohe II, p. 471; Eissenstein to Kálnoky August 15 and 27, 1890 in V. A. In order to reassure the Russians the Kaiser declared at Heligoland early in August that the island represented the "last piece of German soil." The Russians had for some time been apprehensive of German designs on the Baltic Provinces (Cyon: *Histoire de l'Entente Franco-Russe* p. 187; Un Russe: Les Allemands de la Baltique, in *Nouvelle Revue*, August 1, 1890). On the favorable impression made by the Kaiser's utterance see Köhler pp. 269-271.

[56] Eissenstein to Kálnoky September 5, 1890, in V. A.

[57] G. P. VII, no. 1609; Schweinitz II, p. 414. Raschdau in *Deutsche Rundschau* May 1924, pp. 114 ff. Giers had indicated to Schweinitz before the visit that he desired particularly a statement as to the German attitude on the Straits question (G. P. VII, no. 1610).

[58] The Tsar had looked forward to the visit in a mood of passive expectancy (Eissenstein to Kálnoky August 9 and 15, 1890, in V. A. Also Köhler p. 272). On the Kaiser's extreme amiability see the amusing account in Köhler pp. 271-273. Wolkenstein, who was not particularly pleased by the visit, thought he noticed a trace of scorn in Alexander's attitude (Wolkenstein to Kálnoky August 20, 1890, in V. A.).

[59] Wilhelm II: *Ereignisse und Gestalten* p. 15; *Geschichtstabellen* p. 13. The necessity for monarchical solidarity was also discussed (Köhler pp. 273-274; Aehrenthal to Kálnoky September 17, 1890 in V. A.; Schweinitz II, pp. 416 ff).

some discussion of the Bulgarian question, but Alexander showed no inclination to consider concessions.[60]

Most important were the pourparlers between Giers and Caprivi, but here too the German chancellor refused to go beyond generalities.[61] He was willing to admit that the existing regime in Bulgaria was illegal and he declared that Germany still stood by the treaties of 1856 and 1871 regulating the passage of the Straits. But he simply ignored Giers' suggestion that in 1878 the English had placed upon the treaty of 1871 a construction which the Russians could not accept.[62] There was no indication in what Caprivi said that Germany would, as Bismarck had promised, leave the Russians a free hand in the Near East and at Constantinople, or that they would oppose the English interpretation of the Straits agreements, as they had done in 1885.

The Narva visit, then, had no political result so far as Russo-German relations were concerned.[63] At best the Tsar may have

---

[60] Köhler pp. 269-271 (Greindl report quoting Marschall). Eissenstein to Kálnoky September 5, 1890 (V. A.) reported from a reliable source that the Kaiser suggested a settlement of the Bulgarian question between Russia and Austria. Of this the Tsar would not hear, adding: "Die ganze orientalische Frage erschiene ihm wie ein Geschwür, welches mit der Zeit von selbst aufgehen werde—man thue daher am besten, diesen Zeitpunct einfach abzuwarten." These facts leaked out in the *Hamburgische Korrespondent* and were denied by the *Reichsanzeiger* (Schulthess 1890, pp. 149-150). Kálnoky regarded the Tsar's stand as due to his desire to evade German mediation rather than to aversion to a settlement (Kálnoky to Aehrenthal September 11, 1890; Aehrenthal to Kálnoky September 17, 1890, in V. A. See also Waldersee: *Denkwürdigkeiten* II, p. 141; *Briefwechsel* I, p. 402).

[61] Giers was well pleased with Caprivi, whom he described as "einfach, sehr ruhig, sehr verständig" (Wolkenstein to Kálnoky August 25, 1890), and as "un homme loyal" (Aehrenthal to Kálnoky September 3, 1890). Later he spoke of him as "einen sympathischen, offenen Character mit bestimmten und festen Anschauungen." Perhaps not a great statesman "aber gewiss, eine vertrauenerweckende, energische Persönlichkeit" (Aehrenthal to Kálnoky October 2, 1890, in V. A.). Caprivi spoke chiefly of the German emperor's desire to preserve peace in order to devote his attention to "the increasing peril of socialism." The Kaiser spoke in a similar vein (Wolkenstein to Kálnoky August 25, 1890 in V. A.).

[62] Goriainov p. 347; G. P. VII, no. 1612.

[63] On their return both the Kaiser and Caprivi stated that the situation was unchanged (Waldersee: *Denkwürdigkeiten* II, p. 141. Similarly Köhler pp. 271-273; Kálnoky to Aehrenthal September 11, 1890; Eissenstein to Kálnoky September 5, 1890 in V. A.; *Saturday Review* August 23, 1890: "The only possible

been somewhat reassured as to the Kaiser's plans and may have been well-impressed by Caprivi's personality.[64] But there could be no thought of a *courant de confidence mutuelle* such as Giers desired to establish. Even the Russian minister, who was the stoutest adherent of the alliance with Germany, was forced to admit failure. After the visit he attempted to get from Caprivi a written confirmation of what had been said. The paper would have had at least a sort of symbolic value, but even that satisfaction was denied him. Such a confirmation, declared Caprivi, would be "quite useless." "I have not the political strength of Bismarck," he added, "but I am loyal, and you can rely upon our loyalty, which will never fail you."[65] Sincere though they undoubtedly were, these words could hardly be expected to allay the suspicions of the Russians.

After this there could be no further doubt even in the mind of Giers that an agreement with Germany was impossible. Russia was isolated, that was the naked truth, and she shared with every European power the dread of isolation in the face of hostile or potentially hostile combinations. The only possible ally was France, and the Tsar had taken the precaution of inviting General Boisdeffre to the Narva manoeuvres, probably as a sort of silent warning to the Germans. Boisdeffre had formerly been military attaché in St. Petersburg and was well acquainted with army circles. He had numerous talks with Vannovski, the minister of war, and with Obruchev, the chief of staff, both of

relation between Germany and Russia is one of personal friendship tempered by political distrust.").

[64] G. P. VII, nos. 1611 ff. Apparently the Russians were relieved that there was no longer an invisible third person present in the shape of Bismarck (G. P. VII, no. 1613). The Tsar evidently never quite trusted Bismarck (Hohenlohe II, p. 491; Wilhelm II: *Ereignisse* p. 16; Aehrenthal to Kálnoky November 28, 1890 in V. A. etc.; and the discussion of this point by Becker: *Das französisch-russische Bündnis* pp. 290-294).

[65] On this whole matter see G. P. VII, nos. 1611 ff.; Goriainov p. 347; Schweinitz II. p. 416; Lamsdorf pp. 351 ff. After the failure of the negotiations Giers disavowed the Russian ambassador at Berlin, insisting that the whole thing was "une communication de galant homme à galant homme" and that he never thought of asking for a receipt, in bankers' fashion.

whom were known to be advocates of an alliance with France.[66] No doubt the Russian generals were in complete agreement with the French representative, and there is certainly some significance in this contact between the military authorities of the two countries. But politically Boisdeffre's presence was not necessarily of importance. Indeed, the French ambassador appears to have been somewhat uneasy about the whole demonstration, and Boisdeffre himself seems to have felt uncomfortable and a bit superfluous during the festivities.[67] After the visit the French ambassador sent home a glowing account, but the report is rather the exuberant expression of a pious wish than a dispassionate statement of facts.[68] The best commentary to it may be found in Giers' desperate efforts to secure an agreement with the Germans and in the Tsar's declaration to his imperial guest that he would never make an alliance with a republic.[69] The time had not yet come for so desperate a remedy.

Unwilling to conclude an agreement with France, which would have involved an attitude of hostility towards Germany, the Russians had no course open to them excepting that of renewed

[66] *Troisième Livre Jaune Français. L'Alliance Franco-Russe* (Paris 1918) no. 1 (henceforth referred to as L. J.); Schweinitz II, p. 415. On Vannovski and Obruchev see also Cyon: *Histoire de l'Entente Franco-Russe*, p. 377, and G. P. III, nos. 618, 621; V, nos. 992, 1121; VI, no. 1219. The Germans suspected that there was some loose military understanding (G. P. VII, no. 1492).

[67] Wolkenstein to Kálnoky August 19, 20, 21, 26, 1890 in V. A. Boisdeffre was a royalist and may possibly have discussed the question of a restoration in France. There were rumors of this at the time (Aehrenthal to Kálnoky September 10, 1890 in V. A.) and the Tsar spoke to the Kaiser of the desirability of such a step (G. P. VII, no. 1612; Waldersee: *Denkwürdigkeiten* II, p. 142; Schweinitz II, p. 416; Wilhelm II: *Geschichtstabellen* p. 13; the Kaiser's letter to the Tsar November 28, 1905 (*Krasny Arkhiv* V, reprinted in the *Kriegsschuldfrage* November 1924, p. 498).

[68] L. J. no. 1.

[69] The Kaiser told Marschall on his return that he was fully convinced that the Tsar felt more drawn to the rulers of Austria and Germany than to the president of the French Republic (Eissenstein to Kálnoky September 5, 1890). According to Kiderlen the Tsar said to Caprivi: "Quant à moi, je ne ferai jamais une alliance avec une république" (Eissenstein to Kálnoky August 27, 1890 in V. A.). Cf. also Waldersee: *Denkwürdigkeiten* II, p. 170; Köhler p. 270. In June 1890 Pourtalès reported that the Tsar's aversion to the Republic had, if anything, increased during 1889 (G. P. VII, no. 1489).

attempts to bridge the chasm that divided them from Austria. In the last days of April Giers had suggested to the Austrians that Bulgaria had become for the Tsar merely a *question d'amour propre*. All that he desired was the removal of the objectionable Ferdinand.[70] A duly elected Austrian candidate, preferably a Protestant German Prince, would be acceptable to the Russians. But Kálnoky refused to entertain the suggestion.[71] So long as Ferdinand and Stambulov were in control in Bulgaria there was no danger of its becoming a Russian outpost. To accept the Russian hint would have meant arousing the suspicions of the Germans and estranging England.[72]

But Kálnoky had no objection to an improvement of Austro-Russian relations. Such a change would worry the Germans and perhaps induce them to lend more vigorous support to the Austrian policy in order to maintain the alliance intact.[73] Conse-

[70] Wolkenstein to Kálnoky March 25, 1890 (in V. A.) reports Giers as suggesting the desirability of settling the question, which was merely one "d'amour propre" and one for which the Tsar had only "une superbe indifférence." For the proposals of April and May see Aehrenthal to Kálnoky May 2, 1890; Kálnoky to Wolkenstein June 3, 1890 in V. A. See also G. P. IX, nos. 2075, 2084, 2092, from which it appears that Giers envisaged a renewed Three Emperors' Alliance in view of the coming expiration of the Reinsurance Treaty. Apparently the Russians first tried to get the Turks to take measures to remove Ferdinand, attempting to threaten the Porte with the spectre of a Balkan League (G. P. IX, no. 2078).

[71] It does seem, however, that in April 1890 Kálnoky, discouraged by the indifference of England, entertained the idea of limiting himself to the annexation of Bosnia and Herzegovina and the temporary occupation of Serbia, in case the Russians were to land in Bulgaria (G. P. IX, no. 2077). All of which shows that the Austro-Russian antagonism was not insurmountable. An extraordinary letter from the minister of Würtemberg, Count Linden, to Waldersee, April 29, 1890 (Waldersee: *Briefwechsel* pp. 369 ff.) shows what great efforts were being made behind the scenes to further the candidacy of Prince Ernst of Saxe-Weimar, and also shows that Giers was sincere in his proposals to the Austrians.

[72] It was also feared that the Russians were manoeuvring to improve their position in Bulgaria (G. P. IX, no. 2092). The Germans took a downright negative stand, and Kálnoky, of course, was not in a position to appreciate the larger possibilities of the proposals, especially as he knew nothing of the German-Russian negotiations concerning the Reinsurance Treaty.

[73] The Austrians were sure that the Russians felt that a settlement of the Bulgarian question would obviate the need of the Austro-German Alliance in future (Kálnoky to Aehrenthal September 11, 1890; Aehrenthal to Kálnoky September 17, November 12, 1890 in V. A.).

quently the Austrians provided a warm reception for the Russian heir when he came to Vienna in November, *en route* to the Far East. In February, 1891 the Austrians reciprocated by sending the Archduke Francis Ferdinand to Russia. He was given the most gracious treatment and the visit gave rise to much speculation. But there was no tangible result. The chief difficulty lay in the fact that since the question of Bulgaria had become one of *amour propre* for the Tsar he could not bring himself to make concrete proposals. These, the Russians felt, should come from Austria. But in Vienna there was no thought of taking the initiative. If the Russians desired a settlement it was up to them to offer attractive terms.[74]

In any case, an Austro-Russian settlement was not beyond the range of possibility and the Germans distinctly felt the need of bolstering up the existing alliances.

This was the purpose of the meeting of the two allied emperors and their foreign ministers at the Rohnstock manoeuvres from September 17 to 19, 1890. In order to set the minds of Francis Joseph and his minister at rest in regard to German relations with Russia, William here for the first time communicated to his ally the Reinsurance Treaty.[75] More than that, the Germans

---

[74] Aehrenthal to Kálnoky (September 17, 1890 quoting Prince Cantacuzène). The Russian press took the same stand (Aehrenthal to Kálnoky November 10, 1890 in V. A.) On Aehrenthal's report regarding Russian hopes of Austrian advances Francis Joseph noted: "Da können sie lange warten." Whether the Bulgarian question was actually discussed between the Archduke and the Russian statesmen is not quite clear, but both sides were certainly in a more conciliatory frame of mind (Wolkenstein to Kálnoky January 26, 1891; Waldersee: *Denkwürdigkeiten* II, p. 206). Wolkenstein to Kálnoky February 11, 1891 says the visit had a significance "far beyond that of a simple visit of courtesy." The Germans were distinctly uneasy (Széchényi to Kálnoky March 1, 1891) and Bismarck was seriously alarmed. Cf. his utterance to Waldersee: "Ich sehe es ganz klar, es soll jetzt die Kaunitzsche Politik wieder auferstehen: Allianzen zwischen Russland, Oesterreich, und Frankreich" (Waldersee II, p. 202; Cf. also Hofmann I, pp. 314, 363; Köhler pp. 276-279 and the pamphlet: *Was für einen Kurs haben wir?* with the reference to the "double check" in which Germany had been placed).

[75] Eckardt: *Bismarcks Kampf gegen Caprivi* p. 55; Hammann: *Der missverstandene Bismarck* p. 58; Pribram I, p. 209; G. P. XXX[1], nos. 10987, 10998. The revelation of the treaty and its nonrenewal was evidently meant as a reply to numerous Bismarckian interviews of 1890, emphasizing the importance of close Russo-German relations. The German government had repeatedly reassured the

assented to a verbal understanding to the effect that a solution of the Straits question according to Russian desires would be impossible and that any change in the existing treaties, or any concessions to Russia in the Near East, should be made by Germany only with the consent of Austria. This was indeed a revolutionary change in the Bismarckian policy.[76] Of almost equal importance were the discussions carried on between Caprivi and Kálnoky, for it was on this occasion that the German chancellor first broached his plan of consolidating the Triple Alliance by concluding commercial treaties between the various members.[77] The question had become urgent since the general victory of protectionism in many of the European countries. In the United States the McKinley Bill was in the last stage of legislation and in France the commercial treaties, due to expire in January, 1892, were to be replaced by a higher tariff system; Russia had for years been screwing up the duties on imports; and similar tendencies were noticeable in a number of the lesser states. There was, then, a very real danger that a great part of the world market would be virtually closed to the central powers. To meet this problem a series of inter-allied commercial treaties would be of great value.[78] But Caprivi regarded the scheme perhaps even more from the politico-military standpoint. The commercial relations between Germany and Austria had long been unsatisfactory, and the chancellor recognized that a healthy political relationship could not permanently rest on a foundation

Austrian government in regard to these "Expektorationen," as Caprivi called them (Széchényi to Kálnoky May 28, June 4, July 26, August 7, 1890 in V. A.).

[76] G. P. XXX[1], nos. 10987, 10989, 10998.

[77] The Rohnstock meeting is fully recounted in a semi-official article in the *Pester Lloyd* September 17, 1890. Cf. also Waldersee: *Denkwürdigkeiten* II, p. 146; Eissenstein to Kálnoky September 24, 1890, in V. A.

[78] *Reichsanzeiger* March 19, 1891. Perhaps Caprivi's plans went even further. Even before Rohnstock he spoke to the Austrian ambassador of his desire to establish in central and western Europe "eine Art Liga, einerseits gegen die unerträglichen americanischen Arroganzen, andrerseits gegen die Ueberhandnahme der russischen Getreideeinfuhr" (Eissenstein to Kálnoky September 5, 1890). In January 1892 he told a friend of Waldersee that his ultimate object was the creation of a United States of Europe to make the whole continent economically independent of America (Waldersee: *Denkwürdigkeiten* II, p. 230).

of economic rivalry or discontent.[79] Furthermore, he desired to put commercial relations on such a footing that, when the inevitable war should break out, the central powers might be practically independent economically and not subject to the whims of the maritime powers, on whose benevolence they would otherwise be compelled to rely for the importation of food.[80]

Kálnoky was quite ready to open negotiations, because he knew that an agreement would necessarily hinge upon the question of the German duty on Hungarian grain, and he felt justified in supposing that Caprivi was willing to make concessions. On October 20 delegates of the German states assembled to discuss the bases of the projected accord and early in December negotiations were opened in Vienna.[81]

[79] Széchényi to Kálnoky November 30, 1890 in V. A. For earlier attempts at an Austro-German settlement see the *Reichsanzeiger* March 19, 1891.

[80] See his speech of December 10, 1891 (R. Arndt: *Caprivis Reden* [Berlin 1894] pp. 166 ff.) with the prophetic utterance: "Mir ist es eine ganz unerschütterliche Ueberzeugung, dass in einem künftigen Kriege die Ernährung der Armee und des Landes eine geradezu entscheidende Rolle spielen kann." French writers, on the other hand, urged the utilization of their country's financial power to break up the hostile coalition and build up a new combination to include Italy, Spain, Portugal, Switzerland and Belgium (e. g. Fournier de Flaix: La Triple Alliance et les Traités de Commerce, in *Nouvelle Revue* September 15, 1890).

[81] On the whole subject of Caprivi's tariff policy see R. Wuttke: Der deutsch-oesterreichisch-ungarische Handelsvertrag vom 6 Dezember 1891 (*Verhandlungen des Vereins für Sozialpolitik* 1902); A. Zimmermann: *Die Handelspolitik des deutschen Reiches 1871-1900* (Berlin 1901); W. Lotz: Die Handelspolitik des deutschen Reiches (*Schriften des Vereins für Sozialpolitik* XCII part ii, 1901); P. Ashley: *Modern Tariff History* (3rd Edit. N. Y. 1920) pp. 60 ff.

CHAPTER V

THE MEDITERRANEAN PROBLEM AND THE POSITION OF ITALY

THE danger of Austria's deserting her alliance with Germany was probably never very great. On the other hand Italy was a real problem and one which taxed the statesmanship of the allied ministers to the utmost. The position of Italy in international affairs can perhaps best be treated in connection with French policy.

Italy had been literally driven into the Triple Alliance by the French occupation of Tunis in May 1881 and she was kept there by general fear of further French ambitions in North Africa and in the western Mediterranean. King Humbert undoubtedly desired the connection with the central monarchies for dynastic reasons and from considerations of domestic politics. But the alliance with Austria was never popular. The country accepted it only because it recognized the blocking of French expansion as more important than the pursuit of *Italia Irredenta*. There had been great dissatisfaction with the alliance, however, and it was not until Bismarck in 1887 had consented to support Italian policy in the Mediterranean and until he had enlisted the English on the Italian side by the Mediterranean Agreements that the statesmen in the Consulta had agreed to the renewal of the treaty for a second period of five years.

It was not until after the fall of Jules Ferry and the abrupt ending of the Franco-German entente in 1885 that the French action against Italy began in earnest.[1] Ferry himself had been more interested in the Far Eastern problem, and since his un-

[1]For a good conventional summary of Franco-Italian relations between 1885 and 1895 see F. Despagnet: *La Diplomatie de la Troisième République* (Paris 1904) pp. 458-469; from the Italian side: G. E. Curàtulo: *Francia e Italia 1849-1914* (Turin 1915). According to A. Billot: Le Rapprochement Commercial entre la France et l'Italie (*Revue des Deux Mondes* January 1, 1899) it was the advent of Crispi that opened the period of tension.

derstanding with Bismarck was quite complete, especially in the Egyptian question, he was well able to hold his own against England and had no reason to fear a conflict with Germany in which Italy would become involved. But after 1885 the Mediterranean questions came rapidly to the fore. Germany once more supported the British policy, and Italy, always more or less dependent on England's good will, did likewise. It was not long after the defeat of Gordon that the Italians established themselves at Massowah, and it was in the very midst of the French attempts to force the British out of Egypt that the first Mediterranean Agreement, sealing the coöperation of England and Italy, and the renewal of the Triple Alliance, enlisting German support for the Italian aspirations, were concluded. How soon the French learned of the new coalition it is difficult to say, but they must have felt the effects very soon, and before long interpellations in the English House of Commons revealed the existence of some sort of Anglo-Italian engagement.[2] Ignorance of the real terms of a convention frequently gives rise to undue apprehensions and the French certainly imagined both the renewed Triple Alliance and the new Anglo-Italian pact to be more menacing than they actually were.[3]

In any case one can readily understand the uneasiness of the French statesmen in 1887. A conflict with Germany or with England, or with both, was threatening, and the merest common sense dictated that all possible precautionary measures be taken. Hence the coöperation of France and Russia in the Egyptian question, and the intriguing of the French in the region of

[2] The interpellations by Mr. Labouchère in February 1888 and frequently thereafter are well summarized by Luigi Chiala: *Pagine di Storia Contemporanea* (Turin 1898) III, appendix ii. See chapter iv, note 33 above. At the Lord Mayor's banquet (November 9, 1887) Salisbury referred to English interests as in many respects identical with those of Italy and Austria. The renewal of the Triple Alliance was almost immediately announced in the German semi-official press.

[3] The French had, by an indiscretion of the Italian Court, learned in February 1888 of the existence of a German-Italian military convention (Salvemini: *La Politica Estera di Francesco Crispi* pp. 59-60). It should be noted that in the first edition of Chiala's *Pagine di Storia Contemporanea* (1888) it was asserted that the Triple Alliance contained a provision for offensive action, which was, in a sense, true of the separate German-Italian pact of February 1887.

Abyssinia. This policy was the reply to the Anglo-Italian Mediterranean understanding, and to the Italo-Spanish Agreement of May, 1887, which was almost certainly suspected in Paris.[4] It would be useless to trace in detail the various methods by which this policy was carried out. But it is absolutely necessary to recall the attempts made by the French to drive Italy from the Triple Alliance. This policy, if effective, would necessarily result in a great weakening of Italy's continental position and would greatly facilitate the rupture of the Mediterranean coalition, which, in turn, might lead to a complete recasting of the European alignments.

There was considerable prospect of success, for Italy's geographic position gave her an importance out of proportion to her size or resources. There were various possible modes of attack upon the Italian position. A subtle method was that of republican propaganda aiming at the overthrow of the existing form of government and the organization of Italy as a loose federation of independent states. Whether agitation of this sort was ever officially carried on by the French government it is impossible to say. Crispi certainly believed that the French embassy was a center of republican intrigue, and it was generally believed that similar subversive work was being encouraged in Spain and Portugal.[5] In any case there were enough republicans among the Italians themselves, and it is probably safe to say that they were not discouraged by the officials of the French embassy.[6]

Another line of approach lay through the Roman question. Indeed, there were not a few advocates of a solution of this knotty problem based upon the idea of federalization already men-

---

[4] In November 1887 the *République Française* and the *Gaulois* reported Spain's adhesion to the Triple Alliance, from an Austrian source (Mousset p. 72).

[5] Crispi III, p. 184; G. P. VII, no. 1395; Crispi: *Ultimi Scritti* (Rome 1913) pp. 88, 101, 106, 147; G. P. X, no. 2369 (The Italian memorandum of July 14, 1895.) See also Waldersee: *Briefwechsel* I, p. 408, reporting statements of Ratazzi in regard to large sums spent by the French government in support of the Italian republicans.

[6] It is interesting to note that at this time the French ambassador, the Duc de Noailles, was succeeded by republicans like Mariani, Billot and later Barrère.

tioned.[7] It should be remembered that at the time it was generally believed that the treaty of the Triple Alliance involved a guarantee of the possession of Rome by the Italians.[8] It was common knowledge that many French clericals and royalists entertained hopes of a restoration of the temporal power of the Papacy. The republicans probably had no direct interest in such a policy, but it was convenient to possess a lever with which to bring pressure upon the Italian government. After all, it was generally agreed that anti-clericalism was not an article of export. In fact the French republican government was as jealous of its position as protector of Catholic interests abroad as any of its monarchical predecessors.

The French government had for many years had an unusually able representative at the Vatican, M. Lefebvre de Béhaine. He was known to be a keen observer and to be well-posted in matters of papal diplomacy. Until the year 1887, however, he does not appear to have played a very prominent rôle. Leo XIII was still interested in settling the questions arising from the *Kulturkampf*, and his chief assistants were evidently still deluded by hopes of German or Austrian aid in effecting a restoration of the temporal power. The turning point came with the year 1887, and is marked by the appointment of Cardinal Rampolla as papal secretary of state.[9] From that moment the policy of the

[7] This was perhaps the only possibility of a restoration of the temporal power.

[8] The statement was repeatedly made by responsible Italian statesmen, for example, by Crispi in his famous speech at Florence, October 8, 1890, and on other occasions (see F. Salata: La Questione Romana e la Triplice Alleanza, in *Nuova Antologia* March 1, 1923, p. 59, note).

[9] On the policy of Leo XIII prior to 1887 see C. Crispolti and G. Aureli: *La Politica di Leone XIII* (based on Galimberti papers) (Rome 1912); Lefebvre de Béhaine: *Léon XIII et le Prince de Bismarck* (Paris 1898); Kurd von Schlözer: *Letzte Römische Briefe* (Stuttgart 1924); Chiala: *Pagine di Storia Contemporanea* III, appendix; Crispi: *Politica Interna* (Milan 1924); A. di Pesaro: La Diplomazia Vaticana et la Questione del Potere Temporale (in *Rassegna Nazionale* May 1, 1890, pp. 3-129); F. Mourret: *Les Directions Politiques, Intellectuelles et Sociales de Léon XIII* (Paris 1920); H. Bastgen: *Die Römische Frage* (Freiburg 1919) III, pp. 32 ff.; Woodward: The Diplomacy of the Vatican under Popes Pius IX and Leo XIII (*Journal of the British Institute of International Affairs* May 1924, pp. 113-139); Humphrey Johnson: *The Papacy and the Kingdom of Italy* (London

Vatican began to veer. The influence of Lefebvre gradually replaced that of his German colleague, von Schlözer. The first victory of the French came when their ambassador managed to wreck a well-intentioned attempt on the part of certain clerics to effect a reconciliation between the Holy See and the Italian government.[10] From that moment on the Papal question entered upon an acute phase. German influence reached a low point with the unhappy visit of William II to the Vatican in 1888, while the French influence went from one victory to another. As the Boulangist movement gradually collapsed in France Leo became more and more inclined to accept the Republic and to reëstablish friendly relations. The French in their turn were only too ready to exploit this conciliatory attitude, while Crispi, by this time a confirmed victim of "Vaticanophobia," lost his head entirely at sight of this new and dangerous coalition.

The tension reached the most critical stage when, in the summer of 1889, the Italian government allowed the erection of a monument in commemoration of Giordano Bruno. Demonstrations of serious proportions took place, and the Pope himself was so disgusted and alarmed that he permitted plans to be drawn up for a flight to France or Spain. Those who engineered the scheme evidently hoped that the Italian government would offer resistance and that then the Catholic powers would be forced to intervene to liberate the Holy Father from constraint. Lefebvre

1926) chapters iii and iv; Lulvès: Bismarck und die römische Frage (*Deutsche Revue* XLI [2], pp. 145, 289).

It should be noted, however, that the relations between Germany and the Vatican were fairly close until the visit of William II to Rome in October 1888. It was in 1887 that Izvolski was sent to Rome to negotiate a settlement of the Church question in Russia.

[10] This was the famous rapprochement initiated by Tosti's pamphlet *Conciliazione* and the papal allocution of May 23, 1887. On the whole incident see the documents in Crispi: *Politica Interna* pp. 97 ff., and the reports of Engelbrecht, the German military attaché (Waldersee: *Briefwechsel* I, pp. 87-88, 141-143); F. X. Kraus: Spectator-Briefe, in *Beilage zur Allgemeinen Zeitung* July 1, 1896; G. Manfroni: *Sulla Soglia del Vaticano 1870-1901* (Bologna 1920) II, p. 157; di Pesaro p. 89; and especially the excellent summary, with references, in Salvemini: *La Politica Estera di Francesco Crispi* pp. 49 ff. A detailed account is given by S. Cilibrizzi: *Storia Parlamentare, Politica e Diplomatica d'Italia* (Milan 1925) vol. II, pp. 328-332; Bastgen III, pp. 43 ff.

was apparently one of the prime movers, but the plan failed, in part because of the opposition of certain Italian cardinals, in part because of Leo's own indecision. Much as the Pope desired action in his own behalf he could not help but feel that if once he left Rome he might never return.[11]

Finally there was a third method of bringing effective pressure to bear upon the Italian government, and this was of an economic nature. In July, 1886 the French chamber had rejected the draft of a navigation treaty with Italy, and in December of the same year the Italian government, under pressure of the rising protectionist element, had committed the fatal error of denouncing the commercial treaty with France which had been in force since 1881.[12] No doubt it was hoped that more favorable terms could be obtained from France, but of all governments the Italian could least afford to take chances with national prosperity. Italy was very much dependent upon the trade with France and also upon French capital to develop her industries. By denouncing the treaty the Italians had placed in the hands of the French an exceedingly effective political weapon.

During 1887 great efforts were made by the French statesmen to prevent the renewal of the Triple Alliance or effect its disruption, a favorable treaty of commerce being dangled before the Italians as a reward for proper political conduct.[13] Actual

[11] Crispi in the *Contemporary Review* June and August, 1891 (reprinted in his *Ultimi Scritti*, chapter ii); Crispi: *Politica Interna* pp. 120-123; T'Serclaes: *Le Pape Léon XIII* (Paris 1894) volume II, p. 154; G. Giolitti: *Memorie della mia Vita* (Milan 1922) volume I, pp. 47-48; J. de Narfon: *Pope Leo XIII* (London 1899); Cte. de X: Chronique du Vatican (*Revue Internationale* August 10, 1889); Anon (probably W. Stead): The Papacy, A Revelation and a Prophecy (*Contemporary Review* August 1889, pp. 153-154); Manfroni II, pp. 175 ff., 183; Sinapoli di Giunta: Cardinale Mariano Rampolla (1923) p. 123; Johnson pp. 55-59; Waldersee: *Briefwechsel* I, pp. 308-309.

[12] For details see Crispi: *Memoirs* II, chapter vii; Albert Billot: *La France et l'Italie 1881-1899* (Paris 1905) volume I, chapters iv and viii; Chiala III, pp. 519 ff.; *Documenti Diplomatici: Corrispondenza e negotiati par il rinnovamento del Trattato Commercio con la Francia* (1888); Bonfadini: *La France et l'Italie en 1888* (Rome 1888); *Report on Tariff Wars* (Command Paper 1938; 1904); S. Cilibrizzi II, pp. 354 ff.

[13] Crispi II, pp. 246-249. The defunct tariff treaty of 1881 had been extended by provisional agreements till March 1888.

negotiations were opened in December, 1887, but were abruptly broken off in February, 1888, when the French got wind of the military convention concluded between Germany and Italy.[14] By this time the renewal of the Triple Alliance and the conclusion of the Mediterranean pacts had already become known, and the French negotiator, Senator Teisserenc de Bort made his government's position perfectly clear. On leaving Rome he bluntly told the Italian representative, Ellena: "As long as you remain in the Triple Alliance no commercial agreement between Italy and France will be possible."[15]

In the two succeeding years the relations of the two countries went rapidly from bad to worse. Crispi, who became premier in the summer of 1887, was a hot-headed Sicilian, incalculable, spasmodic and undiplomatic.[16] Suspicion of France became the keynote of his policy, and his every action was influenced by an exaggerated pride and obstinate determination not to yield or appear to be beaten. He paraded the German-Italian connection by ostentatious visits to Bismarck and time and again created a veritable panic by his ill-considered speeches and phantastic fears. One incident followed another in the calendar of Franco-Italian relations and more than once in the years 1888 and 1889 war seemed not far in the offing.[17] In the summer of the latter year Bismarck was obliged to intervene in behalf of his ally, and Lord Salisbury sent the English squadron to Genoa to reassure

---

[14] Salvemini: *La Politica Estera di Francesco Crispi* pp. 59-60.

[15] Crispi II, p. 254. The renewal of the Triple Alliance became known unofficially in March 1887 (see Chiala III, pp. 485 ff).

[16] See the remarkable characterization in Salvemini p. 46: "Il vero Crispi fu un uomo sincero, ombroso, vulcanico, incapace di eufemismi diplomatici, avezzo a parlar violento, sensibile alla lode, più sensibile all' offesa...facile a confondere sè con l'Italia e considerare le brutalità dei giornali francesi, come insulti diretti, non tanto a lui, quanto al suo paese, che egli amava di amore ardente e geloso.. "

[17] Crispi II, pp. 275-276, 307-318; Billot I, chapters v, vi; Chiala III, pp. 519-520; Charles, Comte de Moüy: *Souvenirs* (Paris 1909) p. 256; Galli pp. 120-122; Salvemini pp. 61 ff.; Bonfadini: *La France et l'Italie en 1888;* A. Leroy-Beaulieu: La France, l'Italie et la Triple Alliance (*Revue des Deux Mondes* July 15, 1889); also Cilibrizzi II, pp. 356 ff., 377 ff.; *Documenti Diplomatici: Dichiarazione italofrancese sulla inviolabilità degli archivi Consolari* (1889), for details of the various incidents.

Crispi, who had grown almost hysterical with fears of an un-provoked French attack.

There is no evidence and very little likelihood that the French government harbored such evil thoughts. Crispi's alarms were almost always due to ill-founded rumors and illogical deductions. The only real basis for his fears lay in the actual economic pressure being consistently brought to bear by the French. Be-tween 1887 and 1889 Italian exports to France dropped 40%, the export of cheap Italian wines ceasing almost completely. It was estimated that in one year French bankers withdrew 700,-000,000 francs of capital from the peninsula. Economically the situation had become almost intolerable by the end of 1889, and yet Crispi continued to ask larger and larger appropriations for the army and navy.[18]

The result was just what the French desired. Not only did the anti-monarchical feeling in Italy increase rapidly, but there was a growing agitation against the Triple Alliance, which its opponents made responsible for the strained relations with France and especially for the tremendous outlays for armaments.[19] One expression of this hostile sentiment was the recrudescence of irredentist agitation.[20]

Not even Crispi could withstand the pressure any longer. Al-ready in December, 1889 he had spoken before the chamber in very conciliatory terms. At the same time the Italian government took the first step towards better relations by abolishing the

[18] Billot I, pp. 135 ff.; Usigli: La Crise Italienne et ses Causes (*Revue Inter-nationale* December 25, 1889); H. Geffcken: The Economic Condition of Italy (*Contemporary Review* October 1890, pp. 609-625); F. Nitti: *Il Capitale Straniero in Italia* (Bari 1915); A. Plebano: *Storia della Finanza Italiana 1888-1901* (Turin 1902) III, pp. 131 ff.; further figures in Ashley pp. 326-327. Army expenditures rose from 172,000,000 francs in 1875 to 365,000,000 in 1889; naval expenditures from 25,000,000 to 124,000,000 in the same period (*Mémorial Diplomatique* April 26, 1890).

[19] A typical exposition of this view by Testis: La Crise Economique de l'Italie (*Nouvelle Revue* February 15, 1891). See also *Spectator* editorial June 7, 1890; *Mémorial Diplomatique* April 12, 1890; Jacini: *Pensieri sulla Politica Ital-iana* (1889); Outidanos (?Gladstone): The Triple Alliance and Italy's Place in it (*Contemporary Review* October 1889 pp. 469-489).

[20] See especially Cilibrizzi II, pp. 390 ff.

differential tariff against France.[21]   Crispi's position was still further weakened by Bismarck's fall, and it became the more necessary to reëstablish harmony.[22]   When President Carnot visited Toulon in April, 1890, he found an Italian squadron there to receive him.[23]

On March 21, 1890, almost coincident with Bismarck's dismissal, a change of ministry had taken place in France.   Freycinet, for some time minister of war, became premier, while retaining his previous portfolio.   Constans, generally looked upon at the time as the strong man of French politics, became minister of the interior.   Ribot was foreign minister.   All told it was one of the strongest cabinets France had had in a long time, and its advent may be taken to mark the definitive end of the Boulangist period.   There was every indication that in future France would be in control of the moderate republicans, and that the evolution towards stability would proceed apace.[24]

Freycinet tells us in his memoirs (written long after) that he had always favored an alliance with Russia, and that in 1880 he advocated "carefully cultivating all opportunities for developing sympathy between the two governments."   "Let us not trumpet it from the roof-tops, for we must proceed prudently; we are surrounded by ill-will which may lead to the failure of our efforts."[25]   In any case Freycinet was a cautious man.   There is no evidence that, prior to 1890, this policy was more than an ideal or that in his mind the Franco-Russian Alliance was more than a pious wish.   It was Freycinet himself who, in September, 1886, informed the German ambassador of the unofficial suggestions made by the Russians in Paris.[26]

But in 1890 the situation was different.   France had not only

[21] Chiala III, pp. 525-526, where Crispi's conciliatory utterances are reprinted.

[22] Billot I, p. 170; Crispi II, pp. 434-435; Sir Alfred Lyall: *The Life of the Marquis of Dufferin* (London 1905) II, pp. 231-232; Pribram I, pp. 214-215; Waldersee: *Briefwechsel* I, p. 360.

[23] Billot I, p. 170; Chiala III, pp. 528-529; *Mémorial Diplomatique* April 12, 1890.

[24] Cf. Jules Simon: The Stability of the French Republic (*Forum* December 1890, pp. 383-394).

[25] C. de Freycinet: *Souvenirs 1878-1893* (Paris 1913) p. 110.

[26] G. P. V, nos. 1001, 1004, 1007; VI, nos. 1200-1204, 1210, 1211.

overcome the Boulanger crisis, but had built up a strong army and a powerful navy.[27] She had apparently made some progress in her attempts to undermine the Triple Alliance, and was on better terms with the Papacy than she had been since the advent of the republicans to power. She had shown an unexpected readiness to lend money and supply arms to the needy Russians. In short, she was in every way a more desirable ally than she had been before.[28]

The dismissal of Bismarck also profoundly affected the position of France. French writers have themselves confessed that his presence was an insurmountable obstacle to an alliance with Russia.[29] Freycinet implies the same thing in the passage of his memoirs quoted above. After March, 1890 the French statesmen could at last breathe freely, could at last work for the realization of a policy that was more than narrowly self-protective. So far they had contented themselves with opposing England in the Mediterranean. Beyond coöperation with Russia in the Egyptian question they had not dared go. Even the pressure upon Italy was essentially part of this policy. In so far as it was aimed against the Triple Alliance it was very cautiously veiled and only indirect. Now, however, they could come out more openly and make a bid for a Russian alliance of a broader sort, frankly continental and frankly directed against Germany.

Moreover, the need for more vigorous action seemed imperative, for after Bismarck's fall the French, like the Russians, were before the unknown. By 1890 they had come to believe that Bismarck was a force for peace and that there was little likelihood of his provoking a conflict. But it was generally believed that the "warlike" young Kaiser, who had chosen a military man as his chancellor, would attempt to emulate Frederick the Great

---

[27] Cf. especially Freycinet chapters xii and xiii. *Saturday Review* September 26, 1890: "Since the last war they (the French) have been keeping their folly for their politics and their work for their army, with the result that they have a force now which even Germany would be in no hurry to tackle."

[28] G. P. VII, no. 1489.

[29] Daudet: *Histoire diplomatique de l'Alliance Franco-Russe* p. 328. Similarly Mme. Adam in *Nouvelle Revue* June 15, 1890.

and would initiate his personal rule with a foreign war.[30] To be sure, William was very attentive to the French delegates at the Labor Conference in Berlin and made no attempt to conceal his desire to establish cordial relations. But when Ribot suggested that words be followed by deeds and proposed a relaxation of the irritating passport regulations in Alsace-Lorraine the German government turned a deaf ear.[31]

And then, the French, like the Russians, could not help but be alarmed by the Heligoland Treaty. They firmly believed, it seems, that Germany had given a promise of unconditional support of English policy in Egypt. Might not the Anglo-German rapprochement indicate the coming adhesion of England to the Triple Alliance? Might it not signify the enlistment of Germany in the ranks of the Mediterranean powers?[32]

Freycinet and his colleagues determined to redouble their efforts. On May 30, 1890 the government, reversing the policy of its predecessors, arrested a large group of Russian revolutionaries in Paris. The Russian government, at whose request the arrests had been made, was, of course, greatly pleased, and the Tsar ordered the Paris government to be thanked officially.[33] The energetic manner in which Constans had conducted the whole affair was generally regarded as evidence of the strength of the government, and the good impression made in St. Petersburg was enhanced when, a few days later, the Duke of Orleans,

[30] G. P. VII, no. 1541. Freycinet of course insisted that he had never suspected the Kaiser of bellicose plans. See also *Saturday Review* August 23, 1890, editorial; G. Monod in *Contemporary Review* July 1890, p. 29.

[31] G. P. VII, nos. 1541, 1543. The Kaiser's attempts at conciliation are aptly characterized as "une fausse idylle" by P. Albin: *L'Allemagne et la France en Europe* (Paris 1913) pp. 200 ff. and they aroused Bismarck's scorn (*Gedanken und Erinnerungen* III, pp. 132-133). Cf. on the Alsace-Lorraine question W. Mommsen: Die elsass-lothringische Frage 1890-1897 (in *Archiv für Politik und Geschichte* June-July 1924, pp. 583-591).

[32] It is interesting to note that in July 1890 Ribot told Münster that French opinion was becoming more and more hostile to England and less inimical to Germany (G. P. VIII, no. 1703).

[33] Good accounts in Freycinet pp. 442-443; J. Hansen: *L'Ambassade du Baron de Mohrenheim* (Paris 1907) pp. 113-115; Daudet pp. 294 ff.; Albin pp. 276-277; Smith: The Franco-Russian Alliance (*Universal Review* November 1890, pp. 373-386).

imprisoned for violating the law excluding pretenders, was pardoned.[34]

Of course all this was a policy of small courtesies, a *Trinkgelderpolitik* as Bismarck called it. It might or it might not have significance. Like the invitation extended to General Boisdeffre in August 1890 it was nothing more than an exchange of courtesies marking a greater cordiality in the relations of the two countries. Such action on the part of the Russians was advisable if only in order to keep the French money market well disposed.[35]

More significant, certainly, were the renewed onslaughts of the French upon the Italians and their position in the Mediterranean. Crispi had just exhibited a desire to effect a reconciliation. Since the French government had made its position very clear it probably felt justified in believing that, now after Bismarck's fall, Italy would be prepared to reconsider her entire policy.[36] Consequently Billot, the new ambassador to Rome, was sent off posthaste, armed with instructions of a very friendly tenor. France, he was to say, had no desire to place obstacles in the way of Italian colonial expansion and was quite prepared to regulate the Tunis difficulty in accordance with Italy's claims. Crispi hastened to receive the new envoy and spoke in a very satisfactory way. He almost apologized for the Triple Alliance,

---

[34] In June Pourtalès reported Franco-Russian relations as having greatly improved in the previous few weeks, though he correctly pointed out that this in itself meant very little (G. P. VII, no. 1489). On the good impression created see Köhler p. 93, note 1. Wolkenstein to Kálnoky, June 4, 1890 in V. A. reported: "Erfolg der französischen Polizei wird voraussichtlich nicht unwesentlich zur Vervollkommnung der russisch-französischen Beziehungen beitragen, da Kaiser Alexander in diesem Punkte sehr empfindlich und empfänglich ist." Shortly after the Tsar is said to have exclaimed to a French secret agent at Copenhagen: "Enfin il y a un gouvernement en France" (Chiala III, p. 570 note 1; Albin p. 277).

[35] Even before Bismarck's fall the Russians had carried out a number of conversion transactions with the help of Paris financiers, and in 1889 the Russian government had ordered thousands of rifles from a French firm (Freycinet pp. 414-418; Albin pp. 264-266; Daudet pp. 245 ff., and 281 ff.; Koerlin pp. 195 ff).

[36] Cf. *Mémorial Diplomatique* May 3, 17, 1890: "Tant que cette alliance existera, ou plutôt tant que le Cabinet de Rome persistera dans son intention de la renouveler....la reconciliation desirée se heurtera à l'invincible méfiance du peuple français."

which, he said, he had neither made nor approved of and which he observed only from a sense of duty. He vigorously refuted the idea that it was directed against France and expressed the hope that Italy, as a member, might actually serve as a connecting link in effecting a rapprochement between France and Germany. King Humbert, on receiving the new ambassador in audience on April 21, was even more outspoken and insisted upon the necessity of a settlement between France and Italy, at the same time reminding his visitor of the glories of Magenta and Solferino.[37]

Negotiations were actually opened towards the end of April, in the hope of settling the conflicting claims of the two powers in eastern Africa. Ribot was ready enough to define the boundaries of existing possessions, but he refused to recognize the whole of Abyssinia as within the Italian sphere of influence. On this point, so closely connected with the whole Egyptian problem, the French could yield only in return for the renunciation of all Italian claims in Tunis. Apparently the French were willing, if such an arrangement could be effected, to leave Italy a free hand in Tripoli.[38] If Italy were to accept, the inevitable result would be the estrangement of Turkey from the Mediterranean powers, an increase of French influence in Constantinople and, as a corollary, greater readiness on the part of the Russians to consider an alliance with France.[39]

But this involved a strengthening of the French position in the western Mediterranean. This Crispi would not consider, and negotiations broke down in July. Very likely the Italian premier was influenced in his attitude by the Anglo-German Treaty, which necessarily accrued to the interest of Italy. In any case the Heligoland Treaty, following directly upon the Italo-French negotiations, opened the whole Mediterranean problem.

[37] Crispi III, pp. 181-183; Billot I, pp. 183-184, 190. Cf. also Crispi's apologetic speech in the Senate on March 26, 1890 (*Mémorial Diplomatique* March 29, 1890).

[38] On these negotiations see Billot I, pp. 204-208; Salvemini: *La Politica Estera di Francesco Crispi* pp. 72 ff.

[39] Cf. G. P. VIII, no. 1701, where this explanation of the French policy regarding Tripoli is suggested.

The English desired to convert the Egyptian debt in order to provide funds for the reconquest of the Sudan, and the French, suspecting the ultimate plans of the English, had refused to give their approval.[40] By way of counterattack they had effected an understanding with the Russians and the representatives of the two nations had persuaded the Porte to submit various proposals to the English, the chief characteristics of which were the provisions for the evacuation of Egypt within a definite time-limit.[41]

This first indirect assault on the English position was followed almost immediately by very vigorous French protests against the Anglo-German Treaty. The Paris government insisted that the recognition of an English protectorate over Zanzibar constituted a violation of an earlier treaty, and demanded, by way of compensation, certain concessions in Egypt or the abolition of the capitulations in Tunis.[42] The position of the English was a very awkward one. They could not consider concessions in Egypt without abandoning their advantageous position in the Mediterranean. To yield in the matter of Tunis would have had the same effect, and in either case (but especially in the second) Italy would necessarily be estranged.[43] Crispi was already much

---

[40] It appears that at first the Freycinet cabinet was inclined to an agreement (G. P. VII, no. 1543; VIII, nos. 1777 ff.). This may have been due to a desire to gain time in the critical days following Bismarck's fall. In any case French public opinion would not tolerate concessions. Full details of the debt negotiations in the French *Documents Diplomatiques: Affaires d'Égypte 1884-1893* pp. 227-306.

[41] G. P. VIII, nos. 1775 ff. The first proposal of April was a strictly Turkish product and provided for eventual reoccupation by the English. The Russians and French warned the Porte that they would not accept such a settlement. Salisbury insisted that the Turks first secure French and Russian approval of the English right of reoccupation. The French agreed to promise never to occupy Egypt if the English evacuated. On the basis of this the Turks submitted a second proposal in June. It attempted to fix a definite time for evacuation, and was rejected by the English. (See also Freycinet pp. 450-452; Daudet p. 291.).

[42] The English government did not admit the French claim but thought it better to avoid friction (G. P. VIII, nos. 1601, 1866; Deym to Kálnoky July 3, 1890 in V. A.) It was generally recognized that the abolition of the capitulations would be merely the first step towards French annexation. The French also protested against the German acquisition of the East African mainland, but this was a minor matter and was settled with little difficulty (see G. P. VIII, nos. 1691 ff.)

[43] Already on June 26, 1890 Crispi had appealed to the German government to use its influence to prevent England from making concessions in Tunis. This

alarmed by the construction of military works at Bizerta and was attempting to enlist German and English support for a warning to the French.[44] At first neither power had shown enthusiasm for the Italian proposals. Caprivi argued that continued French activity in the western Mediterranean would necessitate the transfer of French ships from the Channel to the Mediterranean and the reduction of military expenditure in favor of further outlays for the fleet. Above all it would keep England and Italy together and make them both more dependent upon Germany and the Triple Alliance.[45] As for Salisbury, he was always apprehensive lest the impetuosity of Crispi might lead to a conflict with France, which the English by no means desired.[46]

But with the French demands the situation became more serious. It should be remembered that in England it was feared that Russia was planning some action against Constantinople, and the British Mediterranean squadron had been given secret sailing orders. Under no conditions could England afford to yield.[47] The result was that England and Germany drew

the German government did (G. P. VIII, nos. 1691, 1865 ff.; details given by Holstein were reported by Széchényi to Kálnoky July 17, 1890, in V. A.). On the importance of Tunis for England's Mediterranean position and English anxiety not to estrange Italy see especially G. P. VIII, no. 1703. Cf. also the warning in the chronique of the *Nuova Antologia* July 16, 1890: "La acquiescenza dell' Inghilterra all'annessione di Tunisi avrebbe segnato la fine delle buone relazioni tra l'Inghilterra stessa e l'Italia," and Engelbrecht's reports in Waldersee: *Briefwechsel* I, pp. 392-393.

[44] G. P. VIII, nos. 1862 ff. He also appealed to the Austrians for support (Kálnoky to Deym and Széchényi May 23, 1890 in V. A.). The Germans had, at the request of Crispi, warned the French about Bizerta in January 1889 (Crispi III, pp. 85-86). In 1890 the French works were apparently being pushed with great vigor. A full account of the involved negotiations in Crispi II, pp. 438-476, III, pp. 85-87; Cilibrizzi II, pp. 412 ff.

[45] G. P. VIII, nos. 1862, 1886. Caprivi consistently held the view that the fortifications of Bizerta would constitute a greater menace to England than to Italy.

[46] G. P. VIII, no. 1703. Salisbury's apparent indifference in the matter of Bizerta was truly remarkable. It was evidently due chiefly to a desire not to encourage Crispi to the point of rashness, and to avoid a revival of Italian demands for compensation in Tripoli.

[47] See above (text chapter II) and G. P. IX, nos. 2073 ff., especially nos. 2082, 2086, 2087, 2095.

nearer together. They decided, in case of necessity, to coöperate in resisting the French demands, and meanwhile England definitely rejected the suggestion of political concessions in Tunis.[48]

Not even this was enough to satisfy Crispi. Just as his negotiations with France in regard to Abyssinia were breaking down he received word that France had concluded with the Bey of Tunis a secret treaty of devolution.[49] The rumor was probably unfounded, but it was enough to excite the feverish mind of the Italian premier. He now demanded what Germany and England intended to do in case France attempted to change the *status quo* in Tunis. He suggested that Italy might be given compensation in Tripoli.[50] Neither England nor Germany desired to create a crisis and both attempted to deny any obligations under the loosely worded Mediterranean Agreement or under the Triple Alliance Treaty of 1887.[51] The limit to which they were willing to go was a promise to help Italy acquire Tripoli if the supposed intrigues of the French proved to be true. But they considered the moment for an Italian occupation of Tripoli very inopportune. Its immediate result would inevitably be the estrangement of the Porte and a corresponding increase of Franco-Russian influence at Constantinople.[52]

German inquiries in Paris brought from Ribot an energetic denial of French plans to change the existing situation in Tunis.[53] Crispi was incredulous and dissatisfied. His ill-humor was increased by the fact that negotiations with England in regard to the delimitation of Italian possessions on the Red Sea were making no progress.[54] He was anxious to acquire Tripoli in any

[48] G. P. VIII, nos. 1700, 1703, 1864. The French had reduced their demands to a revision of the English commercial treaty with Tunis.

[49] G. P. VIII, nos. 1870 ff.   [50] Crispi II, pp. 449-450.

[51] G. P. VIII, nos. 1874, 1877. Caprivi feared German opinion would never support a war waged because of a minor change in the status of Tunis, and he also suspected that England might hang back and let others defend English Mediterranean interests.

[52] G. P. VIII, nos. 1873 ff. especially nos. 1877, 1884, 1892; Crispi II, pp. 445-462.

[53] G. P. VIII, no. 1883. The French made a similar declaration to the English (Crispi II, pp. 447-452).

[54] G. P. VIII, no. 1972. The English objected to the Italian demand for Cassala, and apparently were anxious not to impair their prestige in Egypt by

event and tried to convince the English and Germans of the necessity for such a step.[55]

Recognizing the Italian view the French hastened to exploit it by offering to partition the province in return for Italian recognition of the French annexation of Tunis.[56] There was something attractive about the suggestion and, even though Crispi may not have considered it seriously on account of the English, he knew enough to make use of the French advances. The Germans were particularly anxious and did their utmost to induce the English to give Italy renewed assurances.[57] The spectre of France and Italy coming together and perhaps bringing joint pressure upon the Porte to force concessions was an alarming one.[58] The German government itself was willing to join England in promising Italy that no other power should be allowed to acquire Tripoli.[59] Salisbury himself was uneasy and after prolonged negotiations convinced Crispi that the moment was inopportune for an Italian occupation, but that Italy might reckon upon English support when circumstances were favorable.[60]

In July and August, 1890 European politics had been concentrated on Mediterranean problems and for a time everything was in confusion. The French and Russians were attempting to force a reopening of the Egyptian question and the Russians were evi-

abandoning part of the Sudan. Negotiations between England and Italy were opened in April but had made no progress by August (Billot I, pp. 210-217; *Saturday Review* October 11 and 18, 1890). Negotiations broke down definitely in October (See further Crispi: *La Prima Guerra d'Africa* pp. 225-245; Lyall: *Dufferin* II, pp. 232-233).

[55] G. P. VIII, no. 1887; Crispi II, pp. 449-450.

[56] G.P. VIII, nos. 1701, 1887 ff. Apparently the French offered the Italians only Barka, reserving the rest of Tripoli for themselves.

[57] The German anxiety is clearly reflected in G. P. VIII, nos. 1872 ff., 1888. It was feared that an Italian annexation would open the whole question of the Turkish heritage and lead to a Balkan conflagration. Furthermore it would lead to Italian desertion of the Triple Alliance.

[58] Caprivi apparently feared also that Italy might appeal to Russia for support in extorting Tripoli from the Turks (G. P. VIII, no. 1891, marginalia).

[59] G. P. VIII, no. 1892. Austria also expressed willingness to join.

[60] G. P. VIII, nos. 1893 ff., Crispi II, pp. 445-455. The Germans were delighted to have England take the initiative for hitherto they had been under obligation to support Italy's claims to Tripoli.

dently considering some action on the Bosporus.[61] The French, on their part, had taken a strong line in the negotiations arising from the Anglo-German Convention. Had they secured concessions in Egypt or Tunis they would have succeeded not only in strengthening their position at the expense of England but would have made considerable progress towards estranging Italy from her allies. As it was the policy had not been very successful. Its effect had been rather, as Salisbury predicted it would be, to drive England and Germany even more closely together.[62] This may in part explain the German refusal to give the Russians a written statement in regard to the German attitude on the Straits question and Bulgaria.[63] It may help to explain the greater inclination of Germany to support the anti-Russian policy in the Balkans. It certainly explains the entente between England and Germany in respect to the questions of North Africa. Not only did Germany promise continued support of the English policy in Egypt; the two powers also discussed together the question of the Straits and coöperated in preventing the defection of Italy by giving Crispi the necessary assurances in regard to Tripoli.[64] France was obliged to accept Anglo-German recognition of her protectorate in Madagascar in return for recognition of the new situation created by the Anglo-German Treaty in

[61] There was considerable alarm in England over rumors that the Russians would propose to the Turks a commercial treaty permitting ships of the Russian Volunteer Fleet to pass the Straits without special permission (G. P. IX, nos. 2096 ff). On the general situation in the Near East see the article in the *Internationale Revue über die gesammten Armeen und Flotten* November 1890.

[62] G. P. VIII, nos. 1698-1699. Salisbury was somewhat anxious lest the Germans should take too vigorous a stand and cause serious complications. See Mme. Adam's tirade against the Anglo-German "alliance" which dominated the Near East, supporting the Stambulov regime and checkmating Russian influence at the Porte (*Nouvelle Revue* August 15, September 1, 15, 1890).

[63] The Germans indirectly hinted to the Turks the necessity of strengthening the fortifications of the Straits in order to encourage England in support of Turkey against the Russians. This was a reversal of the earlier German attitude (G. P. IX, nos. 2083, 2090).

[64] See G. P. IX, nos. 2095 ff. for the long discussion as to what should be done about the passage of ships of the Russian Volunteer Fleet through the Straits. England was at first inclined to protest and call upon the Triple Alliance for support. The Germans dissuaded Salisbury from this course in order not to be forced to act in open hostility to Russia.

Zanzibar and in German East Africa. On August 19 Salisbury
definitely rejected the Turkish draft of an evacuation treaty,
the fruit of Franco-Russian endeavor.[65]

But even after the crisis had blown over, its effects continued
to be felt. Crispi seemed determined to realize upon the promises
of support which he had extracted from Germany and England.
"Having convinced the French government that without Italy's
consent it would be impossible to achieve full sovereignty in
Tunis, he turned his attention to extracting from the situation
he had created such advantages as it might offer," says his
biographer.[66] Apparently the Italians now took the initiative,
proposing in Paris some concessions in the Tunis question in
return for a free hand in Tripoli. Ribot was irritated, and
argued that French opinion would never tolerate an Italian occupation, excepting on one condition. His words are worth
quoting, as they reveal the whole French policy:

"Until the Triple Alliance, which constitutes an even greater offence to
the Tsar than to the French Republic, has been denounced, no intimacy
will ever be possible between Russia and Germany or between the Italians
and ourselves. We may not be hostile, but we can never be true friends."

The *Matin* on August 21 echoed the same sentiments.[67]

Franco-Italian relations had become, if anything, worse than
ever before. Late in August King Humbert refused to be
present at the launching of the battleship *Sardegna* at Spezzia
when it became known that the French government intended to
send a squadron to greet him, in return for the visit of the Italian
ships to Toulon in April.[68] Mutual accusations and recriminations began to exceed all bounds, and the dangers of the situation
became greater and greater. For Crispi was as obstinate as
ever. In October, 1890 the Germans feared that he would propose
a treaty to partition Turkey.[69] This failed to materialize but
Crispi continued his usual methods of prodding his allies into

[65] G. P. VIII, no. 1787.
[66] Palamenghi-Crispi in Crispi II, p. 462.
[67] Crispi II, pp. 469-470.
[68] Crispi III, pp. 184-186; Billot I, pp. 241-243.
[69] G. P. IX, no. 2105.

action. Now it was the French fortifications at Bizerta, now it was renewed designs of the French on the hinterland of Tripoli, which led him to appeal for aid.[70]

The Germans and English were in an embarrassing position. They were willing to lend the Italians all reasonable support, but they certainly could not go with Crispi all the way, for they were both very anxious to prevent a conflict with France. On the other hand there was always danger lest Crispi, goaded by the demands of the chamber and under the continuous pressure of a growing agitation against the Triple Alliance, might in the end capitulate to the French. Though the Italian premier still believed that Italy's best chance lay in continued loyalty to the existing treaties, there was no way of knowing how long he would be able to hold out. He himself at times doubted whether the Triple Alliance could be renewed.[71]

Everything depended upon the outcome of the Italian elections in November. For some time Caprivi had considered the advisability of paying Crispi a visit and it was hoped that in this fashion the premier's position could be bolstered up.[72] Just before the elections, on November 7, Caprivi arrived at Milan. The following day was spent at Monza nearby. In the discussions that took place between the two statesmen Crispi did most of the talking and the subject was always the same—the problem of Franco-Italian relations and Italy's position in the Mediterranean.[73] The Italian premier admitted that the Triple Alliance

---

[70] In regard to Bizerta Crispi complained directly to the French, but received a sharp rebuff (Crispi III, pp. 86-90; G. P. VIII, nos. 1897 ff.; Lyall: *Dufferin* II, p. 248). Both the English and Germans advised the Sultan not to consider the French suggestions for a rectification of the Tunisian frontier in the direction of Tripoli. The whole tedious negotiations are recounted in Crispi III, pp. 30-67.

[71] The action of the Austrian government in closing the *Pro Patria* Society in Trieste added to the existing difficulties. See Crispi's long correspondence with Nigra concerning the value of the alliance and the possibility of renewing it, in Crispi III, pp. 139-157.

[72] Crispi III, p. 406; Billot I, p. 250; Waldersee: *Denkwürdigkeiten* II, p. 155. The *Wiener Politische Korrespondenz* (October 29, 1890) defined the purpose of the visit as "die neue Bekräftigung des festen Bestandes des Dreibundes." The Kaiser himself had considered making a visit (Waldersee II, p. 145).

[73] Accounts of the meeting in Crispi III, pp. 6-16; G. P. VII, nos. 1393 ff.;

must be renewed, but he hardly touched this matter. Attention
was concentrated on two points. The first dealt with economic
matters, Crispi insisting that the French tariff changes were
aimed primarily at Italy and urging the formation of a "commercial league" between Germany, Austria and Italy to counteract the economic warfare being waged upon Italy by France.
This, he thought, might be developed later into a "monarchical
league" to ward off French republican propaganda and bolster
up the tottering dynasties of Spain and Portugal. In a political
way Crispi stressed especially the necessity for strengthening the
connection with Spain. In a war with France Spain would be a
useful ally in so far as she could compel France to leave a large
number of troops on the Pyrenean frontier. She might also
prove a valuable ally in opposing French policy in North Africa.

Caprivi assented to all these remarks. He himself was interested in improving the commercial relations between the members of the Triple Alliance and promised to negotiate a treaty
with Italy as soon as Germany and Austria had succeeded in
making an arrangement. He also approved of Crispi's plan to
draw closer the bonds with Spain, but pointed out again and
again that Italy must lay chief emphasis on her relations with
England. The Italian and Spanish navies must be improved,
even at the expense of the army. As for the question of the
Bizerta fortifications Crispi, he thought, need not worry so long
as the English were not alarmed. The reply of the Italian
premier was that he was absolutely sure of England, even if the
Salisbury cabinet were overthrown.[74]

The last months of 1890 were generally quiet. The first
dangerous passage at arms between the various powers was over.
The hopes of the Russians and the French that the Triple Alliance
would disintegrate had proved illusory. If the statesmen in St.
Petersburg had actually planned some sort of action against

Bruck's report in Pribram I, pp. 215-216; and Eissenstein to Kálnoky November
15, 1890 in V. A. Cf. also Billot I, pp. 250-251.

[74] This is a very obscure point. Crispi repeated the assertion later (G. P.
VIII, no. 1896) but there is certainly no indication of far-reaching promises in
Salisbury's letter of August 4, 1890, nor was any further evidence of an extensive
concrete agreement ever discovered.

Constantinople they had been deterred by the questionable attitude of Germany and the apparent willingness of the Germans to coöperate with England and Austria in Near Eastern affairs. Similarly the French had failed to bring about the defection of Italy, either by a policy of conciliation or by a policy of pressure. Here too the Triple Alliance, reinforced by England, had resisted the strain and had prevented an alteration of the *status quo* in the Mediterranean. Crispi had signalized the French failure by proclaiming his loyalty to the alliance, and the elections of November, 1890 seemed to indicate that the country was behind him.[75]

During the months of comparative calm which followed, the attention of Europe was centered upon the spectacular action of the Papacy, which, it was immediately realized, might have important international implications. Leo was still consumed with the desire to improve the position of the Vatican. There was no longer a possibility of an amicable agreement with the Italian government, certainly not as long as Crispi remained in control. Leo's hopes of German and Austrian influence upon Italy in his behalf had been shown to be ill-founded. Evidently no concessions could be expected from a Masonic Italy through the mediation of Protestant Germany and Hebrew Austria. Similarly the collapse of the Boulangist movement in France had rendered futile any expectation of a royalist restoration and direct intervention to restore the temporal power. The plan of a flight from Rome had been considered and found impractical.

In the spring of 1890 the German representative at the Vatican reported that Jesuit circles were urging the need of a general European War and the desirability of a Franco-Russian Alliance as the only means of recovering the temporal power. Cardinal Galimberti remarked in September, 1890 that the Pope was inclining more and more to this view.[76] It seems very unlikely, however, that Leo ever seriously considered so radical a remedy. He was more inclined to rely upon indirect action and a reorien-

---

[75] Crispi's famous speech at Florence October 8, 1890.

[76] Schlözer's reports May 30 and November 12, 1890 (quoted by Becker: *Das französisch-russische Bündnis* pp. 134-135).

tation of policy. Had not Bismarck himself told Galimberti, the papal representative, in 1887 and 1888, that if a republic were established in Italy he would support a restoration of the temporal power?[77] If the French were favoring a republican propaganda in the peninsula there was evidently a point of contact, a common interest here. Towards the end of 1889 and during the early months of 1890 prominent French clerics had repeatedly pointed out to the Pope the hopelessness of relying upon the outworn monarchist movement. The Papacy should recognize the Republic and throw its moral influence on the side of the moderates. The new slogan for French Catholics should be: "accept the constitution, in order the better to influence legislation."[78] If the Catholics could unite and gain control of the French government the position of the Church would be tremendously improved, and in international affairs a much greater pressure could be exerted on Italy. Republican propaganda and direct action by the French government might successfully drive Italy to accept a compromise.[79]

As early as January 10, 1890 the first step had been taken by the encyclical *Sapientiae Christianae*, in which the Pope denied that the Church was opposed to any form of government as such.[80] French cardinals urged a more vigorous and positive policy in this direction. The Archbishop of Rennes was instructed to draw up a pastoral letter advising the clergy and the faithful to drop their opposition to the Republic, but this was not pub-

[77] Woodward p. 135, quoting Crispolti and Aureli. The establishment of the republic in Italy was the necessary first step. Cf. Jules Bonjean, one of the French Catholic leaders who, speaking of Leo says (*Nouvelle Revue* October 15, 1891, pp. 673-690) that at the Vatican "on aspire moins à lui rendre son trône qu'à renverser celui des souverains qui sont venus établir le leur en face de la chaire de saint Pierre."

[78] F. Despagnet: *La République et le Vatican 1870-1906* (Paris 1906) p. 117.

[79] It was evidently hoped that in case of success France would do something to restore the temporal power. See Bonghi in the *Perseveranza*, quoted in what is practically an official work, T'Serclaes: *Le Pape Léon XIII* (Paris 1894) volume II, p. 440. By way of comment T'Serclaes remarks: "C'était voir clair, il faut l'avouer."

[80] F. Tournier: *Le Cardinal Lavigerie et son Action Politique* (Paris 1913) p. 277 (based on the Lavigerie papers).

lished, because it was thought inadvisable to have the appeal issued in royalist Brittany.[81]

One of the chief advocates of the new policy was Cardinal Lavigerie, Archbishop of Algiers and Primate of Africa, a man prominent not only in Church affairs and a leader in the anti-slavery movement, but also thoroughly versed in French politics.[82] He had been a close friend of the Duc de Chambord and had been active in the royalist movements of the 1870's. At heart he was still a royalist, but he had lost hope and as a churchman believed that the continued identification of the Church with a lost cause would eventually prove fatal. As early as March, 1890 he had urged the Pope to take a decisive step.[83]

The French ambassador supported the advocates of this new policy and the moderate ministry of Freycinet was also favorably inclined. No doubt they retained some suspicions as to the ultimate aims of the papal manoeuvres, but they needed the support of the Catholic elements against the rabidly anti-clerical radicals, and the significance of an entente with the Vatican with regard to foreign affairs could not escape them.[84] Approval of the moderate Republic by the Pope would greatly raise the prestige of the government and would enhance its desirability as an ally in the eyes of the conservative monarchies. France might utilize her new influence in Rome to mediate between Russia and the Vatican and thus forge a new link in the Franco-Russian Alliance. And, finally, the effect of French-Papal friendship would inevitably serve to undermine the Italian position. The Italian republicans would be strengthened by the recognition of the French Republic, and it would be difficult for Italy to resist the French if they chose to raise the question of the temporal power.[85]

[81] See Woodward pp. 136 ff.; Cardinal Domenico Ferrata: *Mémoires* (Rome 1920) II, p. 29.

[82] Léon de Cheyssac: *Le Ralliement* (Paris 1906) pp. 71-72.

[83] Tournier pp. 280-282; Mourret p. 87.

[84] Ferrata II, pp. 64-65, 67.

[85] Cf. Cheyssac, p. 74, who thinks that in November 1890 the French government would not have hesitated to make use of the most extreme royalists to start a subversive movement in the former kingdom of Naples or elsewhere. On

Constans, the French minister of the interior, appears to have been the prime mover among the French statesmen.[86] In the summer Lavigerie went to Paris ostensibly to discuss the slavery question with the ministers, but in reality to confer on political questions with Constans, Ribot and Freycinet, as well as with President Carnot. From Paris he went to Rome, and on October 14 had an important talk with His Holiness. He convinced Leo "that it was necessary to break with the old parties, demand that the Catholics adhere to the Republic and organize a union of Catholics upon this basis." Leo listened sympathetically, but pointed out that it would not do for the head of the Church to come out openly against the French monarchists. He suggested that Lavigerie prepare the ground by a declaration. After some hesitation Lavigerie accepted, and immediately informed Constans, stating that he meant to act at the earliest opportunity.[87]

To the Cardinal the favorable moment seemed to have arrived when, on November 12, 1890, the officers of the French squadron visiting Algiers were assembled at his board. The *Marseillaise* was played as the guests took their seats and at the close of the dinner Lavigerie offered his famous toast. In it he developed the idea that it is the patriotic duty of every individual to recognize the existing form of government once this has received the approbation of the people. He closed by saying that he had no fear of being disavowed.[88]

The Algiers toast naturally created a great stir, not only in France, but in all Europe. It was all the more significant be-

the prevalence of fears to this effect see Billot I, pp. 263-264. Cf. also F. X. Kraus in *Allgemeine Zeitung* August 9, 1903.

[86] Cheyssac, p. 74; Ferrata II, pp. 64-65.

[87] The fundamental accounts in Tournier pp. 283-285 (based on Lavigerie's papers) and Louis Baunard: *Léon XIII et le Toast d'Alger* (Paris 1914) pp. 24-36 (giving Leo's own account); cf. also Baunard: *Le Cardinal Lavigerie* (Paris 1912) volume II, pp. 555-559; T'Serclaes: *Léon XIII*, volume II, pp. 336-337; Ferrata II, p. 32.

[88] Tournier pp. 286-287; Baunard: *Lavigerie* II, pp. 563-566; A. Débidour: *L'Église Catholique et l'État sous la Troisième République* (Paris 1900) II, p. 40-42; T'Serclaes II, pp. 332 ff. Baunard: *Léon XIII* p. 42 takes pains to point out that the *Marseillaise* was played before the dinner and was a mere formality, having nothing to do with the toast.

cause the Papal See backed it with its authority. "It is more than a program, it is an event," wrote the *Moniteur de Rome*.[89] On November 14 Lavigerie reiterated his ideas in a pastoral letter, and early in December, in reply to a number of inquiries from French bishops, Cardinal Rampolla in a letter to the Bishop of St. Flour gave full approval to the stand taken by Lavigerie. There could be no doubt as to the attitude of the Vatican.[90]

One can readily understand the excitement that prevailed in Italian government circles. "The letter of Cardinal Rampolla," wrote *l'Italie*, "is, at bottom, nothing less than the unreserved adhesion of the Papacy to the French Republic.... The entente between the Papacy and the French Republic is complete." The *Riforma*, Crispi's paper, spoke in no less certain terms. The whole matter seemed so serious that in the speech from the throne on December 10 King Humbert declared: "I shall not permit my sovereign authority to be infringed upon in the name of religion for political ends."[91]

The redeeming feature was that the French royalists, who formed the backbone of clericalism in France and who were the main support of charity, offered vigorous resistance and refused to accept the new slogan.[92] Leo, therefore, deemed it advisable to remain in the background, though he continued to work secretly through the French bishops who came to Rome.[93] For the time being the ultimate issue was in doubt, but this in no way diminishes the significance of the new policy. Leo XIII, disillusioned in his hopes of support from the Triple Alliance, had

[89] Billot I, p. 265.

[90] Tournier pp. 291 ff., 302-303; cf. also Edmond Renard: *Le Cardinal Mathieu* (Paris 1925) pp. 325-326.

[91] Billot I, pp. 265-267. The semi-official Italian press openly accused the Papacy of conspiring against the Triple Alliance, and in government circles it was suspected that France had made promises regarding the restoration of the temporal power (Schlözer report, quoted by Becker p. 135).

[92] Tournier pp. 290-297; they did not care "to play the inglorious part of political Mamelukes" (Anon: The Policy of the Pope, in *Contemporary Review* October 1892).

[93] Lavigerie's complaints that the Pope was trying to disavow him (Tournier pp. 295, 299-300) seem to have been unjustified (Baunard: *Léon XIII* p. 40; Ferrata II, pp. 37, 41), though there may have been some feeling at Rome that Lavigerie was too stormy (Renard pp. 326-327).

definitely turned to France. It was in his interest to work hand
in glove with the French government in attempting to smash the
Triple Alliance and bring Italy to terms. The French ministers
had been informed of the plan beforehand and had given their approval,[94] and in Lavigerie's correspondence one can find ample
evidence of the motives which underlay this new entente. In a
letter to Cardinal Ferrata of March 27, 1891 the Primate speaks
of the plan as having resulted from the need of a counterpoise to
the Triple Alliance, and Ferrata, in his memoirs, admits the
truth of the statement. Even more interesting is a letter of April
21, 1891 from Monsignor Bourret to Lavigerie, in which it is
plainly stated that "the Pope wishes to isolate Italy and fortify
himself against the Triple Alliance, which has abandoned him and
subordinated him to the interests of Italy."[95] It would be naïve
to deny the political significance of the Papal policy initiated in
November, 1890.[96]

[94] Tournier p. 305. In the early autumn the Jesuits also had sent a representative to Paris to discuss the new departure. This representative had various conversations with Freycinet (Schlözer report, quoted by Becker p. 135).

[95] Tournier pp. 356, 360; Ferrata II, pp. 14-15.

[96] *Moniteur de Rome* quoted by Bonjean in *Nouvelle Revue* October 15, 1891
pp. 673-690: "Le Toast du Cardinal Lavigerie, suivi de près de la memorable lettre
du Cardinal Rampolla, parus à la veille de Portsmouth et de Cronstadt, presageant
sinon préparant l'éclatante rentrée de la France sur le terrain de la politique internationale et son rélèvement diplomatique, ont une marque historique qui defie tous
les denigrements." Cf. also Ferrata II, p. 95; and J. Piou: *Le Comte Albert de
Mun* (Paris n. d.) pp. 130-131, quoting Leo as saying to a French deputy early in
1891 that he had done his utmost to reassure the Tsar on the question of French
piety and that he hoped to induce Francis Joseph not to renew the Triple Alliance.
In September 1893, after Lavigerie's death, the Papacy was particularly anxious
that his papers should not fall into the hands of the French government (*ibid*, pp.
320 ff).

CHAPTER VI

THE RENEWAL OF THE TRIPLE ALLIANCE

THE recognition of the French Republic by the Papacy was a well-deserved tribute paid to the work done by Freycinet and his colleagues. By January, 1891 the position of France was quite different from what it had been a year before. The reorganization of the army and the navy was practically complete, the Boulangist crisis had definitely come to a close, and the authority of the government was firmly established. The senatorial elections of January, 1891 resulted in an overwhelming victory for the governmental group and could be taken as added proof of the stability of the existing regime. In matters of foreign policy no startling success had been scored, but France had once more resumed her legitimate place in Europe. The surprising activity of the French foreign office in the later months of 1890 had shown only too clearly that the Cinderella days were over and that henceforth France could not be ignored or intimidated. Speaking of the equipment of the army with the new Lebel rifles and the wholesale manufacture of melanite shells in the last months of 1890 Freycinet says in his memoirs:

"From that time on we awaited with relative serenity the complications which we thought were threatening us."[1]

And in his campaign speech of December, 1890 he made his thought even more clear. France, he asserted, was immovably attached to a pacific policy, but she now had a military establishment which would enable her to brave aggression of any sort.

So striking and rapid had been the evolution of the Republic that it could not escape the notice of even the most hostile observers. Especially the manoeuvres of the autumn had attracted widespread attention and much comment. Even the

---

[1] Freycinet p. 414. Cf. also Greindl January 7, 1891: "La France gagne confiance en elle-même" (Köhler p. 88).

Tsar was profoundly impressed with the changes which were taking place. At Narva he had still spoken of the possibility of an Orleans restoration and had reiterated his determination never to conclude an alliance with a republic. By January, 1891 he had already begun to modify his views. The policy of the Pope apparently made a deep impression upon him. He came to see that the Republic was fast becoming one of the determining factors in European politics. Its success would prove to be a danger to the monarchical principle generally speaking. France, he said to the German ambassador, now represented immense power and wealth, well-consolidated and with an admirably reorganized army. The Republic would soon become an object of envy to the other states.[2]

Needless to say, the lesson was not lost on the Germans, who watched developments with the greatest attention. Following the presidential New Year's reception Count Münster reported that if the self-confidence of the *Grande Nation* continued in the future to rise as it had risen in 1890 it might well be that France would show a greater inclination than before to take a hand in complications which might arise.[3] The situation in France contrasted distinctly with that in Germany, where internal politics were in a confused state and dissatisfaction with the new regime and with the Kaiser's absolutistic utterances was general.

Such was the European scene when, on January 31, came the startling news that Crispi had fallen from power. With incredible rashness the Italian premier had accused his predecessors of the Right of having pursued a policy of servility to foreign powers during their tenure of office. By this tactless remark he had deprived himself of his parliamentary majority and had been obliged to make way for the leader of the Right, the Marchese di Rudini.

---

[2] Schweinitz II, pp. 418-419. Similarly Wolkenstein to Kálnoky June 8, 1891, reporting the Tsar's remarks to Schweinitz in January: "Die französische Republik prosperiert sehr,—sie ist sehr stark, sehr mächtig (je vous dis elle est très-forte et très puissante) und sie wirkt nicht abstossend, sondern anziehend, verführend." The Russian press also was extravagant in its praises and printed endless variations on the same theme (see the quotations in the *Mémorial Diplomatique* January 17, 1891, letter from St. Petersburg).   [3] G. P. VII, no. 1545.

Crispi was not much regretted anywhere in Europe. The French and the Russians regarded him as impossible and as an inveterate enemy and trouble-maker. The Germans, English and Austrians appreciated his loyalty and his vigor, but they too were glad to be relieved of the constant strain to which the hot-headed Sicilian had continuously subjected them.[4] Nevertheless his fall was an event of the greatest moment, for it placed the whole political future in the balance. Rudini had on numerous occasions declared his adhesion to the policy of the Triple Alliance, but he was known to favor the establishment of better relations with France and to favor a policy of retrenchment which would involve less activity in colonial and foreign affairs, to say nothing of reductions of expenditure for the army and navy.[5]

To the Germans the overturn in Italy seemed well-nigh catastrophic. After Bismarck's fall they had staked everything on the Triple Alliance and now even the famous League of Peace was being placed in jeopardy. The visit of the Archduke Francis Ferdinand to St. Petersburg looked very suspicious, and even the great chancellor in his retreat viewed the situation with considerable apprehension and believed that he saw the famous Kaunitz coalition looming up on the horizon. What good, he asked, would Italy be then?[6] And now even the continued support of Italy was being called in question. If France and Russia could come together it would be more than doubtful whether

---

[4] Of the French feeling about Crispi nothing more need be said. Giers' attitude in G. P. VII, no. 1618; Salisbury's estimate in G. P. VIII, nos. 1703, 1877, 1900, 1981; even Bismarck thought Crispi too spasmodic (Radowitz II, p. 294) and Marschall said to the Austrian ambassador after Crispi's fall: "das ewige Krachelen Crispis mit dieser Macht (i. e. Frankreich) sei doch zum Mindesten recht überflüssig gewesen" (Széchényi to Kálnoky March 1, 1891).

[5] Cf. G. Giacometti: Cinq Mois de Politique Italienne (*Revue des Deux Mondes* September 15, 1891, pp. 389-390); Salvemini: La Politica del Marchese di Rudini, in *L'Azione* January 13, 1924, quoted in Cilibrizzi II, pp. 426 ff.; also *Mémorial Diplomatique* February 14, 1891.

[6] *Hamburger Nachrichten* January 28, 1891 (Hofmann I, p. 314); Waldersee: *Denkwürdigkeiten* II, p. 202; the Belgian reports in Köhler pp. 276-279. The very fact that Marschall on three occasions assured the Austrian ambassador that Germany approved of the visit shows the uneasiness in Berlin (Széchényi to Kálnoky March 1, 1891).

either the Italians or the Austrians could resist the attractive power of this new coalition. Something had to be done, and done soon.

The Kaiser's first thought was of France. Could she still be held from Russia? Ever since Bismarck's fall the young monarch had been following a policy of conciliation, expressed chiefly by marked attentions to French artists and scientists. The international labor conference in Berlin in March, 1890, the medical conference in the summer of the same year, and later the death of the French painter Meissonier had given him the opportunity to demonstrate his feelings.[7] At the same time the passport regulations for Alsace-Lorraine had been used with great leniency.[8] These advances had met with a favorable reception by a large part of the French press. In fact a whole literature advocating a Franco-German rapprochement had sprung up during 1890. The French now felt that they could deal with Germany more as an equal, and the moderate group which had always objected to the idea of an alliance with "barbarous" Russia now pointed out that France and Germany should stand shoulder to shoulder as guardians of the interests of western Europe. The traditional hostility was detrimental to both and disastrous for their interests and for those of European civilization generally.

"France and Germany together," wrote Gabriel Monod, "can save Europe from the hegemony of Russia and can prevent the whole commerce of the world from being monopolized by England and the United States. Their union is a necessary element in the equilibrium of the forces of the globe."[9]

In a much discussed pamphlet Colonel Stoffel, formerly French military attaché at Berlin, advanced the same argument, and the anonymous writer of a pamphlet entitled *Die Zukunft der Voelker von Mitteleuropa* depicted the coming economic crisis in Europe which would result from the tariff policies of the United

[7] On all this see especially Albin pp. 212 ff., and 282 ff. Waldersee II, p. 197. The German ministers by no means approved of this policy, fearing the effects it might have in Italy and England (G. P. VII, no. 1543).

[8] Hohenlohe II, pp. 463, 470; cf. also Mommsen: Die elsass-lothringische Frage 1890-1897 (*Archiv für Politik und Geschichte* II, pp. 583-591, 1924).

[9] Gabriel Monod in the *Contemporary Review* July 1890, p. 33.

States and Russia. Central Europe must band together and the fundamental obstacle in the way of such a union, the hostility between France and Germany, must be overcome. The writer suggested a security compact for five years, to be concluded between France and the Triple Alliance, this agreement to be supplemented by special tariff arrangements.[10]

Of course the almost insuperable barrier in the way of all these schemes was the Alsace-Lorraine problem. All writers recognized that and offered various more or less practicable suggestions. As yet the movement was only in an embryonic state, and it was hardly to be expected that definite steps should be taken by the two governments. The point is that the acrimonious tone had to a large measure gone out of the relations of the two countries and there was greater readiness to appreciate each other's efforts. When, in January, 1891, the French artists were invited to participate in the coming exhibition of paintings in Berlin, many accepted and the French government lent its patronage informally.[11]

Then came the alarming changes in Italy and the visit of the Archduke Francis Ferdinand to St. Petersburg. In his anxiety the Kaiser made a hasty decision. He arranged, or at least approved of a plan for his mother, the Empress Frederick, to visit Paris.[12] Ostensibly she was to travel incognito, and without any particular mission. As a matter of fact, however, the visit was intended to sound out French sentiment and to pave the

---

[10] Cf. M-t-s: Das Verhältnis Deutschlands zu Frankreich (*Preussische Jahrbücher* January 1891, pp. 99-102); Cyon: La France et la Russie (*Nouvelle Revue* April 15, 1890); Anon: L'Italia e la Triplice Alleanza (*Rassegna Nazionale* August 16, 1890, pp. 633-657); Woeste in *La Revue Générale* October 1890. The chronique of the *Preussische Jahrbücher* for 1890 follows the development of the movement (cf. volume LXV, p. 579; LXVI, pp. 200, 424: "Unsere Aussöhnung ist das *hic Rhodus, hic salta*, das die leidende Menschheit uns zuruft.")

[11] G. P. VII, no. 1546; on the exposition see Gaston Routier: *Un Point d'Histoire Contemporaine* (Paris 1901), where the correspondence is reprinted. The Berlin correspondent of the *Figaro* wrote: "On nous cajole au point d'en oublier presque tous les amis de la Triple Alliance. L'Ambassadeur de France est le mieux en cour."

[12] Albin pp. 287-289; Routier pp. 73, 117; *Rheinischer Kurier* and *Vossische Zeitung* February 21, 1891. Waldersee II, p. 197, says the visit was discussed for weeks. See also *The Letters of the Empress Frederick* pp. 422 ff.

way for closer relations, first in the nonpolitical sphere, later in the political.[13] The Empress arrived in the French capital on February 18 and stayed until the 27. It cannot be said that the program was well-arranged or properly carried out. The incognito was not strictly observed, and as a result there was the eternal question as to the attitude which the French government should take. Furthermore the Empress stayed at the German embassy, took part in receptions, visited the art galleries and even the studios of noted painters, in fact went so far as to commit the incredible blunder of going not only to Versailles but to St. Cloud, the ruins of which were a monument to the German invasion of 1870. This was too much for the French patriots and for the Parisian populace generally, which was informed by swarms of reporters of every move made by the Empress. Déroulède mobilized the members of the former League of Patriots and protested loudly against the presence of the Empress as well as against the projected visit of the Kaiser, of which there were repeated rumors in the press.[14] The Empress had undoubtedly outstayed her welcome, and by the time she finally left the city it was deemed advisable to take all sorts of precautions to ensure her safe departure.[15]

The incident caused a tremendous clamor both in the German and in the French press. The *Kölnische Zeitung* called for

[13] The purpose of the visit was so obvious that it escaped no one. Cf. G. P. VII, no. 1545, and note; *Hannoversche Kurier* and *Vossische Zeitung* February 21, 1891; *Magdeburgische Zeitung* February 21, 1891: "Es ist an Frankreich und an dem französischen Volke, das weitgehende Entgegenkommen Deutschlands zu erwidern." The French press saw through the whole scheme. See *Cocarde* February 21, 1891 and *Mémorial Diplomatique* February 21, 1891: "Le noeud de la Triple Alliance se desserre, et Guillaume II est assez clairvoyant pour s'en être rendu compte." Also the excellent summary in the same journal February 28, 1891.

[14] G. P. VII, nos. 1548, 1549, 1551; *Letters of the Empress Frederick* pp. 422 ff.; Routier, chapters i-iii for a detailed account of the visit. Rumors of the intended visit of the Kaiser in Mme. Adam's letters (*Nouvelle Revue* January 15, March 1, 1891).

[15] G. P. VII, nos. 1548, 1551; Széchényi to Kálnoky March 1, 1891; Freyeinet pp. 457-458; Routier chapter iii. Some 600 secret service men were stationed along the route and at the depot, and the departure of the Empress took place an hour earlier than announced.

adequate satisfaction and the *Kreuzzeitung* demanded the use of vigorous language. The Kaiser himself was completely disillusioned, not to say enraged. It has been said that on February 26 he sent out preliminary orders for mobilization, to be put into effect in case the Empress were insulted on her departure.[16] This is probably overdrawing somewhat, but there is no denying that for a time the crisis was very acute. The Kaiser himself told the Austrian ambassador that "peace hung by a hair."[17] From his private agents in Paris he had learned that Freycinet himself was largely responsible for the unfortunate turn which affairs had taken. The French premier, he believed, desired to stir up the dying chauvinism of the French because he needed more money for the army and navy and because he feared the growing popularity of Ferry:

"He has," so the Kaiser said, "far-reaching plans, the object being to reorganize the ministry of war in such a way as to make it independent of a chance vote of the chamber, then to get himself elected president and finally to conduct a war of revenge."[18]

There is no need for believing such fantastic tales. Indeed, there is no denying that the responsibility for the whole affair lay chiefly with the Kaiser and his mother. They had subjected the French to an ordeal which they could not reasonably be expected to suffer. The period of cordial relations had been abruptly brought to an end, and the order to enforce the passport regulations in Alsace-Lorraine with full vigor, which was intended to act as a warning to the French, served only to increase the tension.[19] During the next months the two governments

[16] Freycinet pp. 457-458; Albin p. 300. Both speak of orders given to Waldersee, but this is obviously incorrect, as he had ceased to be chief of staff on February 2. H. Galli: *Dessous Diplomatiques* (Paris 1894) told the same story (pp. 152-160), saying that Marschall had told Herbette that the Kaiser had signed the order for mobilization.

[17] Széchényi to Kálnoky March 12, 1891.

[18] Széchényi to Kálnoky March 7, 1891. Münster also indicated that Freycinet had been engaged in intrigue (G. P. VII, no. 1551). From the Kaiser's marginalia on the documents dealing with this subject there is ample evidence of his suspicions of Freycinet (cf. G. P. VII, nos. 1558, 1563, etc.).

[19] Széchényi to Kálnoky March 1, 1891; Waldersee II, p. 197; G. P. VII, no. 1555, and note.

eyed each other with deep suspicion, and the Kaiser fell entirely under the influence of the military men, who prophesied a French attack in the summer or autumn.[20] His one consolation was in the thought that the fault lay with the French and that the chauvinism of Paris was responsible for the general unrest.[21]

In this, too, he was sadly mistaken. The French government, while expressing regret for the hostile outbreak of the press, disclaimed all responsibility and took steps to prevent the spread of false reports in foreign capitals. In a circular note to the powers the circumstances of the visit were minutely detailed and special emphasis was placed upon the correct attitude of the population as a whole and upon the extensive precautions taken by the government to insure the safety of the Empress.[22] The note was, of course, intended primarily for Russia, but it was superfluous to explain to the Russian government. In St. Petersburg there had been great uneasiness about the visit. The Kaiser's attempt to conciliate France had been looked upon as another step calculated to isolate Russia.[23] Count Münster,

[20] Hohenlohe II, p. 476; G. P. VII, nos. 1560 ff. Major von Huene, formerly military attaché in Paris, was the leading alarmist. The Kaiser accepted his views without reservation and desired to recall Münster, who took the opposite view. The foreign office objected loudly to any radical departure and kept its balance. Caprivi himself viewed the situation calmly and remarked: "Jetzt Krieg ausrufen, ist weiter nichts als *absichtlich* den Kriegsteufel an die Wand malen." As a matter of fact there is no satisfactory evidence that the French were planning action, either with or without the aid of Russia, though the Kaiser and his military friends thought there was a likelihood of the French taking the aggressive without waiting for the Russians.

[21] To Széchényi the Kaiser remarked: "Europa wird jetzt schon erkennen müssen, wo allein das Ferment der ewigen Beunruhigung gelegen ist, und dies wird den Dreibund nur noch mehr festigen und kräftigen, wie es auch England, welches bei der Behandlung, die meiner Mutter zu Theil geworden, in Ihr wohl die englische Prinzessin sehen wird, unserer Gruppe näher bringen dürfte" (Széchényi to Kálnoky March 7, 1891). Similarly the *Norddeutsche Allgemeine Zeitung* February 28, 1891.

[22] Albin pp. 308-309. The French statesmen were very apologetic and profuse in their excuses. Quite evidently they feared that the incident might have tragic results (cf. G. P. VII, nos. 1558, 1559, 1563).

[23] As early as April 1890 Aehrenthal had reported to Kálnoky that the Russians were uneasy about the Kaiser's attempts to conciliate France. On the Russian apprehensions in February and March 1891 see especially G. P. VII, no. 1493.

the German ambassador at Paris, was firmly convinced that the press campaign had been started by Russian agents and supported by Russian gold.[24] Certainly the pro-Russian views of Déroulède and his friends could not be questioned. In any case the debacle was received with unmixed delight by the Russian public as well as by the government. Giers hastened to assure the French government, through Mohrenheim, the ambassador at Paris, that it had acted correctly in every respect, that the Franco-Russian *entente cordiale* was the best guarantee of peace and that the accord was "solid as granite."[25] It was quite clear to the Russian statesmen that they had been sailing somewhat too closely to the wind, and that a little life must be blown into the entente in order to bolster up the French. On March 26 Mohrenheim went to the Elysée to present President Carnot with the insignia of the Order of St. Andrew, the highest Russian decoration.[26] At the same time the visit of the French squadron to Cronstadt in the coming summer was decided upon. No doubt the visit of the Empress Frederick to Paris had given "a new impulse to the Franco-Russian rapprochement."[27]

This exchange of courtesies was watched in Berlin with the greatest distrust. As aforesaid, the Kaiser was apprehensive of a French attack in the near future. There was also some fear that the Russians were preparing to act. The Tsar had

[24] G. P. VII, nos. 1548, 1551, 1558.

[25] On the delight of the Russians see G. P. VII, no. 1493; St. Petersburg letter in the *Mémorial Diplomatique* March 7, 1891. Giers considered the whole affair "ein unbegreiflicher Fehlgriff." He thought it a beneficial warning to the Kaiser, who felt "qu'il n'avait qu'à se montrer et tout serait dit," (Wolkenstein to Kálnoky March 4, 1891). Giers' assurances to the French government in the *Livre Jaune Français* (henceforth referred to as L. J.), no. 2.

[26] Cf. G. P. VII, nos. 1494, 1497; Schweinitz II, p. 421. The incident caused a great stir in Europe and Giers, in speaking to the German and Austrian diplomats, made every effort to minimize its importance (Wolkenstein to Kálnoky April 1 and 2, 1891; also the Belgian report in Köhler p. 97, note 1).

[27] On the preliminaries of Cronstadt see J. Hansen: *L'Alliance Franco-Russe* (Paris 1897) pp. 59 ff.; Daudet: *Histoire Diplomatique* pp. 297-301; Freycinet pp. 443-444, 464-465; Galli pp. 164-166. Evidently the final arrangements were made by Flourens, who was several times received by the Tsar (cf. Un Diplomate (Flourens): M. Ribot au Quai d'Orsay, in the *Nouvelle Revue* November 15, 1893).

neglected to send New Year's greetings, and, at the very time of the Empress' visit to Paris, the Russian ambassador at Berlin, Count Shuvalov, had suddenly paid a visit to Bismarck at Friedrichsruh.[28] The attempt upon the life of Stambulov and the actual assassination of the Bulgarian minister Belchev at this time was, as usual, laid at the door of the Russians and was interpreted as the first move in the resumption of an active policy in the Near East.[29] The anxiety in Berlin was great and the Kaiser, in a speech at Potsdam on April 18, gave vent to his feelings in no uncertain terms:

"Difficult and serious times are before us; I rely on my army and expect the troops stationed on the frontier to maintain a keen lookout."

So impressed was his audience by these words that it seemed as though the country were on the eve of mobilization.[30]

In St. Petersburg it was generally felt that the impetuous Kaiser would seek a way out of the impasse by declaring war on one or the other of his neighbors.[31] It is well worth noting that in spite of the general uneasiness the Tsar was still cautious, and still unwilling to assume commitments towards France. Freycinet and his colleagues were, of course, anxious to make the

[28] Ottmar von Mohl: *50 Jahre Reichsdienst* (Leipzig 1921) p. 252; Waldersee II, p. 198. Shuvalov's visit irritated the Kaiser particularly. To the Austrian ambassador he exclaimed: "Ist das eine Eselei, und gerade in dem allerunpassendsten Momente hiezu, aber ich werde es ihm schon fühlen lassen" (Széchényi to Kálnoky February 21, 1891).

[29] Waldersee II, pp. 203, 206; G. P. VII, nos. 1495, 1496, 1616; Széchényi to Kálnoky April 19, 1891, reporting the Kaiser's remarks to Steininger; Wolkenstein to Kálnoky April 20, 1891.

[30] This part of the speech was not published and does not appear in Penzler's version of the *Kaiserreden* (volume II, pp. 174-175). My quotation is from a telegram in cipher sent by the Austrian ambassador (Széchényi to Kálnoky April 19, 1891). The Kaiser's apprehensions were in part based on rumors of the moving of a Russian division from the interior to the frontier. This rumor proved unjustified and the German officials in Berlin were as much surprised by the Kaiser's utterances as was anyone (Széchényi to Kálnoky March 31, April 20 and 21, 1891).

[31] Wolkenstein to Kálnoky, April 11 and 29, 1891; cf. also N. Notovich: *Alexandre III* (Paris 1895) pp. 241-250. The statements made by Pobiedonostsev somewhat later are also of interest: "Einmal sei ein directer Einfall des deutschen Heeres in Russland—ein kriegerischer Ueberfall *ohne Kriegserklärung*, unmittelbar bevorstehend gewesen" (Aehrenthal to Kálnoky November 25, 1891). Similar utterances by Pobiedonostsev in G. P. VII, no. 1619.

most of the promising advances of the Russians. Sometime in late March or early April (it is impossible to fix the exact date) the French government instructed M. Laboulaye, the ambassador at St. Petersburg, to secure from the Russian government some concrete assurance for the future.[32]. The question was put in something like the following form: "What would be the attitude of the Russian government in case of war between France and Germany?"[33] It is not entirely clear whether on this occasion an assurance of support was given France in case of an aggression by Germany.[34] What we can say with certainty is that the whole move did not please the Tsar and that the reply given did not satisfy the French. The Russian monarch

[32] Laboulaye went on leave on April 11, so that the *démarche* was presumably made before that date. Schweinitz is probably correct in placing it in the days between the bestowal of the Order of St. Andrew on Carnot and the departure of Laboulaye from St. Petersburg (G. P. VII, no. 1500). On the whole incident compare Hansen: *Mohrenheim* pp. 118-119.

[33] Almost all the information we have on this important incident is indirect, based on Giers' account to the Rumanian minister, M. Ghika, and communicated by him to the Germans. It is there stated that "La France nous a proposé de conclure un traité." Cf. the various accounts in G. P. VII, nos. 1498-1501; Marschall's statements to Greindl (in Köhler pp. 281-282); Hoorickx' report from Bucharest (in Köhler pp. 280-281); also Schweinitz II, p. 423; Wolkenstein to Kálnoky May 18, 1891. The incident is also referred to by Stead in the *Review of Reviews* August 1891, p. 135. It was revealed in the press early in June (See *London Times* June 8, 1891; *Mémorial Diplomatique* June 27, 1891, discussing revelations in the *Münchener Allgemeine Zeitung* and the *Kölnische Zeitung*).

[34] According to Marschall: "La réponse aurait été que si la France était attaquée par l'Allmagne, elle serait soutenue par la Russie; mais que si elle attaquait l'Allemagne, ce serait à ses risques et perils" (Greindl, in Köhler pp. 281-282). This was also what the Kaiser told Salisbury in July (Deym to Kálnoky July 15, 1891). It is not quite clear what Marschall wrote Schweinitz (see G. P. VII, no. 1499). According to what Wolkenstein heard, the Tsar replied "durch Fallenlassén des Themas" (Wolkenstein to Kálnoky May 22, 1891). Giers told Ghika: "Nous avons refusé" (Hoorickx, in Köhler pp. 280-281). Schweinitz also learned from a French source: "Der Zar hat...dem Botschafter Veranlassung gegeben, das Gespräch auf einen anderen Gegenstand zu lenken" (G. P. VII, no. 1500). This seems to be the more likely account. Stead (*op. cit.*) puts the matter very baldly: "When the French ambassador ventured to ask him (i. e. the Tsar) whether, if France went to war with Germany, she could depend upon Russian support, he received a rebuff which he is not soon likely to forget." It is worth noting that Laboulaye's recall was almost immediately decided upon, because, with his inadequate position at St. Petersburg, he was able to accomplish nothing (Wolkenstein to Kálnoky May 18, 1891; Albin p. 310).

was fully aware of the value of French friendship and was willing to cultivate it by little attentions, but he feared being dragged into a French war of revenge and above all he could not yet make up his mind to conclude an agreement with a republican government, with one in which instability seemed to be chronic, and violent outbreaks of popular feeling seemed to be the determining factor.[35]

These advances on the part of the French and their rejection by the Russians, which appear to have escaped the notice of most writers on the period, are of great importance, for they show that in spite of the nonrenewal of the Reinsurance Treaty the Russians were not prepared to bind themselves in case of a conflict between the French and the Germans. They knew that if they ever went to war with the Germans they could count upon the French. Meanwhile a policy of small courtesies would keep the Paris government in good humor. "France is at our feet," remarked Giers, "and we should be ungracious to complain of it."[36]

But there was another problem in which the interests of the two powers were much more equally balanced, and that was the policy to be followed towards the Triple Alliance and its corollary, the Mediterranean Coalition. The question of the renewal of the Triple Alliance had suddenly become an acute one for the central powers after the fall of Crispi. Adhesion to the pact had been the keynote of his policy and there could be no doubt of his sincerity and loyalty. The alliance was absolutely indispensable for him as a protection against France and as a foundation for an active policy in the Mediterranean.[37] This fact had been clearly recognized by both Caprivi and Kálnoky, neither of whom was prepared to make further concessions to Italy, since they both realized that in any event Crispi, if he wished to remain in power, would eventually have to renew the treaty on the terms

[35] G. P. VII, no. 1498; Hoorickx, in Köhler pp. 280-281; Greindl, in Köhler p. 96, note 5; Wolkenstein to Kálnoky May 14, 1891. These are all based on the explanation which Giers gave to Ghika.

[36] G. P. VII, no. 1498.

[37] Crispi also believed that if the alliance broke up Austria would immediately ally herself with France and take up the defense of the Pope (Crispi III, p. 153).

submitted by Berlin and Vienna. During his interview with Caprivi at Milan in November 1890 Crispi had spoken of the necessity of maintaining the alliance and the desirability of renewing it, possibly with some "improvements." Caprivi gave his interlocutor no opportunity to develop his thoughts, for he had little desire to open discussions which might lead to Italian demands for an extension of the treaty of 1887 between Germany and Italy at a time when the Italo-French dispute in northern Africa was in an acute phase.[38] The treaty was not due to expire until May, 1892, and it was quite obviously Crispi's hope of securing further support against France in the Mediterranean that induced him to raise the question of a premature renewal.

In 1887 the unwillingness of Germany to assume obligations in regard to the Balkan question and the refusal of the Austrians to promise the Italians support for their aspirations in the western Mediterranean had led to the addition of separate Austro-Italian and German-Italian agreements to the original treaty of 1882.[39] Crispi now hoped to enlist Austrian support in the Tripoli-Tunis complications by merging the three agreements of 1887 and by effecting this change by a premature renewal. This would, of course, have involved the assumption by Germany of the obligations of the Austro-Italian pact of 1887 in regard to the Balkans. Crispi, being at the moment much less interested in this phase of the situation, first approached the Austrian government, calling attention to the necessity for solidarity between the three powers, acting as a bulwark against the republican propaganda of France. He suggested an early renewal of the treaty in order that a "few desirable and slight changes" might be discussed. One of the alterations which he proposed was the consolidation of the three agreements of 1887 into one document:

"By so doing," he declared, "we would attain greater security and a more uniform coöperation; the territories of the various parties would be better

---

[38] Pribram I, pp. 217-218, 221; Crispi III, pp. 7, 12; G. P. VII, nos. 1394, 1397, 1398.

[39] For the negotiations leading to the renewal of the alliance in 1887 see especially Chiala III, pp. 360-495; Pribram I, pp. 169-207; G. P. IV, pp. 179-261.

safeguarded against attack, and, above all, conditions of greater intimacy would be brought about."

He indicated that he had discussed his views with Caprivi and believed that the latter was inclined to agree with him.[40] Whether the Italian premier's vivid imagination served him ill, or whether his statement was part of a tactical manoeuvre is not clear, but Kálnoky immediately sensed the underlying object of the Italian proposals and refused to believe that Caprivi had assented to them lightly. On inquiry at Berlin, it appeared that nothing had been said at Milan about a premature renewal, that Caprivi was not anxious to open negotiations, and that the subject of merging the three agreements had not been touched upon. The German chancellor did, however, suggest to his Austrian colleague that discussion of the last point, in principle, should not be flatly rejected.[41]

The plan evidently was to drag the matter out and finally, at an opportune moment, induce Crispi to renew the treaty as it stood. The agreements of 1887 rested on "an entirely fair basis," as Kálnoky remarked to the Italian ambassador, Count Nigra. In 1887 an attempt had been made to embody all the various obligations in one document and this had proved to be impracticable. If Crispi now desired to reopen the discussion he should make "precise, practicable proposals." To this Crispi made no reply, and when he fell from power on January 31, 1891, no progress had been made towards the renewal of the treaty.[42]

Rudini's position, when he took over the premiership, was not a strong one. In view of the confused nature of Italian politics it was almost impossible for any cabinet to count absolutely upon a parliamentary majority, as the experience of Crispi had shown. Rudini was, in fact, obliged to include in the ministry

---

[40] Crispi III, pp. 11-14; Pribram I, pp. 215-216; G. P. VII, nos. 1396, 1398.

[41] Pribram I, pp. 217-218; G.P. VII, nos. 1396 ff. The Austrians and Germans took the charitable view, and attributed the contradiction as to the Milan conversations to Crispi's vivid imagination.

[42] Pribram I, 218-219; Crispi III, pp. 12-16; G.P. VII, no. 1398, 1399, 1400, especially the illuminating remark of Kálnoky to the German ambassador: "Wir hätten ja noch über ein Jahr Zeit, und man könne nicht wissen, wie sich die afrikanischen Verhältnisse bis dahin gestalten würden."

men like Nicotera, a leader of the Left, and, as undersecretary for foreign affairs, Conte d'Arco, whose opposition to the Triple Alliance was no secret.[43] The new premier himself had frequently declared his adherence to the policy of the alliance, but at the same time he was known to advocate a policy of conciliation towards France.[44] At any rate the advent of the new ministry gave rise to all sorts of rumors and greatly elated the French. The more radical Paris newspapers prophesied the end of the Triple Alliance. More moderate organs expressed the hope that at least the alliance would not be renewed when it expired in 1892. But the authoritative press was more circumspect, and warned the public against being too sanguine. Taken by and large there was, however, a feeling that things were taking a change for the better so far as France was concerned. The hostile attacks upon Italian policy stopped and quotations on Italian securities immediately rose several points.[45]

The French government itself felt that the time had come to resume its attempts to wean the Italians from their allegiance. To be sure Rudini had declared for the alliance without reservations during the election campaign of November, 1890 and in his presentation of the new cabinet's program to the chamber on February 14 he had declared his intention of remaining faithful to Italy's connections. But he had also expressed his determination to improve relations with France, if possible.[46] He was committed to a policy of economy and retrenchment, and the

[43] See especially G. Giacometti: Cinq Mois de Politique Italien, Février-Juin 1891 (*Revue des Deux Mondes* September 15, 1891, pp. 389-390); also Crispi III, p. 187; Billot I, p. 288.

[44] Cf. the *Saturday Review* February 21, 1891: "The new Italian Ministry is going to trim its sails so as to catch the wind both from the Triple Alliance and France, to make at once for the Land of Retrenchment and that of National Defence."

[45] Cf. *Mémorial Diplomatique* February 7, 14, 1891; Mme. Adam in *Nouvelle Revue* March 15, 1891: "Les griefs de forme ont disparu et nous nous trouvons en présence d'un seul fait...la Triple Alliance". See also Giacometti p. 389.

[46] Rudini in the *Opinione* of November 4, 1890; the declaration of February 14, 1891, in Chiala III, p. 534: "Alle nostre alleanze serberemo fede salda e sicura. Mostreremo a tutti con la nostra condotta, che non abbiamo intendimenti aggressivi. E poichè sulle nostre relazioni con la Francia furono a torto sollevati dubbii, sospetti e diffidenze, noi ci sforzeremo ad eliminare ogni falso apprezzamento."

financial aid of France would be indispensable to him. For the time being the French government could afford to await developments.

The statesmen of the central powers were hardly more convinced by Rudini's declarations than were the French. The Germans were especially anxious, and to the general feeling of uneasiness is to be attributed the Empress Frederick's visit to Paris.[47] It was the period of crisis following this unfortunate incident that finally decided the French to make advances to the Italians, as they did a few weeks later to the Russians. The Italian chargé in Paris, Ressman, had been instructed by Rudini to attempt a more conciliatory policy and the premier himself had given his intercourse with the French ambassador a similar touch.[48] On his return to Paris Ressman had a conversation with Ribot, probably during the first days of March, that is, at the very height of the tension between Germany and France. In reply to the advances made by Ressman Ribot stated that before the French government could openly assume a friendly attitude towards Italy it must be given assurances and explicit declarations calculated to dispel the current suspicions in regard to the purpose and extent of the Triple Alliance. What he desired was a positive assurance of the defensive nature of the agreement and of the new treaty which he assumed would be made. If France were certain that the Triple Alliance was no more menacing to France that the Austro-German Treaty of 1879 there would be no further obstacle to close relations between France and Italy, and France would be ready to engage formally not to attack Italy and not to disturb the *status quo* in the Mediterranean.[49]

[47] Pribram I, p. 222. Both the Austrians and the Germans appear to have been suspicious of Rudini's plans of seeking a reconciliation with France, though from the very start Rudini sent assurances that he meant to remain loyal to the alliance (Bruck to Kálnoky February 11 and 16, 1891, the latter reprinted in G. P. VII, no. 1401; Greindl report, in Köhler p. 100, note.)

[48] Bruck to Kálnoky February 25, 1891; Billot I, p. 287. On the Ressman mission see also the important article in the *Mémorial Diplomatique* February 28, 1891.

[49] G. P. VII, no. 1402. Köhler's conjecture (p. 100, note) that negotiations between Italy and France had already taken place early in February cannot be substantiated.

What Ribot was asking for was something of the nature of the declaration given by Italy in 1902. But in 1891 it was impossible for Rudini or any other statesman to give such an assurance. The difference between the situation as it existed in 1891 and in 1902 lay in the changed position of England. In Rudini's time it would have been fatal to Anglo-Italian relations for Italy to have turned her back on the Triple Alliance, which still enjoyed the cordial support of the English government. It would actually have been suicidal for Rudini to effect a rapprochement with France at the expense of other obligations, for at that very moment England and France were once more at daggers drawn because of the Egyptian question, and Lord Salisbury would have regarded the defection of Italy as downright treason. Rudini needed no reminder of the importance of England. If anything, he laid even greater stress than did Crispi on this aspect of Italian policy, and it was his intention to develop the English connection at all costs.[50]

The issue had thus been joined very soon after Rudini's advent. The Italian premier made his reply indirectly in answering a number of interpellations in the chamber on March 4. In the first place he rejected the idea of publishing the treaty of the Triple Alliance, as demanded by some of the deputies of the extreme Left, curiously enough just at this time. Continuing, he pointed out that the ministry had no intention of relaxing the bonds of the Triple Alliance and still less of dissolving them. He regretted only that much distrust had been mistakenly created with regard to the relations of Italy with France, which ought to remain friendly, for it was not true, he asserted, that the Triple Alliance was an instrument of war. Italy desired at all costs the maintenance of the balance of power in the Mediterranean, for if this were disturbed a blow would be struck at the vital interests as well as at the dignity of the country. This statement Rudini offered the French by way of satisfying their curiosity. The Italian chargé in Paris was instructed to tell Ribot that Italy asked nothing of France by way of compensa-

[50] See especially the interview published in the *London Times* April 14, 1891.

tion, and relied upon the French government to take the initiative in establishing better relations.[51]

This reply had, however, first been submitted to the German government for approval, and the Italian ambassador at Berlin had been instructed to say that Rudini intended to uphold the existing connections with the central powers. The attempt to conciliate France was merely an *extra-tour*, so to speak. Marschall had given his approval, while pointing out to the Italian ambassador the implications of the French demand. It was, he asserted, a tactical move to detach Italy from the alliance and then from England, after which Italy, being isolated, would practically become a vassal of France. It was hardly necessary to convince the Italian premier, who fully appreciated the dangers of the situation. This he demonstrated clearly enough by expressing his determination to renew the Triple Alliance and by taking the first steps towards opening negotiations for that purpose. There was a distinct limit to which Italy could go in the policy of conciliating the French.[52]

Unfortunately the Italian declarations were considered insufficient at the Quai d'Orsay. Ribot once more affirmed his desire to effect a rapprochement and to make concessions of a commercial nature to end the tariff war, but, he continued, the Triple Alliance was the obstacle. The text was unknown and simple ministerial declarations were inadequate. Rudini thereupon decided to drop the matter and leave the initiative henceforth to the French.[53] Nevertheless he did, a few days later,

---

[51] The declaration of March 4 in Chiala III, pp. 542-543. G. P. VII, no. 1402. According to the *Mémorial Diplomatique* February 14, 1891, Ressman had told Rudini that no progress could be made unless the treaty of the alliance were published.

[52] G. P. VII, nos. 1402, 1404.

[53] G. P. VII, no. 1407. It appears that Rudini from the first had labored under the impression that the strained relations were due to Crispi personally rather than to deeper causes. This was not true of diplomats like Bruck, who reported to his government on February 25: "Man will in Paris Italien entschieden von der Trippelallianz loslösen, und solange keine handgreiflichen Beweise vorliegen, ist an eine factische Annäherung zwischen diesen zwei Nachbarreichen nicht zu denken." The French press made no secret of the fact that the underlying motive of the foreign office was to drive Italy out of the Alliance (cf. Giacometti

approach M. Billot, the French ambassador at Rome, and express his resentment at Ribot's insinuation that statements of fact made by an Italian premier in the chamber of deputies were not sufficiently reliable. Ribot's implied threat that he would hinder concessions of an economic nature being made to Italy until he was informed of the content of the Triple Alliance was, he asserted, a serious matter. Billot tried to explain away the rather blunt attitude of the French foreign minister, and comforted his interlocutor with the assurance that the French government was planning to accord Italy the advantages of the most favored nation. Then he returned once more to the charge, asking whether, if France became involved in war and reconquered Alsace-Lorraine, Italy would be obliged to come to the assistance of Germany, and whether compensations for Italy, for example in Tunis, had been envisaged. Rudini replied that to answer these queries would be to divulge the content of the treaties, which he had no intention of doing. If the French were so interested in learning the nature of the agreements why did they not make inquiries in Berlin or Vienna?[54]

A few days later Billot approached King Humbert with the same request that the text of the alliance be published. Unless this were done France could make no concessions, for it could not be expected that one country should place its resources at the disposal of another country which, in case of war, would take

p. 398: "L'esprit français, surexcité par trois années de politique italienne aggressive, ne voyait qu'une chose: la fin de la Triple Alliance.") See also Greindl's report in Köhler p. 102, note 1. Evidently the interview with Billot finally convinced Rudini. Bruck, reporting the incident to Kálnoky on March 25 states: "Billot denkt und Rudini weiss es, dass man Italien im Laufe dieses Jahres zwingen müsse, die Allianz nicht mehr zu erneuern, und es kein Mittel gebe, als stürmisch darauf loszuarbeiten mit der Drohung: si vous ne le faites pas, nous n'ouvrirons pas les cordons de la bourse." That the Germans from the beginning saw the direction of the French efforts is shown by G. P. VII, nos. 1402, 1403.

[54] G. P. VII, no. 1408; Bruck to Kálnoky March 25, 1891; Griendl report April 10, 1891, in Köhler pp. 279-280. Billot (I, p. 297) says that he was authorized to tell Rudini that as soon as the new tariff system had become effective in France, the French government would be ready to negotiate a tariff settlement with Italy. Evidently in speaking to Rudini he stretched his instructions a bit and that accounts for his unwillingness to show Rudini the text of his instructions, though he pleaded that they were in cipher (Bruck to Kálnoky March 25, 1891).

sides against it. The King had been forewarned by Rudini and gave the same reply. When Billot became insistent, Humbert referred him back to the prime minister.[55]

Diplomatic pressure had failed completely, so, as a last resort, the French foreign office turned to the use of financial pressure. About the middle of April a representative of the house of Rothschild came to Rome in connection with the negotiation of a loan. With the express approval of the Quai d'Orsay he offered the Italian government the necessary funds, even if Italy remained in the Triple Alliance. In return h e asked that the Italian government give a written statement, to be kept secret if so desired, regarding the conditions under which it would take part in war against France. What the French government desired was that Italy should remain neutral in a Franco-German conflict, or observe a "hands off" policy in the event of the reconquest of Alsace-Lorraine. Rudini rejected this offer with great indignation and was tempted to throw the bearer of the proposal outdoors. The very suggestion that he should follow a policy of duplicity seemed to him vile.[56] From this time on there could be no further talk of an arrangement between France and Italy. The Italians could not meet the French terms, and Rudini now devoted his whole attention to the problem of renewing the treaty with the central powers and developing the entente with England.

Rudini was not in any sense an enthusiastic supporter of the Triple Alliance, and undoubtedly felt that many of Italy's burdens were due to this connection.[57] But he was forced to

[55] Bruck to Kálnoky March 25, 1891; G. P. VII, no. 1418; the incident is also referred to by Crispi, in the *Contemporary Review* June 1891, p. 778, and in a pamphlet by Torraca: *Neutralità od Alleanza?* published May 13, 1891. It was also described by Wolkenstein to Kálnoky May 26, 1891, the Austrian ambassador to Russia having learned of it from his Italian colleague.

[56] G. P. VII, no. 1418; Bruck to Kálnoky April 27 and May 5, 1891; Hoyos to Kálnoky May 21, 1891 (quoted by Pribram I, p. 221). Cf. also Giacometti, who places this *démarche* at the end of March (pp. 398-400). The accounts of Billot I, pp. 290-294, Chiala III, p. 545, and J. von Eckardt: *Berlin, Wien, Rom*, (Leipzig 1892, p. 130) are apparently all based on Giacometti.

[57] Cf. Albert Pingaud: *L'Italie depuis 1870* pp. 161 ff. and especially the interview in the *London Times* April 14, 1891.

continue the existing arrangements for much the same reasons that his predecessors had originally concluded them. Italy could not afford to remain isolated, especially in the face of France, which had, in the Tunis question, showed superb indifference to the desires and aspirations of the Peninsula, and which would, unquestionably, relegate Italy once more to the position of a vassal if Italy were unable to offer resistance.[58] The methods pursued by the French in March, 1891 showed clearly enough that the tension had not been due so much to Crispi's noisy bellicosity as to the desire of the French to detach Italy from the League of Peace. Rudini certainly realized that the Triple Alliance could not be given up, even in return for an entente with France. The pressure brought to bear upon him, however, must have convinced him that in the future French action would assume more and more menacing forms, especially if the rapprochement between France and Russia were to become complete. Under the circumstances there was nothing to do but to maintain the closest relations with the central powers and renew the alliance prematurely in order to cut short the French intrigues and put an end to the agitation of the radicals against the alliance.[59]

Furthermore, the alliance was absolutely necessary to keep open the connection with England, and this was really the crucial point for Rudini. After all, the alliance gave Italy protection in Europe, but that was all. Though the Germans had agreed, in the separate Italo-German Treaty of 1887, to support the Italian policy in the western Mediterranean, little was to be expected from this promise. The Germans could fight only on the Rhine.[60] They played no rôle in the naval situation in the Mediterranean. Only England could protect the Italian coasts and really hold the balance. Italy being in no position to continue the active colonial policy followed by Crispi it had become more than ever necessary to enlist the aid of the British

[58] See especially the development of this argument in the inspired pamphlet by Torraca, entitled *Neutralità od Alleanza ?*, summarized in Wippermann 1891 I, pp. 345-346.

[59] G. P. VII, no. 1409.   [60] G. P. VII, no. 1419.

in case of French aggression in North Africa. Nothing expresses these fundamental ideas more clearly than an interview which Rudini accorded an Italian politician early in April and which was published by the London *Times*:

"Concerning the Triple Alliance, the Italian Premier expressed the view that its renewal or nonrenewal was a secondary matter, particularly for Italy, and that the decision to be taken must depend upon the general situation of Europe, which might change from one day to another. In the opinion of the Marquis di Rudini, Italy's chief interest lies, not in the Triple Alliance, but in such a constant and steadfast agreement with Great Britain that the two countries should never become disunited. On many occasions the policy of the Triple Alliance has harmonized perfectly with that of the British Cabinet. Although Britain, for special reasons, upon which it is unnecessary to dwell, has never adhered to the treaty concluded in 1882 and renewed in 1887, it is difficult to imagine that she could look on impassively while war was being waged by Russia and France combined against Germany and Austria......At bottom the Marquis is not an enthusiastic advocate of the Triple Alliance. He by no means considers it perpetually indispensable. But he fully appreciates its immense value, the more so that on its present footing it is not in any way inimical to the interests or probable policy of Great Britain. The Italian Premier laid great stress on his firm conviction that Italy ought never to come into conflict with Great Britain. Substantially his idea is that Great Britain and Italy ought to be found on the same side, and that when the former sees no cause to intervene, Italy had better be calm and prudent. This is practically his whole programme so far as European politics are concerned."[61]

In brief, then, Rudini intended to renew the treaty, partly because it was, at the moment, indispensable, but chiefly because he regarded it as a stepping-stone to further development of the connection with England. Though he had expressed his determination to renew the pact as early as March 9, no definite steps were taken before the middle of April, when the pressure of the French had shown the Italian statesman the necessity of acting before it was too late.[62] On the whole the negotiations for

[61] *London Times* April 14, 1891, report from Rome April 13. The interview was said to have taken place between Rudini and an Italian statesman, but was more probably given directly to the *Times* correspondent. It was later declared from Rome to be "without foundation," but this *démenti* was not accepted by the European press generally, and it must be confessed that Rudini's utterances are so closely in accord with what we know from other sources that only the most sceptical would call the authenticity of the interview in question.

[62] G. P. VII, nos. 1404, 1410; Pribram I, pp. 222 ff.

the renewal went off smoothly and quickly, the explanation being that all three of the powers were anxious to have the situation cleared up. Rudini from the beginning gave up Crispi's idea of enlisting the support of Austria for Italy's North African policy. Indeed, nothing more was asked of Austria and the treaty in its renewed form laid no additional burdens upon the Hapsburg Monarchy.[63] The negotiations were, in fact, carried on in Berlin. Kálnoky and Caprivi, who originally had not looked upon the idea of a premature renewal with great enthusiasm, were now quite as anxious as Rudini, for the reports of French pressure on Italy and the rumors of a coming entente between France and Russia had shown them the dangers in waiting longer. Rudini's position was not very secure, and there was no knowing what attitude his successor might take. For the same reasons the Vienna and Berlin cabinets raised no further objection to the merging of the three treaties of 1887 into one document.[64] In fact the only real difficulty presented during the negotiation of the new pact arose from Rudini's desire to extend Germany's obligations to support Italy in the western Mediterranean. In article III of the separate German-Italian Treaty of 1887 it had been provided that if France should make a move to extend her occupation, or even her protectorate or sovereignty in the North African territories (Tripoli or Morocco), and Italy in consequence felt obliged to take action herself in those parts or even to "have recourse to extreme measures in French territory in Europe," the resultant state of war would, on the demand of Italy, constitute the *casus foederis*. Rudini pointed out that this clause provided only for the most extreme case. What he desired was a provision for continuous diplomatic coöperation to uphold the *status quo de facto* and *de jure* in Cyrenaica, Tripoli, Tunis and Morocco. If the maintenance of the *status quo* should prove impossible, Germany should support Italy in any action, in the form of occupation or other guarantee, which she might think it necessary to undertake in the interest of the equilibrium or in order to secure compensation.

[63] Pribram I, pp. 222-223; G. P. VII, no. 1416.
[64] Pribram I, pp. 222-225; G. P. VII, nos. 1406, and marginal note, 1411, 1412.

Caprivi did not like this new Italian demand, nor did he consider this new clause necessary. There was considerable discussion on this point, but the Germans at an early date agreed to the principle and the debate turned chiefly on the wording. In the new treaty this article appeared in somewhat diluted form. The Germans agreed to work for the maintenance of the *status quo*, but only the territorial *status quo*, in Cyrenaica, Tripoli and Tunis. Morocco was left out, evidently to avoid the possibility of coming into conflict with the policy of the English. In case the existing situation could not be upheld and this fact were recognized by both parties after a mature examination of the situation, Germany agreed, after a formal and previous accord, to support Italy in any action in the form of occupation or other taking of guarantee which the latter should undertake in those same regions in the interest of the equilibrium or of legitimate compensation. The treaty was signed on May 6 and ratifications were exchanged on May 17.[65]

Rudini's insistence that Germany should extend her support of Italian policy in North Africa is characteristic and instructive. He was thinking chiefly of France and the Mediterranean and he hoped to enlist the help not only of Germany but also of England. One of his first steps in foreign policy had been to re-open the negotiations with England for the delimitation of the spheres of influence in the Red Sea region. These negotiations had been dropped, it will be remembered, because of Crispi's insistence that Kassala should be assigned to Italy. Rudini made no trouble on this point, and on March 24 the agreement was signed, a supplementary clause being added on April 15. By it Italy was allowed to occupy Kassala temporarily, though

---

[65] The details of the negotiations may be found in G. P. VII, chapter xlv *passim*, where the German desire to avoid anything that might estrange England is very clearly brought out. Rudini made a second demand, namely that Germany should undertake to uphold the *status quo*, not only on the Turkish coasts and islands of the Adriatic and Aegean Seas, but throughout the entire Turkish Orient, as provided for in the separate Italo-Austrian Treaty of 1887. To this Caprivi objected, and the point was not pressed.

technically it was recognized as part of the Sudan, which the English claimed for Egypt.[66]

This treaty restored the good feeling between England and Italy and set the seals anew upon the coöperation of the two powers in matters concerning the Red Sea and Egypt. Rudini intended that the entente should be extended to the Mediterranean proper and that England should accept more specific obligations. The Mediterranean Agreement between England and Italy, signed in February, 1887, had been extremely vague. The *status quo* was to be maintained on the shores of the Black Sea, the Aegean and the Adriatic, and on the northern coast of Africa. In case the maintenance of the *status quo* became impossible, both powers desired that there should be no extension of the domination of any other great power over any portion of those coasts. The British government earnestly desired to give its best coöperation to maintain these cardinal principles, but Lord Salisbury had pointed out to begin with that "the character of that coöperation must be decided by them (i. e., by the British government) when the occasion for it arises, according to the circumstances of the case."[67]

Quite evidently this promise on the part of the English was inadequate from the point of view of the Italians. Time and again Crispi had attempted to secure from Lord Salisbury a definite assurance that the British fleet would assist the Italian in guarding the coasts of the Peninsula against French aggression. It appears that during the crisis and war scare of 1888 Salisbury had given some such assurance, but only for this special case. Crispi, however, always maintained thereafter that he was absolutely certain of English protection, and King Humbert himself is said to have made a categorical statement to that effect to Prince Napoleon in 1890. Crispi was certainly overstating the situation and Rudini, when he took over the foreign office, looked in vain for a document to bear out his predecessor's assertions.[68] It was, therefore, necessary for him to take up the

[66] Billot I, pp. 304-305; Cilibrizzi II, pp. 423 ff.

[67] Cf. G. P. VII, chapter xxvi *passim*, and the text in Pribram I, pp. 36 ff.

[68] This whole knotty question was frequently brought up in the Austrian cor-

matter anew, and in the first days of April he approached the Austrian ambassador with the request that Austria and Germany should support him in his attempt to induce the English to assume obligations in the western Mediterranean similar to those laid down for the eastern Mediterranean in the agreement of December, 1887.[69] Both Kálnoky and Caprivi were only too ready to accede to this wish, for they regarded the aid of Italy as dependent on English willingness to protect the coasts while the Italian armies were engaged elsewhere.[70] In the final text of the renewed Triple Alliance the third paragraph of article IX, dealing with North Africa, provided that if the maintenance of the *status quo* proved to be impossible the two contracting powers (Germany and Italy) should seek to put themselves into agreement with England. Furthermore, a protocol was added which stated baldly:

"The accession of England being already acquired, in principle, to the stipulations of the treaty of this day which concern the Orient, properly so-called, to wit, the territories of the Ottoman Empire, the High Contracting Parties shall exert themselves at the opportune moment, and to the extent that circumstances may permit, to bring about an analogous accession with regard to the North African territories of the central and western part of the Mediterranean, including Morocco. This accession might be realized by an acceptance, on the part of England, of the programme established by articles IX and X of the Treaty of this day."[71]

---

respondence (Bruck to Kálnoky December 16, 1890; April 7, 1891; Kálnoky to Bruck April 13, 1891—thinks Crispi's assertions are little more than a "sanguinisches Phantasiegemälde"; Bruck to Kálnoky April 21, 1891). Cf. also G. P. VIII, no. 1707 and note, and especially 1714, where Rudini reports King Humbert as saying that Crispi had a private letter from Lord Salisbury "durch welchen dieser sich Italien gegenüber sehr weit engagiert habe." This letter Crispi refused to show Rudini. The evidence that there was some such assurance rests upon Crispi II, p. 349, upon the reports to Kálnoky (Bruck to Kálnoky November 11, 1891 and Deym to Kálnoky December 22, 1893) and upon the categorical statement of the inspired writer in the *Quarterly Review* October 1902, p. 664: "The limits of his (Salisbury's)relations with the Triple Alliance were marked in February 1887, when, in order to prevent Italy from withdrawing from the Treaty, he guaranteed her against a naval attack by France in an agreement for assuring the *status quo* in the Mediterranean, to which Austria was also a party."

[69] Pribram I, p. 223. Similar advances were made to Germany shortly after (G. P. VIII, no. 1707).

[70] G. P. VII, nos. 1412, 1416; VIII chapter lii *passim*; Pribram I, pp. 222 ff.

[71] G. P. VII, no. 1427; Pribram I, pp. 68-69.

As a matter of fact the preparations for common action in order to attain this goal had already been made during the negotiations for the renewal of the Triple Alliance, and the Austrian and German governments had already broached to Salisbury the question of revising the agreement of February, 1887 in the direction of greater explicitness.[72] The moment for this action was by no means ill-chosen, for the English government was quite as much threatened by the recent developments in European politics as were the central powers. The Egyptian question had once more entered upon a critical phase, with the attempts of the English to reform the judicial system and reëstablish the authority of the Khedive in Upper Egypt. Both the French and the Russian ambassadors at Constantinople were actively engaged in frustrating this policy, and it appeared as though once more, as in 1887, the Egyptian question might prove to be the most convenient bridge to bring the French and the Russians together. At the same time the Newfoundland Fisheries question was once more under discussion, and there were indications that the French were preparing for action in Morocco.[73] Under the circumstances it was essential for the English government to maintain its connection with the League of Peace. The threatened entente between France and Russia, which had caused so much anxiety in Berlin, was equally menacing to the position of the British. For the Germans it opened up the possibility of a war of revenge and an attack upon two fronts. For the British it meant the prospect of united action in the Mediterranean, with the possible loss of Egypt and the severance of the connections with India. Consequently it was distinctly to the interest of the English government to reassure itself of the loyalty of the Ital-

[72] G. P. VIII, nos. 1708 ff.

[73] On the Egyptian troubles see especially G. P. VIII, nos. 1788 ff., which clearly indicate the great anxiety of the Germans to support the English, in the face of the Franco-Russian rapprochement. Cf. also Documents Diplomatiques: Affaires d'Égypte 1884-1893. On Morocco see G. P. VIII, nos. 1914 ff., reflecting the English anxiety respecting French designs and the hopes of the Germans that Morocco would continue to be a bone of contention between England and France and thus keep England within the orbit of the Triple Alliance. Cf. also Haweis: The Coming Crisis in Morocco (Fortnightly Review April 1892).

ians, for the Italian fleet might well prove to be the decisive factor in a naval conflict in the Mediterranean. Salisbury had already shown himself anxious to please the new Italian ministry during the negotiations which led to the delimitation of territory in eastern Africa, and had consented to the temporary occupation of Kassala by the Italians.[74]

So natural was the rapprochement between England and Italy that it has been claimed that Rudini renewed the Triple Alliance only because Salisbury made his continued support conditional on the renewal of the pact.[75] This is a gross exaggeration, but when, after the alliance had been renewed, Count Hatzfeldt approached the English prime minister, about the middle of May, he found him very well disposed. Salisbury once more emphasized the impossibility of concluding an actual alliance with Italy, because English public opinion, wedded to the idea of "splendid isolation," would never consent to a binding agreement of so formidable a nature. He was, however, ready to consider a revision of the notes exchanged in February, 1887.[76] Rudini had already approached the English ambassador, Lord Dufferin, with the suggestion of an alliance, and a few days later he submitted to the German ambassador the tentative draft of a four power pact, to be concluded between the members of the Triple Alliance and England. The agreement was to take the form of an exchange of notes, and, as suggested in the protocol of the Triple Alliance Treaty of May 6, its purpose was formally to enlist the support of the English government for Italian Mediterranean interests. As in the First Mediterranean Agreement of February, 1887, Austria was to be more or less a silent partner.

[74] G. P. VIII, no. 1707.

[75] Eckardt: *Berlin, Wien, Rom* pp. 130-131. It is interesting to note that when Eckardt's book appeared Marschall told the Austrian ambassador that "manches in der Broschüre, besonders aber dasjenige über den Anschluss Englands an den Dreibund gesagte, den thatsächlichen Verhältnissen nicht ganz entspricht" (Széchényi to Kálnoky May 10, 1892). In the autumn of 1891 it was said that Rudini had remarked to a friend that the renewal of the Triple Alliance was necessary in order to keep the friendship of England, which had been made conditional upon it (Giacometti p. 425; Salvemini, in the *Revue des Nations Latines* 1916, pp. 485-486).

[76] G. P. VIII, no. 1710.

In return for a promise on the part of the powers of the Triple Alliance to support the English policy in Egypt, the British government was to promise to work for the maintenance of the *status quo* in North Africa (including Morocco); to approve, after previous agreement, any action which Italy might feel called upon to take in order to uphold the equilibrium, or in order to secure compensation if the existing situation could no longer be maintained; and to take definite action in certain eventualities. Articles IV and V of the Rudini draft read as follows:

"If France should make a move to extend her occupation, or even her protectorate or her sovereignty under any form whatsoever, in the North African territories, or if she wished to trouble the work of England in Egypt, any such attempt on the part of France would be considered by Germany, Italy and England as injuring their common interests. If, in such a case, one of them took the initiative militarily, the two others, after previous formal agreement, would support this action militarily.

"The four powers will exchange, after a previous formal agreement at an opportune time, an analogous declaration to cover the case of French aggression against any one of them in Europe."[77]

The German ambassador immediately pointed out that this draft was more the basis for a quadruple alliance than a mere revision of the agreement of 1887, and that it would entail long discussions between Rome, Vienna and Berlin before it could be submitted to Lord Salisbury. The likelihood that the English would accept such an arrangement was very small. Rudini thereupon withdrew the draft and submitted a new one, less precise in form and designed for Italy and England alone.[78] This project was to be discussed with Salisbury by Count Hatzfeldt, but before there was a good opportunity for taking up the question the negotiations had more or less leaked out and interpellations had been made in the house of commons. In view of these developments Hatzfeldt himself felt it to be inadvisable to press the point.[79]

In one sense the failure of the negotiations was due to Rudini himself. Recognizing the fact that most Italians, even those most bitterly opposed to the Triple Alliance, were advocates of

[77] G. P. VIII, nos. 1713, 1714.   [78] G. P. VIII, nos. 1714, 1715.
[79] G. P. VIII, nos. 1717 ff.

a close understanding with England, he continually went out of his way to emphasize the community of interest between England and the central powers, indicating that the connection with England would be broken if the alliance were not renewed. His statements, reported in the London *Times* on April 14, have already been quoted and discussed. Of much the same nature were the arguments advanced in the chamber of deputies by Chiala on May 14, evidently at the instigation of the foreign office. He emphasized the importance of the agreement of 1887 between England and Italy and reminded the deputies that Depretis had declared that Italy's position was secured by land and sea, and that, so long as Italy and England stood by the central powers, France could not risk taking the aggressive, even if she were certain of Russian support.[80] In a series of articles published by the *Corriere della Sera* on June 6 and 7 a friend of Rudini, the Italian deputy Maggiorino Ferraris, made a special point of Italo-English relations. Declaring that the Triple Alliance might be regarded as having been renewed, he continued:

"England engages to defend Italy even in case the latter becomes involved in a war resulting from her obligations to the Triple Alliance. This disposition is especially important because, by it, England indirectly enters the Triple Alliance, which thereby becomes quadruple."[81]

Inspired by the statements of Chiala, the English radical leader, Labouchère, on June 2 and 4, interpellated the government as to whether special undertakings entered into in 1887 by England and Italy were of such importance as to justify the remarks made in the Italian chamber. The undersecretary, Fergusson, replied skillfully but evasively that England had no engagements involving the use of the military and naval forces beyond those of which the house knew. England would, however, be found on the side of those powers whose aim was the maintenance of the *status quo*. An exchange of notes defining

---

[80] Chiala had made similar statements in the appendix of his book *La Spedizione di Massaua* (1888). See Chiala III, pp. 702-703, 705; also G. P. VIII, no. 1718.

[81] Quoted by Giacometti p. 409.

this policy had taken place between Italy and England in 1887, he admitted.[82]

Even more spectacular was the publication, on June 3, in the *Figaro*, of a letter written by the Boulangist deputy, Millevoye, to Labouchère, in which the writer communicated certain remarks which King Humbert was reputed to have made to Prince Napoleon and which the latter had passed on to the deputy in January, 1890. King Humbert was quoted as saying:

"I have nothing to fear for the security of the Italian coasts, for I have had a formal promise from the Cabinet of St. James that the English Fleet will ally itself with mine, should the necessity arise, in order to protect Italy against all maritime operations." On Napoleon's objecting that this was tantamount to adhesion to the Triple Alliance on the part of England, Humbert was reported to have said: "I have nothing more to say to you about it. But I can state that the English and Italian governments have exchanged despatches which contain certain definite engagements, and I have full confidence in the written word of the English government."[83]

A few days later, on June 8, it was reported from Paris that this supposed agreement of 1887 had been even further extended:

"The Marquis di Rudini is said to have succeeded in securing positive stipulations almost of the character of a protocol. The principal points are that England shall defend Italy with its fleet if Italy is attacked and in particular that she engages to defend Italy if the latter country should be attacked on account of her connection with the Triple Alliance."[84]

---

[82] *Parliamentary Debates* CCCLIII, p. 1466. Labouchère had interpellated the government on several earlier occasions in regard to this same matter (see the excellent summary in Chiala III, appendix ii). The *London Times* and other conservative papers put these interpellations down as party manoeuvres and expressed doubt whether Labouchère himself believed in an agreement. The letter of Gladstone in A. L. Thorold: *The Life of Henry Labouchère* (London 1913) p. 371, shows that Gladstone at least was sincerely suspicious. On these interpellations see also G. P. VIII, nos. 1718, 1719.

[83] From The *London Times* June 4, 1891. The authenticity of the remarks was denied from Rome on June 7, and the conservative press in England ridiculed the idea (cf. editorial of the *Times* June 5, 1891). The *Saturday Review* wrote on June 6, 1891: "A chain with the late revered Plon-Plon for one of its links would not exactly hold an ironclad; but whether any such engagement was given or not, it is to be hoped that no Radical raging will induce the English government to confess it. The whole value of such engagements lies in the power of making them seriously." Salisbury confessed to Hatzfeldt that he believed Humbert to have made the remarks, and there is no doubt that the King believed in them himself, as shown by his statement to Rudini a short time before (G. P. VIII, nos. 1714, 1720).

[84] *London Times* June 9, 1891.

With all this discussion of so fundamental a question it was quite obviously impossible for Salisbury to consider an extension of England's obligations for the time being, and Hatzfeldt was probably wise in not raising the question at all. It was just at this time that the renewal of the Triple Alliance became known, and the European press was full of conjectures. During the negotiations public opinion, especially in Italy, had been kept in a state of uncertainty by the conflicting arguments brought forward by that part of the press which was generally regarded as representing the government policy.[85] But early in May the great event gradually became known. The renewal of the treaty was reported from Vienna and on May 8 the London *Daily Telegraph* stated that the new treaty had been signed. These reports were denied by the semiofficial papers, but the publication, on May 13, of a pamphlet urging the desirability of the alliance, by the influential editor of the *Opinione*, Deputy Torraca, created quite a stir.[86] Rudini himself declared in the chamber on the following day:

"Italy has two objects in view: the balance of power and maintenance of peace. Italy has believed, and still believes, that the Triple Alliance has contributed to the attainment of these objects; we must uphold these ideals firmly. I do not believe it opportune to discuss each day the direction of the foreign policy of a great power, especially as the system of alliances is such that it cannot be changed whimsically from today to tomorrow. We must persevere and the government will persevere in the earnest hope of maintaining intact our friendship with neighboring peoples."[87]

On June 6 and 7 Ferraris, writing in the *Corriere della Sera*, announced that the alliance might be considered as renewed, since the "verbal agreement was already complete." There followed a fairly accurate summary of the substance of the new pact, and the statement that England had practically joined.[88] The Italian

---

[85] Giacometti pp. 401-403. Even the *Fanfulla*, organ of the extreme Right, published articles against the alliance, and Bonghi, the friend of Rudini, declared against renewal (Bonghi: Il Programma di un Partito, in the *Rassegna Nazionale* March 1, 1891).

[86] G. P. VII, no. 1428. The pamphlet by Torraca is summarized in the *Neue Freie Presse* May 15, 1891 and in Wippermann 1891, I, pp. 345-346.

[87] Chiala III, pp. 551-552.

[88] Reprinted in large part in Giacometti pp. 407-409.

radicals, who had not considered the question of the renewal as a very pressing one, were now completely disillusioned. On June 18, a manifesto calling for a meeting of protest was issued by the radical leaders. The meeting was prohibited, whereupon an interpellation in the chamber was arranged for.[89] On June 28, in an extremely stormy session and in the midst of a very sharp clash on a question of procedure, Rudini arose and announced:

"We shall maintain firmly and solidly our treaties of alliance with the Central European Empires. Italy and Europe may rest assured that these alliances will be maintained and that the peace of Europe will long be preserved."[90]

On the following day he told the senate that, in order to cut short the uncertainty, he had considered it opportune to act:

"Long before the old treaties lapse the new agreements will be in force, because in foreign policy there should be no break in continuity. Our alliances, firmly and sincerely maintained, will assure the peace of Europe for a long time to come."[91]

On the very same day the Kaiser, *en route* to Heligoland, announced the renewal of the treaty in rather grotesque fashion by informing the president of the steamship company of this important event.[92]

[89] Chiala III, pp. 555 ff.; Giacometti pp. 411 ff.; Billot I, pp. 328-330.

[90] Chiala III, p. 558. Full descriptions of this tumultuous session, during which Imbriani called Rudini an "Austrian minister," may be found in Giacometti pp. 112 ff.; Billot I, p. 334; *London Times* June 29, 1891.

[91] Chiala III, p. 560; Giacometti p. 414; Billot I, p. 335-336. Rudini added, rather poetically: "Sarà come una giornata estiva nelle regioni polari, dove la notte non porta le tenebre, dove il tramonto del sole si confonde col suo risorgere."

[92] *London Times* June 30, 1891; Chiala III, p. 561; Giacometti pp. 403-404.

CHAPTER VII

CRONSTADT AND THE ENTENTE OF AUGUST
1891

ALTHOUGH the renewal of the Triple Alliance had not involved any material changes in the text, and although there had been no real extension of England's obligations to Italy or alteration of her relations to the Triple Alliance, it could hardly be expected that the uninitiated French and Russians should believe that such was the case. On the contrary they had every reason to feel convinced that the opposite was true, for the central powers and England seemed to be intent on advertising their entente and flaunting it in the face of the isolated states. Rudini himself, in announcing the renewal of the alliance in the Italian senate on June 29, had declared that there had been, some years ago, an exchange of views between England and Italy and that Sir James Fergusson had described this exchange in accurate terms in his replies to Labouchère's interpellations. The two countries, he continued, had proposed to coöperate for the maintenance of peace and the *status quo*. He did not see how the identity of views of Great Britain and Italy could be called in question.[1]

At the same time Labouchère returned to the attack, questioning the government in regard to the statements made by Rudini. Fergusson reiterated his former declarations that any measures to be taken in case of need for the maintenance of the *status quo* in the Mediterranean would be a matter for consideration according to the circumstances of the case. The exchange of views between England and Italy had been occasional, but there had been no change in the English attitude since 1888.[2] On July 6 the undersecretary once more asserted that the purpose of the understanding was the maintenance of the *status quo* in

[1] Chiala III, pp. 559-561.
[2] July 2, 1891, *Parliamentary Debates* CCCLV, p. 210.

the Mediterranean,[3] while on July 9 there was a regular debate on the estimates for the foreign office, the German minister, Marschall, being present. Labouchère once again took up the cudgels, and complained bitterly of the vague and "diplomatic" replies that had been given to his questions. Lord Salisbury, he said,

"loves secret alliances. He goes in a surreptitious manner to one of the Great Powers; he begs that Power to enter into some secret understanding with himself, and what is the result? These understandings with one Power in Europe lead to misunderstandings with other Powers, and when trouble arises we find ourselves absolutely crippled in any effort to bring back Europe to a state of peace."

In regard to the Triple Alliance he declared that

"Lord Salisbury's notion seems to be that just as these three allies are making themselves a police force to maintain the Continental peace, so we with our navy should make ourselves a sort of police force to maintain the *status quo* in the Mediterranean."

To this Fergusson replied by defining England's position once more, this time in unmistakable terms:

"There has been during several years of anxiety which have passed away an interchange of views upon the condition of things in Europe, and with regard to matters in which they, i. e. England and Italy, are particularly interested, namely, the maintenance of the *status quo* and peace in the Mediterranean. It is altogether unnecessary to mix up such a question with the Triple Alliance; we are no parties to the Triple Alliance; we are not even aware of the Treaties so-called which we are informed have been renewed between the central Powers in Europe. We have entered into no agreement or understanding with any Power pledging us to the employment of Her Majesty's forces in any contingency."[4]

The upshot of all this discussion was to show clearly enough that England had no actual part in the Triple Alliance and that there was not and could not be any formal alliance between England and Italy. On the other hand it had been made plain enough that there was an understanding between these two countries and that it aimed at the maintenance of the *status quo* in the Mediterranean. Furthermore the English government had declared that its sympathies lay with those powers whose

[3] July 6, 1891, *Parliamentary Debates* CCCLV, pp. 434-435.
[4] July 9, 1891, *Parliamentary Debates* CCCLV, pp. 771-790.

policy it was to maintain the existing situation, and no effort was made to conceal the fact that even without a written treaty the interests of the English lay in a close connection with the Triple Alliance. On June 23 a British squadron had visited Fiume and had been honored by the Emperor Francis Joseph. The warm toasts of friendship which were exchanged on this occasion were even outdone by the celebrations at Venice on July 6 in connection with the launching of the new Italian battleship *Sicilia*. A group of English officers stood on the deck with King Humbert as the ship went down the ways and on the following day the King attended a luncheon on board H. M. *Benbow*, during which the most cordial good wishes were exchanged.[5]

As a complement to these Mediterranean demonstrations came the visit of the Kaiser to London, from July 4 to 13. In contrast to the earlier family visits, this was a state visit, with all the attendant pomp and circumstance. The reception accorded to the young monarch was almost unparalleled in its enthusiasm, cordiality and heartiness. On July 10, in his famous Guildhall speech, William announced his determination to follow the example of his grandfather and father and to preserve, so far as possible, the historic friendship between the two nations, which had so often stood side by side in defense of freedom and justice. On July 12, in the company of Marschall, he paid a visit to Lord Salisbury at Hatfield. There appears to have been little in the way of political discussion on this occasion,[6] but Marschall had

---

[5] See Geoffrey Rawson: *Life of Admiral Sir Harry Rawson* (London 1914) p. 85. The *Standard* wrote on this occasion: "England knows the peaceful intentions of Austria-Hungary, and that is why she shares and supports the same. We doubt whether England is in similar agreement with any other state" (quoted by Arthur Singer: *Geschichte des Dreibundes* [Leipzig 1914] p. 103). The *Saturday Review* declared (June 27, 1891): "Nationally the two nations (i. e., England and Austria) are almost the only pair in the world between whom rivalry is almost impossible and whose desires mutually assist each other. We might for treaty reasons and auld lang syne object to Austria's expansion southwards, but no interest of England's could be hurt if the Austro-Hungarian flag waved from the Danube to the Gulf of Salonica." On the celebrations in Venice see especially the *London Times* July 9 and 10, 1891. The *Freisinnige Zeitung* declared that it looked like a "prearranged demonstration which would remove the last vestige of doubt as to England's attitude and position towards the Triple Alliance."

[6] G. P. VIII, no. 1727. The Kaiser did not go beyond a few remarks con-

had a long talk with the Prime Minister on July 6. The subjects dealt with by the two statesmen are of particular interest. First and foremost came not the question of North Africa and the western Mediterranean, but the ever-recurring question of the Near East and Russian designs on Turkey. Salisbury was convinced that the Russians had not given up their hopes, but were simply temporizing until their forces had been rearmed and until Gladstone might have returned to power in England. Marschall took the view that a Russian attack would eventually come by sea in the form of a *coup de main* delivered against the Turkish capital. Salisbury was inclined to doubt this, but insisted that in any case the English fleet, possibly reinforced by the Italian squadrons, would be on hand to frustrate such an attempt. The conversation then turned to general Near Eastern problems, Salisbury praising particularly the Stambulov régime in Bulgaria. The German minister took this as a sounding of Germany's eventual attitude towards complications in the Balkans, and seized the opportunity to explain that Germany still regarded it as her prime duty to hold a vengeful France in check. Germany must have consideration for the Tsar and must respect the feeling of the people, which had become entirely converted to the Bismarckian policy in regard to the Near East. But, he said, England could always count on German sympathy and support in asserting her influence in the Orient, presupposing, always, that England were willing to protect her own interests at the crucial moment. "You can count on us;" replied Salisbury, "as long as the present government is in power, we shall be on hand in good time."[7]

The English premier had reason to be satisfied with the imperial visit. At first he had been very apprehensive lest demands

cerning the desirability of close relations between England and Italy and the necessity for pursuing a conciliatory policy towards the Sultan.

[7] G. P. VIII, nos. 1724, 1727; IX, no. 2111. Marschall was particularly impressed with Salisbury's categorical statement that England meant to come to the assistance of the Sultan against Russia, if necessary. In 1907 he said that Salisbury had told him on this occasion: "Kein englischer Minister werde jemals zugeben, dass das Schwarze Meer für die russische Flotte *mare liberum* und für England *mare clausum* sei" (G. P. XXII, no. 7384).

should be made upon him.[8] In view of Rudini's proposals for an alliance it was only reasonable to suppose that the question would be raised again. These demands he could not and would not grant. While sympathizing with the Triple Alliance and especially with Italy in questions of the western Mediterranean, the English government had no desire to come out too openly with an anti-French policy. It might well be doubted whether the country would have accepted such a course.[9] In any case it would have been dangerous and might have resulted in furthering the Franco-Russian policy in the eastern Mediterranean. After all, the English were more interested in Egypt, Suez and the Straits than in what France might do in Tripoli or even in Morocco. What Salisbury stood for was an anti-Russian rather than an anti-French policy, but this was just the reverse of what the Germans desired. Salisbury, in fact, was disappointed with the Kaiser's attitude, bitter as it was towards France and rather too tolerant of the Russians.[10] An actual accord was impossible so long as this fundamental divergence of interests continued, and it was on this rock that Bismarck's advances had been wrecked, just as were the hopes of the German statesmen in 1891. The upshot of the visit was that the Germans had received renewed assurances that the English meant to defend their interests in the Near East against Russia and in

[8] G. P. VIII, no. 1727. Cf. also Solvyns' report July 9 (Köhler p. 89, note 1).

[9] Cf. the reports of Solvyns July 8,9 and 12 (Köhler pp. 89, note 1,90, note 1, and 282, 283). Cf. also the *Daily News*, July 4: "We cannot take part in isolating France nor can we take part in a policy which regards France as an aggressive power, etc." Similarly *Daily Telegraph* July 5 and *Daily News* July 10: "We are faithful friends of Italy, Germany and Austria-Hungary, but also good friends of France."

[10] Cf. Deym to Kálnoky July 15, 1891: "Gegen Frankreich hat sich der Kaiser sehr gereizt ausgesprochen, dagegen hat er der Friedensliebe des Kaisers von Russland volle Anerkennung gezollt. Es scheint Lord Salisbury, dass Seine Majestät den Einfluss und die Macht der slawophilen Partei in Russland unterschätzt." He went on to express disappointment that Germany was unwilling to take a primary part in the defense of Constantinople against the Russians. This disappointment may in part explain Salisbury's belittling remarks about the personality of the Kaiser and Marschall (Köhler pp. 282-283; Lord George Hamilton: *Parliamentary Reminiscences and Reflections 1886-1906* p. 137; also Deym to Kálnoky July 15, 1891).

North Africa against the French, while Lord Salisbury had been told that he could rely upon German support whenever English interests were threatened. There was no agreement, but there was an understanding which, for the moment, at least, had full validity. The visit of the Italian Crown Prince to England during the last week of July was simply the finale of a large-scale demonstration of solidarity and good feeling.[11]

Nothing was more natural than that both France and Russia should have looked upon these proceedings with great apprehension and anxiety. Having no reliable information as to the real state of affairs they were thrown back upon conjecture, and under the circumstances it is quite comprehensible that they pictured the situation as blacker than it actually was. The French government had staked its hopes upon Rudini and had devoted its efforts for weeks to detaching Italy from the Triple Alliance. It had been disappointed in Rudini and had failed in its assault upon the Italian position. Not only had the alliance been renewed, but there seemed good reason to suppose that England had identified herself with the central powers and committed herself to an anti-French policy in the western Mediterranean. The substance of the conversation between Prince Napoleon and King Humbert had been communicated to the French foreign office some time before it was published by Millevoye.[12] After the divulgation of the letter on June 3 Ribot inquired of the Italian ambassador whether or not there was any foundation for the story. General Menabrea replied rather gruffly that he knew nothing of the authenticity of the remarks, nor did he know whether there were written agreements between England and Italy. All that, he went on, was a matter of indifference, for if France were to attempt to disturb the *status quo* in the Mediterranean the English and Italian fleets would coöperate even without such formal engagements.[13] This was plain

---

[11] Rudini had originally desired to effect a meeting between the King of Italy and the Queen of England or the Prince of Wales (G. P. VIII, no. 1715; Lee: *Edward VII*, volume I, p. 628).

[12] *London Times* June 4, 1891; G. P. VIII, no. 1721.

[13] G. P. VIII, no. 1721.

speaking and must have given Ribot food for thought. A few days later the French ambassador at Rome asked Rudini for assurances that the Triple Alliance had not been renewed. The Italian premier's only reply was that "nothing had changed." Quite obviously the French were being snubbed, and they immediately dropped the negotiations which had been opened in March for the delimitation of the territories claimed by the two countries in eastern Africa.[14]

Meanwhile, ever since the beginning of June, the European press had been greatly exercised by the question of the renewal of the Triple Alliance and England's relation to it. One must really re-read the newspaper comment of these days in order to form an adequate idea of the state of the European mind. The Italian, Austrian and German newspapers naturally made the most of the supposed adhesion of England to the Triple Alliance, and the outbursts in the French and Russian press were correspondingly rabid on the other side. Of course the more moderate organs realized that it was unlikely that England had signed a formal written agreement, even with Italy. Fergusson's replies to Labouchère had made that clear.[15] On the other hand Fergusson had admitted that there was an understanding with Italy and he had declared the purpose of the understanding. The cryptic nature of his utterances naturally gave rise to suspicion and anxiety, and even the English newspapers declared *urbi et orbi* that, whether there was an agreement or not, there could be no doubt what England's policy would be in a crisis. England, said the *Saturday Review*, needs only to recognize the side on which her bread is buttered. "We are friends with those powers with whom it is our special interest to be friendly, and with ourselves they are strong enough to play policeman to the others."[16] Even the *London Times*, in a leading article, came out frankly:

"The formal renewal of the Triple Alliance....must dispel any lingering hopes of disruption and unsettlement which may be entertained either in

---

[14] Billot I, pp. 308-312 and 324-327.

[15] *Temps* July 6; *London Times* July 13; *Neue Freie Presse* July 13, 1891.

[16] *Saturday Review* July 4 and 11, 1891.

the East or in the West....England is not a party to the Alliance, absolutely or conditionally, nor is there any separate pact with Italy....At the same time there has been an interchange of views between the two governments, and it is known, not merely to the Cabinet at Rome, but to the public throughout Europe, that the maintenance of the *status quo* in the Mediterranean is not and cannot be a matter of indifference to us. The *status quo* would be, beyond dispute, injuriously affected if the maritime power of Italy were to be attacked..if France, for instance, were to destroy the Italian navy in the course of a general war, or to annex it forcibly to her own.... One of the advantages of the Triple Alliance is that it increases the improbability of this particular infraction of the *status quo*, which, however it might originate, would compel us to put forth our naval strength in order to secure the freedom of the Mediterranean as well as our own interest therein. But, though we stand clear of any positive engagements with the powers composing the Triple Alliance, it is satisfactory to reflect that we have never been on more cordial terms of amity with Germany, Austria-Hungary and Italy....The Union of Germany and England in the cause of peace and civilization may be as solid and valuable as if it were embodied in a formal treaty and supported, as it would be, were the necessity to arise in the future as it has arisen in the past, by a conjunction of the forces of the greatest naval power with those of the greatest military power in the world."[17]

Commenting on the Kaiser's speech in the Guildhall, the same important paper declared:

"This country is drawn to Germany and the Triple Alliance by community of interests.. There is no question here of conscious preferences or capricious selection. It is a simple question of political gravitation, a case of the operation of the laws that override all individual and collective wills."[18]

Writing in a similar strain, the *Neue Freie Presse* referred to England as the fourth member of the League, or at least the reserve of the allies:

"The mighty sea power, England, feels called upon to unite its great interest in the *status quo* in the Mediterranean with the interest in peace of the three Continental Powers, and this union, even without the form of a written treaty, automatically turns against France and Russia, these being the powers which are dissatisfied with the present situation in Europe."[19]

Together with these declarations of policy there went a host of rumors. It was said that the members of the "quadruple" alliance would now act together in regard to the Egyptian question and that they were already bringing pressure to bear upon the

[17] *London Times* July 1, 1891.   [18] *London Times* July 11, 1891.
[19] *Neue Freie Presse* July 4, 1891.

Sultan to induce him to conclude an agreement in regard to Egypt.[20] Other reports said that the four allies were planning to recognize Ferdinand of Bulgaria and to force the Sultan to accept the union of Bulgaria and Eastern Rumelia as an accomplished fact.[21] Marschall's presence in England led to reports that conferences of great importance had taken place and that a formal protocol had been signed.[22]

These few random references will serve to give a general idea of the excitement which resulted from the renewal of the Triple Alliance and the demonstrations of English sympathy for the central powers. "There is something like a storm in the air; the political atmosphere is saturated with electricity," wrote one French paper, accurately diagnosing the situation.[23] But what could the French do? To talk about the treason of England did not help much. Here and there a voice was raised in behalf of a settlement with Germany by compromise, but these were voices crying in the wilderness, and even a truly remarkable statement by Barthélemy Saint-Hilaire, a Nestor of French politics, went almost unnoticed.[24]

[20] *Kreuzzeitung* July 2, 1891; *Mémorial Diplomatique* June 27 and July 4, 1891.

[21] *Estafette* July 3, 1891; *Neue Freie Presse* July 4, 1891; *Mémorial Diplomatique* July 18, 1891.

[22] *Standard* July 6: "The words exchanged at Windsor will have an influence on events as decisive as written treaties." The *Hamburger Korrespondent* July 6, reported from London that a close understanding would be effected, though no treaty would be signed. The *Neue Freie Presse* July 10, reported from London: "Der formelle Ideenaustausch scheint das Verhältnis Englands zur erneuerten Friedensliga für sehr weitgehende Eventualitäten...auf das Genaueste festgestellt zu haben." On July 15 the same paper reported that a protocol had been signed at Hatfield. Cf. also Schulthess 1891, p. 102.

[23] *Mémorial Diplomatique* June 6, 1891.

[24] On June 16, 1891 the *Figaro* published an article by a "European Statesman" in which it was suggested that the hostility of France and Germany should be brought to an end by a compromise: France to receive Lorraine, while Germany should keep Alsace and receive Luxemburg, which it might fortify. In addition France was to give Germany a number of coaling stations in various parts of the world. This article raised a considerable discussion, especially outside France. The Barthélemy interview was published in *Gil Blas* early in July. The substance of it was that England had associated herself with the Triple Alliance and that France too should take her stand with the powers that were opposing barbarian Russia in the interests of European civilization.

For most Frenchmen the only hope of salvation lay in the prospects of an alliance with Russia.[24a] But relations between the two countries had become very cool since the French attempt to secure assurances of Russian support had ended in failure early in April. The Tsar had shown his displeasure by forbidding the Grand Duke Sergius to attend the opening of the French exposition at Moscow. The banquet to the city authorities had been cancelled in order to avoid political speech-making, and the reception accorded to the French representatives was so cool that they, including Flourens, left Moscow on the same day.[25] To this demonstration the French government replied in a very effective manner. At almost the same time the Rothschilds declared that they would be unable to float the new Russian loan which had been arranged for, unless the Tsar altered his policy towards the Jews. Whether this was merely a pretext it is hard to say. In the opinion of contemporary writers the hand of the French government was but ill-concealed.[26]

There followed a period of estrangement between the two countries which lasted for weeks.[27] The Tsar attempted to appease the French by graciously visiting the Moscow exposition on May 30.[28] This led to extravagant panegyrics in the Russo-

[24a] Cf., for example, G. P. VII, no. 1505.

[25] Report of the Belgian consul in Moscow, May 12, 1891 (Köhler p. 98, note 2); for the story of the Moscow exposition see the authoritative anonymous account in the *Nouvelle Revue* April 1, 1891 and August 1, 1891.

[26] Daudet: *Histoire Diplomatique* pp. 261-262; Greindl report May 14, 1891 (Köhler pp. 281-282). Needless to say, this incident called forth a great deal of comment in the press. The sum involved was no less than 500,000,000 rubles, and upon the failure of the loan Russian bonds immediately dropped 2.5 points. On the whole incident see further G. P. VII, no. 1566, note; P. Petit: *La Dette Publique de la Russie* (Poitiers 1912) p. 94, note; Jacob Viner: International Finance and Balance of Power Diplomacy, 1880-1914 (*Southwestern Political and Social Science Quarterly* March 1929, pp. 5, 6).

[27] Cf. *Münchener Allgemeine Zeitung* and *Kölnische Zeitung*, quoted in *Mémorial Diplomatique*, June 27, 1891; *London Times* June 9, 1891.

[28] On this see Un Diplomate (Flourens), in *Nouvelle Revue* November 15, 1892, p. 241; E. Flourens: *Alexandre III* (Paris 1894) pp. 332-334, in both of which places it is stated that the imperial visit was "plus qu'un acte de courtoisie ou de curiosité, c'était un grand acte politique." See also the anonymous article in the *Nouvelle Revue* August 1, 1891, where the visit is brought into connection with the rumors of the renewal of the Triple Alliance. Similarly the *Novosti* wrote:

phil Paris press, but evidently did not satisfy the French government. Freycinet and his colleagues were weary of the exchange of small courtesies. They wanted something tangible, something real and concrete, and so they continued to bring pressure to bear upon Russia.[29] Late in May a dispute arose in Bethlehem between the Franciscans and the Greek monks concerning the use of the door to the Church of the Nativity. As protector of the Roman Catholics in the east the French government was drawn into the quarrel. But, instead of attempting to reach an agreement with Russia, the French government instructed the ambassador at Constantinople, the Comte de Montebello, to take a vigorous stand. A note was handed in at the Porte, in which the Turkish authorities were accused of having given preference to the Orthodox Church. The French ambassador demanded an investigation and the punishment of the culprits. Since this did not suffice, Montebello made representations to the Sultan in person, whereupon the latter yielded and instructed the governor of Jerusalem to give satisfaction to France.[30]

This move was a masterpiece of policy on the part of the Quai d'Orsay. It touched Russia in a most sensitive spot and showed the Tsar once and for all that he could not expect French support unless he gave some adequate return. The statesmen in St. Petersburg were horrified, but at the same time they realized that, however distasteful, some substantial concessions would have to be made to France.[31] The army was about to be supplied

"The existence of the heartiest and most confiding relations between the two peoples, between the two mighty states of eastern and western Europe has now been demonstrated to the world. The existence of such friendly relations is particularly significant just now, when talk of the renewal of the Triple Alliance, the so-called League of Peace, is unending, etc."

[29] Both the *Figaro* and the *Matin* wrote rather bitterly of Russia, saying that the Tsar was laughing up his sleeve and thinking that he could count on the French army and the French funds without himself making any sacrifices.

[30] Wippermann 1891, volume I, pp. 379-380; *Mémorial Diplomatique* June 13, 1891; *Nouvelle Revue* July 1, 1891; the incident created a great stir and was discussed by the press for weeks.

[31] At first it was supposed in diplomatic circles that Montebello had acted after an understanding with Nelidov, but such was not the fact (Wolkenstein to Kálnoky June 19 and 29, 1891). The horror of the Russian foreign office is shown by the following telegram (Wolkenstein to Kálnoky June 26, 1891): "M. Schisch-

with new Lebel rifles and was, at the time, no match for the better equipped armies of the west. At the same time it was becoming evident that there would be a serious crop failure and probably a famine that would tax the financial power of the country. Germany, which had just concluded a commercial treaty with Austria-Hungary, showed no disposition to make concessions to Russia and no great desire to come to a tariff agreement.[32] All told, Russia was badly in need of financial aid, and this aid only the French could give. The failure of the Rothschild loan was a bitter pill for the Tsar. It drove home to him the importance of France and taught him that the statesmen in Paris were not to be trifled with.

Such was the situation when the renewal of the Triple Alliance became known. It has already been pointed out that in the spring of 1891 the Russians were by no means convinced of the pacific intentions of the Germans. Indeed, they thought there was considerable likelihood of an attack. Nevertheless, the Tsar had refused to accept the advances of the French. After all, he probably thought that in a crisis, in the event of a German attack upon Russia, the French would join the conflict in their own interest, no matter what their feelings towards the Russians as such might be. In fact, there was no great surprise in Russia at the renewal of the Triple Alliance. There was no really good reason to suppose that the combination that had been built up almost ten years before would be lightly dropped

kine se serait positivement plaint à chargé d'affaires d'Allemagne de Comte Montebello, dont attitude turbulente aurait mis cabinet de St. Pétersburg dans position essentiellement fausse en forçant M. de Nelidov de s'effacer pour éviter choc des deux gouvernements. Reconnaissance du statu quo à Bethlehem extorqué au Sultan par l'ambassadeur de France serait vexant pour la Russie qui pourrait à la rigeur le tolérer, mais non admettre formellement la legalité." Another official of the foreign office told Wolkenstein: "C'est une bête affaire. Nous avons dit toute la verité à M. le Comte de Montebello, qui a joué un rôle si intempestif. Toutefois il faut céder à la France, car en ne ménageant pas sa situation comme protectrice des intérêts catholiques en Orient, nous risquerions de voir passer cette protection entre les mains de l'Autriche-Hongrie, et avec vous une entente est impossible" (Wolkenstein to Kálnoky July 22, 1891).

[32] See especially G. P. VII, nos. 1626 ff. The Germans showed themselves quite unconciliatory, and the discussions lapsed late in May.

by its members. The Russians had almost reconciled themselves
to the existence of this pact.[33] Indeed, its existence was almost
a guarantee that France would join Russia in a European war,
while the Russians were free to do as they chose in the event of a
conflict between Germany and France or Italy and France.
The new element in the situation in 1891 was the position taken
by England. This was the crux of the whole problem, as has
been pointed out before. After all, if Fergusson declared that
England's sympathies were with the central powers and that
England meant to maintain the *status quo* in the Mediterranean,
what did this mean? So far as Anglo-Italian relations were
concerned it undoubtedly referred to northern Africa and was a
demonstration against France. But did not the *status quo* in
the Mediterranean also include the existing arrangements in
regard to the Straits? After all, the Second Mediterranean
Agreement of 1887, with its outspokenly anti-Russian provisions,
was known in St. Petersburg, and, if the community of interest
between England and Germany was now being so loudly proclaimed during the Kaiser's visit to London, was it not reasonable
to suppose that the Berlin government, which had refused to
renew the Reinsurance Treaty and which had resisted every effort
of the Russians to secure assurances in regard to Germany's eastern
policy, had now identified itself with England, Austria and Italy
so far as Oriental affairs were concerned? It was certainly a
reasonable supposition, and, as we now know, not so far from
the truth, for Marschall had given Lord Salisbury the assurance
in Windsor that, provided England were ready to defend her
interests actively in the Near East, the sympathy and support of
Germany could be relied upon.

The peculiar circumstances attending the renewal of the
Triple Alliance, then, proved to be the decisive factor in the
consummation of the Franco-Russian Entente. The nonrenewal
of the Reinsurance Treaty had made the Russians suspicious of
Germany's policy in regard to the Near East. But it was only
the background of the stage on which the Cronstadt demons-

---

[33] G. P. VII, nos. 1502, 1507; *Mémorial Diplomatique*, June 6, 1891, July
11, 1891 (quoting St. Petersburg letter July 5); *London Times* July 10, 1891.

trations took place. The abandonment of the famous Russo-German agreement had made the Franco-Russian Entente a possibility, but hardly a probability and certainly not an unavoidable necessity. Only the events of May, June and July 1891, brought matters to a head and placed the Tsar before the two alternatives: isolation in the face of a hostile coalition or an agreement with France. That he chose the latter was the most natural thing in the world. It was the German policy that drove Russia into the arms of France, and there is abundant evidence to prove that it was the ill-fated *flirt anglo-triplicien* that led to the conclusion of the entente between the two countries.[34] During the festivities in London the Russian press had

---

[34] The evidence on this point is so overwhelming that Bismarck's attempt to link up Cronstadt directly with the nonrenewal of the Reinsurance Treaty can no longer be regarded as convincing (see *Hamburger Nachrichten* October 24, 1896). He was, however, right in attributing the Franco-Russian Entente to the mistakes of German policy. Conclusive evidence that the apparent association of England with the Triple Alliance was what finally determined the Tsar may be found in the French *Yellow Book* nos. 3, 4, 5; Freycinet p. 465; G. P. VII, nos. 1502, 1507 and especially 1504, emphasizing the fact that the Russians felt not merely isolated, but threatened; VIII, no. 1726; the reports of the Belgian diplomats in Köhler pp. 284, 288, 290-291; Waldersee II, p. 213, and the following unpublished Austrian reports: Aehrenthal to Kálnoky July 7: "Es ist natürlich, dass die Kunde von der Erneuerung des Dreibundes, insbesondere die lärmende Art und Weise wie dieses Ereignis von der Mehrzahl der europäischen Blätter commentiert wird—dann die freudige Genugthuung, mit welcher sich Kaiser Wilhelm diesbezüglich ausgesprochen, in Russland in allen Kreisen verstimmt und irritierend gewirkt hat. Das Wort 'Dreibund' hat hierlands einen schlechten Klang und wirkt wie das rothe Tuch auf den Stier. Man hatte sich in den Gedanken hineingelebt, dass der Bund der Central-Mächte morsch und demnächst ausseinanderfallen würde. Das Triumphgeschrei der deutschen, oesterreich-ungarischen und englischen Blätter wird hier die Enttäuschung und den Ärger über die fehlgeschlagenen Hoffnungen nur vermehren." Aehrenthal to Kálnoky July 21, reporting a conversation with a high official of the Russian foreign office: "In St. Petersburg wird die Situation in Folge der Erneuerung des Dreibundes, des Besuches des Kaisers Wilhelm in England und der accentuierten Stellungnahme dieser Grossmacht, als eine ernste aufgefasst.... Durch die deutsch-englische Freundschaft hat eine Verschiebung der Kräfte in Europa platzgegriffen. Das reiche England mit seiner gewaltigen Flotte verfügt gewissermassen nunmehr über das grösste Heer des Continents und die Verbindung dieser Kräfte könne in ihrer letzten Consequenz nur den Krieg bedeuten.... Die Solidarität der russisch-französischen Interessen liege eben in der europäischen Constellation." Similarly Aehrenthal to Kálnoky August 7; Wolkenstein to Kálnoky August 21; Aehrenthal to Kálnoky August 23: "Was immer Kaiser Wilhelm mit dieser (englischen)

been unanimous in offering a solution for the problem: the time had now come for solidifying the relations between France and Russia by concluding a formal treaty. In fact the way out of the dilemma was so obvious that there was no longer any mistaking it.[35]

On July 23 the French squadron, under command of Admiral Gervais, anchored in the roadstead of Cronstadt, and therewith began a two weeks'demonstration such as the world had never seen. One festivity followed the other in rapid succession, the French sailors were lionized wherever they went, the *Marseillaise* resounded in the streets, and the Tsar himself visited the squadron and listened bareheaded while the battle hymn of the revolution was being played by the Russian band. The world at large was stupefied by this outburst, this "political orgy," which seemed to prove, beyond all shadow of doubt, the close sympathy that existed between the two peoples.[36]

Reise bezweckt, eines hat er bestimmt erreicht, sowohl in Frankreich wie in Russland ein Gefühl der Isolierung, der Beängstigung zu erzeugen, dass der Dreibund unter Deutschlands Führung, noch verstärkt durch den Anschluss Englands, sich allmählich in eine aggressive Coalition verwandle..... Jedenfalls hat das Coquettiren Kaiser Wilhelms mit England das Gefühl der Solidarität zwischen Frankreich und Russland mächtig gefördert." The French chargé, Count Vauvineux, remarked that the Tsar "saw red" (G.P.VIII, no. 1726), and told Aehrenthal: "Le voyage de l'Empereur d'Allemagne en Angleterre a admirablement préparé le terrain pour la visite de notre escadre; nous n'avions qu'à croiser les bras." Cf. also the utterance of Flourens, quoted in Singer p. 102; *London Times* July 30, August 18, 1891.

[35] The demand for an alliance with France began in earnest with a noteworthy article in the *Novoie Vremia* of July 1, in which it was argued that unless something definite were done the central powers would be convinced of the impotence of their adversaries and therefore precipitate a war (*London Times* July 2; *Neue Freie Presse*, July 2 and 5; *Mémorial Diplomatique* July 11). On July 8 the *Politische Korrespondenz* published an equally remarkable letter from St. Petersburg, in which it was demanded that the Franco-Russian Alliance should be concluded and made a nucleus for an association to include all the Balkan states, with the exception of Bulgaria: "Ein engeres Aneinanderschliessen Russlands und Frankreichs bildet nicht blos ein Wunsch des russischen Volkes, sondern angesichts der begleitenden Umstände der Erneuerung des Dreibundes eine unausbleibliche Nothwendigkeit der russischen Politik." Cf. also *Moskovski Viedomosti* July 7, *Novosti* July 13 and *Mémorial Diplomatique* July 18 (St. Petersburg letter July 12).

[36] The best account of the festivities, with the texts of all speeches and toasts, may be found in Philip Deschamps: *Le Livre d'Or de l'Alliance Franco-Russe*, (Paris 1898).

As a matter of fact, however, the Cronstadt Days had a greater significance than that, for they were the external evidences of the Tsar's determination to align himself with France. In a country like Russia, autocratically ruled, the government controlled even the popular manifestations. Had the government so desired, the demonstrations would have been much milder, perhaps nothing more than formal and courteous. But the events of the preceding weeks had determined Alexander to make the visit a counter-demonstration to the Triple Alliance and England.

"When people are in the unpleasant situation of being out in the physical cold, they almost always cuddle together as closely as possible," wrote the *Saturday Review*. "It may be admitted that the Triple Alliance has very ostentatiously proclaimed the fact that these two Powers are out in the cold. It is, therefore, we say, most natural that they should wish to keep each other warm."[37]

The same idea was expressed by Giers himself when he said that it was good to show that one had friends.[38] The French visit came very conveniently for the Russian government, which did its utmost to encourage the populace and create enthusiasm.[39] It is still a question whether the outbursts of joy in St. Petersburg were due more to the presence of the French or more to the letting down of the bars and the liberation from the usual restrictions. The Belgian representative thought that, given the same leniency on the part of the government, the enthusiasm would have been the same had a Chinese squadron appeared instead of a French one.[40]

"The Russians would be a strange kind of Slaves," wrote the *Saturday Review* rather aptly, "if, when the police allow it, and the weather is fine,

---

[37] *Saturday Review* August 8, 1891.   [38] G. P. VII, no. 1504.

[39] The *Marseillaise* was permitted only during the time of the visit, and it is said that the Tsar gave his consent to this concession only with great reluctance (Aehrenthal to Kálnoky July 30, August 23, 1891). It was also noted that the toasts were usually to France, and that the Republic was never mentioned. References to the Franco-Russian Alliance seem to have been completely taboo (Cf. *London Times* July 27, 1891). Aehrenthal repeatedly emphasized the fact that the renewal of the Triple Alliance was responsible for the large scale of the demonstrations (to Kálnoky July 7, 22, 30, 1891).

[40] Köhler pp. 298-300.

and there is plenty of liquor, and a brisk responsive people like the French to answer cheers, they could not get into a state of respectable excitement... It is not often that the weather, the police and the opportunity combine to give the Russians such a capital chance to slap a friend on the back and snub an unfriend."[41]

At first the European press took a distinctly optimistic point of view. There was more raillery than serious discussion. Even the *Vossische Zeitung*, one of the most respected newspapers on the continent, wrote in a humorous vein on July 25:

"The mighty squadron which yesterday cast anchor in Cronstadt Roads, carries instead of an arsenal of bombs and grenades, an inexhaustible supply of bottles and casks, and intends to open such a cannonade of champagne corks against the walls of the Russian fortress that the hearts of the Russians, already half-open, must infallibly capitulate."

But on July 28 there appeared in the *Novoie Vremia* the report of an interview with Admiral Gervais, in which the French commander said that

"the relations between France and Russia were of such a character as to result, whenever necessary, in a political combination which, although not in form, would in substance be perfectly analogous to the Triple Alliance."

This cryptic utterance was followed by an important despatch from St. Petersburg, published in the *London Times* on August 1. The correspondent stated that he had learned from a high authority that pourparlers for an alliance had for some time been carried on in Paris by Baron Mohrenheim and had resulted in a sort of *exposé des motifs* or draft of conditions which Gervais had brought with him to St. Petersburg. It was to be signed by the ministers of foreign affairs, war and navy, but not by the Tsar until the "psychological moment" had arrived. Gervais, it was pointed out, had spent his mornings regularly with Giers, Vannovski and Chikachev.

The Paris *Temps* stigmatized this story as a "diplomatic operetta," but there was at least a kernel of truth in it.[42] Hardly had the Kaiser left England when Giers, in a conversation with

---

[41] *Saturday Review* August 1, 1891.

[42] Paris *Temps*, August 4, 1891. The accuracy of the report was, of course, denied (*London Times* August 18, from St. Petersburg, August 16), and it received no credence in diplomatic circles (G. P. VII, no. 1508).

Laboulaye on July 18, spoke of the renewal of the Triple Alliance and the indirect accession of England to the same, and raised the question whether the new situation created by these events did not make a further step in the direction of a Franco-Russian Entente desirable.[43] The matter was immediately taken up in Paris by Ribot, Freycinet and Carnot, probably in consultation with Mohrenheim, and on July 24 the draft of an agreement was forwarded to Laboulaye.[44] In a covering letter to the ambassador Ribot pointed out that an alliance designed to effect in common certain political aims determined in advance might give rise to more or less delicate discussions, but a more general accord was evidently what Giers desired. The French desires were limited to two provisions: the two governments should agree to act in concert in all questions which might affect the maintenance of peace in Europe, and it should be understood that if the peace were really menaced by one of the powers of the Triple Alliance, France and Russia would, without delay, take the necessary measures to prevent surprise. In other words, France and Russia should even then come to an agreement to mobilize their forces simultaneously as soon as one of the nations of the Triple Alliance should mobilize its forces. These ideas were embodied in the draft of the agreement, where it was also stated in the clearest terms that the renewal of the Triple Alliance and England's apparent indirect adhesion to it had upset the equilibrium and made a closer understanding desirable.

This draft is typical of the views and aims of the French statesmen, for whom Germany was, of course, the chief enemy and the most dangerous opponent. The attitude taken by Giers towards the French proposals was, however, just as characteristic of the Russian stand. Giers desired, in the first place, to make the entente as general as possible, and to avoid specific military obligations. He objected, first of all, to the French attempt to confine the application of the accord to questions concerning the European peace only.

[43] L. J. no.. 3.
[44] L. J. No. 5, annexe, dated July 23; see also Freycinet pp. 466-467.

"Peace," he said, "might be troubled in Egypt or in China by considerations reflected by the situation in Europe. I refrain from speaking of Turkey, since that country is numbered among the European Powers."

Furthermore, the value of the entente would be too restricted if it provided only for the case in which the peace were threatened by one of the powers of the Triple Alliance.[45] He therefore proposed that the second clause of Ribot's draft be recast to provide that, in case the maintenance of peace were threatened, and especially in case one of the two contracting powers were menaced by aggression, the two parties should, if they thought necessary, take counsel in order to concert in advance measures to be taken immediately and simultaneously in case the eventuality contemplated should actually take place.[46] Such a provision, it will be noted, would hardly have changed the existing situation. Under its evasive circumlocutions Giers hoped to conceal his unwillingness to make any real concessions or to abandon Russia's freedom of action.[47]

It may be that the Russians had originally intended to go somewhat further than Giers' proposals would suggest. It appears that there was a change in the Russian attitude just prior to the discussion between the foreign minister and the French ambassador. The Austrian chargé d'affaires noted a distinct tuning down in the enthusiasm on about August 5.[48] The newspapers became less exuberant, and the enigmatic *Grashdanin*, the newspaper of the court circles, wrote:

"Nothing is more natural than the exchange of sympathy which is now taking place in St. Petersburg in honor of the French. But nothing is more unnatural than to try to transform this exchange of sympathy into a political rapprochement or, as some hotheads think, into a political union of the two states. Such an idea is ridiculous."[49]

---

[45] L. J. no. 7. Laboulaye to Ribot August 5, 1891.

[46] L. J. no. 9. Laboulaye to Ribot August 6, 1891; Freycinet p. 467.

[47] An excellent discussion of this interplay of motives may be found in Eugen Fischer's illuminating article: Der Sinn der russisch-französischen Militär-Konvention (*Preussische Jahrbücher* April 1923, pp. 65-98).

[48] Aehrenthal to Kálnoky August 5, 1891, noting "eine katzenjammerliche Stimmung."

[49] *Grashdanin* August 3, 1891.

The explanation for this change in the Russian outlook is not hard to find. On July 28 it had been officially announced in London that the French squadron would, on its return, pay a visit to Portsmouth. On the very next day Lord Salisbury delivered an important address at the Mansion House, in which he declared that he did not know the terms of the Triple Alliance and had not even asked what they were. He doubted whether he would have been told them even if he had asked. These two events, taken together, necessarily affected the policy of the Tsar. He had meant to take precautionary measures in view of the renewal of the Triple Alliance and apparent inclusion of the English in the League. The announcement of the coming Portsmouth visit indicated not only the anxiety of the English to maintain tolerable relations with the French, but also the reverse. It meant that the French desired to avoid taking an outspokenly Anglophobe stand. Through Salisbury's declaration it had at length become clear that the rumors of England's association with the central powers had been grossly exaggerated, and that the English government was still playing a lone hand in all matters of vital importance. In short, it had become evident to the Russians that they need not go to extremes to secure the assurance of French support.

The French, on the other hand, could not be expected to accept the Russian counterproposal. Their object was, of necessity, not to allow themselves to be bound without also binding the Russians. They had had enough of a friendship that was not only compromising, but dangerous. While Ribot raised no objection to the Russian suggestion that they should concert action in any matter jeopardizing the peace, even outside Europe, he did stand firmly by his determination to secure a more specific wording of the second clause. The text was to be made to read that, in case the peace were threatened or one party menaced by aggression, the two contracting parties should *agree to concert measures*, etc. The preliminary negotiations were, in other words, to be compulsory, not optional. The two powers were not to discuss whether measures should be taken, but rather what measures should be taken.[50]

[50] L. J. no. 11, Ribot to Laboulaye August 7, 1891. That the French saw

Giers naturally found this version too far-reaching. The Tsar himself appears to have become hesitant. Nothing, he told Laboulaye, must be done precipitously. It would be too dangerous to try to reach an accord by telegraph. It would be better to initiate Mohrenheim and to settle the matter with the new French ambassador, Montebello. By October or November, he hoped, an agreement might be reached.[51] Mohrenheim was, in fact, summoned to St. Petersburg and apparently argued his sovereign out of his doubts, for he returned to Paris late in August, armed with a draft dated August 19, in which the French suggestions were embodied.[52] It should be noted, however, that the agreement as concluded did not require the Russians to mobilize as soon as one of the powers of the Triple Alliance mobilized. The real wishes of the French had not been realized. The accord of August was, in fact, a compromise between the extreme demands of the French and the extreme desires of the Russians. The *entente cordiale* between the two powers had been called into existence, but it was itself only the first step toward an effective alliance.

The negotiations of August, 1891 are highly instructive, for, in a sense, they were the first passage at arms between the statesmen of the two countries. If an agreement had not been reached in the twenty years since the Franco-German war, the explanation is to be found in the difference of forms of government and above all in the divergence of interests. Only extraordinary circum-

through the Russian policy clearly enough appears from Ribot's letter to Carnot on August 11 (L. J. no. 16).

[51] L. J. nos. 13, 14, 15 (Laboulaye to Ribot August 8, 9, 10, 1891). Giers evidently took advantage of the precise demands of the French to discourage the Tsar (L. J. nos. 5, 16).

[52] Mohrenheim left Paris on August 12 and arrived at St. Petersburg on August 16. He was back in Paris on August 25 (Hansen: *Mohrenheim* p. 119; *London Times* August 14, 27). His call to St. Petersburg was certainly a defeat for Giers, who immediately retired to his estate in Finland, and later tried to make out that Mohrenheim had come on his own initiative. The decisive conferences between the Tsar and the ambassador appear to have taken place on August 18 and 21 (Hansen p. 119; Wolkenstein to Kálnoky August 20, 1891). Apparently the Tsar was especially anxious for assurances that the *revanche* party in France was not likely to get the upper hand (L. J. no. 16). The text of the agreement in L. J. no. 17 and annexe (Mohrenheim to Ribot August 27, 1891).

stances could bring the two together, and even then, in 1891, there was a latent suspicion and circumspection which is apparent in the discussions. The French were naturally enough interested primarily in the European problem, and desired reliable assurances of aid against German attack. Without that an alliance would be more dangerous than beneficial. It might lead to increased hostility on the part of England and Italy and possibly to a general conflagration in which France would be overwhelmed by hopeless odds, while the Russians, if they joined at all, would concentrate their attack upon Austria.[52a] France could not afford such a desperate policy. This explains the fact that as early as May arrangements had been made to send the fleet to some port in Great Britain after the Cronstadt visit.[53] So long as definite assurances from the Russians were not on paper, France could not entirely estrange England or drive her further on the road towards the Triple Alliance. There was nothing to gain and everything to lose by such a policy. After all, the Anglo-French antagonism centered upon Egypt, and so far as that particular problem was concerned the Russians in their own interest had been coöperating with the French ever since 1887. There was no need to buy assistance that was voluntarily offered. All this throws light upon the numerous pacific utterances by the leading French statesmen in the month or six weeks following Cronstadt, and upon the attitude of the saner section of the French press, which welcomed the Portsmouth visit and continued to urge moderation on the part of the French public.[54] There were, of course, French statesmen and thinkers who went even further. In an interview published in the *Manchester Examiner* the veteran Barthélemy Saint-Hilaire pointed out the danger lurking even in the mere conduct of negotiations:

[52a] L. J. no. 16.

[53] Daudet: *Histoire Diplomatique* pp. 308 ff., 316 ff.; Un Diplomate in *Nouvelle Revue* November 15, 1893, pp. 242-243; Freycinet pp 464-465; G. P. VIII, no. 1728; *Temps* July 30, 1891.

[54] *Liberté* August 3; *Temps* August 9; *Journal des Débats* August 9; *Liberté* August 11; *Gazette de France* August 11. See also the summarizing article in the *Spectator* August 15, 1891.

"I have no ill-feeling towards the Emperor of Russia or the Russian people, but we cannot shut our eyes to facts—the Russians want Constantinople, and France wants her lost provinces. . . . Supposing the object were attained, what would happen? France would have sacrificed her independence for Russian dreams of conquest. And if, as is far more likely, the coalition fell through in the face of the Triple Alliance, we should have courted the fate of Poland."[55]

The Paris *Soir* felt equally dubious and emphasized the need of not estranging England:

"The Czar's friendship will not be without danger to us unless it is supplemented by English friendship. One is a necessary insurance against the risks which the other might unexpectedly make us run."[56]

Gabriel Monod, too, raised his voice in warning, and spoke of the entente as a "strange drawing together of two countries the most unfitted for mutual understanding and coöperation."[57]

The Russian attitude has already been discussed at length. Fundamentally the Russians had no interest whatsoever in joining in a struggle to reconquer Alsace-Lorraine for the French. If it should ever come to war with Germany, France could be reckoned on in any case. What the Russians really desired was coöperation in the eastern question and in Asia, and particularly eventual assistance in opening the Straits for Russian warships. No less an authority than Baron Jomini himself had made an important declaration on the subject just before the Cronstadt visit. In speaking to the Boulangist deputy, Millevoye, he had said that Russia did not want Constantinople, but did desire the free passage of the Straits for her own and France's warhips:

"This is a very reasonable claim, which it could not be repugnant to France to support, and, if realized, its consequences would be incalculable in the pacific development of the resources of France and Russia. Moreover, when reassured by the signature of France, Turkey would be able to enjoy the fruits of this alliance. There would not even be anything to prevent France and Russia from undertaking to guarantee the integrity of the Turkish Empire against every contingency. It is only through the Dar-

---

[55] Quoted in the *Spectator* August 15, 1891, and generally discussed in the European press. See also the interview with Barthélemy published in the *London Times* October 21, 1891.

[56] *Soir*, August 21, 1891.

[57] Monod in the *Contemporary Review* December 1891, pp. 915 ff.

danelles made free that France will find the way to an effective alliance with Russia."[58]

The same argument was advanced in various forms by the Russian press:

"The question of the free passage through the Straits is for Russia of far greater importance than that of Bulgaria," declared the *Novosti*, one of the chief advocates of an alliance with France. "It is Russia's Alsace-Lorraine. On this point the interests of Russia and France are identical."[59]

But the French statesmen could not see this argument, though it was pressed upon them repeatedly by the Russophil journals such as the *Nouvelle Revue*. Madame Adam was far too clever a woman not to recognize the fundamental divergence of French and Russian interests so far as Europe was concerned. She had been pressing the need for an Asiatic basis for the alliance for a long time, and had been doing her utmost to give the entente a frankly anti-English bent, which was what the Russians desired:

"Our whole country has understood," she wrote after the Cronstadt visit, "that the policy of France and Russia can not only impose upon the hypocritical League of Peace a loyal peace, but that it holds England in check to such an extent that, instead of being the instigator or the arbiter of a war in which she would attempt to fish in troubled waters, she will be forced to gravitate to the Dual Alliance and discard the Triple; for her interests will be more and more in the hands of France and Russia, once they are united."[60]

Meanwhile Ribot and Freycinet were unconvinced, and feared more than anything the possibility that some of these delicate

[58] Published in the *Nord* (Brussels) and the Paris *Gaulois*, July 16, 1891.

[59] *Novosti* September 11, 1891. Other Russian papers demanded that France should aid Russia in the Far East as well, and there was a good deal of talk about France's ceding some of her coaling stations to Russia (cf. *London Times* July 31, August 25).

[60] *Nouvelle Revue* September 1, 1891; similarly August 15: "L'action combinée de la France et de la Russie dans l'Asie Centrale et en Indo-Chine sera triomphante le jour où elle deviendra effective....La *Nouvelle Revue* n'a cessé de repéter que la solution de la question d'Asie influencera celle de l'Europe." October 15: "Des solutions asiatiques sortiront les solutions occidentales favorables à la France....C'est en Chine et dans les mers de Chine que doit éclater et se faire agissante notre amitié pour la Russie. C'est la que nous travaillerons le mieux aux intérêts de la France et de l'Alsace-Lorraine."

matters might be made the subject of Russian demands.[61] Apparently the Russians realized the hopelessness of making the attempt at that time. As a result the really crucial questions were not even touched on. The two powers shook hands in passing, but did not set out on a promenade arm in arm. While Giers was declaring that Russia would have nothing to do with a warlike or chauvinistic France and would not go beyond defending a pacific and industrious France against aggression, the Paris press declared roundly that France could not afford to give Russia Constantinople or to allow her to come into the Mediterranean. France could support Russia in the east only on the understanding that the integrity of the Turkish Empire should be respected.[62] The London *Times* was not far from the truth when it summarized the general situation in the following terms:

"For the one side there is the vision of a free hand in the Balkans, on the Bosporus, and in Central Asia. For the other there is the resumption of Alsace-Lorraine; there is the restoration of a control in Italian policy; and there is Egypt. . . .A Frenchman is under an extraordinary delusion if he believes that the Czar would wage war with Germany to give the Republic the left bank of the Rhine. Russians are utterly deceived if they fancy that France would hazard its fortunes for the furtherance of their Eastern policy . . . .Englishmen can afford to contemplate with equanimity the attainment by France and Russia of an understanding which, in its positive phases, impresses them chiefly as a picturesque antithesis."[63]

The weeks following the Cronstadt visit were weeks of uneasiness and uncertainty, comparable to those which succeeded the fall of Bismarck. The Germans, who at first had regarded the

[61] L. J. no. 4 and especially no. 10 (Ribot to Freycinet August 6), where the Russian desire to enlist French aid against England is referred to as "L'écueil que nous avons prévu."

[62] Giers' utterances in *London Times* August 24; similarly Aehrenthal to Kálnoky September 2, 1891. On the French attitude see especially the *Siècle* September 9, 1891; *Die russisch-französische Allianz* von einem vormaligen Botschafter (*Deutsche Revue* October 1891).

[63] *London Times* editorial August 8, 1891. Similarly Stead in the *Review of Reviews* September 1891 and October 1891: "The Franco-Russian alliance, so far as such a phantasmal understanding can be called an alliance. . . .is not a thing that increases France's capacity for realizing her longing for revenge." See also Eckardt: *Berlin, Wien, Rom* pp. 15-23, and the much-quoted passage in the *Carnets de Georges Louis* I, p. 136: "Dans l'alliance, Constantinople et les Détroits forment la contre partie de l'Alsace-Lorraine."

whole Cronstadt demonstration as a joke, were dumbfounded when the news came that the Tsar had listened bareheaded while the *Marseillaise* was played.[64]   The announcement that the French fleet would visit Portsmouth could not have been very reassuring either.[65]   In any case the report of the Franco-Russian negotiations as published in the London *Times* on August 1 created a great stir.   It became clear to the statesmen in Berlin that the Tsar had finally cleared the ditch to the edge of which intriguers had thus far pushed him in vain.[66]   Nevertheless, they still relied upon the assurances which the Tsar had given at Narva, and would not believe that an alliance or formal agreement had been concluded.   To quiet their apprehensions they argued that the mass demonstrations in St.   Petersburg might have a greater effect on the domestic developments in Russia than upon the international situation.   The Tsar could not afford to allow the cult of republican France to go too far.[67]

In any case it was felt both in Berlin and in Vienna that there was no immediate danger of Russian action against the central powers.   What danger there appeared to be came chiefly from France, where the celebrations following the Cronstadt days continued to grow in number and in enthusiasm.   In spite of the fact that the French government, like the Russian, gave assur-

[64] G. P. VII, nos. 1502, 1504; similarly Aehrenthal to Kálnoky July 30; Wolkenstein to Kálnoky August 21, 1891; Köhler pp. 285-286.

[65] G. P. VIII, p. 70, footnote.

[66] Waldersee: *Denkwürdigkeiten* II, p. 214.

[67] G. P. VII, nos. 1503, 1504; Aehrenthal to Kálnoky August 5, 1891.   Both Schweinitz and Münster believed that, though no actual treaty had been concluded, military arrangements of a non-binding character had been reached by the French and Russian staffs.   Széchényi to Kálnoky August 6, quoting Caprivi: "Dass eine schriftliche Abmachung irgend einer Form zustande gekommen sei, das glaubt der General nicht.   Wohlaber die pourparlers über das, wie sich die beiden Mächte gegebenen Falls die Hände zu reichen haben würden...einen Schritt weiter gemacht haben."   Also Wolkenstein to Kálnoky August 21, and Greindl August 19, 25 (in Köhler pp. 291-294) who reports Marschall saying that he hoped "que l'espèce d'entente franco-russe établie à Cronstadt est un joujou dont on est engué maintenant, mais dont on finira par se lasser."   Writing retrospectively in 1904 Bülow asserted that the Franco-Russian Alliance had never caused the German government anxiety, because it recognized the fundamental divergence of interests (G. P. XIX, no. 6016).

ances of its pacific intentions, it was feared that the rapprochement between France and Russia might so enhance the self-confidence of the former that the way would be opened for a renaissance of the *revanche* party.[68] After all, the French statesmen, in a series of public addresses given at this time, all sounded a note of triumph along with their declaration in favor of peace. At the great autumn manoeuvres, which made a tremendous impression on military observers from all over the world,[69] Freycinet told the generals and foreign military attachés on September 9 that France owed her influence in the world to her army:

"Today no one doubts that we are strong; we shall now prove that we are also wise and that in a new situation we can maintain that calmness, dignity and moderation which, in evil times, prepared the way for our reconstruction."

At Carpentras, on September 14, Constans referred to

"the complete reconstruction of France, of her return to the world, so to speak." France, he declared, desired peace, but "peace such as can be understood by a great nation, which, without boasting as well as without weakness, preserves at all times the feeling of her strength and the anxiety for her grandeur."

On September 19, at a celebration at Rheims, Carnot in a toast pointed out that France had regained her position in the world. Ribot went even further, and at the dedication of a monument to Faidherbe at Bapaume on September 27, announced that "Europe, which for some time was undecided in regard to us, has at last done us justice." The ovations given the French fleet were the expressions of the general feeling that France was a necessary factor in the European balance of power. The series of

---

[68] G. P. VII, nos. 1505, 1509 ff., 1569; *Norddeutsche Allgemeine Zeitung* August 4, 1891; *Politische Korrespondenz* August 8, 1891. Caprivi considered the danger of war not more acute but more accentuated (Széchényi to Kálnoky August 5, 1891). Marschall went so far as to say to Herbette "Nous avons un nouveau Boulangisme sans Boulanger" and the French ambassador did not deny it (Köhler pp. 291-294). Prominent French writers like Jules Simon and Monod urged moderation, and there is no doubt that the government did its best to keep the demonstrations within reason.

[69] See especially the splendid article by Sir Charles Dilke: The French Armies (*Fortnightly Review* November, 1891).

ministerial declarations was fittingly closed by Freycinet on October 8, when he said in a speech at Marseilles:

"France, isolated and almost obliged to disinterest herself in what was going on about her, has become again an important factor in the European balance, thanks to the reorganization of her army and the wisdom of her diplomacy. Peace is no longer exclusively in the hands of others; it rests also in ours, and consequently is all the more assured."

There was absolutely no denying that the France of 1891 was a new France, and that she could no longer be looked upon as the Cinderella of European politics, no matter what might be the nature of the Franco-Russian relationship. The Germans were not exactly apprehensive, but they could not blink at the fact that something had changed since Bismarck's fall and that on general principles it would be wise to reckon on the new alignment for a long time to come. The very least that could be done would be to keep one's powder dry.[70] The idea of increasing the country's military resources was taken up in Berlin, and at the same time negotiations for commercial treaties between the various members of the Triple Alliance were pressed with renewed vigor.[71] Early in September the Kaiser and Francis Joseph met at Schwarzenau and discussed the general situation. It was evidently decided that a course of calm and conciliation would be most advisable.[72] At any rate, the irritating passport regulations for Alsace-Lorraine were largely abolished shortly after,[73] and on September 27 Caprivi, in a famous speech at Osnabrück, declared that the Franco-Russian rapprochement need not give rise to uneasiness:

"It is nothing more than the expression of a situation already existing; perhaps it means nothing more than the establishment of a European balance of power such as formerly existed."

---

[70] G. P. VII, no. 1505; Széchényi to Kálnoky August 6; Köhler, pp. 289-290.

[71] Waldersee II, pp. 214, 218, 231, 238. Bismarck's criticism of the "Trinkgelderpolitik" in tariff matters in *Gedanken und Erinnerungen* III, chapter xii; also Hofmann I, pp. 263-265. The difficulties on the Italian side were set forth by Rudini in the *Messagero* June 12, 1915 (quoted by Salvemini pp. 1917-1918).

[72] Kálnoky and Caprivi were present at the discussions. On the meeting generally see Chiala III, pp. 580-581, basing his account on the communication made to Rudini.

[73] G. P. VII, nos. 1750 ff.; Hohenlohe II, pp. 481-482; Eckardt: *Aus den Tagen von Bismarcks Kampf gegen Caprivi* pp. 8 ff.

Rudini spoke in almost identical terms at Milan on November 11, saying that the Cronstadt demonstrations had merely made manifest in visible form the existence of an equilibrium which would guarantee the peace of Europe. On November 14 Kál-noky, speaking before the Hungarian delegation, endorsed these views, and asserted that Cronstadt, in his opinion, did not represent the introduction of a new factor in the general situation.

While the Germans regarded the events of July and August with unjustifiable optimism,[74] the English took practical steps to take the edge off the new combination. There can be no doubt that they felt that the combination of France and Russia, if it had any basis in reality, would prove more troublesome to England than to the continental countries.[75] If there was no chance of Russia's joining France in war against Germany, there was at least the prospect of coöperation between the two powers in questions affecting the Mediterranean, the Near East and Asia. Even though France might not be ready to tear up the treaties regulating the passage of the Straits or to countenance the seizure of Constantinople by the Russian forces, there were numerous other problems on which the French and their Russian friends might find it profitable to combine their efforts. In Morocco it was quite evident that the French were preparing for action, and in Siam matters seemed to be drifting towards a crisis.[76] At the same time the Russians had sent an expedition to the Pamirs and were, it seemed, laying the foundations for a

[74] Schweinitz felt very keenly that Caprivi took things too lightly (*Denk-würdigkeiten* II, p. 424).

[75] Cf. for example Lee: *Edward VII* volume I, p. 688, referring to the entente of 1891, "which the Kaiser regarded as aimed at the Triple Alliance and other observers as aimed at England." Similarly Grey of Fallodon (*Twenty-Five Years*, [London 1925], volume I, p. 233) imagines Bismarck as saying: "The Alliance seemed directed more against England than against Germany, so bad were the relations of England with both France and Russia."

[76] On Morocco see G. P. VIII, nos. 1914 ff., especially the situation arising from the French designs on Tuat. It is interesting to note that the English attempted to keep in the background and to send Spain and Italy to the firing line. See also Haweis: The Coming Crisis in Morocco (*Fortnightly Review* April 1892) where the view is taken that France can have everything south of Fez if England can get Tangiers and the region north of the capital. On Siam see Lehaut: La Neutralité du Siam (*Nouvelle Revue* August 1, 1891).

new advance.[77] Even more important were two other questions, Egypt and the Straits, both of which caused much anxiety in London.

Lord Salisbury had, therefore, accepted with alacrity the French suggestion, made in May, that the French fleet on its return from Russia, should call at some Scottish port or at Plymouth.[78] For the moment the English were quite as eager as the French to avoid having their antagonism assume dangerous proportions. In the interval between May and August the situation had undergone serious changes. England had generally been associated with the central powers, and so much had been made of her supposed obligations to Italy and the Triple Alliance that there was reason to fear that the rapprochement between France and Russia might eventually result in a program of common action against England. As aforesaid, Salisbury had seized the opportunity presented by the Mansion House banquet to proclaim to the world that England was not initiated into the terms of the Triple Alliance. At the same time he arranged to have the Queen herself invite the French squadron to visit Portsmouth. Great preparations were made for its reception and Victoria came over from Osborne to review the fleet in person. At the same time courtesies were exchanged between the English and French Mediterranean squadrons at Villefranche.[79]

To the French sailors the Portsmouth festivities may have

[77] Cf. P. Lehaut: Les Echos de l'Extrême Orient. L'Alliance Franco-Russe (*Nouvelle Revue* June 8, 1890): "L'Union Franco-Russe dans toutes les questions de la Chine, c'est l'Angleterre réduite à l'impuissance." P. Lehaut: La Fortune de la Russie en Asie et la Question du Pamir (*Nouvelle Revue* November 1, 1891): "La suzeraineté de la Russie en Asie est une question française. Le Pamir nous touche plus qu'on ne pourrait le croire, et notre indifférence pourrait compromettre la paix du monde."

[78] Daudet: *Histoire Diplomatique* pp. 308 ff., 316 ff.; Un Diplomate in *Nouvelle Revue* November 15, 1893, pp. 242-243; Freycinet pp. 464-465; *Temps* July 30, 1891.

[79] Lord George Hamilton: *Parliamentary Reminiscences and Reflections* pp. 124-126, gives an account of the efforts made to please the French. The newspaper reception was very cordial indeed (cf. *London Times* July 29, August 19 ff.; *Saturday Review* August 15: "Admiral Gervais, it seems, wept at Moscow; and it must be our study, if possible, to draw tears down that manly cheek in London.")

seemed somewhat flat as compared to Cronstadt. It was no use
trying to make them love two women at one and the same time.[80]
Madame Adam scornfully declared that it was like viewing a
pasticcio after having seen a masterpiece, and the whole Boulangist press of Paris followed her in her denunciations of Freycinet and Ribot.[81] And yet the Portsmouth visit was hardly of
less significance than was the Cronstadt celebration. Looked at
from the English point of view it was meant to indicate that
England was not bound and was ever willing to come to an agreement with the French if the latter were willing. For the French
it meant that a real balance had been established in Europe, with
England controlling it. There still remained the possibility of
drawing over England if Russia proved unreliable. That the
English invitation was a masterstroke of policy on the part of
Lord Salisbury was generally recognized throughout Europe, not
only by the leading statesmen, but also by the chief organs of the
press.[82] The London *Times* declared tersely on August 26 that
the meaning of the Portsmouth visit was "that we wish to keep
well with all and to enter formal bonds with none." The *Saturday
Review* on August 8 expressed the same idea with even greater
bluntness:

"The balance of power—which parrot-pedants laugh at as a thing out of
date, and which is about as much out of date as the multiplication table—
is capable of being better preserved by two combinations than by one, if
the Power which holds the middle of the see-saw knows how to use its position. And by history and geography, by interest and temperament, Great
Britain is the Power which ought to hold that middle."

The Paris *Liberté* on August 3 came to the same general conclusions:

"We are at an extremely important moment in the European movement.
The Triple Alliance on the one hand, France and Russia on the other, are

---

[80] Daudet: *Histoire Diplomatique* pp. 316 ff.

[81] Mme. Adam: Lettres |sur la Politique Extèrieure (*Nouvelle Revue* August
1, 15, September 1, 1891). On August 17, there was a great Boulangist demonstration in Paris directed against the Portsmouth visit (*London Times* August 18,
1891).

[82] See especially Kálnoky's opinion, in G. P. VIII, no. 1728.

balanced against each other and constitute the equilibrium. We have every interest that England, placing herself in one of these balances, should not weigh it down with a weight as tremendous as it would be dangerous."

A French correspondent of the *Times* went so far as to declare that the invitation to the French fleet was the cleverest stroke in European politics in twenty-one years.[83]

As a matter of fact the effect seems to have been almost immediate. The French government, fearing lest Russia might inveigle it into an openly anti-English policy, seems to have put the damper on the activity of its representatives in Egypt. Whereas in June and July the French and Russian ambassadors at the Porte had worked hard to induce the Sultan to make demands upon the English and press for the evacuation of the country, the French appear to have done nothing further when, on August 3, Salisbury flatly refused to consider a Turkish project for evacuation and told the Turkish ambassador that the whole thing would have to be postponed until the cabinet ministers had returned from their vacations.[84]

Neither do the French seem to have done anything to assist the Russians to solve their problems. At the time there were many rumors that the Russians were preparing a *coup de main* against Constantinople or at least against the entrance to the Bosporus.[85] Whether there was any truth in these rumors it is impossible to say, but the possibility of a Russian move was generally recognized in the European chancelleries, and was the subject of constant consideration.[86] What lent color to the ru-

---

[83] *London Times* August 18 1891.

[84] G. P. VIII, nos. 1801 ff. The Sultan did, however, approach the English ambassador somewhat later with the proposal that an agreement be concluded in which the recognition of Turkish sovereignty should be the essential thing. This could obviously not have been due to French inspiration. See further *London Times* August 10, reporting the rebuff given to Rustem by Salisbury.

[85] *Hamburger Korrespondent* September 11; *London Times* September 12 (St. Petersburg September 11): A very competent person recently remarked: "To effect a landing and the possession of the mouth of the Straits would be an easy task. Russia is not building a dozen large ironclads of 10,000 tons apiece in the Black Sea for nothing;" *Saturday Review* September 12, 1891.

[86] Hence the German alarm at the loss of influence by England at Constantinople, and the constant efforts to induce the English government to reach an agreement with the Porte (G. P. VIII, nos. 1788 ff.; IX, nos. 2111 ff.).

mors at this particular time was the fact that on August 4 the Russian steamer *Moskva*, of the volunteer fleet, had been stopped by the Turkish authorities as it passed through the Straits with discharged troops from the Far East. To be sure, it was by no means the first time that ships of this class had been stopped. In April, 1891, for example, the *Kostroma* had been detained. The difficulty invariably arose from the peculiar status of the ships of the volunteer fleet, which, while ordinarily serving as transports, were generally ranked as auxiliary cruisers and had been built for use as raiders. As a result of the detention of the *Kostroma* the Russian ambassador, Nelidov, had made a vigorous protest, and the matter had been tentatively settled by the payment of an indemnity by the Porte, the ambassador, on his part, promising to notify the Turkish officials whenever a ship of the volunteer fleet carried munitions or armed convict guards. In the case of the *Moskva* the notification agreed upon had apparently not been given. Nevertheless Nelidov lodged a protest that almost smacked of an ultimatum: the Turks were not only to pay an indemnity, but were to remove the offending officer and to promise not to make trouble for the volunteer fleet in the future.[87]

To the uninitiated outsider the high-handed procedure of Nelidov looked very much like the beginning of a large scale action on the part of the Russians. Rumors began to multiply, and the excitement assumed large dimensions when it was announced on August 31 that Turkey and Russia had reached an agreement by which Russian warships were to be allowed to pass the Straits.[88] This was, of course, exaggeration, but before it became known that the accord dealt only with the ships of the volunteer fleet

[87] On the status of the volunteer fleet see J. B. Esperet: *La Condition Internationale des Détroits du Bosphore et des Dardanelles* (Toulouse 1907) chapter vii; *Neue Freie Presse* August 13, 1891; H. S. Edwards: *Sir William White* (London 1902) pp. 251 ff. On the incidents of 1891 see *Mémorial Diplomatique* May 16, 23, September 5, 12; *Preussische Jahrbücher* June 1891, p. 690; *London Times* August 13, 24, September 2, 1891; Wippermann 1891 part II, p. 360.

[88] *London Times* September 4 (Constantinople September 2); the Constantinople report (August 29) published in the *London Standard* August 31 had given rise to the mistaken version of the agreement (see *Neue Freie Presse* September 1, 3, 1891).

the world was further alarmed by the news that on September 3 the Sultan had dismissed Kiamil Pasha, the grand vezir who was looked upon as the champion of a policy of close relations with the Triple Alliance and England. Throughout Europe this was regarded as a great and resounding first victory for the new Franco-Russian combination and the Sultan's reply to Salisbury's refusal to discuss the evacuation of Egypt.[89] In England there was considerable uneasiness, especially as the reports of a Russian move against the Bosporus were supplemented by rumors of large Russian purchases of Suez Canal shares and of plans for Franco-Russian pressure upon the Porte to reopen the Egyptian problem. At the same time it became known that the Russians were negotiating with Persia for a commercial treaty of so extensive a nature that it would be tantamount to a protectorate, and that the Russian force in the Pamirs had turned back Captain Younghusband, who had been sent to investigate its activities.[90]

There was no denying the fact that on the surface it appeared as though the Franco-Russian demonstrations at Cronstadt had really borne fruit and that the beginnings of a vigorous campaign against England's position were being made. Incredible as it might seem, France was apparently abandoning her traditional eastern policy and supporting Russia in the Dardanelles question in return for assistance in solving the Egyptian problem satisfactorily.[91] If this were actually so, it would create a serious situation for the British. Their force in the Mediterranean was at best the equal of the French Mediterranean squadron and the Russian Black Sea squadron combined. In fact France had concentrated for the naval manoeuvres a larger force than she had brought together at any time since the Crimean War.[92] Lord

[89] G. P. IX, no. 2113; *London Times* September 5, 7, 1891; *Neue Freie Presse* September 4, etc.

[90] *London Times* September 3, 22, 26, 1891.

[91] *London Times* editorial September 8, 1891; this opinion was generally shared by other newspapers.

[92] On the French naval manoeuvres see the authoritative account by the anonymous writer in the *Revue des Deux Mondes* September 1, 1891. For the general naval situation in the Mediterranean see Lord Brassey: *Naval Annual*

Salisbury might insist that in his opinion a Russian attack upon Constantinople, if it came at all, would come through Rumania and Bulgaria, and that the British squadrons could reach the Dardanelles in time to prevent their seizure by the Russians, but this was probably merely camouflage, designed to arouse the Austrians and indirectly the Germans and to induce them to take an active part in opposing the Russian schemes.[93]

On September 13 the European world was startled by the news that a British force had landed on the island of Sigri, a barren rock just west of Mytilene. After a number of conflicting reports it was stated that the foreign office and the admiralty knew nothing of the landing and that presumably a few sailors had landed to stretch their legs or to carry out some manoeuvre. As a matter of fact, however, it appears that guns were landed and torpedoes sunk, and that the whole action was in defiance of a Turkish regulation which refused foreign warships permission to execute manoeuvres within fifteen miles of the Turkish coast.[94]

1890 and 1891. There was considerable difference of opinion as to whether the English could hold their own in a crisis, the difference depending on the stress laid on the imponderables. Hatzfeldt believed that at best the English and Italian squadrons would be equal to the French and Russian (G. P. IX, no. 2109). Admiral Sir Reginald Bacon: *A Naval Scrapbook 1877-1900* (London 1925) says (p. 154) "There is no doubt that had we gone to war with France in those days (1889) we might well have been swept off the face of the globe." On this important subject see further the comparisons of the fleets of the Quadruple Alliance (sic) and those of France and Russia in *La Marine Française* June, July, and October 1891, and the article on England in the Mediterranean (*ibid*. December 1891); G. S. Lefevre: The Naval Policy of France (*Nineteenth Century* October 1891).

[93] G. P. IX, nos. 2109, 2111, 2117. Salisbury was convinced that the Russians still entertained their former designs, but it is hardly credible that he should have seriously thought that an attempt would be made through Bulgaria. The English papers all emphasized the fact that the Straits treaties were international and that therefore it was unjust to expect England to take the initiative in protesting against violations.

[94] The details of the Sigri Scare were never completely cleared up. See the *London Times* September 15, 16, which tried to laugh the whole thing off. The *Morning Post* and *Standard*, both government organs, took the matter far more seriously. It appeared later that troops and guns had actually been landed and torpedoes planted and boats sent to "attack in the face of fire from the shore," but it is not certain whether the British fleet had permission to carry out such manoeuvres (Cf. *Saturday Review* October 3, 1891; *Kreuzzeitung* October 5; and es-

At any rate the English explanations were not taken seriously anywhere on the continent. It seemed extraordinarily queer that, just at the moment when the Dardanelles question was in the forefront and when there was so much talk of the possibility of a Russian attack upon the Bosporus or Constantinople, the English ships should have found it necessary to carry out so spectacular an action just off the coast of Mytilene and at the most strategic point near the entrance to the Dardanelles. There seems to be almost no doubt that the landing was meant as a warning to both Turkey and Russia, and as a reminder that in case of crisis the English could land promptly near the Dardanelles and seize control. At any rate, this was the interpretation given to the incident in both Paris and St. Petersburg.[95] The Sultan, on his part, was so alarmed that he immediately issued a circular note to the powers explaining that the Russo-Turkish agreement regarding the Straits did not involve a new departure from the regulations laid down in the treaties. It simply embodied clean-cut instructions which were designed to obviate further misunderstandings. To this Austria replied on September 30 and England and Italy on October 16 by taking note of the Turkish explanations and by expressing their deter-

pecially Edwards: *Sir William White* p. 253; Le Nocher, in *La Revue Française* October 1, 1891).

[95] *London Times* September 16; *Mémorial Diplomatique* September 19, 26, October 3, summarizing the French and the Russian attitude. The *Novoie Vremia* declared that the debarkation was nothing less that a little sortie against Russia. The German press also took the incident as very ominous, and published reports that Russia had offered to cancel part of the Turkish war indemnity if the Turks would agree to devote the money to fortifying the archipelago. In connection with the incident it should also be noted that the *Standard* immediately announced (September 15) that if Russia were to seize Constantinople, England and the Triple Alliance would drive her out again. The *Saturday Review* had written somewhat significantly as early as September 5 that the paper treaties were of no value, but "there are capital harbors in the North Aegean which would be pleasant change from Villefranche and Venice, even from Malta and Gibraltar, to our Mediterranean fleet. For the rest, what is the use of stretching parchment booms across a channel for ironclad rams?" On September 19 the same journal wrote: "It is by no means ill that people in general should be reminded that England is a Mediterranean Power, that alterations in the balance of power in that sea concern her at least as much, if not more, than they concern anyone else, and that she is both accustomed and able to do a great deal of the police of the seas in that direction."

mination not to allow the treaty provisions to be changed without the consent of the signatory powers. At the same time they reserved for themselves the same privileges which had been granted to the Russians.[96]

[96] Edwards p. 253; G. P. IX, nos. 2113-2116; Aehrenthal to Kálnoky September 30; Schiessl to Kálnoky October 3 and 17, 1891; the British press quite characteristically tried from the beginning to make out that the Straits Treaties were international and that, therefore, England was no more concerned than the powers of the Triple Alliance. The Austrians were considerably worried and the Italians ready from the beginning to second England in any action she might take. The Germans, however, refused to take action and took the stand that England was chiefly threatened and should take the initiative. This pleased neither the Austrians nor the English. Further details in *London Times* September 2, 3, 8, 11, 14, 18, 25, October 13; *Neue Freie Presse* September 13, 16, 19; *Mémorial Diplomatique* September 12, 1891.

CHAPTER VIII

PEACE OR WAR?

THE winter of 1891-1892, while outwardly calm, was a period of great tension and uncertainty. The calamitous famine in Russia occupied the attention of European statesmen, but there was no unanimity of opinion in regard to the possible consequences of the disaster. By some it was thought that the Russian government would attempt to find an outlet in a foreign war for the domestic difficulties which confronted it, while others took the stand that the famine would actually paralyze the great empire for some time to come. The English apparently took the latter view, though they believed in keeping their powder dry and maintaining a keen lookout.[1] All through the winter the question of the Straits and the problem of Central Asia were in the forefront of public discussion and it was generally agreed by experts that a Russian move, if it came at all, would come either in the Near East or the Middle East.[2] Lord Salisbury kept as

---

[1] Gladstone, for example, told Hatzfeldt that in his opinion Russia was so paralyzed that she could hardly be regarded as a decisive factor in European politics (Széchényi to Kálnoky March 10, 1892).

[2] See, for example, the articles by V. Bieberstein in the *United Service Magazine* (December 1891, January and February 1892) on the fortifications of Constantinople and the Russian Fleet in the Black Sea; in the *Revue Française de l'Étranger* (December 1891) on Russia's search for an open port; in the *Internationale Revue über die gesammten Armeen und Flotten* (January 1892) on the various possibilities of a Russian advance on Constantinople, and (February, March and July 1892) on the British position in the Mediterranean and the Dardanelles question; and in the *Neue militärische Blätter* (March, April and May 1892) on the Russian fleet in the Black Sea and the fortifications of Constantinople. See also the interesting anonymous book: *Darf Russland einen Angriff auf den Bosporus wagen?* (Vienna 1892) evidently written by an officer high in the Turkish service. Sir Charles Dilke wrote very frankly (*Fortnightly Review* January 1892): "As matters stand, in the event of a single-handed war at any time with France we should be unable to hold the Mediterranean, could only mask the French fleets at Gibraltar, and might find ourselves forced to undertake dangerous expeditions for the relief of Malta, while Cyprus must be given up and the Suez Canal and Red Sea be sealed."

much as possible in the background, but he left no doubt whatsoever that the English would not evacuate Egypt and that they would not tolerate a Russian advance on India. As a result of the expulsion of Captain Younghusband from the Pamirs the English ambassador at St. Petersburg was instructed to lodge a vigorous protest. Sir Robert Morier had a reputation for harshness, and the indications are that on this occasion he acted true to form. The Russian government was forced to apologize.[3]

As a matter of fact there is no indication that the Russian policy, directed by Alexander III and Giers, was an adventurous policy. Russia was not prepared for action, either by sea or by land, and the famine absorbed all available funds. No evidence is at hand to show that a move on Constantinople was planned, and even the activity in Central Asia seems to have been largely due to the military men on the spot.[4] While the Russians were apprehensive of England, they had done nothing until it appeared that England and the Triple Alliance had actually joined hands, and even then the Russian government had made every effort to avoid a provocatory attitude. When the coming visit of the French squadron to Portsmouth was announced, the Russian press was almost unanimous in declaring that Russia had no objection to the visit and actually welcomed it. It indicated that England was still free and anxious not to be identified too

[3] Sir Francis Younghusband: *The Light of Experience* (Boston, 1927) pp. 58 ff.; Wolkenstein to Kálnoky March 16, 1892; Galli: *Dessous Diplomatiques* p. 176; *St. James Gazette* October 15, 1891, forecasting a very lively exchange of notes. Younghusband himself says that on reporting to Lord Roberts at Gilgit in October 1891 the commander said: "Now's the time to go for the Russians; we are ready and they are not." The seriousness of the situation is attested by Dilke (*Fortnightly Review* January 1892): "Our one most real danger is an eventual advance by Russia on the northwest frontier of India." See further the Russian view in W. B. Steveni: Colonel Grambcheffsky's Explorations and the Indian Government (*Asiatic Quarterly Review* October 1891 and January 1892), and the English view in "An Indian Officer": *Russia's March towards India* (London 1894) II, pp. 252 ff. The Russian apology was made on February 25, 1892 (*London Times* February 26) but passed unnoticed, as no details were published.

[4] Schweinitz: *Denkwürdigkeiten* II, p. 438; G. P. VII, no. 1623; IX, nos. 2114, 2117; *Novoie Vremia*, quoted in *Mémorial Diplomatique* October 3, 1891; Aehrenthal to Kálnoky September 5 and September 16, 1891, and the evidence adduced in the subsequent part of the text.

closely with the Triple Alliance. It has been pointed out above
that even then the Tsar seems to have lost his interest in the
entente with France. In any case the Russian press was instructed to tone down its enthusiasm and hints were also given to
the French newspapers.[5] In Berlin and elsewhere assurances
were given by the Russian representatives that no hostile action
was envisaged, and that the entente signified peace.[6]

The French government adopted a similar policy, not so much
because of Russian pressure or because it knew that the entente
could not at that time be utilized for aggressive purposes, but
because the entente itself was not what the French statesmen
desired.[7] In its existing form it was more of a danger than a
protection. With no precise provisions for common action it
would be downright folly to become involved in difficulties with
a foreign power, especially Germany. Freycinet himself says
that the stipulations were not practical enough. Though common action was prescribed, the methods and conditions of such
action were left undetermined. As a logical complement the
conclusion of a military convention was indispensable. The
agreement of August was at best a *point de depart* for further
negotiations.[8]

After consultation with Mohrenheim it was decided to take up
the matter with Giers when he came to Paris in November, but
by way of preparation it was agreed, at the suggestion of the
Russian ambassador, to approach the Tsar immediately.[9] For
this mission M. Jules Hansen, a personal friend of Mohrenheim
and a sort of liaison officer between the Russian embassy and the

    [5] G. P. VII, no. 1509; Aehrenthal to Kálnoky August 5, September 2, 16, 1891;
London Times July 26, August 12, 1891.

    [6] G. P. VII, nos. 1573, 1577, 1578, 1579; Köhler pp. 111, note 2, 293, note 4;
Aehrenthal to Kálnoky September 21, 1891.

    [7] The French assurances, see preceding note.

    [8] Freycinet pp. 468, 487; L. J. no. 16 (Ribot to Carnot August 11, 1891).
Already in his letter accepting the Russian draft (August 27) Ribot had suggested
the necessity "à confier à des délégués spéciaux, qui seraient désignés le plus tôt
possible, l'étude pratique des mesures destinées à parer aux eventualités prévues
par le second point de l'accord" (Ribot to Mohrenheim August 27, 1891; L. J.
no. 18).

    [9] Freycinet p. 488.

Quai d'Orsay, was selected. On September 1 he departed for Fredensborg, where the Tsar was sojourning with his Danish relatives. The aide-mémoire which he carried with him developed in full the idea of a military convention. The Triple Alliance, it was argued, has at present the great advantage of military agreements. Mobilization by one member automatically means mobilization by the others. So long as Russia and France have no similar arrangement to fall back upon, victory will be jeopardized. Hence an agreement was suggested by which Russia and France should mobilize simultaneously the moment news of the mobilization of the Triple Alliance were received. Furthermore, it was proposed that the general staffs should negotiate in regard to concentration and simultaneous movement of troops.[10]

This aide-mémoire was submitted to the Tsar by Prince Obolenski, the master of the imperial household, on September 4, and on the following day Hansen received the reply. He was to tell Freycinet that the Tsar would consider the matter seriously and would take action upon it as soon as he returned to St. Petersburg.[11] As a matter of fact the Tsar, so far as can be determined, had at the time no intention of involving himself in military agreements. Cronstadt and the agreement of August was about all that the lethargic nature of the Tsar could stand at one time. He was already overcome by anxiety lest what he had done should become known, and lest the result would be an attack by either England or Germany.[12] All this did not prevent the Russian government from floating a loan of 500,000,000 francs in Paris on October 15. Hostile critics at the time went so far as to suggest that the whole demonstration of Franco-Russian solidarity was due to the Russian need of funds, and that the interest of the Tsar was limited by the extent of his de-

---

[10] Hansen: *Mohrenheim* pp. 132-135. Hansen knew a good deal about the military agreements of the Triple Alliance, as shown in his chapter x. Freycinet had already authorized Russian officers to open relations with the French general staff in order to study troop transport and supplies, and he himself corresponded regularly with Vannovski.

[11] Hansen: *Mohrenheim* pp. 135-136; Freycinet pp. 488-489; L. J. no. 19 (Mohrenheim to Ribot September 21, 1891).

[12] So Giers wrote to Mohrenheim (L. J. no. 16; cf. also no. 19).

pendence on French money.[13] This is undoubtedly a gross exaggeration, even though there is a certain element of truth in the theory that financial considerations influenced the course of Russian policy. Had Russian securities not been rejected in Germany the prospects of an agreement between France and Russia would have been distinctly lessened, and even in 1891 the Tsar, anxious as he was to avoid complications, made a definite attempt to reëstablish connections with Germany.

Giers had for sometime been planning a visit to the west. His health was wretched and a change of climate was desirable, so he decided to go to northern Italy, returning by way of Wiesbaden and Berlin.[14] At the same time he intended to accomplish some work while away, and evidently from the beginning planned a meeting with Rudini and with the German statesmen. The visit to Paris was not decided upon until later, but on October 13 and 14 the Russian minister conferred with the Italian premier and with King Humbert at Milan and at Monza.[15] We have no official information as to what was actually said at these meetings. All we know for certain is that Giers gave numerous assurances respecting the nature of the agreement with France and that Rudini reiterated what had been frequently said before in regard to the character of the Triple Alliance in its renewed form. All this is natural and not of particular significance, excepting as an added bit of evidence of Russia's desire to pour oil upon the troubled waters. The cabinets of Berlin and Vienna had been informed beforehand of the coming interview and no doubt were in complete sympathy with the pacific assurances given by Rudini in behalf of the whole Triple Alliance.[16]

[13] Köhler p. 112, note 2.

[14] Schweinitz: *Denkwürdigkeiten* II, p. 428, August 20, 1891.

[15] At the time it was repeatedly asserted that Giers had no intention of seeking interviews with other statesmen (cf. *London Times* November 20, 1891), but it seems almost certain that the Russian ambassador to Rome, Vlangali, sought the interview at Monza (*Times* October 16, 21; *Neue Freie Presse* October 14). Vienna was left out purposely (Schweinitz II, p. 428), though the Austrian ambassador was told that the failure to effect a meeting with Kálnoky was due to a misunderstanding (Wolkenstein to Kálnoky December 31, 1891). The visit to Paris appears to have been made largely in order not to estrange the French (*Times* November 20).

[16] Bruck to Kálnoky October 19, 1891, quoting Rudini; Schiessl to Kálnoky

A more difficult question is whether on this occasion an attempt was made by Giers to detach Italy from the Triple Alliance, and whether any special Italo-Russian agreement was concluded. At the time no statement was given out by the governments, and the whole thing was shrouded in mystery. Partly in view of these circumstances, and partly because of the presence of the Italian ambassadors to Vienna and Paris and the Russian ambassador to Rome, the Monza meeting gave rise to all sorts of rumors. It was claimed by some that Rudini had divulged the text or at least the content of the Triple Alliance and that in return Giers had offered to mediate between Italy and France, possibly to prepare the way for a commercial treaty. Later it was even asserted that Italy was to be protected against loss in case the Triple Alliance were defeated by France and Russia, and that Italy should, in case of war, change her status from that of an ally of the central powers to that of a neutral. All these statements were categorically denied by Rudini, who reiterated that he had acted with the full approval of his allies and that he had not gone beyond assurances of the pacific intentions of the central powers.[17]

On the whole the *démenti* issued by Rudini many years later is

October 31, quoting Marschall and Launay; Greindl report October 26 (Köhler p 105, note 1); L. J. no. 20; Chiala III, pp. 584-585; Billot I, p. 385; *London Times* October 14, 16, 1891; *Corriere della Sera* October 13, 1891; and Rudini's categorical statement in the *Corriere di Napoli* January 24, 1894: "Both before and after the renewal of the Triple Alliance I informed the Russian government as well as the other powers that the intentions of Italy and of the Triple Alliance were sincerely pacific. My interview at Monza with M. de Giers took place in the full light of day, after the visit of the French fleet to Cronstadt and with the full consent of the other allied powers, who were especially interested in allaying any anxiety in the mind of the Russian government."

[17] *London Times* October 20; *Gaulois* October 14; *Hamburger Nachrichten* October 13, 14, 1891; *Hamburger Nachrichten* January 18; *London Times* January 19; *Opinione* January 20, 23, 25, 29, 31, 1894; *Tribuna* November 23, December 2, 3, 10, 13; *Hamburger Nachrichten* December 11; *London Times* December 12, 1896. The denials of Rudini in *London Times* October 23, 1891; *Corriere di Napoli* January 24, 1894; *Neue Freie Presse* January 21, 1894; *Opinione* January 20, 22, 1894; *Italie* December 11, 1896. See further Salvemini pp. 488 ff.; Crispi III, p. 188; "Ex-Diplomat" in *Contemporary Review* December 1894, p. 771; Baron de Stieglitz: *L'Italie et la Triple Alliance* (Paris 1906) pp. 15-16; Wydenbruck to Kálnoky January 24, 1894.

rather evasive and inconclusive. At the time there was considerable uneasiness in Berlin as to what might have taken place at Monza.[18] Rudini appears to have contemplated the establishment of better relations with Russia from the very beginning of his ministry. Crispi had been cordially hated in St. Petersburg and his fall had been greeted with delight, for he had been a self-confessed advocate of the Bulgarian policy of independence.[19] The Russians, in revenge, had done their utmost to frustrate the realization of the Italian plans in Abyssinia.[20] There was no reason why Rudini should continue such a barren policy, and soon after forming his cabinet he instructed the Italian representative at Sofia to do nothing likely to dissatisfy the Russians. This conciliatory move had been received with joy by the Russian press and no doubt had delighted the Russian government, thus preparing the way for Giers' visit.[21]

Surely the Russian minister must have had some object in arranging the meeting with Rudini, and it seems only logical to assume that certain problems were discussed between the two statesmen. After all, it must be remembered that at the time almost all the really dangerous questions were Mediterranean questions, and that in problems of this kind Italy played a rôle quite out of proportion to her actual military and naval

[18] G. P. VIII, nos. 1928, 1932; in 1893, when there were many rumors about the agreement in diplomatic circles, Kálnoky was inclined to lend some credence to the reports, but Caprivi persisted in disbelieving them. Marschall sounded Brin on the subject during the Kaiser's visit to Rome in April 1893, but failed to discover the basis of the rumors (Wolkenstein to Kálnoky April 10, 1893; Szögyény to Kálnoky May 13, 1893, August 19, 1893). The newspapers were divided, the *Hamburger Nachrichten* insisting throughout that there was some agreement, and the *London Times* also (January 18, 19, 1894) writing very harshly about Rudini, who ran with the hare and hunted with the hounds. The *Neue Freie Presse* was inclined to accept Rudini's *démentis* (January 23, 1894).

[19] Wolkenstein to Kálnoky March 12, 1891; G. P. VII, no. 1618. During his visit to Berlin in 1889 Crispi had boasted that the sturdy resistance of the Bulgarians was due largely to the advice given by the Italian cabinet (Schiessl to Kálnoky October 31, 1891; Crispi *passim*).

[20] See especially the illuminating account in the *London Times* July 25, 28, 1891.

[21] Wolkenstein to Kálnoky April 11, 1891; the Austrian ambassador was rather worried to see his Italian colleague coquetting with the Russians with such surprising placidity.

strength. If the Franco-Italian dispute could be settled or at least shelved, there was every prospect that the peace would not be troubled, and |that was the primary object which Giers had in view.[22] Rudini, on his part, must have been eager enough to reach some sort of *modus vivendi*. He was not an enthusiastic supporter of an active colonial policy, like Crispi, but was keenly intent on straightening out the country's finances. Besides, the effort to enlist the aid of England in support of Italy's Mediterranean aspirations had been unsuccessful. In fact, Lord Salisbury was showing no enthusiasm in the Moroccan question, and Italy was being left more or less to her own devices.[23]

Perhaps even more important for Italy was the problem created by the rapprochement between the Papacy and the French Republic. Hardly had the renewal of the Triple Alliance been rumored when the *Osservatore Romano* on June 18 published a startling article forecasting the alliance between the Catholic Church and the French Republic. Both, it was argued, had been deserted and abandoned by all Europe, and the position of the one was similar to that of the other. The two would come together in the future as they had in the past. The Papacy in its isolation would turn to France, united and strong:

"In old Europe will be seen to arise the wondrous union between the Catholic Church and the Catholic democracy."

This article, published in the regular organ of the Vatican, could hardly have appeared without the permission of the Curia, and gave rise to a protracted discussion in the whole European press. The other organs of the Church, like the *Moniteur de Rome* and the *Civiltà Cattolica* supported the view of the *Osservatore* and declared that the Triple Alliance was the prison guard which kept the Church in bondage and servitude, an unholy alliance of Jews and Free-Masons which undermined the whole basis of Christian society.[24] The press of Italy and Germany retorted

[22] In an interview with a representative of the *Daily Telegraph* (October 13) he said that the Tsar shuddered at the mere mention of the word *war*.

[23] G. P. VIII, chapter liii (c) *passim*.

[24] Cf. Anonymous: Le Ragioni della Triplice Alleanza (*Civiltà Cattolica* X, pp. 257-270, August 1, 1891); and the *chronique politique* of the same journal

in like manner, and Crispi himself took up the cudgels, warning his fellow-countrymen that

"France, or at least the French press, wishes our defeat, and wishes to re-constitute the civil rule of the Church, and divide us into as many republics perhaps as there were, in the Middle Ages, States in the Peninsula."[25]

The situation, already difficult, was aggravated on October 2 when a French pilgrim wrote upon the visitors' book at the tomb of Victor Immanuel in the Pantheon the words: "Down with the House of Savoy. Long Live the Pope." The incident resulted in a monster demonstration in the Italian capital and necessi-tated extraordinary measures for the protection of other French pilgrims.[26]

Such was the situation when Giers arrived. Quite obviously Rudini must have been anxious to smooth over difficulties. Since he had, ever since February, asserted his desire for improved rela-tions with France, even to his own allies, there is no reason to suppose that he rejected a Russian offer to mediate in Paris. It seems very unlikely that he divulged the text or the content of the Triple Alliance, or that he concluded any agreement contrary to the obligations assumed by the Italian government under the treaties.[27] On the other hand it seems highly probable that the

volume XI, pp. 741 ff., August 16-31, 1891. In this connection the remarkable letter in Schlözer pp. 167-168 is interesting.

[25] Crispi: Italy, France and the Papacy (*Contemporary Review* August 1891, p. 177). For extensive quotations from the German and Italian press see Wipper-man 1891, volume II, pp. 109-121.

[26] Billot I, pp. 368-378; T'Serclaes II, pp. 205-211; Sir J. Rennell Rodd: *Social and Diplomatic Memoirs 1884-1893* (London 1922) pp. 257-258; *Civiltà Cattolica* XII, pp. 348 ff.; Manfroni II, pp. 194 ff.; Ferrata II, pp. 97 ff., etc. The incident was important because it precipitated the problem involved in the *ral-liement* in France. There is no question that great efforts were made at this time by the Curia to win the support of the French government for its new policy. Both Constans and Ribot were approached, though both were reluctant about coming out openly (see especially J. Piou: *Le Comte Albert de Mun* Paris, n. d. pp. 138-139; Ferrata II, pp. 64-67, 95), but the government attempt to restrict the pilgrimages to Rome led to a conflict with the irreconcilable part of the clergy and forced the issue, with the result that the Freycinet cabinet was finally overthrown on this very question.

[27] *Hamburger Nachrichten* October 14; *Neue Freie Presse* October 18; *London Times* October 16, 1891: *Hamburger Nachrichten* and *London Times* December 11, 1896.

Russian newspapers were right when they declared that Giers was desirous of making clear the true nature of Russian policy in regard to the Straits and that Rudini gave assurances that Crispi's Bulgarian policy would not be followed.[28] After all, neither of these questions had any direct connection with the Triple Alliance, and there was no reason whatsoever why Italy should not follow her own needs in these matters. The Italian government had worked hand in hand with the English in protesting against the passage of Russian ships of the volunteer fleet a few weeks before, and in Russia it was feared that this was merely the prelude to English action as in 1885.[29] Giers had a great interest in convincing Rudini that Russia had no intention of opening the Straits problem, and in securing from the Italian premier an assurance that Italy would not join Austria or England in an attempt to force matters in Bulgaria at a time

[28] *Novoie Vremia*, October 14, 1891: "It is especially important that Italy should be made aware of the real character of the Dardanelles question, which appears to have caused her some anxiety." Similarly *Novoie Vremia* and *Novosti*, October 15, asserting further that the Bulgarian question had been discussed. Compare also the important account in the *London Times* October 20 (Paris October 19), 1891; *Neue Freie Presse* October 14, 1891. All this is borne out by Rudini's own statement to the Austrian ambassador, Baron Bruck. The question of the monarchy in Portugal was discussed, and Giers promised to bring pressure upon France in case of a crisis. He furthermore reiterated that Russia was determined to leave Bulgaria and the whole Balkan problem alone. Rudini stated that the Balkans were only of secondary interest to Italy, but that her obligations required her to support Austrian policy in this respect. He expressed the hope that Russia and Austria would reach an agreement on this matter. Soon after, Vlangali, the Russian ambassador to Rome, came to Rudini and called his attention to the dangers of the Bulgarian problem and to the necessity of assuring the peace of Europe by finding a satisfactory solution. He suggested that Italy make a proposal. Rudini replied that he knew of no arrangement that would satisfy Russia, whereupon the ambassador replied that *he* knew of one, without saying what it was (Bruck to Kálnoky October 19, 1891). Schiessl to Kálnoky October 31, 1891 received a similar account from Marschall and Launay, and somewhat later Széchényi reported (November 29, 1891) that in Berlin Giers had expressed his satisfaction with his Italian stay and his conviction "dass sowohl der König als auch die Regierung der bulgarischen Frage gegenüber in korrektester Weise den Standpunkt des Berliner Vertrages festhalte."

[29] Cf. *Mémorial Diplomatique* September 12, 1891; shortly after, the Italian ambassadors to London and Vienna were called home to confer with Rudini, and it was believed that joint action by the Mediterranean coalition was being arranged for (*London Times* September 16, 1891).

when Russia was quite unable to take an active part. In return it would be only natural for the Russian minister to offer to use his influence in Paris to reëstablish better relations between France and Italy. Both Russia and France would be the gainers thereby, and in the end there was no knowing whether Italy might not eventually be brought over to the side of the new combination. In short, it seems more than likely that the Monza meeting resulted in some sort of verbal understanding which may be regarded as the initial step towards the Franco-Italian accords of 1900 and 1902 and the Racconigi agreement of 1909.[30]

From Monza the Russian foreign minister went to Wiesbaden and eventually to Paris, where he arrived on November 20. Here, too, his object was primarily to counteract any tendency to open the critical problems of European politics, notably the various questions pending in the Near East. The visit of Ferdinand of Bulgaria to Vienna and his reception by Francis Joseph in the summer of 1891, the ostentatious receptions accorded to Charles of Rumania in Italy and Berlin in October, and the constantly recurring rumors of attempts by Stambulov to secure recognition from the Porte naturally created uneasiness, and Giers feared that Austria might take advantage of Russia's weakness to extend her influence in the Balkans and to push on towards Saloniki. Then, too, there was the eternal Egyptian question, which the French regarded as of prime importance. The Russians, who had on previous occasions coöperated with the French in making difficulties for the English, were now anxious to avoid all complications that might lead to war. France must not be allowed to make use of the entente of August to force matters by bringing pressure to bear upon the Sultan. In other words, it would not do to precipitate a war against England for the sake of French interests in Egypt. The opposition to the English policy must, for the moment at least, be kept within the bounds of safety.[31]

---

[30] This is also the well-considered opinion of Salvemini (*Revue des Nations Latines* 1916, pp. 488 ff.). It seems unlikely that such subjects as Albania, Tripoli, or the possession of Rome were discussed, though there may have been some mention of the situation in Abyssinia (see especially de Stieglitz pp. 15-16; *Mémorial Diplomatique* October 24, 1891).

[31] Cf. especially the St. Petersburg letters in the *Mémorial Diplomatique*

During his very brief stay in Paris the Russian minister had two conferences with the French statesmen. The first of these, with Ribot, took place on November 20, and was of minor importance. Giers merely reported the result of his talks with Rudini and King Humbert and expressed the opinion that Germany, though irritated by recent developments, would not take action. Hence, he declared, the Tsar did not consider the necessity for extending the entente of August a pressing one. In closing he expressed the Tsar's satisfaction with the moderation shown by the French government after the Cronstadt celebrations.[32] The second conference was of greater significance, and was attended not only by Ribot, but by Freycinet and Mohrenheim.[33] Characteristically, the conversation turned almost entirely upon the question of the Near East. Giers repeatedly emphasized the fact that Russia's policy in that region aimed at the maintenance of the *status quo*. Russia had no designs on Constantinople and desired only that the Turks should retain it. Only in case the Austrians or the Greeks should make an attempt to gain possession of the city would Russia be prepared to take action. In the question of the Holy Places, too, he hoped that a satisfactory settlement would be arrived at on the basis of the *status quo*. In regard to Egypt, he expressed a willingness to

(January 16, 30, 1892) where it is emphasized that Russia favors "une rigoreuse expectative jusqu'à ce qu'il se présente des circonstances véritablement favorables pour une action tendant à l'évacuation de l'Égypte par les Anglais." In October the Russian representative in Egypt had joined his French colleague in a vigorous and successful protest against the new police regulations (*Affaires d'Égypte 1884-1893* pp. 394 ff.). This move was hailed by Mme. Adam (*Nouvelle Revue* November 15, 1891) as "la première sanction politique de l'entente franco-russe," and it does seem that some attempts were made by the French at this time to enlist Russian aid in inducing the Sultan to reopen the question of evacuation (cf. W. S. Blunt: *My Diaries* [London 1919] I, p. 71; Schiessl to Kálnoky October 9, 1891; G. P. VIII, no. 1807).

[32] Ribot's résumé in L. J. no. 20. Giers also paid brief visits of courtesy to Carnot and Freycinet.

[33] According to the *London Times* November 23, 1891, Flourens was also present at this conference, which lasted about an hour and a half. Flourens was certainly one of the most important workers for the alliance and it is to be regretted that so little is known of his activities.

lend France moral support in maintaining the capitulations, but that was all.[34]

So much we know of the conversations from the official French documents. Evidently the discussion ranged even further, however. For example, the problem of sending a Russian squadron to the Mediterranean was gone into. The Russians feared that England, knowing that in an Asiatic conflict she would fight without allies, would raise the question of the Straits by executing something like the Sigri scare and so precipitate a conflict. A Russian squadron would strengthen the French position and probably would deter the English from taking action at all.[35] Here again the evidence indicates that Giers was anxious to avoid a provocative policy of any kind, but was at the same time intent on securing protection against any attempt by Russia's enemies to take advantage of the famine and the domestic difficulties of the empire. The same point is even more clearly illustrated by the discussions regarding a military alliance. Giers reiterated his conviction that the Triple Alliance was not willing to risk a war. In other words he was forestalling any attempt to

[34] Résumé dated November 21, 1891 in L. J. no. 21. Cf. also Ribot to Cambon December 6, 1891, and Giers to Nelidov, December 14, 1891 (L. J. nos. 22, 24); Freycinet pp. 489-491; Hansen: *Mohrenheim* pp. 137-138. Giers made it plain that Russia did not want to become a party to a vigorous *démarche* at Constantinople and Nelidov was instructed to support France against England, but to avoid "tout ce qui pourrait évoquer le danger d'un conflit." The stress laid upon the necessity of winning over the Sultan to the Franco-Russian combination may perhaps be taken to indicate that Giers or Ribot had learned something of the discussions between the powers of the Triple Alliance and England as to the desirability of drawing Turkey into the Mediterranean agreement (Schiessl to Kálnoky October 9, 1891; G. P. VIII, no. 1805; IX, no. 2117).

[35] Hansen: *Mohrenheim* p. 137 goes so far as to say that the question of establishing a Mediterranean squadron was the chief topic of the conference. Cf. also L. J. no. 24. In January, 1892 the French government decided definitely to keep a permanent squadron in the eastern Mediterranean (L. J. no. 25; *Mémorial Diplomatique* January 23, 1892) and early in February Russia sent a squadron to the Levant (*Temps* February 11, 1892). The two squadrons followed each other closely in visiting Alexandria, and then met at the Piraeus. Naturally this demonstration gave rise to a good deal of comment. The Russian fear that the English would attempt to solve their Asiatic difficulties by precipitating a crisis in the Near East is well expressed by the *Novoie Vremia* (quoted in *Mémorial Diplomatique* October 3, 1891); cf. also Schiessl to Kálnoky August 27, October 3, 1891, quoting Marschall's opinion.

press the point by denying in advance that there was any immediate need for a more extensive agreement. When, notwithstanding this, Freycinet broached the question, he pointed out the difficulties of going into too great detail and "entrenched himself behind his personal incompetence and the desire of the emperor to treat this affair directly with the minister of war and himself (Giers)."[36] The Russian minister was not favorably impressed with his French colleague, and the latter in turn was disgusted with Giers' unwillingness to go beyond generalities or to discuss anything but the *status quo*.[37] The only concrete result of the conferences was the agreement between the two parties to send their representatives at Constantinople instructions to coöperate in convincing the Sultan that the object of the new entente was to uphold the existing situation, that it was not directed against Turkey and that, in case the Porte swerved too much to the side of the Triple Alliance and England, France and Russia would act accordingly.[38]

Giers had every reason to feel satisfied with his visit to Paris. He had gone there with the intention of preaching peace and of putting the damper on French hopes for assistance in a struggle to recover the lost provinces.[39] He had found that the French statesmen were by no means disposed to act so long as the obligations of the Russians were so ill-defined, and that they were quite aware that Russian aid in a war of revenge could not be hoped for. So far as the Russian government was concerned the

[36] L. J. no. 21. It appears that Freycinet succeeded in partially convincing Giers of the necessity for a military agreement (Freycinet pp. 489-491; Hansen: *Mohrenheim* p. 138).

[37] Aehrenthal to Kálnoky December 11, 1891; Wolkenstein to Kálnoky December 9, 1891; G. P. VII, nos. 1512, 1513.

[38] Ribot to Cambon December 6; Giers to Nelidov December 14, 1891 (L. J. Nos. 22, 24, 25). Ribot thus summarizes the policy to be followed: "Amener le Sultan à comprendre que nous ne voulons pas, mais que nous pourrions lui faire beaucoup de mal."

[39] Giers was always accusing his enemy, Mohrenheim, of encouraging French hopes of *revanche*. His own attitude needs no elaboration. In September he had told Aehrenthal clearly enough: "Qu'est-ce-que cela nous fait, si ces deux provinces restent allemandes ou redeviennent françaises?" (Aehrenthal to Kálnoky September 21, 30, 1891; cf. also Vinck's report of September 21, in Köhler p. 301).

entente of August was serving its purpose in restraining France and at the same time giving Russia the necessary assurances that France could be counted on if war were forced by the action of the Triple Alliance or England.

The Russian minister had intended, from the first, to visit Berlin on his return trip to St. Petersburg.[40] He had always been the advocate of good relations with Germany, and the evidence would indicate that he had signed the agreement with France only at his master's behest, and with great reluctance.[41] He was quite ready, then, to do his utmost to restore the former cordiality to the relations of the two countries, and to convince the German government that Russia had entered upon the understanding with France only because driven by dire necessity, and that there was nothing in the way of good friendship of the old kind. The story of the great loan which the Russian ministry of finance had attempted to float in Paris in October supplied him with additional arguments against the conclusion of a closer understanding with the French government. When the new securities were offered on the market they were immediately oversubscribed more than seven times, but within a very short time it appeared that the brokers were unable to dispose of them to investors. The price had fallen so rapidly that in the end the Russian ministry of finance had been compelled to buy back large amounts in order to save itself from a complete debacle. Apparently France could not even be relied upon to supply the funds of which Russia was so badly in need.[42]

The Russian government had anticipated difficulty in disposing of so large a loan and had from the beginning sounded diplomats and bankers as to the possibility of German participation. Jewish banks like Mendelssohn and Warschauer in Berlin, who had had extensive dealings with the Russian government in the period prior to 1887, were quite ready to reëstablish con-

---

[40] Aehrenthal to Kálnoky September 16, 1891.

[41] In speaking to the French statesmen he had insisted that the initiative had come from him, not from the Tsar (L. J. no. 21) but this does not seem to me to be conclusive.

[42] The checkered history of the loan is given in Daudet: *Histoire Diplomatique* pp. 262-279. See also Petit pp. 94-95.

nections, but when the affair became known there was such a popular outcry that the German government, which had only been lukewarm from the beginning, let its disapproval become known to the firms concerned.[43] After the debacle in Paris it was hoped that Giers might be able to bring about a change of mind in the German government, and do at least something towards paving the way for the conclusion of a tariff treaty between the two countries.[44] Russia was bound to suffer from the agreements between Germany and Austria-Hungary, Italy, Switzerland and other powers, concluded in December. Giers raised the subject during his stay in Berlin from November 23 to 25, but received little encouragement. Marschall said that the German government would be ready to examine any proposals that might be submitted, but he did not exhibit any tendency to come even halfway and made it clear that Germany was suffering less from the existing unsatisfactory situation than was Russia.[45]

The attitude of the Germans was no more accommodating when the conversation turned to political matters. The Kaiser, in fact, found it impossible to give the Russian minister more than twenty minutes before hurrying off to a review. Caprivi and Marschall both maintained an attitude of reserve and allowed Giers to do almost all of the talking.[46] Under the circumstances the conversation could hardly go beyond generalities. The Russian minister began by explaining that the entente between Russia and France was the result of the noisy renewal of the Triple

[43] Marschall insisted to Giers that the German government had remained strictly neutral (G. P. VII, no. 1515) but Schiessl to Kálnoky September 28 and October 31, 1891 made it clear that this was not quite the whole truth. See also the inspired article in the Berlin *Post* September 28, 1891. Further press comment against the loan in Wippermann 1891, volume II, pp. 88-90.

[44] Schweinitz was sounded out by M. Sack, the director of the St. Petersburg Banque d'Escompte, but replied that German public opinion was too strongly opposed (Aehrenthal to Kálnoky October 29, 1891).

[45] G. P. VII, nos. 1515, 1633, 1634; Schiessl to Kálnoky November 20, 24; Széchényi to Kálnoky November 29, 1891. Giers was very badly impressed with the attitude of the German press (Wolkenstein to Kálnoky December 9, 1891). An article in the *Novoie Vremia* (see *Mémorial Diplomatique* October 10) had made it clear that the Russians intended the loan as an earnest of good relations.

[46] *London Times* November 25, 1891; *Mémorial Diplomatique* November 28, 1891; Wolkenstein to Kálnoky December 8, 1891. Cf. also Cyon p. 429.

Alliance. He then minimized the importance of the Cronstadt demonstrations and pointed out that the Tsar could not avoid listening to the *Marseillaise* because he could not very well invent a new anthem. The failure of Alexander to visit the Kaiser was due to his peculiar character, and nothing was meant by it.[47] Beyond these explanations Giers spent most of the time in expatiating upon his visit to Paris, which, he insisted, had pleased him immensely. He had found the French statesmen wedded to the idea of peace, which they regarded as necessary for the maintenance of the conversative Republic. The idea of revenge was current only in a small circle of chauvinistic die-hards. It was not even mentioned by the ministers, in fact neither Alsace nor Lorraine had been named in the course of the conversation. The present French government desired nothing more than good relations with Germany. Furthermore, it had no ill feeling towards Italy and had no intention of restoring the temporal power of the Pope or of propagating republican doctrines in either Italy or the Iberian Peninsula.

According to M. Giers the French government was quite as much attached to peace as the government of the Tsar. The famine alone made it impossible for Russia to act, quite apart from other considerations. Besides, the question of French revenge did not even exist for the Russian ministers. As for the problem of the Near East, Russia had largely lost interest in Bulgaria. The whole Bulgarian affair had sunk to the status of a *question de dignité*. Russia would leave Bulgaria alone, and would even agree to recognize a Protestant prince, if he were duly elected in the place of Ferdinand. Finally, in regard to the

[47] On September 25 and again on October 31 the Tsar had passed through German territory without indicating a desire to see the Kaiser. The latter, on the other hand, was very anxious to effect an interview and consequently took the incident very tragically, going so far as to speak of an insult to the German nation and referring to the Tsar as his personal enemy (Schiessl to Kálnoky September 29; Aehrenthal to Kálnoky October 25, 29, November 12, 1891; Waldersee II, p. 223; Johannes Haller: *Aus dem Leben des Fürsten Philipp zu Eulenburg-Hertefeld* [Berlin 1924] p. 78; Wolkenstein to Kálnoky November 23, 1891). The Tsar's real reason for not meeting the Kaiser was probably that he feared being questioned about Cronstadt and did not want to play the hypocrite (L. J. no. 21; Köhler p. 306).

Straits, Russia was quite content with the existing arrangements. All she asked was that the ships of no other power should be let through to the Black Sea. All that was said in the secret protocol of the defunct Reinsurance Treaty was too far-reaching and was due to Shuvalov alone. The Tsar had no designs on Constantinople.[48]

Even with a considerable effort of the imagination it could not be asserted that Giers' visit to Berlin had any effect. Caprivi, it is true, reviewed the European situation a few days later in very optimistic terms and reflected many of the statements made by the Russian minister. Speaking in the Reichstag on November 27 he explained that there was nothing that the German government could have done to prevent the Cronstadt demonstrations. How could the Triple Alliance be blamed for the Franco-Russian Entente, when the former had been in existence for many years and had merely been renewed? There had, to be sure, been too many alarums and excursions connected with the renewal, and that had, no doubt, inspired other nations to stage demonstrations of their own:

"I am firmly convinced," he went on, "that the personal intentions of the Emperor of Russia are the most pacific in the world. No power now has so distinct a preponderance that it could undertake a war light-heartedly.... I am glad that our western neighbors have a government strong enough to hold the reins and I believe our eastern neighbors have realized that they can depend upon that government. The increased self-confidence of our western neighbors need not disturb us, because their nervousness will be thereby diminished."

This utterance seems to have represented the attitude of the German foreign office fairly accurately. Both Caprivi and Marschall appear to have realized that Russia would not assist France in a war against Germany, that France would not start such a war unless certain of Russian support, and that in any case the Russians were not ready to take action of any kind. On the other hand, public opinion was much more apprehensive, and the speech was intended to allay the general uneasiness.[49]

[48] G. P. VII, nos. 1513, 1514, 1515, 1633, 1634; IX, no. 2118. Széchényi to Kálnoky November 29; Wolkenstein to Kálnoky December 3, 1891; Greindl's report, December 6, 1891 (Köhler pp. 304-305).

[49] Marschall's statement to Giers (G. P. VII, no. 1515) is borne out by his

In spite of this reasonable and reassuring speech on the part of the chancellor, the relations between Russia and Germany became steadily worse during the winter, until the tension became so great that it overshadowed the antagonism between Russia and Austria and even the rivalry between Russia and England. The Franco-Russian Entente began to become a continental affair, much to the advantage of the English and the detriment of the Germans, and much to the delight of the French. For this unfortunate development it is hard to make any one person or any one event responsible. It was, in a sense, primarily due to the psychology of the Russian and German rulers. The Kaiser, for example, had been somewhat dubious about the Cronstadt events from the very beginning. The papal policy caused him some uneasiness, and the meeting of Giers and Rudini at Monza looked distinctly suspicious as viewed from Berlin. Not only was the domestic situation in Germany unsatisfactory, but the Triple Alliance itself, upon which everything had been staked in 1890, appeared to be weakening in the face of the new constellation. England showed no disposition to take the lead in Morocco or the Near East, Italy was ready to negotiate with the new combination, and even Austria seemed to be wavering.[50] All these factors had contributed to the Kaiser's nervousness, and the Tsar's failure to stop on his way through Germany seemed like the last straw, like convincing evidence that he did not desire to maintain cordial relations. From that time on the Kaiser regarded Alexander as a personal enemy and a danger to Germany.[51] All Giers' protestations could not alter this feeling, for, whatever the personal convictions of the Russian foreign

later assertion in G. P. XIX, no. 6016. Caprivi was also confident that, in the event of war, the Germans would be able to fight successfully even on two fronts (Wolkenstein to Kálnoky November 24, 1891).

[50] Kálnoky's statement before the Hungarian delegation on November 12 to the effect that Austria had no intention of extending her influence or domination in the direction of Saloniki was a *beau geste* towards Russia, while his remark in the Austrian delegation on November 27 in regard to the temporal power of the Pope created a great deal of ill-feeling in Italy (cf. especially Bastgen: *Die Römische Frage* III, pp. 308 ff.) Kálnoky was also dissatisfied by the attitude of the German government in connection with the Straits question (G. P. IX, no. 2116).

[51] Wolkenstein to Kálnoky November 23, 1891.

minister may have been, it was the Tsar who made the policy and the Tsar who had demonstrated his hostility. As the winter of 1891 to 1892 wore on the apprehensions of the German court became almost morbid, and there was constant danger that Caprivi and the moderate group, which argued that Russia was unable to act because of the famine, would be swept away by Holstein and his friends, who opposed any attempt at conciliation and argued that the famine would drive the Tsar into war as the only outlet from an impossible situation so, that Germany must be ready for an attack at any moment.[52]

At the time Alexander was tortured by the same agonizing fears. War on his part he knew would be impossible and disastrous, but just because of Russia's helplessness he became convinced that either England or the Triple Alliance or both would seize the opportunity to make him pay the penalty for the rapprochement with France.[53] With the eyes of suspicion he watched every little move made by his opponents, while the German policy in its larger aspects served to nourish his distrust even more. For instance, the unwillingness of the German gov-

[52] Wolkenstein, who occasionally went to Berlin as a special observer for his friend Kálnoky, continually emphasized the split in the German foreign office: "Es bestehen eben in dem deutschen auswärtigen Amte zwei Strömungen. Eine kluge, gemässigte, staatsmännische, an deren Spitze der Reichskanzler Graf Caprivi steht,—eine dünkelhaftunkluge, chauvinistisch-masslose, burschikos-unstaatsmännische, deren sichtbares Haupt Freiherr Marschall von Bieberstein ist." Holstein and Raschdau, he says, "sind die entschiedenen Gegner jeder Verbesserung der Beziehungen zu Russland" (Wolkenstein to Kálnoky February 2, 1892; also Széchényi to Kálnoky February 20, and Schiessl to Kálnoky February 30, 1892). Poultney Bigelow (*Prussian Memories* pp. 104-106) admits that at this time he strongly advised the Kaiser to make war on Russia. Cf. also Bigelow's article in the *Century Magazine* for May 1892, in which he says that the Kaiser and the best-informed German generals were convinced that Russia would attack at the earliest convenient moment. See also D. S. Macdiarmid: *The Life of Lieut. General Sir James Moncrieff Grierson* (London 1923) p. 106, for Bigelow's influence.

[53] The unpreparedness of Russia at this time hardly needs further discussion. Even the German generals and military experts admitted that Russia was in no position to attack (Lesczynski: Krieg ?, in the *Deutsche Revue* January 1892; von Engelnstedt: Die russische Kriegsbereitschaft, in *Preussische Jahrbücher* January 1892, etc.; Schweinitz in a classic report in G. P. VII, no. 1623; *Denkwürdigkeiten* II, pp. 434 ff.; Széchényi to Kálnoky February 20; Wolkenstein to Kálnoky March 1, 1892). Cf. also the Belgian correspondence in Köhler pp. 301-302; 112, note 3.

ernment to lend any assistance in the flotation of a Russian loan, while comprehensible in itself, looked to the Tsar like an attempt to precipitate an economic collapse in Russia.[54] This idea was strengthened by the refusal of the German government to consider favorably the Russian attempts to effect a settlement of the tariff question, which was one of the knottiest problems in the relations of the two countries. Russia was by tradition a protectionist nation and had not concluded commercial agreements with other states. In 1876 a regulation had been passed specifying that all revenue on imports should be paid in gold, which, on account of the low standing of the paper ruble, was tantamount to an increase of 33% on import duties.[55] The Turkish War made further increases necessary. In 1881 the tariff was raised 10% and by another increase in 1882 it became almost double what it had been in 1868. Another increase of 20% took place in 1885. Vishnegradski, who was minister of finance from 1886 to 1893, steadily pursued a policy of encouraging exports and discouraging imports. The excess of the former over the latter, which, in the time of Bunge, had amounted to 66 million rubles annually, rose to 307 million. The export of grain was encouraged particularly. As a result a rise took place in the value of the ruble, followed by a natural tendency to import more. In order to check this development, a further increase of the tariff was effected in 1890, and in July 1891 the whole schedule was revised with a view to protecting Russia's infant industries against German competition.

In retaliation Bismarck, intent on protecting German agriculture, had raised the import duty on grain in 1887.[56] But 1891 was a year of famine. There were bread riots in Berlin. Fur-

[54] Marschall admitted that the loan would be an excellent financial proposition and that the German bankers were smacking their lips at the prospect. Furthermore it would do much to reassure the world, but public opinion would not stand for it (Széchényi to Kálnoky January 9, 1892).

[55] The following account is based largely on V. Wittschewsky: *Russlands Handels-Zoll-und Industriepolitik* (Berlin 1905) pp. 135-149; A. Zimmermann: *Die Handelspolitik des Deutschen Reiches vom Frankfurter Frieden bis zur Gegenwart* (Berlin 1901) pp. 162-170.

[56] Count Sergius Witte: *Memoirs* (New York 1921) pp. 62-63 admits that Bismarck had warned Giers of the disastrous consequences of the Russian policy.

thermore, almost all of Germany's commercial treaties were due to expire early in 1892. The agreements of 1891, which are perhaps Caprivi's chief claim to fame, not only estàblished closer economic relations between the members of the Triple Alliance, but saved the day for Germany. Even the conservatives voted for them, though they involved a reduction on grain duties from 5 to 3½ marks per bushel.[57] This move turned the tables on Russia. Shuvalov, who had always been the advocate of friendship between the two countries, did his utmost to effect an agreement which would, once and for all, remove this source of friction.[58] Vishnegradski, hoping in this way to obtain a German loan, yielded. In March, 1892 Shuvalov went to St. Petersburg to arrange for negotiations, but the serious illness of Giers, who had seconded the efforts of Shuvalov, caused the idea to be dropped temporarily. Shuvalov returned to Berlin without instructions and the German government showed no readiness to take the initiative.[59] To make concessions to Russia would only have estranged Austrian agricultural interests, and besides, the Germans were hoping that the Russian menace might be removed by the economic and political disintegration of the country.[60]

[57] The agreements of 1891 are well treated from the economic standpoint by W. Lotz: *Die Handelspolitik des Deutschen Reiches unter Graf Caprivi und Fürst Hohenlohe* (1901) p. 78. See also Ashley: *Modern Tariff History.*

[58] In February 1892 he attempted to induce the Germans to make an agreement, but received a sceptical and cool reply. Shuvalov then went to Russia to arrange for a settlement on very broad and inclusive lines (Wolkenstein to Kálnoky February 29, 1892). It appears that the German government's attitude was largely influenced by the fear of offending the Austrians (cf. G. P. VII, no. 1634; *Mémorial Diplomatique* April 9, 1892).

[59] Hohenlohe II, p. 486; Aehrenthal to Kálnoky April 13, 1892; Széchényi to Kálnoky April 6, 16, 1892, reporting Marschall as saying that the German government was "kühl bis ins Herz hinein" in regard to these Russian advances. Schiessl learned later (Schiessl to Pasetti July 9, 1892) that Caprivi had been willing to grant the Russians the most-favored-nation duty on grain in return for a reduction of the Russian duty on iron and textiles, but that Holstein had opposed all concessions. Cf. also *Mémorial Diplomatique* April 9, 16, 1892; *London Times* December 30, 1891; January 2, April 4, 5, 8, 9, 19, 22, 1892.

[60] Kálnoky outlined the principles of this policy in a long despatch to Széchényi February 25, 1892: "Dieser äusserst schmerzhafte Process sollte jedenfalls *nur durch den inneren Zusammenbruch* und ungestört durch irgendwelche äussere

Another source of the Tsar's distrust lay in the so-called Polish policy initiated by the Caprivi administration. Reversing the policy of oppression pursued so long by Bismarck, Caprivi adopted a more conciliatory attitude.[61] In November, 1891 the new policy was definitely initiated by the election of Dr. von Stablewski to the archiepiscopal chair of Posen and Gnesen.[62] There were several reasons for this new departure. One was that the votes of the Polish deputies in the Reichstag were necessary in order to enable the government to pass certain naval appropriations. At the same time the election of Stablewski was intended as a *beau geste* towards the papacy.[63] Finally there was a military consideration, evidently advanced most urgently by Caprivi himself. While in no sense contemplating the resurrection of Poland, he hoped that if war should break out, the Poles could be induced to throw in their lot with the power which had treated them best.[64] In any case a reversal of the Bismarckian

Einflüsse vor sich gehen, welche alle Leidenschaften gegen das Ausland zum Ausbruche bringen könnten." The Berlin cabinet concurred entirely in this view: "Den kranken Bären nicht reizen und nichts tun, was den Krankheitsprozess stören könnte, damit er so lange er noch nicht ganz entkräftet ist, nicht veranlasst werde, noch in der elften Stunde mit der Tatze zum Schlagen auszuholen" (Széchényi to Kálnoky March 7, 1892). Cf. also G. P. VII, no. 1620.

[61] In the spring and summer of 1891 Polish laborers had been readmitted to Germany and permission had been given for private instruction in Polish in the public school buildings.

[62] The election aroused great opposition in a large part of the German nationalist press (See Wippermann 1891 II, pp. 226-231). A semiofficial article in the *Norddeutsche Allgemeine Zeitung* (November 4) expressed the hope that this concession would do much to strengthen the bonds which united the Polish districts to the rest of the Fatherland.

[63] G. P. VII, no. 1624.

[64] The Kaiser's marginalia on G. P. VII, no. 1624 show that he had no idea of *resurrecting* Poland and the editors say that there is nothing in the archives to show that an anti-Russian policy was intended. On the other hand Caprivi's intentions seem clear beyond question. Cf. Tirpitz p. 26: "Seine Polenfreundlichkeit hatte ihre Wurzel in dem Bemühen, für den Krieg uns dort kein zu feindliches Element zu schaffen." Also Waldersee II, p. 221: "Ich weiss nun wohl, dass Caprivi angefangen hat, mit den Polen zu rechnen, um sie gegen Russland zu verwenden, bin ja auch selbst überzeugt, dass wir ohne polnische Hilfe nur schwer den Krieg gegen Russland zu Ende führen könnten." See also Bismarck in *Hamburger Nachrichten* November 25, 1891; January 20, 1892; January 26, 1892; November 22, 1893, etc. (Hofmann I, p. 392; II, pp. 3,6-8, 233). See also *Preussische Jahr-*

policy could hardly fail to arouse the anger of the Tsar. Time and again it had been pointed out to him by German statesmen that the common interest of Germany and Russia demanded the suppression of the Polish aspirations, and that this common interest formed one of the strongest bonds between the two empires. A change in German policy could mean only one thing, and if the Tsar had any doubts they were quickly dispelled by virulent attacks launched by Bismarck against the government's policy, prophesying the bad impression it would make in St. Petersburg and justifying in advance the suspicions of the Russians.[65]

A third important source of agitation for the Tsar was the development of affairs in Bulgaria. In spite of the strong dictatorship of Stambulov intrigues against the existing regime continued. These were carried on chiefly by pro-Russian Bulgarians who had taken refuge in Belgrade and Constantinople and who received directions from a committee in Odessa, the existence of which was connived at by the Russian government, to say the least.[66] Stambulov, already irritated and impatient with the situation, was determined to take action, and already in August, 1891 there had been numerous reports that both Sofia and Belgrade were making preparations for war.[67] It was feared that the refugees and their supporters in the Bulgarian army would

bücher, December 1891, pp. 907-908: "Wir wollen die Polen weniger erbittern als je, weil wir in ihnen unsere Bundesgenossen sehen."

[65] Bismarck's utterances in Neue Freie Presse June 23, 1892; Hamburger Nachrichten October 24, 1896 (Hofmann II, pp. 372-373); and in many other places. For the effect on the Tsar and on Russian circles generally see G. P. VII, no. 1624; Wolkenstein to Kálnoky January 21, 1892; "Ich glaube aber unbedingt dass wenn es ein politisches Element, einen politischen Factor geben kann, der einen russischen Angriff auf Deutschland zu provozieren vermöchte, dieser Factor in einer gründlich umgestalteten Politik Preussen gegenüber Polen gegeben wäre." Waldersee II, pp. 221; Mémorial Diplomatique February 13, 1892 (St. Petersburg letter February 7). According to Lobanov the Poles themselves had hopes that the kingdom would be resurrected (Schweinitz: Denkwürdigkeiten II, p. 441); see also Preussische Jahrbücher July 1892, p. 122.

[66] Shuvalov, while admitting that the committee existed at Odessa, insisted that the government had nothing to do with it (G. P. IX, no. 2121; Széchényi to Kálnoky January 29, 1892).

[67] London Times August 31, 1891; Schiessl to Kálnoky August 22, 1891.

stage a revolution before New Years (O. S.) but nothing happened, due probably to the extensive precautionary measures
taken by the Bulgarian government.[68] The situation, however,
seemed so critical that shortly afterward Kálnoky instructed the
Austrian representative in Belgrade to protest against the activities of the Bulgarian emigrés and to demand that steps be
taken to check them. The Austrian note appears to have been
couched in very strong terms, and caused a sensation in St.
Petersburg, where it was felt that the Ballplatz, encouraged by
England, was attempting to foment trouble between Serbia and
Bulgaria in order to settle the Balkan problem to the detriment
of Russia and her Serbian client.[69] Shuvalov was instructed to
appeal to the German government to induce Kálnoky to exercise
a moderating influence upon the Bulgarian government and to
put an end to Austrian interference in the domestic concerns of
Serbia. The Germans had not been consulted by the Austrian
government, and in Berlin there was deep dissatisfaction with
the independent way in which Kálnoky had seized the initiative,
but it was not considered safe to drive matters to extremes.
Caprivi assured the Russian ambassador that the German attitude in matters concerning the Near East had not changed, and
that the interests of Germany were distinctly of a secondary
nature. He would not put pressure upon the Austrians

[68] The German government learned that the plot, which had many supporters
in the Bulgarian army, aimed at the overthrow of the government and the murder
of Ferdinand and Stambulov, and that it had been prepared in Belgrade with the
help of the Serbian government (note submitted by Reuss to Kálnoky January 6,
1892). Extraordinary precautions were taken in Sofia and Ferdinand did not
leave the palace for fourteen days (German consular report from Sofia, January
19, 1892—copy in V. A.).

[69] G. P. IX, no. 2120; the *Sviet* wrote that the action of Austria was to be regarded as the first indication of the beginning of the campaign against Russia by
the Triple Alliance (quoted in *Mémorial Diplomatique* January 30; see also the
numbers of February 20 and 27, 1892). The Austrians, at least, were convinced
that the Russian government had promised the Serbs support if matters came to a
head (Wolkenstein to Kálnoky January 23; Kálnoky to Wolkenstein January 27;
Kálnoky to Széchényi January 28; Wolkenstein to Kálnoky February 3, 1892).
See also Schweinitz: *Denkwürdigkeiten* II, p. 433. Both Salisbury in the Guildhall
speech and Kálnoky in addressing the Hungarian delegation had spoken in glowing
terms of the development of Bulgaria.

but at the same time he refused to support the Austrian action in Belgrade by instructing the German representative to protest to the Serbian government. Not until six weeks later did Kálnoky succeed in convincing the German government that some action ought to be taken in the matter, and then the Germans hardly went beyond a mild warning.[70]

Meanwhile negotiations had been opened between Vienna and St. Petersburg. The matter was, of course, a crucial one and greatly impressed the Tsar. On the outside it appeared as though the Austrians were taking the opportunity to punish the Serbs for the rapprochement with Russia which had begun in 1889 and which had found its most eloquent expression in the spectacular visit of the young King Alexander to Russia in the summer of 1891. The Austrians naturally protested loudly that their intentions were honorable and .that they desired nothing but peace, hence their interest in putting an end to the intrigues of the Bulgarian refugees. Finally the Russian government declared itself satisfied, but it may be doubted whether the Tsar was at all convinced.[71] The Crown Prince of Sweden, returning from a visit to Russia early in February, reported that the imperial family was living in a state of perpetual anxiety, as though on the eve of a catastrophe. The Tsar was undecided and obstinate and very much wrought up against the Kaiser, while everyone in St. Petersburg was persuaded that Germany desired war with Russia and was merely seeking a pretext.[72] Every little

---

[70] G. P. IX, nos. 2120-2124; Aehrenthal to Kálnoky January 31. Kiderlen complained bitterly to Aehrenthal of Kálnoky's action. Germany, he said, was inclined to abandon her policy of aloofness in Balkan matters, but would not allow her hand to be forced (Aehrenthal to Kálnoky January 31, 1891; Széchényi to Kálnoky January 29, February 1; Kálnoky to Széchényi March 7; Széchényi to Kálnoky March 11, 12, 1892).

[71] Schweinitz: Denkwürdigkeiten II, p. 433; G. P. IX, nos. 2123, 2124, 2125.

[72] G. P. VII, nos. 1622, 1624, 1625; Greindl report February 13, 1892 (Köhler pp. 305-306). The same thing is borne out again and again by the reports of the Austrian representatives (Wolkenstein to Kálnoky February 4, March 1, 30; Széchényi to Kálnoky February 14, 1892). See also Schweinitz: Denkwürdigkeiten II, p. 439, and the St. Petersburg letters in the Mémorial Diplomatique October 17, November 21, December 26, 1891; February 13, March 5, 26, April 2, 1892. General von Werder, who went to St. Petersburg to attend the funeral of the Grand Duke Constantine, was astonished at the "ungewöhnlich grosse Ani-

incident that could possibly be interpreted as directed against Russia enhanced the general irritability of the court. Thus, for example, the Kaiser's speech before the Brandenburg Landtag on February 24 made a very bad impression. When William announced to his hearers that he would lead the country out of the darkness and into the light, the Russians took this as an indication of coming trouble.[73] The ministerial crisis in Berlin in March, which threatened to end with the resignation of Caprivi, was looked upon in St. Petersburg as an attempt by the Kaiser to rid himself of the one adviser whose good intentions no one doubted.[74]

Meanwhile the Bulgarian question had entered upon a new and very troublesome phase. Ferdinand was becoming impatient with his high-handed minister Stambulov, and the latter himself felt that his political career would soon come to an end unless he could satisfy his master's burning desire for recognition.[75] During the summer and autumn of 1891 repeated attempts had been made to induce the Porte to make some concessions in this direction, but always without result. But in the latter part of March Stambulov adopted new tactics. He sounded the Aus-

mosität und Gehässigkeit gegen die deutschen Majestäten" (Wolkenstein to Kálnoky February 17; Széchényi to Kálnoky February 14, 1892).

[73] Giers was entirely perplexed by this speech and Russian opinion regarded it as a sympton of coming insanity (Pitteurs-Hiegaert's report in Köhler pp. 306-308; *Mémorial Diplomatique* March 5, April 2; and the venomous anonymous article entitled *William* in the *Contemporary Review* April 1892). The English government was apparently very uneasy lest the Kaiser should start trouble (Wydenbruck to Kálnoky March 9, 1892; *Mémorial Diplomatique* March 5, 17, April 2, 1892, reporting Germany and the Triple Alliance as wholly discredited and the Kaiser distrusted in London). According to Waldersee (II, p. 239) the Kaiser repeatedly spoke of how he would whip the Russians, and reports of these utterances undoubtedly reached the ears of the Tsar.

[74] The Tsar's confidence in Caprivi is attested by G. P. IX, no. 2124 and Wolkenstein to Kálnoky March 31, 1892, though there may be some truth in the suggestion made by Bismarck and Waldersee that Caprivi was liked because he was convenient (*Hamburger Nachrichten* March 29, 1892, in Hoffman II, pp. 144-145; Waldersee II, p. 239). According to the St. Petersburg letter of the *Mémorial Diplomatique* (March 26) the Russians were fairly praying that Caprivi might not be dismissed.

[75] Széchényi to Kálnoky March 11, 1892; Ernest Daudet: *Ferdinand I* (Paris 1917) chapter xii; *Mémorial Diplomatique* February 6, 13, March 17, 1892.

trian and German governments as to what their attitude would
be if the question were again raised by the Bulgarian government. Both governments were opposed, not so much to the step
to be taken as to the time chosen for it. It was feared that Bulgaria's action would give Russia an opportunity to open up the
whole question of Bulgaria's status and start a general conflict,
which was just what the statesmen in Vienna and Berlin desired
to avoid.[76] Of course the situation was viewed in the same suspicious way in St. Petersburg, where no motives were too bad
to be attributed to the German and Austrian governments.
Stambulov, however, could not afford to take consideration of
these factors. The pressure upon him was too great, and so, ignoring the advice of the friendly powers, he submitted a note to
the Porte on April 12, in which he complained bitterly of the
support given the Bulgarian émigrés by Russia and also of the
leniency shown by the Turkish government itself in dealing with
Bulgarian offenders. In closing he asked for Turkish support
against the plots of the émigrés and begged the Porte to assist
in consolidating the principality by recognizing the existing regime as legal. The Porte, no doubt after sounding out the powers
and finding that none was ready to urge Bulgaria's demands,
gave an oral reply in which it was declared that the Bulgarian
request for recognition was inopportune and that the Turkish
government could only advise the exercise of patience.[77]

[76] Széchényi to Kálnoky March 25, 1892; Greindl report March 30, 1892
(Köhler pp. 308-310).

[77] Dmitrov, the Bulgarian agent, called upon Nelidov and inquired what
would be the prospects of Russia's recognizing Ferdinand, but the reply was a
categorical "no" (Széchényi to Kálnoky April 16, 1892). The German government likewise took a negative stand (Széchéyni to Kálnoky April 20, May 14,
1892). The French, of course, stood by the Russian view, and the attitude of the
government is reflected in the instructions sent to Cambon on January 16, 1892
(L. J. no. 25). The English government apparently was also opposed to Stambulov's *démarche* (*Mémorial Diplomatique* April 23, 1892).

CHAPTER IX

ALLIANCE OR FLIRTATION?

IN view of the economic crisis in Russia and the government's great desire to avoid complications during the period of the nation's weakness, it was not to be expected that the Tsar would show any readiness to yield to French pressure for the conclusion of a military convention. Montebello was not a little surprised when, on being received by the Tsar in December, 1891, the latter made no mention of the entente, despite the hints dropped by the new ambassador.[1] The French were quite obviously disappointed, but they continued their efforts to further the good cause, because, as aforesaid, the entente of August was not only insufficient but dangerous in the extreme. In December, 1891 the French government had broken off relations with Bulgaria because of the expulsion of Chadourne, a French journalist accused by Stambulov of having systematically misrepresented conditions in Sofia. Chadourne himself does not appear to have been a very reputable character and there was but little sympathy expressed for him in the European press. In taking a strong stand the French government was quite evidently attempting to win the favor of Russia by proclaiming *urbi et orbi* that it did not recognize the existing regime in Bulgaria and meant to hold Stambulov in check. But the effect was absolutely nil. The Russians were genuinely interested in not raising the Bulgarian problem and showed no inclination to encourage or support the French action. In the end the matter was smoothed out through the general mediation of the powers, the Triple Alliance and Italy in particular taking an active part.[2]

The intervention of the Pope in behalf of the Franco-Russian Alliance was no more successful. In the autumn of 1891 exten-

---

[1] L. J. no. 23 (Montebello to Ribot December 11, 1891).

[2] Cf. *Mémorial Diplomatique* January 2, 1892. Ribot mentioned the good services of Italy in the chamber on December 28, 1891.

sive negotiations were being carried on both in Rome and St. Petersburg in the hope that some agreement between the Curia and the Russian government might be reached. In the course of these discussions the Pope unquestionably brought all his influence to bear to convince the Tsar that the so-called atheism of the French Republic was merely external, and that it would be to the interest of all conservative powers to support the existing moderate government in Paris in order to keep it out of the hands of the godless radicals.[3] At the same time His Holiness made no effort to conceal his displeasure with the members of the Triple Alliance, and the European world was, in the winter of 1891-1892, appalled at the growing estrangement of the Vatican and the governments of Vienna and Budapest.[4] In the meanwhile the French policy of Leo was finally brought to fruition. In spite of the unfriendly utterances made by Freycinet in November, 1891 during the cabinet crisis, and in spite of the hostile attitude of a large number of the French royalists, the Pope persisted in the policy which had been outlined by Cardinal Lavigerie in the Algiers toast. On January 21, 1892 the five French

---

[3] See Piou p. 140; K. von Golowin: *Meine Erinnerungen* (Leipzig 1911) pp. 361 ff.; Anonymous: The Policy of the Pope (*Contemporary Review* October 1892). According to an article in the *Figaro* in July 1892 the Russian representative at the Vatican, Alexander Izvolski, played an important part in effecting the agreement between the Papacy and the French Republic (Die russisch-französische Allianz, in *Deutsche Revue* December 1892). In December 1891 it was reported that Russia and the Vatican had come to an agreement (*Mémorial Diplomatique* December 12, 1891).

[4] There was considerable friction concerning the position of the Austrian representative, Count Revertera, and it was said that Rampolla attempted to get him recalled. The tension continued throughout 1892. See especially the vehement accusation against the Vatican, purporting to be written by a Catholic, and probably written by Geffcken, in the *Contemporary Review* October 1892, and the equally warm reply by Father Brandi, the editor of the *Civiltà Cattolica*: La Politica di Leone XIII e la Contemporary Review, in *Civiltà Cattolica* 1892, volume IV, pp. 513-536, 641-67. These articles were published in pamphlet form and translated into all European languages. A reply to Brandi was written by the writer in the *Contemporary*, under the title: The Pope and the Bible (*Contemporary* April 1893) and a rejoinder to this by Brandi: The Policy of Leo XIII (*ibid.* May 1893). The anonymous writer closed the discussion with a final article: The Pope and Father Brandi (*ibid.* June 1893). See also *London Times* August 5 and 6, 1892; *Mémorial Diplomatique* August 6, September 3, 1892.

cardinals issued a collective appeal to the French Catholics to respect the established authority and to do their duty as citizens loyally. On February 18 the *Petit Journal* published an interview with the Pope in which the latter recognized the Republic as a legitimate form of government. Two days later was published the famous encyclical in which the same views were reiterated and developed at greater length. It would be ridiculous to say that Leo was not concerned chiefly with the strengthening of the Church's position in France, but it would also be incorrect to deny the bearing of international politics on the action of the Vatican at this time. The recognition of the French government by the Papacy was meant to encourage the Tsar at a time when he was quite obviously wavering.[5]

Freycinet, in the meanwhile, had been proceeding on the theory that if any progress were to be made towards a military convention the initiative must come from Paris. He had instructed Miribel to draw up a preliminary draft to determine the distribution of forces and the means of coöperation between the two powers in time of war.[6] The draft was quite characteristically based on the assumption that any war engaged in by the two powers would be a defensive war, but it was also based on the fundamental French thesis that only the powers of the Triple Alliance could be considered as possible enemies. England was not considered at all. Miribel figured only that the Triple Alliance would be able to muster 2,810,000 men as against 3,150,000 at the disposal of France and Russia. According to his calculations, however, the forces on both sides would be about equal, because the members of the Triple Alliance would be able to mobilize more quickly than the Russians. In the second part of the draft the French views come out even more

[5] See particularly Freycinet chapter xiv; Tournier pp. 393-395; Billot I, pp. 410-415; T'Serclaes II, p. 403; Piou p. 141. Giers admired the Pope and expressed the hope that he would save France from godlessness (Wolkenstein to Kálnoky February 24, 1892).

[6] The draft is dated February 4, 1892 (L. J. no. 28, annexe). Freycinet (p. 500) gives the date as February 16 and says it was worked out by himself in concert with Saussier and Miribel.

clearly. Miribel argues eloquently that the principal attack
should be directed against Germany:

"Germany once conquered, the Franco-Russian armies can impose their
will upon Austria and Italy."

France would concentrate more than five-sixths of her forces
against Germany. Russia, it was recognized, would be more exposed to an Austrian attack than France to an Italian one, but
Miribel hoped that Russia would be able to concentrate one-half
of her forces against Germany and that particular attention
would be devoted to rapid mobilization against this, the chief
enemy, in order to tie up a part of the German armies in the
east and so weaken the resistance offered to the French forces.

This Miribel draft may be taken as the classic expression of
the French desiderata. The problem was to get the Russians
to accept it. At the time, in February, 1892, the Tsar was by no
means disposed to sign anything, much less a document which
was so far from an embodiment of the Russian view. Montebello
himself considered the draft inappropriate in form and sent a modified version back to Paris, while Giers, when informed that
a note was to be submitted, showed no enthusiasm whatsoever.[7]
After all, what the Russians needed at the moment was money.
The Paris market was glutted and the Berlin market closed. It
will be remembered that at this very time the Russians were
preparing to reopen negotiations with Germany for a tariff treaty, in the hope that once the commercial difficulties had been
removed it might be possible to float a loan.[8] Besides, with the
constant fear of a German attack upon him, Alexander did
not dare conclude a military agreement, the news of which might
leak out and thus precipitate a conflict. What the Russians
were doing at the time was to make use of the entente of August
to hold in check all and any adventurous proclivities of the
French.[8a] It was not likely that they would consent to sign an

[7] L. J. no. 29, annexe.

[8] G. P. VII, no. 1516; see also chapter vii above, note 59.

[8a] Giers had made much of this argument during his visit to Berlin (Széchényi
to Kálnoky November 29, 1891; Wolkenstein to Kálnoky December 3, 1891;
Greindl report, in Köhler pp. 304-305; Stead, in the *Review of Reviews* January
1892).

agreement which might act as a stimulus to action on the part of the French.

Evidently inspired by the Russian foreign office, the press of St. Petersburg and Moscow began a systematic campaign directed against the French demands. The *Viestnik Evropi*, one of the most moderate and reputable of the Russian monthlies, declared that an actual alliance would be a danger to Russia, for the famine made it impossible for Russia to act.[9] The *Novosti*, perhaps the most persistent protagonist of the alliance, pointed out that the agreement with France was never intended as a program of action, either in Alsace-Lorraine or in Bulgaria. It had been concluded only to safeguard the national interests of the contracting parties, and nothing more was necessary.[10] And, as though to strengthen the Russians in their view, at that very moment a serious ministerial crisis occurred in France, precipitated by the very policy through which Leo XIII intended to further the cause of the alliance. The fall of Freycinet made a very bad impression in St. Petersburg and was taken as added evidence that France had not yet reached that degree of stability which the Tsar regarded as the prerequisite for an alliance. The press minced no words in making it clear to the French that in the interest of good relations and the entente with Russia it was indispensable that Freycinet and Ribot should be retained. Mohrenheim himself warned the French authorities that the Tsar did not like "new faces," and undoubtedly considerations of high policy had something to do with the retention of Freycinet as minister of war and Ribot as minister of foreign affairs in the new Loubet ministry.[11]

The Russians thereupon frankly expressed their pleasure, but that did not mean that they were ready to proceed with the conclusion of the military convention. The Miribel draft was submitted to the Tsar on March 8, and he declared himself in agreement with the principle of reciprocal assistance and simultaneous

[9] *Viestnik Evropi* January 1892, pp. 395 ff.
[10] Quoted in *Mémorial Diplomatique* February 20, 1892.
[11] Freycinet p. 497; Wolkenstein to Kálnoky February 24, 29, March 1, 1892; *Mémorial Diplomatique* February 27, March 5, 1892.

mobilization. This in itself meant nothing, and Alexander's decision to talk the matter over with Giers and to have a French officer sent to St. Petersburg to talk over the details after the return of the imperial family from Denmark in July was merely a polite refusal to discuss the matter at that time.[12]   Why should the Russians accept the anti-German draft of the French, when the latter had just exhibited their unwillingness to support the Russians against the English demands for an apology for the ejection of Younghusband from the Pamirs?[13] In other words, the fundamental obstacle to an agreement for common action in anything but the most general terms still lay in the divergent interests of the two countries. The Russians needed the Germans and simply would not listen to any suggestions which might lead to an accentuation of the relationship between the two countries. The situation was bad enough without being made worse. In the opinion of the Russians the least incident would precipitate a German attack. To conclude an agreement against Germany, as the French wished, would be like courting disaster. In much the same way the French refused to come out openly against the English. Mme. Adam and her friends continued in vain their pleas for an alliance with Russia based on an anti-English policy in Asia, and redoubled their efforts to have the Anglophils, Ribot and Waddington, turned out. In December 1891 the *Nouvelle Revue* wrote:

"It is our interest to hasten the day when Russia shall have established her suzerainty at Cabul, at Kashar and at Lhassa....In Asia the consequences of common action are tangible; our minister of foreign affairs could solve the problem of Egypt more easily at Bangkok, at Kashar, in the Little Pamir and at Lhassa than at Cairo."[14]

In January the same arguments were again advanced, with the eloquent plea for an "Asiatic Cronstadt" in 1892. In March it was suggested that the sphere of action should also extend to

[12] L. J. nos. 30 and 31 (Montebello to Ribot March 12, 16, 1892).
[13] Wolkenstein to Kálnoky March 16, 1892; Galli: *Dessous Diplomatiques* p. 176.
[14] *Nouvelle Revue* December 1, 1891.

Africa, and that the two nations should coöperate in Abyssinia against England and her outpost, Italy:

"The Russians established in Africa means the evacuation of Egypt without a conflict, by the mere force of things."[15]

But the French statesmen were too clever to fall into such a trap. A conflict with England could only end in disaster, for it would almost certainly lead to the intervention of the Triple Alliance. However great the antagonism between England and France might be, it would be the merest folly to allow things to go to extremes. The French could no more afford to go to war with the English than the Russians could afford to go to war with the Germans.

Under the circumstances the question of the military convention hung fire for the time being. The Tsar had instructed Vannovski to draw up another project, which the latter did, basing it upon the French draft. After looking it through, Alexander passed it on to Giers and left for a prolonged sojourn in Denmark. Giers himself lay seriously ill in Finland and so long as the draft remained in his hands all the good will of Vannovski and Obruchev availed nothing.[16]

What was in the Tsar's mind when he left for Denmark was not the conclusion of a convention with France but the possibility of improving the relations with Germany. The negotiations of April had failed completely, and apparently Alexander felt that a reëstablishment of personal relations with the Kaiser would help to open up the possibility of a commercial or financial agreement. There may also have been in his mind the idea of a political rapprochement as a means of escape from the hateful French alliance and the possibility of complications in Europe. It is impossible to adduce any specific proof of such intentions, but it should be remembered that the relations between Russia and England in Central Asia were constantly becoming more

[15] *Nouvelle Revue* January 15, March 1, 1892. In the number of March 15 there is an article on the Franco-Russian Alliance by "Un Ermite de l'Oural," who argues that if France wants a real alliance she will have to take the same attitude towards England that Russia takes.

[16] L. J. nos. 32, 33, 38.

tense. In Persia and in Afghanistan affairs were moving towards a crisis and the Russian government was compelled to provide against all eventualities. The French showed no inclination to support the Russian action in the east, and so the logical solution would be the resurrection of the entente with Germany, which would give Russia the all-important assurance that Germany would not side openly with England and would not attack Russia in the rear while she was engaged on the Indian frontier. It might also decide the question as to whether or not the English could get their ships through the Dardanelles in order to attack the Black Sea coasts of Russia.[17]

On the whole the moment was not inopportune for the initiation of such a policy. In Germany domestic matters were in a bad state, and the "new course" was pretty thoroughly discredited. In foreign affairs the situation was equally unfavorable. The attempted rapprochement with England had not ended in anything tangible. In fact the English government seemed to be less anxious to pay for German friendship, since, in the winter of 1891-1892, it had become obvious to all the world that the old connection between the Kaiser and the Tsar no longer existed.[18] In Italy too the financial crisis had entered upon a decisive phase, and it appeared likely that the only solution would be a reduction of the Italian armaments. As a military factor Italy could no longer be reckoned on.[19] As for Austria, there had been nu-

---

[17] I shall return to a discussion of these factors later.

[18] G. P. VIII, no. 1809 betrays the disappointment of the Germans with the English attitude towards Turkey, and no. 1944 the dissatisfaction with the English attitude in regard to Morocco. Cf. also the London letter in the *Mémorial Diplomatique* April 2, 1892, on the strained relations between England and Germany.

[19] See especially G. P. VII, nos. 1435 ff. and the opinions of von Loë and Waldersee on the Italian army, in Leopold von Schlözer: *General-Feldmarschall Freiherr von Loë* (Stuttgart 1914) p. 187; Waldersee II, *passim*. It was generally supposed at the time that the German government was the obstacle to a policy of reduction of military expenditures, and some of the German papers took that stand, but it is clear from the German documents that actually the German government preferred a reduction of armaments to a general financial collapse (see *London Times* April 28; *Norddeutsche Allgemeine Zeitung* and *Berlin Post* May 19, 1892; Billot I, pp. 432-440). During his visit to Berlin in June Humbert voluntarily assured the German statesmen that no reduction was being contemplated (Schiessl to Kálnoky June 28, 30, 1892).

merous points of friction, and relations were none too cordial.[20]
A return to the policy of Bismarck, then, would have been advisable and logical, and the policy of Bismarck would have been exactly what the Tsar desired. To be sure he had great confidence in Caprivi personally, and it was probably never a question for him of Bismarck or Caprivi. It was a question rather of Bismarck or the Kaiser. Without Bismarck the foreign policy of Germany was really under the direction of the Kaiser or of those who succeeded in influencing him. There was the ever-present danger that Holstein and his anti-Russian group would carry the day. If Bismarck were back in power the Kaiser would of necessity be relegated into the background and one would know with whom one was dealing.[21]

There had, of course, been much talk at various times of a reconciliation between the former chancellor and his master. In December, 1891 efforts had been made in that direction, and in May, 1892 the question again came to the fore. The Kaiser seems to have been rather favorably disposed, but Holstein, of course, feared for his own position and for the policy which he sponsored, and induced first Eulenburg and then Caprivi to block the move being made in this direction. The Russians were no doubt very well-posted on all these developments, for it must be remembered that Shuvalov was a close friend of the Bismarcks and had kept up his connection with the former chancellor in spite of the Kaiser's frowns.[22] At any rate it seemed

[20] The German foreign office was particularly offended by Austria's apathy in the Chadourne incident and by her aggressiveness in the question of the Bulgarian refugees in Serbia. There was some very acrimonious discussion between the two cabinets in January and February 1892 (Aehrenthal to Kálnoky January 31; Wolkenstein to Kálnoky February 2, 1892). The Austrians also resented the German negotiations with Russia for a tariff treaty (*London Times* April 6), while the German newspapers criticized the Austrian military machine (*Kreuzzeitung* May 6, 1892). See also *Mémorial Diplomatique* April 9, 1892.

[21] Early in June 1892 the *Novosti*, one of the leading champions of the alliance with France, published an article stating that Russia would in no way object to the return of Bismarck (*Mémorial Diplomatique* June 11, 1892—St. Petersburg letter June 5).

[22] For the efforts made in December 1891 and Holstein's attitude see Haller: *Eulenburg* pp. 99 ff. The documents bearing on the attempts made in May and June 1892 are published in O. Gradenwitz: *Akten über Bismarcks grossdeutsche*

wise to the Tsar to do his share toward eliminating friction between the two countries. He had not yet returned the visit paid
him by William at Narva in 1891 and could hardly postpone
doing so much longer. He had decided, apparently at an early
date, to visit the Kaiser after the celebrations at Copenhagen,
and stuck to his purpose in spite of the pressure brought to bear
upon him by his Danish relatives.[23] The meeting would, he expected, be a rather painful experience, and so he arranged to
spend but one day at Kiel and return immediately to Copenhagen.
In Berlin there was even less enthusiasm. In fact Marschall,
who, of course, reflected the views of Holstein to a certain extent,
declared to the Austrian ambassador that the prospective visit
was regarded with complete indifference. It was at first decided that nothing short of a visit to Berlin would be accepted,
and Kiel was agreed upon only because the Tsar planned to
return to Denmark.[24]

On June 7 the Tsar and Tsarevich arrived aboard the imperial
yacht for a stay of some twelve hours. Both monarchs viewed
each other with distrust and still felt the strain of the previous
winter, but both were anxious to put an end to the crisis and
consequently did their utmost to make the meeting a success.
Political discussion was scrupulously avoided, for it was felt on
both sides that nothing could be gained by attempting explana-

Rundfahrt vom Jahr 1892 (Heidelberg 1922). See also the same author's: *Bismarcks letzter Kampf* (Berlin 1924) chapters xi and xii; Waldersee II, pp.
240-247. *The London Times* reported rumors of a coming reconciliation as early
as May 18, and on June 14 gave a full and essentially correct version of what had
happened. The *Tägliche Rundschau* announced on June 2 that the prospect of a
reconciliation was not bad. See also Hammann: *Der neue Kurs* pp. 25 ff.

[23] The Austrian representatives reported the possibility of a meeting as early
as April 16 (Széchényi to Kálnoky April 16; Aehrenthal to Kálnoky May 16;
Széchényi to Kálnoky May 28, 1892) and believed that it was primarily Shuvalov
and Giers who urged the Tsar to go (Széchényi to Kálnoky May 28; similarly
Waldersee II, p. 242). On the influence of the Danish royal family see Hohenlohe
II, p. 483; Wolkenstein to Kálnoky July 10, 1892. From the German documents
(G. P. VII, no. 1635) it appears that King Christian favored the meeting.

[24] Széchényi to Kálnoky April 16, May 30, June 7, 1892; Waldersee II, p.
241. The German press was unanimously of the opinion that the visit had no
larger significance and that nothing was to be expected of it (*London Times* June
3, 1892).

tions. The result was that the visit was much more successful than either sovereign had expected it to be. The personal contact had been reëstablished and the Tsar seems to have been reassured as to the Kaiser's intentions.[25] Most characteristic was his talk with Waldersee, whom he no longer suspected of anti-Russian intrigue since his dismissal and his rapprochement with Bismarck. The Tsar asked about the former chancellor and requested Waldersee to transmit his greetings. At this time the movement for reconciliation had not yet failed.[26] In any case the Tsar had given a clear indication of his own feelings in the matter, and there can be no doubt whatsoever that the Kiel interview had a very beneficial effect on Russo-German relations, though the effect was not of the tangible kind.

One can easily imagine how these developments were viewed in Paris. From the French standpoint things were going from bad to worse. In Morocco the English seemed to be pushing ahead and the mission to Fez of the notorious English consul in Zanzibar, Sir C. Euan-Smith, was watched with bated breath. It was regarded as certain that the English, probably supported by the Italians, were manoeuvring for an opportunity to seize Tangier and there appeared to be no method of effectively blocking them.[27] In Italy itself affairs were taking an unfortunate turn. Rudini was overthrown in May and succeeded by Giolitti, with Brin as foreign minister. Brin was known to have no love for France, and Giolitti too lost no time in declaring his adhesion to the principles of the Triple Alliance. Of course the financial sit-

---

[25] The numerous reports of the meeting agree in all essentials. See G. P. VII, no. 1636; Waldersee II, pp. 241-242; Széchényi to Kálnoky June 9, 10; Wolkenstein to Kálnoky June 11, 18; Aehrenthal to Kálnoky July 20; Caprivi to Reuss, communicated to Kálnoky, June 10. In parting the two monarchs embraced and Alexander said: "Nun denn, zwischen uns bleibt alles beim Alten," whereupon the Kaiser replied: "Ja, denn dieses entspricht ja ganz den Traditionen unserer Familien."

[26] Waldersee II, pp. 241 ff.; *London Times* June 14; as late as June 9 the *Hamburger Korrespondent* spoke hopefully of the possibility of a reconciliation.

[27] The Smith mission to Fez was one of the chief topics of interest discussed in the whole European press. Cf. G. P. VIII, nos. 1944 ff. Smith himself, in an interview published in the *Pall Mall Gazette* in March, asserted that England meant to open Morocco to commerce, and that Italy would coöperate if need be.

uation was desperate, but there was no consolation for the French in that, for it was felt that the real power behind Giolitti was Crispi and that, when it became evident that Italy was faced by the alternative of reducing armaments or going to war, Crispi would take over the reins and precipitate the conflict.[28] At the same time there was the danger of complications with Germany and a new incident like that of the visit of the Empress Frederick. The students at Nancy were planning an international celebration to which they invited members of all other universities, excepting only the German. It so happened that President Carnot was to be in the eastern departments at the same time and would have to put in an appearance at Nancy. The students themselves made no secret of their desire to turn the affair into a chauvinistic anti-German and pro-Russian demonstration, and the Czech delegation promised to do its level best to make this aspect of the celebration a complete success. In fact it was planned to make an excursion to a neighboring height very close to the German frontier.[29]

Quite obviously an event of this sort might easily lead to dire consequences. The press of Germany called attention to the implications of the meeting and the French press replied in kind. So serious did the matter appear that the German government made inquiries as to whether the French government would undertake to guard the German frontier against violation. Ribot and Freycinet were evidently panic-stricken for the moment and did everything within their power to throw cold water on the plans of the students. The excursion was transferred to another locality and the press was persuaded to put an end to the acrimonious discussion.[30] The celebration began on June 5 and was going forward quite satisfactorily when, on June 6, the Grand Duke Constantine, a close relative of the Tsar, suddenly appeared at Nancy to pay his respects to Carnot. His appearance

[28] L. J. no. 34 (Ribot to Montebello May 25, 1892); *London Times* May 18, 1892. Caprivi himself was not enthusiastic at the prospect of Crispi's return and described him as "ein unruhiger, hitzköpfiger und effecthaschender Politiker" (Széchényi to Kálnoky May 25, 1892).

[29] G. P. VII, nos. 1580 ff.; L. J. no. 34.

[30] G. P. VII, nos. 1580 ff.; Széchényi to Kálnoky May 28, 1892.

was made the occasion for a huge Russophil demonstration on the part of the students, and, coming as it did just before the meeting of the Tsar and the Kaiser at Kiel, it looked very much like a prearranged affair, like a means adopted by the Tsar to reassure the French people and to proclaim to the world the unimportance of the Kiel *entrevue*. The French press was jubilant and for the moment there was a revival of the spirit of the Cronstadt days. No arguments could make the press waver. "Subtract Nancy from Kiel and you have Cronstadt" wrote the *Novoie Vremia*, and this interpretation the French were only too eager to accept.[31] It was as though the Tsar had said: "Frenchmen, have no fear; if my body is at Kiel, my heart is with you," wrote the *Journal de Genéve*.[31a]

But the governments knew better, especially the French government, which had been trying in vain to get something substantial from the reluctant Russians. The French ministers had been so alarmed at the possible results of the Nancy affair that Ribot had redoubled his efforts to get action taken on the French draft. "Europe is calm," he wrote to Montebello on May 5, "but who can vouch that peace will long continue?" He pressed for action in St. Petersburg before July and wrote the ambassador to go over the head of Giers, if possible, and directly to the Tsar.[32] At the same time Freycinet asked Hansen to write directly to Alexander at Copenhagen requesting his consent to the mission of a French officer to St. Petersburg to treat directly with the minister of war and the chief of staff. To this request a favorable reply was obtained, but that was all.[33]

---

[31] *Novoie Vremia*, quoted by Mme. Adam in *Nouvelle Revue* July 1, 1892; similarly *London Times* June 8, which says that Constantine's appearance gave the celebration the character of an international demonstration, and June 9, where the visit is described as a "corollary to Cronstadt." *Mémorial Diplomatique* June 18, 1892; Billot I, p. 438.

[31a] Quoted by Daniel: *Année Politique* 1892, p. 175.

[32] L. J. No. 34 (Ribot to Montebello May 25, 1892); no. 35 (Ribot to Montebello June 23, 1892) speaking bitterly of Giers as "un esprit timore qui craint les engagements trop nets et qui aime les circonlocutions."

[33] Hansen: *Mohrenheim* pp. 138-139. The Tsar had already spoken on several occasions of inviting military men to the manoeuvres in order to discuss the question (L. J. nos. 23, 29, 31, 32).

As for the visit of the Grand Duke to Nancy, it must not be supposed that the French government welcomed it. In fact Carnot attempted at the last minute to dissuade Constantine from coming and the government seems to have been apprehensive of the possible consequences.[34] There were, however, no consequences, for in Germany it was not taken seriously. It seemed incredible that the Tsar should be so tactless as to stage such a counter-demonstration. Mohrenheim was immediately suspected of having been at the bottom of the thing, and the suspicions were justified.[35] It appears that the idea had occurred originally to Mohrenheim, who suggested it to the Grand Duke, a firm advocate of the alliance and an equally consistent enemy of Giers.[36] The matter was referred to the Tsar, who gave his approval, evidently without thinking of the possible implications of the visit.[37] In any case it was a clever move on the part of Mohrenheim or the Grand Duke, though it had no further effect than to throw dust in the eyes of the public. Far from having cold-bloodedly arranged the demonstration, the Tsar was infuriated when he heard of it and feared that it would jeopardize the

[34] G. P. VII, no. 1588.

[35] G. P. VII, no. 1588; in Vienna, however, it was at first believed that the visit had been planned as a counter-demonstration (G. P. VII, no. 1637; *London Times* June 8). The Kaiser learned of the incident on the afternoon of June 7, at Kiel, but was not impressed (*London Times* June 8; Széchényi to Kálnoky June 9; Wolkenstein to Kálnoky June 18, 1892).

[36] *London Times* June 11, 1892. Flourens in an interview claimed that the Tsar asked him a few weeks before to tell Carnot that Constantine would pay the visit, but there is absolutely no evidence to support this statement.

[37] The details in Hansen: *Mohrenheim* pp. 141-142, who, however, assigns the ultimate responsibility to the Grand Duke. Schweinitz and Münster both suspected Mohrenheim from the beginning (G. P. VII, no. 1588; Wolkenstein to Kálnoky June 8, 1892) and most diplomats in St. Petersburg were of the same opinion (Wolkenstein to Kálnoky June 18; Aehrenthal to Kálnoky August 2, 1892). The accounts given by Shishkin (Wolkenstein to Kálnoky June 11) and by a member of the Russian legation at Copenhagen (Aehrenthal to Kálnoky August 2) tally in all essentials with that of Hansen. Constantine's wife later told the Austrian ambassador that the Grand Duke had been led by Mohrenheim to believe that the Tsar wished him to go to Nancy (Wolkenstein to Kálnoky March 16, 1893). Cf. also the article on Mohrenheim by Fortunio (?Flourens) in *Mémorial Diplomatique* December 3, 1892, in which it is plainly stated that Mohrenheim took the initiative.

results attained at Kiel, by "blowing the pollen off the flowers."[38]

The succeeding months continued to be outwardly calm so far as international politics were concerned. But there were two events which aroused considerable interest and which had a direct bearing on the attitude of the Russian government towards the proposals of the French. The first of these was the famous visit of Bismarck to Vienna in the latter part of June to attend the wedding of his son Herbert. The astounding outcome of this incident can only be understood in connection with the attempted reconciliation between the former chancellor and the Kaiser, which, it will be remembered, had been frustrated by the action of Caprivi and Holstein. The men in the Wilhelmstrasse ought to have been satisfied with this success, but they feared that if Bismarck were received in Vienna by the Emperor Francis Joseph it would so strengthen his position and add to the numbers of his adherents that in the end the Kaiser would be unable to resist the pressure of public opinion in favor of reconciliation.[39] Caprivi therefore instructed Prince Reuss, the ambassador at Vienna, who was a personal friend of the Bismarcks, not to attend the wedding. This was the famous "Uriasbrief" and was a fatal error on the part of the government. By way of sup-

[38] The expression is Schweinitz' (Wolkenstein to Kálnoky June 8, 1892). According to a member of the Russian legation at Copenhagen the Tsar, on first hearing of the affair, exclaimed: "Welcher Dummkopf! Was hat er es nötig gehabt, dahin zu fahren." General Kioer, the Danish minister to Russia, who was in Copenhagen at the time, also stated that Alexander was very angry at Mohrenheim (Aehrenthal to Kálnoky August 2, 1892). Constantine himself never forgave Mohrenheim, whom the Grand Duchess referred to as "der abscheuliche Jude" (Wolkenstein to Kálnoky March 16, 1893). The German government officially expressed its displeasure to the Russian foreign office, but was assured that the whole thing was a mere coincidence (Wolkenstein to Kálnoky June 18; Aehrenthal to Kálnoky August 2, 1892).

[39] Marschall, in fact, believed that Bismarck's object in asking for an audience was so to heighten his prestige that the Kaiser would take the initiative in effecting a reconciliation (Széchényi to Kálnoky June 12). Marschall's letter to Eulenburg June 13 (Gradenwitz: *Akten* pp. 33-34) shows that the Kaiser feared Bismarck might induce Francis Joseph to take some step towards bringing the former chancellor back into the government's graces. Similarly the Kaiser's remarks to Steininger (Wertheimer: Ein K. und K. Militärattaché über das politische Leben in Berlin, in *Preussische Jahrbücher* September 1925, pp. 264-282).

plement the Kaiser wrote to Francis Joseph indicating his desire that no audience be granted the ex-chancellor.[40]

When Bismarck learned of the *démarche* made by the German government, his rage knew no bounds. His journey to Vienna had been one long ovation—nothing less than a triumphal procession, which must have convinced him that the country stood with him as against the Kaiser. In this frame of mind he received Moritz Benedikt, at that time a representative of the *Neue Freie Presse*, and granted him the famous interview which appeared on June 23. Up to this time he had occasionally criticized the policy of the government. But now he threw all caution and discretion to the winds and delivered a violent attack not only on the policy of the government, but on the government itself and especially on Caprivi.[41] Aside from his comments on domestic affairs it will suffice to recall here his famous indictment of the government's foreign policy. Germany, he declared, no longer had any influence on Russian policy. The Tsar no longer had any personal confidence in Germany's statesmen and this explained the great change which had taken place in European politics since March, 1890. "The wire which connected us with Russia has been cut"—this was the pregnant summary which he himself gave.[42]

The publication of this interview struck Europe like a thunder-

---

[40] The despatch to Reuss in the *Reichsanzeiger* July 9, 1892, reprinted, together with the original authentic text, in Gradenwitz: *Akten* p. 5. The Kaiser's letter to Francis Joseph published by Schlitter, in *Oesterreichische Rundschau* January 1919, p. 109. Caprivi stoutly denied any intention to prescribe the attitude to be taken by Kálnoky and Francis Joseph (Szechényi to Kálnoky June 13, 1892), but the communication, to Kálnoky, of Reuss' instructions, the Kaiser's remarks to Steininger, and the Kaiser's correspondence with Francis Joseph leave no doubt as to the Kaiser's intentions. Cf. also Hammann: *Der neue Kurs* p. 23.

[41] A friend of Bismarck's told Schiessl that there could be no reconciliation until Caprivi had gone (Schiessl to Kálnoky June 25). Cf. also Hammann p. 22.

[42] Bismarck in all probability had learned of the Kaiser's letter to Francis Joseph, in which William made much of Bismarck's Russophilism (to Steininger he said: "Fürst Bismarck war immer Russe, ist Russe und wird immer Russe bleiben und in seinem Herzen ein entschiedener Gegner Oesterreichs.)" If this is so, the interview in the *Neue Freie Presse* may indeed be taken as a reply (See Gradenwitz: *Bismarcks letzter Kampf* pp. 243 ff.).

bolt.[43] Those who had already disapproved and condemned the policies of the government now had for their views the endorsement of a recognized authority. The great ovations accorded to Bismarck on his return journey show that a large part of the population, notably in south Germany, accepted his dictum. On the other hand there were many who regarded Bismarck's action as unpatriotic to a high degree, not to say treasonable. Such was the attitude generally taken abroad and in diplomatic circles.[44] The general upshot of the incident was that it revealed to the whole world the sad state of German affairs and the existence of what looked like a Fronde.[45] Beyond that it had no noticeable effect. The governing circles in Russia, for example, were in no way influenced in their opinion of Caprivi. The Tsar probably would have liked to see Bismarck return and sweep away the anti-Russian group about Holstein and the Kaiser. It was now obvious that Bismarck's return to power or even to influence was quite out of the question. The press was therefore unanimous in condemning him and ridiculing his remarks, while it lavished praise on Caprivi. As for the Tsar, he had nothing against Caprivi personally, and so he consoled himself with the thought that for some time to come the Kaiser would be so occupied with domestic difficulties that he would not have much time to think of foreign policy.[46] Relations between the two

[43] As an immediate result the Berlin exchange became unsteady and it was believed that Bismarck's utterances meant that war with Russia was imminent (Hohenlohe II, p. 488).

[44] E. g., Greindl's report, in Köhler pp. 310-312; Wolkenstein to Kálnoky, July 6, 1892.

[45] Caprivi feared that, because of Bismarck's arguments, the people would, in case of war, accept it unenthusiastically and feel that it could have been avoided (Schiessl to Kálnoky July 13, 1892). Only consideration for the national welfare, he said, deterred him from publishing documents which would show Bismarck in another light. For example, the archives showed that in his last years Bismarck had considered banning all socialists and eventually deporting them to Africa. He had also considered readmitting the Redemptorists, and had even thought of standing the whole German constitution on its head, abolishing the legislature and doing away with universal suffrage (Széchényi to Kálnoky August 6, 1892).

[46] L. J. no. 71 (Boisdeffre to Freycinet August 18, reporting the Tsar's remarks); Wolkenstein to Kálnoky July 6; cf. also the St. Petersburg letters in the *Mémorial Diplomatique* July 2 and 9, 1892. The Tsar's marginal note referring to

countries continued to be as cordial as could be expected, and before long negotiations for a commercial treaty were once more taken up.

The second great event of the summer of 1892 was the general election in England which resulted in the overturn of the Salisbury ministry and the advent of Gladstone and the liberals. The issue had long been in doubt, and the final victory for the opposition made a profound impression on the continent. In fact, for weeks it crowded almost everything else into the background. To be sure, the delight felt in both France and Russia was considerably tempered by the fact that Lord Rosebery took over the ministry of foreign affairs. He was known to be an admirer and follower of Lord Salisbury in matters of foreign policy, and there was no doubt in Paris that there would be no radical departure from the old course, for example, in such matters as Egypt.[47] But even after making the necessary allowance the advent of the new ministry gave European politics quite a different setting. Gladstone was primarily interested in the Home Rule Bill, and the country would probably become so engrossed in matters of domestic concern that there would be little attention paid to the larger issues of international relations. Besides, Gladstone was known to be very "squeezable," as the conservative *Spectator* remarked on July 16. With a little pressure properly applied he might be brought to make concessions. At any rate, the new cabinet could be more easily talked to and argued with, and there was at least a good prospect that the forward policy of Lord Salisbury in Morocco would be abandoned, that negotiations in regard to the evacuation of Egypt would be initiated, that an end would be put to the English policy of en-

Caprivi: "Diesem Manne muss man Glauben schencken" (G. P. IX, no. 2124; Wolkenstein to Kálnoky March 31, 1892) is characteristic. Shuvalov's remark that Caprivi was "un trop honnête homme" (Hohenlohe II, p. 484) is well-known. See also the very favorable estimate of Caprivi in Daudet: *Bismarck* p.253, reflecting French official correspondence. Francis Joseph's estimate of the two men at this time is equally interesting. Of Bismarck he said to Hohenlohe: "Es ist traurig, wie ein solcher Mann so tief sinken kann." Of Caprivi: "Gott gebe, dass dieser Mann noch lange auf seinem Posten verbleibe" (Hohenlohe II, p. 490).

[47] See especially *Mémorial Diplomatique* July 9, 23, 1892.

couraging Stambulov and Ferdinand to resist the Russians, and that the rivalry of England and Russia in Central Asia would be settled by a delimitation commission.[48] Finally, and this overshadowed everything else, it was hardly to be expected that Gladstone, who had written bitterly of Italy's alliances in the *Contemporary Review* in 1889, who was constantly exposed to the pressure of men like Labouchère, and who was known to have no inclinations towards friendship with Germany, Austria or Turkey, would continue the policy of Salisbury in establishing close connections with the Triple Alliance.[49] In brief, the political change in England might reasonably be expected to lead to a general *détente*, even though there were no concrete change in the policy pursued by the government.

Looked at from the Russian viewpoint, then, the situation in the summer of 1892 showed a marked improvement over what it had been since Bismarck's fall. The Triple Alliance appeared considerably weakened, Germany was involved in domestic problems of power, Austria was confronted with the rising tide of Young Czech agitation and on rather cool terms with her German ally, Italy was threatened with financial ruin or reduction of armaments, apparently on the point of being driven to a reorientation of her policy. On the other hand the close understanding between England and the Triple Alliance was apparently at an end and therewith the greatest threat to Russia's position removed. The Tsar had every reason to be satisfied with recent developments.

No one appreciated the situation better than the French statesmen. A mere perusal of the Russian press was sufficient to show that the entente between the two nations was not as enthusiastically viewed as in the days following Cronstadt. In fact, the chief object of the Russians seemed to be to ridicule and abuse the French. Cartoons pictured the French playing the

[48] This was the general tenor of the press comment. *London Times* July 19, August 13; cf. also G. P. VIII, no. 1733; and Aehrenthal to Kálnoky August 17, 1892.

[49] This was what the Russians and French reckoned on chiefly (see e. g., *Mémorial Diplomatique* August 20, 1892). The uneasiness in Berlin is reflected in G. P. VIII, nos. 1731 ff.

Marseillaise while the Russians were starving. "Politics aside,
let us frankly say we are disappointed; we did not expect that,"
wrote the *Petersburgskaia Gazeta*, while the *Grashdanin* took the
opportunity offered by the cabinet crisis in Paris to picture France
as a hotbed of republicanism, atheism and anarchy.[50] Quite
obviously the chances of securing a military convention were
rapidly diminishing and Ribot therefore redoubled his efforts to
force a conclusion. He had already suggested that Montebello
ignore Giers and go directly to the Tsar, but the Tsar was in
Denmark, and all that he had agreed to was the mission of a
French officer to discuss details. Ribot still hoped that all could
be settled by the end of July, since the Tsar was to return about
July 20. "If war should unfortunately break out before we had
succeeded in establishing a plan of common action between the
two countries, we should be blamed for not having pursued the
negotiations with sufficient energy," he wrote to Montebello.[51]
The immediate need was to learn the text or the principal points
of the Russian draft in order that Boisdeffre could be given the
proper instructions before leaving.[52] In the hope of accomplish-
ing something in this direction Montebello decided to visit Giers
at his estate in Finland. But he found the Russian minister in
bed, tortured with rheumatic pains and suffering from a slight
attack of pneumonia. There could be no thought of a political
discussion. Montebello returned, having learned nothing beyond the fact that Giers wished to resign.[53] All he could do was

---

[50] Wolkenstein to Kálnoky June 8, 1892; *Mémorial Diplomatique* May 7,
1892; *London Times* August 17, quoting the *Den*. The correspondent of the
Débats at the international railroad conference in St. Petersburg in August reported that he could find "not the slightest toy commemorating the Franco-Russian
Alliance" (*Times* August 27, 1892).

[51] L. J. no. 39 (Ribot to Montebello July 8). Cf. also nos. 35, 36.

[52] L. J. nos. 35, 40.

[53] L. J. no. 43 (Montebello to Ribot July 17). Though Montebello went
to Finland secretly, his mission became known and certain words of discourage-
ment which he uttered betrayed to his colleagues that he had had an important
purpose and that he had failed (Aehrenthal to Kálnoky July 27, 1892). The
German government had similar intelligence and Caprivi concluded from it that
there was no written agreement and that the Tsar's pacifism would prove to be
an insurmountable barrier (Széchényi to Kálnoky August 6, 1892; Greindl
report August 13, in Köhler pp. 313-314).

to forward to Paris a note embodying what was thought to be the content of the Russian counter-proposals.[54]

After the Tsar's return the efforts to initiate discussions were renewed, but even Obruchev was unable to obtain more than a formal invitation for Boisdeffre.[55] Ribot continued to press for action and finally resorted to the press to make his standpoint clear.[56] On July 14, while the French were celebrating the national fête and while the French and Russian colors were gayly mingled in the decorations of the capital, the *Figaro* published a remarkable article entitled "Alliance or Flirtation," signed by *Conscius*. At the time it passed almost unnoticed, and was not reproduced in any of the leading European organs. But in St. Petersburg it did not escape attention. Knowing the circumstances of the case, the Russian foreign office immediately realized that the article was inspired and that it was an official declaration of the French position. The argument of the writer in the *Figaro* was that in view of numerous rumors of a coming meeting of the three Emperors it was high time that something definite should be done about Russo-French relations and that the era of coquetting and of bagatelles should be closed by the conclusion of an alliance contract. The Russians had always argued that the instability of the French system made such a procedure dangerous, but the argument might well be reversed and used by the French, for the economic and financial difficulties of Russia, the illness of Giers and Vishnegradski, and the inadequate equipment of the Russian army simply added to the uncertainty of the situation as viewed from Paris, while, to be sure, these same considerations might help to explain the hesitancy of the Russians about concluding a treaty with a nation which had not definitely recognized its defeat by Germany:

"In view of these eventualities has not France the right to demand that her diplomacy enter at last upon the period of action and go beyond the

---

[54] L. J. no. 42, and annexe (Montebello to Ribot July 16, 1892).

[55] L. J. no. 43.

[56] L. J. no. 45 (Ribot to Montebello July 22): "Il faut pourtant sortir d'incertitude. Nos responsabilités sont trop graves pour que nous ne traitons pas cette affaire avec toute la précision nécessaire."

limits of demonstrative phraseology which has contributed more to the interests of the ministry than to the future of the country?......We cannot refuse to recognize that these exchanges of vague promises, these assurances of reciprocal assistance, these intermittent manifestations of Platonic attachment arouse the susceptibilities of certain powers, deprive us of the possibility of other connections, bring about the coalition of certain interests against us, interests which erroneously consider themselves menaced.... Let us leave flirtation to the English, who have an interest in not allying themselves with anybody and who at times exploit the sentimentalism of other nations by this little national game. Let us return to our traditions. We have been courting for the last year; let us raise the question of a marriage contract resolutely, as befits families who respect each other. Just as a Franco-Russian alliance is desirable, so also is a perpetual flirtation without a positive conclusion imprudent."[57]

This was plain speaking, and the Russians recognized it. The Tsar and his advisers were deeply offended by the presumption of the French, and the Russian press replied to the *Figaro* in equally unmistakable terms. The *Novoie Vremia* argued eloquently against a formal alliance, declaring that the sympathies existing between the two nations were quite enough to guarantee mutual support in case of a crisis. The *Grashdanin* characterized the French demands as childish and remarked that, if the French hoped to oblige the Russians to champion purely French designs, they were thoroughly mistaken. The Tsar wished nothing more fervently than to maintain the peace. He had effected the rapprochement with France in the hope of furthering the maintenance of peace and with the idea of strengthening the European balance, but he had no intention of identifying himself with the quarrels of others or of regarding the reconquest of Alsace-Lorraine as a Russian interest, as the *Figaro* had suggested.

[57] Much the same ideas were expressed by *Punch* on April 16, 1892, in a humorous verse, where Miss France says:
> "But six short months ago and I to him
> Indeed seemed all in all.
> A stalwart lover, though *tant soit peu* grim
> I fancied him my thrall.
> And was it after all pretence, or whim?
> Oh prospect to appal.
> Was't but my money he desired to clutch?
> I lent it with delight.
> Were his mere venal vows? His bonds but such
> As Samson snapped at sight?"

Paris must understand that Russia would not go beyond the *entente morale*, established in order to restore the balance of power which had been temporarily upset by an unequal division of power.[58]

Finally, in order to make sure that the French public should understand the position of the Russians, an inspired article was published in the *Mémorial Diplomatique*, presumably by the former editor of the *Nord* who was in close touch with the Russian foreign office. A formal alliance, it argued, would very likely lead to a declaration of war by the Triple Alliance, which would feel itself menaced. The result, then, would be that the remedy proved worse than the disease. After all, no formal treaty was really necessary:

"The question of Alsace-Lorraine, like the question of Bulgaria, must provisionally rest in the shade, must remain a tacit understanding of the Franco-Russian entente, a germ of its future material development."

The whole problem, it continued, was one for the victorious armies to settle, and there was really no need of counting chickens before the eggs were hatched. For the time being Russia's reply to the *Figaro* must be:

"Neither alliance nor flirtation, but simply sincere friendship and full confidence."[59]

---

[58] Aehrenthal to Kálnoky July 20, August 2, 1892; F. H. Geffcken: *Frankreich, Russland und der Dreibund* (Berlin 1893) pp. 166-167.

[59] *Mémorial Diplomatique* July 30, 1892. The discussion of Russian aid in the reconquest of Alsace-Lorraine came about in the following way: At Kiel the German statesmen had come away with the impression "dass für ihn (den Zaren) eine elsass-lothringische Frage nicht existiert, und er trotz Kronstadt für eine französische Revanchepolitik nicht zu haben ist" (G. P. VII, no. 1636). On June 9 the *Kölnische Zeitung* reported that the visit had not left even the slightest doubt "dass, falls es Frankreich belieben sollte, die elsass-lothringische Frage Deutschland gegenüber einmal praktisch aufzurollen, der Zar nicht daran denken wird, Frankreich in seinem Vorgehen zu unterstützen. Die Erklärung, die in dieser Hinsicht der Zar abgegeben hat, ist völlig unzweideutig...." On June 11 the *National Zeitung* replied that there had been no "Erklärung," but the visit had strengthened the impression "dass der Zar weit entfernt ist, sich von französischer Seite einen Krieg aufdrängen zu lassen." On June 13 the *Hamburger Korrespondent* reiterated: "Es darf mit grösserer Sicherheit als bisher behauptet werden, dass der Zar seine friedliche Politik um französischer Revancheinteressen willen nicht verlassen wird." These utterances were evidently inspired by the foreign office in order to dis-

In spite of these exchanges of opinion, Ribot still hoped to make some progress through the mission of Boisdeffre. The French demands, as drawn up in despatches of July 22 and 28, were approximately as follows: a) in case the Triple Alliance or Germany alone mobilizes, Russia and France should do likewise without the need of previous agreement or notification; b) in case of war Russia would place on her German frontier all forces at her disposal minus those necessary to hold Austria in check; c) the forces used against Germany should not confine themselves to observation but should attack, in order to prevent the Germans from transporting their troops to the west and thus crushing France. It was a complete, orderly program that Ribot thus mapped out, and he took pains to state that the French government desired not only the signature of the minister of war, but also of the minister of foreign affairs.[60]

With this draft in his pocket Boisdeffre set out for St. Petersburg, where he arrived on August 1. Through Montebello he was immediately put in touch with Obruchev and Vannovski, with whom he had numerous conferences during the ensuing days.[61] At the very first of these meetings, with Obruchev, Boisdeffre learned to his great disappointment that the situation was by no means auspicious. Even such staunch advocates of an agreement as the Russian minister of war and the chief of staff were obliged to admit that the Tsar did not feel disposed to exchange signatures at that time.[62] The submission of Boisdeffre's draft only made matters worse, and the discussions which took place between August 1 and August 10 at times reached a distinctly acrimonious pitch.[63] The Russian negotiators once more questioned the very need of a formal agreement. Such

illusion the public in regard to the Nancy demonstrations. On the other hand the absence of any *démenti* seems to have caused great uneasiness in Paris, and the *Figaro* article demanded to know what Russia intended to do about Alsace-Lorraine. Hence the Russian replies.

[60] L. J. nos. 45, 47 (Ribot to Montebello July 22, 28).

[61] Boisdeffre's own account is given in two reports to Freycinet dated August 10 and 18 (L. J. nos. 53 and 71). Cf. also the summary in Freycinet p. 501.

[62] L. J. no. 53.

[63] Boisdeffre's report (L. J. no. 53) shows how warm the debate was, and yet he speaks of his account as being "sous une forme très adoucie."

written documents were usually not lived up to. It would be much better to confine oneself to a gentlemen's agreement. In any case they objected to the haste shown by the French, and pointed out that nothing definitive could be done without Giers. Again and again they recurred to the bad impression made on the Tsar by the *Figaro* article and other indiscreet utterances of the French press. All the old objections to a formal alliance were disinterred: the instability of the French ministries, the unconstitutionality of agreements in French law unless approved by the chamber, the impossibility of submitting the agreements to the chamber because of the Tsar's insistence on absolute secrecy.[64] Vannovski even went so far as to express doubts as to whether the French people would really try to maintain the peace once they had the Tsar's signature, and also raised the question whether, if the agreement were concluded, Germany would not be driven by despair to declare war.

Quite as serious were the objections raised by the Russians to the terms of the French draft. They rebelled particularly against the idea of making the mobilization of Germany alone a *casus foederis*. For them Austria was the principal enemy, and no arguments, however apt, could move them.[65] Obruchev declared in unmistakable terms that in his opinion an agreement in two articles would be quite sufficient. Russia and France should agree to mobilize simultaneously if the Triple Alliance mobilized and to carry out a vigorous attack against the troops of the Triple Alliance without fixing the strength or division of forces. In the end Boisdeffre realized that the signature of Giers could not be obtained for the time being. All he could do was to extract from Vannovski a promise to submit the French draft to the Tsar and to hope that the latter's approval might be obtained for whatever was agreed upon.[66] The French project was actually sub-

---

[64] Boisdeffre suggested that the agreement be submitted to the French chamber, whereupon Vannovski "se récria vivement, déclarant que l'Empereur ne redoutait rien tant qu'un éclat" (L. J. no. 53).

[65] Obruchev insisted: "Il n'y a pas d'Allemagne ni d'ennemi principal: Il y a les forces de la Triple Alliance. Si le gros des forces qui nous menacent est autrichien il faut marcher contre lui et le battre; c'est pour nous l'ennemi principal."

[66] In regard to the Russian "project" which had so worried the French and

mitted to Alexander, but, in anticipation of his disapproval, Obruchev and Boisdeffre drew up a new text based on the French draft but taking into consideration the objections of the Russians.[67] The changes made in the original French proposals can best be seen by placing the two versions in juxtaposition:

French Original.	Modified Draft.
1. In case the forces of the Triple Alliance or of Germany alone should be mobilized, France and Russia shall, at the first report of the event and without the need of previous agreement, mobilize immediately and simultaneously all their forces and transport them as near to the frontiers as possible.	1. If France is attacked by Germany or by Italy supported by Germany, Russia will employ all her available forces to attack Germany. If Russia is attacked by Germany or by Austria supported by Germany, France will employ all her available forces to combat Germany.
2. If France or Russia is actually attacked by the forces of the Triple Alliance or of Germany alone, the two Powers will direct against Germany all the forces which are not absolutely indispensable at other points. These forces will be unsparingly engaged as quickly as possible, so that Germany will have to fight in the East and the West at the same time.	2. In case the forces of the Triple Alliance, or of one of the Powers composing it, should mobilize, France and Russia, at the first news of the event and without the necessity of any previous concert, shall mobilize immediately and simultaneously all their forces and transport them as near to the frontiers as possible.
3. In the most unfavorable case... France estimates that she can put 1,300,000 men into the field against Germany and that these forces will be concentrated on the frontier on the 14th day of mobilization. In the same case Russia estimates that she can put into the field against Germany 800,000 men, etc.	3. The available forces to be employed against Germany shall be, on the part of France 1,300,000 men, on the part of Russia 700,000 or 800,000. These forces shall engage to the full with all speed, so that Germany will have to fight on the East and West at the same time.

which had supposedly been submitted to the Tsar, it appeared that no real draft had ever been made.

[67] L. J. nos. 56, 57 (Boisdeffre to Freycinet August 10, no. 4; Montebello to Ribot August 10).

A comparison of the two drafts immediately shows that the second was the result of a compromise, and that there were a number of important changes made not only in the wording but in the sequence of the articles. The two versions, the second of which was the final one, have been so admirably analyzed by Eugen Fischer that one can not do much more than summarize his closely-reasoned arguments.[68] The final draft shows that article I of the French original, which dealt with mobilization, became article II, and that article II of the French draft, dealing with common action in the event of actual hostilities, was given the place of article I in the modified version. The last sentence of article I of the French draft, providing for the speedy engagement of the forces to be used against Germany, is relegated to the end of article III of the final text. Furthermore, in the final form it appears that the French won their point providing for mobilization in case of mobilization by Germany alone ("In case the forces of the Triple Alliance, or of *one of the Powers composing it*, etc."). On the other hand the same clause obliged France to mobilize in case Austria alone mobilized against Russia. To this the French had objected quite as obstinately, because they did not want to become embroiled in the Austro-Russian quarrel any more than the Russians meant to become involved in the Franco-German dispute. In the end the French had yielded in order not to wreck the negotiations, and had consoled themselves with the thought that an Austro-Russian conflict would almost certainly bring in Germany also. Here, then, there was a perfect compromise.

The question arises, however, as to why the Russians should have consented to the compromise. It was the French, not the Russians, who were anxious for the convention. The fact is that the changed sequence of the articles deprived the compromise of most of its force and value. In the original French draft the articles had followed logically one upon the other: 1) mobilization; 2) common action in case of actual hostilities; 3) divi-

---

[68] Eugen Fischer: Der Sinn der russisch-französischen Militärkonvention (*Preussische Jahrbücher* April 1923, pp. 65-98). I am in full agreement with Fischer's reasoning.

sion of forces, etc. In the final draft the cart was put before the horse, and Boisdeffre was quite right when he pointed out that there was a contradiction between the first and second articles of the final version. In the second article France bound herself to mobilize even if Austria alone mobilized, but in article I France was obliged to lend active assistance only in case Russia were attacked by Germany or by Austria supported by Germany. At first this discrepancy does not appear to have struck the French negotiators with full force. Of course the same contradiction applied to Russia's obligations. In article I she was obliged to assist France if the latter were attacked by Germany or by Italy supported by Germany. In article II she bound herself to mobilize not only if the Triple Alliance mobilized, but if Germany or Italy alone mobilized against France. The French statesmen later decided to get out of the dilemma, in case of necessity, by pleading that they could not be expected to mobilize against Austria alone if they were not expected to fight against Austria alone.[69] The evidence would indicate that the Russians, by insisting on the transposition of articles I and II of the original French draft, intended to leave themselves just such a loophole to escape from those obligations to which they objected. They were willing to assist France in case she were actually attacked by Germany, but they were determined not to assume the rôle of the aggressor themselves, by mobilizing against Germany as soon as the latter mobilized against France. In such a case they too could declare that they could not be obliged to mobilize against Germany alone if they were not bound by the convention to fight against Germany alone unless the latter had actually attacked France. This left sufficient room for interpretation of the elusive terms *aggression* and *attack*. Apparently the Russians meant to take only article I of the final draft really seriously, and that may explain their insistence that the last sentence of article I of the French draft should not be included, in fact should not be put into article II of the final draft, but should be relegated to the third article. In addition there were clauses providing for

---

[69] L. J. no. 82 (Montebello to Develle May 20, 1893).

the coöperation of the two general staffs in time of peace, and three articles providing: 1) that France and Russia should not conclude a separate peace with the Triple Alliance; 2) that the convention should have the same duration as the Triple Alliance; 3) that all the clauses should be kept rigorously secret.[70]

For this draft Obruchev desired Boisdeffre's signature, in order that it might inspire more confidence in the Tsar.[71] After some hesitation Freycinet, who still hoped that Alexander might be induced to accept the French draft, granted Boisdeffre permission to sign, but by that time Obruchev had already seized a favorable opportunity and had submitted the document to his master.[72] After thorough consideration, Alexander approved it "on the whole," but in view of the political nature of certain clauses he insisted that it be referred to Giers.[73] Obruchev went to Finland to submit the document to the minister, whom he found still very ill. Giers read the draft and offered no objections. All he asked was that he might be permitted to think the matter over *"à tête reposée."*[74] Therewith the negotiations lapsed. The French realized that there was nothing to do but wait until Giers saw fit to complete the convention by appending his signature. Boisdeffre prepared to return home. In his last audience with the Tsar the latter again impressed upon him the necessity for absolute secrecy. He even went so far as to suggest that only Carnot, Freycinet and Ribot should be initiated, but Boisdeffre pointed out that this would be quite impossible. Alexander made it perfectly clear that he did not want to compromise the negotiations with Germany for a commercial agreement and

---

[70] The Russians could not impress too strongly upon Boisdeffre the necessity for absolute secrecy. The Tsar wished to make the divulgation of the clauses of the convention a reason for nullifying it (L. J. no. 67; cf. also no. 71).

[71] L. J. no. 71 (Boisdeffre to Freycinet August 18).

[72] L. J. nos. 60, 61, 62, 65, 66, 67. Two copies were, however, signed by Obruchev and Boisdeffre (L. J. no. 71).

[73] L. J. no. 67. The Tsar told Boisdeffre that he had read, re-read and studied the convention (*ibid.* no. 71).

[74] Giers "trouve le projet bon et l'approuve d'une manière générale. Toutefois, en raison de son état de faiblesse, il a demandé à l'examiner à tête reposée" (Montebello to Ribot August 17, L. J. no. 69). Cf. also L. J. no. 71, and Freycinet p. 501.

that he could not afford to become involved in difficulties, for Russia required at least two years more of peace in order to complete her army reforms and recover from the famine and the cholera epidemic. He asked for assurances that France would not take action without first consulting Russia in case some such dispute as the Schnaebele incident should take place.[75]

The draft, to which the Tsar had given his approval "in principle" on August 17, was not only quite different in form from the original French project, but was not definitive. The French government, in fact, did not regard itself bound and Ribot complained of the delay in winding the matter up.[76] After Boisdeffre's return to Paris the new text was carefully reconsidered and a few changes suggested. The French statesmen were distinctly worried by the second article, which obliged them to mobilize against Austria alone. They envisaged the situation in which Austria might mobilize a part of her forces against some Balkan state, and argued that obviously it could not be in the interest of the contracting parties to proceed to a general mobilization in such a case. It was also desired that the specifications as to the number of forces to be employed by France should be slightly altered in her favor. Finally, at the insistence of Carnot, it was decided to propose that the secrecy clause should be reworded as so to eliminate the word "secret."[77] These changes were submitted to Obruchev, who had come to France on leave, but the objections raised by him and the doubts of Vannovski as to whether the Tsar would consider the matter at that time induced the French not to press their desires.[78] Early in Sep-

---

[75] L. J. no. 71 (Boisdeffre to Freycinet, August 18).

[76] Boisdeffre told Obruchev "que tant que les ratifications definitives ne seraient pas échangés nous n'étions liés ni les uns ni les autres, et que nous nous trouvions exactement dans la même situation qu'avant le projet." He then adds: "Il (Obruchev) en est entièrement convenu" (L. J. no. 71). Similarly Ribot to Montebello August 27 (L. J. no. 75): "L'approbation donnée en principe par l'Empereur à un projet signé par les chefs d'Etat Major des deux pays n'équivaut pas à un engagement régulier des deux gouvernements."

[77] L. J. no. 75 (Ribot to Montebello August 27).

[78] The Russian general received the French proposals rather gruffly and wanted to know why the French hadn't said what they had to say during the negotiations. He was particularly sensitive about the secrecy clause (L. J. nos. 76, 78).

tember Giers came to Aix to recuperate, and Freycinet and Ribot took the opportunity to pay him a visit, in the hope of inducing him to sign the draft. They found the Russian minister still in very bad health and did not succeed in eliciting from him anything but general statements and benevolent assurances. "It seems to me that we must resign ourselves to being not more anxious than the Emperor," wrote Ribot at the end of this interview.[79] In this spirit of forced resignation he and his colleagues waited for the next favorable opportunity to press for the completion of the military convention.

It is one thing to explain the changes made in the original French draft by the Russian negotiators, and another thing to explain why the Russians should at this time have consented to an agreement at all. To be sure, the agreement come to by Boisdeffre and Obruchev had no validity, and there could be no harm in merely discussing a possible convention. But apart from this there is no denying that the mere fact of the negotiations indicated an unwillingness on the part of the Tsar to drop the projected alliance with France entirely. There were, in fact, good reasons why the wire to Paris should be kept intact. In the first place, the Russians had cause for apprehension in the events which were taking place in Bulgaria. Urged on by Ferdinand, Stambulov was still intent on extorting, from the Porte, at least, a recognition of the legality of the existing government. In June Ferdinand paid a visit to London, where he was received by the Queen and "lionized" by the population.[80] On his return

---

[79] Ribot's account in L. J. no. 79 (Ribot to Montebello, September 7, 1892). Freycinet's account in his *Souvenirs* p. 502. Cf. also Hansen: *Mohrenheim* p. 140, and G. P. VII, no. 1520. Giers kept on saying that all could be settled in a half-hour, but he made no move to do so. It is interesting to note that the *Gaulois* on September 15 stated that negotiations had been going on for three months and that they were almost complete. The *Novoie Vremia* replied on September 23 that a formal treaty might sooner or later become an absolute necessity. In any case it would be strictly defensive, and would be the equivalent of the treaties of the Triple Alliance. It would, however, be preferable not to have to take this step, and only inexorable political events might compel it.

[80] Hatzfeldt reported that Ferdinand had been treated practically as a sovereign, and at Lord Salisbury's *soirée* the representatives of Russia, France and Turkey were conspicuously absent (Széchényi to Kálnoky June 4, 1892). Cf. also Daudet: *Ferdinand* pp. 135-136; *Mémorial Diplomatique* June 4, 11, 18, 1892.

he stopped at Vienna and was granted an audience by Francis Joseph and an interview by Kálnoky. What passed on these occasions it is difficult to say. It is very doubtful whether Ferdinand was in any way encouraged to act, but nevertheless he could not avoid feeling that in any case his prestige had been increased and that, in case of necessity, he might count on support from England and Austria.

The Russians viewed these developments with the greatest concern, and felt outraged by the condemnation and execution of the conspirators who had been responsible for the assassination of the Bulgarian minister Belchev.[81] In the course of the trial Stambulov had caused to be published large numbers of documents purporting to show that it was Russia who had originally instigated and supported the plotters. Whether or not the papers were authentic is immaterial. The important point was the steady accentuation of the Russo-Bulgarian dispute, which reached a very critical phase in August when Stambulov paid a visit to Constantinople. It was rumored at the time that the Bulgarian dictator had suggested to the Sultan a Turko-Bulgarian alliance to resist the encroachments of Russia.[82] This may be an exaggeration, but it is more than likely that Stambulov did his utmost to induce Abdul to recognize Ferdinand.[83] The Sultan's gracious attitude towards his

[81] Cf. the St. Petersburg letters in the *Mémorial Diplomatique* June 18, August 6, 13, 1892.

[82] N. Staneff: *Geschichte der Bulgaren* (Leipzig 1917) II, p. 167; A. G. Drandar: *Les Evénéments Politiques en Bulgarie* (Brussels 1896) pp. 266-267; G. Bousquet: *Histoire du Peuple Bulgare* (Paris 1909) p. 310. A. H. Beaman: *Stambuloff* (London 1895) p. 310, says nothing of these rumors, but the German foreign office received a report to this effect and even suggested to Kálnoky that something should be done to warn the Sultan. Kálnoky, however, feared that such a step might make the Sultan suspicious of Bulgaria (Schiessl to Kálnoky September 11, 1892). See also *Mémorial Diplomatique* August 20 and 27, 1892, and Mijatovich: Turkey and Bulgaria (*Eastern and Western Review* September 15, October 1, 1892).

[83] The *Agence Balkanique* announced (August 13) that the Sultan told Stambulov that he would recognize Ferdinand when the favorable moment arrived, and that Stambulov had agreed to leave the matter to the discretion of the Sultan. The *Saturday Review* (August 20) took the stand that in any case the mere fact of Stambulov's reception constituted a sort of "informal recognition."

visitor made anything seem plausible enough, and reports of the coming visit of Ferdinand himself to the Turkish capital found general credence. The Russians regarded the whole thing as an outrage.[84] They felt certain that England was behind the Bulgarian politicians and that an attempt was being made to solve the Near Eastern problem in spite of the Tsar. To be sure the Turkish foreign office hastened to give assurances and insisted that the visit of Stambulov had been a complete surprise. There had been no change whatsoever in the situation.[85] Nevertheless the Russians thought it advisable to warn the Porte, and they induced France to take a similar step.[86] The Russian note of August 30 stated that Stambulov's reception by the Sultan had raised "just susceptibilities" in St. Petersburg and that it seemed to indicate a desire on the part of Turkey to recognize the Sofia regime indirectly and thus perpetuate a situation which, in the opinion of the world, constituted a permanent danger to European peace.[86a]

The Russian statesmen were not naïve enough to believe that this kind of demonstration would accomplish much. As aforesaid, they suspected England of being at the bottom of the whole thing, and of trying to raise the Near Eastern question at a time when Russia was not in a position to protect her own interests effectively. There was only one satisfactory method of putting an end to the English intrigue, and that was to put pressure on the Indian frontier. Russian newspapers openly stated that Russia must make the English feel in India the necessity of preserving neutrality in Europe, and almost immediately after the visit of Ferdinand to London it became known that Colonel Ianov, who had expelled Younghusband from the Pamirs in 1891,

[84] Aehrenthal to Kálnoky August 3, 1892.

[85] Aehrenthal to Kálnoky August 23, 1892. The Sultan also appealed to Cambon to transmit a similar assurance to the Tsar through Montebello (Aehrenthal to Kálnoky September 1, 1892; Schiessl to Kálnoky September 27, 1892).

[86] Shishkin to Iadovski August 30, 1892 (copy sent to Berlin and communicated from there to Vienna). The text was also published in the newspapers soon after. Cf. *Mémorial Diplomatique* October 1 and 8, 1892.

[86a] After long delays the Porte finally replied by repeating its earlier assurances (Aehrenthal to Kálnoky October 27, 1892; *Mémorial Diplomatique* October 29, 1892).

had been sent with a considerable force to assert the authority of Russia against the encroachments of China and Afghanistan.[87]. Ianov took his task seriously and before long clashes took place between the Russian force and the Afghan detachments. Experienced observers took a serious view of the situation, and the English government had, in fact, sufficient reason for apprehension, for Afghanistan was wracked by insurrections and revolts of various subject tribes and the Amir, Abd-er-Rahman, showed no inclination to accept the intervention of the Indian government. In fact he made it clear that he did not care to receive Lord Roberts or an Indian mission, and it appeared for a time as though he might go over to the Russian side.[88]

After the advent of the Gladstone ministry and the appointment of Rosebery as foreign minister, the Central Asian crisis began to become less acute. Negotiations were opened and explanations exchanged, and Ianov was recalled to Ferghana, leaving only a small detachment to winter in the disputed area.[89] But at the time of the opening of the negotiations between Rus-

[87] *Mémorial Diplomatique* (June 18, 1892) quoting the *Novoie Vremia*. Ianov actually left Ferghana on June 14 (*London Times* August 5, 1892) though naturally the news of events in the Pamirs was very slow in reaching Europe. The *Mémorial Diplomatique* reported on June 25 that a new Russian expedition would be sent out, but the first news of its presence in the Pamirs appeared in the *Times* on July 30.

[88] It is, of course, impossible to go into details, but see, among others, the excellent account by an "Indian Officer": *Russia's March towards India* II, pp. 263 ff.; Lord Roberts: *Forty-one Years in India* (London 1897) II, p. 453; *The Life of Abdur Rahman* (London 1900) II, pp. 135 ff. Of contemporary articles the best are the two accounts by Vambéry: The Situation in Central Asia (*Nineteenth Century* July 1892) and the Russian Advance in the Pamirs (*New Review* September 1892) which sounded the alarm and were much discussed; see also Russia, India and Afghanistan (*Quarterly Review* October 1892).

[89] Cf. *Mémorial Diplomatique* August 27, September 3, 10, 17, 24, October 1, 1892. Serious negotiations do not appear to have been initiated at this time, but Morier, who returned to St. Petersburg about September 20, probably asked questions of the Russian government in such a way as to make the situation clear. Rosebery seems to have been anxious for a pacific settlement. Why Ianov and his 2,000-3,000 men were recalled is not clear. The Russian press attempted to minimize the whole matter, and it seems that Ianov's recall was due to the desire of the Russian government not to cause trouble for the liberal cabinet. On the other hand Ianov may have been recalled in order to guard against the outbreak of an insurrection in Turkestan which was threatening.

sia and France the Asian imbroglio was at its worst, and many people regarded war as inevitable in the near future. This explains why the Russians could not afford to throw over the French entirely, and it also explains in part the text of the final draft of the military convention. It must be recalled that the chief value of the Reinsurance Treaty for Russia had lain in the fact that it guaranteed Russia against Germany's supporting Austria and England in their Near Eastern policy and at the same time guaranteed Russia against a German attack on the Polish front in case Russia and England should come to blows in Asia. With the Reinsurance Treaty gone Russia had to look elsewhere for these guarantees. The Franco-Russian Alliance afforded the necessary assurance, though only in a measure. What the Russians were primarily interested in was to have the French hold the Germans in check in case of an Asiatic conflict. They themselves had no desire to fight the Germans, but they were anxious to know that the Germans would not attack them. That was the chief consideration in the mind of the Tsar in the summer of 1892, and with the completion of the draft he had all that he needed for the time being. He had really committed the French without committing himself. When the time came he could always consummate the alliance by having Giers sign the papers.

CHAPTER X

SHADES OF THE PAST

FOR Alexander III the alliance with France was at most a *pis aller*. The very idea was anathema to him, and it was said that during the spring of 1892 he had literally flown into a rage whenever he read discussions of the subject in the newspapers.[1] The French negotiators had had sufficient opportunity to learn for themselves the true disposition of the Tsar, and they recognized how almost futile it was to attempt further pourparlers. And yet it was imperative that they should spare no effort to release France from the anomalous and dangerous position into which the entente of August, 1891 had placed her. Even after the failure of Freycinet and Ribot to win over Giers during the latter's stay at Aix the French foreign minister had written to his Russian colleague urging the desirability of closing the whole matter, in view of the introduction of the new military bill in Germany and the danger of a cabinet crisis in France, which would jeopardize the secrecy of the agreement. The reply he received was no different from the previous ones made by Giers, who argued that he would be unable to resume the direction of the foreign office for some time and pointed out once more that the whole matter could be quickly settled if the need arose.[2]

At the time when this last desperate effort was made by the French statesmen the situation had already become utterly hopeless. The great Panama scandal, which revealed to the whole world the rottenness and corruption of French politics, had already begun. The republican form of government, which had never met with any sympathy from the Tsar, was now entirely discredited. Alexander was thoroughly shocked and more than ever disgusted with his "ally". The demonstrations attending the funeral of Renan wrung from him the bitter remark

[1] G. P. VII, no. 1524.
[2] L. J. nos. 81, 82, and annexe.

that the French were, after all, nothing but atheists and rascals; in order to be rated as a great man among them one had to suffer a dog's funeral.[3] The Russian press followed suit, and when the Boulangist deputy, Delahaye, made the assertion that the great Russian journalist, Katkov, had received 500,000 francs of Panama money to back the Franco-Russian Alliance, the papers of St. Petersburg and Moscow rose in unison to defend the memory of their dead leader and to vilify the French.[4]

Of course, this was all a matter of sentiment. Had the interests of the two countries been really identical, all the recrimination would have availed little to undermine the relationship between them. But the Russians felt that they could not reckon on the French to support them against England in the Middle East and they were consequently determined not to allow themselves to be exploited in the service of French interests elsewhere. A striking example of the complete debacle of the Franco-Russian Entente in the winter of 1892-1893 may be found by examining the Egyptian crisis which broke out in January. Ever since the accession of the young Khedive, Abbas Hilmi II, in January, 1892, the French had entertained hopes that the new ruler would take a stronger stand in opposition to his English advisers, while both the French and the Turks were sanguine in their expectations that the new liberal cabinet in England would show itself disposed to discuss the eventual evacuation of the Nile country.[5] Abbas himself was distinctly susceptible to the alluring suggestions made to him by the rivals of the English, and there is no doubt that a good deal of intrigue went on at Cairo and that Abbas was encouraged to challenge the authority of Lord Cromer.[6] On the other hand, Rosebery made no move in the

[3] Such was the report of the Prince of Sachsen-Altenburg, who had been hunting with the Tsar at Spala (Aehrenthal to Kálnoky November 10, 1892).

[4] Aehrenthal to Kálnoky December 8, 1892; *Mémorial Diplomatique* December 3, 1892; Cyon: L'Enquête sur le Panama et la Russie (*Nouvelle Revue* January 1, 1893).

[5] G. P. VIII, nos. 1811, 1813; *Mémorial Diplomatique* September 24, 1892.

[6] Earl of Cromer: *Abbas II* (London 1915) chapters ii and iii, is the leading authority on this whole matter, but it should be noted that this supplement to *Modern Egypt* was written during the World War and is therefore very con-

direction of negotiations with France and in fact left no doubt whatsoever that he intended to adhere to the policy of his predecessor. The French therefore decided to go over his head and appeal to Gladstone personally, relying on the fact that the premier in his preëlection speeches had practically committed himself to a policy of negotiation and eventual evacuation. It was the same policy which Ribot had suggested to Montebello in regard to Giers—a foolish policy and a dangerous one. Rosebery naturally learned of the affair and felt deeply hurt. The net result was that he became less than ever inclined to make concessions to the French on any point.[7]

Soon after, the illness of Mustapha Pasha Fehmy, the Egyptian premier, opened up the prospect of a change of ministry. The French seized the opportunity and urged Abbas to make his own choice. Without consulting Lord Cromer the self-confident young ruler appointed Fakhry Pasha, who had been previously dismissed at the instigation of the English because of his opposition to the judicial reforms. It was a slap in the face for the English and a direct challenge to their position. Cromer realized that the time had come to demonstrate to the young Khedive once and for all that England must be reckoned with and that even a liberal cabinet in London did not mean that the English ministry would allow its hand to be forced so easily. A lively correspondence ensued between Cromer and Rosebery with the result that on the morning of January 17 the former was able to present Abbas with what was practically an ultimatum. The Khedive, evidently after consulting with the French and finding them unwilling to go the limit, yielded in good time and Riaz

siderate of France. At the time Cromer was quite positive about the intrigues of the French and Russian consuls-general (A. G. Gardiner: *The Life of Sir William Harcourt* [London 1923] II, pp. 225-226). On the intrigue of the French and Russian consuls-general see Cromer pp. 25-26; further G. P. VIII, no. 1819, footnote, with the reports of the German representative; Blunt: Lord Cromer and the Khedive (*Nineteenth Century* April 1893); Blunt: *Diaries* I, p. 177; Mme. Adam in *Nouvelle Revue* February 1, 1893. Of course all such insinuations were vehemently repudiated by the French at the time (cf. *London Times* January 18, 1893; *Journal des Débats* January 19, 24, 1893).

[7] G. P. VIII, nos. 1813, 1829.

Pasha, a compromise candidate, was chosen in place of Fakhry. This, however, was not the end of the story, for the incident gave rise to considerable agitation in Egypt, and Cromer now demanded of the home government an increase in the forces of occupation. Gladstone objected but after a hot debate Rosebery, who supported Cromer, won his point, and an infantry battalion which was passing through the Suez Canal was immediately diverted to Egypt.[8]

Against these "high-handed" actions of the English government the French loudly protested, arguing that they would be taken throughout Europe as well as in France as a "long step in the direction of actual annexation." It is not unlikely that in Paris the prospect of reopening the whole question was rather welcome and that it was thought the Egyptian imbroglio might serve as a useful diversion from the complications arising from the Panama revelations.[9] At any rate the French foreign office exerted itself to the utmost to induce the Sultan to lodge a vigorous protest and demand explanations, if not to issue an appeal to the powers. That Abdul Hamid was very much irritated by the action of the English there can be no doubt, but the Sultan was too wary to allow himself to be dragged into deep waters. He first sounded out the governments of Berlin and Vienna as to their probable attitude, and, finding no encouragement in either quarter, refused to be inveigled by the French.[10]

[8] On this whole incident see Cromer, *loc. cit.*; *Egypt, no. 1, 1893* (Command no. 6849); *Affaires d'Égypte 1884-1893*, chapter xviii (Crise Ministérielle 1893); S. H. Jeyes: *The Earl of Rosebery* (London 1906) pp. 13 ff.; Anon: The Foreign Policy of Lord Rosebery (*Contemporary Review* August 1901, pp. 154-156); G. P. VIII, nos. 1819 ff. Gladstone was violently opposed to Cromer's demand and told Harcourt "that they might as well ask him to put a torch to Westminster Abbey as to send more troops to Egypt." Rosebery almost resigned as a result of the quarrel in the cabinet, and an agreement was patched up only with difficulty (Sir Algernon West: *Private Diaries* [London 1922], pp. 123-137).

[9] Gladstone in the house of commons, January 31, 1893. The correspondence between France and England is to be found in the Blue Book and Yellow Book referred to above. Rosebery's attitude is best brought out by his despatch to Cromer of February 16, 1893, published as *Egypt no. 2, 1893*, (Command 6956), and reprinted in Jeyes p. 144 and Cromer pp. 39-41.

[10] The Sultan's anger is well brought out in the extracts from the report of Sir Clare Ford, printed in Cromer p. 31. The negotiations at Constantinople

Even more important, however, was the attitude of Russia. It may be that the Russian representative in Cairo had coöperated with his French colleague in encouraging the Khedive, but it is certain that the Russian government as such had no intention of becoming embroiled. No inclination whatsoever was shown to support the French protests. The Russian government merely took note of the declarations made by Rosebery to the effect that the strengthening of the British forces did not involve a change in English policy.[11] Under the circumstances the French were absolutely isolated. They reserved the right to consult with the other powers and with the Sultan as to the steps to be taken in case of further developments, but Rosebery ignored this mild menace, knowing full well that the French would find no support for their pretensions.[12]

The French had chosen the worst possible moment for taking action and for appealing to the Russians for support. It was at the very height of the Panama scandal, and at the very time of the Egyptian crisis accusations were being published in Paris against Mohrenheim, who was reputed to have accepted sums from the Panama funds.[13]   Far from thinking of the alliance

dragged on for a long time and may be most easily studied in G. P. VIII, nos. 1821, 1822, 1824, 1826, 1828, 1830, 1831, etc.   See also *London Times* January 27, February 4, 6, 9, 13, 1893.

[11] Cromer p. 26: "Russia was prepared to drive pins into England in order to please the French, but was not inclined to risk a serious quarrel out of sheer love for the Franco-Russian Alliance." An official of the Russian foreign office admitted to Wolkenstein that the French had made "ouvertures assez pressantes" while the French chargé confessed that all efforts to interest the Russians had failed (Wolkenstein to Kálnoky February 8, 15, 1893). In speaking to Morier, Shishkin characterized the Khedive's action as "imprudent" and recognized the desirability of maintaining the *status quo* (Wolkenstein to Kálnoky February 4, 1893). Though the Russian press fulminated against the English policy, it also complained that the French could not expect the Russians to act when the French themselves were in no position to do so (*Mémorial Diplomatique*, letters from St. Petersburg, January 28, February 4, 18, 1893; *London Times* January 23, 26, February 9, 13, 1893).

[12] The French press was rabid, especially after the announcement that the English garrison would be increased.   The *Figaro* on January 25 went so far as to suggest the seizure of Tangier in retaliation.   But it was well-known at the time that the powers of the Triple Alliance were firmly behind England (cf. *London Times* January 26, February 6, 9, 1893, and the sources mentioned above).

[13] Cf. especially Hansen: *Mohrenheim* pp. 143-154. It appears from Cyon's letter to Pobiedonostsev, November 21, 1893, that Mohrenheim received about

with France or of coöperation with France the Tsar's mind was preoccupied with ideas of a very different kind. The tension in Central Asia and the possibility of a clash with the English in itself emphasized the value of the connection with Germany which was no more, and in like fashion the development of the Bulgarian question demanded the undivided attention of the Russian statesmen. Quite obviously the prospect of ever getting rid of Ferdinand was becoming slighter and slighter. The existing situation simply could not last, and the Russian protests against the policies of Stambulov were becoming ridiculously monotonous. If eventual recognition was becoming inevitable the only sensible course open to the Tsar was to reach an amicable agreement with Austria and, through Austria, with Germany.

The matter had been discreetly broached by the Russian statesmen on various occasions since the fall of Bismarck and the nonrenewal of the Reinsurance Treaty, and it was evidently felt in St. Petersburg that everything was to be gained and nothing lost by a pursuance of this policy. An arrangement with Austria would either weaken and eventually wreck the Triple Alliance, or else it would frighten the Germans sufficiently to induce them to resume their former relationship with Russia. Already in the summer of 1892 there had been numerous rumors of a coming visit of Francis Joseph to the Tsar, and it was said that a meeting at Skiernievice had actually been arranged for September but had been frustrated by the sudden announcement that the Kaiser would visit Vienna at that very time.[14] The truth of the matter was probably that both sides desired the interview, but that neither was willing to take the initiative. In any case Francis Joseph spoke very warmly of Russia in his speech to the delegations on October 3 and the Russian foreign office seized the opportunity to give assurances as to Russia's

750,000 francs of Panama money from Freycinet (C. Pobiedonostsev: *Mémoires*, [Paris 1927] pp. 637 ff.).

[14] *London Times* June 9, 1892; *Mémorial Diplomatique* September 24, October 15, 1892; Mme. Adam in *Nouvelle Revue* November 15, 1892; E. de Cyon: La Fin de la Triple Alliance (*Nouvelle Revue* December 1, 1892).

good intentions.[15] What was even more important was the Tsar's decision to send the Tsarevich to Vienna in November. The unusually hearty reception accorded to the Russian heir by the Emperor Francis Joseph and the Austrian court made an excellent impression in St. Petersburg and led to considerable discussion of the desirability of an Austro-Russian agreement. Even then it was pointed out that the two governments might conclude a pact by which the one should be allowed to annex Bosnia and Herzegovina and the other to secure the free passage of its warships through the Bosporus and Dardanelles.[16] Of course this was shooting very wide of the mark, but it illustrates the persistence of the idea of an arrangement in the political writing of the time. In diplomatic circles no one expected the visit of the Grand Duke to have an influence except upon the personal relations of the dynasties, because the Bulgarian problem was still looked upon as a well-nigh insuperable barrier to a sincere rapprochement.

No doubt the Tsar would have welcomed a settlement of this wearisome question, but it is unlikely that he would have agreed to any proposal which did not involve the expulsion of Ferdinand. To the Austrians this was too far-reaching and the game did not seem worth the candle. It was, after all, a question of comparative values, and opinions were divided. Aehrenthal, for example, was at that time first secretary of the Austrian embassy in St. Petersburg and repeatedly urged the desirability of an entente, even at the expense of considerable sacrifices in Bulgaria. He was convinced that the Russians were not planning action in the west and declared that, so long as the Austrian foreign office did not irritate the Russian "epidermis" in Bulgarian matters, there would be no need to fear aggression. In view of the Tsar's disgust with recent events in Paris a favorable opportunity was being offered, perhaps for the last time, to draw him away from the French alliance and reconstitute the Alliance of the Three Emperors:

[15] Aehrenthal to Kálnoky October 5, 13, 1892.
[16] Aehrenthal to Kálnoky November 17, 1892; G. P. VII, no. 1638; *Mémorial Diplomatique* November 19, 26, 1892.

"Between orthodox and autocratic Russia on the one hand and the two neighboring monarchies on the other there are certainly more factors making for union and common interest than for separation," he wrote on November 10, 1892. "All three of these states are based on Christian and monarchical foundations and against these foundations the forces of republican socialism are directed. In view of the increasingly violent attacks of these elements on the authority of the crown, an agreement is necessary between those who are threatened by the common danger. The character of the Russian autocrat is certainly a considerable, though I think not insuperable obstacle to such an agreement; of course both sides would have to make sacrifices: we should have to consider the Tsar's *amour propre* in the Bulgarian question and in a general way the principle that subordinate interests must yield to higher political considerations would have to be recognized by both sides."[17]

Aehrenthal was not rebuked for his daring suggestions. In fact his chief, Count Wolkenstein, held very similar views and Kálnoky himself was apparently favorably inclined.[18] But the men at the Ballhausplatz could not quite bring themselves to take the final plunge. Of course they realized the possible implications of the Franco-Russian combination, and they made little effort to conceal their dissatisfaction with the policy of their German ally. But there were other considerations which must have weighed heavily; above all, the problem of the English attitude. So far there was no reason to complain of Rosebery's policy, which was merely a continuation of that of his predecessor. As for the future, that was of necessity uncertain, and consequently the Austrian statesmen felt it advisable to maintain the best possible relations with St. Petersburg without actually making concessions which might estrange Germany or England. The policy can be clearly seen in action if one reviews the developments of the Bulgarian problem in the winter and spring of 1892-1893.

Ferdinand and Stambulov had failed to induce the Porte to take any steps in the direction of recognition, and they had found

[17] Aehrenthal to Kálnoky October 27, November 10, 27, 1892.

[18] In a forty-two page despatch dated December 20, 1892, Wolkenstein reviewed the whole situation and came to the conclusion that the Tsar could never feel real sympathy for France. All the concessions he had made were the result of supposed menaces. In view of the scandals in Paris, a rapprochement between Russia, Germany and Austria would be possible if the Tsar could be convinced that the Triple Alliance involved no offensive designs against Russia.

that all hopes of action by any of the great powers were entirely
illusory. Pending the solution of this problem Ferdinand devoted
himself to the consolidation of his position within the country.
He determined to secure himself by marrying and establishing
a dynasty. The main hindrance to the scheme was, however, the
provision of article 38 of the Constitution of Tirnovo, which spe-
cified that only the elected ruler might retain his own faith, if
other than orthodox. There was no hope of contracting a marriage with a Catholic family unless some guarantee were given
that the children would be brought up in the Roman Catholic
faith. This point had, perhaps, been made clear to Ferdinand in
London and Vienna. However that may be, he realized its importance and on December 20, 1892 the government introduced
a bill altering the Constitution of Tirnovo in a number of details.
Article 38 was made to read:

"Only the prince who ascends the throne by election and his first successor may, if they belong to a confession other than the orthodox, retain
their faith if they wish."

In spite of some opposition on the part of the Bulgarian clergy,
this measure was forced through by Stambulov and was then
ready for reference to the grand sobranje, which alone could
make the final decision in matters affecting the constitution.[19]
Having removed this great obstacle, Ferdinand immediately
set out in search of a bride, and in February, 1893 Stambulov
was able to announce his master's engagement to Princess Marie
Louise of Parma. On April 20 the wedding took place on the
Italian Riviera and on May 11 Ferdinand and his bride arrived
in Bulgaria. On May 28 the grand sobranje accepted the
changes in the constitution. The union of Ferdinand with a
princess belonging to one of the old royal families of Europe was
a tremendous success for the existing regime in Bulgaria. More
than anything else it helped to secure Ferdinand's position and to
increase his popularity among the Bulgarian people, by whom the
event was regarded as a turning point. Uncertainty was over
and the future looked very much more hopeful now that a real

[19] Cf. Staneff part ii, pp. 174-175.

national dynasty had been founded. The tremendous advantage gained was no doubt worth even the sacrifice involved in the constitutional change, and Ferdinand was acclaimed with great enthusiasm when he returned home. He had, indeed, succeeded in shifting the responsibility and the odium to Stambulov while he himself received the laurels.

From the standpoint of international relations this turn in the history of the Bulgarian question was of considerable importance. Ferdinand and his minister had acted quite independently and neither one of the friendly Austrian or English cabinets had been consulted. Neither, in fact, was at all well-impressed by the plan, for it was a matter of importance to both that the Bulgarian question should not be raised at that time.[20] Fortunately the submission of the constitutional changes to the sobranje in December 1892 did not make a very deep impression in St. Petersburg, partly because the provision regarding the confession of the future heir was concealed amid a number of other clauses and partly because it was believed that the opposition of the orthodox clergy in Bulgaria would prove sufficiently strong to crush the measure in the grand sobranje.[21] In any case Kálnoky seems to have had no difficulty in convincing the Russian foreign office that he was not behind the scheme, and Shishkin, the assistant foreign minister, declared that Russia had no intention of abandoning her policy of watchful waiting.[22] Austro-Russian relations therefore remained unaffected, and in

[20] Kálnoky to Aehrenthal December 9, 1892, shows that, while the Austrian minister was informed somewhat in advance, he was in no way consulted. On December 5, 1892 the *Neue Freie Presse* published a strong article against Stambulov's plan, and on December 7 the *London Times* published a report from Vienna stating that the Austrian government had had no inkling of what was being prepared, and that it probably would have disapproved, if asked beforehand.

[21] Kálnoky to Aehrenthal December 9; Schiessl to Kálnoky December 10; Szögyény to Kálnoky January 3, 1893.

[22] Wolkenstein to Kálnoky January 3, 1893. Kálnoky seems to have been genuinely irritated with Stambulov's independence of action (Kálnoky to Aehrenthal December 9, 1892) while the English feared that the Russians might seize the opportunity to march (Wolkenstein to Kálnoky December 21; Szögyény to Kálnoky December 29, 1892; G. P. IX, no. 2129). According to the *London Times* December 19, England opened negotiations with the powers of the Triple Alliance, but Germany refused to join the others in a warning to Sofia.

February 1893 it was reported from Vienna that the relations between the three eastern monarchies had not been better in the previous decade.[23]

The announcement of Ferdinand's betrothal, on the other hand, necessarily complicated matters and completely changed the situation, at least in the eyes of the Russian statesmen. It was now clearly recognized what the object of the constitutional changes had been, and it had become evident that the acceptance of the amendments by the grand sobranje must be practically assured. The Russian government acted promptly and on March 5 issued a circular note to the powers protesting against the proposed change in article 38 of the Bulgarian constitution. It was argued that there was nothing in the Treaty of Berlin which could be interpreted as making the Bulgarian throne hereditary, and that

"The imperial government, standing strictly on the principle of non-interference in the internal affairs of Bulgaria, does not intend to examine the motives, evidently interested, which induced the Prince of Coburg and those actually in power at Sofia, to have recourse to this deplorable measure. But in view of the religious and racial ties which unite Russia and Bulgaria, it cannot remain a silent spectator to an attempt destined to shake the dominant religion in the principality."[24]

At the same time the Russian press opened a violent campaign against the Bulgarian statesmen and against Austria as well, accompanying the usual denunciations with threats that Russia would tear up the whole Treaty of Berlin upon which the Austrian control of Bosnia and Herzegovina rested.[25]

By some it was feared that the Tsar, who was fanatically orthodox, had at last made up his mind to act, especially since he could hope to find support in a religious question among a great many Bulgarians.[26] But Kálnoky knew that the whole question had become a matter of personal honor for Alexander and that

[23] *London Times* February 8, 1893 (Vienna February 7).

[24] Copy in Vienna Archives. The circular had been published in part in the *Messager Officiel.* Cf. also G. P. IX, no. 2130; Drandar pp. 273-274; Bousquet p. 313.

[25] *Mémorial Diplomatique* March 18, 1893.

[26] Wolkenstein to Kálnoky March 23, 1893; Daudet: *Ferdinand I,* pp. 153-154.

the protests, while inevitable, were not very seriously meant and would not be followed by action.[27] In reply to the Russian note he reasserted his complete innocence, though he did not let pass the opportunity to combat the new Russian theory as to the non-hereditary nature of the Bulgarian throne.[28] Now that Stambulov had executed a *coup* he thought that Russia ought to realize the debacle of her Bulgarian policy and accept a reasonable settlement, by which, no doubt, he meant the recognition of Ferdinand in one way or another. The prospects of Giers' return to the Russian foreign office were very slight and Prince Lobanov, the Russian ambassador at Vienna, was regarded as the most likely candidate for the position. Lobanov was well-disposed towards the idea of a settlement of the Balkan difficulty by way of an agreement with Austria, and clearly recognized that with the construction of the Trans-Siberian Railway the centre of Russia's interests would shift to the Far East. Through him Kálnoky reopened the question of a possible revival of the Three Emperors' Alliance, but apparently the Tsar himself could not be induced to admit his complete failure in the Near East.[29]

At the same time Kálnoky felt the need of retaining some influence in Sofia. The agreement with Russia was, after all, uncertain, and on the other hand Ferdinand and Stambulov had

[27] Lobanov told him: "Nous ne pouvons reculer d'un pouce dans l'affaire bulgare et nous laisserons faire par conséquent sans sortir de notre réserve et sans nous mêler de cette aventure du 'Petit Ferdinand' " (Kálnoky to Wolkenstein March 9, 1893). In Berlin also it was thought unlikely that the protest was seriously meant (Szögyény to Kálnoky March 13, April 16, 1893).

[28] Kálnoky to Wolkenstein March 13, 1893. Similarly, despatch from Vienna in the *London Times* March 16, 1893.

[29] Kálnoky to Wolkenstein March 9 and July 7, 1893, reporting long talks with Lobanov. Kálnoky assured the Russian ambassador of the good will of Austria and Germany and complained of the Tsar's distrust of his neighbors. He warned Lobanov of the spread of French revolutionary principles and spoke of the Panama scandal as revealing "eine Fäulnis, die Giftstoffe genug enthält, um ganz Europa zu vergiften." The only remedy would be a new *Dreikaiserbund*. Shishkin seems to have been in favor of a solution of the Bulgarian question, and the Tsar appears to have been the great obstacle to a settlement (Wolkenstein to Kálnoky March 22 and April 20, 1893; Kálnoky to Wolkenstein May 4, 1893). That Wolkenstein himself was an ardent worker in the same cause appears clearly from G. P. IX, no. 2130.

acted entirely too independently to suit the authorities in Vienna. Ferdinand, it was rumored, was planning to return to Bulgaria by way of Constantinople.[30] He must not be allowed to precipitate a crisis which might end in war for the Dual Monarchy. A recognition of the legality of his government by the Sultan would almost certainly arouse the Russians to action and thus compromise all prospects of an Austro-Russian agreement. These considerations probably conditioned the reception of Ferdinand and Stambulov by Francis Joseph on April 10 and 11, as they were passing through Vienna on their way to the wedding. There is no reason to suppose that they received anything but good advice. Ferdinand and his minister were urged not to complicate matters by a trip to Constantinople or by any other steps looking towards recognition or independence.[31] As a result Ferdinand promised to return to Sofia without stopping in the Turkish capital.[32]

It may well be imagined how great was the displeasure of the Tsar and of Russia generally at the reception accorded Stambulov by the Austrian Emperor.[33] Stambulov, who, according to the Russian press, was the murderer of Panitza and other conspirators and whose hands were still dripping with Russian blood, was a regular bugaboo to the Tsar and his advisers. At the time it was still feared that the "Coburger" would pay the Sultan a visit and that then complications would become unavoidable.[34] On the other hand the Russians had long been losing their sympathy even for the Bulgarian people, and the

[30] The Russian ambassador at Constantinople was immediately instructed to protest to the Sultan (Szögyény to Kálnoky April 16, 1893).

[31] Kálnoky to Wolkenstein July 7, 1893, says that he told Stambulov and Ferdinand that Austria could not undertake a war to support Bulgarian pretensions, and that they ought to consolidate the gains they had made rather than embark on further adventures. Cf. also G. P. IX, no. 2133; Beaman: *Stambuloff* pp. 179-180.

[32] Kálnoky to Szögyény April 19, 1893, says that Ferdinand gave up the idea "wegen entschiedenen Bedenken des Sultans," but the representations of Russia and of Germany undoubtedly influenced the Porte just as Kálnoky influenced Ferdinand. Cf. *London Times* April 19, 1893.

[33] Wolkenstein to Kálnoky April 28, 1893.

[34] Wolkenstein to Kálnoky April 20; Szögyény to Kálnoky April 29, 1893.

government sincerely desired a settlement of the problem if only its own face could be saved. Lobanov, who was in St. Petersburg at the time, no doubt threw all the weight of his influence into the scales, and before long the Russian press took the cue from the foreign office. Giers was returning from the Riviera to resume control of affairs and fully sympathized with the new movement. On his way he stopped at Vienna and both Francis Joseph and Kálnoky took the opportunity to pay their respects. Giers opened his heart to his visitors and bitterly complained of the Bulgarians. Every one of them, he maintained, had cost Russia 456 rubles and not one of them was worth it:

"We have had enough of the Bulgarians," he continued, "and we do not want to hear them mentioned. Let them do what they like. After all, they will not succeed in constituting themselves without Russia's consent. The Bulgarian question can become dangerous only in the future."[35]

This was evidently a strong bid for an agreement, which Kálnoky does not appear to have followed up, probably because he felt that the first concrete proposals should come from the Russian side. After all, the Austrians were satisfied with things as they were in Bulgaria. Nevertheless, the attention paid to Giers in Vienna made a very good impression in Russian circles.[36] Russia could have nothing to do with Ferdinand and Stambulov, but at any rate she was no longer accusing Austria of the Bulgarian trouble. The celebration of the twenty-fifth anniversary of the Slavic Welfare Society gave the Russian press sufficient opportunity to express the new attitude of Holy Russia towards her brother Slavs in the Balkans. The *Grashdanin* declared the jubilee to be

"sinful towards God, in whose name we have told so many falsehoods and inflamed so much hatred, and an insult to the remains of our Russian brethren who have fallen as a sacrifice to Slav imposture."[37]

---

[35] Kálnoky to Wolkenstein May 4, 1893. Giers also spoke very deprecatingly of the French and asserted that the Tsar had full confidence in the Kaiser. Cf. further G. P. VII, no. 1655, 1656; IX, no. 2134.

[36] Wolkenstein to Kálnoky May 9, 1893; Szögyény to Kálnoky May 13, 1893); *Mémorial Diplomatique* May 6, 1893. From G. P. VII, no. 1657 it appears that Kálnoky regarded Giers as done for, and that he was probably waiting for Lobanov to take over the reins.

[37] Quoted in the *London Times* May 31, 1893.

In the *Viestnik Evropi* Professor Pipin wrote as follows:

"Russia has sacrificed enough money and blood in the Slav cause. It is time to inquire what equivalent has been received. Economically nothing, absolutely nothing; politically next to nothing, as was found by the results of the last Eastern War. Has something, then, been gained in the way of civilization? This is, for the present, questionable. There is, it is true, a kind of Panslavist movement in Russia. It is much talked-of in Europe, because the Western European press look upon it and its aspirations as essentially dangerous. As a matter of fact, however, the party is not numerous and has so far not achieved anything extraordinary." Russia's real mission, he went on, is to attend to her own domestic affairs. She cannot associate herself with the whole of Slavdom. "That idea is Utopian." The Poles were hostile to the idea and the other Slavs promoted it only artificially. "They think of the Russians when they want a bogey to frighten their enemies, the Germans and Turks."[38]

In the *Russki Viestnik* the well-known writer, Tatischev, went so far as to characterize Russia's past policy in Bulgaria as *childish* and to advocate a settlement even with Stambulov.[39]

Nothing was left of the Pan-Slav movement, at least for the moment. No agreement had been made with Austria, because the Austrians were unwilling to make great concessions and because the Tsar was unable to swallow his pride. But there was no longer any real danger that the Bulgarian question would lead to war between the two powers. In June 1893 Kálnoky declared in the delegations that "it could only be a matter for congratulation that Austria's relations with Russia, which had previously been good, had now improved." These relations were, he repeated, "very friendly." Both the Tsar and the Russian government were, he felt convinced, well-disposed towards the Dual Monarchy, and an agreement between them in regard to the Balkans was indeed but a matter of time.[40]

[38] Quoted in the *London Times* May 25, 1893. Compare also the quotations given in Becker pp. 152 ff.

[39] These articles were later published in book form. In June the Russian press, even the *Sviet* on June 11, began to ask the question whether it would not be better to recognize the *status quo* in Bulgaria and so avoid further humiliation (Wolkenstein to Kálnoky June 21, 1893).

[40] These declarations were hailed with great delight in the Russian capital (Wolkenstein to Kálnoky June 7, 13, 1893). Cf. also Kálnoky's remarks to the French ambassador Decrais (in Köhler pp. 317-319). From Kálnoky's despatch to Wolkenstein (July 7, 1893) it is clear that he intended to pave the way to a settlement of the Bulgarian matter.

The Austro-Russian agreement, had it materialized, would have been regarded by both sides as only a first step in the direction of something resembling the old Alliance of the Three Emperors. The Austrians, no matter how disappointed and irritated they may have been with the course of events in Berlin since the fall of Bismarck, would never have entrusted their fate to the Russians alone, and it is unlikely that a new Kaunitz coalition between Russia, Austria and France could have been effected.[41] The Tsar would have lost interest in France if an arrangement with the central powers had proved possible, and the Austrians themselves would have thought twice before assuming a hostile attitude towards Germany. Public opinion, too, would have made such a coalition quite impossible. What the Tsar was really after was an agreement with Germany such as had existed before 1890, or else a new Russo-Austro-German Entente. It must be constantly borne in mind that good relations with Germany were almost imperative for Russia if she hoped to make progress anywhere. In the Near East they were almost essential, while at the same time an active policy in Asia was almost unthinkable unless Russia could count on the neutrality of both Germany and Austria, or at least of Germany.

The revival of the Three Emperors' Alliance in 1892-1893 was, in a sense, rendered impossible because of the Austrian attitude on the Bulgarian question, but this is only part of the story. The relations between Germany and Russia were infinitely more complex and proved even more incapable of a satisfactory solution. Since the meeting of the Kaiser and the Tsar at Kiel the relations between the two courts had certainly improved. On the Russian side the old friendship with Germany would still have been preferred to the new entente with France, especially in view of the development of the Russo-English antagonism

[41] In all the material now available there is, so far as I know, no indication that the Austrians ever seriously considered abandoning the alliance with Germany. On the contrary, the Austrians seem to have been worried as much about the bad relations between Germany and Russia as about the relations between the Russians and themselves.

in Central Asia. Furthermore the Russians were badly in need of money. They desired a tariff agreement, in part because the commercial treaty between Germany and Austria put Russian agricultural products at a great disadvantage at a time when Russia was trying desperately to recover from the effects of the famine, and in part because it was hoped that a tariff treaty would prove the first step to the readmission of Russian securities to the German market and the flotation of a loan. It is quite interesting to note that as early as August, 1892 the tariff negotiations were reopened, though they made little progress because of the coolness of the Germans towards the Russian proposals. But the Tsar made it perfectly clear to Boisdeffre during the negotiations for the military convention that he required secrecy and could not afford to jeopardize the prospects of an agreement with Germany.[42]

On the German side there was also a distinct desire to contribute to the establishment of better relations. It may be that the tirades of Bismarck had something to do with the attitude of the foreign office, and that it was thought necessary to do something to convince the country that the government could not be held responsible for any eventual complications between the two countries. It may also be that the debacle of the efforts made to reconcile the Kaiser and his former chancellor had removed the chief reason for the anti-Russian policy of Holstein. There was no longer the slightest possibility of Bismarck's return to power, and consequently no obstacle to the resumption of the policy with which he had identified himself.[43] But beyond these minor considerations there were very good and important reasons for the German change of front. The change of ministry in Eng-

---

[42] L. J. no. 71. According to E. J. Dillon: *The Eclipse of Russia* (New York 1918, p. 352) the negotiations for the military convention were actually held up on account of the pourparlers with Germany. On the negotiations themselves see Witte pp. 65-66; Aehrenthal to Kálnoky August 17, 1892; Széchényi to Kálnoky August 20, 1892; Széchényi to Kálnoky, October 15, 1892; Aehrenthal to Kálnoky August 13, 1892.

[43] From Holstein's letter to Eulenburg January 29, 1893 (Haller: *Eulenburg* pp. 85-86) it appears that Holstein had been in favor of the Kiel meeting and that he had become converted to the policy of better relations with Russia.

land was, for Germany, of the utmost significance. Whatever the attitude of Rosebery personally might be, there was no longer the slightest assurance that the cabinet would support the foreign minister in continuing the policy of Salisbury. Gladstone was a person to be reckoned with. He was known to favor an agreement with France and there were fears in the hearts of the Germans that he might attempt an arrangement with Russia in the affairs of Central Asia.[44] Besides, Gladstone was the classic opponent of the Turks, and he had made it clear that he had no intention of allowing England to intervene on behalf of Italy in case of a conflict between the latter and France. Men like Morley made no secret of their desires to see Egypt evacuated as early as possible, and the abandonment of Egypt would, quite obviously, revolutionize the whole Eastern question and necessitate a revamping of the whole European alignment.[45]

The Italians were particularly anxious about the possible development of English policy, and even the Germans considered the advisability of a return to the Bismarckian policy of 1884.[46] At that time the great chancellor had forced Gladstone into making concessions by taking the side of France and deserting the English in the Egyptian question. The most immediate problem was to secure from the new cabinet a clear statement as to its attitude towards the Mediterranean agreements and especially towards the assurances given to Italy by Lord Salisbury. Rosebery's own views and intentions were quite satisfactory, but the question was whether he could give the necessary declarations without creating a cabinet crisis which might lead to his overthrow and the substitution of Labouchère and Dilke. Through the extremely tactful handling of this problem by Hatzfeldt the Italian apprehensions were finally quieted. Rosebery could not give a written declaration of the intentions of the government, but he did go so far as to give the German ambas-

---

[44] Compare the rumors to this effect in *Mémorial Diplomatique* August 27, September 3, September 10, 1892.

[45] See especially G. P. VIII, no. 1732.

[46] G. P. VIII, no. 1735; Schiessl to Kálnoky, August 31, 1892. On the German calculations see G. P. VIII, no. 1733.

sador written confirmation of their conversation, with permission to communicate it to the Italian government. The important passage of this document was as follows:

"My personal view was this, but it must be held to be nothing more, that in the event of France groundlessly attacking Italy, the interests of England as a Mediterranean and Indian Power would bring her naturally to the rescue of Italy, while her sympathy, as having so long and ardently coöperated in the cause of Italian freedom, would lead her in the same direction. That was my personal conviction, but beyond that I could say nothing, and in any case I could not make an authoritative communication as from the British Cabinet to the Italian government. My belief was simply this, that in the eventuality that was dreaded and contemplated, the natural force of things would bring about the defensive coöperation they desired."[47]

This declaration, though binding only Rosebery personally, was almost more than could have been expected, and it appears to have satisfied the Italians.[48] They had, in fact, helped to bring it about by the outspokenly Francophil tinge given to the Columbus celebrations at Genoa early in August, at the very time when the French were beginning to indicate their intention of reopening the Egyptian question.[49]

The position of England was, in fact, a difficult one. In foreign policy the liberal cabinet did not enjoy the prestige of its predecessor and was constantly exposed to daring advances on the part of its opponents. So long as Gladstone had anything to say

[47] G. P. VIII, nos. 1737 ff. for details. The conversation between Rosebery and Hatzfeldt took place on September 6, and the words used by the foreign minister were somewhat stronger than those committed to paper, according to the ambassador. In view of this declaration it is hard to understand the statement in a memorandum of Lord Lansdowne November 11, 1901: "Lord Rosebery, on coming into office, refused to recognise this (Mediterranean) agreement" (British Documents on the Origins of the War II, p. 78).

[48] G. P. VIII, nos. 1741, 1742; Schiessl to Kálnoky October 1, 1892. As Brin pointed out, however, the question as to whether England would support Italy, if the latter went to war with France after France had attacked Germany, was still an open one.

[49] On the Genoa celebration see *Mémorial Diplomatique* September 10, 1892, where it is gleefully argued that the Triple Alliance was losing all influence in Italy and the Italians had become disillusioned about the English as well. Gladstone had sent only three English ships where Salisbury had planned to send seven (*Saturday Review* September 10, 1892).

there could be no thought of far-reaching commitments to Italy or the Triple Alliance.   In fact, it would be difficult to persuade the "Grand Old Man" of the necessity of taking even ordinary precautions.   The cabinet was inclined to concern itself almost exclusively with the Irish question, to take but little interest in naval affairs, and to dissociate itself almost completely from a forward policy anywhere.   Meanwhile the French were intriguing in Egypt and the Russians pushing on in Central Asia. England was isolated between them, and since no satisfactory or reliable assurances of support could be given to the central powers, the position of Rosebery was by no means an enviable one.

In the Wilhelmstrasse the implications of the situation were clearly recognized and at this very time began the policy of playing one side off against the other.   It was, in fact, easier for the Germans to play off the Russians and even the French against England than for England to play off the new Franco-Russian combination against the Triple Alliance, for the very good reason that the Franco-Russian Entente was not sufficiently secure to make a program of action possible and the Russians were unwilling to antagonize the Germans in any case.   On the contrary they were courting the good will of the Germans and the latter found themselves in a stronger position than at any time since the fall of Bismarck.   While desirous of not estranging England and of maintaining the wire to London intact, the statesmen in the Wilhelmstrasse had decided to reëstablish the connection with St. Petersburg.   One might almost say that in the next decade this policy remained essentially unchanged, the Germans selling their support now to the one side, now to the other, until the two sides put an end to this method by the Anglo-French Entente of 1904 and the Anglo-Russian Agreement of 1907.   In a sense it was a return to the Bismarckian system of holding the balance between England and Russia, but there were important differences.   In the first place Bismarck's primary object was to preserve the peace and to secure for Germany an opportunity to consolidate and develop.   With his successors the policy still aimed at preserving the peace, but a great deal more effort was

devoted to expansive tendencies. The policy of Bismarck in
1884-1885 became continuous after 1892. The other important
difference lay in the fact that Bismarck, while keeping open the
connection with both London and St. Petersburg, inclined rather
to the latter. His successors, who had started by throwing
themselves almost entirely upon the mercy of England, continued, even after 1892, to direct their sympathies to England
while attempting, nevertheless, to reëstablish contact with the
Russians. In any case the German position was strong and was
bound to remain strong as long as the rivalry of France and England and of Russia and England continued to exist. In 1892
there was no prospect of their coming to an end and the German
statesmen were safe, if not wise, in adopting the policy of the
two irons in the fire.

So far as England was concerned this new policy of the Germans was eloquently and effectively expressed in the winter of
1892-1893 in connection with the Egyptian affair. Bismarck
had always regarded the Egyptian question as the most reliable
bond holding England and Germany together and he had consistently supported the English policy in order to maintain
the contact between England and the Triple Alliance. This
policy had, of course, been faithfully followed by his successors,
who had, during the last two years of the Salisbury ministry, laid
even greater stress upon the connection with England. It seemed
like the A. B. C. of foreign relations to avoid creating difficulties
for the English in this all-important matter, which, in a sense,
was the very crux of the Mediterranean problem. Failure to do so
might well have resulted in an Anglo-French arrangement and a
veritable revolution in the European alignment. Even after the
advent of Gladstone and Rosebery this policy was continued,
though rather half-heartedly and with the distinct feeling that
England, no longer entirely trustworthy as a friend of the Triple
Alliance, must be prepared for a change in the German attitude
the moment she showed an inclination to swerve from her support
of the central powers. It has already been pointed out that
Hatzfeldt, soon after the downfall of the Salisbury cabinet, had
called the attention of his government to the possibility of such

a return to the extraordinary policy of Bismarck towards the Gladstone ministry in 1884-1885. At that time the Russians were threatening the English in Central Asia and so Bismarck could afford to assume a stern tone. In 1892 the situation was similar. The Germans were safe so long as there was no prospect of an Anglo-Russian understanding.[50]

In December, 1892 the English asked the powers to approve an increase in the numbers of the Egyptian army, pleading the renewed danger of an attack by the dervishes. To this proposal the Germans unhesitatingly assented, only to learn immediately after that English interests in Constantinople were doing their utmost to oppose the award of the concession for a railway to Konia to a German syndicate.[51] Bismarck had never taken great interest in the expansion of German enterprise in the Near East, or at any rate he had taken care to divorce such purely economic undertakings from political considerations. In fact he took the view that the competition of the French and English in matters of Anatolian railway construction might well develop into acute antagonism and that this might be exploited by the Germans in the same way as the Egyptian question.[52] In spite of the comparative indifference of the government German interests had secured the concession for a railway to Angora and had completed it by the autumn of 1892. The Sultan was greatly pleased by the efficient way in which the undertaking had been carried through, and intended to have the line continued to Bagdad by way of Sivas. The Kaiser, too, had shown his sympathy with the project, though he had not actively intervened in the matter.[53]

In December, 1892 a three-cornered fight developed in Constantinople. Herr Kaulla, representing the German group, was negotiating directly with the Sultan for the Angora-Sivas-Bagdad concession. French interests, under the direction of M.

[50] Cf. G. P. VIII, no. 1733.

[51] G. P. VIII, nos. 1814, 1815; XIV (2), nos. 3963 ff.

[52] G. P. XIV, no. 3958, note; cf. also H. Holborn: Deutschland und die Türkei 1878-1890 (Archiv für Politik und Geschichte August 1925).

[53] G. P. XIV, nos. 3961, 3962; Earle: Turkey, the Great Powers and the Bagdad Railway (New York 1923), chapter iii.

Nagelmakers, were negotiating with the Porte for a concession to connect Eskishehir with Konia, by way of Kutahia. Thirdly a British syndicate, led by Mr. Staniforth, desired to build a line from Heraclea on the Black Sea to Angora and thence to Bagdad. For one reason or another, probably because of engineering difficulties, the Sultan, in conference with Kaulla, seems to have decided to abandon the northern route to Bagdad *via* Sivas, and to run the line to Konia and thence, *via* the southern route, to Bagdad.[54] Since the negotiations between Kaulla and the Sultan were absolutely secret and unknown even to the grand vezir, the English and French did not at first know of what was brewing. When the news leaked out, the alarm was immediately sounded. The London *Times* on December 26 announced that a German railway to Konia would constitute an encroachment on the English sphere represented by the Smyrna-Cassaba and Smyrna-Aidin lines. This seems like a rather far-fetched interpretation unless one remembers that it was clearly understood in Constantinople that the Sultan meant to run a railway to Bagdad and presumably to the Persian Gulf, and that the English were much worried by the prospect of such a route falling into the hands of another power, even though friendly. Be that as it may, the English ambassador, Sir Clare Ford, protested against the award of the concession to Kaulla, urging consideration of English interests.[55]

News of this English protest appears to have reached Berlin on January 6, 1893, and immediately created a storm. Marschall turned to Malet, the English ambassador, and pointed out in no uncertain terms that Ford's action had placed the whole matter on a political plane. The English protest was not only discourteous, he went on, but actually hostile, and struck at the very basic principle of Anglo-German coöperation, especially in Near Eastern matters. Why should England object to the Indian

---

[54] The reason for this change of plan is still obscure, but I find no evidence to substantiate the claim sometimes made that Russian opposition influenced the Sultan at this time.

[55] On this whole incident compare G. P. XIV, nos. 3963 ff.; K. Helfferich: *Georg von Siemens* (Leipzig 1923) volume III, pp. 63 ff.; *The Memoirs of Ismail Kemal Bey* (London 1920) pp. 239 ff.

route being in the hands of the Germans, when there was no rivalry between them?[56] Not satisfied with this the German government took a very serious step. Without awaiting the reply of the English in regard to the railway negotiations Marschall telegraphed the German representative at Cairo to withhold the consent of the German government to the increase of the Egyptian army and instructed him to inform Lord Cromer that this change of attitude was due to the hostile stand of the English in respect to the Anatolian railway concession.[57] The English position in Egypt was at best a precarious one, and Cromer, who was probably anticipating trouble from the Khedive and had just been informed of the French refusal to sanction an increase of the forces, was horror-stricken at the idea of being deserted by the Germans. He wired to Rosebery urging the necessity of Anglo-German coöperation.[58]

It appears that the British foreign minister had been taken entirely by surprise in the matter of the Turkish railways. In any case he had not the slightest intention of antagonizing the Germans. On the contrary he was quite aware of the dangers which beset the English course at that time. With commendable promptitude he telegraphed to Berlin on January 9 explaining that the English government had no desire to obstruct the German concession for a railroad from Angora to Bagdad, and had only made representations to the Porte, pointing out that an extension of the Ismid line to Konia would injure British lines running inland from Smyrna. All the English government had asked for was delay, so that the English interests might be duly considered. "Her Majesty's Government have no desire to take any step inimical to German influence or interest at Constantinople."[59] To the German ambassador Rosebery explained that he had had no intention of crossing the Germans and had been entirely surprised by the affair. The English ambassador at Constantinople had never been instructed to transfer these commercial projects to the political field.[60] At first the

---

[56] G. P. XIV, no. 3966.

[58] G. P. XIV, no. 3967.

[60] G. P. XIV, no. 3974.

[57] G. P. VIII, no. 1816.

[59] G. P. XIV, nos. 3967, 3969.

noble Lord was inclined to be rather sulky, and spoke of the increased difficulty he would have in advocating in the cabinet a
policy friendly to the Triple Alliance.[61] But a few days later the
acute Egyptian crisis came on, and he hastened to complete the
satisfaction of the Germans in order to secure their renewed
support. In the course of the negotiations he spoke of the possibility of laying the whole Egyptian problem before a European
congress, whereupon Hatzfeldt pointed out that the alignment
of the powers on such an occasion would make it appear that
England had joined the Triple Alliance. The reply of the foreign
minister was characteristic. After remarking that this aspect of
the affair did not worry him and that the Egyptian crisis had
converted some of his colleagues to his policy, he continued:

"What a position England would be in if the Triple Alliance were shattered and we were then to find ourselves alone in the face of the Franco-
Russian group."[62]

This remark speaks volumes and should be closely noted. We
know from Lord Grey's memoirs what a deep impression the
abrupt and rather harsh action of the German government in the
matter of the Anatolian railway concession made upon the men
in the English foreign office. To Grey, at least, it appeared as a
case of crude blackmail. He resented it and never forgot it.
But at the time there was nothing to be done. England needed
Germany and had to submit.[63]

On February 6, 1893, the concession for the Konia line was
finally signed by the Sultan and his ministers.[64] Like most of
these agreements it involved a kilometer guarantee, and the
question immediately arose as to where the necessary funds were
to come from. The German syndicate greatly desired that the
revenues set aside should be administered by the council of the
Ottoman Public Debt. To this the English bondholders violent-

[61] G. P. VIII, no. 1818; XIV, no. 3972.

[62] G. P. VIII, no. 1823.

[63] Viscount Grey of Fallodon: *Twenty-Five Years* (New York 1925) volume I,
pp. 7-10. Cf. also H. Lutz: *Lord Grey und der Weltkrieg* (Berlin 1926), pp. 6-8.

[64] The decision was come to by the Turkish cabinet on January 19, the irade
granting the concession was published on February 6, and the contracts were signed
on February 16 (*London Times* January 23, February 7, 17, 1893).

ly objected. It is hardly likely that the English government had anything to do with this, but the German government evidently expected that Downing Street would see to it that the Germans got what they desired. The *Kölnische Zeitung,* in an article that was obviously inspired, wrote on March 10:

"If the English prefer to wage obstinate war against us in economic questions of this kind, the present moment is singularly rich in opportunities for Germany to retaliate upon England; and we are quite convinced that the German Government will not hesitate to accept the challenge."

This extraordinary effusion created quite a stir in London. The *Times* pointed out that the Germans should distinguish between the English government and the English colony in Constantinople, and should realize that the former could not be held responsible for the actions of the latter. But, in the end, the administration of the revenues was assigned to the Public Debt Administration. Rosebery understood the German threat and was wise enough to yield. The upshot of the whole affair was that it showed clearly that the German government had now placed Anglo-German relations on a business basis, and that it was determined to utilize its position, to take advantage of England's weakness, in order to make gains for itself. The two irons were already in the fire.[65]

The other iron was Russia. By the autumn of 1892 the German statesmen had frankly gone over to a policy designed to cultivate better relations with their eastern neighbor, a course which was dictated by common sense rather than sentiment, and was one of the logical results of the cabinet change in England.[66] Not being able to reckon entirely upon English support for the Triple Alliance, the German diplomats recognized the necessity of reëstablishing the connection with Russia. There was nothing the English dreaded more than a close understanding between the two empires, and that accounts in part for the weakening of the English position after Salisbury's fall and for Rosebery's

[65] *London Times* March 10, 13, 15, 25, 1893.

[66] Schweinitz: *Denkwürdigkeiten* II, p. 443, reporting a conversation with Marschall. Cf. also Salisbury's remark to Hatzfeldt in November 1892 that if Gladstone controlled English foreign policy he should expect to see Germany in the arms of Russia.

helplessness against German pressure in the winter of 1892-1893. However that may be, the Germans had begun to put themselves out to impress the Tsar favorably. Whereas they had shown an unusual inclination to take an active part in Balkan affairs in 1890 and 1891, they now returned to a thoroughly Russophil policy in the Bulgarian question. The Russian press repeatedly expressed its great satisfaction at this change of heart, while the English government was quite evidently alarmed lest the Russians should become over-confident and precipitate a crisis.[67] When, in December, 1892, rumors got abroad that the Russians were including demands for the free passage of their ships through the Straits in the negotiations for a commercial treaty with the Porte, the English were very much exercised. Some of the papers, like the *Standard*, were so outspokenly alarmist that copies of them were confiscated in Constantinople. It was, in fact, reported that the English government had made representations to the Porte and had reserved for itself all rights which might be granted to the Russians.[68] The Turks, meanwhile, summoned General Brialmont, the "fortifier of Europe," and set to work reorganizing the defences of the Bosporus, at the same time drawing as close as possible to Bulgaria, which was an indispensable barrier against Russian advance in the Balkans.[69]

All these developments were viewed with the greatest serenity in Berlin. The Germans were through playing the English game unquestioningly. Of supporting Austria in her Balkan policy there could no longer be any question either. The following

---

[67] *Mémorial Diplomatique* August 13, 1892 (St. Petersburg August 7). In August 1892 the German government discouraged all hopes of Ferdinand's being received in Berlin (G. P. IX, no. 2126). The alarm of the English appears from G. P. IX, no. 2129.

[68] *Mémorial Diplomatique* October 29, November 5, 26, December 24; *London Times* December 15, 22, 1892. It was rumored that the Triple Alliance might sell its approval of the Russian Straits policy for the abandonment by Russia of the rapprochement with France.

[69] *Mémorial Diplomatique* September 24, November 5; *London Times* December 6, 16, 1892. The uneasiness of the English is further illustrated by the fact that the secret sailing orders given to the British Mediterranean squadron by Lord Salisbury were not revoked by the liberal cabinet (G. P. IX, no. 2128).

letter of Holstein to Eulenburg, dated January 29, 1893, is a characteristic and succinct formulation of the new German attitude:

"We desire good relations with Russia, *but without committing political adultery*. The existing treaties must be observed, as long as they last and as far as they go. But to go beyond that, there is no call. If Russia attacks Rumania, Austria would *certainly* be on the defensive if she advanced against Russia. If Russia attacks Bulgaria, Austria would *perhaps* be on the defensive. But Austria would *not* be on the defensive if Russia delivers a direct attack by sea against Turkey proper. In that case let those fight who wish; *we* are under no obligation to fight. No *casus foederis*."[70]

This doctrine, coming from Holstein, is truly noteworthy. It was a return to the Bismarckian policy of strict interpretation of the German obligation to Austria. A short time after, the German foreign minister wrote to the ambassador at St. Petersburg explicitly recalling to him that the Austro-German Alliance did not extend to Bulgarian problems, or, indeed, to any Balkan affairs.[71] While Kálnoky continued to cultivate the connection with Sofia, the German statesmen entirely washed their hands of the Bulgarian question. The Kaiser went even further. It was through his intervention that Ferdinand's suit for the hand of a Bavarian princess in January, 1893 was completely wrecked.[72] In April, 1893 Caprivi refused unconditionally to receive Stambulov in Berlin, either secretly or publicly.[73] The Austrians were left to solve their Near Eastern difficulties in their own way.

The Tsar, of course, appreciated this return of German policy

---

[70] Haller: *Eulenburg* pp. 83-84. Holstein in this letter even goes so far as to contemplate a German-Russian alliance without Austria, to be concluded after the existing treaties had expired.

[71] G. P. IX, no. 2131.

[72] Wolkenstein to Kálnoky March 11, 1893; G. P. VII, no. 1651; Daudet: *Ferdinand I*, p. 137.

[73] G. P. IX, no. 2132. At the time of the Russian protest against the change in the Bulgarian constitution the German government repeated its determination not to recognize Ferdinand and expressed to the Russian government its willingness to consider any proposals for a settlement of the question which the latter might wish to make (Szögyény to Kálnoky March 13, 1893). A month later, when there were rumors that Ferdinand would visit Constantinople, the German ambassador to the Porte was instructed, at the request of the Russian government, to warn the Sultan against taking any step in the direction of recognition (Szögyény to Kálnoky April 18, 1893; Wolkenstein to Kálnoky April 28, 1893).

to the old lines. In need of a commercial treaty and a loan, he was quite prepared to accept the German advances in any case. Troubles in Central Asia and unrest in Bulgaria made the friendship of Germany all the more desirable. Furthermore, the beginning of the Panama crisis in France boded no good for the future. The troubles in the French chamber might well enough end in the streets of Paris, and 1893 might see a repetition of 1793.[74] Alexander decided to make a grand gesture in the direction of Germany and open the road toward conciliation. The German ambassador to St. Petersburg, General von Schweinitz, was retiring from his post in December, 1892, and the problem of finding a suitable successor had long occupied the statesmen in Berlin. The Tsar, as far back as the days of the Kiel interview, had talked the matter over with Shuvalov and had instructed him to speak for General von Werder, a personal friend of Alexander II and of the Russian ruling house generally.[75] Apparently this preference of Alexander was not made known to Schweinitz, who suggested Alvensleben as his successor. Learning indirectly of the Tsar's desires in the matter, Count Eulenburg induced the Russian minister at Munich to suggest that the Russian Emperor himself intercede with the Kaiser. Eventually Alexander wrote directly to the Kaiser asking for Werder's appointment. The request could not, of course, be refused. As a matter of fact Holstein was strongly in favor of it, and political circles in Berlin generally regarded this unusual procedure as striking evidence of the Russian desire for better relations. Together with the Panama crisis it was felt that this incident should finish the French and the Franco-Russian Alliance.[76]

From this time on, for several months, cordial relations continued to exist between Berlin and St. Petersburg. The Panama

---

[74] *London Times* December 21, 1892, in a rather interesting article.

[75] Aehrenthal to Kálnoky December 8, 1892; Hohenlohe II, p. 494; Haller: *Eulenburg* p. 82.

[76] G. P. VII, nos. 1639-1642; Schweinitz II, pp. 442 ff.; Haller: *Eulenburg* pp. 82-83; Szögyény to Kálnoky November 21, 24; Aehrenthal to Kálnoky November 25, December 8, 1892. The Austrians were not very well pleased by the appointment. On a despatch from Aehrenthal on November 8 Francis Joseph noted: "Wäre Werder nicht gar zu russisch?"

scandal supplied an excellent basis for the Russo-German rapprochement, and the German statesmen were determined to exploit it to the full. On January 12, 1893, the Ribot cabinet was
reorganized as a result of Freycinet's implication in the affair.
This was the end of the famous "Cronstadt Ministry" even in
its modified form. The famous war minister, who was, in a
sense, the very soul of the alliance policy, resigned and Develle
became minister of foreign affairs. The crisis went from bad to
worse, and soon afterward the Paris *Journal* published an article
insinuating that Mohrenheim himself had received a large sum
from the Panama funds.[77] Then the other ambassadors were
drawn in, and France became "one wild sea of denunciation,
suspicion and mutual recrimination," as Lord Dufferin said.[78]
Even more serious was the situation when the newspapers began
to hint that the accusation against Mohrenheim had been started
by representatives of the Triple Alliance, the object being to sow
discord between France and Russia. On January 15 a certain
Szekelyi, correspondent of the *Budapesti Hirlap*, was arrested
and expelled from the country for his supposed guilt in the
matter.[79] In Austria-Hungary this action raised a storm of indignation and anger. But no one became quite as excited about
it as the Kaiser. To be sure, the German ambassador alone
among the representatives of the great powers had been spared
by the virulent French press. But the Kaiser evidently believed
that the time had come for a crusade against the Republic and
for a decisive campaign against the Franco-Russian combination.
The Tsarevich had just come to Berlin on a visit and William
felt more confident of success than ever.

On January 22 the *Kölnische Zeitung* published a noteworthy

[77] See Hansen: *Mohrenheim* pp. 143-154.

[78] Sir Alfred C. Lyall: *The Life of the Marquis of Dufferin and Ava* (London
1905) volume II, p. 264. It had been repeatedly hinted that Lord Dufferin had been
sent to Paris with unlimited funds to spend in undermining the Franco-Russian
Alliance. See his clever and caustic reply, in a speech before the British Chamber
of Commerce in Paris, February 13, 1893 (*London Times* February 14, 1893).

[79] G. P. VII, no. 1590; Hansen: *Mohrenheim* pp. 143-154; Cyon: *L'Entente
Franco-Russe* pp. 445 ff.; *London Times* January 16, 1893.

article in which it was pointed out that, in view of the insults offered to several of the ambassadors to France,

"it might be judicious if the foreign ambassadors were to watch the develop-ment of things from outside France as long as the Panama scandals and this apparently insatiable love of calumny continue."

To this the *Norddeutsche Allgemeine Zeitung* added that, to be sure, Münster had not been attacked, but that, if the other monarchical powers decided to take the step suggested, Ger-many would undoubtedly join. As a matter of fact the Kaiser actually suggested to the powers that they consider the plan of withdrawing their ambassadors from Paris and reducing the post to the rank of a legation.[80] This would have been an intolerable insult to the French and would probably have resulted in war. To this extreme none of the powers was willing to go. Kálnoky, having received satisfactory explanations and apologies from the French foreign office, opposed the German suggestion, and Münster himself recommended a more cautious attitude.[81]

No doubt the Kaiser's excitability was in part due to domestic difficulties, and possibly even to the critical situation that had developed in the Near East.[82] But at bottom his eagerness was undoubtedly occasioned by the prospect of dealing a telling blow at France and destroying the entente of August, 1891.[83] In this

[80] G. P. VII, nos. 1590 ff.; Szögyény to Kálnoky January 23, 1893.

[81] Herbette had evidently gotten wind of what was occurring in Berlin and had warned his government. It appears that Caprivi was from the start opposed to magnifying the affair (G. P. VII, nos. 1593 ff.; Szögyény to Kálnoky January 26, 30, 1893; *London Times* January 27, 28, 1893).

[82] The domestic difficulties were due in large part to the opposition aroused by the projected military bill. It appears that about New Years' the Kaiser was con-sidering a *coup d'état* and the abolition of representative government. Cf. his re-marks to his generals (Waldersee II, p. 274), and his conversation with the Austrian ambassador (Szögyény to Kálnoky January 7, 1893):"Er riet mir, dahin zu wirken, dass das oesterreichisch-ungarische Botschaftspalais, welches seinem Zwecke nicht entspreche, verkauft werde; Er würde bald in die lage kommen, uns ein bedeutend grösseres Haus anzubieten, und zwar das im Baue begriffene Parlamentsgebäude, indem Er entschlossen sei, den Reichstag, wenn er fortfährt, sich so ungefügig und 'unpatriotisch' zu benehmen wir bisher, 'für lange Zeit, oder auch ganz,' zum Teufel zu jagen."

[83] Since the mission of Boisdeffre to St. Petersburg and the visit paid by Frey-cinet and Ribot to Giers at Aix, the Germans were no longer so certain that some

connection the visit of the Russian heir to Berlin opened up new vistas. The mission of Werder to St. Petersburg had been rather disappointing. Not that the new ambassador was not *persona gratissima* at the Russian court, but he proved too anxious not to compromise his own personal position by indiscreet and hasty steps. Besides, not being a professional diplomat, he could hardly be more than a *drapeau*, as the Austrian representative put it.[84] Under the circumstances the visit of Nicholas was all the more welcome. He arrived on January 24 for the wedding of Prince Frederick Charles of Hessia and the Kaiser's youngest sister, Margaret. For six days he was made the object of flattering attentions on the part of the Kaiser, who promised himself a rapprochement between Russia and the Triple Alliance as a result of his efforts to impress his cousin.[85] On January 26, while visiting the Emperor Alexander Grenadier Guards with his guest, William made the following instructive remarks:

"We all regard your Imperial Father not only as the noble chief of the regiment, not only as our most distinguished comrade, but, above all, as the representative of old and approved monarchical traditions of well-tried friendship, and of close ties of intimate relationship with my illustrious predecessors—traditions which, in days gone by, both Russian and Prussian regiments sealed with their blood on the field of battle."

This was the public expression of the Kaiser's policy, and its significance was not overlooked:

agreement had not been made between the two states. There were many rumors in the newspapers to this effect. See Chiala III, p. 593; G. P. VII, no. 1522; and Caprivi's utterance in the parliamentary commission on the military bill, January 11, 1893: "Ob ein schriftlicher Allianz Vertrag zwischen Russland und Frankreich bestehe, wissen wir nicht; sonst unterrichtete Personen sind in der Auffassung, dass ein solcher Vertrag nicht bestehe, in letzter zeit wankelnder geworden; wahrscheinlich aber bestehen zwischen Russland und Frankreich militärische Abmachungen für Land und Wasser" (Official version sent by Szögyény to Kálnoky April 29, 1893). It should also be remembered that Caprivi as well as Marschall was apprehensive lest the French Republic should be overthrown and succeeded by a monarchy which would be much more dangerous for Germany. As a matter of fact there were Orleanist intrigues going on at the time (Szögyény to Kálnoky December 29, 1892; January 21, April 29, 1893).

[84] Aehrenthal to Kálnoky November 25, 1892; Wolkenstein to Kálnoky January 19, 20, February 13, March 11, May 10, 1893.

[85] Szögyény to Kálnoky January 21, 1893.

"The toast is beyond question the most important political event of
recent times,"

wrote the *Hamburger Nachrichten* on February 1, and other
newspapers expressed similar opinions.[86]

In private the Kaiser made every conceivable effort to seduce
his guest with facile arguments. On the very evening of the
Grand Duke's arrival and on numerous other occasions the two
men had long conversations on the state of Europe. The centre
of the discussion was, of course, France. After assuring his
guest of the utter corruption and complete rottenness of the
French government and painting a lurid picture of the inevitable
spread of anarchy and the consequent menace to the social order
in Europe and to the monarchical system, the Kaiser listened to
his guest tell of the Tsar's disillusionment and anger. Questioned
as to the views held in St. Petersburg in regard to future developments, Nicholas replied that a military dictatorship was regarded
as probable and that war would then be likely. This, incidentally, was also the opinion of the German foreign office,
which greatly feared that a monarchical restoration might take
place and that Russia would more readily conclude an alliance
with a French king than with a French republic. Under the
circumstances the words of the Grand Duke were more than
soothing. He declared that if a military dictatorship were actually established in Paris it would be necessary to build up a
coalition like that of 1813 to combat France. This gave the
Kaiser the necessary opening. He pointed out that this very
idea lay at the bottom of the Triple Alliance, the purpose of
which was to guarantee the territorial possessions of its members,
to maintain the monarchical principle against the attacks of
radicalism, socialism and nihilism and to effect an economic
rapprochement in the interests of peace and with the idea of
uniting Europe against the economic policies of the United
States. The Triple Alliance was wholly defensive, and was not
directed against any nation, least of all against Russia. In fact,
any nation ready to subscribe to its general principles could

[86] Cf. *Mémorial Diplomatique* January 28, 1893; *London Times* January 30,
January 31, February 2, February 8, 1893.

easily be admitted. Salvation, according to the Kaiser, lay only in steps similar to those taken to combat the revolution in 1815—in short, the solution of the problem would be the reëstablishment of the "Holy Alliance," of the "League of the Three Emperors."[87]

Nicholas appeared to be deeply impressed by his host's eloquent arguments and ended by expressing his full conviction that the Triple Alliance had no other than defensive objects in view. He then outdid the Kaiser in violently denouncing and condemning the situation in France and subscribing to the plan of reconstructing the agreement between the three monarchies. The Kaiser felt that he had been entirely successful. He urged Nicholas to lay the situation before the Tsar and even supplied him with a written memorandum of the arguments to be used. This memorandum, incidentally, was carefully worked over in the foreign office, and though unsigned, was seriously intended.[88] After Nicholas's departure further efforts were made to win the favor of Russia. Condolences were sent on the death of General Cheremetiev; Yorck, the Russophobe military attaché in St. Petersburg, was withdrawn; the Kaiser wrecked the hopes of Ferdinand of Bulgaria for a union with the Wittelsbach family; and during the Bulgarian crisis of March, 1893 the German

---

[87] On these important conversations see G. P. VII, nos. 1526, 1527. I have supplemented these with the extensive reports of the Austrian ambassador, Count Szögyény, who obtained his information from the Kaiser, from Caprivi, and from Marschall (Szögyény to Kálnoky January 30, February 4, February 18, 1893). See also Waldersee II, p. 284; and the important letter of Holstein to Eulenburg in Haller pp. 83-84.

[88] The text of the memorandum in G. P. VII, no. 1527; it is also discussed in Szögyény to Kálnoky February 4, 1893. The optimism which prevailed in Berlin official circles is most clearly expressed in Holstein's letter to Eulenburg (Haller pp. 83-84), where plans for a whole recasting of the alliance system are advanced. The same attitude comes out clearly in the inspired articles of the press, e. g., *Kölnische Zeitung* February 3, 1893. The *Münchener Allgemeine Zeitung* and the *Kreuzzeitung* insisted that the Grand Duke had assured the German statesmen that no Franco-Russian Alliance existed, but this was denied in the *Berlin Post* on February 6. A Vienna despatch to the *London Times*, published on February 8, declared that "it may confidently be stated that for the last ten years at least there has never been less chance of a conflict between any of the Great Powers." There evidently is no Franco-Russian Alliance and no longer any prospect of one.

government went so far as to express its willingness to consider any proposals Russia might wish to make for the solution of the problem.[89]

As a matter of fact, nothing substantial ever came of this rather curious interlude. Day by day the Kaiser waited anxiously for a report on the results of Nicholas's conversations with his father, but no report came, and the Tsar himself never even mentioned the discussions which had taken place in Berlin.[90] There can be little doubt that Nicholas sincerely accepted the Kaiser's arguments, and it may well be that the Tsar, too, was sympathetic. At any rate he appears to have convinced himself that the Kaiser was not as bellicose or dangerous as had been at first supposed.[91] But there were very good reasons why he could not change his policy overnight. The version of the Triple Alliance as given by William was indeed a novel one, and so far no definite offers had come from Berlin. The Tsar would have to know first what the German attitude would be in case of an Anglo-Russian crisis in the Middle East or in the Near East. Of the German policy towards France there could be no question. Furthermore, Alexander quite naturally desired to see whether the honeyed words spoken in Berlin would be followed by more concrete evidence of good intentions. It has already been pointed out that the Tsar had, in a sense, taken the initiative in preparing better relations with Germany, and that one all-important consideration for him was the conclusion of a commercial treaty and eventually a loan in Berlin. It did him no good to be told that the Triple Alliance, in its economic aspect, was directed against American encroachments. What the Russians wanted was an equal chance for their cereals, which had been put at a

[89] Szögyény to Kálnoky February 18 and March 13; Wolkenstein to Kálnoky March 11, 1893; G. P. VII, no. 1651.

[90] The Austrian ambassador reported the growing disillusionment in Berlin very faithfully (Szögyény to Kálnoky February 18, 26, March 18, April 16).

[91] G. P. VII, no. 1647; cf. also Wolkenstein to Kálnoky January 28, 1893; Giers spoke in similar terms to Kálnoky in Vienna somewhat later (Kálnoky to Wolkenstein May 4, 1893).

great disadvantage by the tariff treaties between Germany and Austria and Italy.[92]

Negotiations between the Russians and the Germans had been reopened in Berlin shortly after the Kiel visit, but had made almost no progress. Finally, in March, 1893, the German government presented its demands to Shuvalov.[93] Russia was offered Germany's conventional tariff in return for most-favored-nation treatment by Russia, equal treatment for land and sea imports into Russia, and a reduction of 40 to 80 percent on 77 articles of the Russian tariff. A reduction of the Finnish tariff was also demanded. These terms were admittedly so far-reaching that an early agreement was not expected by the Germans.[94] The reply of Witte, submitted in April, offered a reduction of 56 items but demanded that an agreement should be reached in regard to diseases of cattle. He suggested a conference to consider the demands of both parties. It was not until the middle of June that the German government replied, declaring that a cattle convention would be impracticable and insisting on a reduction of the Finnish tariff, while rejecting the reductions in the Russian tariff offered by Witte. The Russian government promptly rejoined by expressing its willingness to drop the cattle convention and by suggesting again that a conference be called. On June 28 the German government stated that a conference could be successful only if Russia satisfied all the German demands, and declared that in any case the conference could not be summoned before October 1. The Russian suggestion that

[92] It is interesting to note that Kálnoky, who sympathized with the Kaiser's conciliatory policy, had from the beginning pointed out that Alexander would not be so easily convinced (Kálnoky to Szögyény February 10; Kálnoky to Wolkenstein February 12, 1893). The same attitude is expressed in Francis Joseph's letter to the Kaiser (G. P. VII, no. 1648).

[93] Cf. the outline of the negotiations from July 1892 to February 1893 in G. P. VII, p. 443, footnote; further details were given, from the Russian side, in the reports of Aehrenthal to Kálnoky August 17, August 20, October 13, October 15, 1892. See also the detailed résumé of the negotiations which was presented to the Reichstag in July 1893 (reprinted in Schulthess 1893, pp. 99 ff.).

[94] Szögyény to Kálnoky February 26, 1893. The account of the negotiations is taken from the German résumé (Schulthess 1893, pp. 99 ff.) and from the memorandum of Witte, published in the Russian *Messager Officiel* on August 12, 1893.

in the meanwhile both powers should accord each other most-favored-nation treatment was rejected by Germany. Witte, the Russian minister of finance, realizing that the prospect of a settlement was small, succeeded in persuading the Tsar to approve a differential tariff, by which the existing rates were to become the minimum, accorded to nations favoring Russia, while other nations were to pay import duties 15 to 30 per cent higher. The scheme aimed particularly at wounding Germany's trade in manufactured articles, and was carried through the imperial council in spite of the opposition of Shuvalov and Giers. It appears that Germany was first warned that the new system would be enforced if she did not cut down her demands, and that Germany accepted the challenge.[95] On June 26 the new Russian tariff was announced, and therewith began the tariff war between the two countries. The important point to note here is that the Germans showed no inclination to make sacrifices or even concessions, and that the continued tension in the economic field was a serious obstacle in the way of an agreement between the two governments.

Of even greater immediate effect on the Tsar's attitude was the history of the important German military bill. As introduced by the government in November, 1892 it provided for an increase of the German forces by some 80,000 men and the reduction of the term of service to two years in the infantry and artillery. It should be particularly noted that this plan of reorganization had not been called forth by any immediate danger threatening the country, and that it can hardly be attributed to the new Franco-Russian Entente of 1891. Apparently it was primarily due to the reëstablishment of the French military system under Freycinet in the period following 1887. Even before Bismarck's fall the matter had been considered, but it had been repeatedly postponed because of the Kaiser's obstinate resistance to the idea of reducing the term of service. Only after much persuasion and long arguments had his consent finally been obtained, and here the rumors of a Franco-Russian

[95] Witte pp. 66-67.

understanding very probably played a part in bringing about the decision.[96] In any case the introduction of the bill in the Reichstag marked the beginning of a period of great tension in the domestic affairs of Germany. Both the conservatives and the Centre had been estranged by the previous action of the government, and most of the liberals were opposed to any augmentation of the country's military forces. Almost from the start it was evident that the existing Reichstag would not pass the bill. On the other hand its obstinate attitude irritated the Kaiser in the highest degree. He felt that he had made a tremendous concession in giving his approval to the two-year-service clause, and evidently for a time in January, 1893 he had half made up his mind to effect a *coup d'état* and abolish representative government. Only the steadying hand of Caprivi saved the country from serious complications.[97]

Naturally the development of the situation in Berlin was watched with great interest abroad, especially in Russia. The Tsar's armies were by no means in fighting trim and he had reason for apprehension. Almost from the very beginning the Russian press had voiced grave misgivings.[98] If the bill fails in the Reichstag, it was argued, it will lead to chaos in Germany. If it succeeds, it will be necessary for France and Russia to take precautions, with the ultimate result that Germany and her allies may be driven into war by sheer desperation.[99] By others the opinion was expressed that the passage of the bill would necessitate the immediate conclusion of a military convention between Russia and France, and that it would involve the transfer of more Russian troops to the western frontier.[100] In brief, Russian government circles were absorbed by the German military plans,

---

[96] Cf. Caprivi to Schneidewin March 17, 1895 (*Deutsche Revue* May and June 1922, p. 145); Waldersee II, p. 206; Hohenlohe II, p. 494; and Caprivi's great speech in the Reichstag November 23, 1892, introducing the bill.

[97] Cf. footnote no. 82, above.

[98] The Tsar himself seems to have regarded the projected bill with equanimity at first (Wolkenstein to Kálnoky December 13, January 13, 1893; G. P. VII, no. 1644).

[99] *Mémorial Diplomatique* November 5, 1892 (St. Petersburg letter, October 30).

[100] *Mémorial Diplomatique* November 19, 1892.

the situation becoming more serious with the outbreak of the Panama crisis in France, which temporarily paralyzed the country. No doubt the realization of Russia's helplessness had something to do with Alexander's readiness to seek an entente with Germany, but these very efforts for the establishment of better relations were made under the shadow of a serious contradiction. While the Tsar was asking for the appointment of his friend Werder as ambassador, Caprivi made his first great speech on the military bill in the Reichstag, discussing frankly the danger of war on two fronts in the future and pointing out that Russia could always count on France even though the reverse might not be true. At the very moment that Werder arrived in St. Petersburg in January, and just before the departure of the Grand Duke Nicholas for Berlin, the German chancellor made an even more startling address to the committee of the legislature:

> Conditions in France, he pointed out, were drifting towards a dictatorship, and this would probably make for war. The Russian and German governments were on good terms, but public opinion in the two countries was hostile. The Russian tradition demanded the advance to the Straits and Constantinople, even if the road were through Berlin. Under the circumstances the German government felt obliged to preserve the position of Austria as a great power. "We cannot sacrifice Austria to gain temporary concessions from Russia. In these circumstances we must be prepared for a war on two fronts. We do not know what engagements exist between France and Russia, but in all probability arrangements have been made in view of military operations both by land and by sea. Nor must we omit Denmark from our calculations, notwithstanding the personal friendliness of King Christian."

This speech was made in committee, behind closed doors, but that does not mean that the full details did not become known to the newspapers.[101] In fact, the very secrecy led to all sorts of exaggerations, and the effect was, of course, to increase the general uneasiness, especially in Russia. The Tsar himself took an eminently reasonable viewpoint, and while complaining to the

---

[101] Caprivi in the committee, January 11, 1893. I am relying chiefly on the official version sent by Szögyény to Kálnoky April 29, 1893. The reports which were published in the leading newspapers were substantially correct (see especially the text in the *London Times* January 13, 1893).

German ambassador that the chancellor had said too much, he recognized that it might be necessary to put the case strongly in order to put the bill through, and admitted that he still had the greatest confidence in Caprivi.[102]

It is not surprising, however, that Alexander should have become dubious about the development of affairs in Berlin, for the Kaiser, while flattering the Tsarevich, was not ready to throw over his former friends the English. Just before the arrival of Nicholas he toasted the Duke of Edinburgh, who was in the German capital, and suggested publicly the possibility that the English and German fleets might sometime fight shoulder to shoulder against a common enemy.[103] A few days later General von Schkopp, commander of the forces stationed at Cologne, made an address in which he said:

"The clouds are gathering blacker and blacker on our political horizon, and before long the storm is sure to break.[104]

All this was rather in contradiction to the seductive utterances of the Kaiser to the Russian Grand Duke, and one can hardly blame Alexander for wanting to see what the ultimate outcome would be.[105] Evidently he expected that the military bill would fail to pass the Reichstag and that the government would eventually drop it. As the German government's chances of success diminished, his optimism increased.[106] When the bill was rejected and the Reichstag dissolved on May 6, 1893, the Tsar hailed the news with delight, hoping that the new Reichstag would prove even more recalcitrant and that the German government would eventually have to agree to a settlement with Russia on any terms.[107] The crisis in Berlin was acute, and the

---

[102] G. P. VII, no. 1645; Wolkenstein to Kálnoky January 28, 1893. For the profound impression made on the Russian public see the St. Petersburg letter in the *Mémorial Diplomatique* January 21, 1893.

[103] Text in Penzler: *Reden* II, pp. 221-222.

[104] Text in Wippermann 1893, I, p. 112.

[105] Werder complained bitterly of these utterances and was enraged at the inconsistency of his government (G. P. VII, no. 1650, and Caprivi's defence in no. 1651; similarly Wolkenstein to Kálnoky February 13, 1893).

[106] G. P. VII, no. 1653; Wolkenstein to Kálnoky March 24, 1893.

[107] Wolkenstein to Kálnoky May 9, 1893.

Kaiser so far lost his head as to complain of Kálnoky's pacific utterances in the delegations on June 3 and 5, because he feared that undue emphasis on the good prospects of peace would make military increases seem superfluous.[108] But by June 15 it seemed obvious that the new Reichstag would pass the bill in modified form. The elections had been a crushing defeat for the liberals, who lost thirty-two seats, while the more conservative groups as well as the Poles showed substantial gains. On July 4, the bill was reintroduced and on the 15 it was passed by a vote of 201 to 85, the Poles proving the decisive factor. The impression produced by this event, on the Russians in general and upon the Tsar in particular, was a profound one, and directly influenced the later course of events. Here it is only necessary to stress the fact that, through the whole winter of 1892-1893, the Germans made efforts to draw the Russians from France and to the side of the Triple Alliance, but that these efforts were bound to remain barren of results so long as such important issues as the commercial agreement and the military law hung in the balance.

[108] Szögyény to Kálnoky June 8 and 10, 1893. The Kaiser took the stand that a second rejection of the bill would be tantamount to a revolution and he was determined, in that case, to effect a *coup d'état*, though no one knew what form he intended his action to take (Szögyény to Kálnoky May 27, 1893). Cf. also his remarkable speech to the generals at the review at Tempelhof on May 9, in which he voices the expectation that the new Reichstag will pass the bill and then goes on to say: "Should this expectation be again disappointed I am determined to use every means in my power to achieve my purpose."

CHAPTER XI

TOULON AND TARANTO

WHILE the Kaiser was directing his efforts to the improvement of Russo-German relations in the winter of 1892-1893, it must not be supposed that the statesmen of the Wilhelmstrasse were so blind as to stake everything on this one play, nor must it be imagined that the Tsar was under any illusions regarding the possible extent of an agreement with Germany. After all, in Berlin due consideration had to be given to the needs of the Triple Alliance, which was still the sheet anchor of German policy, and in St. Petersburg it was rightly felt that the entente with France could not be discarded until something substantial had been obtained to replace it. At the Quai d'Orsay every effort was being made to wipe out the bad impression made by the Panama scandal. Ribot gave explicit assurances that steps would be taken to protect foreign ambassadors from vicious attacks in the press, and on March 6 the government introduced a bill providing against the possible repetition of the Mohrenheim incident. The new foreign minister, Develle, even induced Carnot to apologize directly to the Tsar, and before long the press was declaring that Russia was getting over the estrangement which had resulted from the recent crisis.[1] Some of the newspapers even spoke of a coming visit of the Russian squadron to French waters, though all announcements of this sort soon proved to be premature.[2] Nevertheless, Alexander appeared at a grand ball given by the French ambassador in St. Petersburg on February 21 and in this fashion indicated his readiness to forgive and forget. In the succeeding months the French statesmen showed exemplary tact and moderation in the handling of matters

[1] Hansen: *L'Alliance Franco-Russe* pp. 105-106; Hansen: *Mohrenheim* pp. 153-154; Albin p. 258; *Mémorial Diplomatique* January 21 and 28, 1893.

[2] *London Times* February 9, March 8; *Mémorial Diplomatique* February 4, March 18, 1893.

which might disturb the peace of the continent. For example, when, in April, 1893, a German named Kurtz was arrested in Rouen and deported as a spy and it appeared that the local authorities had delayed for some time an appeal which he had written to the German ambassador, the government gave the Kaiser no opportunity to make capital of the incident, but readily recognized the error of the French officials and promised that in future greater care should be exercised.[3] In the same way the French press, probably at a word from the government, carefully abstained from provocative comment on the German army bill, and gave the Germans no opening whatsoever for faultfinding.[4]

So satisfactory had been the development of Russo-French relations in the spring of 1893 that the ambassador at St. Petersburg already saw the prospect of resuming the negotiations for the conclusion of the military convention. There was no doubt in Paris that the Kaiser had been pursuing a policy extremely hostile to France and that he was still exerting himself to the utmost to establish an entente with the Tsar. Such a situation could not be regarded with equanimity, and one cannot find fault with the French statesmen for attempting to parry by exploiting the difficulties at issue between Germany and Russia. The French *Yellow Book* tells us almost nothing about the correspondence of these months, but we know that the French government painted the German army law in the blackest colors and urged the necessity for precautionary measures on the part of France and Russia.[5] In the same way the tariff treaty concluded between France and Russia in June was intended to contrast the

---

[3] *Norddeutsche Allgemeine Zeitung* April 9, 1893. Münster was instructed to protest vigorously and even to threaten a rupture of diplomatic relations, while the Kaiser told the Austrian ambassador: "If such incidents are repeated too frequently and the French government exhibits its ill-will too ostentatiously, the Germans will have to assume a severer tone. France is at present entirely isolated and it would be a political mistake not to show the authorities of that rotten state who is the master" (Szögyény to Kálnoky April 8 and 10, 1893).

[4] *London Times* May 8 and 11; *Mémorial Diplomatique* May 20, 1893.

[5] See especially *Bourgeois and Pagès* pp. 248-249, Develle's despatch of July 17, 1893 to Herbette. Naturally the French press laid great stress upon the change implied in the new German law.

goodwill of the French and the obstinacy of the Germans. Economically the treaty was of very little significance.[6]

Montebello had already been urging the desirability of preparing for the possible reopening of the negotiations for the military convention. On May 20 he wrote to Develle suggesting that, in order to minimize the chances of opposition on the part of the Russians, the alterations proposed by Ribot in 1892 should be dropped for the present and that the draft as signed by Boisdeffre and Obruchev should be taken up again.[7] Apparently Develle was not prepared to go so far. Carnot was still president and was still insisting that the convention must be constitutional. Some correspondence followed. Montebello's idea was that the changes might be discussed after the agreement had been formally signed by the two foreign ministers, and that then they might be embodied in a supplementary clause. The main point, he argued, was that the negotiations should be taken up immediately, for he suspected that after the German election Giers would reopen the subject of his own accord.[8] For the time being nothing seems to have been done by the authorities in Paris, but the situation was rapidly changing for the better. Early in July there were extensive riots in Paris, which the government suppressed with a stern hand. The vigor of the authorities in this case undoubtedly did much to convince the Tsar, as it convinced the rest of the world, that the Panama crisis was really over and that the temporary weakness of France was a thing of the past.[9] Then, on July 15, came the passage of the German military law, the success of which was largely due to the vote of the Polish deputies. The enthusiastic

---

[6] *London Times* June 19 and 22, 1893. In the St. Petersburg letter published in the *Mémorial Diplomatique* on July 1 it was stated that the Russian government had forbidden the press to discuss the possible political implications of the treaty, in order that Germany might not be offended. This did not prevent the French press from hailing it as a great political victory (see *Mémorial Diplomatique* June 24, July 1, 1893).

[7] Montebello to Develle May 20, 1893 (L. J. no. 82).

[8] Montebello to Develle June 27, 1893 (L. J. no. 83).

[9] Albin p. 362; Wolkenstein to Kálnoky July 5, 17; Aehrenthal to Kálnoky September 5, 1893; *Mémorial Diplomatique* July 15, 1893.

message of thanks sent by the Kaiser to Koscielski, the Polish
leader, served only to strengthen the Tsar in his suspicions that
the German government was pursuing a policy which might
eventually prove detrimental to Russian interests.[10]   On top of
all this came the breakdown of the Russo-German tariff negotiations and the opening of the tariff war.   Giers and his
friends, who had always championed the understanding with
Germany, were very downcast, for there was now every likelihood that the Tsar would feel called upon to take precautionary
measures in the shape of a further rapprochement with France.[11]

It may well be questioned, however, whether the turn for the
worse in the relations between Russia and Germany would have
decided the Tsar to take the final step and conclude the military
convention with France.   After all, the commercial negotiations
were to be resumed on October 1, and it is not likely that Alexander would have jeopardized the success of the pourparlers by
a policy which might be interpreted as hostile to his neighbor.
Furthermore, it cannot be too often repeated that there was no
doubt that Russia could count on the aid of France in the event
of complications between Germany and Russia.   No statesman
at the time would have questioned this even for a moment.
The Tsar's reply to the German military bill was to mass more
and more troops in Poland, until, in September, the French am-

---

[10] Text of the Kaiser's remarks in Wippermann 1893, part II, pp. 16-17.   Giers
told Werder that this flirtation with the Poles was particularly offensive to the
Russians (Wolkenstein to Kálnoky July 15 and 19, 1893), and somewhat later the
Tsar himself made the significant remark to Werder: "Stablewski, c'est notre plus
grand ennemi," (Wolkenstein to Kálnoky February 3, 1894).   The Russians' fears
are clearly reflected in Cyon pp. 475-477, who claims that a great revolution in
Poland, to be led by Koscielski, was being planned with the approval of the German
government to meet the possibility of the Russo-German tariff war ending in
political hostilities.   Cf. Waldersee II, pp. 294, 298, who thinks that the Franco-
Russian Entente was forced on the Tsar "durch unser fortwährendes Betonen des
Dreibundes und durch unsere Polenpolitik," and who seems to indicate that in October 1893 there were negotiations with Koscielski as to Poland's rôle in a future war.

[11] G. P. VII, nos. 1663, 1665; Wolkenstein to Kálnoky July 5, 17, 20, 1893;
Aehrenthal to Kálnoky September 5, 1893.   The Austrian ambassador bitterly
complained of the German attitude, which threatened to put an end to the rapprochement between Russia and her western neighbors (Wolkenstein to Kálnoky
August 3, 16, 1893).

bassador could speak of this region as "a vast entrenched camp" with more than 650,000 men on the border and almost as many more who would be ready within a short time to form an army redoubtable in strength and in quality.[12] The transfer of Russian troops from the interior to the west front had been going on uninterruptedly ever since the Near Eastern crisis of 1885-1887, until in 1893 the nineteen army corps were distributed as follows: one in the Caucasus, three in the Moscow district, three in the St. Petersburg district, two in and about Odessa, four about Kiev, four in the vicinity of Vilna and four in the Warsaw district. In other words, of the total peace strength of about 975,000, about 500,000 were in the Warsaw, Vilna and Kiev regions, 285,000 in and about St. Petersburg and Moscow, 80,000 at Odessa and 50,000 in the Caucasus. The facts were well-known and no one was under any illusions as to what they signified. They meant simply that Russia was prepared for any attack from the west. "And so," wrote Alfred Rambaud, one of the most enthusiastic supporters of the Franco-Russian Alliance, "at the western extremity of the vast empire, the whole force of the empire is concentrated; all the swords have been converged on a single point."[13]

But the French statesmen knew perfectly well that this in itself was no proof that Russia would take the aggressive. It was even less proof that the forces of the Tsar would be set in motion in defence of the French, least of all if the French were to make themselves guilty of a provocative policy aimed at the recovery of the lost provinces. One must, after all, credit the Russian statesmen with as clear an appreciation of their own interests as others are credited with. Russia had no interest in a war with Germany. There was nothing to be gained and everything to be lost by such a policy. It may indeed have been to the interest of the Russians not to allow the Germans to demolish the power and position of France, but this was a very different

---

[12] Montebello to Develle September 7, 1893 (L. J. no. 88).

[13] Alfred Rambaud: L'Armée du Tsar Alexandre III en 1893 (*Revue Bleue* October 7, 1893). See also Flourens: *Alexandre III, sa Vie, son Oeuvre* (Paris 1893) pp. 193 ff., and the interesting account by General Sir Archibald Alison: Armed Europe (*Blackwood's Magazine* December 1893, pp. 755-764).

thing from encouraging the French to throw down the gauntlet
to the Germans. As a matter of fact it is probably quite safe to
say that no responsible French statesman at the time had any
idea of precipitating a war. The French army had been built up
and reorganized and was about as strong as it could be made at
the time. The Russian forces had been moved to the front, ready
to act if the occasion arose. But these were protective measures
and cannot be interpreted as signifying the intention of launching
an attack.

One need not go far afield to find adequate evidence to prove
this contention. In the spring and summer of 1893 the attention
of the world was not focussed on the "hole in the Vosges" but on
the Mediterranean and on Asia. It was not the hostility of
Russia towards Germany and Austria or the antagonism of France
and Germany that was most prominent in the thoughts of the
statesmen of Europe, but the acute rivalry of the Russians and
English and the French and English. On the high plateaus of
Central Asia the English and the Russians eyed each other with
profound suspicion, and there were not a few influential people
who believed that a conflict between the whale and the elephant
was merely a matter of time, in fact of a short time. While the
leading European newspapers hardly mentioned Bulgaria, they
were full of alarms about the Pamirs, where the Russians had
left a small force during the winter and whither they announced
their intention of sending another expedition in the spring.[14]
The Trans-Siberian Railroad was in process of construction and
the Transcaspian was being extended. Quite obviously Russia
had put the Balkans "on ice" and was concentrating on the advance to the east. To Germany and Austria this was a matter of
supreme indifference. Bismarck had, in fact, repeatedly sent
the Russians to Asia in order to relieve the tension in Europe.
William II was to do it after him. Indeed, the Germans had
every reason to applaud. It was the English who had reason to

---

[14] *Mémorial Diplomatique* April 8, 1893; *London Times* May 19, 1893. The
Russian expedition actually left Ferghana on June 13, and it was announced that
its purpose was definitely to annex the Pamir region and establish a permanent
garrison (*London Times* July 11, 20, 1893).

lose sleep over this diversion of Russia's energies. Between them and the Russian colossus there lay only the buffer state of Afghanistan, ruled by the clever but thoroughly unreliable Abd-er-Rahman. Since the summer of 1892 attempts had been made to induce him to receive an English mission, but even Lord Roberts had been rebuffed. No man living could tell what action the Amir would eventually take, especially if some fine day a Russian force were to appear at Herat. And no one denied that the Russians could appear at Herat whenever they chose. India was threatened — seriously threatened, and no one less than Lord Roberts himself proclaimed the fact to his countrymen whenever the opportunity offered.[15]

On the other hand there was the Anglo-French antagonism, not nearly so crystallized and perhaps not so profound, but very acute at the time and particularly dangerous because the final decision rested not with a few calculating men but with the un-accountable population of the boulevards. The hostility be-tween the two powers was originally due to the English occu-pation of Egypt, and this knotty problem was still the prime factor in the whole complex. With the French it had become a *question d'amour propre* to effect the evacuation of the Nile Land by the English, and they continued to raise up every con-ceivable obstacle to the English policy in this question. After the failure of Abbas' offensive in January, 1893 the French sent a squadron first to Alexandria and then to Constantinople in order to proclaim to the world that France had no intention of re-treating.[16] It can hardly be doubted that the French representa-tives were behind every move that was made in the Egyptian question at this time, and that they persuaded the young Khe-dive to make a pilgrimage to Constantinople in July, 1893. With

[15] For example, in his speech at Dundee November 23, 1893. See also Sir Lepel Griffin: Is India Safe? (*Asiatic Quarterly Review* July 1893, pp. 26 ff.) and the same authority's excellent article entitled England and France in Asia (*Nineteenth Century* December 1893).

[16] This was a very spectacular performance, some twenty French warships taking part. Nothing like it had been seen in the eastern Mediterranean for a long time (see Mme. Adam in the *Nouvelle Revue* May 1, 1893; *London Times* April 13, 1893; *Mémorial Diplomatique* May 27, 1893).

him came a delegation of Notables with a petition to the Sultan couched in the following terms:

"We hereby implore you, O Khalif, to consider our position with the stranger who, under specious pretexts, has established himself in our country and persists in encumbering our sacred soil with his abhorred presence, after many fallacious promises to quit it."

No one doubted that the visit would be made the point of departure for a great diplomatic action, and it was generally feared in England that the Sultan would take the occasion to appeal to the European powers to effect a settlement of the Egyptian question.[17] The English cabinet was by no means blind to the possible dangers of the situation and Lord Rosebery had himself approached the Turkish ambassador in April with the suggestion of an Anglo-Turkish agreement which would postpone the discussion of evacuation for some five years. To this the Sultan did not even deign to give a reply until three months later, on the eve of the Khedive's visit. He was on the worst possible terms with the English, especially after Gladstone's unexpected announcement in the house of commons on May 1 that no date could be fixed for the evacuation of Egypt.[18] In the meanwhile the English and the Turks had fallen out further in the discussion of the Armenian question. But the Sultan was no fool. While he distrusted the English and was thoroughly at odds with them, he could not help but fear that the French were simply using Abbas as a tool, and that the evacuation of Egypt by the English might well be followed by a declaration of Egyptian independence, the rights of the Porte being entirely ignored and the influence of the English being replaced by that of the French. And besides, the French were, from the Turkish standpoint, in bad company. The shadow of Russia in the background was enough to strike terror into the heart of Abdul Hamid. With the French established in Egypt, either officially or un-

---

[17] See Cromer: *Abbas II* pp. 43-47; *London Times* July 12, 1893; *Mémorial Diplomatique* July 1 and 8, 1893; W. S. Blunt: Lord Cromer and the Khedive (*Nineteenth Century* February 1894).

[18] G. P. VIII, nos. 1832 ff.; *London Times* May 3, 4; *Mémorial Diplomatique* May 6, 13, 1893; *The Memoirs of Ismail Kemal Bey* (London 1920), chapter xiii.

officially, there was every reason to apprehend the early appearance of the Russians before Constantinople. The Sultan was certainly wise in steering a middle course between Scylla and Charybdis. While making no secret of his feelings towards the English, he took care not to encourage Abbas or even to receive the Notables. By this policy he saved not only himself but the English, whose position was anything but enviable.[19]

One of the great obstacles to the success of the French in the Egyptian question had always been the support given to England by the Triple Alliance. The policy of Germany and Austria, on the other hand, had not been dictated by love of England but by consideration for Italy, the weakest member of the coalition and the only member which was deeply interested in the contest of powers in the Mediterranean. The agreements of 1887 had been specially designed to enlist the aid of England for the protection of Italy. The common interest of England and Italy in checking the expansion of French power in the Mediterranean was the connecting link between the Island Empire and the the Triple Alliance. Conversely the French policy of driving the Italians out of the Triple Alliance by one method or another was simply one aspect of the balance of power in the Mediterranean, upon which, in turn, the solution of the Egyptian question depended. In the spring of 1893 the question of Italy became one of the major problems of European politics. Economically the country seemed to have come to the verge of ruin and bankruptcy, and there seemed to be no way out but a reduction of the

---

[19] Cromer pp. 45-47, report of Sir Arthur Nicolson; early in July the Turks finally replied to the English proposal of April by submitting a draft of their own, providing that the English should recognize Turkish sovereignty in Egypt and that they should agree not to increase the British force without preliminary understanding. A definitive agreement as to the evacuation of Egypt was to be reached in two years. Rosebery took a decided and negative stand on this proposal, in part because the Turks had kept him waiting so long and in part because it had become evident that the Sultan would not allow himself to be influenced unduly by Abbas or the French. His attitude was so pronounced that the Germans became anxious lest the Turks, in despair, would turn entirely to France and Russia. They therefore induced the Porte to abstain from opening the Egyptian question at so critical a time. Therewith the matter was temporarily dropped (G. P. VIII, nos. 1838-1846).

military forces. The government appeared to be quite unable
to cope with the situation and once again, as in 1891, the danger
that Italy would have to capitulate, because of French pressure,
loomed on the horizon.[20] In April the Kaiser went to Italy to
attend the wedding jubilee of the King and Queen, taking the
opportunity to visit also the Vatican, where he had a long talk
with the Pope. Baron Marschall, who had accompanied the
Emperor, likewise spent much time in discussing the possibilities
of the situation. Ever since the Panama crisis the Pope had
been tortured with doubts as to the wisdom of the policy he had
pursued in favoring the French Republic. The opposition in the
college of cardinals had closed ranks and, under the leadership
of Cardinal Galimberti, loudly demanded that the current policy
be abandoned and replaced by a policy of rapprochement with
the central powers. Rampolla, the heart and soul of the Francophil policy, of course remained firm and, as secretary of state,
was in an extremely powerful position.[21] At any rate His Holiness was more or less at sea and in his conversation with the
Kaiser and Marschall he denied firmly that he had any innate
sympathy with republicanism. The French statesmen of the
day were, he asserted, "demagogues and atheists of the worst
sort." He spoke of himself as a monarch and insisted that
Papal interests were identical with those of the great monarchies.
With Italian unity he strongly sympathized, though he could not
understand why Florence would not do as a capital just as well
as Rome. For the moment, then, the Papacy was wavering in
its policy, and there can be no doubt that the Kaiser entertained
hopes that some sort of *modus vivendi* could be established between the Vatican and the Quirinal, thus strengthening the posi-

---

[20] Cf. Giolitti: *Memorie* I, pp. 69 ff.; Billot I, pp. 479 ff.

[21] On the struggle of parties in Vatican circles see *London Times* December
20, 30, 1892; March 30, April 1, 3, 10, 1893; *Mémorial Diplomatique* December
31, 1892. Mme. Adam claimed that prominent German Catholics were bom-
barding the Pope to induce him to give up Republican France, which had been
"delivered up to Babylonian corruption" (*Nouvelle Revue* January 15, 1893).
The difficult position of the Papacy is well discussed by Debidour: *L'Église Catholique et l'État sous la troisième République* II, pp. 94-101. See also Hohenlohe II,
pp. 496, 500; T'Serclaes II, pp. 229-232.

tion of the Italian government and depriving the policy of the French of much of its force.[22] But this hope was doomed to disappointment. As the French government reëstablished its position the Pope once more looked favorably upon the Republic while in the meantime the position of Italy became more and more critical. The French were resuming their activities on the Tripolitan frontier and were encouraging the Spaniards in Morocco. By June, 1893 the Germans were considering the advisability of reopening the discussion of the agreement of 1887 between England and Italy. It may well be that the English would have refused to extend the agreement at that time, for small consolation was to be gotten from Italy. At best the connection was worth keeping up because it established contact with the Triple Alliance.[23]

Taken by and large the position of England was as unfavorable as it could conceivably be. The one hope of safety lay in the continuance of good relations with Germany and her allies. The Germans themselves had shown clearly enough during the winter that they had no intention of supporting the English without a *quid pro quo*, but they were bound to take a fairly lenient attitude if only because of the fact that they knew that a complete break might leave them at the mercy of Russia, and their ally, Italy, at the mercy of France. *Der Neue Kurs*, a periodical published in Berlin, which was supposed to receive inspiration from the German foreign office, wrote quite characteristically in the May number that too much reliance could not be placed upon Russia, for Russia resembled a wolf rather than a

[22] Marschall's account to the Austrian ambassador (Szögyény to Kálnoky May 8, 13, 1893); Haller: *Eulenburg* pp. 63-64; *Mémorial Diplomatique* April 29, May 27; *London Times* April 28; *Civiltà Cattolica* May 20, 1893.

[23] On the Tripolitan difficulties cf. G. P. VIII, nos. 1904-1908; on Morocco G. P. VIII, no. 1953; according to Marschall's account to the Austrian ambassador the question of a written agreement with England had been broached by the Italian statesmen during the Kaiser's visit to Rome, but the Germans evaded by pointing out once more the impossibility of obtaining a formal treaty with England. Marschall consoled Brin by expressing his conviction that in a crisis England could be counted on, provided Italy did nothing to estrange her (Szögyény to Kálnoky May 8, 13, 1893). On the Anglo-Italian relations in May and June 1893 see G. P. VIII, nos. 1745-1748.

dog. Russia might keep Germany's enemies away, but would also scare off Germany's friends. In the end the beast might, in fact, turn upon its master. On the whole England's friendship was of value, and the Triple Alliance really ought to be supported by the power of the British fleet.

As for the English, they spared no effort in cultivating the good graces of the members of the Triple Alliance. Rosebery did his utmost to make a favorable impression upon the Italian ambassador and to make it clear that the English sympathized with the Italians, even though Gladstone might refuse to consider the conclusion of a binding agreement.[24] The English statesmen likewise went out of their way to cultivate the good will of the Austrians. On May 14 the ambassador at Vienna, Lord Paget, in addressing a group of English residents, made the following noteworthy remarks:

> "It has always been my conviction....that a cardinal principle of our foreign policy should be the cultivation of the closest friendship with our ancient and natural ally, Austria-Hungary....There is not a single question, so far as I am aware, on which their interests and views are divergent. They both desire the maintenance of peace and are willing to employ their good offices for its preservation. They neither of them, I am convinced, entertain the faintest notion of self-aggrandizement at the expense of any other power. They both desire the continuance of the present *status quo* in Europe and especially in the East, where they wish the freedom of the Balkan states from foreign influence...."

This declaration was, of course, greeted by the Viennese press with the greatest jubilation, and when, in the last days of June, the Emperor Francis Joseph went to the British embassy to pay his respects to the wife of the departing ambassador, the *Neue Freie Presse,* in an apparently inspired article, took the opportunity to acknowledge once more the identity of English and Austrian interests in the Near East, and asserted that the relations between England and the Triple Alliance were such that, in certain eventualities, they would assume the force of an alliance. The Emperor's visit showed "that England's relations

[24] G. P. VIII, nos. 1745, 1746.

to the Triple Alliance and in particular to Austria-Hungary have undergone no change under the Gladstone administration."[25]

Now what was the attitude of the Russian government towards these developments? In the first place the Tsar could not help but notice that the connection between England and the Triple Alliance still existed and that it would have to be recognized as a factor in any European complication. This being so, it would be almost impossible for Russia to reëmbark on an active policy in the Near East, and there would be always the danger that, if a clash between the English and the Russians took place in Central Asia, the former might succeed in shifting the centre of gravity to Europe by opening the Near Eastern question and so bringing in the Triple Alliance. Under the circumstances a Franco-Russian Alliance would be of indifferent value unless the French were willing to relegate their differences with Germany to the background, take a frankly anti-English standpoint and support Russia in Asiatic questions. This the French, under the leadership of Ribot, had always refused to do, and the out-and-out protagonists of the alliance in Paris, like Madame Adam and her group, had never tired of accusing the foreign minister of yielding too much to England, of pursuing a pusillanimous policy in the Egyptian question and of persistently ignoring the importance of Asiatic questions.[26] It was, then, a matter of the greatest significance that Ribot, who had in the meanwhile become premier, resigned on March 30, 1893, and that Develle became foreign minister in the new Dupuy cabinet.

With the advent of Develle an important change immediately became noticeable. As aforesaid, every effort was made to prevent the outbreak of a crisis in Franco-German relations, while at the same time the French government embarked actively

---

[25] *London Times* May 15, July 1, 1893. Rosebery told the German ambassador that he entirely shared and approved the sentiments expressed by Paget (G. P. VIII, no. 1747).

[26] In addition to references already quoted see Mme. Adam in *Nouvelle Revue* April 1, June 1, 1893, but especially March 1, 1893: "Les Russes travaillent pour nous dans le Pamir, en Mongolie, dans le Thibet, dans le Kan-sou, en Corée; travaillons pour eux dans le Setchuan, dans le Yunnan, l'Interland du Tonkin...La Russie et la France doivent marcher la main dans la main en Asie."

upon an anti-British policy. We have already examined the various expressions of this new attitude in so far as it related to Mediterranean matters, but of infinitely greater importance was the initiation of an active policy in Asia. Ever since the establishment of the French in Cochin China and Tonkin, efforts had been made by them to extend their frontier westward towards the Mekong, at the expense of the Kingdom of Siam. These efforts had met with opposition not only from the Siamese themselves, but from the English, who desired to maintain Siam as a buffer state between the English possessions in Burma and the French colonies to the east. Siam, in other words, was to be an eastern Afghanistan, and the encroachments of the French were the exact counterpart to the Russian advance on the northwest frontier of India. The matter had been hanging fire for several years. Ribot had shown little interest in the whole affair and had been careful not to estrange the English. But hardly had Develle assumed control than the question entered upon an acute phase. In May there were clashes between the French and the Siamese troops, and in both France and England the press became so rabid that many people regarded a war between the two nations as almost inevitable. The French government made no move to send an ambassador to London to take the place of Waddington, who had retired, and the English called back Lord Dufferin on extended leave, making it quite clear that the real reason for this action lay in the repeated and vitriolic attacks that had been launched against the ambassador by the French press.[27]

---

[27] *London Times* May 29, July 12, 13, 1893; the earlier history of the Siamese question may be followed in the newspapers and in the following books and articles: *British and Foreign State Papers* volume 87, *Correspondence respecting the Affairs of Siam 1887-1894* (pp. 189-390); *Documents Diplomatiques: Affaires de Siam* (1893); Capitaine Séauve: *Les Rélations de la France et du Siam* (Paris 1907); A. de Pourvoirville: *L'Affaire de Siam 1886-1896* (Paris 1897); G. Maurel: *Histoire des Rélations de la France et du Siam* (Paris 1906); H. W. Smyth: *Five Years in Siam* (London 1898) volume I, chapter xii; J. G. D. Campbell: *Siam in the Twentieth Century* (London 1902) chapter xi; G. N. Curzon: *The Siamese Boundary Question* (*Nineteenth Century* July 1893); D. C. Boulger: *The Crisis in Indo-China* (*Nineteenth Century* August 1893); H. Norman: *The Future of Siam* (*Contemporary* July 1893); Temple: *French Movements in Eastern Siam* (*Fort-*

Into the pros and cons of the Siamese question it is hardly necessary to enter here. Suffice it to say that Lord Rosebery took an extremely indulgent attitude from the start and announced that England recognized the right of France to settle her account with Siam as she saw fit, though England could not recognize the French claim to the left bank of the Mekong on its upper reaches. Not only that, but Lord Rosebery on several occasions warned the Siamese government not to drive matters to extremes, but to yield to the French demands before they became too extensive. The attitude of the English foreign minister was no doubt conditioned in large part by the opinions of Gladstone, Harcourt and other violently anti-imperialistic members of the cabinet, but it did not save the Siamese from the results of their folly, neither did it save the English from repeated attacks by the French press, which insisted loudly that the English government was underhandedly encouraging the Siamese to resist the just demands of the French.[28] After months of acrimonious debate on both sides the whole question entered upon a very acute phase when, on July 13, the two French gunboats *Inconstant* and *Comète* forced their way up the Menam River, past the forts at Paknam, and anchored off Bangkok itself. The Siamese had fired on the French ships and there had been some casualties. In any case the French considered themselves justified in submitting a very harsh ultimatum to the Siamese government, and

nightly July 1893); R. S. Gundry: France, England and Siam (*National Review* July 1893); A. Merignhac: L'Incident Franco-Siamois de 1893 (*Revue de Droit Public* April 1894, pp. 197-241).

[28] Abundant evidence of the moderate attitude of the English government may be found in the British *Blue Book, passim.* So pronounced was this indulgent attitude that the *Bombay Gazette* in March 1893 published a statement to the effect that some three years before Lord Salisbury and M. Waddington had come to an understanding by which the right of India to occupy the Shan States and the right of the Empire of Annam to control the country between the Annamese Hills and the Mekong was recognized. The statement was repeated in the *Asiatic Quarterly Review* (July 1893 p. 64) and in the *Spectator* of July 22. Lord Salisbury categorically denied that an understanding concerning Siam had been arrived at by the conservative government (see the details of the matter in the *Asiatic Quarterly* October 1893, pp. 462-465, and January 1894, p. 202.). French press opinion may be well followed in the *Mémorial Diplomatique* March 4, July 22; and *London Times* May 29, July 18, 1893.

when this was rejected the French agent withdrew and a blockade was instituted.

The English government had been promised information as to the mission of French ships to Bangkok. It had, however, not been informed and no effort was made by Develle to give a satisfactory explanation. Though the blockade was officially announced from Paris to begin on July 31, reports were being received in London which showed that the French commanders on the spot had put it into effect several days earlier. The very fact of the blockade was a serious matter, for it injured no one but the English, who had fully ninety per cent of all the trade.[29] Lord Dufferin was immediately rushed off to Paris to negotiate with the French in regard to their claims on the upper Mekong and to reserve the rights of the British. In the meanwhile Lord Rosebery, who apparently regarded war as almost inevitable, began to sound out the Italians as to their attitude in the event of a crisis, while at the same time he approached the German ambassador, hinting that if matters took a turn for the worse an opportunity might present itself for bringing about the quadruple alliance which had been so frequently discussed, but which had always been vetoed by Gladstone.[30] "What can Frenchmen expect from provocation carried beyond a certain point except to drive us fairly into the arms of the Triple Alliance," wrote the *Times* in a leading article on July 18. The problem was whether the continental powers would now consent to act as shock-absorbers, when England had so long preserved her splendid isolation. The Italians appear to have been not entirely averse to taking a strong stand, but the Germans were much more circumspect. Germany, wrote the *Berliner Tageblatt* on July 24, can afford to look at the Siamese crisis with the greatest serenity,

---

[29] British *Blue Book* no. 181. Lord Dufferin observed to M. Develle that "such a blockade would be like riding another man's horse with one's own spurs" (*ibid*. no. 185). Full details as to the blockade may be found in the *Blue Book* nos. 190-266, *passim*, and in Hansard: *Parliamentary Debates*, fourth series, volume XV, pp. 657, 763, 884. The French explanations are given in the British *Blue Book* no. 268. The actual proclamations by the French commanders on the spot in the *Blue Book* no. 331.

[30] G. P. VIII, nos. 1749-1751.

and should aim to play the part of the *tertius gaudens* in the
whole matter. "There can be no question of our pulling even
the smallest chestnuts out of the fire for the English," it concluded. Two days later the same newspaper wrote in an almost
cynical vein:

"England loses no opportunity of making it clear to the world that she
stands aloof from the Triple Alliance. The events in Siam afford a welcome
opportunity for showing England by a concrete example that under certain
circumstances she may be very glad of the moral support of Germany. She
must not, however, look for this help if on other occasions she wraps herself
up in her island haughtiness and lets us know that she does not require our
aid."

The same note was struck by most of the other German papers,
and it appears from the German documents that this attitude
was substantially that of the German foreign office. The Italians were warned to stand off and wait either until the English
cannon had already gone off or else until they had in hand a
definite and specific treaty, signed by Gladstone himself.[31] It
so happened that on July 27 the Kaiser himself arrived at Cowes
to take part in the yacht races. On July 29 the Siamese finally
accepted the terms of the French ultimatum, including the cession
of the left bank of the Mekong. News of this reached Paris and
London on the same day, but before there was any let-up of the
international tension, Lord Rosebery received, on July 30, a
telegram from the British minister at Bangkok saying that the
French commander had ordered the British gunboats at the
capital to leave the river and remain outside the blockade limits.
The English government had not recognized the "pacific blockade" announced by the French, and besides, Develle had fixed
the date of the beginning of the blockade as July 31. In any
case there could be no question of England's abandoning her
nationals at the behest of the French, and so, on the afternoon of
July 30, the dreaded crisis seemed to have arrived. Rosebery
sent a note to Paris stating that the English government
could not withdraw the British warships, and apparently
expected the rejection of the note by the French. But in

[31] G. P. VIII, nos. 1750-1751.

the course of the evening a second telegram came from the senior naval officer at Bangkok, through the admiralty, stating that the earlier message was founded on a misunderstanding, and that in reality the English gunboat at Bangkok was to stay inside the blockade. The full details as to what actually happened at Bangkok on July 29 and 30 have never become known, but it is quite clear that the French authorities acted high-handedly, one of the French gunboats outside the bar sailing past the English ship *Pallas* with guns trained for action. Only the good sense of the French commander in chief, who sent his subordinate to apologize for this appalling breach of naval courtesy, prevented this incident from assuming dangerous proportions.[32]

[32] There has always been much uncertainty as to the details of the Siamese crisis of July 30, 1893, and the version given by Sir Sidney Lee in his biography of Edward VII (vol. I, p. 707) is so incomplete and misleading that it is worth while to go to the bottom of it. There is no doubt that the French ship *Lion* steamed down on the English ship *Pallas* in menacing fashion and that the French admiral ordered his subordinate to apologize (*London Times* August 4, 1893; letter of an officer of the *Pallas* to the Earl of Dudley [*London Times* October 7, 1893]; Grey: Twenty-Five Years I, pp. 13-15; Sir W. L. Clowes: *The Royal Navy* [London 1903] VII, pp. 413-414). The real question is whether the British ship sent to Bangkok to protect British lives and property was ordered by the French commander to leave. The situation was as follows: On July 25 France broke off relations with the Siamese government and the three French ships at Bangkok, the *Lutin*, the *Inconstant* and the *Comète* left the river (Dartige du Fournet: *Journal d'un Commandant de la Comète* [Paris 1897] p. 237; A. Pavie: *Mission Pavie: Indo-Chine, 1879-1895, Géographie et Voyages* [Paris 1906] volume II, pp. 244-245); on July 26 the commander of the French ship *Forfait*, lying at the mouth of the river, declared the blockade, whereupon the English merchantmen at Bangkok left the river escorted by the warship *Swift*. Only the *Linnet* remained at Bangkok (Dartige p. 240; Pavie p. 245; *Blue Book* no. 203). On July 29 Admiral Humann himself arrived from Saigon and ordered that the blockade be made effective. An English ship from Hongkong carrying Chinese was detained but finally allowed to go to Bangkok to discharge its cargo (*Blue Book* nos. 220, 231; *Hansard* XV, p. 885). At the same time the French admiral notified the commander of the *Pallas* that the British ships of war must either leave the zone of the blockade or be blockaded. Thereupon the *Pallas* and the *Swift* left the scene and did not return until they were informed that the blockade had been lifted some days later (Dartige pp. 246-247; letter from an officer of the *Pallas*, in *London Times* October 7, 1893; Sir Edward Grey in the house of commons November 7, 1893 [*Hansard* XVIII, p. 340]; Clowes VII, pp. 413-414). Apparently the commander of the *Pallas* was not well-versed in the French language, for he sent a warning to the commander of the *Linnet*, which was still at Bangkok, telling him to be ready to leave the river within

The report that British ships had been ordered to leave Bangkok proved to be a false alarm, but it gave rise to an interesting incident which was not to be without its effect on the future development of the situation. The Kaiser had arrived at Cowes for the yacht races on July 27 and Count Hatzfeldt had left London to attend his sovereign. When the alarming news from Bangkok became known at the foreign office on July 30 Rosebery sent notice to the Queen and asked that someone should be sent to Cowes to request that the German ambassador return to the capital as soon as possible. Rosebery expected war within a few hours, and it is said that at least one London paper had already set the type to announce to the city the great catastrophe.[33] Since all the.English statesmen were out of the city for the holiday, the foreign minister was obliged to act solely on his own res-

the additional day of grace which had been allowed for departures. This would have left British lives and property in the Siamese capital at the mercy of events (Jones to Rosebery July 30, received in London on the same day, *Blue Book* no. 233). The reports of these developments, including an alarming despatch from the commander of the *Pallas* (G. P. VIII, no. 1754, and note), was what caused the panic in London. In reality no attempt had been made by the French to interfere with the gunboat (Vice-Admiral Ballard in the *London Times* January 9, 1924). Rosebery immediately telegraphed to the British minister at Bangkok saying that "the *Linnet* must on no account leave under present circumstances" (*Blue Book* no. 234). The story of his ultimatum to Paris on the same day is rather overdrawn. His despatch to Dufferin, after recounting the circumstances, instructs the ambassador to state to the French government "that it would be impossible that Her Majesty's Government should allow British subjects to be left at the mercy of an unruly Oriental population, and that, therefore, they cannot withdraw Her Majesty's ship now stationed off the city" (*Blue Book* no. 235). It was only late in the day that the earlier report from Bangkok was rectified by a telegram from the senior officer (Rosebery's letter to the Earl of Dudley, printed in the *London Times* October 14, 1893). Meanwhile the crisis had become very acute, the cabinet had been summoned, and in initiated circles it was believed that the country would be at war the next morning (see G. P. VIII, nos. 1752, 1753, 1754, and footnotes; Grey I, pp. 13-15; A. J. Gardiner: *The Life of Sir William Harcourt* [London 1923] volume II, pp. 240-241; Gwynn and Tuckwell: *The Life of Sir Charles Dilke* II, pp. 453, 486; Le Myre de Vilers in the *Revue des Deux Mondes* November 1, 1902; Blunt: My Diaries I, pp. 138-139; and the declarations in parliament August 1, 3, 4: "We are informed that no demand was made by the French admiral that British war vessels should leave Bangkok and their removal outside the blockade limits would never have been permitted by Her Majesty's government" [*Hansard* XV, pp. 982, 1209, 1347; XVIII, p. 341]).

[33] Gardiner II, pp. 240-241.

ponsibility, and naturally enough his first impulse was to establish contact with the German government and to attempt to secure the aid of the Triple Alliance. It was a policy which he had evidently been tempted to follow for some time past, but which had always been shelved at the insistence of Gladstone and his immediate followers.

Sir Arthur Ponsonby, the secretary of the Queen, arrived at Cowes late on the evening of July 30, and immediately made his way to the Kaiser, who was dining with the Prince of Wales. Count Eulenburg, a close confidant of the Kaiser, who was present at the time, has left us a vivid account of this rather dramatic incident. The Kaiser was entirely unnerved, and declared that the French had obviously chosen a favorable moment to embark upon a policy intended to provoke war at a time when the English fleet was not in the best condition and the German army had not yet reaped the advantage of the increase provided for in the military bill. It was his old distrust of the French which once more dictated his attitude, and it is quite clear that on the spur of the moment his own inclination was to take the part of the English and assume a leading rôle in the whole action. Since Hatzfeldt was sick in bed, Count Metternich was immediately sent up to London in his stead. He arrived early on July 31 only to learn that the crisis had blown over and that the danger of war was past.[34] In the meanwhile the Kaiser's advisers had gone over the whole problem with their sovereign and persuaded him that it would be a mistaken policy to offer the English the aid of Germany and the Triple Alliance before the terms of assistance had been clearly laid down. There is every likelihood that if war had actually broken out the Germans would have come to the assistance of the English even without a definite agreement, for they realized that an initial English defeat would have been almost fatal to the position of the central powers as well as to England herself. But they were determined to conceal this fact from Lord Rosebery and, if possible, to wait until England was irrevocably engaged militarily before definitely committing them-

---

[34] Haller: *Eulenburg* pp. 84-87. See also the accounts of Rosebery in G. P. VIII, nos. 1752-1754, and notes; and Lee: Edward VII, volume I, p. 707.

selves. Once an English warship has fired the first shot, wrote Caprivi on a report from Hatzfeldt, we can be certain that the Triple Alliance can be transformed into a Quadruple Alliance.[35]

In actual fact the whole problem became academic just as soon as the second telegram arrived from Bangkok on the evening of July 30. Rosebery knew that his colleagues would never consent to a war in behalf of the Siamese and that the matter would have to be straightened out as best it could. At almost the same moment word came from Lord Dufferin in Paris that the French government had recognized the principle of a buffer state on the upper reaches of the Mekong, thus satisfying English public opinion in the most essential point.[36] The outcome was that the English foreign office seized the opportunity to withdraw gracefully from the whole matter, but the crisis left a very poor impression on the governments of other nations. "Eh bien, l'Angleterre ne joue pas un beau rôle," said Signor Brin to the German ambassador a day or two later.[37] He did not know of the exciting developments of July 30 in London and at Cowes, but it was clear that the English were pursuing an extremely pusillanimous policy in throwing Siam to the wolves and allowing the French to take what they wanted while ruthlessly pressing the Siamese to the wall. Even the recognition by the French of the desirability of a buffer state on the upper Mekong could not alter the impression, for this principle had been recognized over and over again by the French on earlier occasions.[38] To have ignored it in the hour of victory would have amounted to an outright repudiation of past engagements, and it may be doubted whether even Gladstone, Harcourt and their ilk could have ac-

---

[35] G. P. VIII, nos. 1752-1757. Schiessl to Kálnoky July 22, 1893; Szögyény to Kálnoky March 17, 1894.

[36] *Blue Book* no. 242.

[37] G. P. VIII, no. 1755. It appears from the German documents that the Italians were by no means loath to join in an adventure with the English, and that the German government was much concerned lest the Italian government should commit itself too easily.

[38] *Blue Book passim*, especially no. 309, which is a résumé of the negotiations from 1887 on. A telling criticism of the settlement was made by Curzon in a speech at Crosby in October, referred to by the Earl of Ronaldshay: *The Life of Lord Curzon* (London 1928) volume I, pp. 197-198.

cepted such action without recourse to war. As for the Kaiser and his friends, they could never forget that dramatic scene at Cowes and the nervous excitement which turned the face of Ponsonby to a ghastly white as he came into the Imperial presence on the evening of the 30. Poor Rosebery, who was evidently quite ready to take a strong stand and who fully appreciated all the implications of the situation, never heard the end of this unfortunate matter and attempted again and again to explain his conduct to the Germans. But in the Wilhelmstrasse no faith was put in his account, and it was evidently believed that the English had actually been ordered by the French to withdraw their ships from Bangkok and that they had acquiesced.[39]

Looked at from the broadest point of view the Siamese crisis of 1893 was the most serious crisis in Anglo-French relations before Fashoda. Excepting for Gladstone and a few other rabid anti-imperialists well-informed people in England felt certain that the action of the French represented the beginning of a new era of acute tension. In view of the rising tide of French sentiment against England and the advance of the Russians in the Pamirs, it looked very much as though the two powers were beginning to join forces for a united assault on the British Empire and were wisely planning to direct the attack against the most vulnerable point, the Indian Empire, in the hope that England would find no support among the other nations for a campaign in Asia. Lord Curzon gave a classic formulation of this viewpoint in an article entitled *India between Two Fires*, which was much commented on at the time. Even supposing that the French and Russians were not to attempt an actual attack on India as such, he presented the following situation for the consideration of his readers:

"Russia might be advancing upon Constantinople, and England might be deploying her full strength to resist that movement. Is it inconceivable that

---

[39] G. P. VIII, nos. 1752-1754. The publication of the letter of an officer of the *Pallas* in the *London Times* on October 7 and Rosebery's reply on October 14 created quite a stir in Germany, where Rosebery's explanations were regarded as quite inadequate (*London Times* October 28, 1893).

at such a moment news of an outbreak might arrive from Upper Burma, or that the French should be reported as having crossed the Upper Mekong? Or again, France might decide to invade Egypt, and England might be involved in a fierce struggle for the mastery. What would be our position if at such a juncture there flashed across the wires tidings that the Russian flag was flying from the citadel of Herat, or that a dozen squadrons of Cossacks were encamped amid the ruins of Balkh?"[40]

In other words, if complete coöperation between Russia and France could be established, sufficient pressure could be brought to bear upon England to make her yield not only in Asia but in the Mediterranean. In Asia she would find no support. In Europe it would be difficult to find allies in a war which had its origins in a Far Eastern problem. And even if the Triple Alliance were disposed to fly to the aid of the English in defending the *status quo* in the Near East, there was one very effective method of discouraging the statesmen of the central powers. The reorganized French army and the Russian forces massed in Poland were, if taken together, quite sufficient to make a war on the part of the Triple Alliance an extremely risky proposition, especially while Italy was in so critical a financial condition. The policy of the Russian government, once the French had clearly demonstrated their readiness to adopt a firm tone in their dealings with England, was perfectly obvious. The course of conciliation with both Austria and Germany might with profit be followed even further and the Balkan question shelved so far as possible. To make doubly sure it might be advisable to conclude the military convention with France, which would be entirely defensive and designed to protect Russia and France against the possibility of the Germans or their allies taking the side of England, in the event of a struggle between Russia and France on the one hand and England on the other. An im-

<hr />

[40] G. N. Curzon: India between Two Fires (*Nineteenth Century* August 1893); cf. also Ronaldshay I, pp. 195 ff. This was also the view of the Kaiser at the time (Haller: *Eulenburg* pp. 84-85). The argument is forcefully presented also by D. C. Boulger: The Crisis in Indo-China (*Nineteenth Century* August 1893); by Stead in the *Review of Reviews* August 1893; and by Sir Lepel Griffin: England and France in Asia (*Nineteenth Century* November 1893). There were even rumors that Russia was negotiating for the acquisition of a naval base in the Bay of Bengal (*London Times* July 24).

portant point in this program, however, was to avoid rousing
the suspicions of the central powers. A Franco-Russian demonstration, if not properly managed, might very well drive
Germany into the arms of England and so defeat the very object
which was to be attained.

During the second half of 1893 one can see this policy slowly
taking shape. Its gradual evolution is one of the most interesting
phenomena in the pre-war history of Europe. While the relations
between Russia and her neighbors on the west continued quite
unruffled, and while preparations were being made for the resumption of the tariff negotiations which were to lead to the
Russo-German treaty of 1894, the French on their part continued to avoid, so far as possible, every occasion for friction. In
fact a large number of articles and even books appeared in Paris
suggesting the possibility of settling the Alsace-Lorraine question
by a compromise, and there was every indication that the French,
in their rabid hostility to the English, were quite ready to turn
their eyes from the hole in the Vosges, at least for the time
being.[41] Meanwhile the tension in Anglo-French relations continued undiminished. The French were negotiating the treaty
with the Siamese, while the English looked on with the greatest
apprehension, constantly fearing that the French, once they had
extorted what they wanted from the Siamese, would refuse to
make concessions to the English in the matter of the buffer state.
During the months of September and October the press campaign
became more and more acrid, the English papers declaring that
the French were going far beyond the provisions of the ultimatum accepted by Siam, and the French journals vehemently de-

---

[41] Cf. e. g. the remarkable report of the German representative in Bangkok,
September 18, 1893, who quotes the French plenipotentiary, Le Myre de Vilers, one
of the most influential figures in French colonial circles, as saying that the plan of
the French was to prevent Germany joining in an eventual Franco-English conflict
by effecting an understanding with Germany: "England's humiliation is our immediate aim" (G. P. VIII, p. 126, note). On the subsidence of the revanche
feeling see Charnay: *L'Alsace-Lorraine Vingt Ans Après* (Paris 1892); Arendt:
France et Allemagne (Lausanne 1893); Patiens: *L'Alsace-Lorraine devant l'Europe*
(Paris 1894); Anon.: Deutschland und Frankreich (*Grenzboten* 1893, pp. 289-294);
Pichon: L'Alsace-Lorraine devant l'Europe (*Nouvelle Revue* February 1, 1894).

nouncing the English for their attempts to interfere in what they insisted was strictly a Franco-Siamese transaction.

In all these critical weeks the French showed no inclination to yield, and they were right, for they held the whip hand, and the English were quite helpless. Within a week of the great crisis in the Siamese question the Russian government acceded to the request of the French government and announced that a Russian squadron would visit Toulon late in September or in October, and that some of the ships composing the squadron would be permanently established in the Mediterranean. The French ambassador had been for months urging the desirability of a Russian visit to repay that of Cronstadt, and there is evidence that the French government had urged also the necessity for the establishment of a Russian squadron in the Mediterranean.[42] The French *Yellow Book* tells us nothing of these negotiations, probably because, at the date of publication in 1918, the French government was eager to show that the coalition had, from the

[42] There had been rumors in the spring that the Russian fleet would repay the Cronstadt visit, and these have already been referred to. Montebello had evidently continued to press the point, but had met with little encouragement, as he himself told the Austrian ambassador (Wolkenstein to Kálnoky May 30, 1893). On June 11 Montebello was able to report to his government that the visit would take place, but no date had been set (L. J. no. 83) and the French government was not satisfied. Giers told General von Werder: "Die französische Diplomatie habe ihn mit Anfragen überlaufen" (Wolkenstein to Kálnoky July 15, 1893) and later said to Aehrenthal: "dass Graf Montebello ihn während des Sommers wiederholt mit der Frage gelangweilt habe, wann endlich die Kronstädter Visite zurückgegeben werden würde. Er—der Minister—habe alle Mühe gehabt, die Ungeduld des französischen Botschafters und seiner Regierung zu zügeln" (Aehrenthal to Kálnoky October 22, 1893). There had also been vague reports that a Russian squadron would be established in the Mediterranean (Wolkenstein to Kálnoky July 5, 1893), and it is evident from Hansen's *démarche*, made at Develle's instigation, that the French government strongly advocated this measure (Hansen: *Mohrenheim* p. 157, with the reference to the two reports he had submitted to the Russian government "concernant le rétablissement d'une flotte russe dans le Méditerranée"). On July 15 Giers denied any knowledge of the formation of such a squadron, but the Austrian naval attaché got the full details from Admiral Krahmer (Wolkenstein to Kálnoky July 15, 1893). The Toulon visit and the establishment of the Russian squadron became known on August 6 (*London Times* August 7, 19, 21; *Mémorial Diplomatique* August 12, St. Petersburg letter August 6, 1893). The French ambassador reported it August 10 (L. J. no. 86). The specific date was not fixed until September 1 (*London Times* September 4, 1893).

very beginning, been designed for protection against the sombre plans of the Hun. In reality every well-informed person in 1893 could see that it was directed, not only by the Russians, but by the French as well, against England. The significance of the Toulon visit lay in the fact that it was to be followed by the establishment of a Russian squadron in the Mediterranean, and this was an event of supreme political as well as naval importance, for it was bound to disturb the whole balance of sea power in the Mediterranean and might lead to the checkmating of England in all parts of the world.[43]

The seriousness of the move decided upon by the Russians becomes quite apparent when the question of naval strength is considered. The Naval Defence Act of 1889 had brought to an end a rather prolonged period of lethargy, during which the British navy, not seriously challenged by any near competitor, had been allowed to deteriorate. As is well known, the act was designed to establish firmly the principle that the British fleet must be equal to its two nearest rivals taken together. During the years 1889-1892 new ships had been built at a feverish rate, but the French and Russians had both followed suit, and the result was that the situation became rapidly more critical than ever.[44] The liberal cabinet, intent on economy and com-

[43] Cf. *Mémorial Diplomatique* September 16, 1893, St. Petersburg letter September 10; *Daily Telegraph* September 11, 1893; Baron de Chambourg: Réponse aux Injures et aux Menaces de l'Angleterre (*Nouvelle Revue* August 15, 1893); Anon.: Deutschland und das Mittelmeer (*Grenzboten* 1893, volume IV, pp. 196-206); Admiral F. A. Maxse: The European Outlook (*National Review* November 1893): "A war is just as likely to be made by the Double Alliance against England alone as against the Triple Alliance....such a war would be as popular as one with Germany." Sir Lepel Griffin: England and France in Asia (*Nineteenth Century* November 1893): "The hatred to the Germans is faint when compared with that the French feel and on every occasion proclaim to England." Anon.: Naval Armaments (*Edinburgh Review* April 1894): "All available evidence seems to show that whilst the hatred of Germany is yielding to the soothing balm of time, the jealousy of England tends to become more acute."

[44] See the admirable review of developments by Captain S. Eardley-Wilmot in Brassey's *Naval Annual* for 1894 (chapter viii); Sir John H. Briggs: *Naval Administrations 1827-1892* (London 1897) chapters xxiii and xxiv; C. M. Mc-Hardy: *The British Navy for 100 Years* (London 1897) *passim*, but especially the charts of expenditure on pp. 28-32; Lord George Hamilton: *Parliamentary Reminiscences and Reflections 1886-1906* (London 1922) *passim*.

paratively indifferent to matters of foreign policy, had neglected to lay down even one new battleship in the first twelve months that it was in office. In vain had Lord Spencer, the first lord of the admiralty, laid before his colleagues long lists of statistics showing the comparative strengths of the world's navies, and in vain had he urged the necessity for action. The chancellor of the exchequer, Sir William Harcourt, was one of the most inexorable opponents of an imperialistic policy and gave no encouragement. While he was willing to say that he advocated English maritime supremacy as ardently as any jingo, he admitted that he took some delight in "confounding the panic-mongers." It is quite clear that he sincerely believed that there was no cause for alarm, and that Gladstone fully shared this conviction. But with these two exceptions there were few people in authority and even fewer experts who did not consider the situation very dangerous. In August, 1893 Lord Rosebery warned both the army and navy officials that the prospect for the autumn was stormy, and before long a systematic campaign was begun, in the course of which some very interesting facts were brought prominently to the fore.[45]

The opening gun was fired by that *enfant terrible* of the time, Lord Charles Beresford, who, on July 20, addressed the London chamber of commerce on "The Protection of the Mercantile Marine during War," and pointed out that, while England had only one cruiser for every 71 merchant ships, France had one for every 30, and had in addition a large swarm of torpedo boats that could do great damage as commerce destroyers. It appears that he also supplied the chamber of commerce with a program, which was not published until later but which was dated March, 1893, in which he called for the expenditure of £23,000,000 for the navy, and pointed out that, because of the ease with which the Russian squadron could come through the Straits and into

[45] See especially Gardiner: *Life of Sir William Harcourt* II, pp. 201-202, 230, 245 ff.: Harcourt to Spencer, September 28, 1893: "It is quite obvious that there are not six vessels if you put the whole world together that could meet our fleet, which is more than three times that number." See also J. A. Spender: *The Life of Sir Henry Campbell-Bannerman* (London 1923) I, p. 140, for Rosebery's warning.

the Mediterranean, the British government should buy or otherwise acquire Lemnos or some other base in the eastern Mediterranean, since Cyprus was strategically of almost no use.[46]   The views of Lord Charles may have been somewhat overdrawn, as they frequently were, but there is no difficulty in obtaining statistics to show that the English had good reason to view the situation with uneasiness.   It is not proposed to go into the technical details of naval matters here, nor to examine the various methods used by experts in estimating the comparative strengths of different sea powers. A mere count of ships is, of course, quite insufficient, but with certain allowances an adequate idea can be gained, the rest being left to the opinions of authoritative persons.

From the official figures published by the British government at the time it can be shown that England had only a very slight superiority, if any, over the combined fleets of France and Russia. At the same time both the French and Russian governments were appropriating much larger funds to shipbuilding and had many more keels laid down than the English.   Unless the Engglish program were extended and hastened, there would not be the slightest doubt as to British inferiority within two or three years.[47]   More serious by far was the situation in the Mediterranean, where the French alone had a superiority over the English.   The former had thirteen battleships in commission and a large squadron at Toulon which would be ready to go to sea within a few months.   In addition they had a huge flotilla of

---

[46] *London Times* November 21, 1893; *The Memoirs of Admiral Lord Charles Beresford* (London 1914) II, pp. 386 ff.   Eardley-Wilmot in Brassey (1894).

[47] In the debate on the naval estimates in the house of commons on August 28 Lord George Hamilton insisted that England had only twenty-two first class battleships, while France had fifteen and Russia ten.   In spite of this Harcourt asserted that "he would undertake to say that the superiority of the British Navy was never so great as it is now."   That he stood almost alone in this view is shown by the statistics given in Brassey (1894) who reports that England had 43 battleships of all kinds and 3 building, France had 25 and 9 building, Russia had 9 and 8 building.   See also the figures in McHardy *passim*; L. Renard: *Carnets de l'Officier de Marine* (Paris 1893); and the excellent critical study of comparative strengths by Nauticus: The Official Estimate of Rival Navies (*New Review* March 1894, pp. 385-399).   Cf. also the special articles in the *London Times* November 6, 13, 17, 20, 1893; Admiral Sir Thomas Symonds: The Needs of the Navy (*Fortnightly Review* August 1893).

torpedo boats and other fast craft, the general policy of the preceding years having been to construct large numbers of smaller
craft of great speed to act as commerce destroyers. These
alone, according to the writer of a remarkable article in the London *Times*, could "torture the English fleet into despair in a
week." Behind the French fleet was the great naval port of
Toulon, with its marvellous docks and its wonderful harbor, and
behind Toulon was the whole of French territory. As a base it
was second to none in the world.[48]

As against this force the English had only eleven battleships,
one of which was called home soon after. Roughly, the ships
were of about the same value as those of the French, and the total
tonnage of the two forces was about equal, but the French had a
considerable advantage in the number of guns, a slight advantage
in speed, and a distinct superiority in the number of men. In
torpedo boats the English were far behind. The dozen or there-
abouts which were in the Mediterranean were mostly aged and
could not be compared to the new French craft.[49] Neither did
England have any reserves at hand, nor was there any Toulon.
In fact there was no repair dock between England and Malta.
Strategically Gibraltar was almost useless, as it had no dockyard
and no adequate coaling facilities. Some naval officers con-

[48] Special article in *London Times* October 31, 1893: The French Mediterranean force "could not only wipe out or drive into port the Mediterranean Fleet,
fine though it is, which we maintain, but could also for a considerable period prevent any reinforcements from reaching it and its bases from England.. For the
moment we are at Malta, in Cyprus, in Egypt and at Gibraltar on sufferance."
W. L. Clowes: Toulon and the French Navy (*Nineteenth Century* December
1893): "France is much stronger in the Mediterranean than we, and, further, she
is much readier." W. L. Clowes, in Brassey (1894) chapter v; Nauticus: Sea
Power, its Past and its Future (*Fortnightly* December 1893): "England's sea-power
has ceased to be convincing, undoubted, recognised. To-morrow it would be shattered, perhaps immediately, by France alone, if only France had no other preoccu-
pations and if she were assured beforehand of Italy's non-interference." Captain
Gambier: An Exchange for Gibraltar (*Fortnightly* May 1893): "The Mediterranean, as now held by our fleets and armies, is a standing danger to the British Empire." Cf. also the figures in the *London Times* November 13, and the letters of
the Earl of Pembroke in the *Times* November 10, 20, with the numerous other
letters printed under the latter date, and the figures in the *Times* December 26 and
27, 1893.

[49] See preceding note.

sidered it of no value whatever, and suggested that it be exchanged for Ceuta or some other place. on the Moroccan coast which could be further developed.[50] Taken by and large there was no doubt in the minds of responsible naval officers that the French were far superior to the English in the Mediterranean, and that under the circumstances the junction of the Brest and Toulon squadrons could be carried through with no great difficulty.

The really alarming feature of the situation was, however, the establishment of the Russian Mediterranean squadron, for this would give the French an overwhelming superiority if coöperation between the two could be effected. If England could be driven out of the Mediterranean or even engaged in the western part of it, there would be nothing to prevent the Russians from coming through the Black Sea and throwing the whole weight of the Black Sea squadron into the balance. This Black Sea fleet was by no means a negligible quantity in 1893. There were six battleships, all built since 1886 and without exception fast, heavily armored, and particularly formidable. In addition there were two battleships under construction in the yards on the Black Sea, to say nothing of cruisers, twenty-two first class torpedo boats and twelve fine steamers of the volunteer fleet.[51] The Turks had nothing to oppose to this splendid force, for the Turkish navy had only one armored ship built later than 1875, while the others dated from the early 'seventies and the 'sixties. The Turkish fleet had been lying in the Bosporus for years, and the bottoms of the ships were so overgrown with marine vegetation that it would have been difficult to move them. Militarily

[50] W. L. Clowes: The Uselessness of Gibraltar (*Fortnightly* February 1893); Captain Gambier: An Exchange for Gibraltar (*Fortnightly* May 1893); Letter of H. O. Arnold-Forster (*Times* September 2); letter of G. F. Bowen (*Times* September 7); letter of S. W. Baker (*Times* September 11, 1893).

[51] See especially the excellent review of Russian naval power in the *London Times* October 14, 1893; and the special article in the *London Times* November 15, 1893. Further figures in Brassey, 1893, 1894, and the article by Fauvel in the *Revue Française de l'Étranger*, November 1, 1893. Cf. also Flourens: *Alexandre III* pp. 247 ff.

there was nothing whatsoever to prevent the Russian ships from coming through the Straits or attacking Constantinople.[52]

While the English were outnumbered by the French in the Mediterranean and the Russians were preparing to despatch a force to the same region, considerable importance had to be attached to Italy, for the Italians had a good fleet of over twenty armored vessels, including ten ships of over ten thousand tons, among which were the largest battleships afloat at that time. Opinions varied as to the quality of the Italian fleet as a fighting force, but it was quite obvious that it might sway the decision one way or the other.[53] In 1893 it was not quite clear whether the Italians or the English would be the first to feel the pressure of the combined French and Russian naval force in the Mediterranean, for the relations between France and Italy were quite as bad as those between France and England. On August 17 a number of Italian workers at Aiguesmortes were attacked and severely maltreated by a superior number of French laborers, enraged because the Italians worked for lower wages. As a result of this lamentable clash, in which seven Italians lost their lives, there was a tremendous anti-French demonstration in many Italian cities. In Rome the enraged populace assaulted the French embassy and the French seminary, while in Turin, Naples and other large centers French shops were sacked and crowds paraded the streets shouting cheers for the Triple Alliance and denunciations of France. Only the energetic action of the Italian authorities prevented the disturbances from leading to serious consequences.[54]

The French realized that they were in the wrong, apologized, and later indemnified the families of those who had been killed or injured in the Aiguesmortes catastrophe. But public opinion

[52] Opinion of the British naval attaché in Constantinople, reported by the Austrian ambassador to Turkey (Calice to Kálnoky, December 25, 1893, January 1, 1894). Brassey (1894 p. 330) shows that in 1894 Turkey had not a single armored ship built later than 1885 and only one under construction.

[53] See Brassey 1893, 1894. The three great battleships were the *Re Umberto*, the *Sicilia* and the *Sardegna*, all of over 13,000 tons displacement.

[54] By far the most complete account may be found in Billot I, pp. 467-474. See also Curàtulo: *Francia e Italia*, 1849-1914, chapter x.

in France was hardly less excited than in Italy, and there was, for some time, real danger that the pent-up hostility of the two nations would end in war. The French were convinced that the Italians were seeking an opportunity to get out of their domestic difficulties by waging war, and the Italian idea that the French were straining every nerve to ruin Italy financially and force her to give up the Triple Alliance was becoming more firmly rooted than ever.[55] Feeling in France ran even higher when, in the early days of September, the Prince of Naples appeared in Lorraine to attend the annual German manoeuvres. When the Kaiser declared at Metz that the city and its army corps formed the cornerstone of Germany's military power, destined to protect the peace of Germany and of all Europe, and when he told the Lorrainers that they were Germans and should remain Germans by the help of God and the good German sword, the French took this braggadocio as a matter of course, for they were accustomed to it. What they could not become reconciled to was the sight of the grandson of Victor Immanuel marching side by side with the conqueror. The demonstration was, in fact, quite gratuitous and was generally condemned in the European press. The one consolation for the French lay in the fact that the coming visit of the Russian fleet to Toulon was made public at the very moment when the Kaiser and his guest entered Metz.[56]

It may well be doubted that the French had any desire to pick a quarrel with the Italians at so critical a moment, for it

[55] Billot I, pp. 474; Crispi III, p. 188-189; the documents in G. P. VII, nos. 1442-1456 show clearly how great the tension was. See also W. L. Alden: The Italian Case against France (*Nineteenth Century* August 1894).

[56] According to Billot (I, pp. 466-467) the Prince had been invited by the Kaiser during the latter's visit to Italy in April, at which time the place of the manoeuvres had not yet been decided upon. When the facts became known the Italian royal family thought it better to leave matters as they stood rather than cause friction. The same explanation was given Montebello by the Tsar, who asserted that Italy was not to blame, but that on the part of Germany the affair was a "manque de tact unqualifiable" (Montebello to Casimer-Perier, December 17, 1893—L. J. no. 90). The same story in *Mémorial Diplomatique* August 19, 1893. Giers, of course, took great pains to explain that the publication of the announcement in regard to the Russian visit and the visit of the Prince to Metz was a mere coincidence (Aehrenthal to Kálnoky September 13, October 22, 1893).

was quite clear that a war in the Alps would bring in the Germans and the Austrians as well. In such a case there would also be the danger for France that the English might intervene and seize the opportunity to settle old scores. But in any case it is quite apparent that Italy once more occupied a pivotal place, located as it was in the very centre of the Mediterranean and therefore forming the connecting link between England and the Triple Alliance.

"The old phrase, *balance of power in Europe,* is not wholly obsolete," wrote a keen critic of the situation in the *Edinburgh Review.* "It merely needs a slight amendment to bring it up to date. The words should run now, *balance of power in the Mediterranean.* What has been called *the rising belief in the power of navies* is the inarticulate expression of a widespread conviction that pre-eminence on the Continent is of less moment to the world at large than pre-eminence on the sea. As before intimated, the international *pole* has moved from Central Europe, and is now situated on or near a line drawn from Gibraltar to Alexandretta."[57]

With this very important change from the continental policy of the Bismarckian period to the world policy of the later period England's position was *ipso facto* weakened. It would appear from the documents available that Lord Rosebery was personally quite willing to accept the implications of the situation, that he was prepared to conclude a more specific agreement with the Italians, and that he would probably have taken at least the first steps toward a junction with the Triple Alliance. Here again, however, his colleagues, notably Gladstone and Harcourt, proved to be insurmountable obstacles, and the English foreign office was obliged to muddle along as best it could, while its leader was exposed to the accusations of weakness which continental statesmen were always too ready to direct against the English ministers, who were hedged about with constitutional forms and obligations.[58]

"To the plain man of ordinary observation it must be evident that the virtual annihilation of Italy as a naval power will have a prodigious effect

---

[57] Mediterranean Politics (*Edinburgh Review* October 1892).

[58] Cf. the *Private |Diaries of Sir Algernon West,* chapters xv-xvii *passim;* Gardiner: *Life of Harcourt* II, pp. 245 ff., 252 ff.; Deym to Kálnoky December 23, 1893; G. P. VIII, nos. 1755-1762.

on the affairs of the United Kingdom as well as on those of the rest of Europe," wrote the critic of the *Edinburgh Review* in discussing the Mediterranean situation. "It would be about as necessary and as sensible to give formal recognition to this by a binding engagement as it would be to enter into a bond undertaking, whenever we may have occasion to add two and two, that the sum shall be made to come out four. French vituperation of England because of this supposed agreement means, in polite language, simply this: 'We know that the disappearance of the Italian navy would be of great importance to your interests; and we are convinced that you have good sense enough to know it yourselves.' "[59]

Now this kind of reasoning would all have been very well had it been merely a question of England and Italy. The Italians were compelled to rely upon English aid for protection against France whether the English chose to give a written promise of assistance or not. As for the English themselves, their only hope was that the Italians, in an Anglo-French crisis, would see where their interests lay and fly to the assistance of the British fleet.[60] Neither side could really afford to see the other defeated in the Mediterranean, because neither could tolerate French preponderance in that region. The great difference came, however, from the fact that England was a free agent, while Italy was not entirely mistress of her own fate. Before joining the British, the Italian statesmen would of necessity have to secure the approval of the German foreign office, because Italy was obliged to prepare for a war on land as well as a war on sea. Her case was, in a sense, hopeless unless she had the support of both England and Germany. In other words, nothing short of a quadruple alliance could meet the actual needs of the situation.

It must not be supposed that all this is mere speculation. The careful student can find more than enough material in the contemporary sources. The German documents, for example, illustrate the crucial point very well indeed. They show how very anxious the Germans were to prevent the Italians from coming

[59] *Edinburgh Review* October 1892, pp. 398-399. The same attitude taken by the *London Times* (October 17, 1893): "There is, at all events, no question of a naval compact with Italy, still less of our entering the Triple Alliance," though England values Italian friendship highly.

[60] It has already been noted that the Germans were always anxious lest the Italians should act before England had been tied down by a definite agreement, if possible with the whole Triple Alliance.

out in support of the English at the time of the Siamese crisis, and how the German statesmen again and again urged the necessity of waiting until the English had fired the first gun and had irrevocably committed themselves to action. There can be little doubt that, if it had actually come to war between the French and the English, not only the Italians, but also the Germans and probably the Austrians would have aligned themselves with the United Kingdom, treaty or no treaty, provided only that the English themselves were actually engaged.[61] It was a policy of common sense, for if the Italians or the Germans were to wait until the English had suffered an initial defeat in the Mediterranean, there would be little use of intervention at all. The essential point for the Germans was that Italy should not move first and that the provocation should not come from her. During the critical days following the disaster at Aiguesmortes the Germans left no stone unturned to calm the Italians and to urge them not to move until the English had come out. It would have been unpardonable for the Italians to have shouldered the whole responsibility and in this way to have relieved the English of the crushing burden of French hostility.

To say that the French were preparing for war against their neighbors in 1893 would be an extremely daring assertion and one impossible to prove. The evidence would indicate rather that they were quite as pacifically inclined as the Germans or the English, although, like other powers, they were anxious to score points in a game which might conceivably lead to a cataclysm. Reduced to the lowest terms the situation on the eve of the Toulon visit was this: The French had been isolated for twenty years, during which their efforts to secure the support of Russia against Germany had ended in egregious failure. The Russians had no interest in picking a quarrel with their neighbors on the west and they were too wise to pull the chestnuts out of the fire for the French Republic. Progress towards an alliance had been made only since the danger of a quadruple alliance had become acute and since the French, more and more estranged by the

[61] See especially G. P. VIII, no. 1757.

failure of the English to evacuate Egypt, had shown a readiness to shelve the question of the lost provinces and to embark on an actively hostile policy towards the English.

The French in 1893 had a splendid army, which some experts considered quite the equal of the German military machine. It would, however, have been foolhardy to launch this army against Germany in an aggressive war, for the military issue would have been in doubt even as between the two antagonists, while on the other hand the Germans would be able to count on the support of the Italians and probably the Austrians, and the French could by no means reckon with certainty on the assistance of the Russians unless the Germans provoked the crisis. On the other hand the French could rely upon the Russians to protect them against attack, and the French forces, taken together with the huge concentrations of the Russians in Poland, were a sufficient guarantee that the Germans would not take the initiative. In the meanwhile the French fleet had been so far developed and enlarged that England could not lightly ignore it. Siam had shown to the satisfaction of everyone that the British government, especially the liberal government, was unwilling to take up the challenge. The road was open to revenge for Egypt, and in the crusade against the United Kingdom the Russians were only too eager to take an active part. Not that either party wanted war. What they did intend to do was to put an end to the British preponderance in colonial affairs. With the Russians in the Pamirs and the French on the Mekong, India was indeed between two fires, and pressure could be brought to bear upon England in Asia just as soon as England made a move of resistance in Europe.

As for the European end, that was infinitely more complicated, for in Europe the English might find allies. Apparently it was hoped that the military pressure on Germany, carefully regulated by a military convention between France and Russia, would induce the statesmen of the Wilhelmstrasse to exercise a moderating influence on Italy and keep the Triple Alliance from becoming a quadruple alliance. On the other hand the mission of the Russian squadron to the Mediterranean was intended to intimidate the Italians and at the same time to press the English to the wall.

If they opposed the French or Russian policy in the Mediterranean or the Near East, the threat to India would prove effective; if they opposed the French or Russian policy in Asia, they
could easily enough be brought to terms by an appropriate
demonstration in the Mediterranean.[62] Later writers have been
so fascinated by the experiences of the World War that to some
the Franco-Russian Alliance appears as a coalition directed from
the beginning against the central powers.[63] This was undoubtedly what the French would have preferred, but even a casual examination of the history of the alliance from 1894 to 1912 will
show that, when the agreement functioned at all, it functioned
until 1904 against the English in Asia, the intervention of Shimonoseki being the classic example, with the Germans standing
shoulder to shoulder with the new allies.[64] When, in September,
1893, it became known that the Russians would establish a
squadron permanently in the Mediterranean, the German chancellor declared that no event of the preceding twenty years had
so seriously threatened the peace of Europe. But he was not
thinking of Germany so much as of her friends. Germany's
direct interests in the Mediterranean were almost nonexistent
at that time. As Caprivi himself pointed out, the new naval
combination menaced the vital interests of Italy and England
and so promised to displace the whole balance of power in favor
of France and Russia.[65] That neither the English nor the Italians missed the point is most clearly shown by the fact that

[62] See the St. Petersburg letters in the *Mémorial Diplomatique* September 9,
16, 1893; cf. also the *Neue Freie Presse* November 3, 1893; the letter of Admiral
G. H. Richards in the *London Times* November 14, 1893: "The remarkable demonstrations across the Channel lately cannot be ignored; they are far more connected with affairs in the East than with any European alliances, and therefore
concern us the most."

[63] Robert L. Owen: *The Russian Imperial Conspiracy* (New York 1927) may
be taken as the extreme statement of this view.

[64] See the excellent survey by Georges Michon: *L'Alliance Franco-Russe*
(Paris 1927).

[65] Caprivi's remarks to the Austrian ambassador (Szögyény to Kálnoky August 19, 1893); similarly the remarks of Marschall somewhat earlier (Schiessl to
Kálnoky July 22, 1893) and those of the Kaiser (Szögyény to Kálnoky August
19, 1893); cf. also G. P. VIII, nos. 1756 ff.

they immediately arranged for a counter-demonstration and announced on September 17 that the British squadron in the Mediterranean would visit Taranto at the very time the Russian ships lay at Toulon.[66]

Meanwhile elaborate preparations had been made in Toulon and Paris for the reception of the Russian ships. On October 13 Admiral Avellan arrived in the roadstead with his five ships. During his two weeks' stay he visited Paris, Lyons and Marseilles with a delegation of his men, and everywhere he met with the greatest enthusiasm and joy. Demonstration followed demonstration, banquet followed banquet, and fête followed fête, until disinterested observers expressed grave doubts as to whether, as human beings, the Russian sailors could stand the tremendous strain. Gifts were showered upon the guests of France wherever they went, Mme. Adam herself presenting some two thousand bracelets, bought for the wives and sweethearts of the men by the women of France. Of course there can be no object in cataloging here the innumerable celebrations which took place, or in quoting the countless toasts offered by delegations and officials, but it should be remembered that the Toulon-Paris demonstration was quite without precedent. Nothing of its kind had been seen in Europe within the memory of man, and the spectacle made a very profound impression upon the inhabitants of the other countries. The significance of the thing was enhanced by the fact that on October 13, the very day on which the Russian squadron arrived at Toulon, the Tsar, who was then staying with his relatives in Denmark, went aboard the French warship *Isly* which was lying in the harbor, and spent over an hour in carefully inspecting the ship. Once more the *Marseillaise* was played, and the Russian Imperial yacht even fired a salute in honor of the occasion.[67] Compared with all this the Anglo-Italian demonstration at Taranto was a tame affair. It

[66] *London Times* September 18, 1893. It appears that the visit was requested by the Italian government (G. P. VIII, no. 1760).

[67] See Deschamps: *Le Livre d'Or de l'Alliance Franco-Russe*; Lyall: *The Life of Lord Dufferin* II, pp. 270, and the extended accounts in the newspapers, in Schulthess and in the *Annual Register*.

seemed, indeed, as though the English commander scrupulously
avoided saying anything that might give offense to other nations,
and the Italians themselves acted rather reserved. No one paid
much attention to what was going on in the Italian ports, and
even the English newspapers devoted as little space as they de-
cently could to this secondary event. As for Toulon, everyone
felt that, in a sense, it marked the beginning of a new chapter in
European international affairs, and everyone was more or less
keyed up with expectation as to what the next step would be.
Considering the character of Alexander III no one had the tem-
erity to suggest that the demonstration was of little significance.
Rather was there a tendency to overestimate the importance of
the event and to read too much into the telegrams exchanged
between the Tsar and the French president. In any case the
message sent by Alexander to Carnot just as the Russian squadron was leaving Toulon was sufficiently vague to allow of
various interpretations:

"The evidences of sincere sympathy, which have once again been mani-
fested so eloquently, will add one more link to the chain which unites our
two countries and will, I hope, help to strengthen the general peace, the
object of our constant efforts and prayers."[68]

---

[68] For the interpretations placed on this Gatchina telegram see the discussion
in the *London Times* October 30 and October 31, 1893.

CHAPTER XII

THE AFTERMATH OF TOULON

DEMONSTRATIONS like those of October, 1893 are apt to be not without danger for the participants. The French were especially exposed, for as yet they had not been able to induce the Tsar to accept the military convention and it was by no means inconceivable that the Italians, relying on the eventual aid of Germany and England, might seize the opportunity to launch a preventive war and so cut the Gordian knot of their domestic difficulties.[1] Considerations of this kind undoubtedly occupied the French statesmen even in the days before the Toulon visit of the Russian squadron. At any rate it appears that they meant to tie up the negotiations for the naval demonstration with the negotiations for the acceptance of the military convention. Montebello had already provided himself with a note drawn up by General Miribel in which the French chief of staff expounded the significance of the new German military law and set forth the dangers resulting therefrom for France and Russia. In view of the rapidity of Germany's mobilization, it was argued, it would be impossible to make arrangements for action at the last minute. France was already taking steps to improve and increase her forces and it behooved both powers to leave nothing to chance—

---

[1] Billot II, p. 30; Crispi III, p. 189. As a result of the Aiguesmortes crisis the French had already greatly increased their troops on the Italian frontier, and the Duke of Cambridge, in the winter of 1893-1894, said it appeared "as if the whole region, from Cannes to Ventimiglia, had suddenly become the scene of a military occupation." Cf. also Lord Dufferin to Lord Rosebery November 3, 1893: "There is no doubt that a little while ago there was a desperate inclination on the part of the Italians to run amuck at France at any hazard, in the expectation that neither their allies nor England would allow them to be destroyed" (*British Documents on the Origins of the War*, volume II, p. 287). The genuineness of these fears is also brought out by the utterances of the Italian ambassador in Paris (see G. P. VII, nos. 1450, 1451, 1452).

the convention of August, 1892 should be concluded without delay.[2]

Giers probably received this communication with mixed feelings and was no doubt glad that his master was, at the moment, in Copenhagen. He promised to forward the French note to his sovereign, knowing full well that nothing would be done about the question for some time.[3] Certainly the Tsar was anxious to avoid encouraging the French by taking so vital a step. He had no desire to become embroiled with Germany, especially at a time when a tariff war was in full swing and when Russia's economic future depended so largely on the success of the negotiations with Germany which were to begin within a few weeks. Consequently the Russian press and, at the suggestion of the Russian government, the French press too, were instructed not to treat the visit in bellicose or menacing terms, but to emphasize the pacific nature of the entente.[4] In actual fact the celebrations were so orderly and so carefully supervised that no one could find an excuse to complain. There were no anti-German utterances such as Caprivi had at first feared, and no expression of warlike spirit. The newspapers vied with one another in setting forth the peaceful objects of the entente and emphasizing its importance for general European peace. The *Figaro* on October 13 published an article evidently inspired by the Russian embassy in which it was said that the Tsar wished Europe to know that Russia would support France if she were attacked but that Russia would not take part in any aggressive action unless justified by considerations of vital interest to herself. The Russian press went even further, many papers stressing the fact that Russia, in spite of the warm sympathy felt for France, wished to

[2] L. J. nos. 85, 87, 88.

[3] L. J. no. 88. Cf. also Cyon p. 459, for Giers' lack of enthusiasm.

[4] Hansen: *Mohrenheim* pp. 159-160; Aehrenthal to Kálnoky September 14, 28, October 12, 1893; and especially the St. Petersburg letter in the *Mémorial Diplomatique* September 30, 1893: "Le grand souci du gouvernement russe est effectivement que tout se passe à Toulon et à Paris avec une calme parfait, sans moindre incident capable d'être interpreté par la Triple Alliance comme une contradiction au caractère essentiellement et sincèrement pacifique de l'entente franco-russe."

regard the Germans too as friends.   The French people were
warned again and again not to hope for Russian support in an
attempt to reconquer Alsace and Lorraine.[5]

Taken all in all the Tsar had every reason to be satisfied.[6]   Not
only had there been no "untoward incidents," but the French
clergy had joined whole-heartedly in the demonstrations, much to
the gratification of orthodox feelings.   "France, the real France,
is deeply Christian and has prayed for Russia with all her heart,"
wrote Canon Joucquet of Boulogne to Protopresbyter Ianyshev,
the head of the court clergy.   Archbishop Richard of Paris had a
Te Deum sung in the churches, for which he received a letter of
thanks from the Tsar himself.[7]   Best of all the visit did not result
in friction with Germany.   The German press viewed the situation with complete calm and composure, and the *Norddeutsche
Allgemeine Zeitung* wrote in an inspired article on October 29
that the German attitude was one of perfect tranquillity.[7a]   The
negotiations for a tariff treaty were opened in due course and
proceeded with unexpected smoothness so that by January, 1894
the great treaty was finally ready.[8]   Far from drifting apart,
Russia and Germany were, if anything, on closer terms in the

---

[5] Report on the press by Aehrenthal October 24, 1893.   See also *Viestnik
Evropy* and *Russkaia Zhizn* for October 15, 1893.

[6] Hansen: *Mohrenheim* p. 163; L. J. no. 90; Aehrenthal to Kálnoky November 11, 1893; G. P. VII, no. 1534; St. Petersburg letter in *Mémorial Diplomatique*
October 21, 1893.

[7] Aehrenthal to Kálnoky November 22, 1893; St. Petersburg letter in the
Mémorial Diplomatique November 4, 1893.   The Germans also had reports as to
the profound impression made on the Tsar by the attitude of the French clergy,
and believed that the Papacy, particularly Cardinal Rampolla, was again actively
furthering the Franco-Russian Entente (Szögyény to Kálnoky December 9, 1893).
As a matter of fact M. Piou argued in the *Figaro* on November 13 that the Pope
was to be thanked for the Franco-Russian Alliance, and we know from Cardinal
Ferrata's *Mémoires* (volume II, pp. 327 ff.) that Rampolla instructed him to enlist
Montebello's aid in smoothing out the difficulties between Russia and the Vatican.
Ferrata talked also to Develle and Dupuy and found them both sympathetic towards the policy of the Papal See and both ready to recognize the great value of
the Papacy's moral support: "Ces messieurs se rendaient compte que la politique
du Saint Père n'avait pas été étrangère à l'alliance entre la France et la Russie..."

[7a] Cf. also the *London Times* October 16, 1893.

[8] G. P. VII, nos. 1665, 1666; *London Times* December 25, 1893; Aehrenthal
to Kálnoky January 6, 1894.

winter of 1893-1894 than they had been since the dismissal of
Bismarck. Even the relations between France and Germany
seemed to be gradually improving. During the very days of the
Toulon festivities Marshal MacMahon had died and the Kaiser
had instructed Münster to place a wreath on the former president's grave. William himself sent a telegram of condolence to
Mme. MacMahon, which made a very favorable impression on
the French.[9] Perhaps more important was the conciliatory
policy adopted by the German government in matters of colonial
concern. In November, 1893 Germany and England had signed
an agreement delimiting the frontiers of Kamerun, by which the
Germans received access to Lake Chad and theoretically at
least were enabled to extend their possessions as far east as the
borders of the Egyptian Sudan. The treaty had been concluded
without reference to French claims, and the French government
protested its rights in parts of the region so liberally abandoned
by England to Germany. The German government immediately
consented to negotiate and pourparlers began in Berlin early in
December, 1893. An agreement was soon reached and a treaty
concluded on March 15, 1894, by which, in return for minor
concessions on the part of France, Germany handed over the
whole region between Kamerun and the Egyptian Sudan, thus
giving France access to Lake Chad and enabling her to extend
her influence to the Nile Basin, exactly what the English had
been anxious to avoid when they signed the convention with
Germany.[10]

In view of the general tranquillity on the continent it was quite
impossible for the Tsar to resist longer the demands of the French
that the military convention should finally be ratified. We know
nothing of the negotiations which took place in the autumn of
1893, but it is more than unlikely that the French did not make
the most of the situation. We know only that when Montebello

[9] G. P. VII, nos. 1599, 1600, 1601.

[10] Cf. *London Times* November 23, 1893, on the French attitude towards the
Anglo-German agreement; also G. P. VII, no. 1598, and explanatory note; Darcy:
France et Angleterre p. 267; Raymond Ronze: *La Question d'Afrique* (Paris 1918)
p. 220; Schefer pp. 182-183; Friedjung I, pp. 129-130, and Bourgeois and Pagès pp.
244-245.

returned to his post on December 13 he found the cordon of the Alexander Nevski Order awaiting him and that on the same evening he was tendered an elaborate banquet by the nobility of St. Petersburg.[11] On December 16 the Tsar received him in audience and for the first time really opened his heart in speakiug of the Franco-Russian Entente. The outcome of the Toulon festivities had given him great satisfaction, and the enthusiastic and at the same time discreet reception of the Russian sailors had exceeded his own expectations. In face of such a demonstration by two great nations which felt themselves spontaneously drawn the one to the other no one, he thought, would dare stir:

"I often hear speak of ideas of revenge which exist in your country and which are said to be a menace, but I see no justification whatsoever for this statement. You would not be Frenchmen if you did not cherish the belief that the day would come when you might regain possession of your lost provinces; but between this very natural sentiment and the idea of a provocation to effect its realization, the idea of *revanche*, in a word, there is a great difference, and you have frequently proved, you have just shown again, that you desire peace above all and that you will know how to wait with dignity."

The only point that still troubled the Tsar was the instability of the French ministries, but even in this matter he seemed very ready to listen to the arguments of Montebello.[12]

The conversation between the Tsar and the French ambassador meant the definitive acceptance of the August Convention. So far all the impatience and all the importunity of the French had failed to move the Russian autocrat. He had, as Montebello himself put it, followed his program mathematically, and had refused to act before he was convinced that the proper time had come.[13] On December 30 the French ambassador was able to forward to his government the letter of Giers dated December 27, by which the Russian government formally adhered to the draft which had been worked out and signed by Boisdeffre and Obruchev more than a year before. On January 4, 1894 Monte-

---

[11] Aehrenthal to Kálnoky December 15 and 16, 1893; *London Times* December 14, 1893.

[12] L. J. no. 90.

[13] L. J. no. 91. Similarly Kálnoky's remarks to Eulenburg and the Kaiser's assent (G. P. IX, no. 2138).

bello replied by a note couched in almost identical terms and therewith the Franco-Russian Alliance, consisting of the agreement of August, 1891, supplemented by the military convention of August, 1892, became a reality.[14]

The Franco-Russian Alliance of 1894 was a purely defensive arrangement, and nothing could be more mistaken than to regard it as a "Russian Imperial Conspiracy" directed against Germany. The last thing the Tsar desired at the time was trouble with Germany, and it is only fair to say that the French statesmen themselves, in 1894, were eager to maintain peace and avoid complications. Such certainly was the opinion of many diplomats and writers, including even the Germans themselves.[15] We cannot know for a certainty why the Tsar concluded the agreement at just that time until we have all the Russian documents, but it is not difficult to understand the implications of the alliance if one bears in mind the general situation and particularly the acute tension which had developed between England on the one hand and France and Russia on the other. Observers at the time were almost unanimous in regarding the whole Toulon episode as a

[14] L. J. nos. 91, and annexe, 92. Georges Démartial has advanced the argument that the so-called Franco-Russian Alliance was not an alliance at all, but merely a military understanding like the Anglo-French conversations of later date. The Russians, he thinks, never intended to give it the force of an alliance (L'Alliance Franco-Russe et l'explosion de la guerre mondiale, in *Die Kriegsschuldfrage* VI, pp. 593-594, June 1928). I confess that this argument does not seem to me convincing.

[15] Giers certainly signed the treaty without enthusiasm and perhaps with distinct regret (cf. G. P. VII, nos. 1534, 1535). To the Danish minister he said, just after the audience granted Montebello by the Tsar: "Nous avons accepté l'entente avec la France, mais avec une France pacifique. Nous ne voulons qu'une chose, c'est la paix et toujours la paix. Je ne suis pas sans savoir que derrière ces manifestations de joie, d'enthousiasme pour nous se cache l'idée de la revanche. Cependant ces aspirations populaires n'ont aucune prise sur la politique éminemment pacifique des deux gouvernements.... Vous pouvez me croire, que nous avons certifié aux Français: l'entente serait pacifique ou elle ne serait pas du tout" (Aehrenthal to Kálnoky December 20 and 21, 1893). Giers spoke in a similar vein to Werder, referring to the demonstrations as "eine wahre Plage" (Aehrenthal to Kálnoky December 29, 1893; G. P. VII, no. 1535). Cf. also Marschall's opinion in Köhler pp. 322-325; Caprivi regarded the only danger as lying in the increased self-confidence of the French (Szögyény to Kálnoky October 28, 1893; Schiessl to Kálnoky November 18, 1893).

huge demonstration against England, and it was England that
felt chiefly menaced by the Franco-Russian Entente:

"Englishmen hardly ventured to show themselves while the delirium
lasted, which it did unabated for seven days," wrote Thomas Barclay, who
witnessed the celebrations in Paris. "It meant in the eyes of the Parisian
public an entente against England with England's Asiatic enemy."[16]

In a leading article of October 28 the London *Times* struck the
keynote of the English attitude:

"All that we know is that we have just beheld perhaps the most remarkable outburst of international feeling ever witnessed, and that the demonstration points directly to joint action between the fleets of France and
Russia in the waters of the Mediterranean. Despite all the assurances which
reach us that peace and peace only is contemplated by both parties, that is
a fact which no true Englishman can afford to think of otherwise than
gravely."

More instructive even than this is a long general report forwarded
by Lord Dufferin from Paris on November 3, 1893, of which only
a few extracts can be given here:

"I am afraid that I can only describe the sentiments of French people of
all classes towards us as that of unmitigated and bitter dislike." "In view
of the strong feelings of hostility towards England which prevail in this
country; of its enormous armaments; of the innumerable occasions when
we shall be compelled in the future to run counter to some of France's most
cherished wishes and ambitions, I should not be fulfilling one of the first
duties incumbent upon me as Her Majesty's Ambassador accredited to the
Republic did I not call the serious attention of Your Lordship to the desirability of being prepared to meet, and successfully cope with, all eventualities....At all events I believe that, if war were inevitable, a war with England would be as popular, and would be considered less dangerous, than a
single-handed encounter with Germany."[17]

Punch, which can always be relied upon to reflect English opinion in a truthful and unsparing fashion, had begun by taking the
whole Toulon demonstration light-heartedly and laughing away
the Franco-Russian love scene. A cartoon in the number of

---

[16] Sir Thomas Barclay: *Thirty Years, Anglo-French Reminiscences 1876-1906*
(Boston 1914) p. 111. See also Solvyns' report in Köhler pp. 329-330. The Austrian ambassador reported Rosebery as taking a very pessimistic view and regarding the demonstration as directed primarily against England (Deym to Kálnoky November 15, 1893).

[17] *British Documents on the Origins of the War* (London 1926—) II, no. 351.

October 21, showing the Russian Bear and Miss Republic dancing, was accompanied by the following verses:

"Beauty and Beast vis-à-vis in the dance
Were scarce funnier partners than Russia and France.

* * * * *

Autocrat Bruin, can he really relish
The larkish high-kick, the tempestuous twirl
That risky Republican dances embellish?
And she—a political 'Wallflower', poor girl—
Can she truly like the strange partner that Fate
Apportions her, lumpish, unlovely and late?"

But within a short time the attitude of the famous London comic had changed. In the number of November 11 appeared the following verses:

"The Tzar, on peace and friendship all intent
To France his Admiral Avellan has sent.
'Twere pity if this Russian olive-branch
Portended merely General Avalanche."

One could multiply instances of the uneasiness of the English, but let it suffice to bring these quotations to a close with the words of Sir Lepel Griffin, published in November:

"Englishmen who have carefully followed the course of events in the East; who have watched, year after year, the shadow of the Russian eclipse sweeping across Persia and Central Asia until it has reached the frontiers of India and Afghanistan; and who now see France reviving her old ambition of an Eastern Empire and fanning in every direction the hatred and jealousy of England among her ignorant and passionate people, realise with sufficient distinctness that the alliance of Russia and France is directed as much against England and her Eastern Empire as against the Powers of the Triple Alliance........The hatred to the Germans is faint when compared with that the French feel and on every occasion proclaim to England."[18]

The immediate preoccupation of the English was with the naval situation, especially as it affected the Mediterranean.

[18] Sir Lepel Griffin: England and France in Asia (*Nineteenth Century* November 1893); see also *Review of Reviews* January 1894; the anonymous articles Europa und England, and Deutschland und das Mittelmeer, in *Grenzboten* 1893, IV, pp. 145-163, 196-206; Frederick Greenwood: A new Drift in Foreign Affairs (*Contemporary* September 1894) predicting that the Franco-Russian Alliance would result in "a resolute squeezing of England by Russia and France in regions a long way off from Charing Cross." See also G. P. VII, no. 1533.

Since there was no question of the hostility of the French and since observers were agreed that the hatred of the English far exceeded hatred of the Germans, beyond the Channel there seemed to be every reason to suppose that the French had put their naval forces at the disposal of the Russians and that a general overturn would not be far off.[19] Nothing could stop the Russian squadrons from coming out of the Black Sea and joining the French forces. In that event there would be no staying in the Mediterranean. It would simply be a question of evacuating at once or being locked up in some corner of the great sea.[20] Obviously the first need was for an increase in English naval power, and in the autumn of 1893 a systematic campaign was carried

[19] On the hostility of the French towards the English compare the following, in addition to those already mentioned: Admiral F. A. Maxse: The European Outlook (*National Review* November, 1893): "A war is just as likely to be made by the Double Alliance against England alone as against the Triple Alliance.... Such a war would be as popular as one with Germany." So also Marschall: "La haine que nourrissent les Français contre elle (l'Angleterre) est plus profonde que celle dont ils sont animés contre l'Allemagne," and Caprivi (Köhler pp. 322-325; Szögyény to Kálnoky October 28, 1893); Ex-Diplomat: Peace and the Quadruple Alliance (*Contemporary* December 1894): "France would tomorrow forego her quarrel with Germany to unite with her in the overthrow of England." Anonymous: Naval Armaments (*Edinburgh Review* April 1894): "All available evidence seems to show that whilst the hatred of Germany is yielding to the soothing balm of time, the jealousy of England tends to become more acute." On January 22, 1894 Balfour made a great speech at Manchester in which he said: "My conviction is this, that at the present moment the French are, as a nation, hostile to us." With this a leading article in the *London Times* on February 7 entirely agreed, but Mr. J. E. C. Bodley, in a long and able letter published in the *Times* on the same date, took exception to the statement, though he admitted that the Paris press and the boulevards were rabidly Anglophobe. A letter by *Traveller* in the *Times* of February 9, asserted that hostility to England was widespread even in the provinces, and a French deputy, M. André Lebon, in an article entitled French Feeling towards England (*National Review* March 1894) admitted that relations were bad, though he denied that the Franco-Russian Entente was intended by France for use against England.

[20] See especially Frederic Harrison: The Problem of Constantinople (*Fortnightly* May 1894): "If the Tsar gives the word, his eagles may float over the Seraglio within a month..." Cf. also the excellent discussion of the problem in the article entitled Naval Armaments (*Edinburgh Review* April 1894). The Kaiser told Colonel Swain in the autumn of 1894 that "Russia could have seized Constantinople at any time in these last five or six years if she had been desirous to do so." (Gardiner: *Life of Harcourt* II, p. 324).

on to that end. The London *Times* in a leading article on October 14 had stated categorically.

"Whatever government or whatever party may be in power, the English people are determined never to forfeit the maritime predominance in the Mediterranean which their fathers have handed down to them for one hundred and fifty years, and which cannot be shaken, as they well know, without imperilling the Empire."

In the subsequent agitation the *Times* played a leading part, publishing articles by experts, correspondence from naval officers and important leading articles:

"We must shape our naval policy in the future on the assumption that a formidable combination of hostile fleets may, in certain circumstances, confront us in the Mediterranean and due weight must be given to this contingency not only in the shipbuilding programme of the Admiralty, but in the management of our diplomatic relations."[21]

That Lord Rosebery and Earl Spencer were quite convinced of the seriousness of the situation and the need for immediate remedies seems certain, but it is equally clear that neither Gladstone nor Harcourt were impressed with the public anxiety. In reply to a question in the house of commons on November 7, Gladstone stated that "Her Majesty's Government are perfectly satisfied as to the adequacy and capacity of the British Navy to perform all the purposes for which it exists."[22] *Punch* made fun of the prime minister who was buried under the Employers' Liability Bill and the Parish Councils Bill, and Sir Samuel Baker wrote to the *Times*:

"It is to be trusted that our Premier is not playing Irish melodies and Home Rule ditties while England is sinking in the respect and estimation of the civilized world."[23]

In spite of all this Gladstone once more declared in the house on November 17:

"I think that I may venture to assure the House, on the responsibility of the Government, that neither the House nor the country need entertain, in the existing circumstances, the smallest apprehension as to the maintenance of the distinct naval supremacy of Great Britain."[24]

---

[21] *London Times*, leading article November 1, 1893.
[22] *Hansard* series 4, volume xviii, p. 349.
[23] *Punch* November 18, 1893; *London Times* November 20, 1893.
[24] *Hansard* series 4, volume xviii p. 1151.

In the meanwhile the situation had developed further. Naval experts were debating the Mediterranean problem, the one group, known as the Channel School, led by Admiral Colomb and Lord Brassey, arguing that a strong and ever mobile Channel squadron would effectively prevent action by France in the Mediterranean, while the so-called Mediterranean School, represented by Admiral Hornby, Lord Beresford and others, insisted that England must always have in the Mediterranean a fleet at least equal to any single foreign fleet in those waters.[25] At the same time it was reported in the press that Russia had been given use of the port of Bizerta by the French government, and that the Russians were negotiating with the Greek government for a base in the eastern Mediterranean. The island of Poros, in the Aegean Sea, had been used by the Russian government as a storage place for arms and supplies in the earlier part of the century, and it was rumored that the Russian representative had now demanded from the Greek government access to the abandoned warehouses. How much truth there may have been in these reports it is hard now to say. What we do know is that in the days just preceding the Toulon celebrations M. Nelidov, the very capable and active Russian ambassador at Constantinople, had made an extended visit to Mt. Athos, where he had negotiated with the monks for certain concessions, while the embassy ship had carefully reconnoitred the neighboring coasts.[26] To top it all, attention was called to the fact that one of the Russian ships which had taken part in the Toulon festivities belonged to the

[25] See especially W. L. Clowes: The Naval Manoeuvres (*Nineteenth Century* September 1894); Admiral P. H. Colomb: Our Strategic Position in the Mediterranean (in Brassey's *Naval Annual* 1894, chapter vii); Admiral P. H. Colomb: England in the Mediterranean (*North American Review* May 1894); Anonymous: The British Navy (*Quarterly Review* April 1894); Lord Brassey: Our Naval Position in 1894 (Brassey's *Naval Annual* 1894 part v.)

[26] Szögyény to Kálnoky August 19, 1893; Schiessl to Kálnoky, September 16, 1893; two reports by Mr. Blunt, English consul at Saloniki, to Sir Arthur Nicolson, English ambassador at Constantinople, dated October 26 and 28, 1893 (communicated to Kálnoky by Baron Calice January 22, 1894). See also *London Times* October 24, 31, November 4, 1893, January 16, 25, 1894; according to the anonymous writer of the article Naval Armaments (*Edinburgh Review* April 1894) the Russian squadron actually spent the four months from January to April at Poros.

Russian Black Sea fleet and had come through the Straits, no one knew just how.[27] From this it was natural to infer that the Russians were preparing to reopen the thorny Straits question and to attempt to bring the whole Black Sea squadron into the Mediterranean.[28] And yet, when the government was questioned in the house on these points on November 28, Gladstone replied that nothing was known of any proceedings for the acquiring by Russia of a port or rendezvous in the Mediterranean. As for the passage of the *Teretz* through the Straits the prime minister stated that this had repeatedly happened and that

"with regard to the general question, it must be clearly understood that in the view of Her Majesty's Government the exclusion or the passage of foreign warships through the Bosphorus affects all nations alike; and with regard to any privilege granted to any one nation, if such privilege were granted, it would be claimed by the British Government to be enjoyed by us also."[29]

As a matter of fact both Gladstone and Harcourt refused to take the situation seriously. We know from Harcourt's correspondence that he did not believe the Russians wanted to come out of the Black Sea at all and that in his opinion an attempt by the Russians to do so would result in war with Germany, Austria and

[27] *London Times*, special article November 15, 1893; W. L. Clowes: Toulon and the French Navy (*Nineteenth Century* December 1893).

[28] Aehrenthal to Kálnoky September 23, 1893; Spender: *Life of Campbell-Bannerman* I, p. 140; Kálnoky to Szögyény December 10, 1893; Kálnoky to Calice, December 15, 1893: "Es ist zweifellos dass Russland nur auf den ihm passendsten Moment wartet, um in Konstantinopel für seine Kriegsflotte die freie Durchfahrt durch die Meerengen zu erhalten oder zu erzwingen, und aus der bisher mehr theoretischen Errichtung einer Mittelmeer Escadre erst die wirklichen politischen Consequenzen zu ziehen." Kálnoky memorandum of a talk with Sir Edmund Monson, January 18, 1894. See also G. P. IX, nos. 2140 ff., and the amusing verses in *Punch* November 25:

"Who says that Franco-Russian gush
   Means naught, to reason's optic?
The Russian will help the Frank to rush
   England, from regions Coptic;
And—here John Bull must surely flinch,
   While Gallia's bosom swells!—
The Bear, if but allowed an inch,
   Will take—the Dardanelles."

[29] *Hansard* series 4 volume xviii, p. 1915.

Italy. In other words, he was still relying upon others to defend English interests.[30]

In December, 1893 the agitation in England reached the climax. The London chamber of commerce had appointed a committee to report on the naval situation and a paper had been drawn up on "The State of the Naval Defences of the British Empire in 1893." A public meeting was convoked for December 12, and was called to order in the Cannon Street Hotel. After speeches by various leaders Lord Roberts expressed the opinion that the enormous expenditures of France and Russia could be intended only for aggressive purposes, and it was then resolved

"That this meeting views with deep concern and anxiety the present state of our navy and urgently presses upon the Government the necessity of taking immediate steps to provide such additional means of defence as shall afford that security which our Empire and our commerce demand."[31]

There followed on December 19 a great debate in parliament. Lord George Hamilton, who had been first lord of the admiralty in the Salisbury cabinet and had been chiefly responsible for the Naval Defence Act of 1889, moved a resolution

"That, in the opinion of this House, it is necessary for the maintenance of the security of the Country and the continued protection of British interests and commerce, that a considerable addition should at once be made to the Navy. This House, therefore, calls upon Her Majesty's Government to make before the Christmas Recess a statement of their intentions in order that immediate action may be taken thereon."

In the speech moving the resolution Lord George reviewed the the entire situation and asserted deliberately that British supremacy of the sea was at the moment in jeopardy:

"The danger which threatens the future naval supremacy of this country is of so insidious a character that neither the Government nor the House can control or counteract it."

---

[30] Harcourt to Spencer, November 20, 1893 (Gardiner: *Life of Harcourt* II, p. 247).

[31] Full report of the meeting in *London Times* December 13, 1893. A member of the house of commons, referring to the meeting shortly after, said he thought it "represented more Income Tax than he ever saw in one room before" (*Hansard* series 4 volume xix, p. 1827). See also Captain S. Eardley-Wilmot: The Agitation in 1893 for the Increase of the Navy (Brassey's *Naval Annual* 1894, chapter viii).

"It is impossible to ignore the fact that the more insight one gets into Naval plans and Naval operations of foreign nations, the more it becomes apparent that they have but one object—and that is to act against us."

Sir Charles Dilke, in what was perhaps the best single speech of the evening, insisted that "as matters stand there are all the elements of a national catastrophe," and expressed the opinion that, in the event of a single-handed war between England and France, the English Mediterranean fleet would immediately have to evacuate that important area. Joseph Chamberlain spoke even more boldly:

"Will it be questioned that if war were declared tomorrow the British Navy in the Mediterranean would have to cut and run—if it could run?"

This merciless statement created quite a stir among the members and Sir William Harcourt rose to defend the government. According to his figures England had in the Channel and the Mediterranean nineteen first-class battleships, while France had ten and Russia had one:

"You are to cut and run from the Mediterranean. Why, if you have got 19 ships are you to cut and run? (Cries of *Russia*)......It is said that Russia has other ships in the Black Sea; and that is true. But how are those ships coming into the Mediterranean? They must break the ban of Europe; for the Russian Fleet cannot come through the Bosphorus into the Mediterranean without, in the first place, I suppose, capturing Constantinople, and at any rate arraying against itself the Powers of Europe."[32]

The resolution was finally lost, because Gladstone had insisted on making the question one of confidence in the government and the division consequently was along strictly party lines. But the whole incident served to force a climax. In the *Times* Admiral Hornby denied that Russia could not come through the Straits without first capturing Constantinople, while a leading article on December 22 ridiculed the idea that Russia would hesitate to break the ban of Europe.[33] Not only that: Harcourt had insisted in his speech that he was "speaking the opinion of the responsible professional advisers of the British Admiralty" when he said that the existing condition of things was satisfactory. This

[32] The debates in *Hansard* series 4 volume xix, pp. 1771-1886.
[33] *London Times* December 22, 1893.

led to a vehement protest on the part of the members of the naval board, and in order to prevent their resignation Harcourt was obliged to state in the house on December 28 that he was referring only to "the relative forces of England, France and Russia during the present financial year in respect to first-class battleships.[34]"

Meanwhile an acute crisis had developed in the cabinet. Lord Spencer had been confronted with demands of the naval board for greatly increased expenditure, especially for new construction. Admiral Richards, the first naval lord, was positively obstinate and refused to consider anything less than an increase of three million. The rest of the board stood with him and threatened to resign if the views of the naval authorities were not met. Spencer himself was by no means unsympathetic and a majority of the cabinet realized that the popular demand was justified and therefore should be satisfied. Harcourt, however, insisted on substantial reductions in the proposed estimates and Gladstone was inexorable in his opposition. When Spencer brought before the cabinet his tentative figures the premier remarked in an aside: "Bedlam ought to be enlarged at once." He would not, he said, be associated with a militaristic policy and refused to entertain the proposals made to him. By January, 1894 a deadlock had been reached and Gladstone's resignation was a foregone conclusion. "It is the Admirals that have got their knife into me," he complained bitterly, but he received no support from his colleagues, most of whom, according to Lord Morley, were "this-weekers" rather than "next-monthers" so far as the resignation of their chief was concerned. Nevertheless the decision was not come to for some time. Gladstone went to Biarritz for several weeks and the matter remained undecided. It was not until March 1 that the veteran statesman finally handed in his letter of resignation, and even then it was not known what the real reason for his action was. The cabinet had decided that it would wreck the party to advertize Glads-

---

[34] *Hansard* series 4, volume xx, pp. 339-340. Gardiner II, p. 251; Hamilton: *Parliamentary Reminiscences and Reflections 1886-1906*, p. 224; article on Lord Spencer in the *Dictionary of National Biography*, Second Supplement, p. 371.

stone's opposition to naval increases and the dissension in the cabinet, and so the public was allowed to believe that physical infirmities had necessitated the retirement of the liberal leader.[35]

There was now no further obstacle to the introduction of the estimates for 1894-1895. The Spencerian program called for the expenditure of £17,366,100, which was more than £3,000,000 in excess of the estimates for the preceding year. Sixty-seven hundred men were to be added to the personnel of the navy, and provision was made to commence the construction of seven battleships of the first-class, six cruisers of the second-class and two sloops, all independent of the ships already provided for in the Naval Defence Act of 1889. The scheme for construction in 1894-1895 was part of a larger five-year program, the details of which were not published for fear that it might result in competitive building on the part of France and Russia.[36] At any rate the English people had shown that they were alive to the implications of the Toulon visit and that they would not tolerate laxity on the part of the government in matters of national defence.

But a mere increase of the navy, however substantial, was not sufficient to solve England's problem. What made the British position especially precarious in the autumn and winter of 1893-1894 was the changing attitude of the great powers towards her. While the hostility of France and Russia was assuming undreamed-of proportions, England's former friends of the Triple Alliance were turning their backs upon her. The nonchalant attitude of the German government has already been commented on. One might almost say that in Berlin there was felt a mild sort of satisfaction at England's embarrassment, which was regarded as just retribution. England had always prided herself

[35] The details of the crisis may be found in John Morley: *The Life of Gladstone* (London 1903) III, chapter viii; John Morley: *Recollections* (London 1917) II, chapter vi; Gardiner: *Life of Harcourt* II, chapter xiv; and especially in Sir Algernon West's *Private Diaries*, chapters xiv-xvii. See also Hamilton, chapter xxiv, and the article on Lord Spencer in the *Dictionary of National Biography*, Second Supplement.

[36] First Lord's Memorandum and the Estimates, both reprinted in Brassey's *Naval Annual* 1894, pp. 421-442.

on her splendid isolation, now let her make the best of it, and not expect other powers to pull the chestnuts out of the fire for her. The Kaiser found it particularly difficult to forget the events of July, when, during the Siam crisis, the prospect of England's joining the Triple Alliance had loomed large on the horizon, only to disappear with provoking suddenness.[37] After all, the Germans had no direct interests in the Mediterranean. If they could engage the Russians in conflict with the English in Asia and the French in North African enterprises, the pressure on the German frontiers would be relieved and the general situation much improved.

Only one consideration prevented the Germans from unceremoniously deserting the English, and that was solicitude for the position of Italy. As aforesaid, the new developments in the Mediterranean affected Italy quite as much as England, and, with the very strained relations existing between Paris and Rome, there was every likelihood that the great crisis would, in the beginning, take the form of a Franco-Italian conflict. While continually urging the Italians to remain calm until the English had taken the initiative, the German government therefore resumed its efforts to convince Lord Rosebery that England could not count upon Italian assistance unless a formal agreement were made between the two countries. But these discussions, carried on by Count Hatzfeldt, lacked the force and sincerity of earlier *démarches* with the same object in view. Hatzfeldt himself was eager to save the Anglo-German friendship from shipwreck, but the Kaiser took the view that England was not looking for allies but for lightning rods, and that nothing could be hoped for.[38] When, on December 10, Crispi succeeded Giolitti as Italian premier and the danger of action by Italy or capitulation to France became more acute, the German ambassador in London was instructed to approach the English statesmen with the idea of securing new assurances of support for the

[37] G. P. VIII, no. 1762; Szögyény to Kálnoky August 19, 1893, reporting the attitude of Caprivi; Schiessl to Kálnoky September 16, October 14, 1893, reporting remarks made by Marschall; Szögyény to Kálnoky, December 23, 1893.

[38] G. P. VIII, nos. 1757-1764.

Italians. But apparently even this step was to be unofficial in character and led to nothing.[39]

Meanwhile the Austrian foreign office had been viewing the situation with considerable uneasiness. Kálnoky regarded the future of Italy with the greatest misgiving. The credit of the country was ruined and the nation was suffering severely from the commercial and financial boycott of the French.[40] In October there were great strikes and riots in Sicily which, by December, developed into a genuine revolution and led to severe clashes between the population and the troops. The demonstrations, which took on a distinctly republican tinge, were regarded as a menace to the monarchy, and Crispi himself was suspected of flirting with the idea of being elected first president of the Italian Republic.[41] At the same time the agitation in the Italian press against the Triple Alliance, which was held responsible for the huge military expenditures, was growing apace. There really seemed to be no solution except war with France or reconciliation with France.

These apprehensions took Kálnoky to Italy in November, 1893. At Monza on the 14 he engaged in long conferences with King Humbert and Brin and Nigra, the Italian ambassador at Vienna. He found the Italians profoundly discouraged by the hopelessness of the domestic situation and exceedingly anxious about recent events and displacements in the Mediterranean. As before, they looked to England and asked themselves whether or not that power could be counted on in case Italy were attacked. Kálnoky's assurances that the interests of England and Italy in the Mediterranean were identical and that, in case of need, the English fleet would certainly coöperate with the Italian forces

[39] Szögyény to Kálnoky December 16, 23, 1893; Deym to Kálnoky December 23, 27, 1893; Szögyény to Kálnoky January 6, 1894. Since there is hardly a trace of this *démarche* in the German documents it is possible that Hatzfeldt acted entirely without direct instructions from Berlin.

[40] Even the German government was so anxious about the Italian situation that it secured from the German bankers a loan of 40,000,000 marks, though it had to give the bankers a guarantee (Szögyény to Kálnoky October 28, November 11, 1893).

[41] Cf. Giolitti: *Memorie* I, pp. 82 ff.; Billot II, pp. 30 ff.; Cilibrizzi II, chapter xviii; G. P. IX, no. 2138.

in defending the peninsula, made but a slight impression upon his auditors. What they wanted was a concrete promise, and nothing else would do.[42] So Kálnoky returned to Vienna convinced that unless some such assurance could be obtained from the English cabinet, or at least from Lord Rosebery, it was likely that Italy, in despair, would give up her resistance to French pressure and throw herself into the arms of France and Russia. This in itself would have constituted a severe blow at the Austrian position. In the first place it would have made France supreme in the Mediterranean and in the second place it would have exposed Austria entirely to Russian designs in the Near East. Without the certainty that she would not be attacked in the rear how could Austria hope to stand out against Muscovite policy in the Balkans? Austria from that day on would be existing as a great power only on sufferance.[43]

Kálnoky, who does not appear to have rated the Italians very highly, decided nevertheless to do his utmost to save the situation. On December 7, 1893 he forwarded to Count Deym, the ambassador at London, three very long despatches in which he reviewed the course of events in the past few months, and pointed out the critical condition of Italy and the danger of that country's falling into the hands of France. The Franco-Russian Entente, he argued, was unmistakably a menace for England rather than for the central powers. A mere increase of the British naval forces seemed to him inadequate:

"I cannot help expressing my conviction that the psychological moment has come for England not only to increase her navy, but also to make up her mind whether she intends to assert her traditional political authority or whether she will allow herself to be crowded out of the Mediterranean, where British power has hitherto been predominant."

He then expressed the hope that Rosebery would face the situation and act energetically. For the time being no concrete sug-

---

[42] Kálnoky to Deym, December 7, 1893, despatch no. 2, gives a full account of the discussions at Monza. Billot I, p.478, as usual tries to minimize the importance of the visit.

[43] G. P. IX, no. 2138, Kálnoky's remark to Eulenburg: "Für den Fall eines Krieges sei die Sicherheit, keinen Feind im Rücken zu haben, von unberechenbarem Wert." Cf. also G. P. IX, no. 2143.

gestions were made, though they were indicated clearly enough. England's interest in assuring herself of Italian support in the Mediterranean was especially emphasized.[44]

On December 13 Deym laid the situation before the English minister, who said that he realized the full significance of recent developments and the importance of Italy's policy. He expressed the hope that the Italians would be reassured by the coming naval bill, but rejected Deym's suggestion that he, personally, should give the Italian government "assurances for special cases." It would be impossible to do so, he said, without weakening his position in the cabinet, and there was no hope of securing the approval of the cabinet for such a policy. England's sympathies, he continued, were all on the side of Italy and there could be no question but that, in case of an unprovoked attack by France upon Italy, the government would immediately declare its readiness to stand by the latter. General assurances of this nature he had frequently given the Italian ambassador, and England's policy left no room for doubt on this point. But there was no hope of concrete promises.[45]

Kálnoky was ill-pleased with this first result of his efforts. On December 20 he wrote Deym rather sharply pointing out that, if the repeated general assurances given Italy by England had not satisfied the Italian government in the past, there was no reason to suppose they would prove sufficient in the existing crisis.[46] He then came back in more specific terms to the danger of a separate Franco-Italian understanding which would deprive England of Italy's support in the Mediterranean. He did not believe that France had aggressive plans directed against Italy, but was convinced that the French were attempting by pressure to make their neighbors more pliable and to show them that

[44] Kálnoky to Deym December 7, 1893, nos. 2 and 3.

[45] Deym to Kálnoky December 13, 1893.

[46] Kálnoky was particularly anxious as to the future policy of the new Crispi ministry. In his opening declaration Crispi had said not a word about foreign affairs, while Baron Blanc, the new foreign minister, remarked that he would try to right past mistakes. This seemed like the announcement of a new policy towards France (Kálnoky to Szögyény December 10, 1893; Kálnoky to Bruck, December 28, 1893).

they would be better off in the company of France than in that of England. France, he argued, might offer Italy a guarantee against attack from the west; financial assistance; a settlement of the commercial war; and finally, an amicable agreement with respect to the Mediterranean problem. In return, France might demand merely that Italy show her good will by reducing her army and that she remain neutral in an eventual Franco-English conflict in the Mediterranean. Is Rosebery sure, he asked, that Italy will remain firm in her adhesion to England if such proposals are made?[47]

But all these arguments failed to move Rosebery. He was having a hard time in the cabinet, struggling against Gladstone's opposition to increased naval expenditures. It was obvious that, if the question of further concessions to Italy were brought before the cabinet the divergence of opinion would become greater yet, and in the end Rosebery might be obliged to resign.[48] He told Deym that he had no faith in the possibility of a separate Franco-Italian agreement. English and Italian interests in the Mediterranean are identical, he argued, and the coöperation of the two countries is natural, especially if England, by increasing her navy, shows her determination to maintain her position in that region. Then again, the French chamber is too protectively inclined to think of making commercial concessions to Italy, while French chauvinism would be firmly opposed to any sacrifices in northern Africa.[49] It is hard to say how sincerely these arguments were meant. There is some evidence that Rosebery's distrust had been aroused by the successive *démarches* of Hatzfeldt and Deym and that he suspected that a concerted attempt was being made to drag England into the Triple Alliance.[50] In any case it should be quite clear that the British foreign minister could never have

[47] Kálnoky to Deym December 20, 1893.

[48] Deym to Kálnoky December 27, 1893.

[49] Deym to Kálnoky December 29, 1893; G. P. VIII, no. 1763.

[50] Sir Philip Currie's remark to Baron Calice, reported by Calice to Kálnoky February 26, 1894. Currie had carried on much of the discussion with Hatzfeldt while he was still undersecretary for foreign affairs.

secured the approval of Gladstone to any projected agreement with Italy. All he could do under the circumstances was to stick to generalities. He had put off Hatzfeldt with the reminder that he had not revoked the Mediterranean Agreements concluded in 1887 by Lord Salisbury and that he had not withdrawn the secret orders issued to the English admiral in the Mediterranean for certain eventualities.[51] He was even more circumspect in discussing the matter with the Austrian ambassador, and yet it appears that, early in January, the English minister did give the Italian ambassador some comfort. He agreed to take over the arrangements made by Lord Salisbury and gave the assurance "that the English cabinet could not regard with indifference the defeat of Italy by France."[52]

Kálnoky's efforts in behalf of Italy were only the first moves in a larger campaign to clear the atmosphere and to make the adjustments necessitated by the new Franco-Russian Entente. The problem, as it confronted the Austrian statesman, centered about the question of the Near East. If England were to pursue a pusillanimous policy and beat a retreat in the face of French or Russian threats in the Mediterranean, the position of the Dual Monarchy would be seriously jeopardized. Having systematically opposed the Russian schemes in the Near East, Austria might suddenly find herself abandoned in the face of the Russian colossus. Under the circumstances Kálnoky was obliged to sound out both the Germans and the English as to what policy they intended to pursue in the event of complications in the Near East.

Apparently the subject was discussed by the Austrian minister and the German Emperor during the latter's visit to Güns, in Hungary, to attend the manoeuvres in the middle of September. The Kaiser took a very definite stand: a Russian occupation of Constantinople would not be a *casus belli* for Germany, he said, suggesting at the same time that Austria might square accounts

---

[51] Deym to Kálnoky December 22, 1893.

[52] Deym to Kálnoky January 14, 1894; December 13, 1894; Calice to Kálnoky January 22, 1894; February 26, 1894; Szögyény to Kálnoky January 31, 1894.

by taking compensation, Saloniki, for example.[53]   In other words, the Kaiser, disillusioned about England after years of courtship, was returning entirely to the pro-Russian policy of Bismarck, and was not only ready to abandon the Turkish capital to the Tsar but was adopting the great chancellor's suggestion that Russia and Austria should settle their differences by partitioning the spoils between them.

In the last years of the Bismarckian regime it had been Austria more than Russia that had rejected the idea of spheres of influence in the Balkans.   Apparently the same attitude still characterized Viennese circles.   It was felt that Russia, once entrenched in the Balkans, would act as a magnet so powerful that the Slavic states in the western parts of the peninsula and even in the Daul Monarchy itself, would be unable to resist the attraction.[54]   At any rate Kálnoky appears to have evaded the question and to have determined to save his former policy, if possible.   In December, 1893 the world was full of rumors of Russia's intention to secure a naval base in the Mediterranean and of her designs upon Constantinople and the Straits.   Kálnoky himself was convinced that Russian action would not be long delayed, for, he argued, the establishment of a Russian squadron in the Mediterranean would be hardly more than a "myth" unless ingress to and egress from the Black Sea were obtained.[55]   There appeared to be no obstacle to the realization of these designs, for the Turks were militarily helpless and the French and Russian ambassadors at the Porte, M. Paul Cambon and M. Nelidov, both men of exceptional ability, were evidently in complete control.   The English ambassador, Sir Clare Ford, lacked entirely the aggressiveness and the great authority of his predecessor, Sir William White, and the German ambassador, Prince Radolin, had no instructions to take an active part in Near Eastern affairs.   The German government, which, a few years before, had shown a disposition to support the Austrian

[53] Kaiser's marginalia in G. P. IX, nos. 2138, 2145.

[54] Cf. especially G. P. X, no. 2497; XI, no. 2680; XII, no. 2931.

[55] G. P. IX, no. 2138. Kálnoky to Szögyény December 10, 1893; Kálnoky to Calice December 15, 1893, quoted in note 28 above.

and English policy, or even to take the initiative in matters concerning the Near East, now confined itself to attempts to extract economic concessions from the Porte.[56]

The dangers inherent in the situation at Constantinople were called to Lord Rosebery's attention during the negotiations concerning Italy's position. Rosebery admitted that the English influence at the Porte had sunk very low and said that he hoped to correct this weakness by sending a vigorous ambassador to replace Sir Arthur Nicolson, the chargé d'affaires. Kálnoky did not press the point, because he was anxious first of all to determine the German attitude.[57] His position in the negotiations with England would be greatly strengthened if he could count on the support of the Berlin authorities:

"It will be necessary to have a frank discussion with Germany," he wrote the Austrian ambassador at Constantinople, "so that we may know whether Germany intends *under all circumstances* to treat Eastern affairs according to the Bismarckian recipe and means to leave the dangers and cares of the watch on the Golden Horn entirely to her allies and friends."[58]

The correspondence between Vienna and London was therefore communicated to Berlin. Caprivi expressed his complete approval of the efforts which had been made to secure for the Italians some sort of concrete assurance from the English, but it was evident from the first that in other matters he would be a hard man to work with. He was extremely sceptical as to the possibility of early action on the part of the Russians. Russia, he said, always works slowly, and now that a Mediterranean squadron has been established she will make a long pause. The prospect of her attempting to force the Straits he regarded as very remote. As for the preponderant influence of France and Russia at Constantinople he appeared to be dubious; he could

[56] G. P. IX, no. 2140; Calice to Kálnoky November 20, 1893; Kálnoky to Szögyény December 14, 1893. Sir Vincent Corbett (*Reminiscences* [London 1928] pp. 144-145) who was a secretary at Constantinople, says that under Sir Clare Ford British influence "sank to a depth hardly to be distinguished from extinction." See also pp. 171 ff.

[57] G. P. IX, nos. 2137; Kálnoky to Deym December 7, 1893, no. 3; Deym to Kálnoky December 22, 1893.

[58] Kálnoky to Calice December 15, 1893.

not believe that the Toulon celebrations had made a deep impression on the Sultan and seemed to be not at all dissatisfied with the nonpolitical rôle which the German government was playing in the Turkish capital. As for England, there seemed, he thought, no prospect that she would adopt a more vigorous policy in the Near East, at least as long as Gladstone continued at the helm.[59]

To the Austrian ambassador it appeared as though the statesmen in Berlin took little interest in international affairs. They were wrapt up in the negotiations for the important tariff treaty with Russia and had no thoughts or sympathy for England's difficulties. Not only that. They regarded with the most profound suspicion the initiative which had been taken by Kálnoky. Bismarck and others after him had already fallen too much into the habit of saying that, since 1890, the leadership in the Triple Alliance had passed into the hands of Germany's Danubian ally. Now it appeared as though the attempt were really being made, and the German statesmen set their teeth against it. Furthermore, they seem to have feared that, in view of the critical condition of Italy, Austria was attempting to pave the way for a separate understanding with Russia and planning to abandon the Triple Alliance if such an agreement could be effected.[60] The depth of these suspicions appears from the fact that Count Eulenburg, a personal friend of the Kaiser and at that time minister to Munich, went to Vienna evidently with the sole object of sounding out Kálnoky as to his intentions. The Austrian minister laid the situation before him in great detail, pointing out that the Russian squadron in the Mediterranean was bound to remain a "myth" unless Russia were to open the Straits for her Black Sea fleet. Whether this problem could be solved by peaceful methods he did not know. At any rate he had

[59] Szögyény to Kálnoky December 9, 1893; Kálnoky to Szögyény December 10, 14, 1893; Szögyény to Kálnoky December 23, 1893; Wolkenstein to Kálnoky January 3, 1894, reporting his talk in Berlin with Caprivi and Marschall on December 21.

[60] This suspicion seems to have gone back to Kálnoky's Russophil statements in the delegations in June 1893 (Wolkenstein to Kálnoky February 3, 1894. See also G. P. VIII, no. 1757).

told Lord Salisbury in times past that the Dardanelles lay outside the sphere of Austrian interests and that Austria would not
feel called upon to defend them single-handed. Eulenburg tried
to feel him out on the question of a possible Austro-Russian
agreement, and, though Kálnoky insisted that he was not even
thinking of such an arrangement, the German diplomat carried
away the impression that he was considering, or had been con-
considering, the possibility of a peaceful solution of the Near
Eastern question.[61]

The suspicions of the German authorities could only be strengthened by their discussions with Count Wolkenstein, the Austrian
ambassador to St. Petersburg, who passed through Berlin
about December 20 on the way to his post. Wolkenstein had
long been known as an advocate of an understanding between
Russia and Austria in matters of the Near East, and took the
stand that Vienna should regard passively any move made by
Russia in the Straits question. He had set forth this argument to his friend Kálnoky, but, he said, the Emperor Francis
Joseph was still firm in his conviction that a strengthening of
the Russian position in the Mediterranean would threaten
Austria's possessions on the Adriatic. Nevertheless, with Germany indifferent and Italy helpless, Austria would have to guard
against a forced retreat.[62]

A day or two later the same subject was taken up again by
Prince Reuss, the German ambassador at Vienna. Kálnoky
once again set forth his arguments: Russia had given up her
designs on Bulgaria and had fixed her eyes on the Straits. The
troops massed on the German and Austrian frontiers were obviously intended to bring pressure on the central powers in case
they should offer resistance to the Russian desires. Austria
alone could not attempt to block the way, and therefore he had
adopted a conciliatory tone in his references to Russia. Since

[61] G. P. IX, no. 2138; Haller: *Eulenburg* pp. 131-132. Kálnoky's version in
his despatch to Szögyény December 29, 1893.

[62] G. P. IX, no. 2140; Wolkenstein to Kálnoky December 25, 1893, January
3, February 3, 1893. On Wolkenstein's rôle see also G. P. IX, nos. 2136, 2138, and
G. P. X. no. 2499.

Bulgaria was no longer exposed to Russian domination, the Straits were no longer within the sphere of Austrian interest.

"You know," replied Reuss, "we Germans still maintain our old standpoint, namely that we approve of any understanding you may reach with Russia on Balkan questions; only we must know what agreements you make with Russia."

Whereupon Kálnoky, with a twinkle in his eye, reminded his visitor that Bismarck had not been so particular on that point and had always treated with Russia behind the back of Austria: "But you need not fear a similar policy on our part," he added.[63]

In all these conversations Kálnoky had made it clear that, even though he might be considering an eventual arrangement with Russia, no action would be taken if England continued to play an active rôle in the Near East. But before he had the opportunity to open negotiations himself the English took the initiative. The explanation of this development is rather interesting. Lord Rosebery, evidently deeply impressed with the precariousness of the English position, had given the Italians what reassurance it was possible for him personally to give. At the same time he had decided to send as ambassador to Constantinople the permanent undersecretary for foreign affairs, Sir Philip Currie, who had been Lord Salisbury's secretary at the time of the Constantinople Conference of 1876 and had been a member of the British staff at the Congress of Berlin. Currie was to devote his efforts to the reëstablishment of the English position at the Porte and to enlist, if possible, the assistance of the German, Austrian and Italian ambassadors in an effort to reduce the influence of Cambon and Nelidov. Before leaving for his post, however, he talked the situation over with Hatzfeldt, the German ambassador, who seized the opportunity to urge upon his auditor the necessity for considering the Austrian position. Currie began the discussion by asserting that England still maintained her traditional attitude toward Russian designs in the Near East, but he insisted that an attempt of the Russians upon the Dardanelles would probably result in a European war and that

[63] Kálnoky to Szögyény December 29, 1893. Reuss' version in G. P. IX, no. 2141.

England could not accomplish much at Constantinople if the Germans were to declare themselves completely disinterested. It was a bid for German support which Hatzfeldt carefully evaded. Instead he turned the tables upon Currie and impressed upon him the fact that Austria could not be blamed for considering an arrangement with Russia if England could not be relied upon to take a strong stand against Russian pretensions. Personally Hatzfeldt, who was distinctly an adherent of the English orientation for German policy, regretted the turn which events had been taking in the past months, and in corresponding with his government he raised the question whether it would be wise to abstain entirely from Near Eastern affairs and run the risk of England's becoming discouraged, thereby hastening the possibility of a Franco-Italian rapprochement and the danger of a separate Austro-Russian agreement. But in talking to Currie he put the case as strongly as he could in order to induce the English to satisfy the Mediterranean and Near Eastern needs of Italy and Austria, in which Germany was not directly interested.[64]

The arguments of the German ambassador evidently made a strong impression on Currie and Rosebery, neither one of whom was ready to abandon the traditional policy of the English in the Near East. On January 17 Sir Edmund Monson, the British ambassador at Vienna, came to Kálnoky to ask what information the Austrian foreign office had in regard to Russian plans to secure from the Porte a coaling station in the eastern Mediterranean. No doubt the question was merely intended to give the Austrian minister an opportunity to declare himself, which he did. While admitting that he had no specific information as to Russian intrigues at the Porte he pointed out that action by Russia in the Straits question was practically inevitable. What should be done in such a case? Since Russia had had stations in the Mediterranean before, a protest might be impossible, unless an attempt were made to erect fortifications on territory over which Russia did not exercise sovereignty. The future attitude

---

[64] G. P. IX, nos. 2142, 2143, the first being Hatzfeldt's report to Caprivi, the second the more detailed and confidential letter to von Holstein.

of the powers should be discussed before complications arose. Russia had a large fleet in the Black Sea and this was obviously not intended for pleasure cruises. If she wished to open the Straits France would probably lend her support, for the French statesmen were now so intoxicated by the Toulon festivities that they would not realize the menace to French interests if the Russians were allowed to establish themselves in the Mediterranean. Italy, for the present, is paralyzed; Germany is uninterested in the Near Eastern problem; Austria is obliged to defend the *status quo* on the land side. All, therefore, depends upon England, for the Sultan is too weak to oppose Russia. England must realize what an effect the appearance of the Russian fleet in the Mediterranean would have upon the situation in the Balkans, in Anatolia, in Syria and in Egypt. What would become of the English fleet and even of Malta, if the Russian fleet were in the Aegean and the French fleet between Toulon and Bizerta? To all this Monson listened in silence, though when Kálnoky had finished he admitted that such a situation would mean the end of the eastern question.[65]

Having broken the ice, the Austrian minister wrote to his ambassador at London, instructing him to discuss the matter with Rosebery and reëmphasizing the fact that, unless England were determined to maintain her traditional policy of defending Constantinople and the Straits against Russia, Austria would be compelled to recast her own policy, to abandon the Straits to Russia and to confine herself to the defence of her interests in the Balkans.[66] At the same time he made inquiries in Berlin and London regarding the possibility of protesting against the eventual erection of a Russian coaling station in the Mediterranean.[67] On this last point both the Germans and the English were of the opinion that a protest to Turkey would not be in order and that in any case it would be inadvisable, because, if

---

[65] Kálnoky memorandum of the conversation January 18, 1894. See also G. P. IX, no. 2145, Kálnoky's account to Reuss.

[66] Kálnoky to Deym January 25, 1894, no. 1.

[67] Kálnoky to Deym, January 25, 1894, no. 2; Kálnoky to Szögyény January 25, 1894.

the protest were successful, Russia would simply accept a station from France, thus making the coöperation of the two powers all the more intimate.[68]

But the danger of Russia reopening the Straits question and the idea of a possible Austro-Russian agreement appear to have made a deep impression on Lord Rosebery. His reply to Count Deym must have been pondered over a long time, for it was very adroitly phrased and very cleverly put:

> "I assure you that I am absolutely determined to maintain the *status quo* in the Straits question and that I would not recoil from the danger of involving England in a war with Russia; but I must tell you frankly that if France should take sides with Russia, it would be impossible for England to defend Constantinople against both powers; in any case we should be unable to allow our Mediterranean fleet to run the risk of a catastrophe by finding itself between the Russian and French fleets. In such a case we should require the assistance of the Triple Alliance to hold France in check. I, and not the British Cabinet, am giving you these assurances, and you may count upon my word."

In spite of Deym's importunity Rosebery refused to bring the question before the cabinet, saying that the ministers would make no definite decision on a question which was still in the future, but that in a crisis the cabinet and the country would be united against Russia.[69]

There is much of interest in this reply of Rosebery's. When one recalls the occasions on which Bismarck had sounded the English in regard to an alliance against France and had elicited nothing but offers of support against Russia, the attitude of the English foreign minister in the spring of 1894 may be taken as symptomatic of the distinct change for the worse in the English position. On the other hand Rosebery had exhibited unusual adroitness in framing his reply. In a sense he had turned the tables on Kálnoky. The latter had declared that Austria could maintain her traditional attitude in the Near East only if English aid were assured. In reply the English minister had

[68] Deym to Kálnoky January 31, 1894; Szögyény to Kálnoky January 31, 1894.

[69] Deym to Kálnoky, January 31, 1894. Rosebery begged for secrecy, saying: "C'est qu'il y va de ma tête si on apprenait ici que je vous ai donné ces assurances." See also G. P. IX, no. 2147.

stated that England would maintain her past policy only if the Triple Alliance would lend support. Kálnoky expressed himself as satisfied with this first result, but immediately extended the discussion by raising the question as to what should be done if Russia, instead of attempting to open the Straits by force, were to rely upon the aid of her French ally and request the powers to accept an alteration in the regulations of the Straits previously agreed upon by Russia and Turkey.[70] Another point was to find out exactly what Rosebery meant when he referred to "the assistance of the Triple Alliance to hold France in check."

According to Sir Philip Currie, who was a close friend of Rosebery and who had been initiated into all the pourparlers, the English minister had in mind the support of the Italian and Austrian fleets.[71] If this were so, it would simplify matters very much, for it would obviate the necessity of bringing Germany into the negotiations. While pointing out that Austria had no large ships and that the Austrian navy was organized primarily for coast defence, Kálnoky was ready to promise coöperation with the English fleet in any well-planned action by the Triple Alliance and England. Of course, England would have to secure the support of the Italian fleet.[72] It soon turned out, however, that Currie had expressed merely a personal opinion. Rosebery's idea was a very different one. He believed the English fleet would be quite sufficient to defend the Straits against Russia and did not even desire the coöperation of Italy or Austria because such common action would lead to a general conflagration. All he asked was that the Triple Alliance should exercise pressure on France and declare to her that she must remain neutral in case she showed any disposition to go to the assistance of Russia.[73] Count Deym was agreeably surprised at the renunciation of military or naval help on the part of the English and had a hard

[70] Kálnoky first raised this point in discussion with Sir Philip Currie as the latter was passing through Vienna *en route* to his post (Kálnoky to Calice February 8, 1894).

[71] Calice to Kálnoky February 19, 1894.

[72] Kálnoky to Deym February 21, 1894.

[73] Deym to Kálnoky February 26 and 27, 1894. Rosebery ended by saying: "Eh bien, maintenant vous connaissez le fond du sac." See also G. P. IX, no. 2148.

time explaining this strange generosity, but his more experienced German colleague immediately pointed out to him that England was thereby reserving for herself the decision as to what should constitute a *casus belli* with Russia. There was not even the guarantee that England would in all circumstances go to war on the Straits question.[74]

At any rate Rosebery's definition of his stand made it necessary to approach the German government. Though he realized that in Berlin the old Bismarckian dictum in regard to Near Eastern questions once again swayed the minds of the German statesmen, Kálnoky hoped to convince them that, if Russia succeeded in extending her power to the Mediterranean, the position of Austria, Italy and England would be effected in a way indirectly detrimental to German interests.[75] Hatzfeldt had already been unofficially informed of the negotiations and the conditions laid down by Rosebery. In his instructions to the Austrian ambassador at Berlin, Count Szögyény, Kálnoky insisted that he desired for the present merely a friendly discussion of the problem. The questions he asked were: How does the German cabinet regard the prospect of Russia's reopening the Straits question? What reply will the German cabinet give to Rosebery's appeal for the support of the Triple Alliance in case France should join Russia in taking action in the Mediterranean? What does the German government think of the consequences likely to arise if England should abandon the Mediterranean?[76]

Szögyény had already predicted that the Berlin cabinet, while perfectly willing to coöperate in persuading England to strengthen her fleet and support Italy, would maintain a passive attitude in case Russia took action to open the Dardanelles for her warships.[77] The Kaiser had made this clear to Kálnoky at Güns in September, and Marschall had restated the German position in

[74] G. P. IX, no. 2150. Deym made this argument his own in his report to Kálnoky February 27, 1894.

[75] Kálnoky to Deym February 19, 1894, no. 3.

[76] Kálnoky to Szögyény February 27, 1894.

[77] Szögyény to Kálnoky January 31, 1894.

speaking to the Austrian ambassador in October.[78] Yet the
reception given the Austrian proposals in Berlin was even more
discouraging than had been expected. First of all, Caprivi refused to discuss the matter before the commercial treaty with
Russia had passed the Reichstag.[79] When, soon after, the Austrian ambassador succeeded nevertheless in drawing him into
conversation on the question, Caprivi would go no further than
to recognize that the Straits question must be regarded as a
European one which could not be altered without the consent of
the powers. With respect to Rosebery's declaration he declared
his satisfaction at England's determination to resist alone any
move which Russia might make. But he was not at all pleased
by the English suggestion that the Triple Alliance should hold
France in check, if that power took her stand by Russia. Under
such an arrangement England alone might decide the moment to
take action and in that way assume the leadership, he remarked,
repeating the argument brought forward by Hatzfeldt.[80]

After this conversation Caprivi worked out a memorandum,
which was submitted to the Kaiser and which was made the
basis of the chancellor's discussion with the Austrian ambassador
on March 8. Caprivi argued that Russia could almost certainly
rely upon France for aid, and that England under the circumstances could hardly risk leaving her squadron in the eastern
Mediterranean while the French fleet was intact in the west.
This meant that a mere warning to France to remain neutral
would hardly be sufficient. The Triple Alliance would have to
be prepared to go to war, and under the circumstances the brunt
of the action would devolve upon Germany. The whole question
would not be worth that much, and German public opinion,
educated by Bismarck, would certainly not approve a war waged
because of the Straits question. Not only that: under the Rosebery proposal England would be getting the promise of the

---

[78] Schiessl to Kálnoky October 14, 1893. Caprivi spoke in the same terms to
Wolkenstein in December (Wolkenstein to Kálnoky January 3, 1894). See also
G. P. IX, no. 2135.

[79] Szögyény to Kálnoky February 28, 1894.

[80] Szögyény to Kálnoky March 4, 1894.

support of the Triple Alliance without in any way binding herself. If she were formally to join the League of Peace and assume definite, permanent obligations, the situation would be quite different. As it was, the only point to be considered by Germany would be the question of her allies' interests. In their behalf efforts must continually be made to secure English support for Italy and to induce England to maintain her traditional Near Eastern policy. If Russia were actually to raise the Straits question, it would be better if the problem could be peacefully solved on the basis of reciprocal compensation.[81]

This was the gist of the remarks made by the chancellor in speaking to Szögyény on March 8. He advised the Austrians to treat the Rosebery proposal dilatorily and emphasized the fact that Germany and Austria should induce Russia to appeal first of all to the Triple Alliance, whereupon the question could be amicably solved and adequate guarantees secured for Austria. It was quite obvious to the Austrian ambassador that there was little, if any, hope of drawing the Germans into an arrangement, nor did the underlying reasons for Caprivi's attitude escape him:

"The chancellor as well as the Kaiser himself," he wrote to Kálnoky, "is deeply impressed by the approaching conclusion of the commercial treaty with Russia; they are convinced that this treaty will lead to a political rapprochement of far-reaching importance between the two empires and that this rapprochement, if skillfully exploited, may alienate Russia and France....Under these circumstances the German government desires to avoid all complications with Russia and regards the Straits question and all it implies from this standpoint."

Besides, Caprivi distrusted England, just as did the Kaiser. He feared that, as in the Siamese crisis, the English government would at first take a vigorous stand in the Straits question and then yield, leaving the associated powers to their fate or allowing them to draw the chestnuts out of the fire for England.[82]

The events of the following weeks diminished even further the chances that Germany could be brought into any combination directed against Russia or France. The Kaiser and his advisers

---

[81] Caprivi Memorandum in G. P. IX, no. 2152.
[82] Szögyény to Kálnoky March 10, 1894.

had definitely embarked upon a policy designed to take the life out of the Franco-Russian Entente by depriving it of every opportunity to express itself in action.[83] It was on March 15, 1894 that the Kamerun Treaty was signed between France and Germany, much to the disgust of the English, who regarded the whole thing as a betrayal of their interests.[84] More important yet was the great Russo-German Tariff Treaty, signed on February 10, 1894. Both parties had been very anxious to have the negotiations end successfully, not only because of economic considerations, but also because of the political implications. It was generally felt that failure to reach an agreement would lead to war.[85] Consequently it was of prime importance that the treaty should be accepted by the Reichstag, where the agrarian interests, organized in the League of Agriculturalists, was preparing for a trial of strength. In the crisis the Kaiser himself took an active part, throwing his influence into the scale against the agrarians. "I have no desire to wage war with Russia on account of a hundred crazy Junkers," he said at a dinner given by the chancellor on February 5. If the treaty were rejected, war would break out in three months, he continued.[86] It was an open secret that the passage of the treaty through the Reichstag on March 16 was due largely to William's efforts. At any rate it supplied the occasion for a very cordial exchange of telegrams between the two sovereigns.[87] The Kaiser hoped that from this time onward the Franco-Russian Entente would lose what vitality it had, and in Berlin all reports of the disillusionment of the French and the gradual cooling of Franco-Russian relations were followed with the greatest attention.[88]

[83] G. P. IX, no. 2155.

[84] Deym to Kálnoky April 14, May 8, 1894.

[85] Cf. Wittschewsky pp. 160-163, reporting statements made by Witte; Massow p. 138; Cyon: M. Witte et les Finances Russes p. 32.

[86] Waldersee II, p. 306. The Kaiser's remarks were reported in the newspapers in very diluted form.

[87] G. P. VII, nos. 1666,1667,1668. Szögyény to Kálnoky February 17, 1894; Witte pp. 70, 403-404; Waldersee II, p. 310.

[88] Szögyény to Kálnoky February 17, March 12, 14, 17, 1894; G. P. VII, no. 1604. The disillusionment of the French was much commented on at the time (Wolkenstein to Kálnoky January 4, 10, 16, February 3, 1894). The decision of the

In view of the new German policy the other members of the Triple Alliance were practically compelled to follow suit and attempt to avoid complications until the situation had become clarified. Both Austria and Italy applied themselves to the rehabilitation of good relations with France or Russia, or both. Early in March Francis Joseph arrived on the French Riviera to visit the Empress, who was at Mentone. He stayed for some time, and soon after his return to Vienna the Grand Cross of St. Stephen was conferred upon President Carnot.[89] The same policy was followed in respect to Russia. Negotiations for an Austo-Russian commercial treaty were initiated, and brought to a successful close on May 18.[90] The new agreement was hailed with delight in both countries, and even in Balkan affairs the two governments seemed determined to avoid friction. King Milan of Serbia had returned to Belgrade in January, 1894, and on April 29 the ordinance providing for his banishment was abrogated. On May 21 the whole liberal constitution of 1889 was declared abolished. The situation might easily have led to serious complications, but both Austria and Russia, while maintaining the illegality of Milan's presence in the country, expressed their desire to abstain from all interference.[91] These events were followed shortly after by Stambulov's dismissal. Instead of leading to difficulties this development, too, contributed towards relieving the situation in the Balkans. Ferdinand, im-

French to raise the tariff on grain made a very bad impression in Russia. On February 25, 1894 the *Figaro* published an article entitled *France and the Danish Court*, in which the influence of the Princess Waldemar of Denmark upon the Tsar was discussed. Carnot was charged with having used the French naval attaché at Copenhagen to obtain through the Princess certain information as to the Tsar's desires and intentions. The publication of this story, which probably contained a grain of truth, enraged the Tsar and the Russian court (Köhler p. 131, note 1; Albin pp. 366-367; Galli p. 171; Szögyény to Kálnoky March 12, 17, 1894).

[89] Kálnoky to Szögyény March 21, 1894, points out the political significance of the award. Similarly Kálnoky's remarks in the Austrian delegation, September 17, 1894. The German government expressed its entire approval (Szögyény to Kálnoky March 31, 1894).

[90] Kálnoky to Szögyény March 21, 1894; Wolkenstein to Kálnoky May 29, 1894; G. P. VII, no. 1669.

[91] Giers to Lobanov April 23, 1894, communicated to Kálnoky; Szögyény to Kálnoky May 26, 1894; Wolkenstein to Kálnoky May 29, 1894.

mediately his undesirable minister was gone, began to apply himself to the preparation of a reconciliation with Russia. Most political offenders were granted an amnesty, and the Metropolitan Clement was recalled, much to the delight of the population. We now know that no formal agreement was reached at the time between Austria and Russia, providing for reciprocal abstention in Bulgaria and Serbia, but in practice the two nations followed a policy which expressed the same idea.[92]

In Italy Crispi, too, was seeking salvation, without too much regard for the allied powers. During the first half of 1894 repeated attempts were made to initiate negotiations for a commercial settlement with France. The French premier, Casimir-Perier, was favorable, and Rouvier was sent to Italy in a semi-official capacity. Nothing came of the pourparlers, but by the summer of 1894 there was a distinct strain of cordiality in the relations between the two countries. They were on better speaking terms than they had been for years.[93]

Of course all these measures were merely precautionary in nature. Neither Kálnoky nor Crispi had any desire or intention of abandoning the Triple Alliance. Both preferred the continued support of England to an agreement with Russia or with France, as the case might be. Crispi made it perfectly clear that there was no prospect of a reduction of expenditure for armaments on the part of Italy, and Kálnoky, in spite of his first rebuff, continued his efforts to win the Germans for his projected Mediterranean agreement and so secure the renewed support of the English. In resuming the negotiations after the German refusal of the English terms he changed the emphasis somewhat and no longer spoke of the probability of a Russian attack upon the Straits. What he now asked was merely a discussion of possible policies to be pursued in the event that Russia should raise the question in a diplomatic way. But the conversations carried on at Berlin by the Austrian ambassador on the one hand and the

[92] The statement that such an agreement was concluded in 1894 is made by Richard Charmatz: *Geschichte der auswärtigen Politik Oesterreichs im 19ten Jahrhundert* (Leipzig 1918) II, p. 126; by B. Molden in his article on Kálnoky in the *Deutsche Allgemeine Biographie* LI, p. 20; and by Kaindl, in *Handbuch der Politik* II, p. 40.   [93] Crispi III, pp. 190-201.

Kaiser, Caprivi and Marschall on the other showed no signs of progress. The Germans repeated the arguments they had already advanced: England would have the advantage under the proposed agreement; England's own interests demand that she pursue a vigorous policy in the Straits question; the English suggestions should be treated dilatorily and the central powers should take counsel when the problem actually arose; in that event an effort should be made to induce Russia to negotiate first with the Triple Alliance and then to ask the approval of England for the settlement agreed upon; if free passage of the Straits must be granted to Russia the members of the Triple Alliance could easily secure adequate guarantees for themselves; in any case Austria could count on the loyal support of Germany in all questions involving the Near East.[94]

Kálnoky's attitude was that the chance to secure the support of England in the Near East should not be allowed to slip by, that Germany herself was largely, though indirectly, interested in the balance of power in the Mediterranean, that it would be unfair to England to negotiate separately with Russia, and that Russia would never discuss a European problem with the Triple Alliance powers alone. As for Austria, she did not desire compensation, but wanted merely to uphold the balance of power.[95] When the Kaiser paid a visit to Francis Joseph at Abbazia on March 29 and received Kálnoky in Vienna on April 13, a concerted effort was made by the Austrian Emperor and his minister to revive the discussion. But the Kaiser replied evasively. He approved the attempt made by Austria to encourage England in her traditional policy toward Russia and promised to do his utmost in the same direction. If Russia should raise the question of the Straits and a member of the Triple Alliance should become involved in the conflict, the Triple Alliance would do its duty, though it was to be hoped that the first shot would be fired by

[94] Szögyény to Kálnoky March 12, 1894, reporting a conversation with Marschall; March 17, reporting his talk with the Kaiser; March 31, reporting a very long discussion with Caprivi, in which all the pros and cons were gone over. See also G. P. IX, no. 2153, and annexes.

[95] Kálnoky to Szögyény March 21, 1894, also printed in G. P. IX, no. 2153, annexe I.

England.[96] To purely academic discussions of the problem the Kaiser seemed to have no objection, and consequently Kálnoky instructed Szögyény to make one last effort to obtain a clear declaration from the German chancellor. Rosebery is becoming restless, he wrote, and the German answer must be definitive. Let Germany consider carefully what a rupture of negotiations may involve. Nothing would so effectively check Franco-Russian designs as the knowledge that, in a crisis, England would stand by the Triple Alliance. It would be a tremendous mistake not to take advantage of the moment while public opinion in England was favorable to closer coöperation with the Triple Alliance. Rosebery had not given any definite assurances and could not expect any in return. But an agreement on general principles could and should be reached. Would Caprivi give a declaration similar to that made by Rosebery? That alone would suffice to keep England by the side of the Triple Alliance, but, if England were allowed to feel isolated, public opinion would undoubtedly veer about and demand a separate arrangement with Russia, which would be welcomed by the latter.[97]

In the conversation between Caprivi and Szögyény on April 23 the German chancellor absolutely refused to yield ground. After repeating the old arguments he stressed the fact that Germany's aim was to wean Russia from the alliance with France and that therefore Germany could not afford to make any statements which England might exploit in eventual negotiations with Russia. So far as Austria was concerned, he expressed willingness to enter into a discussion of principles, which could be more accurately defined once Russia made her demands, but he was sceptical as to the value of such discussion so long as no one knew which course of action Russia would take. He did not agree entirely with the Bismarckian dictum regarding Germany's interests in the east, but the authority and respect enjoyed by his predecessor was so great that it hampered the present government considerably. But, he declared, the position of

---

[96] G. P. IX, no. 2154; also Szögyény to Kálnoky April 19, 1894; Kálnoky to Szögyény April 20, 1894, nos. 1 and 2, giving a full account of the conversations in Vienna.   [97] Kálnoky to Szögyény April 20, no. 3.

Austria-Hungary is absolutely and indisputably of vital interest to Germany, and therefore Germany must and will defend that position in all eventualities.[98]

Kálnoky had desired a definite reply. He now had it, and realized the futility of further discussion. Szögyény was instructed to drop the matter for the present.[99] But it was not until June that the Austrian minister finally announced his intention of giving up the attempt to effect an agreement between England and the Triple Alliance to check Russia's policy. In a despatch to Szögyény, dated June 8, he declared that, while the danger of a peaceful *démarche* by Russia in the Straits question was by no means over, the prospect of a combined action by France and Russia had been much diminished:

"Nothing more is heard of the renowned Admiral Avellan and his Mediterranean fleet and in St. Petersburg there has taken place, instead of the Franco-Russian Alliance hoped for in Paris, a decided rapprochement with the central powers, the foundation of which rests upon the commercial treaties concluded with Germany and Austria."[100]

He therefore proposed to reply to Rosebery in the following terms, for which he desired the approval of the German government: 1). Austria appreciates the declarations given by Lord Rosebery, which, though personal, are important enough to induce Austria to maintain her traditional policy of defending the *status quo* in the Near East. At the same time, Austria's stand will necessarily influence her allies, whose vital interests would also be affected by a change in the balance of power in southern Europe. 2). Austria and Germany agree with England, and Italy undoubtedly would agree, if asked, that the Straits question is a European one and cannot be altered without the consent of the Powers. This attitude on the part of the friendly powers will unquestionably do much to deter Russia from opening the question, and in any event it will guard the friendly powers against surprise by a peaceful *démarche* on the part of Russia. 3). In view of the peaceful development of the international situation the German government does not consider the time ripe for such assurances as Lord Rosebery desires, but the

---

[98] Szögyény to Kálnoky April 24 and 28, 1894, nos. 1 and 2; G. P. IX, no. 2155.
[99] Kálnoky to Szögyény May 3, 1894. [100] Kálnoky to Szögyény, June 8, 1894.

agreement of the friendly powers, as stated in the first point, is sufficient guarantee to England that a diplomatic move by Russia will not be accepted in Berlin and Vienna to the detriment of English interests. Furthermore, it is unlikely that, in case of action by Russia, France will stand aloof, and, if France should interfere, the attitude of the German government would necessarily be influenced in a sense favorable to England.[101]

Caprivi thoroughly approved of Kálnoky's intention to bring the negotiations to a close. There was nothing in the proposed reply to Rosebery that could in any way be interpreted as binding the German government to any course of action, and so no objection was raised to the Austrian draft.[102] The Austrian note was sent to London on June 15, but, on account of the dispute which had arisen between the English and German governments on the question of the Congo Treaty, it was not actually handed to Rosebery until July 9. The English premier, who had at first waited anxiously for word from Berlin, had probably given up hope of a favorable outcome. Both Rosebery and Lord Kimberley, the new foreign minister in the Rosebery cabinet, expressed themselves as satisfied, especially by the declaration that Germany meant to stand by Austria and England in maintaining the international character of the Straits question and in rejecting any possible Russian suggestions for a separate agreement. It was perhaps more than they had hoped for, and they could always reopen negotiations, at least with Austria, if the occasion arose.[103]

Thus ended a series of discussions which had extended over more than six months. Its importance can hardly be exaggerated. In the first place the negotiations show how critical was the situation after Toulon, and how acutely menaced was the English position. For a time the whole European system threatened to undergo a profound transformation, the keynote of which would have been the isolation of England and the return of Ger-

---

[101] Kálnoky to Szögyény June 5, 1894; G. P. IX, no. 2157, and annexes.

[102] G. P. IX, no. 2157; Szögyény to Kálnoky June 10, 1894.

[103] Kálnoky to Deym June 15, 1894, nos. 1 and 2; Deym to Kálnoky July 9 and 12, 1894; G. P. IX, no. 2160.

man policy to the channels marked out by Bismarck.[104]   But
the Russian orientation of German policy had always been anathema to the Austrian statesmen, whose preferences had always
been for England, the bulwark of defence against Russia in the
Near East. Kálnoky therefore tried to save the situation by
bringing England closer to the Triple Alliance. But the very
nature of the changes wrought by Toulon involved English
hostility not only to Russia, but also to France. The German
statesmen flatly refused to be made the catspaw. They had for
years been courting England, until the Siamese crisis of 1893 had
shown them not only the weakness and danger of the English
position, but also the pusillanimity of English policy. They had
definitely returned to the Bismarckian idea, denied any interest
in Near Eastern affairs except as they affected Austria and Italy,
were ready to abandon the Straits and Constantinople to the
Russians, and concentrated on sapping the vitality of the
Franco-Russian Entente by cultivating the friendship of Russia.
Had England been willing to join the Triple Alliance officially
even then the German attitude would have been different, for a
real quadruple alliance would have been irresistible. But clearly
there was no prospect of such an arrangement. So the German
statesmen refused unconditionally to allow Austria to purchase
English support in the Near East by engaging Germany's support against France. By such a policy England would keep her
hands free but her back covered, and Germany would be reduced
to the position of a vassal, obliged to furnish support without
having any influence on the decisions.[105]   Clearly the out-and-
out Anglophil phase of German policy had come to an end.

[104] The first steps towards a reconciliation between the Kaiser and his fallen
chancellor, taken on William's initiative in January 1894, may be taken as symbolic
of the change in course.

[105] See especially G. P. IX, no. 2158. In G. P. VIII, no. 1769 England is described as desiring to play the part of the standard bearer in the Triple Alliance, itself
unarmed, but protected by all the others. Even Hatzfeldt, who had nothing of an
anti-English bias, appears to have regarded the English stand as untenable. In
December, 1894, he spoke of Germany's having avoided the trap which Rosebery
had set for her (Deym to Kálnoky December 13, 1894). Even Lord Kimberley,
who became foreign minister in the Rosebery cabinet in March, 1894, recognized
the justice of the German position. If England and France were to become involved
in war, he said, and Russia chose that moment to open the Straits question, it was
hard to see how England could be in a position to defend the Straits (Deym to
Kálnoky April 20, 1894).

CHAPTER XIII

LOOKING FORWARD

KÁLNOKY'S apprehensions, even if they were genuine, proved to be unfounded. The Russians did not attempt a descent upon Constantinople or the Bosporus; they did not establish a naval base in the Mediterranean; they did not even raise the question of an alteration of the treaties regulating the passage of foreign ships of war through the Straits. All Europe expected some such action in the autumn of 1893 and continued to expect it for some years to come. How is one to explain the passivity of the Russian government under these circumstances?

A definite answer is, of course, impossible so long as the complete Russian documents are not available. The writer's own opinion is that the Tsar had no intention of initiating a forward policy in the Near East, in spite of the evidence which led the statesmen of the time to a very different conclusion. It may be that Nelidov, the Russian ambassador at the Porte, a very energetic and aggressive personality, had hopes of reopening the Straits question and immortalizing himself by securing for his country the free passage to the Mediterranean. Russian ambassadors had a dangerous way of pursuing their own schemes, and Nelidov is known in history chiefly for his famous scheme for an attack upon the heights of the Bosporus in December, 1896. But it seems unlikely that the Tsar himself should have harbored ideas of aggression in 1894. It was not at all like Alexander III to act precipitately or rashly. Many have put him down as lethargic and of mean mentality, but he appears to have been rather a well-balanced, careful and calculating monarch, as the diplomats of the day recognized. He cannot possibly have been under illusions as to the nature and value of the alliance he had just concluded with France. He knew only too well that at the back of the mind of every French statesman was the thought of hostility to Germany and the hope of ultimately recovering the lost provinces. The men who made the alliance on the French side did not desire war and hoped to utilize the connection with Russia in order to establish a more conservative régime in France.[1] But the men of 1887 would undoubtedly have made use of an understanding with the Tsar to force the issue. Even in 1896 Clemenceau complained of the alliance, because it was based on the peace of the *status quo* and *that* peace was the peace of French dismemberment, a German peace.[2] It was appreciation of the dangers of an agreement with France that had made the Tsar hesitate, even after the nonrenewal of the Reinsurance Treaty in 1890. He had made a special point of speaking to Montebello about the question of revenge at the time the military convention was ratified, and the Russian undersecretary for foreign affairs, M. Shishkin, remarked shortly after:

"We went to Toulon only in order to return the Cronstadt visit. This has nothing whatever to do with French claims in regard to Alsace and Lorraine."[3]

A few months later Giers himself stated categorically:

"It is a fixed principle of Russian policy that Russia should have nothing to do with French lust for revenge and reconquest. Russia has absolutely nothing to do with questions touching Alsace and Lorraine. If it was necessary to tell the French this, it was done unequivocally."[4]

The statesmen in Paris had certainly not been left under illusions on this question. They knew quite well that nothing was to be hoped from Russia so far as claims against Germany were concerned:

"Doubtless the Franco-Russian Alliance was not an alliance formed for revenge," says André Tardieu. "Its object was not to give us back Alsace-Lorraine. But it insured us in Europe a moral authority, which, since our defeats, had been wanting to us. It augmented our diplomatic value. It opened to us the field of political combinations, from which our isolation had excluded us. From mere observation we could pass to action, thanks to the recovered balance of power."[5]

---

[1] Cf. G. Michon: *L'Alliance Franco-Russe* (Paris 1927), especially chapter iv.

[2] *Dépeche de Toulouse* October 13, 1896 (quoted by Michon p. 69).

[3] Wolkenstein to Kálnoky, January 10, 1894.

[4] Wolkenstein to Kálnoky April 25, 1894.

[5] A. Tardieu: *France and the Alliances* (New York 1908) p. 13.

In other words, the French government was relying upon the imponderables. With no immediate gain in view, it was hoped that the alliance would increase the bargaining power of France, at the same time protecting her against unprovoked attack on the part of Germany.

As for the Tsar, he had no need of an alliance against Germany, for Germany was in no sense a rival of Russia:

"At bottom," says Prince Bülow, "the Dual Alliance lacked a permanent conflict of interests with the German Empire, common to both allied powers."[6]

Neither could the Tsar have hoped to further Russian interests in the Ottoman Empire through his alliance with France. In the course of the negotiations it had become only too clear that the French statesmen were averse to the idea of war resulting from the conflict of Russian and Austrian interests in the Balkans. They had, in the end, accepted the Russian wording of the military convention only with mental reservations, because they could do no better.[7] Technically speaking M. Poincaré is unquestionably right when he says:

"No French government ever thought of excluding the East from the normal scope of the alliance. It was merely agreed that, in a case not directly provided for in the pact, that is, the attack of Germany or the attack of Italy and of Austria supported by Germany, Russia and France should concert in advance all measures to be taken."[8]

But M. Poincaré is here referring merely to the Balkans, not to the question of Constantinople, the Straits or the eastern Mediterranean. On these last matters the French attitude had been consistent for generations. French diplomacy had resisted the encroachments of Russia on the Ottoman Empire, and even the great Napoleon could not bring himself to abandon the Turk capital to his Tilsit ally. In more recent times Napoleon III had fought shoulder to shoulder with the English to block the Russian advance, and at the Congress of Berlin the French policy was certainly more closely related to that of England and Austria

[6] Fürst Bernhard von Bülow: *Deutsche Politik* (Berlin 1916) p. 85.
[7] See above, chapter viii.
[8] Raymond Poincaré: *Au Service de la France* (Paris 1926) I, p. 335.

than to that of Russia. No wonder that Giers remarked to Bülow in 1886 that an alliance with France would compromise Russia both in her domestic policy and in her Near Eastern policy.[9] Giers' repeated assurances to Freycinet and Ribot in 1891 to the effect that Russia had no designs on Constantinople and desired only the *status quo* in the Near East would almost indicate that the French ministers had some hesitancy about concluding an agreement which was not specific on this point.

Whether or not this question actually came up for discussion in the days following Toulon it is hard to say. In spite of the assertion of M. Poincaré to the contrary, the French *Yellow Book* is so fragmentary and incomplete that no adequate idea of the subtleties of the situation can be gained from it.[10] According to M. Hanotaux, who became minister of foreign affairs shortly after the conclusion of the alliance, this all-important aspect of Franco-Russian relations had not been left out of consideration:

"In the exchange of views which took place at the very time of the agreement, and on many later occasions, it was always, *always*, stipulated that the alliance excluded the affairs of the East, Constantinople and the Balkans, that it was expressly opposed to any Russian enterprise in this region and that, consequently, far from encouraging Russian ambitions in this direction, it pacified and *immobilized* them by the most formal reminders."[11]

By way of example M. Hanotaux quotes his conversations with Prince Lobanov in 1895, when he made the French attitude perfectly clear and secured from the Russian minister renewed assurances that Russia had no intention of acquiring possession of the Turkish capital.[12] Soon after, when Nelidov's plan for an attack on the Bosporus was under discussion, the French govern-

[9] G. P. VI, p. 105.

[10] Cf. Poincaré's statement in *Foreign Affairs* (New York) IV, p. 6 (October 1925): "All the documents relating to the negotiations and to the conclusion of this alliance...have been published in their entirety in a *Livre Jaune* and they admit of no misinterpretation." Michon p. 47 catalogs some of the more obvious omissions in the *Livre Jaune*.

[11] G. Hanotaux: La Prétendue Conjuration Franco-Russe, in the *Revue des Deux Mondes* January 15, 1928.

[12] G. Hanotaux: *Histoire Illustrée de la Guerre de 1914* (Paris 1915) I, p. 203; Hanotaux: La Prétendue Conjuration [Franco-Russe *loc. cit.* Cf. also G. P. XI, no. 2676; XII, no. 2916; XVIII, no. 5916.

ment was approached for an expression of its attitude, and Hanotaux wrote to Montebello on January 12, 1897, reporting his conversation with Mohrenheim:

"I told him that if a conflict should break out on the question of the Black Sea and the Straits, our country appeared in no way disposed to take an active part in the military events which might take place, since the risks would be so great and the advantages for France so far from evident."

A little later yet the same question was broached by Muraviev, whereupon Hanotaux once again formulated the French view:

"I recalled to him the true character of this policy, which consists in the obstinate maintenance of a defensive attitude and abstention on the part of the allied powers from any separate initiative.. Germany will push you to the Straits and Constantinople. She has already offered, first to Prince Lobanov, then to the Emperor Nicholas, the Bosporus, which, to tell the truth, costs her nothing. But take care, Germany is an expert tempter. You would have the support of our diplomacy, but have no illusions in regard to our military support. The real service we should render to Russia would be to observe neutrality, which would oblige Germany to do likewise."[13]

No wonder, then, that M. Sazonov, looking back, complains that

"In spite of our twenty years' alliance with France, we could never quite agree about our policy in the Near East."[14]

The French were taking the attitude so well expressed by François Coppée during the Tsar's visit to Paris in 1896:

"Is the young Emperor secretly tormented by the traditional ideal of the Slavic world? Does he dream of casting the Turkish barbarism back over the Bosporus and making the Greek cross gleam on the dome of St. Sophia? Why not? But the day when the Cossacks gallop into the narrow streets of old Stambul, it is well understood that at Strassburg a French batallion shall present arms at the statue of Kléber."[15]

The same idea is expressed by Georges Louis, who was only too well-versed in the history of Franco-Russian relations and was

[13] Hanotaux: La Prétendue Conjuration Franco-Russe *loc. cit*; quoted also by E. Judet: *Georges Louis* (Paris 1925) p. 146.

[14] S. Sazonov: *Fateful Years* (New York 1927) p. 246.

[15] François Coppée, in the book entitled *Hommage au Tsar*, quoted by Michon pp. 68-69, note.

determined to make no dangerous concessions without a *quid pro quo*:

"In the Alliance, Constantinople and the Straits form the counterpart of Alsace and Lorraine.

"This is not written in any agreement, but it is the supreme end, of which one thinks without talking. If the Russians should open the question in their conversations with us, we should reply: 'Yes, the day when you can assist us to acquire Alsace-Lorraine.' "[16]

The French attitude in this matter remained absolutely unchanged, and even after the outbreak of the World War they offered greater resistance to the Russian demands in regard to Constantinople and the Straits than did the English.[17] The Near East was surely the weakest point in the Franco-Russian Alliance.[18]

If mutual assistance in the event of a German attack was the common denominator of the Franco-Russian Alliance, it was a miserable thing from the start, especially if looked at from the French standpoint. After all, it was just as clear that Russia would not allow another defeat of France by Germany as that France would intervene in a conflict between Germany and her eastern neighbor. There was no need for the signature of a formal agreement in order to provide for such a contingency. The only advantage was that the fundamentals of military action were established by the convention of 1893-1894. But for this the French paid an inordinate price. Not only were they obliged to send over four billions of dollars in loans to Russia in the period between the conclusion of the alliance and the outbreak of the World War, it being quite clear to the statesmen in Paris

[16] Judet: *Georges Louis* p. 143.

[17] See especially B. Shatzky: La Question de Constantinople et des Détroits (*Revue d'Histoire de la Guerre Mondiale* October 1926, January 1927). Cf. also Poincaré: *Au Service de la France* I, p. 336.

[18] Letter of Georges Louis April 10, 1912 (Judet p. 179). Cf. also G. P. XVIII no. 5916, Bülow to William II October 19, 1903: "Eine russisch-französische Freundschaft ist nur dadurch ermöglicht worden, dass Russland 25 Jahre lang vor den Meerengen Halt gemacht hat.... Die Orientfrage ist der Keil, welcher den Zweibund langsam aber sicher auseinandertreiben wird."

that most of this money would eventually be lost;[19]   not only
were they obliged to assume the unenviable position of supporting the odious Russian autocracy in its struggle with
the liberal movement;[20] but they actually exposed themselves
to additional danger by accepting a formal accord with Russia.
It has already been pointed out in a previous chapter that,
after the conclusion of the general agreement of 1891, the
French position was an extremely precarious one, for there
was no telling whether the Germans might not take advantage of the situation to declare war upon France in order to
break up the threatening coalition before it had actually come
into effect.   In a sense this situation continued in a modified
way even after 1894, because, with the completion of the alliance between France and Russia, the Germans could be certain
that a future war on the continent would be a war on two fronts.
It was merely a question of time when the Germas would revise
their plan of campaign and reorganize their strategy, for clearly
they could not think of attacking Russia first in a future conflict.
Common sense dictated that they should direct the brunt of the
attack against the enemy that was militarily the stronger.   In
other words, it is evident that, as a result of the alliance with
Russia, France would be the first power attacked in any future
struggle with the central powers, and that France would have
to face the first shock, much as though Russia were not in the
conflict at all.   No wonder, then, that the writers of the Margaine report on the alliance in 1918 complain bitterly that the
negotiations were left to the military men and that the purely
political accord of 1891 was allowed to be transformed into a
military convention.   In any case the situation was bad enough:

"The diplomatic agreement established a bond the danger of which was
determined by the vagueness of the terms itself.   It engaged France without
telling her what road was to be followed, and, even if this road led to a

---

[19] See especially M. Margaine: *Rapport sur le Livre Jaune Rélatif à l'Alliance
Franco-Russe* (Chambre des Deputés, Session de 1919, no. 6036), and also Michon
chapter ix.

[20] Michon, chapters vi-viii, has an excellent discussion of this aspect of the
problem.

catastrophe, the military convention would knit closer the bonds the nearer the catastrophe came."[21]

No one appears to have discovered what concrete advantages the alliance brought to France. Added prestige there may have been, and also a certain psychological satisfaction in putting an end to French isolation, but it has been aptly remarked that the one thing worse than isolation is an alliance based upon diverging interests. President Grévy had always taken the stand that if France were to stay quietly at home no one would come to attack her, and Jaurès once reminded his hearers that from 1872 to 1890 France had been able, without humiliation or abdication, to remake her finances and her army, to organize republican liberty and to establish a great colonial empire, and that the alliance which was to save France had come only after it had become clear that France was capable of saving herself.[22] Surely the rising prestige of France after 1890 was as much due to her splendid army and navy as to the alliance with Russia, and surely France made no substantial gains as a result of the agreement with Russia. In all the great crises—Fashoda, Morocco, Agadir, the Balkan Wars—there was no indication of Russian assistance, and the Russian government made it more than clear that France need not hope for support in a question which did not directly interest Russia.

On the other hand the Russian government secured many and varied advantages from the pact. The promise of assistance in a war with the central powers was quite secondary, because, as aforesaid, the intervention of France in such a situation went almost without saying. The Tsar concluded the alliance for very different reasons. In the first place it secured for him the continued financial support of the French money market, without which the Russian government and the whole Tsarist regime would probably have been doomed. In the second place it pro-

---

[21] Margaine report pp. 67, 128 ff. It is interesting to note that even in the crisis of 1886-1888 Bismarck, in contrast to the general staff, advocated the attack of France first, in case of war (E. Heller: Bismarcks Stellung zur Führung des Zweifrontenkrieges, *Archiv für Politik und Geschichte* VII, pp. 677-698, 1926).

[22] Quoted by Michon pp. 11, 53.

vided the Russian government with a free hand in its extra-
European enterprises. Even if the French refused to countenance a Russian advance on the Straits or Constantinople, they
were bound by the letter of the treaty to stand by Russia in case
of an attack by Austria arising from a conflict between the two
old rivals in the Balkans. The sequel was to show that French
aid could be enlisted in such a case even if Russia took the initiative in championing one of the southern Slav states against the
Danubian Monarchy, that is, when Russia really assumed a rôle
of provocation. In 1894 the Tsar probably had no idea of taking
any such road. Since the beginning of the construction of the
Trans-Siberian Railroad, Russian policy had been definitely
shifting to Asia. The Mediterranean coalition of 1887 had
blocked the way in the Near East, and the points of conflict were
the Indian frontier and northern China, where England was the
enemy. Here again the French may have been unwilling to
accord real assistance or military and naval support. But the
alliance with France gave Russia the inestimable advantage of
securing her western frontier while she was engaged in the Far
East. If the Mediterranean coalition of 1887 paralyzed Russian
action against the Ottoman Empire, so did France paralyze any
action against Russia in that region. England alone would not
venture an attempt to force the Straits and attack Russia in the
Black Sea so long as the French squadrons were in her rear at
Toulon. Neither would Germany pursue so insane a policy as
that of supporting England by threatening France. The French
army served the purpose of discouraging the German government from action against Russia and from countenancing an
active anti-Russian policy on the part of Austria. It might almost be said that from 1893 onward the Mediterranean coalition
itself began to fall to pieces. Attempts made to rejuvenate it
were doomed to failure from the start.[23] Only the active participation of Germany could have saved it and such participation
was not to be thought of. The upshot of it all was that Russia
received a free hand to go forward in Asia, relying upon French

[23] See particularly G. P. X, nos. 2538 ff.; XI, nos. 2659 ff.

money and French military and naval forces, leaving France entirely in the lurch in Europe, and finally becoming involved in the conflict with Japan, which left the Russian government face to face with the revolution and the Russian forces in a state of complete disruption.[24] The position of France was never more exposed than it was after 1904. Only the understanding with England served to mitigate the danger somewhat, and even then the British fleet could never save Paris. In the following years further sacrifices were demanded of France in order that the alliance might be saved. The huge loan of 1906, which saved the Russian government, was only the first step. There followed further expenditures for the reorganization of the Russian forces and the construction of the necessary strategic railways and finally Poincaré's extension of the applicability of the alliance by giving Russia practically a free hand in her anti-Austrian policy.

From an alliance based upon divergent interests Germany had little to fear. An attack upon either one of the two allied powers would have resulted in a war on two fronts in any case, even if there had been no agreement between them. It was not until the Franco-Russian Alliance had been extended by the Anglo-French and Anglo-Russian agreements that the situation became dangerous for Germany and only after the advent of Poincaré that it became critical. Speaking in 1908 M. Tardieu pointed out quite rightly that:

"Without much trouble she (Germany) recognized that the conclusion of the Dual Alliance did not constitute an immediate threat." "Germany could put up with the Dual Alliance on condition that it did not escape from her control and turn against her."[25]

A noteworthy article in the *Hamburger Nachrichten*, published on October 30, 1893, made the situation at the time of Toulon perfectly clear. The Franco-Russian Alliance, said the writer,

[24] Tardieu (pp. 17, 18) bitterly bemoans the diversion of the alliance to the east; see also Michon chapter vii.

[25] Tardieu pp. 149, 150.

is the result of Russian suspicion of German intimacy with
England:

"The Triple Alliance as such does not in any way threaten Russia or her
policy and cannot, therefore, provoke her into hostile demonstrations. But
as soon as the suspicion arises that its influence is to be exercised for the
defence of England's anti-Russian interests, Russia's resentment is at once
aroused. If the Russian visit to Toulon and Paris has any political significance, it is directed not against Germany and the Triple Alliance, but
against England and the possibility of the Triple Alliance being made sub-
servient to English interests....England will always shape her action according to her own ideas of what may be most useful to her at the moment
without wasting a single thought on the remembrance of friendly services
asked for and granted in the past....If the ghost of a Franco-Russian Alliance has taken a tangible shape at Toulon and has not been laid at Taranto
and Spezia, there is one very simple way of disarming it, and that way lies
open to German diplomacy. It has only to dispel the impression that Germany no longer observes as in the past strict neutrality between England
and Russia. Once that impression dispelled, *cessante causa, cessat et effectus*,
and the Franco-Russian Alliance will shrink back to the modest proportions
to which it was originally restricted. Our traditional good relations with
England need not be on that account impaired. All we want is to restore
the *status quo ante*."

This article does not appear to have been directly inspired by
Prince Bismarck,[26] but it might just as well have been, for it is
nothing more nor less than a brief formulation of the well-known
Bismarckian policy. From the days of Toulon onward it became
the program of the German government, which was pursued unswervingly for the next decade or more. The *mot d'ordre* was no
longer the alliance with England, but good relations with Russia,
and secondarily with France as well. It does not appear that the
statesmen in Berlin intended by this new departure to work for
an alliance with Russia or to break entirely with England, though
in practice that seemed to be the trend during the next several
years.[27] And after all, it was ever impossible for Germany to
hold an exact balance between Russia and England. Even Bismarck's regime had had its Anglophil-Russophobe as well as its
Russophil-Anglophobe periods. To the Kaiser, disillusioned by

[26] It does not appear in either the collection of Penzler or in that of Hofmann.
I am quoting from the *London Times* October 31, 1893.
[27] See, e. g., G. P. XI, no. 2676.

his attempts to associate England with the Triple Alliance, it was much more important in 1894 to win the favor of Russia and to sap the life of the new Franco-Russian Alliance by the reëstablishment of the old relationship with his eastern neighbor than it was to continue the hopeless task of courting perfidious Albion. Already at that time he appears to have entertained the idea of a coöperative union between Germany, Russia and even France to further their own interests as against those of the English.[28]

The new German policy began with the commercial treaty between Germany and Russia, followed soon after by the betrothal of the Tsarevich Nicholas and the Princess Alexandra of Hesse, which had been engineered by the Kaiser and which he regarded as a victory of the first order.[29] At the same time the new relationship with France had been inaugurated by the Franco-German Kamerun Treaty of March, 1894, reaching its zenith a few months later when Germany and France collaborated in protesting against the treaty concluded between England and the King of the Belgians in regard to the Congo.[29a] The complete success of this move boded well for the future and was followed within a year by the famous intervention against Japan after her war with China. In this manoeuvre the new Tsar, Nicholas II, played the leading rôle, while the Kaiser, who had instigated him, appeared as a powerful second, and France trailed behind as an unwilling and reluctant third. England, in spite of her enormous interest in the Far East, was conspicuously non-participant.[30]

[28] G. P. XI, chapter lxiv, *passim*.

[29] Szögyény to Kálnoky April 22, 28, 1894; Wolkenstein to Kálnoky April 26, 1894.

[29a] Bourgeois and Pagès: *Origines et Responsabilités de la Grande Guerre* pp. 252-255.

[30] The best general account is in Otto Francke: *Die Grossmächte in Ostasien* (Hamburg 1923) pp. 31-105. The German policy is well expressed in Holstein's remarks to Chirol, who had asked why Germany had allowed herself to be dragged in. Holstein replied that Germany had done the dragging: "But, anyhow, we had looked for some time past upon the Far East as the Achilles' heel of the Franco-Russian Alliance and the opportunity was too good a one to be lost of driving in a German wedge between St. Petersburg and Paris. The French disliked it im-

It was apparently this successful action in the Far East, staged by the German foreign office for the avowed purpose of preventing the Franco-Russian Alliance from enjoying a baptism of fire, that inspired Holstein and the Kaiser with the idea of a coalition of the continental *big three*, a *continental combine*, as William himself once called it, which would *ipso facto* have operated to the detriment of England.[31] With Russia there would have been comparatively little difficulty if the Germans had been willing to go the whole way. They had already thrown overboard the Polonophil policy of the Caprivi time, and they had rescinded the vexatious measures taken by Bismarck against Russian securities.[32] Caprivi himself had been sent away, in part because the man who regarded the war on two fronts as inevitable and advocated close coöperation not only with Germany's allies but with England, could no longer guide the ship of state on its new course. Prince Hohenlohe, the Bismarckian, was much more suitable, especially because his advanced age was a sort of guarantee that he would not, like Caprivi, insist upon his own ideas.[33] Beyond that the Germans had begun to give every en-

mensely, but they simply could not afford not to come in" (Chirol in *London Times* December 15, 1922 and his *Fifty Years in a Changing World* [London 1927] p. 191).

[31] G. P. XI, chapter lxiv, *passim*.

[32] The change in the Polish policy of the government is clearly indicated by the Kaiser's famous speech at Thorn on September 22, 1894. The lifting of the prohibition on Russian bonds was Caprivi's suggestion (See G. P. V, pp. 336-337). Wolkenstein to Kálnoky November 7, 1894 reports the profound and very favorable effect produced in Russia by this measure.

[33] The immediate cause for Caprivi's dismissal was disagreement between him and the Kaiser in regard to measures to be taken against the subversive parties (see Ebmayer: Caprivis Entlassung, in *Deutsche Revue* December 1922), but there had been a good deal of intrigue against him on the part of the Junker elements, and with these tactics the straightforward General was quite unable to cope (see Theodor Barth: *Politische Porträts*, Berlin 1904, p. 36, and Kálnoky to Szögyény November 14, 1894; Haller: *Eulenburg* pp. 145 ff.). Behind all this there was disagreement in matters of foreign policy. Caprivi was anxious to prevent the Congo dispute from assuming larger proportions and was opposed to magnifying the Samoa conflict (Szögyény to Kálnoky May 12, July 7, 1894) and had no use for the Kaiser's naval schemes, which developed as soon as the Anglophil phase of German policy came to an end (Friedjung I, p. 148; Eckardstein I, p. 130; Caprivi's letter to Schneidewin February 22, 1896 in *Deutsche Revue* 1922, p. 250). Finally

couragement to the Russian designs in the Far East, had promised
to observe a benevolently neutral attitude and act as a rear guard
in case Russia should become involved in complications or conflicts in the east, and had abstained from raising the suspicion
that they would ever oppose Russia's aspirations in the Near
East.[34]

With France, of course, the case was different, and it may be
doubted whether anyone but the Kaiser ever thought the Ger-
man-Franco-Russian combine a practical possibility. Hanotaux
and President Faure may have toyed with the idea at times, but
not very seriously.[35] Nevertheless it is worth noting that there
was a steady falling-off in the revenge sentiment during the last
years of the dying century.[36] The position of Germany, while pursuing the policy of the free hand, was never stronger. In Berlin
it was said that the Franco-Russian Alliance was a positive advantage for Germany, for by it Russia held France in check.[37]
Besides, the French, left to be humiliated at Fashoda and unable

the personal relations between the chancellor and the Emperor had become rather
acrimonious. The Kaiser complained of Caprivi's obstinacy and schoolmastering
way (Szögyény to Kálnoky November 24, 1894; Waldersee II, p. 329) and Caprivi
himself admitted that perhaps he had been too outspoken and insistent in maintaining his views (Szögyény to Kálnoky November 10, 1894). Certainly the traditional characterization of Caprivi as a mere clerk carrying out the Kaiser's will
is about as far from the truth as one can get.

[34] See the writer's article on the origins of the Russo-Japanese War in *Europäische Gespräche* June 1926.

[35] It is said that the Kaiser approached Obruchev at the manoeuvres in 1896
and 1897 and that the latter mentioned the project to President Faure, who thought
it worth studying (Kuropatkin Diary, in *Krasny Arkhiv* II, p. 10).

[36] There is much evidence on this point in the relevant volumes of the *Grosse
Politik*. See also the admirable discussion in Theodor Wolff: *Das Vorspiel* (Munich
1924) *passim*.

[37] Wolff p. 14. Millerand, in a speech in the chamber February 5, 1898, asked
the question whether France had not concluded a fool's bargain: "Est-ce que par
hasard le résultat le plus immédiat et le plus clair de cette alliance ne serait pas
simplement, en dégageant de toute inquiétude la grande puissance qui est votre
voisine, de lui laisser les mains libres partout ailleurs?" (Quoted in the Margaine
report p. 60). Clemenceau even went so far as to say that Russia would approve of
an understanding between Germany and France along colonial lines because the
Franco-Russian Alliance had been intended by the Russians as the prelude to a
Franco-German rapprochement on the basis of the *status quo* (Clemenceau in
Aurore November 4, 1899, quoted by Wolff p. 124).

to prevent the deflection of Russia from Europe to the Far East, were of little account so long as the Dreyfus scandal and the problem of church and state kept the country in uproar. "The Dual Alliance had no more life than a stuffed tailor's dummy," says one of the keenest observers of French affairs.[38]   In the famous Björkö Treaty of 1905 the Kaiser's ideas came nearest to fruition, but the whole move came too late.   France had already found a friend in England and had once more become estranged from Germany by the aggressive Moroccan policy of Holstein. Russia, on the other hand, had been defeated and was in the throes of revolution, quite unable to risk losing the alliance with France entirely.   It is interesting to note, however, that the French were actually approached with the suggestion that they join the projected combine.[39]

The days of the Boer War and the Russian invitations to intervene would have been much more appropriate for the realization of the Kaiser's scheme, but the fact of the matter was that he never could bring himself to take the necessary final step in antagonizing England.   The policy of the free hand and the two irons in the fire was good enough if not driven to extremes.   The Germans so overdid it that they drove both sides to desperation, with the result that before long they were themselves being encircled.   Nothing came of the projected combine of the continental nations, but it must be remembered that it was still possible for Germany and Russia to get along.   In 1908 there would have been no opposition to Izvolski's Straits scheme in Berlin.[40] Even the so-called German ultimatum to Russia of March, 1909 appears to have been meant in good faith, as a golden bridge built for the Russian retreat.   In 1910 came the Potsdam Agreement, which threatened for a time to throw the whole Triple Entente out of gear.   And so it went right down to the time of the World War.   Antagonisms there were, of course, between

[38] Wolff p. 14.

[39] See the documents published in the *Krasny Arkhiv* V, pp. 5-49 (1924) A. Savinsky: *Recollections of a Russian Diplomat* (London 1927) pp. 119-123.

[40] See the writer's article: Russia, the Straits Question and the European Powers 1904-1908, in the *English Historical Review*, January 1929.

Germany and Russia, but the same could be said of any two European powers at the time, even those that were allied to each other. The antagonisms could probably all have been ironed out by compromise had it not been for the unfortunate development of the conflict between Russia and Austria which eventually led to the cataclysm. As we look back from our point of vantage it seems incredible that Russia should ever have taken the field against Germany excepting possibly to defend France from an unprovoked attack, which probably would never have taken place. When the Franco-Russian Alliance did finally function, it was in a conflict between Russia and Austria-Hungary.

While the decade following the Toulon demonstrations was the most brilliant and successful period of Wilhelminian diplomacy, it was the most critical period in the history of modern England's international relations.[40a] Lord Rosebery and his associates at the foreign office appreciated the implications of the Franco-Russian fraternization from the very start, and their insistence on taking the necessary precautions led to the resignation of Gladstone. Under Rosebery's leadership the effort was made to secure England's international position by enlisting the aid of the Triple Alliance, but, as shown in the last chapter, the German attitude had changed, and the men in the Wilhelmstrasse were more determined than ever not to allow themselves to be made the catspaw of the English. Not only did they advertise and parade their new friendship with Russia, but they concluded with France the Kamerun Treaty which threw open to England's rival the road to the Sudan. The agreement signed by England and the King of the Belgians in May, by which the whole of Lado and the greater part of Bahr-el-Ghazal were to be leased to the Congo Free State, was nothing more nor less than a desperate attempt on the part of the English government to block the French advance.[41] The great error made by the men at Downing Street was in trying to kill two birds with one stone by leasing

---

[40a] Cf. Harcourt's letter to Kimberley November 16, 1894: "We have never been so destitute of friends or so 'mal vus' by the Powers." (Gardiner: *Life of Harcourt* II, p. 324).

[41] See Gardiner: *Life of Sir William Harcourt* II, pp. 313 ff.

from the Congo a strip of territory twenty-five kilometers in width running from Lake Albert Edward to Lake Tanganyika. In 1890 the Germans had refused to cede such a strip, which the English desired in order to connect their possessions in Egypt with those in central and south Africa. The effort made in 1894 to realize the old scheme was badly timed, for it brought the Germans upon the scene and led to the famous protests of Germany and France.[42]

The vigor and acerbity of the German stand in the Congo affair was a revelation to the English.[43] It threw a lurid light upon the new situation and the reorientation of the powers, while the Germans mercilessly drove home their advantage by withdrawing support of the English policy in Egypt and by initiating the long drawn out agitation about the Samoan settlement.[44] Before long they opened up connections with the Transvaal and embarked upon the road that was to lead to the Kruger despatch and the crisis of 1896.[45] What were the English to do under the circumstances? There was no knowing at what moment the Russians might launch an attack upon the Bosporus or Constantinople. Not a few influential English politicians were in favor of abandoning the Turkish capital to the enemy and even leaving the Mediterranean before it was too late.[46] The

[42] See G. P. VIII, nos. 2022 ff.; *Accounts and Papers 1894*, volume LVII, Africa no. 4 (C-7360), with an excellent map; volume XCVI, Africa no. 5 (C-7390); Bourgeois and Pagès: *Origines et Responsabilités de la Grande Guerre* pp. 245-248; Sir J. Rennell Rodd: *Social and Diplomatic Memoirs*, volume I, pp. 345-348; Grey: *Twenty-Five Years* I, p. 22; Gardiner: *Life of Harcourt* II, pp. 313 ff. The English always claimed that article III, providing for the lease of the strip of territory by the Congo Free State was really only an inadvertence, but it appears from Rodd's memoirs that the whole matter had been carefully planned.

[43] Deym to Kálnoky June 28, 1894.

[44] G. P. VIII, nos. 1847 ff.; 2024 ff. Rosebery and Kimberley complained to the Austrian ambassador that in Cairo the German agent was more French than the French (Deym to Kálnoky July 12, November 1, 1894).

[45] G. P. XI, chapter lxiii; in the autumn of 1894 the German government coöperated with the Transvaal government with a view to checking possible action by the Cape government in the matter of a rising in the Delagoa Bay district (Velics to Kálnoky October 26, 1894; Deym to Kálnoky November 1, 30, 1894).

[46] The whole circle about Lord Randolph Churchill took this view. See the discussion of the advisability of evacuating the Mediterranean in the *Nineteenth Century* February, March, April and May, 1895.

British naval manoeuvres of 1894 were based entirely upon the problem of Mediterranean strategy and showed conclusively that in the event of war the British Channel squadron would be unable to come to the assistance of the inferior Mediterranean fleet. What happened in the manoeuvres was that the commander of the enemy fleet based on Toulon immediately made for Gibraltar, effected a junction with the Brest squadron, then defeated the inferior British Channel fleet as it was hurrying to reinforce the Mediterranean squadron. After that it was an easy matter to dispose of the British forces in the Mediterranean itself.[47] Under the circumstances nothing much was to be hoped from the aid of Italy or Austria. Unless Germany were willing to assist in keeping France in check, the English position in case of a conflict would be well-nigh desperate.

There was only one faint hope, from which Rosebery and his friends drew what consolation they could. Could it be possible, they argued, that France should throw over her traditional Near Eastern policy and aid the Russians in dealing a deathblow to the Ottoman Empire? It seemed incredible that this should happen, although Kálnoky argued that the French statesmen and people were so intoxicated by the Toulon festivities that they had lost, at least for the time being, all sense of proportion and all appreciation of their own interests, and Hatzfeldt argued that, after all, Russia would be in a position to offer France substantial compensation, in Syria, in Egypt and possibly in Tripoli, to say nothing of the advantages of naval supremacy in the Mediterranean.[48] Nevertheless, Rosebery decided to bide his time. He hoped that his friend, Sir Philip Currie, would retrieve the British position at Constantinople, but as a matter of fact Currie showed himself quite unequal to the task. With the coming of the Armenian massacres the British influence at the Porte fell lower and lower, and during the last years of the century the English ambassador was of no account at all in the Sul-

---

[47] See the admirable study by W. L. Clowes: The Naval Manoeuvres, in the *Nineteenth Century* September 1894.

[48] G. P. IX, nos. 2142, 2143, 2145.

tan's calculations.[49]   At the same time Lord Rosebery made desperate efforts to break down the new Franco-Russian Alliance by buying off one or the other of the members.   After the Congo conflict approaches were made to France, which, however, ended in egregious failure.[50]   The French saw no advantage whatsoever in making concessions to the English at a time when the English position was exceptionally weak.   On the contrary, they were already laying plans for the advance to the Nile which was to end in the Fashoda crisis.   The idea of an entente with France having failed, the English turned to their even more uncompromising enemy, Russia.   The negotiations regarding the Pamirs, which had dragged on half-heartedly for years, were pushed ahead vigorously and resulted in an agreement in November, 1894, because the English gave way to the Russian demands on almost every point.   At the very same time Alexander III died, thus giving the English government a further opportunity to display sympathy and good will.   The Prince of Wales was sent to represent the Queen at the funeral and stayed in Russia for weeks, acting as an unofficial "ambassador extraordinary," as the London *Times* put it.   Rosebery himself, at the Lord Mayor's banquet on November 9, 1894, pointed out that in the Far Eastern crisis England and Russia had proceeded hand in hand and that the relations between the two countries had never been "more hearty."   The recent Pamir settlement, he went on, had removed almost the last obstacle to friendly coöperation.[51]

As a result of this famous utterance the European press was full of rumors of an impending Anglo-Russian entente.   Kálnoky was greatly exercised and did his utmost to smooth out the differences between London and Berlin in an effort to restore the old friendly relations between England and the Triple Alliance.   But in Berlin the whole thing was looked upon as a

[49] See Sir Vincent Corbett: *Reminiscences* pp. 207 ff.

[50] Barclay: *Thirty Years* pp. 123-124; G. P. VIII, nos. 1766, 1769.

[51] *London Times* December 6, 1894. See also Lee: *Edward VII* volume I, pp. 688 ff.; Pallavicini to Kálnoky December 15, 1894; G. P. IX, nos. 2161 ff., from which it appears that in the Anglo-Russian pourparlers even the Straits question was touched upon.

hoax, designed to drive a wedge into the new Russo-German friendship.[52] In a sense the German statesmen were right. The antagonism between Russia and England was well-nigh insuperable, and an agreement would have been possible only at the expense of great sacrifices, which neither side could afford to make. It was not long before Russia went her own way in the Far Eastern question, refused English proposals for intervention in favor of China, and finally settled the question to her own liking, leaving England out of account and relying upon her new ally, France, and her new friend, Germany. After the intervention at Shimonoseki the English position in the Far East was hardly better than it was in the Near East.

In the spring of 1895 the Rosebery government fell from power and was succeeded by the last Salisbury cabinet. If anyone had been able to save the British situation Lord Salisbury, with his great prestige, would have been the man. But his efforts, too, were to prove futile. One of his first moves was to retrieve the old relationship with Germany if possible and at the same time to clarify the situation in the Near East. His proposals for the partition of the Turkish Empire in Europe in the summer of 1895 were designed for this purpose, but he too met with grievous disappointment.[53] The Germans, secure while holding

---

[52] Szögyény to Kálnoky December 8, 1894. Kálnoky called the attention of the Germans to the danger of an Anglo-Russian agreement (Kálnoky to Szögyény November 30, 1894, four despatches). Apparently rather heated discussions took place between Hatzfeldt and Rosebery and Kimberley. Rosebery told Deym that, if Germany meant to change her policy and effect a rapprochement with Russia and France, England would also have to change her course, even if this involved the abandonment of Egypt and the Mediterranean (Deym to Kálnoky November 30, 1894, two despatches). Kálnoky then spoke to Eulenburg in no uncertain terms, accusing Germany of "systematic provocation" of England (Kálnoky to Deym December 1, 1894), but Eulenburg insisted that the Kaiser, though offended at England, had no intention of changing his policy (Kálnoky to Deym December 4, 1894, no. 3). At the same time the English ambassador to Berlin was instructed to inform the German government that the British cabinet had no intention of deserting the Triple Alliance or changing its policy (Szögyény to Kálnoky December 8, 1894). He carried out his instructions on December 14, and on this occasion a general peace was concluded (Szögyény to Kálnoky December 15, 17, 22, 1894; see also the documents in G. P. IX, nos. 2167 ff.).

[53] See G. P. X, chapter lx *passim*.

the balance between England on the one hand and the Franco-
Russian Alliance on the other, had no mind to compromise
their position. Salisbury, like his predecessor, was obliged to
see the English influence sink lower and lower at Constantinople,
and before long he appears to have considered a complete capitulation. At any rate he talked of abandoning the Straits and
Constantinople to the Russians, evidently in the hope of checking
the Russian advance in the Far East, with which England was
quite unable to cope.[54] But the Russian advance continued uninterruptedly, supported by the Germans. The taking of Port
Arthur in the spring of 1898 was a severe blow at the English
position, for which the leasing of Wei-Hai-Wei was but little
consolation. Once again the English considered an agreement
with the Russians, and in the settlement as proposed by Lord
Salisbury the English suggested their willingness to abandon
that portion of Turkey which drains into the Black Sea, together
with the drainage valley of the Euphrates as far as Bagdad. But
even these far-reaching concessions were rejected by the Russians
and no progress was made.[55]

Few ministers have been confronted with a situation so fraught
with danger as that with which Lord Salisbury was obliged to
contend. He was not a timid man, nor one who would become
nervous and panicky. On two occasions he spoke out and by
sheer exhibition of grit and courage won resounding victories for
England. The first occasion was in 1896 when he practically
scared the Germans into an apology in the matter of the Kruger
telegram, thereby preventing the exuberance of the Germans from
going too far. The second occasion was in 1898 when he forced
the retreat of the French in the Fashoda crisis. In both instances
he no doubt reckoned on the unwillingness of the Germans to
commit themselves completely to the Russian side, and on the
unwillingness to the Russians to support the French in a matter
which did not concern them directly. But after all, both these

---

[54] See G. P. X, nos. 2381, 2387, 2392, 2463, 2573; XI, no. 2664; XII, nos. 2918,
2919; XVIII, nos. 5640, 5642; and the article by W. N. Medlicott: Lord Salisbury
and Turkey, in *History* October 1927.

[55] *British Documents on the Origins of the War* I, nos. 5 ff.

victories were essentially of a negative character. One result of the Kruger incident was the hastening of the German naval program, which, in the future, was to embitter Anglo-German relations more than ever. One result of the Fashoda crisis was that the French put hostility to England over and above everything else in foreign affairs. During the Boer War England was constantly exposed to the danger of intervention on the part of the Russians and French. What saved the English was the hesitation of the Germans. They had never intended to go the whole way in antagonizing England, but were interested chiefly in making capital of the English difficulties. They rejected the Russian suggestions for intervention, but at the same time they turned their backs upon the repeated efforts made by the English to establish an alliance. The result was that the English had to pay. They could not stop the Russian advance in Tibet, much less the Russian advance in Manchuria after the Boxer rebellion. As for the Germans, they extracted concessions in the Samoan settlement as in the matter of the Portuguese colonies, to say nothing of the Bagdad Railway. The British experience in these years was indeed an unenviable one.[56]

There is no need for continuing this review of the evolution of England's international position in detail, but it should be noted that the change for the better, which came after the decisive phase of the Boer war, coincided almost exactly with the period of greatest weakness of the Franco-Russian Alliance. The French government, in the hands of men like Combes, disillusioned by the experiences of the Dreyfus period, wrapped up in great questions of domestic politics and at the same time disgusted with the attitude of the Russians in the days of Fashoda and with the diversion of the alliance to the Far East, had gotten over the sentimental "honeymoon" stage, as one writer aptly

[56] The history of Anglo-German relations in this period is well treated by Brandenburg: *Von Bismarck zum Weltkriege*, and by Meinecke: *Geschichte des deutsch-englischen Bündnisproblems, 1890-1901* (Berlin 1927); cf. also the impressive memorandum of Sir Eyre Crowe, January 1, 1907 (*British Documents III*, pp. 397 ff.), especially p. 416: "....The action of Germany towards this country since 1890 might be likened not inappropriately to that of a professional blackmailer....."

calls it. Delcassé himself, who in 1887 had had the greatest
hopes for a Franco-Russian Alliance, now declared that he would
have preferred an alliance with England to an alliance with
Russia and expressed the hope that eventually a triple agreement between England, France and Russia would become possible.[57] The initiative in the negotiations with England for the
settlement of 1904 came from him, but there can be no doubt
that the English statesmen, successors of Lord Salisbury, welcomed the French advances. In any case they made great
sacrifices in order to effect the agreement, thereby removing the
hostility of at least one member of the troublesome coalition.
They had already succeeded in enlisting the aid of Japan against
the Russian menace in the Far East. Now the entente with
France practically removed the danger of French intervention
in favor of Russia and in that way spared England the necessity
of participating in the conflict.

But even then the British position was far from favorable, for
the entente with France obliged the English to come out much
more strongly than they would have wished in the Moroccan
crisis and thereby inaugurated the period a tension in Anglo-
German relations. Not only that. The entente with France
could never be satisfactory so long as England and Russia were
still enemies. Delcassé had seen that and had worked consistently to effect an agreement.[58] After Russia's defeat by Japan one
of the greatest obstacles, conflicting interests in the Far East,
had been gotten out of the way, and the Russian statesmen
themselves were more favorably inclined. When the agreement
was finally consummated in 1907, however, it was anything but
complete. The fundamental problem of the Near East was not
touched upon, though Sir Edward Grey realized that sooner
or later it would have to be faced and that England would be
obliged to make concessions of a far-reaching nature.[59]

[57] Michon p. 9; *British Documents* I, nos. 198, 262.

[58] Cf., among others, Sazonov p. 23.

[59] The question of the Near East was touched upon during the negotiations,
but was not pursued. See Grey I, pp. 155 ff., 179; G. P. XXII, no. 7383; XXVI,
nos. 9005, 9075.

And then, a review of the history of the Anglo-Russian Entente from 1907 to 1914 will show that it was an unedifying relationship. The Russian government was one which almost defied control. Like France, England was not consulted beforehand when Izvolski bargained with Aehrenthal at Buchlau. Like France, England was not let into the secret of the Balkan League before it was too late to do anything about it. Instead, there was constant friction in connection with the Persian question, which was supposedly settled by the terms of the 1907 agreement. In the end it turned out that the entente with Russia was as costly or more costly for England than the entente with France. The latter involved England more and more in the rivalries and antagonisms of the continent, and out of the Moroccan crises grew obligations which, even though they were only moral, were none the less binding. The former dragged England further and further along the Balkan road, and in the end England, like France, entered a conflict over a question in which she had no direct interest.

The Franco-Russian Alliance had made England's traditional policy of isolation an impossible one and had given control of the balance of power into the hands of Germany. In a sense Germany retained this control clear down to the outbreak of the World War. She bargained with Russia in the Potsdam Agreements and with England in the agreements on the Portuguese colonies and the Bagdad Railway in 1914. But in the twenty years between the conclusion of the Franco-Russian Alliance and the catastrophe of 1914 the German position was never handled with real statesmanship. With Bismarck international politics were a sort of chess game, requiring infinite patience, sound judgment, farsightedness, and a sure touch. With his successors the game assumed more the character of bowling, as one German writer has aptly remarked. The policy of the two irons in the fire was hopelessly overdone, and both sides were exploited in merciless fashion. When Germany in 1914 gave Austria a blank check it was merely the crowning error in a long series of bad and unfortunate blunders, the first of which was the nonrenewal of the Reinsurance Treaty. Certainly the relationship with England could have been handled more adroitly. An actual treaty of alliance would not even have been necessary, for it was to England's own interest to stand by the side of the Triple Alliance and to defend the *status quo* as she had done in Bismarck's time. As it was, German policy almost drove the English into the agreements with France and Russia, both of them powers interested in upsetting the *status quo* in Europe and therefore rather dangerous company for a country like England. Had the Germans utilized their great advantages more skillfully they would never have felt obliged to give their last ally a free hand in 1914 and thus involve themselves in a Balkan conflict. In the same way England would have been able to avoid an association which, in the last count, left the decision of war or peace in the hands of the Russians and in the end resulted in the cataclysm.

This brief review of the developments of the international situation after 1894 does not pretend to be a survey of all the factors which entered into the problem of European alignments. The question of Franco-Italian relations and the evolution of Austro-Russian rivalry in the Near East has not been considered, nor has the distinctly Anglo-German problem of naval armaments been touched upon. In the preceding chapters an attempt has been made to show how the Franco-Russian Alliance evolved in the years 1890-1894 and to set forth the circumstances and motives which made possible so anomalous and ill-fated an accord. The evidence adduced should show conclusively that France was the soliciting party and that Russia, deprived of the reinsurance given her by the treaty of 1887 with Germany, finally yielded to the importunities of the French, not with the idea of immediate or even eventual hostility to Germany, but solely with the thought of obliging Germany to maintain the neutrality which had been freely offered in the treaty of 1887. For Russia this neutrality was the *sine qua non* for all action abroad, either in the Near or the Far East. In this last chapter a mere glance has been cast at the succeeding events, which, it appears to the writer, may be taken as unanswerable evidence that the alliance was from start to finish a Russian instrument which operated to Russia's advantage almost exclusively. No attempt was ever made to use it against Germany or even to use it to intimidate Germany. Its effect was essentially what the Russian government intended it should be; that is, it made really close coöperation between England and the Triple Alliance more difficult than it had ever been, it obliged Germany to maintain at least a policy of benevolent neutrality towards Russia, it gave Russia a free hand in the Far East, and it finally pressed England into the agreement with Russia, with the result that in 1914 England could be enlisted in support of Slavic designs against Austria in the Near East.

BIBLIOGRAPHY

OFFICIAL

Austria-Hungary. Extensive use has been made throughout of the correspondence of the Austrian foreign office during the years 1890-1895. Of this correspondence the reports from St. Petersburg, Berlin and Rome were found most useful, as the representatives of the Dual Monarchy in these capitals were all men of considerable ability and influence. Count Wolkenstein, the ambassador to St. Petersburg, was a personal friend of Kálnoky, had excellent connections in Berlin and was well liked in St. Petersburg, where he was known as an ardent advocate of good relations between Russia and Austria. When absent from his post his place was taken by the chargé d'affaires, Freiherr von Aehrenthal, later Austrian foreign minister. Aehrenthal, even at this time, showed by his reports that he was a man of exceptional ability, and both Wolkenstien and Kálnoky appear to have attached considerable value to his opinions. Count Széchényi, the ambassador to Berlin in the first years of the period, was not an outstanding personality, but was on terms of close friendship with Marschall and reported faithfully to his government. His successor, Count Szögyény, won the favor of the Kaiser almost from the start. His reports are penetrating and very informative. The ambassador to Rome, Baron Bruck, was a diplomat of average ability, who succeeded in keeping well-posted and in sending to his chief reports of considerable interest. The Austrian representatives at London and Paris were hardly of average calibre. Count Deym, at London, appears to have had few connections during the Salisbury period, though he was on good terms with Hatzfeldt and later on apparently enjoyed the confidence of the liberal cabinet. Hoyos, in Paris, confined himself almost entirely to reports on domestic developments. His despatches were least helpful in this study of the period.

France. Ministère des Affaires Étrangères. *Documents Diplomatiques. Affaires–d'Égypte*, 1884-1893. Paris, 1893.

France. Ministère des Affaires Étrangères. *Documents Diplomatiques. Affaires de Siam*, 1893-1902. Paris, 1902.

France. *L'Alliance Franco-Russe. Troisième Livre Jaune Français*. Paris, 1918. Cited as L. J. This is the only official collection dealing directly with the alliance. It is obviously very incomplete and must be read in connection with other available material.

France. *Rapport sur le Livre Jaune rélatif à l'Alliance Franco-Russe*. By M. Margaine *et al.* (Annexe au procès-verbal de la Séance du 18 avril 1919. Chambre des Députés, 11 ième législature, session de 1919, no. 6036, Paris, 1919). This report is of considerable value. It was the outcome of numerous interpellations addressed to the government after the publication of the *Yellow Book*. The socialists bitterly accused the government of having made a disastrous agreement without consulting the chamber, and this argument lies at the botton of the present report. The Margaine committee reviewed the whole *Yellow Book* and adduced statistics and other information to show that at the time when the alliance was concluded the French government was fully aware of the wretched condition of the Russian finances, but nevertheless persuaded the French people to invest their money, while allowing the military men to conclude an agreement which in many respects was to prove dangerous rather than salutary.

GERMANY. *Die Grosse Politik der Europäischen Kabinette, 1871-1914.* Edited by Johannes Lepsius, Albrecht Mendelssohn Bartholdy and Friedrich Thimme. Berlin, 1922-1927. Cited as G. P. The great German publication of documents, indispensable for the study of any phase of pre-war diplomacy, and without doubt the most important single source. The volumes dealing with the period under consideration are VII to IX, but the earlier and later volumes have been freely drawn upon when necessary.

GREAT BRITAIN. *Parliamentary Papers. Further Correspondence respecting Affairs in the East.* Turkey no. 2 (1891) Command 6259. Turkey no. 3 (1891) Command 6319. Turkey no. 6 (1891) Command 4393.

GREAT BRITAIN. *Parliamentary Papers. Further Correspondence respecting the Affairs of Egypt.* Egypt no. 1 (1893) Command 6849. Egypt no. 2 (1893) Command 6956.

GREAT BRITAIN. *Parliamentary Papers. Correspondence respecting the Affairs of Siam 1887-1894.* Siam no. 1 (1894) Command 7395.

GREAT BRITAIN. *British Documents on the Origins of the War 1898-1914.* Edited by G. P. Gooch and Harold Temperley. London, 1927 *et seq.* Volumes I and II of the British collection of material on the origins of the war, containing a few papers of interest in connection with the earlier period.

UNOFFICIAL

No attempt is made to classify the material as source or secondary, in view of the fact that so many of the works referred to are inspired or otherwise particularly well-informed, frequently only in respect to some special point. No reference is made to works quoted only once or twice, as this would enlarge the bibliography to unreasonable proportions. In such cases the full reference will be found in the footnotes. Contemporary periodical articles are not listed excepting in special cases where they have some historical approach. Full references may be found in the footnotes.

Adam, Juliette. *Guillaume II, 1890-1899.* Paris, 1917. A selection of the writer's letters on foreign policy, published regularly biweekly in the *Nouvelle Revue.*

Albers, Martin O. *Het Ontslag van Bismarck.* Haarlem, 1926. A dissertation dealing with Bismarck's fall.

Albin, Pierre. *La Paix Armée. L'Allemagne et la France en Europe, 1885-1894.* Paris, 1913. Though written before the appearance of the important source material, Albin's book is still one of the best treatments of the period, thoroughly done and remarkably impartial. Some use was made of the reports of the French ambassador to Berlin.

(Amadori-Vergili, G.). *La Politica Estera Italiana, 1875-1916.* By Un Italiano. Bitonto, 1916. An enormous exhaustive treatment, written from an extreme Crispian standpoint, but not original or suggestive.

Ambrosini, G. *L'Italia nel Mediterraneo.* Foligno. 1927.

Andrássy, Count Julius. *Bismarck, Andrássy and their Successors.* Boston and New York, 1927. A brilliant but poorly balanced survey of the period to about 1905. The writer is particularly harsh in his treatment of Kálnoky.

Ashley, Percy. *Modern Tariff History.* New Third Edition. New York, 1926.

Bächtold, Hermann. Der einheitliche Zusammenhang der modernen Weltpolitik. *Weltwirtschaftliches Archiv* volume XVI, pp. 459-472, April, 1921. One of the most suggestive essays on pre-war international relations.

Ballod, C. Die deutsch-russischen Handelsbeziehungen. *Schriften des Vereins für Sozialpolitik, volume* XC, part 4, 1900.

Bastgen, Hubert. *Die römische Frage.* Three volumes. Freiburg, 1919. A great collection of material bearing on the problem.

Baunard, Louis. *Le Cardinal Lavigerie.* Two volumes. Paris, 1912. The standard biography, based in part on unpublished material.

Baunard, Louis. *Léon XIII et le Toast d'Alger. Souvenirs et Documents de Deux Audiences Pontificales Intimes,* 24 et 26 avril, 1896. Paris, 1914. The Pope's own account of the circumstances attending the famous toast.

Beaman, A. Hulme. *Stambuloff.* London, 1895.

Becker, Otto. *Bismarck und die Einkreisung Deutschlands.* Part I. *Bismarcks Bündnispolitik* Berlin, 1923. Part II. *Das französisch-russische Bündnis.* (Berlin, 1925). These two volumes constitute about the best single account of the Bismarckian system and the policies of the New Course after 1890. The subject is approached from the standpoint of German policy and the views of the writer are distinctly Bismarckian. But the treatment throughout is scholarly and impartial, revealing an unusual grasp of the problem and exceptional penetration in suggesting solutions. In the second part some use has been made of material from the Austrian archives.

Benoist, Charles. *La Question Méditerranéenne.* Paris, 1928.

Beresford, Admiral Lord Charles. *Memoirs.* Two volumes. London, 1914. Of some value in connection with England's naval policy.

Bernhard, Ludwig. *Die Polenfrage, Der Nationalitätenkampf der Polen in Preussen.* Third Edition. Leipzig, 1920.

Biermer, M. *Die deutsche Handelspolitik des neunzehnten Jahrhunderts.* Second edition. Greifswald, 1899.

Billot, Albert. *La France et l'Italie. Histoire des Années Troublées,* 1881-1899. Two volumes. Paris, 1905. The reminiscences of the French ambassador to Rome. There is nothing in the way of revelation, the account being thoroughly systematic and conventional.

Bismarck, Otto Fürst von. *Gedanken und Erinnerungen.* Stuttgart, 1898-1921. Three volumes. English translation of volumes I and II under the title: *Bismarck, the Man and the Statesman,* London and New York, 1899. English edition of volume III entitled *New Chapters of Bismarck's Autobiography.* London, 1921; American edition entitled *The Kaiser vs. Bismarck.* New York, 1921. Volume III is of prime importance for the study of the period from the accession of William II to the fall of the great chancellor.

Blunt, Wilfrid Scawen. *My Diaries.* Two volumes. London, 1919-1920. Of interest in connection with Egyptian affairs.

Boguslawski, A. von. *85 Jahre preussischer Regierungspolitik in Posen und Westpreussen von 1815 bis 1900.* Berlin, 1901.

Bonjean, Jules. Le Mouvement Catholique et la Politique Générale. *Nouvelle Revue* October 15, 1891, pp. 673-690. An important essay by the leader of the Association Catholique Française.

Bornhak, Conrad. *Deutsche Geschichte unter Kaiser Wilhelm II.* Leipzig and Erlangen, 1921.

Bornhak, Conrad. Das Rätsel der Nichterneuerung des Rückversicherungsvertrages. *Archiv für Politik und Geschichte* volume II, pp. 570-582, 1924. An admirable treatment of the nonrenewal of the Reinsurance Treaty.

Bourgeois, Émile. *Manuel Historique de Politique Etrangère.* Volume IV. *La Politique Mondiale* 1878-1919. Paris, 1926.

Bourgeois, Émile, and Pagès, Georges. *Les Origines et les Responsabilités de la Grande Guerre.* Paris, 1921. Contains much unpublished material from the French archives, but passes over this period very lightly.

Bousquet, Georges. *Histoire du Peuple Bulgare.* Paris, 1909.

Brandenburg, Erich. *Von Bismarck zum Weltkriege.* Second Edition. Berlin, 1925. English translation entitled: *From Bismarck to the World War.* London and New York, 1927. The authoritative history of German foreign policy, but treats this period rather briefly.

Brassey, Lord T. A. *The Naval Annual.* Portsmouth, 1886, 1890 et seq. Indispensable for a study of naval armaments and policies.

Caprivi, Graf Leo von. *Reden im deutschen Reichstage, preussischen Landtage und bei besonderen Anlässen,* 1883-1893. Edited by R. Arndt. Berlin, 1894.

Cardella, G. P. Crispi e la Politica Mediterranea e Coloniale. *Politica* volume X, pp. 150-180, 387-432, April and June 1928.

Charmatz, Richard. *Geschichte der auswärtigen Politik Oesterrichs im 19 ten Jahrhundert.* Second edition. Leipzig and Berlin, 1918. Brief popular survey.

Cheyssac, Léon de. *Une Page d'Histoire Politique. Le Ralliement.* Second Edition. Paris, 1906.

Chiala, Luigi. *Pagine di Storia Contemporanea.* Volume III. *La Triplice e la Duplice Alleanza* 1881-1897. Second Edition. Turin, 1898. Still the best general treatment of Italian foreign policy.

Cilibrizzi, Saverio. *Storia Parlamentare, Politica e Diplomatica d'Italia da Novara a Vittorio Veneto.* Three volumes. Milan, Rome, Naples, 1925. An exhaustive systematic history, rather inadequate on diplomatic questions.

Claar, Maximilian. Italien, der päpstliche Stuhl und die Lösung der römischen Frage. *Zeitschrift für Politik* volume IX, pp. 321-370, 1916. Surveys the problem from 1870 to the world war.

Clowes, Sir William Laird. *The Royal Navy.* Volume VII. Boston, 1903. The official history of the British Navy.

Coates, Thomas F. G. *Lord Rosebery, his Life and Speeches.* Two volumes. London, 1900.

Corbett, Sir Vincent. *Reminiscences, Autobiographical and Diplomatic.* London, 1927.

Corti, Count Egon C. *Alexander von Battenberg. Sein Kampf mit den Zaren und Bismarck.* Vienna, 1920. Based on the papers of the Prince and on material in the Austrian archives. A very important contribution to the history of the Near East in the later 'eighties and of great value for the study of Bismarck's policy.

(Crispi, Francesco). Italy and France. *Contemporary Review* volume LIX, June 1891.

Crispi, Francesco. Italy, France and the Papacy. *Contemporary Review* volume LX, August 1891.

Crispi, Francesco. *Politica Estera. Memorie e documenti raccolti e ordinati da T. Palamenghi-Crispi.* Milan, 1912. English translation entitled: *Memoirs of Francesco Crispi.* New York and London, 1912-1914. Three volumes. Consists largely of material from the Crispi archives, presented with running comment by the former premier's nephew. One of the most important sources for the history of Italian foreign policy.

Crispi, Francesco. *Politica Interna. Diario e Documenti.* Edited by T. Palamenghi-Crispi. Milan, 1924. Contains important material on the problem of Italy's relation to the Papacy.

Crispi, Francesco. *Ultimi Scritti e Discorsi extraparlamentare* 1891-1901. Edited by T. Palamenghi-Crispi. Second Edition. Rome, 1913. Reprints a number of articles and speeches of the Italian statesman.

Crispi, Francesco. *La Prima Guerra d'Africa. Storia diplomatica della colonia Eritrea dalle origini al* 1896. Edited by T. Palamenghi-Crispi. Milan, 1914. Contains much unpublished material.

Crispolti, Crispolto, and Aureli, Guido. *La Politica di Leone XIII, da Luigi Galimberti a Mariano Rampolla.* Rome, 1912. Based on the Galimberti papers. An important contribution to the story of papal diplomacy, though dealing primarily with the period prior to 1890.

Cromer, Earl of. *Abbas II.* London, 1915. A supplement to the author's *Modern Egypt.* One of the most important sources for the history of the Egyptian question in the period from 1890-1894.

Curàtulo, Giacomo E. *Francia e Italia, 1849-1914.* Turin, 1915. A conventional account, written with an anti-French bias.

Curàtulo, Giacomo E. *La Questione Romana da Cavour a Mussoloni.* Rome, 1928.

Cyon, Élie de. *Histoire de l'Entente Franco-Russe, 1886-1894. Documents et Souvenirs.* Third Edition. Paris, 1895. Written by one of the most active proponents of the Franco-Russian Alliance. Cyon was a Russian naturalized in France, a collaborator of Katkov and one of the owners of the *Nouvelle Revue.* His account is vainglorious and distorted by very strong prejudices, but the writer was in a position to know a good deal and his account must be taken into consideration.

Cyon, Élie de. *M. Witte et les Finances Russes.* Fifth Edition. Lausanne, 1895. A diatribe against the finance minister, in which may be found some interesting and important bits of information.

Cyon, Élie de. *Où la Dictature de M. Witte Conduit la Russie.* Paris, 1897.

Daniels, Emil. Der Rückversicherungsvertrag vom 18 Juni 1887. *Preussische Jahrbücher* volume CLXXVIII, pp. 178 ff., October 1919.

Darcy, Jean. *France et Angleterre. Cents Années de Rivalité Coloniale.* Paris, 1904.

Darmstaedter, Ludwig. Die Vorgeschichte der russisch-französischen Allianz, 1891-1894. *Preussische Jahrbücher* volume CLXXVI, pp. 393-407, June 1919. Essentially an analysis of the French *Yellow Book.*

Dartige du Fournet, Louis. *Journal d'un Commandant de la Comète.* Paris, 1897. Of importance in connection with the Siamese crisis of 1893.

Daudet, Ernest. *Histoire Diplomatique de l'Alliance Franco-Russe, 1873-1893.* Paris, 1894. One of the earliest and still one of the best books on the subject. The author is apt to be sensational and uncritical, but was in a position to know a good deal of what was going on. His book has distinct source value.

Daudet, Ernest. *Bismarck.* Paris, 1916. A book of slight value excepting for the fact that the reports of the French ambassador to Berlin are utilized in discussing the dismissal of the great chancellor.

Daudet, Ernest. *Guillaume II et François Joseph.* Paris, 1916.

Daudet, Ernest. *Ferdinand I, Tsar de Bulgarie.* Paris, 1917.

Daudet, Ernest. *Alexander III.* Paris, 1920.

Dawson, William H. *The German Empire 1867-1914.* Two volumes. New York, 1919.

Debidour, Antonin. *L'Église Catholique et l'État sous la Troisième République.* Two volumes. Paris, 1909. A standard work on the subject, reliable and exhaustive.

Debidour, Antonin. *Histoire Diplomatique de l' Europe depuis le Congrès de Berlin jusqu'à nos jours.* Two volumes. Paris, 1916-1917. Inferior to the author's other books, but the account of the making of the alliance is rather interesting.

Delbrück, Hans. *Bismarcks Erbe.* Berlin and Vienna, 1915. A brilliant essay defending the New Course.

Delbrück, Hans. Kaiser und Kanzler. *Preussische Jahrbücher* volume CLXXX, pp. 43-53, April 1920. The writer tries to show that the new course and the old were really one and the same thing.

Delbrück, Hans. Von der Bismarck Legende. *Historische Zeitschrift* volume CXXXIII, pp. 69-82, 1925.

Démartial, Georges. L'Alliance Franco-Russe et l'Explosion de la Guerre Mondiale. *Die Kriegsschuldfrage* volume VI, pp. 593-594, June 1928.

Deschamps, Philip. *Le Livre d'Or de l'Alliance Franco-Russe.* Paris, 1898. The author was a rich manufacturer who undertook to collect all the speeches and toasts exchanged during the Cronstadt and Toulon celebrations.

Despagnet, Frantz. *La Diplomatie de la Troisième République et le Droit des Gens.* Paris, 1904.

Despagnet, Frantz. *La République et le Vatican, 1870-1906.* Paris, 1906.

Drandar, A. G. *Les Événements Politiques en Bulgarie depuis 1876 jusqu'à nos jours.* Brussels, 1896. Written by a violent opponent of Stambulov.

Ebmayer, Major von. Caprivis Entlassung. *Deutche Revue* volume XLVII, pp. 193-213, December 1922. The author was Caprivi's adjutant.

(Eckardt, Julius von). *Berlin, Wien, Rom. Betrachtungen über den neuen Kurs und die neue europäische Lage.* Leipzig, 1892. The best known apology for the New Course. The author was a Baltic German and was distinctly opposed to Bismarck's Russian policy. The work is not exactly inspired, but admittedly represented the views of Caprivi in many respects.

Eckardt, Julius von. *Aus den Tagen von Bismarcks Kampf gegen Caprivi.* Leipzig, 1920. An important source, written after the author had been called into the German foreign office and allowed to see the documents dealing with Bismarck's dismissal and the nonrenewal of the Reinsurance Treaty.

Edwards, H. Sutherland. *Sir William White. His Life and Correspondence.* London, 1902. Less important for this period than for the one immediately preceding. White was English ambassador to Constantinople until his death in 1891.

Egelhaaf, Gottlob. *Bismarck, sein Leben und sein Werk.* Stuttgart, 1911.

Egelhaaf, Gottlob. *Geschichte der neuesten Zeit.* Two volumes. Eighth edition, Stuttgart, 1920. Both of Egelhaaf's books are solid and reliable. The writer was one of the first to point out the importance of questions of foreign policy in bringing about Bismarck's dismissal, and was given some information on the subject by Herbert Bismarck.

Eppstein, Georg Freiherr von. *Fürst Bismarcks Entlassung.* Berlin, 1920. Based largely upon the papers of von Boetticher, and important for the story of Bismarck's last months in office.

Espéret, J. B. *La Condition Internationale des Détroits du Bosphore et des Dardanelles.* Toulouse, 1907.

Eulenburg-Hertefeld, Philip, Fürst zu. *Aus 50 Jahren.* Berlin, 1923. One of the most important sources for the history of Bismarck's later years and the period of the dismissal. The author was a confidant of the Kaiser, was on excellent terms with the Bismarcks, and had good connections with Holstein and the foreign office generally, so that he was in an exceptional position to see many sides of the question.

Ferenz, Joseph. Der Bismarcksche Rückversicherungsvertrag zwischen Deutschland und Russland. *Vergangenheit und Gegenwart* volume XVII, pp. 477-484, 1927.

Ferrata, Domenico, Cardinal. *Mémoires.* Three volumes. Rome, 1920. A source of great interest for the study of the diplomacy of the Church. Ferrata was papal nuncio to Paris.

Fester, Richard. Verantwortlichkeiten. III. *Deutsche Rundschau* volume CLXXXIV, pp. 204-244 (August, 1920); IV, *ibid.* volume CLXXXV, pp. 91-103 (October, 1920); Bismarck Renaissance, *ibid.* volume CLXXXIX, pp. 343-351 (December, 1921); VII, *ibid.* volume CXCV, pp. 239-259 (June, 1923). Brilliant discussions of the most important new material as it came out.

Fischer, Eugen. Der Sinn der russisch-französischen Militärkonvention. *Preussische Jahrbücher* volume CXCII, pp. 65-99, April 1923. A very penetrating and suggestive study of the text of the agreement.

Fitzmaurice, Sir Edmond. *The Life of Granville George Leveson Gower, Second Earl Granville.* Two volumes. London and New York, 1905.

(Flourens, Émile). M. Ribot au Quai d'Orsay et à la Présidence du Conseil. *Nouvelle Revue* volume LXXXV, pp. 225-250, November 15, 1893. A scathing indictment of Ribot and his policy. The former French minister is accused of opposing the alliance with Russia and of being obsequious to England.

Flourens, Émile. *Alexander III, sa Vie, son Oeuvre.* Paris, 1894. Contains an important chapter on the foreign policy of Alexander, in which are recounted the attempts made by Flourens, while French foreign minister, to effect an alliance with Russia.

Frahm, Friedrich. England und Russland in Bismarcks Bündnispolitik. *Archiv für Politik und Geschichte* volume VIII, pp. 265-431, 1927. The best general summarizing treatment of the much debated question of Bismarck's policy.

Frankenberg. Richard. *Die Nichterneuerung des deutsch-russischen Rückversiche-rungsvertrages im Jahre* 1890. Berlin, 1927. An exhaustive monograph on the nonrenewal of the famous treaty.

Frederick, Empress. *Letters of the Empress Frederick.* Edited by Sir Frederick Ponsonby. London, 1928.

Freycinet, Charles de. *Souvenirs 1878-1893.* Paris, 1913. One of the most important sources prior to the publication of the *Yellow Book.* The former premier by no means tells all that he knows, but he gives a skeleton outline of the development of the alliance, which seems to have been followed in the compilation of the *Yellow Book.*

Friedjung, Heinrich. Graf Kálnoky. In *Bettelheims Biographisches Jahrbuch* volume III, 1909. Reprinted in the author's *Historischse Aufsätze*, Stuttgart, 1919.

Friedjung, Heinrich. *Das Zeitalter des Imperialismus, 1884-1914.* Three volumes, Berlin, 1919-1922.

Fuller, Joseph Vincent. *Bismarck's Diplomacy at its Zenith.* Cambridge, 1922. An excellent and exhaustive treatment of the critical period from 1886 to 1888.

Gagliardi, Ernst. *Bismarcks Entlassung.* Volume I. *Innenpolitik.* Tübingen, 1927. The most exhaustive treatment of the subject, based in part on unpublished archival material.

Galli, H. *Dessous Diplomatiques. Dix Ans de Politique Étrangère, 1884-1893.* Paris, 1894. The writer was an official in the French foreign office and a close friend of Flourens, from whom he evidently got some material. The book is neither well-balanced nor entirely trustworthy, but cannot be completely ignored.

Gamazo, Gabriel Maura. *Historia Crítica del Reinado de Don Alfonso XIII durante su Menoridad.* Barcelona, no date.

Gardiner, A. G. *The Life of Sir William Harcourt.* Two volumes. London, 1923. A source of great value for the history of English policy during the liberal administrations of Gladstone and Rosebery.

Geffcken, Heinrich. England, Russland und Frankreich in Asien. *Deutsche Revue* volume XVIII, pp. 327-352, December 1893.

Geffcken, Heinrich. *Frankreich, Russland und der Dreibund.* Second edition, Berlin, 1893. A bitter indictment of Bismarck, who is made responsible for the development of the Franco-Russian intimacy. The writer was a member of the circle of Frederick III and was well-informed.

Giacometti, G. Cinq Mois de Politique Italienne, Février-Juin, 1891. *Revue des Deux Mondes*, 3 ième période, volume CVII, pp. 388-452, September 15, 1891. Giacometti was a journalist, with excellent connections both in Paris and in Rome. This long and exhaustive article is exceptionally well-informed, and most later accounts of the renewal of the Triple Alliance in 1891 were based upon it.

Giunta, Sinopoli di. *Cardinale Mariano Rampolla.* Rome, 1923.

(Gladstone, William Ewart). The Triple Alliance and Italy's Place in It. By Outidanos. *Contemporary Review* volume LVI, pp. 469-489, October 1889. Important for an understanding of the attitude of the Liberal cabinet towards the Italian problem and the Triple Alliance.

Goblet, René. Souvenirs de ma Vie Politique. *Revue Politique et Parlementaire* volume CXXXVII, November 1928 to March 1929.

Gooch, George P. Baron von Holstein. *Cambridge Historical Journal* volume I, pp. 61-84, 1923.

Gooch, George P. *History of Modern Europe, 1878-1918.* London and New York, 1923.

Gooch, George P. *Franco-German Relations 1871-1914.* London, 1923. Gooch's studies are all characterized by thoroughness, scholarliness and scrupulous impartiality.

Goriainov, Serge. The End of the Alliance of the Three Emperors. *American Historical Review* volume XXIII, pp. 324-350, January 1918. The author was formerly archivist of the Russian foreign office, and his article, in which the text of the Reinsurance Treaty was first published, is based largely upon Russian documents. It is incomparably the most valuable Russian source we have.

Gothein, Georg. *Reichskanzler Graf Caprivi. Eine kritische Würdigung.* Munich, 1917. A popular sketch, based largely upon Caprivi's speeches.

Gradenwitz, Otto. *Akten über Bismarcks grossdeutsche Rundfahrt vom Jahre 1892.* Heidelberg, 1922.

Gradenwitz, Otto. *Bismarcks letzter Kampf, 1888-1898.* Berlin, 1924. These two monographs contain a number of new documents bearing upon the chancellor's dismissal and the relations between him and the government in the period following 1890.

Grey, Viscount, of Fallodon. *Twenty-Five Years, 1892-1916.* Two volumes. London and New York, 1925.

Guichen, Comte de. Les Rélations Politiques Russo-Allemandes du XIX au XX Siècle. *Académie des Sciences Morales et Politiques. Séances et Travaux* volume CLXXXIX, pp. 503-529, 1918.

Guichen, Comte de. Les Rélations Commerciales Russo-Allemandes du XIX au XX Siècle. *Académie des Sciences Morales et Politiques. Séances et Travaux* volume CXCI, pp. 356-375, 1919.

Gwynn, Stephen, and Tuckwell, Gertrude. *The Life of the Rt. Hon. Sir Charles W. Dilke.* Two volumes. New York, 1917.

Haake, Paul. Die deutsche Aussenpolitik von 1890-1898. *Forschungen zur brandenburgischen und preussischen Geschichte* volume XXXVII, pp. 77-123, 1925. One of the keenest studies of the subject, based upon the German documents.

Haake, Paul. Der neue Kurs 1890. *Zeitschrift für Politik* volume XV, pp. 320-347, 1925. An excellent analysis of the nonrenewal of the Reinsurance Treaty.

Haake, Paul. *Bismarcks Sturz.* Berlin, 1922.

Hagen, Maximilian von. *Geschichte und Bedeutung des Helgolandvertrages.* Munich, 1916.

Halévy, E. Franco-German Relations since 1870. *History,* April 1924.

Haller, Johannes. *Aus dem Leben des Fürsten Philipp zu Eulenburg-Hertefeld.* Berlin, 1924. May be taken as a continuation of Eulenburgs *Aus 50 Jahren.* One of the most important contributions to our knowledge of the Wilhelminian period.

Hamilton, Lord George. *Parliamentary Reminiscences and Reflections, 1886-1906.* London, 1922. A candid and interesting account by the first lord of the admiralty in the Salisbury cabinet.

Hammann, Otto. *Der neue Kurs.* Berlin, 1918.

Hammann, Otto. *Zur Vorgeschichte des Weltkrieges. Erinnerungen aus den Jahren 1897-1906.* Berlin, 1919.

Hammann, Otto. *Der missverstandene Bismarck.* Berlin, 1921..

Hammann, Otto. *Deutsche Weltpolitik 1890-1912.* Berlin, 1925. English translation entitled: *The World Policy of Germany 1890-1912,* London and New York, 1927. The Hammann books must be included among the important sources for the period. The writer was for many years chief of the press bureau of the German foreign office and was well-informed. The books are detached and free from all recrimination. The last two are based in large measure upon the first two, but are revised to accord with later revelations.

Hanotaux, Gabriel. La Prétendue Conjuration Franco-Russe. *Revue des Deux Mondes* 7 ième période, volume XLIII, pp. 415-424, January 15, 1928. An interesting contribution, by the former French foreign minister. The point discussed is the Near Eastern aspect of the alliance, which has always been obscure.

Hansen, Jules. *L'Alliance Franco-Russe.* Second Edition. Paris, 1897.

Hansen, Jules. *Ambassade à Paris du Baron de Mohrenheim, 1884-1898.* Second edition. Paris, 1907. Hansen, a Dane naturalized in France, was one of the unofficial agents of the French government and played a considerable rôle in the history of the Franco-Russian Alliance. Recent publications, especially the French *Yellow Book,* show that his account was much more accurate than had previously been supposed. The later work is an expansion of the earlier one, but there are some things in the first that are omitted from the second. Taken together these works are important as supplementing the official account.

Harden, Maximilian. *Köpfe.* Two volumes. Ninth edition. Berlin, 1910. A series of biographical sketches, by the well-known journalist. By far the most important for this study is that of Holetsin, with whom Harden associated after his dismissal from office.

Hartung, Fritz. *Deutsche Geschichte, 1870-1914.* Berlin, 1920.

Hartung, Fritz. Der deutsch-russische Rückversicherungsvertrag von 1887 und seine Kündigung. *Die Grenzboten,* 1921 (1), pp. 12-17.

Hasenclever, Adolf. Zur Geschichte des Helgolandvertrages. *Archiv für Politik und Geschichte* volume III, pp. 507-524, November 1925. A stimulating and suggestive study, taking due consideration of the English aspects of the problem.

Heller, Eduard. Bismarcks Stellung zur Führung des Zweifrontenkrieges. *Archiv für Politik und Geschichte* volume VII, pp. 677-698, 1926.

Heller, Eduard. *Das deutsch-oesterreichisch-ungarische Bündnis in Bismarcks Aussenpolitik.* Berlin, 1925.

Hofmann, Hermann. *Fürst Bismarck 1890-1898.* Three volumes. Stuttgart, Berlin, Leipzig, 1914. A collection of articles written and inspired by Bismarck and published in the *Hamburger Nachrichten.* Hofmann was at the time editor of the paper and was in the confidence of the former chancellor.

Hohenlohe, Alexander von. Eine Graue Eminenz. *Deutsche Revue* volume XLIV, pp. 97-112, February 1919. An interesting study of Holstein, but deals chiefly with the later period.

Hohenlohe-Schillingsfürst, Fürst. Chlodwig zu. *Denkwürdigkeiten des Fürsten Chlodwig zu Hohenlohe-Schillingsfürst.* Edited by F. Curtius. Two volumes. Stuttgart and Leipzig, 1907. One of the oldest and most interesting sources for the period. The writer's wide connections and his own position in the official world make his notes exceedingly valuable.

Hohenthal, see Richter, Hubert.

Holborn, Hajo. Deutschland und die Türkei, 1878-1890. *Archiv für Politik und Geschichte* volume III, pp. 111-159, August 1925. An important contribution, based in large measure upon new material.

Horn, A. E. A History of Banking in the Russian Empire, in volume II of *A History of Banking in all the Leading Nations*, New York, 1896.

Jäckh, Ernst. *Kiderlen-Wächter, der Staatsmann und Mensch. Briefwechsel und Nachlass.* Two volumes. Stuttgart, 1924. Contains very little material on the earlier period.

Jeyes, Samuel H. *The Life and Times of the Rt. Hon. the Marquis of Salisbury.* Four volumes. London, 1895-1896. A reliable conventional account, based upon official publications.

Jeyes, Samuel H. *The Earl of Rosebery.* London, 1906.

Johnson, Humphrey. *The Papacy and the Kingdom of Italy.* London, 1926. A convenient introductory account.

Judet, Ernest. *Georges Louis.* Paris, 1925. Based on the papers of the former French ambassador to Russia, and important for the later history of the alliance.

Keller, Karl. *Deutschlands auswärtige Politik von Caprivi bis Bethmann-Hollweg.* Detmold, 1921.

Kjéllen, Rudolf. *Dreibund und Dreiverband.* Leipzig and Munich, 1921.

Köhler, Wilhelm, editor. *Revanche-idee und Panslawismus.* Volume V of the collection: *Zur europäischen Politik*, edited by Bernhard Schwertfeger. Berlin. 1919. The documents taken from the Belgian archives during the war. Though merely a selection intended for use as propaganda, this volume is still a source of prime value, because Baron Greindl, the minister to Berlin, was pro-German in his sympathies and was in the confidence of Marschall. His reports were detailed and invariably correct.

Koerlin, Kurt. *Zur Vorgeschichte des russisch-französischen Bündnisses, 1879-1890.* Halle a S., 1926. The only systematic study of the background of the alliance based upon the new material. It is to be regretted that the writer relied so largely upon German material.

Korff, Baron S. A. *Russia's Foreign Relations during the last Half Century.* New York, 1922.

Laloy, Émile. *La Diplomatie de Guillaume II.* Paris, 1917. Based upon very few authorities, prejudiced and quite inadequate.

Lamsdorf, Count Vladimir N. *Dnievnik V. N. Lamsdorfa, 1886-1890.* Moscow, 1926. Next to Goriainov this is the most important contribution to the story of the nonrenewal of the Reinsurance Treaty as seen from the Russian side. Lamsdorf was at the time one of Giers' assistants and kept careful notes of what took place from day to day in the Russian foreign office. This volume is full of valuable and interesting material.

Langer, William L. The Franco-Russian Alliance. *Slavonic Review* volume III, pp. 554-575, March 1925; volume IV, pp. 83-100, June 1925.

Larmeroux, Jean. *La Politique Extérieure de l'Autriche-Hongrie.* Two volumes. Paris, 1918. A wretched piece of work. The writer apparently consulted almost none of the literature in German.

Lee, Sir Sidney. *King Edward VII. A Biography.* Two volumes. London and New York, 1925-1927. These volumes, based upon the personal papers of the late King, are full of interesting documents, but the work is seriously marred by the writer's pronounced Germanophobe bias.

Lefebvre de Béhaine. *Léon XIII et le Prince de Bismarck.* Paris, 1898. Written by the French representative at the Vatican and essential for an understanding of the papal policy, especially in 1887.

Le Glay, A. *Les Origines de l'Alliance Franco-Russe.* Paris, no date.

Lenz, Max. *Deutschland im Kreis der Grossmächte, 1871-1914.* Berlin, 1925. A series of brilliant and suggestive lectures.

Lerchenfeld, see Müller, Karl Alexander von.

Leroy-Beaulieu, Anatole. *La France, la Russie et l'Europe.* Paris, 1888. One of the most penetrating studies of French policy and the problem of French relations to Russia.

Leroy-Beaulieu, Anatole: *Études Russes et Européennes.* Paris, 1897.

Liman, Paul. *Fürst Bismarck nach seiner Entlassung.* Leipzig, 1901.

Lotz, W. Die Handelspolitik des deutschen Reiches unter Graf Caprivi und Fürst Hohenlohe. *Schriften des Vereins für Sozialpolitik* volume XVII, part II, 1901.

Lucius von Ballhausen, Robert, Freiherr. *Bismarck-Erinnerungen.* Stuttgart and Berlin, 1920. A source of the first order. The writer was one of the Prussian ministers and took notes on all the cabinet meetings as well as on conversations which he had with Bismarck and other celebrities.

Lyall, Sir Alfred Comyn. *The Life of the Marquis of Dufferin and Ava.* Two volumes. London, 1905. A good biography of the English ambassador, but does not reveal much of the fundamentals of British policy.

Macdiarmid, D. S. *The Life of Lieutenant-General Sir James Moncrieff Grierson.* London, 1923. Grierson was, for a time, one of the British military attachés abroad.

Mahn, Paul. *Kaiser und Kanzler.* Berlin, 1925. A study of the crisis of 1890, with emphasis on the personal aspects.

Manassewitsch, Boris. *Fürst Bismarck und das deutsch-russische Verhältnis.* Second edition. Leipzig, 1891. The author attempts to show that Bismarck was primarily reponsible for the strained relations between Russia and Germany.

Manfroni, Giuseppe. *Sulla Soglia del Vaticano, 1870-1901.* Two volumes. Bologna, 1920. The writer was an Italian official who acted as a liaison officer between the government and the Vatican.

Marin, P. *Bulgares et Russes vis-à-vis la Triple Alliance.* Paris, 1891.

Marvaud, A. La Politique Extérieure de l'Espagne. *Revue des Sciences Politiques* volume L, January-March, 1927. A survey of recent literature on the subject.

McHardy, C. McL. *The British Navy for 100 Years.* Second Edition. London, 1897. A propagandist publication issued by the Navy League, but well-done and usable.

Medlicott, W. N. The Mediterranean Agreements of 1887. *Slavonic Review* volume V, pp. 66-88, June 1926. Deals primarily with the making of the agreements, but adduces some interesting material from the Russian Embassy archives in London and the Vienna archives.

Medlicott, W. N. Lord Salisbury and Turkey. *History* volume XII, October 1927. Concerned chiefly with Salisbury's attitude in 1878.

Meinecke, Friedrich. *Geschichte des deutsch-englishen Bündnisproblems, 1890-1901.* Munich and Berlin, 1927. The most recent study of the Anglo-German problem after Bismarck's fall. Brilliant and suggestive throughout.

Meisner, H. O. Der neue Kurs. *Preussische Jahrbücher* volume CXCVI, pp. 41-71, April 1924.

Mendelssohn Bartholdy, Albrecht. Der Wille zum Krieg in Europa 1890-1898. *Archiv für Politik und Geschichte* volume II, pp. 36-53, 1924. Deals with a few select problems, considered in the light of the German documents.

Mevil, André. *De la Paix de Francfort à la Conférence d'Algéciras.* Paris, 1909.

Meyer, Arnold O. *Bismarcks Orientpolitik.* Göttingen, 1925.

Michon, Georges. *L'Alliance Franco-Russe, 1891-1917.* Paris, 1927. The only systematic treatment of the history of the alliance as a whole. The viewpoint is radical and the author is distinctly hostile to the alliance, but the book is scholarly and valuable as a study of the evolution of French public opinion.

Molden, Berthold. *Kálnoky.* In *Allgemeine deutsche Biographie, Nachträge* LV, Leipzig, 1906.

Mommsen, Wilhelm. Bismarcks Sturz. *Archiv für Politik und Geschichte* volume I, pp. 481 ff., 1923.

Mommsen, Wilhelm. *Bismarcks Sturz und die Parteien.* Stuttgart, Berlin, Leipzig, 1924.

Mommsen, Wilhelm. Die elsass-lothringische Frage, 1890-1897. *Archiv für Politik und Geschichte* volume II, pp. 583 ff., 1924.

Morley, John. *The Life of William Ewart Gladstone.* Three volumes. London and New York, 1903.

Morrow, I. F. D. An Unpublished Memorandum on the Straits Question by Baron von Aehrenthal. *Cambridge Historical Journal* volume II, no. I, pp. 83-88, 1926. A memorandum dating from the spring of 1894 and reviewing the history of the question.

Mourret, Fernand. *Les Directions Politiques, Intellectuelles et Sociales de Léon XIII.* Paris, 1920.

Mousset, Albert. *L'Espagne dans la Politique Mondiale.* Paris, 1923. The best general account of Spanish foreign policy in the modern period.

Müller, Karl Alexander von. Die Entlassung. Nach den bayerischen Gesandschaftsberichten. *Süddeutsche Monatshefte* volume XIX, pp. 138-178, December, 1921. The reports of Count Lerchenfeld, dealing primarily with the domestic aspects of the Bismarck crisis.

Narfon, Julien de. *Pope Leo XIII, his Life and Work.* London, 1899.

Niemann, Alfred. *Wanderungen mit Kaiser Wilhelm II.* Leipzig, 1924. Contains one of the Kaiser's versions of the dismissal of Bismarck.

Nitti, Francesco. *Il Capitale Straniero in Italia.* Bari, 1915.

Noack, Ulrich. *Bismarcks Friedenspolitik und das Problem des deutschen Machtverfalls.* Leipzig, 1928. The most recent exhaustive treatment of Bismarck's policy.

Notovich, Nikolai. *L'Empereur Alexandre III et son Entourage.* Nouvelle édition. Paris, 1895. The writer was editor of one of the less reliable Russian newspapers, but occasionally received communications from the Russian foreign office and had many connections in diplomatic circles.

Oncken, Hermann. *Das alte und das neue Mitteleuropa.* Gotha, 1917. Still one of the most interesting and stimulating discussions of fundamental problems of German policy.

Packard, Laurence B. Russia and the Dual Alliance. *American Historical Review* volume XXV, pp. 391-411, April 1920. A careful study of the background of the alliance, with a discussion of the light thrown by the French *Yellow Book* upon the negotiations for the agreement.

Papowski, Josef. *Die französich-russische Allianz.* Vienna, 1891.

Penzler, Johannes. *Fürst Bismarck nach seiner Entlassung.* Seven volumes. Leipzig, 1897-1898.

Penzler, Johannes. *Die Reden Kaiser Wilhelms II, 1888-1912.* Six volumes. Leipzig, no date.

Pesaro, A. A. di. La Diplomazia Vaticana e la Questione del Potere Temporale. *Rassegna Nazionale* May 1, 1890, pp. 3-129. An exhaustive and fundamental study of papal diplomacy in the period from 1870 to 1890.

Petit, Pierre. *La Dette Publique de la Russie.* Poitiers, 1912.

Pingaud, Albert. *L'Italie depuis 1870.* Paris, 1915.

Pinon, René. *France et Allemagne, 1870-1913.* Nouvelle Edition. Paris, 1913.

Piou, Jacques. *Le Comte Albert de Mun.* Paris, no date. An excellent biography of the great Catholic leader. Throws considerable light on the background of the *Ralliement.*

Plebano, Achille. *Storia della Finanza Italiana dalla Costituzione del nuovo Regno alla Fine del Secolo XIX.* Three volumes. Turin, 1902.

Plehn, Hans. *Bismarcks auswärtige Politik nach der Reichsgründung.* Munich and Berlin, 1920. A pioneer work which, though out of date so far as facts are concerned, is still of interest. The publication of new material has only served to set the writer's keenness of observation into higher relief.

Poincaré, Raymond. *Les Origines de la Guerre.* Paris, 1921.

Pourvoirville, Albert de. *L'Affaire de Siam, 1886-1896.* Second edition. Paris, 1897.

Preller, Hugo. Zur Entstehung und Struktur des russisch-französischen Zweibundes von 1890-1894. *Archiv für Politik und Geschichte* volume II, pp. 463-475, 1924. A stimulating essay, though somewhat hasty in its conclusions.

Preller, Hugo. Der russisch-französische Zweibund. *Archiv für Politik und Geschichte* volume III, pp. 65-77, 1925. A reply to criticism of the author's first article.

Pribram, Alfred Franzis. *Die politischen Geheimverträge Oesterreich-Ungarns, 1879-1914.* Vienna and Leipzig, 1920. English translation entitled: *The Secret Treaties of Austria-Hungary.* Two volumes. Cambridge, 1920-1921. One of the fundamental sources for the pre-war history of European diplomacy, containing not only the texts of all treaties concluded by the Dual Monarchy, but also the detailed account of the negotiations for the Triple Alliance and its various renewals.

Pürschel, Erich. Das Ende des Rückversicherungsvertrages. *Vergangenheit und und Gegenwart* volume XV, pp. 144-159, 1925.

Raab, Gerhard. *Der deutsch-russische Rückversicherungsvertrag in dem System der Bismarckschen Politik, vornehmlich des Jahres 1887.* Wetzlar, 1923.

Rachfahl, Felix. Der Rückversicherungsvertrag, der "Balkandreibund" und das angebliche Bündnisangebot Bismarcks an England vom Jahre 1887. *Weltwirtschaftliches Archiv* volume XVI, pp. 28-81, 1920.

Rachfahl, Felix. *Bismarcks englishe Bündnispolitik.* Freiburg, 1922.

Rachfahl, Felix. Die Umwälzung der neuesten Geschichtsschreibung durch die letzten Quellen der Bismarckzeit. *Archiv für Politik und Geschichte* volume I, pp. 193-224, 1923.

Rachfahl, Felix. *Die deutsche Aussenpolitik in der Wilhelminischen Ära.* Berlin 1924. A series of scholarly monographs, in which the late German historian attempted to defend the thesis that the Reinsurance Treaty was merely a makeshift and that Bismarck's ultimate object was to consummate an agreement with England.

Radowitz, Josef Maria von. *Aufzeichnungen und Erinnerungen.* Edited by Hajo Holborn. Two volumes. Berlin and Leipzig, 1925. One of the most important sources. Radowitz was German ambassador to Constantinople and happened to be in Berlin at the time of the Bismarck crisis. It is to be regretted that the papers of the ambassador for the period following 1890 have not been published.

Raschdau, Ludwig. Der deutsch-russische Rückversicherungsvertrag. *Die Grenzboten* April 12, 1918, pp. 25-32.

Raschdau, Ludwig. Das Ende der deutsch-russischen Rückversicherung. *Der Tag* October 17, 1920.

Raschdau, Ludwig. Der deutsch-russische Rückversicherungsvertrag. Eine Entgegnung. *Die Grenzboten* 1921, nos. 4-5, pp. 117-118.

Raschdau, Ludwig. Zur Vorgeschichte des Rückversicherungsvertrages. *Deutsche Rundschau* volume CXCIX, pp. 113-126, May 1924.

Raschdau, Ludwig. Zum Kapitel Holstein. *Deutsche Rundschau* volume CCI, pp. 237-248, December 1924.

Raschdau, Ludwig. Zur Bewertung des Rückversicherungsvertrages. *Die Kriegsschuldfrage* volume V, pp. 57-58, January 1927; pp. 1106-1107, November 1927. Raschdau is the last surviving member of the group in the German foreign office after Bismarck's dismissal. As such he was in part responsible for the nonrenewal of the Reinsurance Treaty. In a long series of articles he has attempted to justify the policy of the New Course, and to defend his own attitude.

Renard, Edmond. *Le Cardinal Mathieu, 1839-1908.* Paris, 1925.

Renouvin, Pierre. L'Allemagne et la Conclusion de l'Alliance Franco-Russe. *Bulletin de la Société d'Histoire Moderne*, June 1924.

Reventlow, Ernst Graf zu. Die Frage der türkischen Meerengen und ihre Entwicklung. *Süddeutsche Monatshefte*, volume XIV, pp. 432 ff., January 1917.

Reventlow, Ernst Graf zu. *Deutschlands auswärtige Politik, 1888-1914.* Eleventh edition. Berlin, 1918.

Richter, Hubert. Aus kritischen Tagen. Berichte des königlich-sächsischen Gesandten in Berlin, Grafen Hohental und Bergen, aus den Jahren 1889-1892. *Deutsche Rundschau* volume CXC, pp. 151-173, February 1922. In reality these reports cover only the months of the Bismarck crisis of 1890. They add comparatively little to our knowledge of the questions of foreign affairs.

Richter, Hubert: *Sachsen und Bismarcks Entlassung.* Dresden, 1928.

Ritter, Gerhard. *Bismarcks Verhältnis zu England und die Politik des "Neuen Kurses."* Berlin, 1924. One of the best discussions of the policy of the New Course.

(Robolsky, Hermann). *Die mitteleuropäische Friedensliga.* Leipzig, 1891.

Rodd, Sir James Rennell. *Social and Diplomatic Memoirs, 1884-1893.* London, 1922. Contains much interesting information on the writer's stay in Berlin in the 'eighties', but is rather scant on the later years.

Ronaldshay, Earl of. *The Life of Lord Curzon.* Three volumes. London and New York, 1928. The authoritative biography.

Rothfels, Hans. Zur Bismarck Krise von 1890. *Historiche Zeitschrift* volume CXXIII, pp. 267-296, 1920.

Rothfels, Hans. Zur Geschichte des Rückversicherungsvertrages. *Preussische Jahrbücher* volume CLXXXVII, pp. 265 ff., March 1922.

Rothfels, Hans. Bismarcks Sturz als Forschungsproblem. *Preussische Jahrbücher* volume CXCI, pp. 1-30, January 1923.

Rothfels, Hans. Bismarcks englische Bündnispolitik. Stuttgart, Berlin, Leipzig, 1924.

Rothfels, Hans. Das Problem der Schuldfrage und der neue Kurs. *Die Kriegsschuldfrage* volume II, pp. 192-200, June 1924.

Rothfels, Hans. Das Wesen des russisch-französischen Zweibundes. *Archiv für Politik und Geschichte* volume III, pp. 149-160, 1925.

Rothfels, Hans. Der russisch-französischer Zweibund. *Archiv für Politik und Geschichte* volume III, pp. 78-80, 1925. Rothfels' articles and monographs are among the keenest and most penetrating studies of the period. Done with great impartiality and scholarly thoroughness, they leave nothing to be desired.

Routier, Gaston. *Un Point d'Histoire Contemporaine. Le Voyage de l'Impératrice Frédéric à Paris en 1891.* Paris, 1901. A useful compilation of press comment and other data, supplemented by a report of a conversation with Herbette.

Roux, M. S. *La Vérité sur l'Alliance Franco-Russe.* Paris, 1895.

Salata, F. La Questione Romana e la Triplice Alleanza. *Nuova Antologia* volume CCXXIII, pp. 49-63, March 1, 1923.

Salvemini, Gaetano. La Triple Alliance. *Revue des Nations Latines* July, August, October 1916, and February 1917. A series of very able studies, particularly useful for the wealth of press comment and for the Italian viewpoint.

Salvemini, Gaetano. *La Politica Estera di Francesco Crispi.* Rome, 1919. Indispensable as a commentary on Crispi's memoirs.

Savin, A. Chetire Pisma Vilgelma Prusskovo k Alexandre III. *Krasny Arkhiv* volume II, pp. 118-129, 1922.

Schefer, Christian. *D'Une Guerre à l'Autre. Essai sur la Politique Extérieure de la Troisième République.* Paris, 1920.

Schlitter, Hans. Briefe Kaiser Franz Josephs I und Kaiser Wilhelms II über Bismarcks Rücktritt. *Oesterreichische Rundschau* volume LVIII, pp. 97 ff., February 1919.

Schlözer, Kurd von. *Letzte römische Briefe.* Stuttgart, 1924. The correspondence of the German minister to the Vatican.

Schneidewin, Max. *Das politische System des Reichskanzlers Grafen von Caprivi.* Danzig, 1894. An uninspiring and dry, though honest attempt to defend Caprivi's policies.

Scholz, Adolf von. *Erlebnisse und Gespräche mit Bismarck.* Stuttgart and Berlin, 1922. Reminiscences of one of the ministers in Bismarck's cabinet.

Schüssler, Wilhelm. *Bismarcks Sturz.* Leipzig, 1921. The best general study of Bismarck's dismissal.

Schweinitz, Lother von. *Denkwürdigkeiten des Botschafters General von Schweinitz.* Two volumes. Berlin, 1927. A source of prime importance, containing the correspondence and papers of the German ambassador to St. Petersburg. To a certain extent this material had already appeared in the German publication of documents.

Schweinitz, Lother von. *Briefwechsel des Botschafters General von Schweinitz.* Berlin, 1928.

Séauve, Capitaine. *Les Rélations de la France et du Siam, 1680-1907.* Paris, 1907.

Sell, Manfred. *Das deutsch-englische Abkommen von 1890.* Berlin, 1926. A study of German public opinion in respect to the treaty.

Silva, Pietro. Aspetti e Fasi del Problema del Mediterraneo Occidentale nel XIX Secolo. *Nuova Rivista Storica* volume VIII, pp. 408 ff., 1924.

Simon, E. *L'Allemagne et la Russie au XIX ième Siècle.* Paris, 1893.

Singer, Arthur. *Geschichte des Dreibundes.* Leipzig, 1914.

Stählin, Karl. Aus den diplomatischen Akten des auswärtigen Amtes, 1871-1914. X. Von der Thronbesteigung Wilhelms II bis zum Sturz Bismarcks. *Zeitschrift für Politik* volume XIV, pp. 29-49, 1924.

Staneff, N. *Geschichte der Bulgaren.* Leipzig, 1917.

Stieglitz, Baron de. *L'Italie et la Triple Alliance.* Paris, 1906.

Stieve, Friedrich. Die Verschiebung des europäischen Gleichgewichts nach Bismarcks Entlassung. *Archiv für Politik und Geschichte* volume II, pp. 53-61, 1924.

Stieve, Friedrich. *Deutschland und Europa, 1890-1914.* Berlin, 1926. Essentially an analysis of the German documents.

Tardieu, André. *France and the Alliances.* New York, 1908.

Thorold, Algar L. *The Life of Henry Labouchère.* London, 1913.

Tirpitz, Alfred von. *Erinnerungen.* Leipzig, 1919. English translation entitled: *My Memoirs.* Two volumes. New York, 1919.

Tischert, L. *Fünf Jahre deutscher Handelspolitik, 1890-1894.* Leipzig, 1898.

Tournier, J. *Le Cardinal Lavigerie et son Action Politique, 1863-1892.* Paris, 1913. Based in large part upon the private papers of Lavigerie, this is one of the most important contributions to the history of Church policy in the period under discussion.

Toutain, Edmond. Origines de l'Alliance Franco-Russe. *Revue d'Histoire Diplomatique* volume XLII, pp. 400-431, October 1928. Interesting on the period from 1885-1888.

Tramond, Joannès M. *Éléments d'Histoire Maritime et Coloniale Contemporaine, 1815-1914.* Paris, 1924. An admirable survey, but too general to be of much use on any particular point.

Trubetzkoi, Prince Grigorii. *Russland als Grossmacht.* Stuttgart and Berlin, 1913.

Trützschler, Heinz von. Die Politik der freien Hand. Ein Blick auf die deutsche Aussenpolitik von 1890-1897. *Die Kriegsschuldfrage* volume I, pp. 109-118, December 1923.

Trützschler von Falkenstein, Heinz. *Bismarck und die Kriegsgefahr des Jahres 1887.* Berlin, 1924.

T'Serclaes, Monsignor de. *Le Pape Léon XIII. Sa Vie, son Action Religieuse, Politique et Sociale.* Two volumes. Paris, Lille, 1894. Practically an official biography, very detailed and thorough.

Uebersperger, Hans. Abschluss und Ende des Rückversicherungsvertrages. *Die Kriegsschuldfrage* volume V, pp. 933-966, October 1927. A competent summary and study of the material contained in Lamsdorf's diaries.

Valentin, Veit. *Deutschlands Aussenpolitik von Bismarcks Abgang bis zum Ende des Weltkrieges.* Berlin, 1921.

Vermeil, M. E. *L'Empire Allemand, 1871-1900.* Paris, 1920. Really a general survey of European history during these years.

Vigo, Pietro. *Storia degli Ultimi Trent'Anni del Secolo XIX.* Ten volumes. Milan, 1913.

Vitali, G. Guglielmo II e Bismarck. *Nuova Antologia* January 16, 1929.

Waldersee, Alfred Graf von. Aus den Erinnerungen des General-Feldmarschalls Grafen Waldersee. Edited by H. O. Meisner. *Deutsche Revue* volume XLVI, pp. 208 ff., June 1921.

Waldersee, Alfred Graf von. *Denkwürdigkeiten des General-Feldmarschalls Alfred Grafen von Waldersee.* Edited by H. O. Meisner. Two volumes. Stuttgart and Berlin, 1922. English condensed translation entitled: *A Field Marshal's Memoirs* London, 1921.

Waldersee, Alfred Graf von. *Aus dem Briefwechsel des General-Feldmarschalls Alfred Grafen von Waldersee.* Volume I, 1886-1891. Berlin and Leipzig, 1928. An outstanding source. Waldersee was chief of the general staff from 1888 to 1891 and was in close touch with the Kaiser during the first critical years of his reign. His notes, made from day to day, are very full and of the greatest significance. Even after his dismissal he maintained connections with governing circles in Berlin and played a certain rôle.

Waldteufel, E. *Six Mois de Paix Armée.* Paris, 1893.

Welschinger, Henri. *L'Alliance Franco-Russe.* Paris, 1919. An analysis of the French *Yellow Book* and the Margaine Report.

Wertheimer, Eduard von. Bismarcks Sturz. *Preussische Jahrbücher* volume CLXXXIV, pp. 300 ff., June 1921. Based upon the reports of the Austrian ambassador in Berlin.

Wertheimer, Eduard von. Ein k. und k. Militärattaché über das politische Leben in Berlin 1880-1895. *Preussische Jahrbücher* September 1925, pp. 264-282. Based upon reports and memoranda of Baron von Steininger, the Austrian military attaché in Berlin.

Wertheimer, Eduard von. Neues zur Geschichte der letzten Jahre Bismarcks, 1890-1898. *Historische Zeitschrift* volume CXXXIII, pp. 221-257, 1925. Based upon material from the Austrian and smaller German archives, but dealing primarily with the relations between Bismarck and the government.

West, Sir Algernon. *The Private Diaries of Sir Algernon West.* Edited by Horace G. Hutchinson. London, 1922. West was Gladstone's secretary, and his very detailed diaries throw some light on what went on in the inner councils of the cabinet.

Wilhelm II. *Ereignisse und Gestalten aus den Jahren 1878-1918.* Leipzig and Berlin, 1922. English translation entitled: *The Kaiser's Memoirs.* New York and London, 1922.

Windelband, Wolfgang. *Herbert Bismarck als Mitarbeiter seines Vaters.* Stuttgart Berlin, 1921.

Witte, Count Sergius J. *The Memoirs of Count Witte.* New York, 1921. The memoirs of the Russian minister of finance, who was in part responsible for the commercial treaty with Germany. These memoirs must always be used with caution.

Wittschewsky, V. *Russlands Handels-Zoll-und Industriepolitik von Peter dem Grossen bis auf die Gegenwart.* Berlin, 1905. Based in large part upon Russian material, and emphasizing Russo-German relations.

Woodward, E. L. The Diplomacy of the Vatican under Popes Pius IX and Leo XIII. *Journal of the British Institute of International Affairs* May 1924, pp. 113-139.

Younghusband, Sir Francis. *The Light of Experience.* Boston, 1927.

Zaiontchovsky, A. *et al. Les Alliés contre la Russie.* Paris, 1927. Chapter I: Relations Franco-Russes avant la Guerre de 1914, by A. Zaiontchovsky. An authoritative Russian account.

Zaiontchovsky, A. *Podgotovka Rossii k mirovoi voine v meshdunarodnom Otnoshenii.* Moscow, 1926. A general account of Russian foreign policy after 1870, based in part upon Russian archive material.

Zévort, E. *Histoire de la Troisième République.* Volume IV: *La Présidence de Carnot.* Paris, 1901.

Zimmermann, A. *Die Handelspolitik des deutschen Reiches vom Frankfurter Frieden bis zur Gegenwart.* Second Edition. Berlin, 1901.

Zweig, E. Die russische Handelspolitik seit 1877. *Staats-und sozialwissenschaftliche Forschungen* Heft 123, 1906.

ANONYMOUS.

Warum der russische Draht zerriss. By Vindex Scrutator (?Johannes Haller). *Der Tag* November 4, 1920. Very important letters from Holstein to Eulenburg in the days of the Bismarck crisis.

Fürst Bismarck und Russlands Orientpolitik, von einem dreibundfreundlichen Diplomaten. Berlin, 1892.

L'Alliance Franco-Russe devant la Crise Orientale. Par Un Diplomate Étranger. Paris, 1891.

M. Develle au Quai d'Orsay. Par Un Diplomate. *Nouvelle Revue* volume LXXXVII, pp. 449-468, April 1, 1894. A scathing criticism, probably written by Flourens.

The Foreign Policy of Lord Rosebery. *Contemporary Review* volume LXXX, pp. 1-13, 153-177, July and August 1901. An inadequate and in many respects ill-informed account.

The Marquis of Salisbury. *Quarterly Review* volume CXCVI, pp. 647-676, October 1902. Pending the appearance of the later volumes of Lady Cecil's authoritative biography, this inspired article is still the best general account of Salisbury's foreign policy. Many of the statements made in it have since been borne out by new publications.

INDEX

Abbas Hilmi II, khedive of Egypt (1892-1914), 271, 272; visit to Constantinople of, 317 f.

Abder Rahman Khan, amir of Afghanistan (1880-1901), 317.

Abdul Hamid II, sultan of Turkey (1876-1909), 273, 318 f.

Abyssinia, 97, 98, 112, 122, 213.

(Adam), Madame Juliette Lamber, Franco-Russian Alliance and, 193, 240, 323; Portsmouth festivities and, 200; at Toulon celebration, 348.

Adriatic Sea, 7, 22, 161, 375.

Aehrenthal, Alois Lexa, Freiherr von, secretary of the Austrian embassy at St. Petersburg (1888-94), 276 f., 415.

Afghanistan, 4, 41, note, 242, 268, 317.

Africa, other countries and, 10, 22, 72, 76, 81, 93, 97, 110, 122, 127, 130, 149, 160.

Agadir, 399.

Aiguesmortes, attack on Italian workers by French at, 34.

Alexander I, prince of Battenberg, prince of Bulgaria (1879-86), kidnapping of, 21.

Alexander III, tsar of Russia (1881-94), Bulgaria and, 107, 280 ff.; France and, 138, 146 ff., 179, 181, 183, 184 f., 195, 348 f.; Franco-Russian Alliance and, 210 f., 235, 238 ff., 256, 258, 263, 265, 269, 270, 353 ff., 392 ff., 399; Germany and, 31 ff., 54 f., 91, 211, 225 ff., 241-245, 297 ff., 304, 306 ff.; visit to Berlin of, 36 f.; visit to Kiel of, 244 f.; William II and, 38 f., 56, 80, 102 ff., 225, 241, 244 f., 298.

Alexandria, 317.

Algiers, 134.

Alsace-Lorraine, 14, 89, 90, 91, 141, 156, 192, 194, 393; passport regulations in, 30, 120, 140, 143, 197.

Anatolian railway, 291 ff.

Andrássy, Count Julius, Austro-Hungarian minister of foreign affairs (1871-79), 13, 16, 84.

Angora, question of railway to, 291 ff.

Arthur, Port, 412.

Asia, England and, 316, 332, 333, 347; Russia and, 192, 194, 198, 316, 400.

Athos, Mount, visit of Russian ambassador to, 360.

Austria, general foreign policy of, 7 f.; England and, 4, 15, 85 ff., 376 ff.; Germany and, 107 ff., 231 f., 374 ff., 381 ff.; policy of Bismarck toward, 11 f., 16 f., 21 f., 24, 31, 60, 75; William II and, 44 f., 80; Italy and, 7, 22, 110, 149 f., 162; Russia and, 13 ff., 83 ff., 106 f., 231 ff., 385 f.; efforts of Russia to reach agreement with, 275-284; Near East interests of, 83 ff.; Bulgaria and, 231; Serbia and, 19, 231; in Three Emperors' Alliance, 18; in Triple Alliance, 19, 159. See Francis Joseph, Kálnoky.

Austro-German Alliance of 1879, v, 17, 23, 26, 28, 31, 49, 83, 152, 297.

Austro-Russian commercial treaty (1894) 385.

Avellan, Admiral, 348.

Bagdad, question of railway to, 291 ff. 415.

Baker, Sir Samuel, 359.

Balkan states, 7 ff., 16 ff., 63, 75, 127, 194; Austrian interests in, 8, 83 ff.; English interests in, 86; Germany's lack of interest in, 37, 83, 149, 296 f.; Bismarck and, 17, 20, 37, 60, 75, 83; Italian interests in, 216, note; Russian interests in, 82 ff., 216, note. See Near East.

Bangkok, blockade of French at, 325 ff.